SALMOND

Against the Odds

David Torrance

BIRLINN

For my father, with whom I've often disagreed politically
but without ever doubting his sincerity

This edition first published in 2011 by
Birlinn Limited
West Newington House
10 Newington Road
Edinburgh
EH9 1QS

www.birlinn.co.uk

ISBN: 978 1 78027 066 1
eBook ISBN 978 0 85790 101 9

British Library Cataloguing-in-Publication Data
A catalogue record for this book is available from the British Library

Typeset by Hewer Text (UK) Ltd, Edinburgh
Printed and bound by Clays Ltd, St Ives plc

SALMOND

Against the Odds

Also by David Torrance

The Scottish Secretaries
George Younger: A Life Well Lived
'We in Scotland': Thatcherism in a Cold Climate
Noel Skelton and the Property-Owning Democracy

With Steven Richmond

Inside Edinburgh: Discovering the Classic Interiors of Edinburgh

CONTENTS

LIST OF ILLUSTRATIONS

ACKNOWLEDGEMENTS

It is curious that this should be the first biography, authorised or other-wise, of Alex Salmond. First elected to Parliament in 1987, he first became leader of the SNP 20 years ago and has been a major figure in Scottish politics ever since. Now, as First Minister, his place in history is guaranteed as the first Nationalist to lead the devolved Scottish Government.

There have, of course, been previous attempts. The writer and jour-nalist Alan Taylor began such a project back in 1999, the fruits of which have yet to appear in print, while at around the same time another Scot, the celebrity biographer Brian Robb, planned an authorised life. Salmond, unsurprisingly, was not interested ('It's up to him', commented an SNP spokesman, 'if he wants to write an unauthorised biography'[1]). I managed to resist, meanwhile, Rab McNeil's suggested title for Taylor's project, 'Mein Banff'.[2]

Salmond himself has written little of an autobiographical nature beyond a few newspaper columns and a series of ghosted articles for *Scotland on Sunday* shortly after he announced his resignation as SNP leader in 2000. These demonstrated that even in semi-retirement he was not prepared to give much away, although it seems clear he is planning a memoir. When, for example, a story emerged about a 2001 meeting between Salmond and the US President George W. Bush, a spokesman declined to comment further, simply stating that 'the First Minister would set the record straight in his memoirs'.[3]

The journalist Iain Macwhirter was also informed, perhaps in jest, that he was keeping a diary ('It's a brilliant read,'[4] Salmond told him). 'He's always working on his book,' a former aide told me, 'it's about the life of Alex ... that's how he relaxes, either by reading a book or writing his own.'[5] As an enthusiastic student of history, it appears Salmond is intent upon preserving his place within the story of modern Scotland, even as he continues to shape it. He is well known for hoarding the scraps of paper beloved by historians; when clearing out his Westminster office in 2007 staff were astonished at the extent of printed material gathered over the previous 20 years.

I am sorry, therefore, to have beaten Salmond to it, although his autobiography will obviously enjoy innumerable advantages over an unauthorised work such as this. While my subject did not wish to co-operate directly, he neither hindered my research nor made any attempt to stop me speaking to friends and colleagues. Indeed, I would like to record my appreciation of this attitude, which the political writer John Campbell said was 'probably the ideal relationship between a biographer and a living subject'.[6] That said, this is no hagiography. 'It is a journalist's duty to both himself and to his readers to be unflinchingly truthful about the flaws of the powerful,' observed Andrew Rawnsley. 'It is equally an obligation to give credit where it is due.' This book, therefore, strives to offer a balanced account of the SNP and Alex Salmond, 'highlighting the achievements as well as exploring the failures'.[7]

Beyond that, what can an unauthorised biography of a serving politician hope to achieve? Alan Taylor reckoned the best biographies were 'idiosyncratic, subjective and selective', revealing 'as much about the biographer as the biographee'.[8] That much is true, and readers of my other tomes will no doubt recognise trademark quirks. The late Sir Bernard Crick, meanwhile, argued that a biographer had 'a duty to show how he reaches his conclusions, not to pretend to omniscience', while sharing 'things that are moot, problematic and uncertain with the reader'.[9]

There is much that is either moot or uncertain about Salmond's long career, and most, in keeping with Crick's advice, have been flagged up in the text. As another fine political writer, Ben Pimlott, put it in 1995, the 'aim of the biographer is not to build an exact photographic likeness – that is logically absurd'.

It is to build an impression, using evidence as the paint. The impression should be recognizable and revealing, and the portrait is of particular interest if the sitter is well known ... Focusing on the subject, the author attempts to build, not a distillation of important facts, still less a logical argument, but a verbal image, using a *pointillisme* of detail and comment. The aim is to create a picture, not to display the paint: the choice of colours and their arrangement will be highly selective. In the process of creating the image, public and private details will be mingled according to need and the artist's fancy.

'The aim should be to understand an individual life,' added Pimlott, 'the forces that shape it and the motives that drive it, in the context in which it is placed.'[10] Indeed, although this is primarily a work of portraiture, the text often ranges beyond the relatively narrow confines of Salmond's life on to the broader canvass of Scottish political history. Even now, this area is not blessed with a preponderance of sources while, as the Nationalist politician and writer Mike Russell lamented, the SNP in particular 'has always been poor at celebrating its own past'.[11] So like Geoffrey Barrow's account of Robert Bruce, this book seeks to 'present the story not only of a man but also of an idea',[12] for it is impossible to separate all but Salmond's earliest years from his pursuit of Scottish independence.

'If the quest is for understanding, then public and private facts clearly cannot be put in separate boxes,' Pimlott also observed. 'Real life accepts no such partition. It is apparent that every publicly expressed passion – of patriotism, class sentiment, concern for the poor or whatever, has a private dimension; and that "political character" is always a package in which public and private traits are intertwined.'[13] That is as true of Salmond as it was of Harold Wilson, of whom Pimlott wrote an accomplished life. Where I have delved into that seldom charted 'private dimension' of Salmond, I trust I have done so with tact and care.

Now for dutiful thanks. My fellow scribe John MacLeod has to be singled out for proof reading, suggesting sources, offering insights and structural guidance, and sustained encouragement throughout the whole process despite heavy commitments of his own. My friend Andrew Kerr and brother Michael also offered various comments on the typescript – particularly concerning the historical nomenclature of the European project – as did Colin Mackay, Colin Faulkner, Douglas Pattullo and Ian Swanson on certain chapters. Kevin Pringle, the First Minister's eyes and ears, was unfailingly generous when it came to dealing with inquiries, as was Peter Murrell, the SNP's chief executive. Jim Eadie, meanwhile, happily imparted recollections and VHS copies of Scottish political programming from years gone by. I had great fun, for example, watching coverage of the 1992 general election while the 2010 contest was in full swing (a lot, it has to be said, has not changed). Special thanks must also go to Peter Brunskill, a university contemporary whose affection for Salmond imbued all his recollections, the veteran SNP activist Ian O. Bayne, who dug up some sources that had passed me by, and finally Dr Jason Davies, who offered guidance on the life and work of R. S. Thomas.

Others who agreed to speak to me in person, by telephone or via email were, in no particular order, Andrew Wilson, Duncan Hamilton, Jennifer Dempsie, Charlie Woods, Pam Chesters, Chris McLean, Iain More, Cllr Tim McKay, Colin Bell, Colin Pyle, Dave Smith, Jamie Stone MSP, Gordon Currie, Grant and Glynne Baird, Gordon Wilson, Henry McLeish, Iain Lawson, Ian Blackford, Isobel Lindsay, Lord McConnell, Jim and Margaret Cuthbert, Jim Fairlie, Lord Wallace, John Fellowes, Jonathan Mitchell QC, Kenny Farquharson, Lord Elis-Thomas, Margaret Henderson, Margo MacDonald MSP, Jim Sillars, Peter Clarke, Stephen Maxwell, Stewart Stevenson MSP, Tam Dalyell, Malcolm Anderson, Malcolm Kerr, Martin Sime, Michael Crick, Peter Bainbridge, Rod Cross, Tom Gallagher, Alistair Hicks, Antoni Chawluk, Julie Davidson, Colin Mackay, Ian Swanson, David Cobham, Desmond Swayne MP, Professor Geoffrey Barrow, Professor James Mitchell, David Cairns MP, Brian Wilson and many others who wished, for obvious reasons, to remain anonymous.

Scotland's excellent archives, meanwhile, proved invaluable, particularly Gordon Wilson's hitherto unexplored run of papers at the National Library of Scotland (NLS), which also preserves several boxes of SNP material, as well as those of prominent Nationalists past and present. The staff at the NLS, particularly Maria Castrillo, as well as those at Edinburgh's splendid Central Library were, as ever, unfailingly helpful. An excellent online archive of articles from the journal *Scottish Affairs* (*www. scottishaffairs.org*) also saved me a lot of time and work, as did Eberhard Bort's comprehensive 'Annals of the Parish' series in the same publication. Thanks to Lilly Hunter and Kirsty Malcolm for providing translations of foreign interviews with Salmond

Thanks also to Hugh Andrew and his long-suffering team at Birlinn, who tolerated the usual deadline extensions and preponderance of words. His production team, particularly Jim Hutcheson, Kenny Redpath and Andrew Simmons, did their usual professional job, while Philip Hillyer was a diligent and sympathetic copy-editor. For help tracing pictures I must thank – among others – the *Scotsman*, Aberdeen Journals, the Royal Bank of Scotland (and in particular Andrew Henderson), Peter Brunskill (for the snaps of Salmond as a student), Gordon Smith (for locating the photograph of Salmond's maternal grandfather), Stewart Stevenson MSP, St Andrews University, Peter Adamson, Andrew Taylor and Colin Pyle.

Finally, I would just like to say that I had fun writing this biography, fun because most of the events described within these pages took place within my lifetime, and fun because my father, to whom this book is dedicated, was often a participant, having joined the SNP during one of Billy Wolfe's recruitment drives in the mid-1960s. He was, for example, present in Ayr when Gordon Wilson threatened to expel Salmond and six others from the party, present again eight years later in Perth when Salmond was elected leader, and in the audience during the 'Great Debate' of 1992. I clearly remember peering at BBC coverage of SNP conferences in the mid-1980s, hoping to spot my Dad among the delegates. I also remember sitting among earnest groups of Nationalists in various campaign rooms around Edinburgh as they pasted posters, bundled leaflets and discussed tactics. My father has often joked over the past year or so that he will probably end up being thrown out of the party as a result of his son's latest biography. For his sake, I hope that does not happen. The SNP would not exist, nor would Alex Salmond be First Minister, if it was not for people like him across the country, dedicated men and women who constitute what they often refer to, a little vaingloriously yet sincerely, as the 'National Movement'.

David Torrance
Edinburgh, August 2010
www.davidtorrance.com

FOREWORD TO THE PAPERBACK EDITION

No biography that describes the career of a politician before his career has, as Enoch Powell put it, ended in failure or been cut off at a happy juncture is ever written at the right moment. By the time the author's observations are published, that career will always have moved on, and the reader's perspective will inevitably have changed. 'In this respect,' observed the historian Norman Davies, 'the work of the contemporary historian is more akin to the shifting assignments of the leader writer than to that of the dispassionate analyst of completed histories.'[1]

Yet although the hardback edition of *Salmond: Against the Odds* (a title, happily, that seems more appropriate the second time around) ended rather abruptly in the autumn of 2010, it was not a bad time to assess the career of a politician just months away from an extraordinary electoral triumph. Re-reading it now, however, this author cannot help but flinch. Mercifully, I did not seek to predict the outcome of May's election, but the final chronological chapter ('It's time') did rather give the impression that its protagonist, as Michael Fry put it to me, was 'running out of steam'. I am grateful that this paperback edition has enabled me to put that right.

It is fair to say that reactions to the first edition were mixed. Although most reviewers reckoned I had been thorough and, on the whole, balanced, others thought it had not really got to the 'heart' of Alex Salmond. Such is a biographer's life. From the man himself I had little feedback beyond a phone call in response to a newspaper story on the suicide of Salmond's paternal grandfather, which of course was in the book. Although his tone was that of a disappointed schoolmaster rather than a bullying politician, in the space of ten minutes the First Minister managed to be both reasonable and unreasonable, charming and mildly threatening. As someone (who knew him well) later remarked to me, that phone call had been a pretty good microcosm of Salmond the man.

Otherwise press coverage focused on details of Salmond's aggressive behaviour towards staff (and, indeed, others). Sensibly, his official spokesman chose not to contradict what I had written, but instead issued a statement that followed the 'groove' of the story. 'Alex is a passionate person, and also an extremely compassionate man, with a great drive and ambition for Scotland,' it read. 'I think people would expect these qualities in their leaders, which is why Alex is such a popular First Minister.'[2] Asked about his temper since, Salmond protested that he was 'more charmer than bully', while stressing the loyalty of those who work for him.[3]

In the first edition of this biography I compared the formation of a minority SNP government in 2007 to Labour's first UK administration, also a minority, in 1924. Both established themselves as competent before gaining an overall majority. The difference, of course, is that it took Labour more than 20 years to make that leap; the SNP managed it in just four. The story of how that was achieved forms the first of two new chapters in this paperback edition; the second – a postscript – looks ahead to the 'independence' referendum.

I have also endeavoured to correct as many mistakes as possible, and thanks must go to everyone who took the trouble to point these out. Any remaining typos or factual errors are, of course, my own. Indeed one correspondent, Kenneth Fraser, was remarkably prescient, concluding his letter to me thus: 'I hope these few notes may be of some use to you if a second edition should ever be called for – which I hope it is, as that would probably be because the SNP had "against the odds" won the 2011 election.'[4]

I know little of Salmond's reaction to the book, although he did tell the journalist James McIntyre that it made him 'seem a bit boring', adding that his autobiography would 'be better'.[5] Although I revealed last year that the First Minister had already begun work on a memoir, it has subsequently emerged that it will in fact be 'ghosted' by the journalist-turned-SNP MSP Joan McAlpine (who performed a similar task for Tommy Sheridan and his 1994 anti-Poll Tax polemic, *A Time to Rage*). This, according to the journalist Paul Hutcheon, will 'focus heavily on Salmond's time in power', while also giving 'a blow-by-blow account, through Salmond's eyes, of the SNP's rise'.[6]

Naturally, I look forward to reading the First Minister's take (or rather someone else's take on his take) on his own career, but until then here is Salmond Redux. Please direct feedback – constructive or otherwise – to the email address below. Who knows, I might even get another phone call.

David Torrance
Edinburgh, September 2011
www.davidtorrance.com
Follow @davidtorrance on twitter

'SCOTLAND WILL FLOURISH'

Let the Scots be a nation proud of their heritage
With an eye to the future and a heart to forgive
And let us be rid of those bigots and fools
Who will not let Scotland live and let live.

Let us govern over country wisely and fairly
Let each man and woman work with a will
And Scotland will flourish secure in the knowledge
That we reap our own harvest and ring our own till[1]

Written for The Corries by Ian Richardson

'I've been involved in tens of campaigns over the last 25 years,' reflected SNP chief executive Peter Murrell a few weeks after the 2011 Holyrood election. '[But in] that time I encountered very few that actually had a clear strategy.' He continued: 'As robust as any military strategy, as carefully thought out and as detailed. A strategy that took five times as long to develop as it did to implement, a strategy that covered every aspect of the "battlefield", every "weapon" at one's disposal, and every eventuality; a strategy that was delivered consistently and in detail to, and through, every participant . . . We had a race plan, we knew our speed, our tactics, how to compete, when to hit the front, when to sprint and most importantly, what victory would look like.[2]

Angus Robertson, the Moray MP who ran the campaign, preferred a golfing comparison. 'The analogy I've been using is that of a social golfer': You work hard on the swing and practise a lot, get a good set of clubs, then get on your favourite course with your favourite tee and the best ball you can get. You then get the biggest driver out of the bag, adopt the perfect stance, breathe perfectly, swing, and hit that ball straighter and harder than you've ever hit it before, and the ball keeps going up and up and up. That's how I've been explaining it.[3]

Robertson's golfing analogy was apt. Not only was Alex Salmond a keen golfer, in the run-up to May 2011 he played the political game straight down the middle. As his father Robert used to tell him, 'play the ball as it lies'.[4] The SNP leader and First Minister did precisely that, never for a moment allowing his opponents' louder applause to distract him from a pre-determined strategy. 'The SNP campaign team,' wrote Ewan Crawford in the *Scotsman*, 'can reflect on the greatest achievement in modern Scottish political history.'[5]

Planning in that respect began the moment the dust settled on the 2010 UK general election. Although the SNP pulled out all the stops in that contest, they were never actually in the game. In a campaign dominated by televised leaders' debates that did not include Alex Salmond, Scotland's party was reduced to carping from the sidelines, including a legal challenge contrived to attract attention. Money was also lacking, donors having recognised – like the SNP – that a Westminster election was not the main prize.

Nevertheless Election 2010 was, as one key player put it, 'a useful planning exercise'.*

A countdown clock went up in SNP HQ, near the Scottish Parliament, and attention quickly switched to candidate vetting and selection for Holyrood constituencies, 'probably the most important single factor', according to a senior campaigner, 'in the party switching its mindset from Westminster to Holyrood'.

Throughout June and July, meanwhile, the party started to do some detailed polling, just as it had done in the same period prior to the 2007 election. Comprising traditional canvassing as well as focus groups, it was probably the most extensive research ever conducted by a political party in Scotland. Also pivotal, as in 2007, was the SNP's bespoke computer database Activate, a record of every voter in Scotland: whom they had supported in 2007, and how they fitted into 44 consumer types identified by postcode, family type, income and age. The SNP reckoned it could win by appealing to around 20 of these demographic groups, and therefore targeted them zealously. At the same time,

---

* If a quote is not referenced in this chapter then it comes from an off-the-record interview.

£100,000 was invested in a 'campaign hub infrastructure', bringing the most up-to-date computer technology into party HQ. Finally, in early October the SNP launched its 'Be Part of Better' survey (also a website, bepartofbetter.net), which reached a million voters via letterboxes and a trio of Sunday newspapers.[6]

This polling, taken together, allowed focus group expert Mark Cuthbert (who had worked for the party for more than a decade) to tell the party what he had discovered about the public's attitude towards the Scottish Government and Alex Salmond as First Minister. It gave a sense of 'where people were' and revealed, for example, that voters generally recognised the SNP's 'team' but not Labour's, while voting intentions changed depending on the question. Asked who they would vote for in an election, the response was generally 'Labour', but asked who they would like to see in government, the response was generally 'the SNP'. These findings were crucial to the electoral messaging that followed, not least the party's emphasis on promoting the Scottish Government not only as a team, but also as incumbents seeking re-election.

'[F]ocus groups and community days had allowed us to get under the skin of voters, understanding their fears and aspirations, their propensity to vote and the clues as to what was needed from any campaign to achieve success,' reflected SNP chief executive Peter Murrell the following year. 'We did not use research to "mark" creative work: we used it to determine tone of voice, messaging and detail. From this research, brilliant creative work could then be developed.'[7] 'In effect,' assessed one newspaper after the election, 'the party tried to extend the positive message of its 2007 election, and turbo-charge it with a record of achievement in government and a first-class team at the helm.'[8]

By August 2010, recalled several of those involved, 'everything was pretty much in place', the research having constituted phase one of the party's 'Six Gears' strategy. Kirk J. Torrance,[*] a South African Scot who had joined the team earlier that year, developed the party's new media strategy, while an advertising team led by marketing guru Ian Dommett of the Cor agency worked on the visual side of the campaign. External advisers were also brought in to deal with photography and copywriting, while the media team was beefed up with figures like Joan McAlpine, a candidate and former deputy editor of the *Herald*, and Andy Collier, formerly of the *Scottish Sun*. Accounts later revealed that between July and December the SNP spent £250,000 on communica-

---

[*] No relation to the author.

tions 'positioning' for the election. To Peter Murrell's evident surprise, 'everything we hoped to do we were able to do' over the following eight months. This, he added in a radio interview, 'was surprising'.9 The SNP had expected something called opposition.

From August onwards, the Cabinet began meeting in two capacities, initially as the executive of the Scottish Government on Tuesday afternoons, and afterwards as a 'political Cabinet' in order to plan for the election. 'Some of the Cabinet hadn't thought about politics with such intensity for some time,' reflected a senior figure, 'so on Tuesday the political Cabinet would meet, then on Thursday we'd have our campaign meeting.' The Thursday meetings took place at party HQ at around 5.15 p.m., just after decision time at Holyrood. Before the Scottish Parliament resumed in September 2010, the Cabinet was also presented with the findings of the research conducted that summer.

'What we needed was a strategy that would last until the election,' recalled a senior Nationalist. 'There was to be some flexibility but it was broadly mapped out at that point.' Indeed, so detailed was that map that for the second Holyrood election in a row the party decided in September what the final poster of the election campaign in early May would be. In 2007, it had been a picture of Alex Salmond and his deputy, Nicola Sturgeon; in 2011, it was a solo image of Salmond with the slogan 'together we can make Scotland better'. The target throughout this process had been the autumn conference – phase two of the campaign strategy. 'That,' recalled one adviser, 'was kick off.'

Unusually, Alex Salmond was absent from conference for the first two days, as he was in New Delhi for the official handover of the 2014 Commonwealth Games to Glasgow. 'That Alex arrived late at conference was an indication of strength,' observed a senior figure, 'that he felt he could leave conference in others' hands.' Instead, the First Minister had pre-recorded a video message, while Nicola Sturgeon handled the big policy speech, announcing that the Council Tax freeze – which SNP research showed was hugely popular with voters – would be extended for another two years.

When Salmond got back to the UK from India, he was tired and jet-lagged. He arrived at conference late on Friday night, so his duties were more or less limited to his big speech the following day. The long flight back had given him an opportunity to revise the speech – mainly the work of Alex Bell, an adviser who had rejoined the SNP team shortly after the general election – more than he might otherwise have done. So while Sturgeon's speech had dealt with policy, Salmond's concentrated on the bigger picture, what his aides called 'the vision thing'.

They saw the first phase of the campaign – from the conference until Christmas – as setting out what the party meant by 'independence'. This might sound strange for a party committed to that goal since 1934, but constitutional issues had always been difficult to communicate to the electorate. 'It was seen as important for us all to translate independence into real life for people,' said one adviser. 'People have to feel they understand it if they're going to vote for it.' Alex Bell was particularly keen on phrases like giving the Scottish Parliament 'job-creating powers' (as opposed to 'tax-raising powers', which gave the impression that the SNP wanted to put up taxes).

This was all part of the wider personalisation of the SNP's communications strategy, while the summer research had also informed how the party ought to 'present' its independence message. Salmond's conference speech would be the first time voters heard the party's election goals, so they had to be loud and clear. Drafting and redrafting, therefore, 'went down to the wire', with special adviser Geoff Aberdein shuttling between the party leader's room at the George Hotel in Perth and the city's Concert Hall with drafts of the speech until about 15 minutes before Salmond was due on stage. 'He was very calm before giving that speech,' recalled one adviser. 'He knew what he wanted to say and how he wanted to say it.' The speech's tone was at times defiant ('as you know, I fight and I do not give up'), at points curiously valedictory, and also very bold: 'I am the First Minister of Scotland, and I intend to continue to be.'[10]

But the last 15 minutes of Salmond's speech were the most important, and included the 'vision' the party's media advisers hoped the press would notice. 'Too often independence is talked about in terms of the "how" or the "what" rather than the "why",' blogged Stephen Noon a few months later. 'And the why is the most important.'[11] Salmond's conference speech admitted that 'perhaps when we have spoken of independence, we have assumed everyone else knew what we meant', before explaining that what he meant was 'jobs – to protect and create them'.

'The Independence I seek is the independence to create jobs,' Salmond told delegates. 'This is not an arcane question removed from the people – it is the people, you and me, and how we protect our society, and grow our economy.'[12]

'The idea of the speech,' explained one adviser, 'was to try and reflect that Scotland needed a serious leader for serious times.' Yet the confident tone of Salmond's conference address masked concern among certain advisers that Labour was still ahead in the polls, although the First Minister did not share in this. 'I think now, looking back,' reflected one key aide, 'there was a sense that he knew something we didn't.'

'There was a frustration,' recalled one adviser, 'we thought we were doing good things, that we were popular, yet the polls refused to budge. There was still a Westminster mindset, and although we didn't believe the wilder polls putting Labour 20 points ahead, there was a feeling that they couldn't all be wrong. We started to think: "What do we have to do to turn this around?" We were throwing the kitchen sink at it, with jobs announcements after the conference – big picture stuff. Yet it had no effect.'

Even so, the SNP's annual conference had achieved its purpose as a slick showcase for the party's campaign launch. 'At the conference we had to make the party feel like it could win,' recalled a figure at HQ, 'demonstrate our message, and prove that we still had the same spark we had in 2007.' Indeed, the upbeat (and slightly ironic) campaign theme – 'Let's Work Together' – was unveiled in Perth,[13] while Salmond closed his address with the optimistic refrain: 'I, we, have the purpose to make this a better land. Join us, be part of this, be part of better.'[14] The slogan launched at that conference was the similar: 'Together we can make Scotland better.'

The key figure in this respect was Stephen Noon, a youthful 40-year-old who was 'enormously influential in looking to ensure the party's campaign remained positive and upbeat'.[15] A Jesuit-educated former Young Conservative, Noon joined the SNP in the wake of the 1992 general election via the pro-devolution umbrella group Scotland United. He first came to Alex Salmond's attention after he and two fellow Edinburgh University students draped the Lion Rampant over the railings in front of the Coronation chair at Westminster Abbey (Noon did not, unlike his friends, chain himself to the railings). Salmond congratulated 'these young Scots on their non-violent action on St Andrew's Day'[16] and, after Noon chained himself to the gates of Downing Street following the 1993 Budget, invited him for a drink in the House of Commons.

Although Noon had left his position as senior policy adviser to the Scottish Government in mid-2010 (replaced by Alex Bell) to do a Masters in European law, he had remained in charge of drafting the SNP's manifesto for the 2011 election. 'There was a real advantage in Stephen having time and space to be thoughtful,' reflected a senior campaign figure, 'so he was very applied. He's the keeper of the light;

keeper of the positive vibe.' Throughout late 2010 Noon oversaw a massive consultation process and personally engaged with more than 100 civic groups.

'One of the most powerful lessons I learnt in the run-up to the 2007 campaign is that positive campaigning will beat negative,' explained Noon in one of his semi-regular blogs. 'This only works when the positive message is strong and consistent: a mixed message, sometimes up, sometimes down, does not work as well.' An analysis of 20th-century US election campaigns also revealed that the most optimistic campaign generally won and, indeed, 'the more optimistic the campaign was, the bigger the eventual majority'. Labour, meanwhile, was accentuating the negative rather than the positive, continually talking of 'the Salmond slump'.[17]

On 30 November 2010, St Andrew's Day, the SNP took out a full-page advert in the popular commuter free sheet *Metro*, which built upon Noon's positive messaging and Alex Bell's desire to articulate the independence message in a more punter-friendly manner. Showing a 2007 portrait of Alex Salmond under the headline 'Forget politics, let's talk about Scotland', the advert declared that 'Scots are crying out for a better society. Not a bit better, not a wee change, not some tinkering at the edges, but a better land full stop. To make real change happen, we need independence.'

The ad, in keeping with another emerging aspect of SNP strategy, also sought to contrast the Scottish Government's approach with that of the new Coalition government in London. 'It has taken a Westminster public spending crisis to make the choice stark', it read, 'between doing something to protect our society, as we advocate, and doing nothing, which is for others.'[18] The 'others' Salmond had in mind were, naturally, Conservatives. On 20 October, Chancellor George Osborne's Comprehensive Spending Review had cut devolved spending by 7 per cent. Prior to that announcement, and at Salmond's instigation, the three leaders of the UK's devolved administrations had dispatched a joint letter to Osborne asking him to think again about the scale of public sector budget cuts. As Salmond explained to *Holyrood* magazine: 'We are the only party with a narrative; we are the only people that can say we can make it better and we have a clear idea of how we can improve our circumstances.'[19]

The tone of the *Metro* advert was also unusually personal, reflecting a conscious decision by SNP advisers to 'humanise' the First Minister. 'All my life I have fought for fairness for this country,' read Salmond's message. 'I govern not for the SNP, but for Scotland. The welfare of the nation, of its five million people, is what guides my actions.'[20] This effort to focus on 'the lighter side of Alex' also manifested itself in a wider communications strategy. Salmond recorded an edition of the popular BBC Radio 4 series *Desert Island Discs*, where he talked about his late mother and wife Moira, while also engaging with the influential online forum Mumsnet, both of which got extensive follow-up media coverage. 'No one had ever doubted his credentials as a politician,' explained one senior Nationalist, 'but what they had doubted was him as a person. We needed to sell him as a good guy. To his credit, he agreed to that, considering he's a very private person.' Indeed, as Michael Portillo noted in his BBC profile of the SNP leader, there remained 'a shiver of discomfort at any mention of Alex Salmond's private life'.[21]

The last few weeks of 2010 were dominated by what Harold Macmillan wearily termed 'events, dear boy, events', but curiously, at no point did a trio of superficially bad political crises look likely to derail Alex Salmond, his party or its carefully prepared election strategy. On the contrary, once the furore inside the Holyrood bubble had subsided, the Nationalists emerged, if anything, in better shape than before (although this was yet to be reflected in the polls).

To an extent this can be explained by the SNP's deliberate 'disassociation'. As one party aide put it, 'stuff happened to the Scottish Government, but it didn't happen to the SNP'. So while ministers were under attack for their handling of the Homecoming event, the lapsed Scottish Variable Rate and, latterly, their response to extreme winter weather, there was a Scottish Government team dealing with that, and another team over at party HQ working on the election campaign. 'There's always this frenzy of activity that happens in Holyrood but the real world goes on,' reflected one senior adviser. 'What's important in Westminster and Holyrood bubble terms isn't really important in terms of how people vote.' Or, as another senior party figure put it: 'None of what happened at the end of last year reached the public.'

Indeed, Labour advisers now concede that given their party's impregnable poll lead, at this point they 'were maybe over-confident'. They were certain of an easy victory in May and, as one (now former) Labour MSP put it to colleagues: 'It's like we're walking across a highly polished ballroom floor carrying a priceless Ming Dynasty vase.' This produced a certain reticence in the Labour ranks, a reluctance to move in for the kill. The prospect of no-confidence votes in certain ministers were constantly raised but never followed through, perhaps because Salmond had made it clear that any such vote would amount to a vote of no confidence in his whole administration. As one Parliamentary staff member recalled: 'Bruce Crawford's private office was on constant alert for something that never happened.'

Even so, dealing with these issues took up a lot of valuable time. 'We were under the cosh at that point,' recalled one aide. 'A First Minister appearing before a Scottish Parliamentary committee [regarding the Homecoming] is always a big deal, and we had to do a lot of preparation for that.' Then came the SNP's winter of discontent. With heavy snow bringing much of Scotland's transport network to a halt, the Transport Minister Stewart Stevenson sealed his fate by praising the authorities' 'first class response' during an interview on *Newsnight Scotland*.[22] Despite a damage-limitation exercise led by the First Minister, within days Stevenson had offered Salmond – a long-standing friend – his resignation, sensing that he had become an unwelcome distraction so close to an election. After a brief period of reconsideration, Salmond reluctantly accepted it, appointing Keith Brown in Stevenson's place. Ironically, what should have marked a low point for the Scottish Government actually had what one aide called 'a reinvigorating effect'. Labour ended up looking a little churlish for having effectively forced Stevenson to resign, while Brown attracted positive press coverage. On 15 December the *Scotsman* splashed with an old photograph of the new Transport Minister as a young marine in the Falklands alongside the headline: 'Minister reveals plans to beat the weather.'[23]

'It kind of refreshed us a little,' admitted one adviser. 'There was no more fire fighting; Stewart's resignation automatically put all the fires out. It got us off the agenda of being the Scottish Government and back to being the SNP.' The First Minister spent Christmas and Hogmanay, as he always did, in the North-East of Scotland. He had invited staff and activists to watch 'The Sleeping Beauty' pantomime at Her Majesty's Theatre in Aberdeen as Christmas approached, but the heavy snow meant the outing had to be delayed until early January. Interviewing him for a relaunched *Sunday Herald* before the curtain went up, the journalist Alan Taylor found Salmond relaxed and optimistic. 'Our team is better than their team and we're not the only ones who believe that,' he said, touching upon what would become one of the election campaign's key themes. 'The people believe that as well.' Salmond was sure the SNP in May 2011 would attract a higher level of public support than the SNP in May 2007. Labour's continued ten-point poll lead, meanwhile, was not by any means 'an unbridgeable gap'.24

If Stewart Stevenson's resignation had drawn a line under the SNP's winter of discontent, there remained concern that the opinion polls had yet to turn in the party's favour, as some key figures expected it would before the Christmas recess. 'When the polls didn't turn, there were lots of voices saying we need to point out the negatives [about Labour],' said one adviser, 'but everything we've ever planned said we didn't need to do that.' Even so, on 9 January *Scotland on Sunday* ran a piece signed by Alex Salmond which repeated his line about the SNP team being superior to Labour's. For the people of Scotland, wrote Salmond, 'the choice is clear – a second rate Labour party, or a second term with a talented, positive SNP team'.25 Even this mild critique made some keepers of the 'positive' flame uneasy.

The *Scotland on Sunday* story coincided with a strategy meeting that had a cathartic effect on Team Salmond, boosting internal confidence and convincing many that all was not yet lost. The venue was the Park Inn Hotel in Aberdeen. 'It was a starting point,' reflected someone who was present. 'The October conference had been a starting point of sorts, but what happened at that meeting was the team as a whole became focused on the election.' Acting as chairman was Claire Howell (née Newall) of the London people-coaching firm Red Co., another key figure invited to reprise her role from the 2007 campaign. Howell's profile on the Red Co. website cited her favourite film as *Mary Poppins*, which conjured up an image of her flying in and out, although helping political parties rather than unhappy children.

At the Aberdeen meeting – attended by Alex Salmond, ministers, party and Scottish Government advisers – she started the discussion by asking how the SNP wanted to do in the election. Those present said 'well' (the expectation at this point was 49–55 seats), so Howell asked 'how well?' Some ventured that it would be good to have an overall majority, so that goal went up on a white board, although it should be noted that the London-based Howell probably did not realise that this was supposed to be an electoral impossibility. 'No one thought it was frankly mathematically possible,' recalled one of those present. 'We had in mind the October 1974 general election and that seemingly insurmountable gap between 33 per cent of the vote and the 45 per cent needed to get an overall majority at Holyrood.'

'It was a goal,' said another of those present. 'Did I expect it to happen? No. Was I going to work towards making it happen? Yes.'26

Beyond this election goal, which was not made explicit outside the party, the two-day Park Inn session framed the parameters of the forthcoming campaign. Team Salmond reflected upon the party's research from the previous summer, as well as focus group findings, and decided to emphasise its 'team, record and vision', although Salmond only crystallised it ('in a moment of clarity') in those terms shortly after the Aberdeen session. 'It reflected the responses people had to us,' said one senior party figure. 'They thought Alex was a good leader, our Cabinet was more recognised, so we went with "team", and while people couldn't give you a list of everything we'd done – they talked about the Council Tax freeze, prescription charges, stuff like that – so "record" it was.' The final component, 'vision', was also firmly in Salmond's mind that weekend, as the thing 'that every election has to be about'. 'Aberdeen created the context,' observed one participant, 'that this was about electing a Scottish Government.'

As several people noted, the normally private Salmond always entered into the spirit of these team-building meetings. 'He really gets involved in things like that, particularly that weekend,' said one. 'He really opened up, when you'd expect him to do the opposite.' The Aberdeen session also relieved some pent-up frustration within the team of Salmond's advisers. 'Working for him [Salmond] is extremely challenging at the best of times,' observed one senior figure, 'so the fact that all the special advisers get along well together is good, it helps us let off steam.' Once formal proceedings were finished (Salmond, or 'The Boss', as some staffers call him, had left early to meet the Chinese vice-premier at Edinburgh Airport), they all hit the town to get, as *Private Eye* would put it, tired and emotional. 'But we came out of that weekend feeling that we were all in this together, it really strengthened the team thing.'

'It was quite significant,' recalled another. 'We came out of that meeting with a real lift.'

After the Aberdeen meeting, the party's chief executive, Peter Murrell, circulated an email with the following three objectives:

1) We are winning the election
2) We are winning it with an overall majority
3) We are winning an independence referendum

'That was the mission statement, if you like,' recalled one recipient. 'I wouldn't say I looked at that [email] and laughed, but me and others looked at it and thought, "Well, ok".'

Beyond an internal bounce, something else to emerge from the Aberdeen meeting was the SNP's cutting-edge new media campaign, masterminded since 2010 by Kirk J. Torrance. Ewan McIntosh, one of the world's leading digital entrepreneurs, had recently been brought in as an external consultant and his major contribution was a candidate presentation before the Aberdeen session, demonstrating social media and how to promote yourself online. This constituted what one senior party figure called 'a Eureka moment'. At Aberdeen, meanwhile, SNP deputy leader Nicola Sturgeon instructed all her ministerial colleagues to 'get tweeting'.

Sturgeon had taken the plunge several months before, her iPad allowing her to respond personally to tweets from thousands of followers, while Mike Russell – a long-standing Facebook user – soon followed suit, and following Aberdeen most of the Cabinet. The SNP, meanwhile, had promoted a free membership offer to students via Twitter and Facebook, refreshed its website to make it the most integrated in the UK and also launched a private iPhone 'app', which brought back-end campaigning power to activists. 'The value of creating online advocates who spread a candidate's messages is priceless,' judged Jennifer Dempsie in an article for *Scotland on Sunday*. 'Those who embrace new communication channels online will reap the rewards.'[27]

Although the official 're-elect Alex Salmond as First Minister' campaign was also launched on Twitter, the man himself was not really part of the social media generation (at the media launch of the Scottish Government Robert Burns app, he confused his iPad with an iPhone). Salmond did use email but only sparingly, his preferred medium remaining face-to-face meetings or the telephone (on occasion he even asked for material to be faxed). When it came to Twitter, therefore, Salmond would occasionally suggest a message without actually typing it himself. Some of the SNP's media advisers feared that social media would simply cause trouble, mindful that 'tweeting' had cost one Labour candidate his career at the 2010 general election. But Twitter did not cause any major difficulties in the run-up to the election, while its pros largely outweighed its cons. It was, explained Ewan McIntosh, 'the brevity machine'. 'Having an onus to present every policy in 140 characters helps an entire team eek out the essence of the point they are trying to make.'[28] Importantly, the SNP had been ahead of the curve in terms of social media – so important in the 'Arab Spring' ongoing since the beginning of 2011.

*   *   *

Also present at the Park Inn Hotel in January had been the SNP's ad men from the Cor agency, formerly Golley Slater, and again figures who had worked on the 2007 campaign. Building on the previous summer's research, they had worked up what would be the first poster of the election, the simple yellow-on-black statement 'A Scottish Government Working for Scotland', which pushed the 're-elect' message.

This – phase three of the election campaign – was launched outside St Giles' Cathedral in Edinburgh on Burns Night, which marked 100 days until polling day. Alex Salmond and Nicola Sturgeon were photographed standing in front of the poster, while later at a press conference they confirmed that the Council Tax would be frozen for another two years, that 1,000 additional police officers would be maintained, and that the NHS budget would be protected. Labour launched its 100-day campaign the same day, promising to tweet the SNP's '100 broken promises', but it demonstrated that all the major parties realised, as Stephen Noon put it in a blog, that the 'reality of modern political campaigning is that the run-up to election day is a slow-burn process'.[29] The campaign theme and overall message had been launched at the party conference in October, while activity on the ground had been increasingly steadily ever since.

From the beginning of 2011 there had been a definite sense that things were slotting into place for the SNP. 'Things did seem to go better,' reflected one adviser. 'There was a feeling from then on [late 2010] that this is going absolutely as well as it could – we're pushing all the right buttons, we're getting him [Salmond] in all the right places at the right times, being photographed with the right people, and making all the right announcements on jobs and investment.' From the beginning of 2011, Salmond also started stressing the 'vision thing', which, judged one aide, served to 'highlight the paucity of vision on the Labour side'. Party activity was, according to another, 'absolutely relentless', mostly driven by Peter Murrell at SNP HQ.

But still the opinion polls showed a significant Labour lead, although key strategists continued to believe this would soon change. 'Labour's lead in the polls is like the house built on sand,' blogged Stephen Noon, predicting that when the 'questions came, the scrutiny increased, [and] the focus changed', it would fall 'with a great crash'.[30] Fall it did in mid-February, when a MORI poll in *The Times* put the SNP in the lead for the first time in more than a year. Salmond got wind of this on his way back from a meeting with David Cameron in London. It had, recalled one adviser, a 'reassuring effect' and provided a 'huge boost to morale'. The commentator Gerry Hassan reckoned it gave the SNP campaign 'a deep sense of purpose and fight, of playing the populist underdog, and choosing to emphasise their refound vision of the potential of Scotland'.[31] The SNP's Activate software, which by this point was assessing the voting intentions of more than 1,000 Scots a week, also told the party that polls were not reflecting its true level of support.

Not only did Scottish Labour voters not recognise Iain Gray, but SNP canvassing suggested that they did not like Ed Miliband, the relatively new UK Labour leader. This issue of leadership was considered to be extremely important, the SNP believing that as soon as the debate became about who was going to be the next First Minister, then the polls would shift accordingly. At around this time, Team Salmond were also pulling out all the stops in terms of good news stories – usually involving new jobs – taking care to associate the most high-profile directly with Alex Salmond, who was ever keen on generating and maintaining political momentum. 'Alex's interest is in the rolling story within the Scottish Parliament, within the party, and within the media,' observed one senior Nationalist. 'It's all about where we're going next.'

Immediately after the MORI poll, the SNP, at considerable cost, decided to commission ICM – a pollster the party generally considered accurate – to conduct a poll ahead of its spring conference. When ICM delivered its findings in early March, it still showed the SNP trailing Labour by around five points, something that concerned senior strategists – and, for once, Alex Salmond – given its proximity to the dissolution of Holyrood. 'We took that [poll] as an accurate indication of where people were at that point,' recalled one aide. 'So I was concerned that by that stage we hadn't done enough.' Another was even gloomier: 'I remember thinking, what else can we do as a team? We've had all this good news. So at that point I just didn't think we could win this, and the announcement locker was almost bare.'

For obvious reasons, the SNP did not draw attention to this poll as it gathered for its spring conference – phase four of the campaign – on 11–12 March, although there was a general feeling that things were 'on the up' for the party. In the middle of the previous month the Stagecoach co-founder Brian Souter had donated £500,000 to the campaign ('I believe Alex deserves another kick of the ball'),[32] while at conference there were two high-profile endorsements, from the artist Jack Vettriano and the daughter of the late Jimmy Reid. The party election broadcast, unveiled that weekend, provided another boost. 'In my view it is the best party political broadcast we have produced,' gushed Stephen Noon on his blog, 'certainly in my memory.'[33] The concept emerged from a discussion including Noon and Jennifer Dempsie, both big Monty Python fans, one of whom suggested using the 'what have the Romans ever done for us' sketch from *Life of Brian* as a basis for the broadcast. The SNP's advertising consultants liked the idea and developed it into a memorable film with the theme, 'what has the Scottish Government ever done for us?' Cleverly, it used real people (played by actors) rather than politicians to convey the achievements of the SNP over the previous four years.

Alex Salmond's conference address, meanwhile, did both policy – the Christie Commission on the future of public services in Scotland, the 'social contract' and the living wage – and vision. 'The Scottish National Party speak for all of Scotland,' he declared, becoming almost messianic as the speech drew to a close:

> This movement, this nation, has been patronised, talked down, told it wasn't good enough. And yet this party has risen from a few MPs and a land without a Parliament, to a Scotland with a Parliament, and an SNP government. We never lost the strength of hope – and we fought on to triumph. But we, in our mix of the national and the international, of the personal and the political, we fought not to govern over people, but for the people to govern over themselves. It is for that reason and that reason above all that we are the Friends of the People of Scotland and for that reason we shall prevail.[34]

Indeed, Salmond remained 'serenely and supremely confident' that the election would be won, in spite of the ICM poll. 'I remember Alex having meetings with civil servants and him talking matter-of-factly about stuff happening in June, July and August,' recalled one adviser. 'It was either the biggest act in the world or there wasn't a scintilla of doubt in his mind that he would still be First Minister on May the 5th.'

But Salmond was frustrated, as were many of his advisers, that the polls had not yet moved into line with the SNP's private polling; he simply understood that, as leader of a team, he needed to appear utterly confident. 'We were in campaign mode,' remembered an aide, 'and allowing doubts to creep in would have been disastrous.' Launching the SNP's election campaign at Edinburgh's Dynamic Earth on 22 March,

Salmond said the party was now in 'touching distance' of the 40 per cent of the vote it needed to win the election.[35]

Stephen Noon had submitted the first draft of the SNP's manifesto to Nicola Sturgeon at the end of February. Its structure was based on a corporate annual report, with a statement from the chairman (or leader), chief executive, statement of accounts and then a detailed look at each part of the business (or policy area). 'It was about emphasising team-work and a professional approach,' said somebody involved in its preparation, 'the people in charge, their performance, then a bit about all of them.' Amusingly, it had been the 2010 Wiseman Dairy corporate report that had originally caught Noon's eye.

Although the final draft could not have been described as policy-heavy, the 2011 SNP manifesto basically consolidated existing policies while extending others. The Council Tax freeze, already pledged to continue for another two years, was extended to the whole of the next Holyrood term, while the party reiterated its intention to keep university education free of charge for Scottish students. On both these points, Labour was left exposed. Some SNP policy advisers were bemused that their main opponents had not done more to put a clear dividing line between them and the Scottish Government, perhaps by arguing that the freeze and free tuition were unrealistic and counter-productive (polls, for example, indicated public support for some sort of graduate contribution). It came down to, as one Labour adviser put it, 'a failure of nerve'. 'The feeling was that we had to match them, so we didn't have a clear dividing line during the campaign.' As a Labour candidate later told the *Sunday Herald*, the Council Tax policy was 'symbolic of Iain's short-termism'. 'Instead of having a policy of his own that was rooted in Labour values, developed over time, he opted for a last-minute fudge.'[36]

Just as Alex Salmond's October conference speech attempted to link independence to people's lives, the party tried to do the same with individual policy areas. As the First Minister put it shortly after the election:

> You could have a public sector worker just now, let's say in Dunfermline, commuting to Edinburgh, who's on a wage freeze, therefore times are tough, times are difficult, but on the other hand he or she won't pay bridge tolls to get into work, if they have children they won't have to worry about tuition fees, which might prevent them from going to university, their Council Tax is frozen and will continue to be frozen, if they were paying prescription charges, let's say for a chronic condition, then they won't have to worry about that any more.[37]

It was all about, in crude terms, 'what's in it for me'. 'The reality of a modern political campaign is that most voters do not engage with every aspect of a party's policy pitch,' explained Stephen Noon in his blog, 'but they do pick up on those issues which mean something tangible to them.'38

Salmond, meanwhile, remained absolutely driven until the dissolution of the Scottish Parliament on 23 March. The day before, it was announced that the First Minister had secured R&D commitments from three major wind turbine manufacturers, Mitsubishi, Gamesa and Doosan. 'You think these companies would commit if they didn't believe Scotland is the world leader in these technologies?' Salmond asked an interviewer from *The Big Issue Scotland*. 'They don't think we're playing about, they think we're absolutely committed. It [the 100 per cent target] can be met.'39 Beyond independence, energy had always been Salmond's major policy interest. 'From the moment he was elected First Minister, there's been 100 per cent commitment; he's still very driven by energy,' reflected an aide. 'He's always very hard working and never takes anything for granted.'

Nothing, that is, except the election result. On that front, SNP canvassers began to find that voters' minds were finally moving out of 'Westminster mode', while a subtle question, 'do you think any of the other parties could have done a better job than the SNP since 2007?', established that more than 90 per cent of those asked (cutting across party lines) thought not. In answering this question, blogged Stephen Noon, 'it was as though a light had been switched on' for a lot of voters who had hitherto not thought of letting this positive perception of the SNP's record influence their voting intention.40

There were also, although Labour did exaggerate these, genuine 'broken promises', not least on class sizes, local income tax, an independence referendum and writing off student debt. But Labour failed to capitalise on these, no matter how hard they tried. Only in terms of leadership was everyone of one opinion: Alex Salmond had been on top form as First Minister, rarely putting a foot wrong despite being in government for the first time. Stephen Noon could not help thinking of a memorable Hilary Clinton ad in the United States, when the phone rings in the President's bedroom at 3 a.m., a new crisis having emerged: so who would you want to answer it? 'The answer for the past four years in Scotland, it seems, is a resounding one,' judged Noon. 'Alex Salmond. And, for the next four years? Well, of course, that is for the voters to decide on 5th May.'41 For nearly the past year, the SNP had operated parallel teams, one dealing with the business of government led by the youthful Kevin Pringle ('a calm figure at the heart of the storm, and an expert in damping down stories without antagonising or picking fights with journalists'[42]), and another led by Peter Murrell, whose staff were not involved at Holyrood and were completely focused on the campaign. At this point, the dissolution of Holyrood, the two 'came together like a dream'. A 24/7 war room was set up at party HQ with an 'electronic wall' displaying different constituencies, showing what level local support was at, which seat needed a visit, an extra leaflet and so on (Salmond took a close interest in this), while the remaining special advisers, including Pringle, quit their government posts and joined the party campaign.

Angus Robertson, meanwhile, continued to chair regular campaign meetings, which became more frequent as the campaign progressed. The Thursday meetings were, recalled one of those involved, 'nuts and bolts affairs', while those on Sundays dealt with the political dynamic. Both were generally held at HQ in Edinburgh, with some – for example, the party's vice-convener for organisation, Willie Sanquhar – joining in by telephone. Although not initially a member of the campaign team, Marco Biagi, a trained statistician, was frequently called in to meetings to update Salmond on recent polls. Mark Cuthbert, meanwhile, continued to try out the SNP's key messages on focus groups, checking that what he had gleaned from the previous summer's research remained pertinent. Many people noticed that Salmond was visibly more relaxed during this process, although more directly involved than in 2007. 'He'd done it before,' said one, 'and there was less on the line.'

'We were in a much different position in 2011,' recalled another. 'We had the space to do things in a much more rigorous and planned way.'

Early in the campaign there was a council by-election in Wick, in which the SNP gained a seat from an independent with more than 45 per cent of the vote, an increase of 28.6 per cent. Sensing that 'something big' might be happening in the Highlands, if not nationally, Angus Robertson arranged for Salmond to visit the constituency, and indeed during the six-week campaign the First Minister generally visited seats if local intelligence or Activate indicated that it might be winnable. In this respect there were two distinct campaigns, one focusing on possible wins from Labour, and the other concentrating on likely gains from the Liberal Democrats, whose supporters were, according to the 2010 research, ripe for the taking. The Wick by-election fitted into the latter category, while North-East Fife also emerged as a likely gain, prompting another Salmond visit. 'The aim was to make enough progress in seats to open up a gap,' recalled a key figure in the campaign. 'In those seats we had a stronger media and logistical focus – we had to take advantage of the opportunity that was there.' A special advert even appeared in the Aberdeen *Press and Journal*: 'If You're A Liberal Democrat Here's Why You Should Vote SNP.' An added bonus came from the endorsement by outgoing Liberal Democrat MSP John Farquhar Munro of Alex Salmond as First Minister.

Third-party endorsements – although of the non-politician variety – were a key element of the long campaign, another idea that had emerged from the Aberdeen meeting in January. Party strategists saw them as psychologically important in offering voters a lead, while 'legitimising' a shift in allegiance, all the more potent when those doing the leading, such as former steel-worker Tommy Brennan and the hitherto Labour-supporting actor Brian Cox, were casting off old political ties. Others were counter-intuitive, for example that of the arch-Unionist businessman Sir David Murray (cultivated since 2007 by Salmond), while each endorsement would back a key SNP achievement, pledge or minister, underpinning the 'team, record, vision' triumvirate in the process. Jennifer Dempsie worked on the celebrity endorsements while another staffer, Jennifer Erickson, handled the business side. The party actually ran out of time to pitch them all before polling day, but they were useful during such a long campaign, maintaining a sense of momentum from the spring conference until 5 May.

The SNP's cutting-edge social media campaign was also launched at the spring conference. Led by Kirk J. Torrance, his links to IT professionals involved in Obama's 2008 presidential campaign hit upon NationBuilder, a computer package – costing just £3,000 – that allowed the party to integrate Facebook and Twitter within a new snp.org party platform. This was launched as a concept 90 days before the election, and allowed Torrance's small but dedicated team to identify every social media user who typed 'SNP' into Twitter, or mentioned an SNP candidate or policy. Activists then interacted with them, reeling in potential supporters. 'The internet is like the wild Scottish Highlands of yesteryear,' explained Torrance. 'There are no roads, but you know where you're going; you know where your village or croft is (the website you want to visit), but it's wild and untamed.' What the SNP did amounted to providing new infrastructure to where people live online, 'in order to transport goods, information and services'. The aim was to create the impression that 'the SNP are everywhere', 'because in many areas you can't even put up lamp-post posters any more, so in some parts of the country they didn't even realise there was an election on. Our digital channels reflected and then reinforced the real world sense that something was happening in Scotland with the momentum behind the SNP.'[43] Once someone clicked on an SNP-related link, they were awarded 'political capital', enabling Torrance and his team to discover individuals who were not SNP members but were enthusiastic and good at distributing information.

Although Torrance was careful not to make wild claims about how effective all this was (it was, he said, 'not a magic bullet'[44]), the initial statistics spoke for themselves. When it launched in March, the SNP's new website had 13,031 users (around the same as the SNP's membership), but it soon grew to 35,879 users via social media accounts; during March and April the SNP's Facebook site had 2.2 million hits, while party membership also increased by a couple of thousand. Every morning of the campaign, Torrance and Ewan McIntosh would meet with Peter Murrell, Kevin Pringle and Liz Lloyd, the SNP's press manager, to come up with ideas. More than a hundred of these were put into action. The politicians, wrote McIntosh later, 'gave us permission to go with what our guts, and our data, told us felt right to do. "If you ever need anything" was the most common phrase I heard, which, as an external consultant, is a gift.'[45]

By general agreement, the first two weeks of the election campaign were pretty unremarkable. All that changed, however, when on 3 April the *Sunday Times* carried a dramatic poll that showed the SNP taking the lead for the first time. When two further polls turned this into a trend, an initially lacklustre campaign moved up a notch. To an understandably 'excited' Alex Salmond and his campaign team, this long-anticipated turnaround was a terrific boost to morale, although the campaign – planned in broad terms the previous August – continued as intended. 'We did nothing differently after they [the polls] switched,' reflected one strategist. 'We simply carried on.' Always confident of victory, Salmond said he was surprised by 'only the speed' of the sudden swing in the polls.[46] At around this time, the SNP's internal polling also indicated that an overall majority looked possible. 'In tight circles it was talked about, but in an improbable way,' recalled one aide. Winning a majority of seats had, since January, been the party's campaign 'goal', but no one really believed it was possible.

The fifth phase of the campaign – at which point activity dramatically accelerated – was marked by the manifesto launch in mid-April, deliberately a week later than the other parties to avoid any risk of further 'triangulation'. A few weeks before Peter Murrell had taken his press advisers aside and sketched a picture of Alex Salmond at a podium in front of a massive sign saying 'Re-Elect'. This formed the basis of a slick manifesto launch at the Royal Scottish Academy of Music and Drama in Glasgow. The large screen was borrowed from the SNP's conference set, and was deliberately designed to ensure, as Murrell later put it, 'that even the *Daily Telegraph* spread the word!'[47] 'Re-elect', which along with January's poster, did not explicitly mention the SNP, was also emblazoned upon the manifesto's cover.

The first part of the long and short campaigns had focused on 'team' and 'record', but with the manifesto launch it moved more firmly on to 'team' and 'vision'. The manifesto's design, as Stephen Noon wrote on his blog, contained features that had 'never appeared before in any Scottish or UK manifesto'.[48] Indeed, it resembled a copy of *Hello!* magazine, with its glossy pictures of ministers' families and weddings (including that of Peter Murrell and Nicola Sturgeon the previous year). Conscious that few voters would actually read the 39,000-word document, Noon, together with the press team, created mini-manifestos, each one no more than 400 words, and carefully crafted to reach 14 different sections of the electorate, including carers, small businesses and students. Labour's manifesto launch the week before, by contrast, had been marred by a fire alarm and elementary spelling mistakes. Labour's manifesto began with the words, 'Now that the Tories are back . . .'[49] and indeed much of their campaign was contrived with the UK political context in mind.

It had been quite a week for the SNP, beginning with John Farquhar Munro's endorsement of Salmond, and continuing with Scottish Labour leader Iain Gray's unfortunate confrontation with anti-cuts protestors at Glasgow's Central Station. 'You couldn't plan for things like that,' said one SNP media adviser. 'It was an added bonus.' Crowning it all was an appearance by Salmond on the BBC's popular current affairs debate programme *Question Time*. The First Minister headed to Liverpool to record this immediately after the manifesto launch, and it struck many members of Team Salmond as a key moment in the campaign. 'The preparation we did for that was incredible,' recalled one aide. 'He was just in a zone.' Curiously, there had been a discussion about whether Salmond should participate at all, but given the programme's large audience and its timing, it was considered too important an opportunity to miss. Initially, the audience was lukewarm, but by the end Salmond had them eating out of his hand, particularly his warning not to let English politicians destroy 'their' NHS. 'We knew health would come up, and the point we wanted to make was not that we do things so much better in Scotland, but to make the contrast,' recalled an adviser. 'But that was the key moment – he spoke to them as if they were Scottish voters.' *Question Time* provided a neat counterpoint for the election campaign thus far, the contrast between a confident, authoritative Salmond, and a weak Labour leader, reduced to running away from protestors at Central Station.

Media support, compared with 2007, was of substantial help to the SNP campaign. Most significant was the support of the *Scottish Sun* and the *News of the World*, both staples of the Murdoch media empire (with which, by coincidence, the SNP shared its HQ building in Edinburgh). The *Sun*'s support was probably secured when Alex Salmond met James Murdoch, chairman of News International, in London in early January. The meeting, subsequently played down by the First Minister's official spokesman as 'no big deal', was ostensibly to 'discuss jobs and business opportunities in Scotland',[50] but it seems unlikely the forthcoming election did not also figure. Indeed, when Salmond agreed to publish all his correspondence with News International in August 2011, it revealed an at times obsequious four-year charm offensive. Asked during the campaign if it did not concern him that *News of the World* executives might be facing criminal charges, Salmond replied obliquely: 'I think we should let the courts decide who's broken the law or not.'[51] But that was to come later. During the campaign itself there were two memorable *Sun* headlines, 'Play it again, Salm'[52], announcing the newspaper's support, and, on polling day, 'Keep Salm and Carry On'.[53]

The sixth phase of the campaign saw the SNP go full throttle on the 'both votes' message to maximise list, as well as constituency, seats. This message was repeated online, on leaflets and in the national press in a campaign 'designed to reach out to every single household in Scotland'. 'My view is that the SNP will be doing more over these final few days,' blogged Stephen Noon, 'than all the other political parties in Scotland put together.'[54] One leaflet was dispatched to an astonishing 1.9 million households containing swing voters, particularly Liberal Democrats, as identified by Activate. A key theme was the SNP's determination to build a 'fairer Scotland', which focus group research suggested had resonated strongly with people voting Liberal Democrat at the 2010 general election. The SNP repeatedly stressed competency and incumbency. 'If people were generally satisfied – not ecstatic – then the key issue was to create that sense of continuity,' said one strategist. 'What gave us comfort was that at no stage did Labour communicate a message that we were so bad that voters had to get rid of us.'

Initially, Labour did not even raise the independence issue, preferring to concentrate on the bigger UK picture. The SNP's referendum policy also acted as a convenient device to close it down during the election, although the proposed referendum date seemed to get further away as the campaign progressed. Interviewed on STV's online *Face to Face* series on 21 April, Salmond argued he had made a mistake four years previously by setting out a timescale. Yet by the end of the campaign he had U-turned, pronouncing that a referendum would not come until the second half of the new Parliamentary term. Then, for a profile in the *Sunday Times*, someone briefed Gillian Bowditch to the effect that it would actually be 'well into the second half of the five-year term', signaling that Salmond's constitutional priority upon re-election would be giving the Scotland Bill 'economic teeth'.[55]

Indeed, another key moment in the campaign came as Labour relaunched its campaign with less than two weeks to go until polling day, warning voters that backing the SNP meant electing a government that would then contrive everything it did with an independence referendum in mind. While Iain Gray would wake up every morning thinking about how to fight for jobs, the argument ran, Salmond would wake up and think about breaking up Britain. But this message was too subtle, and also much too late. As one SNP adviser observed: 'Labour began the campaign fighting a Westminster election and ended it fighting a referendum campaign. We, however, fought a Scottish election campaign.' Not only that, but Labour's change of tone smacked of panic. 'It was only when Labour changed tack in those last two weeks that I knew we'd won,' recalled one SNP aide. 'It was as if they were admitting their campaign was wrong.' As one Labour candidate told the *Sunday Herald* in the penultimate week of the campaign, the party's only hope of winning was if the SNP leader 'disgraced himself in a public toilet'.[56]

Team Salmond were persistently surprised by the lacklustre nature of the Labour campaign. Stephen Noon, for example, did not hesitate in spelling out the SNP's strategy on his blog because he was sure Labour would not take any notice of his 'good advice'.[57] 'We knew what they were going to say; we knew the game they were going to play,' recalled one SNP adviser. 'The quality of their stuff didn't change, it was almost by-election standard.'

'I'm not convinced that the opposition was useless as such, it was just the same,' said another. 'We'd seen it all before; we knew that confronted with "x" that we would say "y".' A senior Nationalist said simply: 'We weren't challenged as an election campaign, we just weren't challenged.'

Labour sources blame Scottish Labour HQ at John Smith House, which believed it 'had a successful blueprint for fighting an election'. 'They wanted to skirt around Alex Salmond,' said one. 'Overall we were organisationally prepared, but politically under-prepared. Our focus groups were embarrassingly small compared with the Nats.' Giving his assessment, Salmond momentarily ignored Stephen Noon's positivity doctrine. Labour, he told a journalist, were a 'two-dimensional party for a 3D age . . . They're out of date.'[58]

The contrast between Salmond and Gray was also played out in three televised leaders' debates, two on STV and the other on BBC Scotland. Although these did not dominate in the manner of the 2010 general election, SNP advisers felt they were useful in reminding voters that they rated Salmond as more 'competent' than his main opponent. 'The words, what Alex said,' observed one aide, 'were not as important as how he came across, which was calm and confident.' This was the initial impression following the first debate on STV, and it was maintained thereafter. One point against Salmond's appearance was his weight, his usual election diet having proved less than successful. He claimed to have 'lost some weight since using a cross trainer',[59] but otherwise he yielded 'too easily to temptation'.[60] Helping Salmond prepare for television appearances was Joan McAlpine, as well as Geoff Aberdein, a talented amateur footballer and favoured golfing partner of the SNP leader, who looked after the diary. The most important figure in the campaign, however, was chief executive Peter Murrell. 'He's quiet, hard to gauge at first, even,' judged Ewan McIntosh, 'but is the smartest mind in political campaign management in the UK, quite possibly in Europe.'[61] Murrell's meticulous planning had begun as soon as the 2007 election ended, while the campaign proper had been organised to the nth degree right across the whole country.

In the last week of the campaign, the prospect of an overall majority was discussed again. Although an STV/TNS poll conducted for the final televised leaders' debate had shown the SNP within touching distance of this, most commentators dismissed it as a rogue poll. Strategists, however, took it seriously, not least because it was much closer to where internal polling suggested public support was. The tracker at party HQ had passed the critical 40 per cent mark by Christmas, and a fortnight before polling it had reached 46 per cent. Then, with less than a week to go, Activate revealed that Labour support was haemorrhaging, intelligence that directed Salmond to Labour seats in Glasgow, the Central Belt, Edinburgh and Aberdeen in the last few days of the campaign. A YouGov survey later disclosed that as many as 80,000 voters switched from Labour to the SNP in the last few days. Mark Shaw, one of the SNP's resident number crunchers, started telling colleagues that it meant the party was set to win a lot more seats than previously thought.

If the SNP's formidable campaigning machine resembled a well-rehearsed orchestra, then Salmond was its star conductor. There were, of course, a few discordant notes, but these were more than compensated for by the sheer vigour of the overall performance. No longer could the SNP leader be accused of being a 'one-man band'. 'I am not saying we have a whole orchestra,' he explained, but 'we certainly have a very good front row and a bit more besides'. Indeed, since his student days Salmond had always had a knack for surrounding himself with talented individuals. 'While I undoubtedly have my faults and foibles,' he admitted in a rare moment of humility, 'I have never found it difficult to get people to work together.'62

There was, as in 2007, an element of luck, but then luck was not to be dismissed in the endless adventure of governing men. Salmond was lucky in his opponents, and lucky in the context of UK politics, from the veritable gift of George Osborne's 'tax raid' on North Sea oil to the psephological likelihood that the votes of increasingly toxic Liberal Democrats would play a large part in determining the result. On Allied action in Libya, the SNP leader adopted a 'safety first' strategy; there was to be no echo of the 'unpardonable folly' from the 1999 election.

On his only campaign visit to Scotland, the Prime Minister accused the First Minister of behaving like 'El Presidente Salmondo' and treating the Holyrood race like a presidential election,63 but only occasionally did hubris creep into Salmond's public pronouncements. 'All of Scotland', he informed the *Daily Telegraph* towards the end of April, 'is backing the SNP now.'64

Wednesday, 4 May, the day before polling, was the first time Alex Salmond and others got an inkling that not only were things looking very good, but that an overall majority might just be possible. Planned for that day was Salmond's final helicopter tour, moving from marginal seat to marginal seat in Saltire One with a view to 'maxing out' every possible vote. The SNP's Activate software, as ever, guided the itinerary, which took in Edinburgh, Glasgow, Clydesdale, Kilmarnock and, at the last minute, East Lothian. 'On the basis of Alex going to all these places,' recalled an aide, 'he believed that an overall majority was possible.' Indeed, most of the seats Salmond visited that day went to the SNP, while even cautious estimates put the SNP's likely tally of seats in the mid-to-late 50s.

On polling day itself, Salmond's first appearance of the day was at the St Andrews Church polling station in Inverurie, and by just after 10 a.m. he was on the road, blaring out his recorded message, urging constituents to vote SNP, accompanied by the campaign tune 'Let's Stick Together'. Unlike in 2007, only one journalist, the *Scottish Sun*'s Matt Bendoris (together with photographer Andy Barr), was with Salmond that day. Bendoris recorded his reaction to a newspaper claiming the SNP leader had already written his victory speech: 'No I bloody haven't,' snapped Salmond. 'Not even I would be that cocky.' The speech, of course, had been prepared.

At around noon information started coming in from Clydesdale, where the SNP had arranged exit polling. 'We knew from that it was looking good,' recalled an aide. 'We knew even then we were well ahead.' Salmond, as usual, remained in his constituency, only leaving at around 5 p.m. to help out Kevin Stewart, an SNP candidate in Aberdeen. The First Minister was still going more than two hours later. 'I only get six hours of sleep at night and never go to bed before 2 a.m.,' he explained to the *Scottish Sun*. 'It's all I need.' Matt Bendoris also captured something of Salmond's relationship with his wife of nearly 30 years when Moira called asking what he was bringing home to Strichen for dinner. 'Would you like a fish supper or how about lasagna?' recounted Salmond, before sighing: 'You can't imagine Barack Obama having the same dilemma on election day.'[65]

Down at SNP HQ in Edinburgh an electronic clock installed the previous year was counting down to '0'. Shortly before it did, there had been two conference calls for MSPs or MPs doing radio or television to agree their approach. Angus Robertson, the campaign chairman, reminded everyone that the SNP had never managed to get more than 33 per cent of the vote in an election. Come 10 p.m., however, Robertson started making some phone calls and reading Post-It notes people were handing to him, while he kept a minute-by-minute diary of what was happening on his iPad. 'It was obviously clear that something big was happening,' he recalled, 'something very big.'[66] When two Labour frontbenchers in Hamilton (a constituency of symbolic importance to the SNP) and East Kilbride lost their seats to the SNP, something 'big' did indeed begin to take shape. At around 2.30 a.m. Robertson had to drive to Glasgow to do his share of election night television, while a message went out not to say, on any account, that the party believed it was heading for an overall majority.

By this point, Salmond had been in a suite at the Holiday Inn near the Aberdeen Exhibition & Conference Centre (AECC) for several hours, along with Moira, Geoff Aberdein, Alexander Anderson (a long-serving member of Salmond's constituency staff), local party workers and Kirk J. Torrance, who made a series of high-definition stills and films of the gathering for the 'historical record'. There, Salmond had visibly relaxed as he digested initial swings. Still not knowing how good the overall result would be, aides delayed the timing of Salmond's arrival at the AECC several times. Ever the showman, the SNP leader also ordered a media blackout ('you've got to keep them wanting more'), having previously planned to do some media interviews before his own declaration. Conscious that he had to set the agenda on the night, the agenda started setting itself. 'Initially we had regular phone calls from Peter Murrell, but they quickly became pointless because we knew what was happening,' recalled one staffer. 'Alex was obviously excited, he kept saying, "Yes, yes!" We basically had to try and calm him down.'

At 3.53 a.m., Salmond finally arrived at the count amid a scrum of cameras, forcing BBC Scotland to quickly wrap up a live interview with Scottish Labour leader Iain Gray ('Coincidence?' wondered the *Scottish Sun*[67]). Surrounded by reporters, Salmond – never normally short of something to say – struggled to adhere to his decision not to give any interviews. 'Are you surprised?' asked Sky News' James Matthews. 'People [are] talking about it being historic.' Salmond patted him on the back and replied: 'Well, it seems pretty reasonable, doesn't it?' Matthews tried again, asking once more if he was surprised. 'Well, people seem quite cheerful about it, don't they?' Meanwhile Salmond walked hand in hand with Moira, smiling quietly without looking at each other. 'Ten more yards,' instructed Geoff Aberdein, meaning to say feet, 'then to the left.'[68] Kirk J. Torrance followed behind with a digital camera, filming what everyone else was filming.

On the counting floor Salmond embraced, with big bear hugs, long-standing party workers, some of whom had campaigned for him since he first stood in Banff and Buchan back in 1987. Lingering behind the podium before his declaration, the SNP leader chatted with aides. 'He was clearly excited about it, but was also incredibly calm,' recalled one. 'He'd been awake right through but while everyone was tired he was just getting sharper and more energetic.' At 4.16 a.m., Salmond was re-elected with a massive majority, his eighth successive election win in the North-East of Scotland:

Alex Salmond (SNP)	19,533
Alison McInnes (Liberal Democrat)	4,238
Geordie Burnett Stuart (Conservative)	4,211
Peter Smyth (Labour)	2,304

With a majority of 15,295 votes in the new Holyrood constituency of Aberdeenshire East, Salmond's result was one of the most decisive in Scotland at nearly 65 per cent of the vote. In his victory speech he thanked Moira and, with obvious affection, his veteran election agent Stuart Pratt, who had 'guided me, and I think that's the right word, through eight elections in the North-East of Scotland . . . it's time he got the credit for these election campaigns'. Scotland, continued Salmond, had 'outgrown negative campaigning', while the SNP, alluding to an old name for the party, could 'finally claim that we have lived up to that accolade as the National Party of Scotland'. He then linked his over-whelming mandate to extending Holyrood's powers: 'Which is why in this term of the Parliament we will bring forward a referendum, and trust the people with Scotland's own constitutional future.'[69]

The plan had been for Salmond to make his victory speech and then leave the hall, in order to keep up 'momentum' and, of course, leave the Scottish press corps hungry for more. But such was the scale of the SNP's likely victory that Salmond decided to stay put until the rest of the constituency seats in the North-East had declared. 'This is a spec-tacular result for the SNP,' he told a reporter shortly after his declaration. 'It's likely that the SNP has been restored in a way that no other party has been before in Scottish elections.'[70]

Not only was Salmond's personal victory in Aberdeenshire East impressive, but so too was that of his friend Stewart Stevenson in Banff-shire and Buchan Coast, who despite his winter of discontent achieved the highest share of the vote in Scotland (67.24 per cent). Most emotional was the election of Dennis Robertson, Scotland's first blind MSP, who dedicated his victory in Aberdeenshire West to his teenage daughter Caroline, who had died of anorexia. Salmond was in tears as he and party activists surrounded Robertson as he left the stage. At 6.45

a.m. Kevin Stewart's victory made it a clean sweep for the SNP in the region. Salmond watched some of the results from the media platform, his head jerking gently from side to side as those deep black eyes took in the results.

An hour and a half after winning his seat, Salmond was still giving a string of interviews, as the *Scottish Sun* observed, 'with no hint of running out of steam'.[71] After a lot of persuasion from reporter Claire Stewart, Geoff Aberdein agreed to bring Salmond to STV's camera first, recognition that the commercial broadcaster had 'had a good campaign'. Having miked him up, Stewart told the SNP leader they were about to come to him for a live interview. 'You'd better,' he responded, letting a little of his well-known arrogance slip through, 'hundreds of people want to speak to me tonight.' Asked about the result, Salmond explained that his party had 'polished down the campaign from 2007 . . . after that the Labour votes just started to melt like snow off a dyke'. Anchor Bernard Ponsonby also reminded him about STV's poll the week before, recounting that he had told newsroom colleagues he would 'eat his hat' if the SNP got as many as 59 seats. 'Will I be eating hats in the morning?' he asked Salmond. 'Depends what size your hat is, Bernard,' he replied. 'You could be in severe danger of indigestion.'[72]

Asked by another journalist about Labour's losses, Salmond momentarily went off message, forgetting Stephen Noon's dictum to remain positive at all times. 'This idea that Labour had ownership over parts of Scotland, well that's gone forever, hasn't it?' he said. 'I suppose it's a bit like the American bison – I mean, I dare say we'll still see one or two dotted about here and there, but the great herds of Labour have gone forever.'

'Scotland,' added Salmond for good measure, 'has now outgrown the Labour Party.'[73]

Although this was an overstatement, one accepted rule of Scottish politics had indeed perished that night – no longer did Labour automatically benefit in Scotland from Conservative rule at Westminster. Amid dramatic scenes in Haddington's Corn Exchange, Scottish Labour leader Iain Gray learned that he had retained his constituency seat by just 151 votes.

At 6.02 a.m. a 'very gracious' Gray called Salmond on his mobile to congratulate him on an historic win. Indeed, the scale of that result clearly came as a shock even to the SNP leader, who admitted to the *Scottish Sun* that he was 'finding it difficult to catch up with the amazing movements towards the SNP'.[74] His audible disbelief was almost broadcast by the BBC after he was told the SNP had beaten Labour in Clydebank and Milngavie. 'F★★★ me,' he whistled in an unguarded moment, later asking an aide to check no fewer than three times if it was true. Before heading home to Strichen for some sleep at 6.50 a.m., Salmond told the *Scottish Sun*: 'I may cancel that chopper, as I've no need to rush back to Edinburgh and claim the crown like last time. After this result I could cycle to Holyrood.'[75]

Just a few yards from Holyrood, SNP officials had already realised they were on course for an overall majority, but, as per the plan, that prospect was not communicated to anyone beyond HQ. (Importantly, the SNP's concept of a majority was 65 seats *including* the Greens and Independent Nationalist MSP Margo MacDonald.) Ironically, one of the party's chief number crunchers, Marco Biagi, had unexpectedly won his own contest in Edinburgh Central. 'I texted him,' joked his boss Liz Lloyd, 'and said: "Congratulations – you're fired".'[76] Based on information coming in from counts, and from Activate, Mark Shaw had settled on 66 seats, although he later revised that upwards to 69. A more cautious Peter Murrell preferred to stick with the lower figure, realising that Holyrood's election system had been designed to prevent any party gaining an overall majority. Either figure, however, constituted a majority. This was what Murrell later called the '6.24 a.m. moment'. Realising someone ought to inform Salmond, Murrell informed him of their thinking at around 6.30 a.m. Sharing his chief executive's caution, Salmond simply murmured, 'that's not possible'.

But it was. 'He hadn't even thought about it,' reflected an adviser later, 'so at that point something was happening that all of us were struggling slightly to get our heads round. He was somewhat overwhelmed; we're used to it now, but at that point we just thought "this can't be right".' Indeed, the result that officially 'broke the system' was that in the North-East of Scotland, Salmond's home region. There, the SNP had already won all ten constituencies and as Friday progressed won a regional list seat, too. (The victorious candidate, Mark McDonald, had turned up at the count dressed in jeans and a T-shirt, so remote was his expectation of victory.) That the SNP had managed to win a list seat in a region where it had already taken every constituency seat mortified the respected psephologist Professor David Denver. Not five minutes earlier he had confidently told BBC Radio Scotland listeners such an outcome was impossible.

Next the SNP awaited confirmation that it had won a crucial 65th seat. Now at SNP HQ, having got an early train from Aberdeen, at around 2.15 p.m. Kirk J. Torrance pointed towards the giant wall-mounted television screens in the war room and shouted: 'It's coming now!' Tickertape at the bottom of the screen confirmed that after a recount the SNP's candidate David Torrance★ had won Kirkcaldy, ostensibly the party's 65th seat. Before the BBC feed had even cut to the voice of Fife Council's returning officer, the room was in uproar. 'Everyone is on his feet,' recorded Mike Wade of *The Times*, who was present almost by accident.

> Many, like Kevin Pringle, Alex Salmond's special adviser, are staring at the screen, smiling, clapping their hands and shaking their heads in joy and disbelief. People are falling into each other's arms, hugging and kissing. Nicola Sturgeon, the deputy leader, has cupped her face in her hands and is on the verge of tears. 'Look,' says Peter Murrell. 'The sun's come out.'

Sturgeon then stepped forward to make a speech, 'propping herself up on the desk as if still overwhelmed by what has unfolded before her'.

'This operation in here is mind blowing,' she said, straightening herself up. 'The effort you put in day in, day out, night in, night out has been way beyond the call of duty,' she went on. 'Without the effort and contribution that all of you have made, we wouldn't be standing here today making history. Thank you all so much. Enjoy it. You are history makers.'[77]

It is often said that the victors write history, and of course even victors can make mistakes. Although the SNP genuinely believed, and continued to believe until after Salmond made his victory speech later that day, that Kirkcaldy was the party's 65th seat, it was in fact Clackmannanshire and Dunblane, which declared at 2.40 p.m., 25 minutes after Kirkcaldy. Indeed, Keith Brown, the victorious MSP, said as much in his acceptance speech, as did some news outlets. Nevertheless, the SNP had done it, and within an hour the Prime Minister had issued a statement congratulating the SNP on 'this emphatic win' (characterised by one Coalition adviser as 'Thistlenacht') but warning that if it wanted to hold a referendum, then he would 'campaign to keep our United Kingdom together with every fibre I have'.

Alex Salmond, who wanted to radically reconstitute that United Kingdom if not exactly break it up, had gone home for some rest. Later, when all the results were in, it became clear the SNP had seized a remark-

★ As with Kirk, no relation to the author.

able 45.4 per cent of the constituency vote to Labour's 31.7 per cent, and
44 per cent of the regional list to Labour's 26.3 per cent. This translated into
69 SNP MSPs to Labour's 37. Even more remarkably, when the regional
list vote was later analysed by constituency, it revealed the Nationalists had
won 69 out of 73. Salmond's long campaign to position the SNP in the
'mainstream' of Scottish political opinion while challenging Labour's dominance in west-central Scotland had finally come to pass, a mere 21 years
after the fledgling party leader had first promised his members precisely that.
But then Salmond had always been one to play the long game. In 2007,
voters had been apprehensive but willing to give the SNP and its leader a
chance; in 2011, they knew what they were getting: a First Minister they
respected, a ministerial team they reckoned had done a good job, and a
series of populist policies which were, well, popular. Of the 'team, record,
vision' triumvirate, 'record' had been crucial. 'It was about competence,
not the constitution,' said Professor James Mitchell, explaining the findings
of the 2011 Scottish Election Survey. 'They [the SNP] won because they
were seen to be competent.'[78]

After a few hours' sleep, aides picked Salmond up at Longside, and
from a small airfield outside Inverurie he, Moira and Geoff Aberdein
boarded Saltire One for the short flight to the Scottish capital. Salmond
was understandably excited, the flight allowing him to survey, as
Stephen McGinty put it in the *Scotsman*, 'the nation, from each corner
of which his party drew support'.[79] He also went over the final draft of
a speech to be delivered outside Prestonfield House Hotel, as in 2007.
Although the chopper left on time and the journey usually took an
hour, it had to stop at Edinburgh Airport and circle, and thus arrived
slightly late at 5.25 p.m.

Waiting on the dappled lawn for his party leader to arrive, even the
normally reserved Peter Murrell allowed himself a moment of exuber-
ance. 'Wow! Wowww!' he said of a result he had played a big part in
helping achieve. 'We missed this coming,' remarked another of the
SNP's inner circle. 'We didn't even plan for this scenario.'[80] Then the
distinctive whir of helicopter rotors could be heard and Saltire One,
otherwise known as G-CYRS, appeared in overcast Edinburgh skies,
coming in low over the trees on the edge of Prestonfield Golf Course in
the shadow of Arthur's Seat. It seemed to take an age to actually land,
longer still for the blades to stop spinning, and even longer for the First
Minister to emerge.

Finally, Salmond stepped onto the grass and embraced his deputy
Nicola Sturgeon (re-elected in Glasgow Southside), while staff and

supporters cheered from a distance. He looked overwhelmed, and played nervously with his right-hand suit pocket as he zigzagged over to the crowd while giving a thumbs-up. The former Conservative Cabinet minister Michael Portillo, meanwhile, was recording a piece-to-camera for a BBC profile. 'When I started making this documentary about Alex Salmond, I thought it might be his political obituary,' he said, 'because Labour were then ahead in the polls, favourites to win this election.' Instead, Portillo noted, Salmond had returned to Edinburgh triumphant, the only First Minister of Scotland to win a second term, the only First Minister to win an overall majority. 'How did he do it?'[81]

It was a good question. As Salmond and Sturgeon made their way through the scrum, which was much larger and more aggressive than that in 2007, Angus Robertson said, to no one in particular, 'C'mon, folks'; Geoff Aberdein chipped in with 'Take it easy, guys,' while another minder asked to 'clear a path here'.[82] The duo headed towards the hotel to sign off his speech, drafted by Alex Bell and Joan McAlpine. 'It was a very quiet atmosphere,' recalled one of those present. 'There was no jubilation, just a feeling of let's get this over and done with.' Descriptions of Salmond's mood at this point ranged from 'energised' and 'obviously ecstatic' to 'elated, about as high as the helicopter he'd just come down in'. 'He's unusually calm in situations like that,' reflected one aide. 'Sometimes it's the minutia rather than the big moments that gets him exasperated.' Nevertheless, another had never seen Salmond 'so overwhelmed'. 'He was having difficulty – we were all having difficulty – taking it all in. He was calm but it would be wrong to say he took it all in his stride; I think he was quite emotional about the level of trust voters had put in him.'

This time they stuck to the plan, that Salmond would say relatively few words to the press and then retreat to the hotel. He emerged to milk the crowd some more, giving another trademark thumbs-up sign, which gave the following day's newspapers a memorable image. 'It's a walk of about 70 yards,' wrote Michael Portillo later, 'and you could see him trying to control the look on his face. He had quite a lot to be smug about, but he does have a natural boyish smug expression.'[83] In 2007, Salmond had urged Scots 'to work as if you live in the early days of a better nation', and almost exactly four years later little had changed as he positioned himself in front of a Saltire and behind a yellow lectern, this time emblazoned with the call to 'be part of better'. 'The gardens of Prestonfield House, that most stately of Edinburgh hotels, are home to peacocks,' wrote Lindsay McIntosh in *The Times*. 'Yesterday afternoon, the First Minister of Scotland was the proudest of them all.'[84]

'Kirkcaldy is my kind of town,' he began. 'It gave us Adam Smith, Jack Vettriano and Gordon Brown. And earlier today, it gave the SNP our 65th and winning seat in the Scottish parliamentary elections. I am, therefore, delighted to confirm that I will be seeking re-election by the Scottish Parliament as the First Minister of Scotland.' Otherwise Salmond struck a statesmanlike tone, confident enough to speak for the country as a whole but also careful to appear conciliatory, for 'although the SNP has a majority of the seats, we don't have a monopoly of wisdom'. He also looked to the future:

> Later this evening, I will be speaking to the Prime Minister and laying down markers as to what this result and this mandate means in terms of Scotland's relationship with the United Kingdom . . . I believe the SNP won this election because Scotland wants to travel in hope and to aim high. Scotland has chosen to believe in itself and our shared capacity to build a fair society. The nation can be better, it wants to be better, and I will do all I can as First Minister to make it better. We have given ourselves the permission to be bold and we will govern fairly and wisely, with an eye to the future but a heart to forgive.

The last line was a quote from the Corries song 'Scotland Will Flourish' and was Salmond's own idea, something he had used a number of times over the years. With that, he retreated back to the hotel to have tea with Moira and watch continuing television news coverage of the election.

'Scotland slept on a victory, awoke to a landslide, and by last night was contemplating a political avalanche of hitherto unthinkable proportions,' opened Eddie Barnes' memorable report in that day's *Scotsman*. 'A fresh chapter in the country's story was written yesterday, as the 2011 Scottish election results were made clear. And in Alex Salmond, a nation had found its History Man.'[85] As the *Guardian* noted, calling political events seismic was usually hyperbole, but Salmond's re-election was a 'remarkable' exception. 'Incumbents seldom increase their support so resoundingly, least of all in times of increased hardship.'[86]

All of this was still sinking in as the First Minister made a brief stop at Bute House, his Edinburgh residence, before heading to the Jam House on Queen Street for the SNP's victory party. There, The Proclaimers' 'I'm On My Way' ('from misery to happiness') belted out from large speakers as MSPs old and new mingled with activists, business backers like Sir Tom Farmer, and journalists from those sympathetic to the cause to Alan Cochrane, the arch-Unionist commentator for the *Daily Telegraph*, and this author, pleased that his father – a lifelong SNP activist – was pleased. Kevin Pringle, noted Alan Taylor, 'stood by the bar, sipping water, like a snooker player forced to watch as a rival compiled a threatening break. He had the look of a man to whom sleep was alien.'

As the evening progressed, there was still no sign of Salmond, whose 'concept of time is always elastic', but by 8.30 p.m. it was clear he had arrived. Angus Robertson introduced him to an expectant crowd, noting that as he had driven from Glasgow to Edinburgh that morning it had occurred to him 'that every single seat in central Scotland is now held by the Scottish National Party'. Then it was Salmond's turn. 'I've heard another rumour,' he said, referencing his speech to the same gathering four years earlier. 'We won another election.' Echoing Robertson's introduction in his catch-all Scottish accent, he added: 'A' was thinking that a' the seats a' flew over in ma helicopter were yellow.'[87]

Alex Salmond, who had gone into politics with no realistic expectation of savouring such a moment, could be forgiven a moment of modest triumphalism. Winning an overall majority under an electoral system designed to prevent precisely that was, to return to a golfing analogy, the 19th hole of Scottish politics. But Salmond did not stay long at the Jam House. 'Usually he would have stayed to mingle,' explained an aide, 'but he was just knackered, so we pulled him out the back entrance.' Salmond then went on to one of his favourite restaurants to have dinner with Moira, whom he had married on 6 May 1981. It was their 30th anniversary, although neither of them could have anticipated such a memorable present.

Chapter 1

'A REAL BLACK BITCH'

> Linlithgow, the appearance of rude decayed, idle grandeur – charmingly rural, retired situation – the old rough royal palace a tolerably fine, but melancholy ruin – sweetly situated on a small elevation on the bank of a Loch – shown the room where the beautiful injured Mary Queen of Scots was born.
>
> Robert Burns, 25 August 1787

Alexander Elliot Anderson Salmond was born on Hogmanay, 1954, in the midst of a particularly cold winter. The historic West Lothian town of Linlithgow, and the surrounding countryside, was covered with snow. Forty years later, Salmond reflected on the moment through the eyes of his grandfather, Alexander (known as Sandy) Salmond, in an untypically personal, and at times mystical, column for the *Herald* newspaper:

> It was hardly the preparation for Hogmanay that Sandy had expected. With pipes frozen all over town times were busy even for a semi-retired plumber and besides his new grandchild was due. Indeed overdue. And here he was on the hill trudging through the snow to a lonely farmhouse. Still the weather would mean that the wean would more than likely be born in the royal burgh, for there was no safe route to Edinburgh on a day such as this. And just think if it were a boy, a namesake, and a real Black Bitch, born within the sound of St Michael's bells. He turned to look at his town from the hill. It was a grand sight at any time but tonight in the frost and snow the palace, the great church with the frozen loch beyond and the high street in front were majestic. Even the new town hall at a mere 70 years old didn't look quite so much out of place as normal amid the rest of the medieval grandeur.

Salmond then linked his birth with the final hours of a recluse called Bob Jamieson, whom Sandy was visiting at his farmhouse that night. A young doctor called McKay arrived just as Jamieson slipped away. 'Well, that's a blessing,' he said to Sandy. 'One going and one coming, because you'll have a grandchild before this day's over.'[1]

This story not only drew upon Alex Salmond's obviously fond memories of his grandfather, but also suggested a heightened sense of his Linlithgow roots, and perhaps his place in the wider sweep of Scottish history. He did, after all, share a birthday with Bonnie Prince Charlie. The Scotland of 1954/55, however, was more than two generations away from having a devolved Scottish Parliament, let along one controlled by the Scottish National Party which, in two spells beginning in 1990 and 2004, Salmond would lead.

Rather, Scotland was at the height of its political Unionism. In the weeks preceding Salmond's birth, Winston Churchill, whom Mary Salmond, Alex's mother, adored and his father, Robert, despised, was being urged to resign as Prime Minister by a 'hanging jury' comprising his seven most senior Cabinet colleagues, including the then Secretary of State for Scotland, the aristocratic James Stuart, son of the Earl of Moray. 'My mum thought Churchill was the greatest man who ever lived,' Salmond later recalled, 'and my dad wanted to hang him because of what he did to the miners.'[2]

By the beginning of 1955, the ageing premier accepted that resignation was unavoidable and announced his retirement that April. Anthony Eden – who had played a long waiting game akin to that of Gordon Brown half a century later – took over as Prime Minister and immediately called a general election. The Conservative Party was rewarded with a unique result for a political party in Scotland: a majority of both seats and (albeit narrowly) the popular vote. Salmond's mother, whom Alex described as a 'Winston Churchill Conservative', undoubtedly played her small part in that historic poll.

The SNP, by contrast, barely registered in electoral terms. The party contested just two seats, Stirling and Falkirk Burghs and Perth and East Perthshire, only retaining its deposit in the latter. The SNP's share of the national vote was a pitiful 0.5 per cent. The glory days of a decade earlier, when Robert D. McIntyre had triumphed in Motherwell as the first Nationalist Member of Parliament, were but a distant memory. The SNP was still perceived as a romantic movement, a collection of cranks who meant well but achieved little.

It was another two years before Harold Macmillan would famously declare that 'most of our people have never had it so good',[3] but this sentiment had as much resonance in 1950s Scotland as it did in the rest of the UK. Unemployment, the curse of the inter-war period, was at an historic low and the income of the average working-class household – which included Salmond's family – was almost three times greater than in 1938. Linlithgow, which occupied a prime location along the southern shore of Linlithgow Loch in a broad agricultural valley, would not have escaped this relative prosperity.

The town boasted an illustrious past, its much-favoured royal palace (the birthplace of Mary, Queen of Scots) ensuring the town's historical prominence. During the 15th and 16th centuries Linlithgow reached its height in terms of influence, prosperity and architectural achievement. It was then that the pre-Reformation church of St Michael's and the Palace were both completed, but when the 1603 Union of the Crowns removed the royal court to England, the town began to decline. But the Linlithgow Salmond would have been familiar with in the 1950s and 1960s was no longer charmingly rural, its road and rail links having transformed it into a busy residential settlement.

There was also ongoing redevelopment. Two large tracts of the northern side of the High Street – where Salmond's grandfather had been born – were demolished in the 1960s and replaced by flats and public buildings in a contemporary style. Although these were a vast improvement on what must have been cramped and dilapidated traditional accommodation, they were poorly conceived and had a rather brutal impact on the appearance of the town's main thoroughfare. In 1964 came the most controversial addition of all, a modernist aluminium spire – representing Christ's crown of thorns – which was added to St Michael's.[4]

The young Salmond obviously took a keen interest in the history of his home town and even decades later a friend conducted round Linlithgow's magnificent ruins was surprised by the eloquence and feeling of 'Alex's guided tour'.[5] In the early 1970s he devoured Angus Macdonald's 1932 book, *Linlithgow in Pictures*, and used it as the basis of a knowledgably articulate letter to the local newspaper when he was just 17. It concerned a street in the town called 'Beinn-Castle Brae', of which he enclosed a print:

The 'Beinn' in Beinn-Castle comes not as 'Incomer' seemingly suggests from 'Bean', the leguminous plant but from the Scots' 'Beinn' meaning 'rich'or 'well to do'. The term probably has most truth when applied to the West Port House ... which was completed by one of the Hamiltons [in] about 1600. It possessed extensive grounds, and is, not to become too involved, the largest and oldest inhabited property in town. The three mid-17th century houses in the foreground were demolished by the Town Council, showing a surprising, if somewhat familiar, lack of vision, in 1930, and made way for the incongruous, though no doubt necessary, public conveniences.[6]

The letter is signed, formally, 'Alexander Salmond'. Prominent characteristics are already present: a love of history, confidence and a straightforward – if youthfully clumsy – writing style with a humorous turn of phrase. 'Politicians gain by cultivating the local,'[7] observed Christopher Harvie, and indeed Salmond would assiduously cultivate Linlithgow, just as Lloyd George did Criccieth, Bevan Ebbw Vale and Gordon Brown Kirkcaldy.

Salmond also admired the 'confidence and certainty' of the Forth Rail Bridge, which stood ten miles away from Linlithgow. 'My main preoccupation with the bridge ... was being allowed to fling a penny out of the train carriage window,' he recalled in 2006, 'The penny had to reach the water for the wish to come true. In such a venture, timing is all and I used to wait until the join of the two cantilevers in the middle, which provides by far the best opportunity for negotiating an old penny through the webs of steel.'[8] Salmond also walked across the new Forth Road Bridge – which, as First Minister, he would seek to replace – when it first opened in 1964.

However handsome these two bridges were, Salmond much preferred his home town. A university friend remembered Salmond making a point of going back home for the riding of the marches, 'which was very important to him. He wasn't a romantic at all but felt that where he came from was very important.'[9]

There had been people by the name of Salmond – a 'Crusader' name of Hebrew origins – in Linlithgow since the 16th century, and members of Alex's family since at least the 18th century. His great-great-great grandfather, John Salmond, shows up as a ploughman in the old parish records held at the National Archives of Scotland, while the forename Alexander, or Alex, appears to have become a family favourite when John's son was christened in 1816. The Salmonds were modest citizens, mainly working as ferrymen or flour millers, while Alex's grandfather, the aforementioned Sandy, became a plumber.

His son (and the future First Minister's father), Robert Dobbie Salmond,[10] was born on 21 August 1921 in an area of Linlithgow known as Low Port. Robert was by instinct a Labour voter, and indeed during his stint in the Royal Navy was nicknamed 'Uncle Joe' because of his Stalinist leanings. During the Second World War, Robert was an electrician on the aircraft carrier *Indomitable*, which was torpedoed (but not sunk) in the Mediterranean. Later he moved to the Civil Service, working as an executive officer at the Ministry of Pensions and National Insurance where, in 1961, a young Margaret Thatcher was appointed a junior minister. A miner called Willie Wilson later told Alex that his father had 'a reputation in the mining community as . . . the one and only person who will hunt down a reason to allow a mining appeal'.[11]

In September 1950 Robert married Mary Stewart Milne, who also worked at the local National Insurance office as a 'clerical officer' but came from a more middle-class background. Her father, William Milne, was a former headmaster and her mother, Margaret Hamilton, also a schoolteacher. Robert and Mary eventually had four children, the second of which was Alex, a baby-boomer born at 4.30 p.m. on 31 December 1954 at 101 Preston Road, the Salmonds' family home.

Following a local church tradition Alex's two middle names came from the minister who christened him, (Gilbert) Elliot Anderson, who was inducted into the united congregation of St Ninian's Craigmailen on 15 February 1955. 'I have tried to bear that name with pride,' Salmond told the General Assembly of the Church of Scotland in 2009, 'and make no mistake as to the extent that my roots lie with this Assembly.'[12] Both his father and grandfather, meanwhile, were elders at St Ninian's.

The Rev. Elliot Anderson appears to have made quite an impression on the young Alex, who later gave serious thought to becoming a minister himself.[13] 'I thought he was a terrific preacher,' he recalled in 2008, adding:

He had a great liking for what Professor [William] Barclay[14] used to do and looked at the exact meaning of words in Latin [and] Greek. He used to do sermons about what was meant by . . . the apostles or what did it mean when Jesus said such and such to this group of folk. I used to think it was fantastic. I used to demand to listen to sermons rather than go to Sunday school. I would be sitting in rapt attention listening to the full thing. He was not a great preacher in the Barclay spellbinding nature but he was a good minister and wholly good.[15]

Salmond attended church almost every Sunday until he was 18. At university, however, a friend remembered that 'Alex wasn't particularly interested' in religion, 'although he didn't rubbish it either'.[16] However, like many politicians seeking to broaden their appeal, Salmond would later talk up his Kirk background.

Those trying to pin down the formative influences on the young Salmond need look no further than his grandfather, Sandy. 'I was ... instructed in the Scottish oral tradition,' he reflected in 2002, 'literally from my grandfather's knee, and I have little doubt that this was the strongest influence in my life in determining my attitude to nationality and identity.'[17] But whether or not this actually made Salmond a Nationalist is a moot point. Interestingly, when pushed on this point in a television interview, Salmond's father said a love of history rather than support for independence had been his father's enduring influence upon Alex.

Alexander Salmond liked to impart Scottish historical tales and, as his grandson later recalled, 'the way my granddad told it gave it incredible local colour'.[18] 'If he was telling a story about the wars of independence,' Salmond elaborated, 'he didn't tell it like a history book. For example, Bruce's men captured Linlithgow Castle. They did it by using a hay-cart and stopping the drawbridge and charging in. But what my grandfather used to say was, there were a couple of Davidsons ... an Anderson [and] the Oliphants were involved. The Oliphants were the local bakers, so at four years old I had this image of the local bakers, covered in flour, dusting themselves off and charging in. It was personal, colourful, vital. It would have won more Oscars than *Braveheart*.'

In retrospect, Salmond realised his grandfather had embellished these stories but in Linlithgow, 'where much of Scottish history was made and unmade, this task was far from impossible'. 'He showed me, for example, the ground where he said Edward I had camped before the Battle of Falkirk,' he recalled, 'He showed me the window from where the Regent Moray was shot dead in the High Street.' It was because this oral history was 'unofficial, almost subversive' that made it so 'irresistible' to Salmond. He was detached enough to realise that while his grandfather 'did get the sweep of things about right', his '*Braveheart* version of Scots history may have been vulnerable in the occasional point of detail'.[19]

Nevertheless, Salmond's grandfather did at least sow the seeds of Alex's Nationalism: 'Of course, a pro-Scottish inclination goes a lot deeper than economics. Robert Burns put it best when he wrote that the story of Wallace kindled a fire in his veins "which will boil along there till the floodgates of life shut in eternal rest". Burns got his inspiration from Blind Harry's epic poem, Wallace. I got mine, literally, from my paternal grandfather's knee.'[20] 'The fire that he lit still burns,'[21] Salmond concluded. 'Each of us is the product of all our experiences and I do believe there is a link between these early memories and the support I developed in later years for the Scottish cause.'[22]

This latent Nationalism was not, however, cultural. Salmond wore a kilt for the first time when he attended a family wedding at Harrogate in 1959; an experience that meant the garment was not part of his wardrobe until nearly 50 years later. It seems he found the 'shortbread tin' and 'white heather club'[23] image of the kilt in 1950s Scotland disagreeable.

By contrast to his family experience, Salmond was 'taught little or no Scottish history at schools – perhaps a smidgeon at primary level, while Scots was reserved for third-degree Burns every January'.[24] His first school was Linlithgow Primary, where he was once belted for making farmyard noises. 'I kept clucking in class, which I thought was very amusing, but my teacher thought it was less so,' Salmond recalled nearly 40 years after his first painful lashes. 'Mrs Baird was a formidable woman, but an extremely good teacher,' he added. 'I had the belt six times in primary one, but not very often after that – I was a bit more careful about making animal noises.'[25] The experience, added Salmond, had not done him any harm.

It was also at primary school that Salmond experienced his first foray into populist politics, standing for the SNP in mock elections. 'It was the only party left,' he explained later. 'I had a landslide victory because I advocated half-day school and the replacement of free school milk with ice cream.'[26] Margaret Henderson, who taught Alex in Primary 6, reckons there may have been another, possibly subconscious, influence during this period. 'At the time I was teaching the BMC car factory came up from Birmingham to Bathgate and lots of English workers said they were coming up to "civilise the Scots". Now that did not go down at all. It put my back up, and perhaps the whole atmosphere rubbed off on the boys.'[27]

Henderson also remembered the young Salmond's health problems: 'Alex had very bad asthma and so did my son and she [Mary Salmond] was always very nice to me because our boys had similar problems. I could hear him breathing from the front of the classroom because his asthma was so bad, but it didn't stop him joining in the fun. He was also terribly untidy. If you remember the chap in the Persil advert with his shirt hanging out, then that was Alex. His desk looked like it had been stirred by a stick, but he was a very clever lad.'

'There was never any bother with Alex,' added Henderson, 'although I didn't see him as a politician but more a scientist, someone who was serious but clever.'[28] Because of his health, meanwhile, he was off school a 'great deal' and 'just read everything'. 'My dad bought an encyclopaedia in 1960, when I was five,' Salmond recalled. 'There were 12 volumes, and I read them from cover to cover. I knew something about everything.'[29] Whenever he suffered an attack he was moved from his small room at the back of the house to his parents' bedroom at the front. 'It had a fantastic view over the swing park,' remembered Salmond. 'I used to lie there, read and ponder. My passion was [also] DC comics. I had the whole range: *Batman*, *Superman*, *Captain Marvel*, that sort of stuff.' His love of Enid Blyton also led to a family cairn terrier being christened 'Shadow'.[30]

Salmond has often spoken about his paternal grandfather, Alexander Salmond, but said nothing about his mother's father, William Milne. This is understandable, for Milne died nearly 14 years before Alex was born, although he was an impressive figure from whom one might have expected the future First Minister to derive some inspiration.

Milne moved to Linlithgow in 1929 to become Rector of the town's academy, the same school his grandson would later attend. He hailed from a comfortable background in Kirriemuir (his father had been an insurance agent) and moved from Webster's Seminary, where he was dux medallist in 1906, to St Andrews University – again like Salmond – from which he graduated with honours in 1910. 'This considerable "lad o'pairts",'[31] as one newspaper described him, then worked as classics master at Bo'ness Academy for 19 years, interrupted only by a commission in the 10th Royal Scots during the First World War. When war broke out Milne was drafted to France as a captain, and taken prisoner in the spring of 1918, spending the remainder of the war in a German camp.

Milne took over as Rector at Linlithgow Academy as the school became an 'omnibus' institution, or prototype comprehensive. The abolition of the primary fee-paying department provoked a storm of criticism but, as another newspaper later noted, 'Mr Milne was a man who always said that difficulties and obstacles could be overcome'.[32] In 1935 – in addition to his duties with the local Educational Institute of

Scotland, the Freemasons[33], local Boy Scouts and the church – Milne was elected to Linlithgow Town Council as a Unionist (or Conservative). 'One cannot live long in an old "city" like Linlithgow without falling in love with it,' he said upon his election. 'I have no experience at municipal work, but will do my best to serve the town.'[34]

In 1937 Milne was appointed treasurer and successfully decreased local rates during a four-year tenure. A talented orator, he was also president of the West Lothian Discussion Club. At one notable meeting in February 1939 he presided over speeches by Sir William Y. Darling, the National government's prospective candidate for Linlithgow (and great uncle of Alistair), and Lieutenant-Colonel Dalyell of The Binns (father of Tam). Decades later, Milne's grandson would spar with different generations of the same families.[35] Too old to serve in the Second World War, Milne instead became commander of Linlithgow's Home Guard.

Then on 31 March 1941, quite out of the blue, the *West Lothian Courier* carried the following story: 'On going to the school before the usual hour of nine o'clock, a cleaner found the dead body of Mr Milne lying on the floor of his room in a pool of blood with wounds in the head and body, and a firearm lying nearby.'[36] As a mark of respect Linlithgow Academy was closed for the day and, in keeping with contemporary editorial etiquette, no speculation as to what lay behind Milne's apparent suicide was offered. His death certificate noted that he had last been seen alive at 11 p.m. the previous evening, adding simply 'Gunshot wounds (suicide)' under cause of death.

Tributes were glowing. 'There never could have been a more considerate or understanding headmaster,' observed the *Linlithgowshire Journal and Gazette*. 'Indeed, it was not too much to say that he was universally beloved by staff and pupils. A man of clear vision, he was, from his long experience, well fitted to advise parents in the directions best suited to the bent and ability of the pupil.'[37] Milne had been, noted several reports, one of the best-known men in West Lothian. His grandson Alex would eventually become one of the best-known men in Scotland.

Why, then, no public reference from Salmond? The primary reason must have been the stigma associated then, as now, with suicide. Any reference to the death of her father must also have been acutely distressing to Salmond's mother Mary, only 19 at the time of her father's death. Indeed, when asked to comment on the story in 2008 (although it never appeared in print), Salmond told the journalist Tom Gordon that the death had never been discussed at home. 'I found out about it because my dad told me when I was growing up,' he said. 'I'm not callous or uncaring about it, but he died more than ten years before I was born so I never knew him.'

Salmond also believed the tragedy had helped shape what Gordon called his mother's 'compassionate but pragmatic approach to life . . . she became a tireless volunteer who tried to instil a can-do attitude in her son'.[38] Salmond also revealed a little more to a university friend. 'Alex spoke of him as a man of honour,' he recalled. 'The story he told was that as treasurer of Linlithgow Town Council his grandfather had become aware of a discrepancy in the finances which he had rectified immediately; however he felt bound to report the error although at the time it had not been discovered. As a man of honour he then took his own life.'

Salmond, however, never spoke of his Tory grandfather, which is odd considering he was far from coy when talking about other aspects of his family background. 'I see no purpose whatsoever in dwelling on a 70-year-old family tragedy,' he said when asked to comment on the first edition of this biography. 'It only risks hurt to those old enough to remember what actually happened. My maternal grandfather . . . died many years before I was even born. I have never speculated on the reasons for his death in 1941.'[39]

Salmond's childhood appears, by all accounts, to have been a happy one ('great childhood; fantastic'[40] he said in 1998). His parents were loving, encouraging and delighted not just in Alex's progress, but also that of his brother and two sisters, although there was quite an age gap. 'Effectively my parents had two sets of family,' Salmond later reflected. 'Margaret and me three years apart and then, ten years later, Gail and Bob.' Indeed, Margaret Salmond had been born in 1951, followed by Alex in 1954, Gail in 1963 and, finally, Robert in 1967.[41] The two Salmond families inhabited 101 Preston Road, what Alex later called 'the best kind of council scheme in Scotland'. 'The houses were nicely spaced out with a decent bit of garden,' he explained. 'My parents started their married life in that house. They had the downstairs and my aunt and uncle had the upstairs. A lot of folk lived like that back then.'[42]

The journalist Ian Jack noted that had Salmond been an English politician, he might have made more of the fact that he had been 'born in a council house . . . to stress his knowledge of another social reality, but in Scotland it goes unremarked. Most of his Scottish generation grew up in council houses. Two-thirds of the population lived in them.'[43] 'We weren't poor,' Salmond stressed in 1990, 'but money was tight. Education was important to my family and they managed to send all four of us to university. It can't have been easy.'[44]

'He was a very happy child,' recalled Mary Salmond in 2001, 'We never had any worries with him, he was quite happy to go to school, but very happy to come back and play.'[45] Salmond himself recalled: 'As a boy growing up in Linlithgow, I was hugely fortunate in having an incredibly secure family background. If there were any problems during my childhood – at school, with friends, etc – I had a loving family of both parents and three siblings, and grandparents within 200 yards, to go greetin' to. The extended family was very close – indeed, Linlithgow was a sort of extended family in itself.'[46] 'His [Salmond's] parents had a very gentle calm influence on all the family,' remembered one of Alex's teachers, 'that all of them should work hard and study hard, which they did.'[47] Journalists would later remark upon Salmond's 'serenity', a rootedness that probably stemmed from a stable childhood in which his mother was the predominant influence.

When not playing with friends, Salmond was a devotee of the original *Star Trek* series then showing on British television. In 2001 he outed himself as a 'Trekkie', confessing to having stood in front of a mirror with a clothes peg on his eyebrow in order to impersonate Spock, a character from the science fiction show whom friends had told him he resembled. 'I sat in front of a mirror and I'd say things like, "Captain, we have a 2,499,999-to-one chance of surviving this" in his Vulcan voice,' he told the comedienne Elaine C. Smith. 'I sat there until I could do that. I was going to describe it as a normal childhood, but maybe it wasn't.'[48]

Sport was also an early enthusiasm, and certainly predated that for politics. Despite his asthma ('He never let that get him down,'[49] recalled Mary), Alex played golf, usually every Saturday evening, from the age of five. Robert Salmond, meanwhile, idolised the veteran pro 'Gentleman John' Panton,[50] which puzzled his son, who thought it would be better 'to support a Palmer, Player or a Jackson – someone in that elite group challenging for the golfing majors'. 'Faither's passionate support for Panton was something of a family curiosity,' recalled Salmond in one of his more memorable *Herald* columns, 'rather like being the son of a Third Lanark fan. Even when Panton dusted off Sam Snead in the world seniors in that otherwise disastrous sporting summer of 1966 I remained to be convinced; despite being posted newspaper cuttings of the Scot's triumph all the way to the school camp in darkest Lanark-shire. It wasn't until the 1970 Open that I finally became a convert.'

The 1970 Open took place at the Old Course in St Andrews, where Salmond would later play as a student, and he remembered accompany-ing his father to follow Panton and his partner Bob Charles ('still near the peak of his powers'). From 'the first drive to the short iron at the last,' he recalled in the *Herald*, 'Panton's ball was never off the fairway . . . it only gradually dawned on the crowd that we were witness-ing something exceptional.'[51] At the St Andrews Open of 2005 Salmond had 'the enormous pleasure of having lunch with the great man',[52] while following Panton's death in July 2009 aged 93, he penned a warm tribute, again for the *Herald*.

Another sport was also a steady fixture during Salmond's childhood. Both Alex's father and grandfather were great supporters of the Edin-burgh-based football team Heart of Midlothian, or Hearts, and ensured, in Robert's words, that 'Alex would be brought up in the faith'.[53] 'I have been a Hearts supporter all my life,' declared Salmond in 2005, 'ever since my faither lifted me over the turnstile at the Gorgie Road end.'[54] The Salmonds travelled all over Scotland watching Hearts in action, favourite players including Donald Ford, who was signed to Hearts in 1964 and hailed from Linlithgow. 'I watched Hearts home and away all season, every season,' Salmond recalled in 1993. 'I even saw Willie Bauld although the King was old and I was young. I cried all weekend when we threw away the league to Kilmarnock on goal average and went to the Texaco Cup final in Wolverhampton the night before my higher chemistry exam.'[55] He also remembered watching 'Jim Jefferies when I went to see Hearts play every week in the seventies'.[56]

Blessed with a good memory, Salmond took a train-spotter's delight in memorising footballing facts and figures, although there was disappointment when his teacher did not include him in the school team. It was, after all, his dearest wish to play for Hearts.[57] Following Hearts also took Salmond south of the border for the first time. His team had reached the final of the Texaco Cup (later the Anglo-Scottish Cup) and had to play Wolverhampton Wanderers, or Wolves, over two legs in 1971. Hearts lost 3–1 at home on 14 April 1971, but beat the Wolves 1–0 on 3 May, losing 3–2 on aggregate. 'The latter was the game Alex travelled down to see,' recalled a university friend. 'He went down and back in the same day and expressed no desire to travel south again.'[58] Indeed, it is possible that Salmond did not visit England again until he worked for the Scottish Office in the late 1970s. 'Given the choice,' he remarked in 2005, 'I would rather travel west than south.'[59]

Robert Salmond was also a 'huge' cricket fan, although his son was less so. 'I used to open the batting at Linlithgow Academy', Salmond later recalled, 'and because we had hand-me-down full-size bats from West Lothian County, it was very difficult to play flowery shots. I used to play a lot of defensive shots and edges, and was famous for batting for the whole innings and only scoring about four runs.'[60] Alex also started indulging in 'the sport of kings' aged just nine, after his uncle Andrew told him that 'an Irish horse called Arkle was going to humble the pride of England, a horse called Millhouse in the Cheltenham Gold Cup'.[61] A rapt Salmond watched in 'grainy black and white' as Arkle won the 1964 Gold Cup. 'My half-a-crown became seven-and-six,' he recalled in 2003, 'and I suddenly started to become interested in horse racing.'[62]

Future flutters were funded 'by doing a round for Vernons [football] Pools'.[63] 'On my round I had a customer called John, with whom I shared an interest in the gee-gees,' Salmond recalled in 2001. 'One Thursday night John told me that his "speed figures" showed Bronze Hill nailed on for the Lincoln handicap. I followed John's advice, and lo and behold Bronze Hill turned my silver into gold at an awesome 50–1.'[64] Greyhounds did not hold the same allure. 'There was hardly a race where it was not clear that some were "in the know" as to which dug [dog] could be expected to perform and which greyhounds were merely out for exercise,' explained Salmond in 2001. 'As a result, I have not seriously backed a greyhound in my adult life.'[65]

Betting also gave rise to the first moral dilemma of Salmond's short life, as a result of having to place bets on behalf of his grandfather. 'He was a church elder and never had a bet in his life until he retired, when he went on to sixpenny three-crosses,' Salmond recalled in 2000:

> One day his three horses came up, but one was disqualified. He'd put his initials at the bottom of the slip, which the girl behind the counter read, wrongly, to be FPP. She took it to mean 'first past the post' and paid me the bet in full. My grandad was the most honest man I've ever met and I knew that if I mentioned this to him, he'd have sent me back to repay the money. I solved the dilemma by saying to myself that my grandad wouldn't know the horse had been disqualified – there was no such thing as teletext in those days – so when I got home I told him they'd all come in.[66]

Interviewed by the television chef Clarissa Dickson-Wright before the 1999 Scottish Parliament elections Salmond also confessed that his grandfather 'took to the bottle in his old age',[67] although he does not appear to have mentioned this to anyone else. Alexander Salmond died, aged 83, in September 1975, at which point his grandson would probably have been on holiday from university and therefore in Linlithgow at the time.

Perhaps as a consequence alcohol seems to have held little appeal for Salmond, either as a young man or throughout the rest of his life, although the consumption of food certainly formed the basis for other childhood memories. Salmond's father called him 'skink' (as in Cullen Skink) as a child because he was so skinny, while Alex later recalled his mother's Christmas cakes being the talk of the town. 'She would make some 50 each year to give out to extended family, friends and old folk,' he said. 'I used to dispatch them. These were serious cakes and they lasted for ages.' His favourite dish, however, was rice pudding made with goats' milk because of a 'severe'[68] allergy to cow's milk.

Although current affairs were discussed at home, Alex's parents were not immediately aware of his interest in this arena. 'I'm not political and I didn't see it,' recalled Mary Salmond, 'but the lady next door who Alex used to pop in and see a lot said to me, "I can see him in Parliament one day", and I thought, "what rubbish". He was always interested in things, but football mostly.'[69] The lady next door was Nan Borthwick, 'who figured very large in Alex's life', recalled a university friend. 'She was almost a surrogate grandparent. I often stayed at Nan's when I went over to see Alex as their own house was usually full to bursting!'[70] One of Salmond's favourite lines about post-independence relations with England, 'England will lose a surly lodger and gain a good neighbour', might also have come from Borthwick.[71]

Another experience when Salmond was 15 also ensured he would stay on at school and eventually go into politics. Seeing his friends earning cash at Steins Brickworks, where his uncle was foreman, Alex managed to get a holiday job and was determined to stay permanently. 'I announced to my startled parents that for me it was Steins Brickworks,' recalled Salmond. Mary Salmond appeared to play along with this modest ambition, but when Alex was given the 'dirtiest, smelliest, most ridiculous backbreaking work at the entire brickworks' he decided to return to school after all.[72] It was only years later that he learned his mother had contrived the whole thing with Salmond's uncle.

★　　★　　★

Robert Salmond had been, by his own admission, 'very left at one time', and was still voting Labour at the 1964 general election, at which his wife remained loyal to Sir Alec Douglas-Home's Unionists. Then, most likely at the 1966 election, a Labour canvasser came to the Salmonds' door. His father joked that the party would have his vote, but that his wife's was lost to the Conservatives. 'That's OK,' said the canvasser, or so Alex recalled. 'Just as long as she's not voting for the Scottish Nose Pickers.'[73] It so happened that Robert's golfing partner was a miner and staunch Nationalist. Reacting badly to the indirect slight on his friend, he told the Labour activist he would never vote for the party again. 'Like so many Scots who love their country and its traditions,' Salmond said of his parents in 1990, 'they were nationalist with a small "n".'[74]

Robert instead backed the SNP, whose candidate, Billy Wolfe, would later take Alex under his wing. Wolfe had secured nearly 10,000 votes at a by-election in 1962, but the Old Etonian and occupant of the nearby House of Binns, Tam Dalyell, won both that and the two elections that followed. Dalyell too would later befriend Alex who, despite his developing political proclivities, was impressed by Labour's Harold Wilson, Prime Minister from 1964 to 1970. A skilful media operator, orator and tactician, Wilson had obvious appeal to the young Alex. 'What tends to get lost in the fog of his dubious behaviour in office is the inspiration Wilson provided as Opposition leader,' he reflected in 1994. 'For example Wilson went into the 1964 election campaigning against Polaris.'[75]

Billy Wolfe, meanwhile, was a local accountant, church member and Scout leader.[76] Following the by-election a proper SNP constituency association was formed and membership boomed both locally and nationally. For Wolfe, the SNP's future 'lay in developing coherent policies, addressing the socio-economic conditions of ordinary Scots and explaining how self-government would deliver economic growth and social justice',[77] an analysis consistent with Salmond's as a future SNP activist, MP and party leader. Wolfe increased his share of the vote from 23.3 per cent in the by-election to 30.4 per cent at the 1964 general election, going on to mastermind a party reorganisation that endured for the next few decades.

In his second year at secondary school, Salmond most likely followed news of Winnie Ewing's spectacular victory at the Hamilton by-election in November 1967. Within weeks every West Lothian branch of the SNP had reported an increase in membership and Wolfe was telling the *Linlithgowshire Journal and Gazette* that it 'was obvious that the SNP could win any seat in Scotland given the opportunity'.[78] This optimism proved misplaced but, nevertheless, the '1960s was the decade in which the SNP arrived as a serious political force'.[79]

Salmond's new school, Linlithgow Academy, had roots in a much older educational establishment dating back centuries. Initially Alex would have been in what was known as the 'Old Academy', an early Edwardian building in the tranquil setting of the loch-lapped Low Port (the area in which his father had been born in 1921). However by the late 1960s the school roll had risen to around 600 and the facilities became cramped, so in December 1968 a new school building opened on Braehead Road, not far from Salmond's home, 'dominated by a slaughter house, a cemetery, the rooftops of Braehead and a railway'.[80]

The teenage Salmond stood out even then. 'He was confident, didn't go with the pack,' remembered a contemporary. 'He wasn't a loner but certainly stood out as an individual, he also wasn't afraid of standing up to teachers. In fifth and sixth year we all used to play cards in the common room and Alex played a big part in that.' Salmond had clearly added another gambling hobby to his growing interest in the sport of kings, while another fellow pupil recalled Salmond – known as 'Wee Fish' – once bringing a loaded roulette wheel into the sixth-year common room. There was, however, 'no interest in girls at school', while a popular rumour was that Salmond had 'sub-contracted his paper round'.[81] This love of gambling together with an aptitude for delegation pointed clearly to a career in politics.

Back in his first year, however, Salmond had surprised his parents by revealing himself to be a talented boy soprano. Mary remembered arriving late at the school for a 'little concert' and being struck by a moving performance of the traditional Irish folk song, 'The Lark in the Clear Air'. 'I thought it was the most beautiful thing I'd ever heard,' she recalled, 'but I didn't know it was Alex.' He sang a lot at home and on the way to school, and it seems that when the organist at St Michael's Church decided to start a boys' choir, a teacher at the Academy 'pointed Alex out'. 'He took us completely by surprise,'[82] added Mary. 'I used to sing in choirs and things and I took a wee bit of ribbing about it,' Salmond recalled in 2009. 'But on the other hand I was quite good at it so it was a strange thing – on the one hand you kind of kept it quiet because some of my pals would have made a bit of a fool of me; on the other hand once you did it and everybody clapped and said that's terrific and you felt good about that.'[83]

Salmond's vocal talent reached a wider audience when an Edinburgh organist called Dr E. F. Thomas, who also taught at Callendar Park College of Education (a teacher training college), sought out a boy soprano for what would be the only Scottish touring production of Gian Carlo Menotti's *Amahl and the Night Visitors*, an hour-long one-act opera which was then a popular Christmas classic. Alex did two performances in the lead role at Callendar Park and St Michael's Church over the Christmas of 1967/68 and was, according to his mother, 'absolutely marvellous'.[84]

Covering the first performance at the end of 1967, the *Linlithgowshire Journal and Gazette* noted that Salmond was co-starring with 20 girls (Menotti had stipulated that Amahl must be played by a boy) but 'did not seem overawed in the slightest by his female company'. Jean Graham of the *Falkirk Herald*, who had formed part of the 'fine turnout', also observed that 'Alex is a fine wee singer. He has a very pleasant voice and carried the part very well indeed.'[85] The second performance, at St Michael's on 21 January 1968, was directed by Dr Thomas and produced by Mr A. C. Simpson. The story goes that Salmond's music teacher recognised his talent and wanted to export it, to Australia, but that his voice broke at the crucial moment. 'I used to be able to sing lots of octaves and I ended up being able to sing about four notes, so I wasn't good at it anymore,' Salmond recalled. 'But the one thing it left me with was being able to be in front of audiences.'[86] He did not, however, stop singing in public. In 1999 Salmond sang one of his favourite songs, 'O Rowan Tree', with the Scots-Gaelic music star Anne Lorne Gillies for an SNP Christmas CD, while in February 2009 he performed another favourite, 'Caledonia', live on stage with the Scottish pop singer Sandi Thom.

Otherwise Salmond's school reports were 'satisfactory without being brilliant'. He preferred to sit at the back of the class, and took his studies seriously without larking about. Although he did not excel at technical subjects, in his second year he got the prize for history, no doubt aided by his grandfather's early tutorials, while for Sixth Year Studies English Salmond chose to study the poetry of R. S. Thomas, a cleric who became a committed Welsh Nationalist on leaving the ministry in 1978. A difficult man, he refused to support Plaid Cymru because he believed they did not go far enough in their opposition to English rule. He did, however, support the Meibion Glyndwr fire-bombings of English-owned holiday cottages in rural Wales, and also the CND. His poetry, meanwhile, largely concerned his twin passions, the Welsh landscape and the Welsh people, with graphic descriptions of the harsh working conditions many of them had to endure.

Evidence of how his prose and poetry shaped Salmond's thinking can be found in Thomas's essay, 'Some Contemporary Scottish Writing', which first appeared in 1946. Alex was clearly familiar with this, quoting from the following passage in one of his *Herald* columns in the 1990s: 'And so we come full circle back to the crude reality, the necessity for politics, distasteful as they may appear. For it is England, the home of the industrial revolution, and the consequent twentieth-century rationalism, that has been the winter on our native pastures, and we must break their grip, and the grip of all the quislings and yes-men before we can strike that authentic note.'

Thomas was an admirer of Hugh MacDiarmid, the Scottish Nationalist poet, whom he saw as a 'new Don Quixote' and likened to 'the unacknowledged legislator'. Thomas also quoted William Power's description of MacDiarmid as someone who wanted to see 'Scotland "respected like the lave," not for her ships and engines, banks and investment companies, prize bulls and sporting estates, Empire-builders and "heids o' depairtments"; not even for her kirks and her Sabbath; but for her intellect and art, her developed national culture, her social justice and equity'.[87] It is easy to see the appeal of such prose to the teenage Salmond.

So appealing, in fact, that Salmond contacted Thomas directly, displaying typical self-confidence. 'When I was 16,' he later recalled, 'I wrote to R.S. Thomas to tell him what his poems meant. He had a reputation as being an iconoclast with a celebrated short temper. In my limited experience – which consists of two letters, both of which he replied to – he was one of the most patient and forgiving people on God's earth. I never cease to be amazed that such a celebrated poet would take the time to write to me. I got an A [in his Sixth Year Studies English] – and no wonder – because Appendix one was letter one and Appendix two was letter two. That's his letters to me, of course, not mine to him!'[88] Interestingly, Salmond made contact just as Thomas's poetry was undergoing a stylistic shift. Whereas his early period, 1942–68, focused on his portrayal of the Welsh hill farmer and was more overtly political, from 1972 onwards he became increasingly preoccupied with the search for what he called the 'ultimate truth'.

Salmond studied Thomas's most recent volume, 1968's *Not That He Brought Flowers*, which included hard-hitting Nationalist (and some might say anti-English) poems on the investiture of Charles as Prince of Wales and other contemporary issues. Salmond, however, also explored Thomas's earlier works, which concerned a Welsh hill farmer called Iago Prytherch. Indeed, Salmond later told a close university friend that he even identified with Prytherch. This is interesting, for although Prytherch is presented as a symbol of Wales he remained an 'Enigma' to the poet, who confessed that 'there was something else that would worry me as I saw him sweating or shivering hour after hour in the fields: "What is he thinking about? What's going on inside his skull?"'[89] The same question would later be asked about the enigmatic Alex Salmond.

'He loved poetry,' recalled a university friend, 'I think that's where his Nationalism came from and I think he was a Nationalist before he got to university. He spoke about R. S. Thomas a lot to me, it was very important to him. I think when he was first developing political thoughts he did his dissertation on Thomas. Alex gave me a copy of "Not That He Brought Flowers" which I still have, and introduced me to Prytherch, although neither of us knew how to pronounce his name.'[90]

Salmond's other Sixth Year Studies topic was history. He opted not to take the Wars of Independence as his dissertation subject, instead choosing the American Civil War. 'It was my first year [1971] teaching at Linlithgow Academy and Alex chose the topic himself,' recalled Gordon Currie, Salmond's history teacher. 'I think I would have told him to make his dissertation more interesting, to give it more bite, but when I spoke to him he knew more about it than I did. He helped me as a teacher instead of it being the other way round.' They also discussed current affairs. 'When we spoke about politics it was obvious he wasn't a novice,' said Currie, 'he was very keen on it. I told him that in politics you've really got to capture the imagination of the people you're trying to get on board.'[91]

By then Salmond's hero, Harold Wilson, had been replaced by the Conservative Edward Heath following the 1970 general election. The SNP's popularity had peaked in 1968 and when Jim Sillars, author of the arch-unionist polemic, *Don't Butcher Scotland's Future*, convincingly won the South Ayrshire by-election on behalf of Labour, the omens for the general election were not good. While Sillars – within the decade a key influence on Salmond – held on, Winnie Ewing, the victor of Hamilton in 1967, did not. The SNP scored 11.4 per cent of the vote but returned just one MP, Donald Stewart in the Western Isles. Billy Wolfe again failed to secure West Lothian, even though he had been elected chairman of the SNP at the 1969 Oban conference.

Again, Salmond undoubtedly followed these developments and was by this point politically engaged, although not yet a member of the SNP. The Upper Clyde Shipbuilders action of 1971, for example, captured his imagination. 'A youngster at school like myself,' Salmond later reflected, 'was fully behind the work-in.'[92] Salmond also overlapped at the school with a future political ally, the Edinburgh-born Kenny MacAskill, who was four years younger than Alex.[93]

In the summer of 1972 Salmond left Linlithgow Academy, not yet certain what his future held in store, although there appears to have been vague talk of applying to St Andrews University. Not only was the Rector of Linlithgow Academy, James Liston, a St Andrews graduate, but he recruited fellow St Andreans as staff and encouraged senior pupils to study there. Gordon Currie, also a prominent local Tory, was one such Liston recruit and actively encouraged Salmond to follow in his footsteps. 'I studied modern history at St Andrews', recalled Currie, 'and encouraged him to go there because it was good for history.'[94]

That encouragement must have come after Salmond left Linlithgow Academy, for the next year was spent at the Edinburgh College of Commerce, an Edinburgh Corporation institution established in 1966 to provide the city and its surrounding area with vocational education. Salmond studied for an Higher National Certificate in industry, or business studies, at the College's Sighthill campus. Curiously, this year of Salmond's life has seldom been mentioned since, frequent accounts of his education giving the impression that he moved seamlessly from one medieval town to another. There was, however, a racing anecdote:

Back in 1973 I put the whole of Sighthill College HNC Business Studies course on Crisp, who was the best chaser I had seen since Arkle and the most imposing horse I had ever seen. Sure enough off went the giant Crisp from the start and with Richard Pitman hanging on for dear life dismissed the Aintree fences as if they were mere twiglets. Twenty, even 30 lengths clear, Crisp powered past fence after fence only to falter just after the very last. Crisp didn't so much hit the wall as almost hit the elbow on the famous finishing straight and in the shadow of he post was caught by the young Red Rum, to whom the gallant Australian horse was conceding 24lbs in weight. I thought that my fellow students would be suitably grateful that they had had such a memorable run for their money not to mention their each-way profit. Not a bit of it – they were all cheesed off that my tip had got beaten![95]

For the next four years, Salmond backed Red Rum every time. Business studies, meanwhile, does not appear to have engaged him and he considered switching to either advertising or journalism instead. Above all, however, he had arrived in Edinburgh with – as a 1997 profile put it – 'a burning desire to be a somebody';[96] like the young Robert Bruce, Salmond was determined to play a leading role. The first stage in his determination to fulfil that ambition would take him to the University of St Andrews.

Chapter 2

'ACT OF REBELLION'

The stature and the statesmanship of King Robert I appears enhanced rather than diminished when we see him grappling with political difficulties and often failing to find an easy or brilliant solution ... Above all, he had to manage the community of the realm, impalpable, inarticulate, yet always a force to be reckoned with; wayward to lead, yet impossible to drive.[1]

Geoffrey Barrow in *Robert Bruce and the Community of the Realm of Scotland*

St Andrews, wrote the Nationalist Douglas Young in a 1969 history, is a 'town at the centre of three great facets of Scottish life – learning, religion and golf'.[2] These were three facets that, to varying degrees, interested the 18-year-old Alex Salmond when he arrived at the town's university, taking particular advantage of the Old Course with its special rates for undergraduates.[3] Appropriately enough, as Young also noted, St Andrews had also been the 'Headquarters of Militant Nationalism'. The 3,000 students studying at St Andrews in 1973, however, were more likely to preach Conservatism than Nationalism, while it remained 'a relatively small and intimate university'.[4]

'I just absolutely loved it,' Salmond recalled in 2009, 'and if it hadn't been for the money and the lack of it, I'd still be there.' There had been an element of chippiness in his choice, as he later admitted. 'St Andrews is a very Anglicised University, a very socially select university and so I went as a kind of Scottish punter because I wanted to demonstrate something.'[5] There is a side to Salmond that likes tradition, be it Scottish or British, and he therefore had no problem donning the university's red gown, particularly when he realised it earned him bigger tips when conducting tours of campus.

Salmond's choice of subjects was also traditional, although carefully selected. Medieval History was an obvious choice given his grandfather's influence, while Economics was probably chosen with an eye on his future career. 'I think he did economics because it was a good thing for a politician to do,' reflected Peter Brunskill, who became perhaps Salmond's closest friend during this period. 'I think he did medieval history because he loved it.' But, added Brunskill, 'he never seemed to do any work. He was bright and if he had an essay to do he would just do it, although his degree took him longer – five years rather than four – because he had to get extra credits to do honours.'[6] Similarly, Pam Chesters (née Beveridge) remembered Salmond sitting 'in the SRC office reading the *Racing Post* rather more diligently then any economics notes'.[7]

The pleasures of the turf provided an obvious distraction. Dave Smith, another university contemporary, remembered Salmond 'corrupting' him by introducing him to the sport of kings. 'Alex had a revenue forecast which he admitted he was particularly fond of,' he recalled, 'so he was hedging his bets even in those days.'[8] Salmond had an account with his local bookies, which was just off Lade Braes. 'Thanks to him I'm still ahead of the bookies years later,' said Brunskill, 'even after backing Lucky Sovereign in the Derby in Jubilee year (it came 7th). Alex also introduced me to Sea Pigeon which earned us both a fair bit in 1977 and '78. One good tip on Hogmanay 1978 paid for a splendid night out.'[9] 'There was a bookie there [in St Andrews] who used to give a quarter the odds place-only,' recalled Salmond in 2000. 'That was extreme value – it certainly helped finance my studies.'[10] Punting, like politics, was invariably a question of timing, unlike the art of economics.

'The [economics] department was a bit moribund,' recalled Peter Jones, who did first- and second-year economics at around the same time as Salmond, 'and very Keynesian.'[11] 'When Alex was a student the department was going through a few changes,' recalled Rod Cross, one of Salmond's tutors. 'Recently appointed lecturers like myself, Antoni Chawluk and David Cobham [who taught Salmond in the last year of his degree] were trying to introduce more up to date and challenging courses. The older staff tended to [believe that] Marx was a nutter, Keynes was a heretic and mathematics and statistics were not on the menu – the outcome being that the department had been teaching stuff that was out of line with what we younger lecturers – and Keith Shaw – had absorbed at LSE, Manchester, Oxford etc.'[12] There was also

Professor Peter Robson, whose field was developmental economics, and the regional economist Stuart McDowall. The department, however, lacked a visionary leader.

The same could not be said of Salmond's other chosen subject, history. There, Professor Norman Gash was leading a monetarist revolution with the help of figures like Madsen Pirie and Eamonn Butler, who went on to found the monetarist think tank, the Adam Smith Institute, in 1977. Although the so-called St Andrews 'school' owed more to a chance gathering of like-minded economists than any distinctly 'Scottish' tradition of thought, it nevertheless comprised a lively arena of which Salmond would certainly have been aware. Charlie Woods, who studied economics with Salmond, however, recalled that he 'and I both leaned towards the Keynesian viewpoint'.[13] That, however, did necessarily mean that Salmond attended lectures. 'My most embarrassing moment', he admitted in 2006, 'was when I attended a senior modern economics class and the entire class got up and applauded because it was the first time I'd been there.'[14]

Studying economics also consolidated Salmond's pre-existing interest in Nationalism, as fashioned by his grandfather's tales and R. S. Thomas's poetry. 'Looking back, my views when a student about independence were no doubt similar to some Scots now', he later told the journalist Ian Jack. 'I had a natural sympathy with the idea – but it was the economic arguments that convinced me.' 'So there had been no epiphany', enquired Jack, no moment when he saw his life's work as achieving Scottish independence? Salmond replied: 'No, but studying economics was important. I'd grown up with an assumption that Scotland was a poor, wee deprived place that had never had a fair kick o' the ball and could certainly never stand on its own two feet. I started to question that assumption. And then I read a lot and thought a lot and decided that assumption was based on hee-haw apart from an ingrained indoctrination and pessimism.'[15]

Stephen Maxwell, then the SNP's press officer, remembered being invited by Salmond to speak at various university gatherings and recalled him subscribing to the 'dependency theory' of Andre Gunder Frank, predicated on the notion that natural resources flowed from a 'periphery' of poor and underdeveloped states to a 'core' of wealthy states, enriching the latter at the expense of the former. As Keith Webb observed in his 1977 book, *The Growth of Nationalism in Scotland*, the SNP's view was that the 'UK Government has acted, either through malignity, neglect or incompetence, to exploit Scotland and deny her the means of advancement'. Furthermore, from 'the nationalist point of view the exploitation of North Sea oil by the United Kingdom rather than Scotland becomes one more example of the economic rape of Scotland'.[16] This theme would feature prominently in Salmond's political pronouncements, with an inevitable link to the constitutional question. 'It's true that I've never been fascinated by independence as a constitutional abstraction,' admitted Salmond in 1992. 'I simply became more and more convinced that Scotland would be better off running its own economy.'[17] He was, nevertheless, a pragmatist even at this early stage, and frequently quoted the maxim 'politics is the art of the possible' to political contemporaries.

History, however, was probably Salmond's main preoccupation as a student, and must also have contributed to his political beliefs, at least in terms of national identity. The notion of studying Scottish history in its own right, however, was some way off. Salmond complained 'loudly about the difficulty in pursuing studies in Scottish history as anything other than an option in British (i.e. English) constitutional history'. He eventually succeeded in 'weaving it into' the honours year of his degree by taking a 'special subject' class but later reflected that he might not have been so keen on pursuing it had it not 'been made so damned difficult'. 'If, as now, I could have completed a degree course in Scottish history without any bother then I don't know if I would have been half as keen. I was (and am) thrawn in such matters and I suspect most Scots are.'[18]

It was the Nationalist-inclined Geoffrey Barrow, Professor of Scottish History at St Andrews from 1974 to 1979, who taught Salmond about the Wars of Independence in this 'special subject' class. Barrow's book, *Robert Bruce and the Community of the Realm of Scotland*, was a consistent bestseller and highly valued by Salmond ('the best book about Scottish history ever written'), who was particularly attracted by its emphasis on the phrase 'Community of the Realm' as 'one of the first expressions of national feeling in medieval Europe'.[19]

'Alex was a very bright student who took an active part in the class', recalled Barrow, 'and was fond of teasing some of the English students when they jumped to the defence of King Edward I, and thought that Wallace and Bruce were rather a bad thing.'[20] Barrow later told the SNP's Paul Henderson Scott that Salmond had been his 'star student'; to him it was obvious Salmond 'was going places'.[21]

St Andrews, however, was not an obvious context in which Salmond could go places politically, unlike 'Mike' Forsyth, Michael Fallon and

Desmond Swayne, a trio of student contemporaries who all ended up in Parliament as Conservative MPs. Conservatives not only dominated campus politics, but the local MP, Sir John Gilmour, was an old-school knight of the shire who had represented East Fife since 1961. 'The student left was small and divided, with at least five different Socialist and three feminist groups,' remembered Greg Michaelson, a postgraduate student in computational science. 'Most activity was focused on the Students Representative Council [SRC], with shifting alliances jousting with a well-oiled Tory machine.'[22]

When Salmond arrived at St Andrews in the autumn of 1973, members of the SRC included Forsyth, Fallon and two future *Scotsman* journalists: Joyce McMillan (who was treasurer) and Peter Jones. The 'small and divided' student left included the future Labour MP Mark Lazarowicz and Kevin Dunion, who later became Scotland's freedom of information commissioner, while the student newspaper, *Aien*, was edited by both the future Green MSP Chris Ballance, and Brian Taylor, who rose through the ranks at BBC Scotland to become its political editor. He remembered an image of Salmond as 'a lean and energetic individual who wore what I was later to lampoon as a Maoist cap while he rushed about the old town pursuing the cause of Scottish Nationalism. Clearly on the Left, he could easily have been an influential figure within the university Labour Club. Indeed, he confessed to me that he had once voted Labour at St Andrews in a contest where there was no SNP candidate. He neutralized this, however, by also registering to vote in his home town of Linlithgow – where there was an SNP candidate to gain his support. Such options were available to wandering students.'[23] Salmond, however, appears to have remained aloof from SRC and journalistic activity for at least his first year at St Andrews, and his name does not appear in *Aien* until 1976, lampooning Liberals who believed 'in a federal Scotland, in a federal Britain, in a federal Europe, no doubt in a federal world'.[24]

But by Salmond's own account he wasted no time in joining the SNP. It was the era of the three-day week, quadrupling oil prices and the dying days of Edward Heath's Conservative government through militant strike action. 'I can remember [at] Andrew Melville Hall I had a poster supporting the miners' strike stuck to my window,' Salmond recalled in 2001, 'with a light shining behind it so that people coming into St Andrews could look up at night to ... see this "back the miners" poster.'[25] Following a return visit to his old halls of residence as First Minister, he remembered being 'ensconced' there 'for a week', because it was 'so much colder than Lithgae'.[26] Salmond's student digs were also decorated, fittingly, with a copy of the Declaration of Arbroath.

The story of precisely how Salmond came to join the SNP is well known, but not exactly solid. Following an argument with an English girlfriend, Debbie Horton from Hackney,[27] who was secretary of the St Andrews Labour club, she apparently said: 'If you feel like that, go and join the bloody SNP.'[28] Salmond took up the story in 2008:

> The next day, that is precisely what I did, trekking to Dundee from St Andrews. The reason for going to Dundee is that I had absolutely no idea how to join a political party, these being the days before websites made the process very simple. Arriving in Dundee at the local SNP office in 1973, a companion and I were promptly given an address in St Andrews – and hitch-hiked back again, finally to sign on the dotted line. It may not have been the most auspicious and organised beginning to a political career but I like to think that at least it did display a degree of enthusiasm and fortitude.[29]

That same evening Salmond and his 'companion', Tony Lawson, turned up at a sparsely attended AGM of the St Andrews branch of the Federation of Student Nationalists (FSN). As the only two paid-up members, according to another account, they were duly elected president and treasurer. Within a few years, Salmond would also be elected vice-president (to Malcolm Kerr) of the national FSN.

Later, Salmond would depict his student membership of the SNP as an unplanned act, 'more a kind of act of rebellion than anything else',[30] with a political career far from his undergraduate mind. 'My view on this has always that most people who're aware have a political inclination,' he told Ian Jack, 'but the act of joining a political party is an accident. The moment presents itself . . . and then you kinda get sucked in.'[31]

Salmond got sucked in, he claims, in November 1973, in which case he must have moved quickly in terms of acquiring a girlfriend. But Peter Brunskill, Salmond's best friend (together with the Leven-born David Hunt) at St Andrews, remembered a slightly different version of events:

> A day or two [after joining the FSN in September 1974] I was sitting in my room one evening when there was a knock on the door and it was Alex. Sartorially he was quite scruffy and wore a denim jacket and cap with an SNP badge on it. He was very skinny then despite putting away

lots of food. He sat there and talked to me for about two-and-a-half hours and a lot of it went way over my head, because this was a guy with a highly developed political philosophy even at the age of 19. He spoke about his influences, all left-wing radicals, then he spoke about the St Andrews FSN, which he said had been controlled by a right-wing group, so he and some mates had got some people elected and staged a coup. Thereafter a bunch of us followed the Salmond whip, but we were happy to do so. He was the best sort of evangelist; he made you feel happy to be helping out.[32]

If this version is correct, then it seems unlikely that Salmond was elected president at his first meeting of the St Andrews FSN in late 1973, and nor would he have joined the SNP without a shred of ambition. Indeed, Brunskill remembered that the St Andrews FSN, 'a right wing drinking club', was actually 'purged'[33] at the 1974 AGM, after which Salmond, Brunskill and another member called Lawson Brown built up its membership and, according to Alex, made the club 'substantially bigger'.[34] Salmond's later presentation of this story, together with significant omissions from his family background and early life, demonstrate a remarkably thorough approach to the presentation of his public image.

Salmond's friendship with the Burnley-born Brunskill is interesting. 'One thing that emerged over the few years we were at university was that I never once detected a trace of anti-Englishness in him, which was unusual,' recalled Brunskill. 'We used to go along to [SNP] meetings where I was regarded with suspicion for being English, but Alex always accepted my explanation for why I was involved.'[35] In Peter Brunskill, Salmond spotted the potential for winning converts from the unlikeliest quarters.

The political backdrop of the times must also have influenced Salmond. The SNP's high-profile 'It's Scotland's Oil' campaign had begun the year before while at the Dundee East by-election of March 1973, in which the SNP's future leader Gordon Wilson was the candidate, the campaign appeared to bear fruit.[36] Indeed, when Salmond arrived on campus for the first time, the local SNP association and university FSN were actively promoting the oil campaign, while the *St Andrews Citizen* speculated about what the oil boom might mean for the town's economy.

A cultural influence may also have been the BBC's adaptation of a political thriller by Douglas Hurd and Andrew Osmond called *Scotch on the Rocks*, in which separatist guerrillas briefly take over Fort William as a prelude to Scottish independence.[37] It is also likely Salmond saw John McGrath's influential play, *The Cheviot, the Stag and the Black, Black Oil*, in Cumbernauld during its 1973 tour.

Then, on 31 October that year, the long-awaited Royal Commission on the Constitution, chaired by the Scottish judge Lord Kilbrandon, published its report, the most important recommendation being the creation of a directly elected Scottish Assembly. Finally, on 8 November Margo MacDonald scored a sensational win in the Glasgow Govan by-election (Billy Wolfe, contesting Edinburgh North the same day, came third). As a political party the SNP had advanced significantly in the preceding decade, and in 1973 was broadly social democrat in tone though not yet taken seriously by political opponents. It was, in short, an exciting time to be a Nationalist student at St Andrews.

So what sort of student was Salmond? On one level, he was relatively normal. He drank, enjoyed himself and probably spent too little time actually studying history and economics. One indulgence was a board game called 'Diplomacy', also a favourite of Henry Kissinger and John F. Kennedy, which he 'sometimes stayed up all night playing'.[38] Based upon a geopolitical map of Europe, Diplomacy required strategy and negotiation as well as bluff and backstabbing, so was good training for a future politician. Dave Smith, a Labour activist, also remembered playing 'postal Diplomacy' with Salmond, in which participants would record their moves and comments on slips of paper later typed up as a 'press' by whoever was in charge.

Each person played the game as a country, and while Smith remembered Salmond representing Germany, he also suffered the ignominy of having to be England. As Germany, however, Salmond displayed his sense of humour and fondness for Churchillian quotes. 'If I was asked to choose between Eurpoe [*sic*] and the sea, I would choose the sea', he wrote on one slip, with this clarification the following week: 'Mr. Salmond wishes it pointed out that last week's press was a quote from one Churchill W. sometime Prime Minister of Great Britain, as this information will fill the players with greater awe than if they believed the quote to be merely from the works of Chairperson Salmond.' He also could not resist introducing political themes. 'The series of until now, secret talks between the S.N.P. and the Imperial German Government today resulted in a 'small naval detachment' moving into the North Sea simultaneously twith [*sic*] the Scottish declaration of independence,' reported Salmond. 'The Imperial Navy has orders to act as an interim administration and peacekeeping force ... until the new independent government is set up. This could be as soon as 1984 according to reliable sources in the German Ministry of Overseas Aid.' The final 'press' simply records: 'Congratulations, I presume Mr Salmond.'[39]

Another obsession was pinball, which Salmond would often play throughout the night at David Russell Hall. 'We all had our own shots,' recalled Peter Brunskill. 'Alex didn't have a shot, but he did have something called the "Salmond bum-up" in which his first ball would knock down everything, producing the biggest score possible.' He continued:

At that point, just when he had everything, he would want that little bit more; tilt the machine and then lose the game. I mention that because that's Alex all over. He just had this idea that there was no limit to what he could do. I was the same as him, brought up in a council house and from a modest background, but while I reckoned I'd done pretty well to get into St Andrews; while the rest of us were pleased with position 'A', Alex was already thinking about position 'C'. It wasn't just ambition, he had this feeling that the whole world was out there and that he could do what he wanted. This was really inspiring stuff and that's how he persuaded people to follow him.[40]

The same trait manifested itself in Salmond's approach to bridge, a card game that, like politics, required a good short-term memory and strong tactical skills. Brunskill, his bridge partner, remembered him playing bridge 'like he played pinball, always tried to go for more than his cards really warranted, and often succeeded':

Alex was a calculating bridge player who would often bid a contract he knew we couldn't make just so his opponents wouldn't get the chance. He would gamble with the plus and minus scores and often kept us in the game with another chance to win. This meant we sometimes won games when we shouldn't have done, though occasionally we went down so spectacularly that we ended up buying the pies at 6 a.m. As with everything in life he calculated the odds in his head without apparent effort. I've never enjoyed Bridge as much with any other partner, he was exasperating to his opponents who never seemed to get chance to make their contracts, or had to overbid in order to have the opportunity to play them (and often then didn't make them).

As well as this gambling instinct, there was a superstitious side to Salmond's character. 'In his late teens Alex had a very vivid dream that

the next time he walked down Sauchiehall Street, he would die,'
recalled Brunskill. 'As a result when we were in Glasgow we always had
to detour to ensure we didn't do this (although it was OK to walk
up!).'[41]

Salmond also indulged in more serious activities, not least the
direct action typical of students in the 1960s and 1970s. 'I launched
a campaign once to occupy the Hall of Residence as a protest,'
Salmond later recalled, 'but I did lots of stuff like that, lots of daft
stuff and quite a bit of student activism which seemed important at
the time, and some of it was.'[42] But St Andrews, according to Mark
Lazarowicz, was 'certainly never a hotbed of student radicalism or
anything like that'. 'Other places had massive sit-ins,' he recalled,
'but at St Andrews 25 of us marched on the registry, had a cup of tea
with the registrar and then went away.'[43]

It was at this stage that Salmond's parents back in Linlithgow must
have become aware that their son had caught the political bug. In the
long summer holidays and at other points outwith term time Salmond
would base his political activities at 101 Preston Road. Brunskill remembered him being 'massively devoted to his family'. 'I once took him
home on my motorbike and we crashed on the A9, so it sat in his
parents' back garden for ages. Gail and Bobby [Alex's sister and brother]
were both still at school and his elder sister [Margaret] had been over in
Tanzania.'[44]

'I used to sit here and they [Alex and his friends] would traipse
through out to this old car,' recalled Salmond's father Robert, 'there
was hardly room for them because of SNP banners.' He also remembered his son going 'about with Billy Wolfe a bit, being in Linlithgow'.[45]
Indeed, Wolfe's brand of Nationalist social democracy, as well as his
emphasis on professional organisation, must have had a strong influence
on the young Salmond. He later remembered advice Wolfe had given
him 'as a young lad in West Lothian': 'Always remember that the SNP
stands for two things – independence for Scotland and home rule for
Bo'ness!'[46]

Salmond's first major political campaigning experiences were the
general elections of February and October 1974, at which Wolfe was
once again the SNP candidate for West Lothian. Peter Brunskill recalled
standing outside Linlithgow Academy on a freezing cold night at the
latter poll, handing leaflets to those about to vote, and then supporting
Wolfe at the declaration, where he lost, for the sixth time, to Tam
Dalyell.

The following year Salmond was also active in the referendum on the UK's continuing membership of the European Economic Community (EEC). Although the SNP formally campaigned for a 'no' vote, its opposition hinged upon being compelled to join as part of the UK rather than on Scotland's own terms. 'Feeling was also heightened by European centralisation that was anathema to SNP members who had been fighting London control', wrote Gordon Wilson in his history of the party, 'and saw little benefit in exchanging that jackboot for a European model.'[47]

Indeed, Salmond's speeches from this period reveal him to be both informed, and vehemently opposed to continued EEC membership. 'Scotland's bright economic future will be jeopardised by the remote and centralised policies of the Common Market,' he declared at one gathering. 'Already the fishing and steel industries are under pressure from Brussels' regulations. With no Scottish representation on the Council of ministers, oil will be next when the Scottish interests of controlled, planned development conflict with the exploitative, "boom-and-bust" proposal of the EEC Common Energy Policy. The Common Market will drain jobs and investment away from Scotland to the "Golden Triangle" of London, Paris, and the German Ruhr. Scotland knows from bitter experience what treatment is in store for a powerless region of a common market.' 'Within the UK common market,' continued Salmond, 'Scotland suffers a constant drain of its economic lifeblood to London and the South East – the centres of political power ... The same pattern will be repeated on a larger scale in the Common Market.' In stark contrast to his later support for 'independence in Europe', Salmond clearly envisaged Scotland's role as being outwith the EEC. 'Our economic future does not lie with that small segment of Europe called the Common Market,' he continued. 'It lies with the wider world and it is there that the best trading prospects are to be found. If we in Scotland are to take full advantage of our tremendous economic potential, we must break the Brussels stranglehold.'[48]

Salmond was also prepared to work with other parties to ensure that it did. In May 1975 he joined Mark Lazarowicz, chairman of the university's Labour club and later a Scottish Labour MP, to form the 'Students Against the Common Market' committee. Indeed, Lazarowicz recalled campaigning closely with Salmond. 'The only time when Alex Salmond put up a Labour poster and I put up an SNP poster,' he recalled, 'was when he had his SNP "vote no" posters and vice versa, so we'd take it in turns holding the ladders and so on.'[49] Harold Wilson, of course, had, in a cleverly pragmatic move, encouraged members of his party and government to campaign for whatever result they desired.

More than two years later, and despite a decisive 'yes' vote in the referendum, Salmond's opposition had barely dimmed; although it now had a structural, rather than a political, focus. Describing plans for only eight Scottish seats in forthcoming elections to a European Parliament as 'insulting', he reiterated his party's concerns: 'We in the SNP have grave reservations about the Common Market and during the referendum campaign warned of the dangers, dangers which have now been realised, to fishing, farming and industry implicit in EEC membership. However, until the people of Scotland can decide, after independence, whether to remain in membership, as an independent country, it is vital that we have the maximum protection from the excesses of the Brussels bureaucracy. This means campaigning for as large a representation in the European parliament as possible.'[50]

The dominant political issue of the mid 1970s, however, was that of home rule, or rather 'devolution' for Scotland. At this stage all four of Scotland's main political parties were committed to some degree of autonomy in the form of a Scottish Assembly, although the SNP obviously wanted to go much further. In November 1975 the Labour government finally responded to the Kilbrandon Commission by publishing a white paper, *Our Changing Democracy*, which promised directly-elected Assemblies in Scotland and Wales.

Tam Dalyell, Salmond's MP back in West Lothian, was already emerging as his own party's principal devolution rebel. In a polemical text entitled *Devolution: The End of Britain?*, which Salmond would certainly have read in 1977, Dalyell articulated his opposition in uncompromising terms. 'National self-assertion has not done much for the cause of peace or the improvement of living standards in this century,' he wrote. 'It is out of tune with man's struggling attempt to gather himself into slightly larger groupings than before for the better use of his limited resources.'[51]

While staying with his parents in the summer of 1976, Salmond launched the first of several attacks on the West Lothian Labour Party's flip-flopping when it came to devolution. Criticising Dalyell's 'extreme Unionist standpoint' he noted that at the last election both the MP and his local party appeared to have been 'ardent devolutionists': 'I trust this remains their position, for if, as implied by your report, they have committe[d] yet another devolutionary U-turn it could have serious electoral consequences. For while the public might be able to accept (admittedly with some difficulty) that one man might honestly change his devolution stance once, or even, as in Mr Dalyell's case, twice, it would be inexcusable if the entire local Labour Party were to desert the devolutionary platform on which they secured their candidate's election. A devolution somersault now would associate the local Labour Party with the same blatant political expediency which characterises the Party nationally.' Salmond signed himself, rather grandly, 'Editor, "Free Student Press"', of which more later.[52] His reference, meanwhile, to 'serious electoral consequences' was not without foundation, for the SNP had made several gains from Labour in district and regional council by-elections during that year, doing so well that Dalyell even publicly questioned whether he would hold on to his seat.

The wider Labour movement had also experienced a split in January 1976, when Jim Sillars quit the party to establish the ostentatiously pro-devolution 'Scottish Labour Party'. Donald Robertson, a resident of St Andrews, was the new party's chairman and Peter Brunskill remembered he and Alex going 'round to his place one night to discuss the SLP and possible links. It was very friendly but didn't amount to much, sadly.'[53] It is also possible that Salmond met Sillars as early as December 1975, when he visited St Andrews to speak about the devolution white paper, just weeks before he resigned the Labour whip.

Salmond's mentor Billy Wolfe had been responsible for the SNP's October 1974 manifesto, *Scotland's Future*, which gives a fair representation of the party's thinking at the time. Billed as an 'introduction to a practical programme of social justice for the people of Scotland', it showed 'how the wealth of the oil and gas fields off the Scottish coast, added to other natural resources and assets, offers opportunities for greatly improved living standards to the people of Scotland – when they have a *Scottish Government*.'[54] It is difficult to imagine Salmond disagreeing with much of this, although he was probably a little to the left of both Wolfe and the manifesto's definition of social democracy.

Even at this point, meanwhile, there was no overtly cultural dimension to Salmond's Nationalism. 'Alex wasn't a cultural Nationalist at all,' recalled Brunskill. 'I learned to play the bagpipes when I was at university but he hated the sound of them, and especially the sound I made. He also abhorred tartan of any sort.' Salmond did, however, like the music of Paul Robeson, a big hero of the left whose LPs could be purchased via the SNP. 'He was big on Paul Robeson and would quote him,' remembered Brunskill. 'It wasn't just the music and the voice, he admired the dignity of the man.'[55] 'Paul Robeson is a hero of mine,'

Salmond later admitted, 'both musically and politically.'[56] As with most students there were figures he looked up to. Another was John F. Kennedy, whom Salmond would frequently quote using a small book of his eloquent pronouncements.

It is important to remember that Salmond's political consciousness developed, or coincided with, two big growths in Nationalism, between 1967 to 1968 when he was still at school, and from 1973 to 1977 when he was at university. During most of Salmond's university career the SNP were not a fringe concern, they were Scotland's second-biggest party and seemingly on the cusp of a great breakthrough. So although he was in a minority on the St Andrews campus, Salmond was not alone, particularly among young people. Indeed, Keith Webb observed that 'the party has for some years been disproportionately gaining the allegiance of new and young voters ... nearly half of these voters between the ages of eighteen and thirty-four declare for the SNP, compared with around 20 per cent for Labour and Conservative'.[57]

Most contemporaries from this period remember being impressed by perhaps the brightest of this youthful crop of Nationalists. To Mark Lazarowicz, Salmond 'was actually quite normal'. 'Most [Nationalist] activists at that time were quite mad,' he added, 'but he [Salmond] had quite a coherent political philosophy.'[58] Michael Forsyth, meanwhile, remembered always having 'the greatest respect for Alex, and even at St Andrews, where he was a bit of a lone voice, he has always had the courage of his convictions. We used to think he was a bit amusing but he has always believed in an independent Scotland and always believed he could get there.'[59]

Indeed, Forsyth and Salmond make for a fascinating comparison. Both arrived at St Andrews from modest backgrounds (Forsyth's father owned a garage), and both were initially socialist by inclination; but while St Andrews transformed Forsyth into an evangelical Thatcherite, it consolidated Salmond's nascent Nationalism. 'Michael only became a Thatcherite', said a dismissive Salmond in 1990, 'when he saw that was the way forward in the party ... it was more ambition than ideology'.[60]

Forsyth's respect for Salmond, however, was not reciprocated, although relations between the pair appear to have been good as undergraduates. 'Although they were at opposite ends of the political spectrum they had a lot in common,' remarked Brian Taylor in 1992. 'They were clearly both going to be high flyers, but they also shared a similarly wicked sense of humour. They were both masters of the scurrilous satire, and fought for space in the [student] magazine.'[61]

Following one of their clashes in the university debating chamber, Forsyth invited Salmond and Brunskill to his 21st birthday party. This, recalled Brunskill, was 'an excellent evening'. 'He was drinking G&T which Alex questioned, getting the reply that he was learning to like it as it was politically a good thing for a Young Conservative to drink. Forsyth then asked what we were drinking – we had to admit it was Drambuie.'[62] 'He arrived at St Andrews drinking pints of heavy and left drinking gin and tonic,' Salmond later said scathingly. 'People change their minds, of course, but he [Forsyth] changed his drinking habits, his politics and his accent for social emulation.'[63]

Throughout the next 30 years – as both became MPs and rose through their parties' respective ranks – Salmond's distaste for Forsyth did not diminish. Rather sharp barbs about Forsyth litter Salmond's Hansard entries; in 1997, for example, he described Forsyth as 'the Mekon, a malign influence in Scottish politics'.[64] Only occasionally did he admit to grudging admiration for Forsyth, reflecting in 1995 that 'then and now his real talent has been for ferocious backroom organisation ... a determination to pick an opponent's weakness and then devote all resources to pursuing ruthlessly the point to destruction'.[65] Salmond somehow regarded Forsyth as beyond the pale, someone from a modest background who had betrayed his class by opting for the elitist and 'anti-Scottish' Conservative Party.

Rather snide references to 'Mike' Forsyth also litter the pages of the *Free Student Press* (FSP), the publication of which marked Salmond's first substantial foray into front-line student activism. Peter Brunskill remembered 'getting visions of this student paper from Alex, which he wanted to give a free copy of to every student at a halls of residence in Scotland, which he calculated to be 20,000. He had no money, no support from the party, no journalists, no advertising, nothing. I think he needed to raise £2,000 to publish each edition. Undeterred, Alex called in favours from various people for advertising, for instance the Lea Rig Bar in Bo'ness was one of his locals and they agreed to place an advert, as did various party people. Then we distributed 20,000 newspapers on our own, using my beat up old car.'[66]

The first edition duly appeared on university campuses across Scotland in October 1975. 'This paper, as the name implies, is an independent journal,' asserted an editorial presumably written by Salmond. 'Financially and organisationally we are free from reliance on any group or individual. As editor, I am accountable only to the rest of the editorial staff. Having said that, we make no claim to being impartial. We have a definite political position and we make no apology for that.'[67]

That 'definite political position' was avowedly Nationalist. Salmond wrote many of its articles himself, including the mischievous 'McSlickley' diary column. He was a natural writer, if a little rough round the edges, and enjoyed the business of gathering quotes. Brunskill can still picture Salmond buttonholing Margaret Thatcher during a visit to St Andrews in 1976. 'She had amazing security and his interview lasted 5 seconds,' he recalled:

Q: Do you think it right that the universities will not be devolved to the Scottish Assembly? (This was the suggestion of the Kilbrandon Commission and was a hot topic at the time.)

A: That seems to be what people want ... (demonstrating she had no idea what a Nationalist was!)[68]

Brunskill also tried to photograph Salmond interviewing Mrs Thatcher but with unusable results. Another snap taken later that day shows a rather coy Alex, sans 'scruffy cap' but with shoulder-length hair and sporting his trademark beige jacket adorned with FSP and SNP stickers.

A regular target for the FSP was the National Union of Students (Scotland), then dominated by what was known as the 'Broad Left', a coalition of Labour and Communist students, 'a political grouping which, in theory, exists as a forum for left discussion, but in practice is a shabby clandestine electoral device for securing the elevation of hacks and careerists'. Salmond, however, believed that 'the policies of the "broad left" are not the fundamental issue. What really is at stake is two different concepts of how our Union should operate. One (the 'broad left' one) is to treat students as passive consuming units to be bombarded with propaganda and instructed on what to think. The other, and the one supported by this paper, is the idea of a union structure which will allow real involvement by the members, and thus a strong union which will express genuine student concern about education and about society.' Without the Broad Left's 'blundering incompetence', concluded Salmond, 'the F.S.P. would not have been necessary.'[69] The battle lines were thus set for a long-running battle over the heart and soul of NUS Scotland that would culminate in St Andrews disaffiliating and voting on whether or not to join a new Scottish Union of Students, of which Salmond was one of the principal architects.[70]

Tim McKay, who chaired the St Andrews FSN before defecting to the Liberals, remembered the FSP being Salmond's 'big baby'. 'He told me that there was even a copy on the desk at the United Nations,' he recalled, 'which I found very impressive.'[71] Editing the FSP also brought Salmond into contact with Stewart Stevenson, who would become a lifelong friend (and ministerial colleague) despite being eight years his senior. 'He'd heard that I could take and develop photographs so he got in touch,' recalled Stevenson. 'It was typical of the way he approached things, he was able to draw people in, that was his absolutely key skill.'[72]

The FSP's inaugural edition, meanwhile, captured the lively Scottish student scene in which Salmond was now a player. There was major coverage of an FSN report condemning government and universities of 'betraying the ideals' of Scottish education, while demanding changes to 'autocratic and obsolete' university governance. A poster boy in this latter campaign was the student rector of Edinburgh University, Gordon Brown. Commenting on Senate proposals that included the removal of the rector as chair of the university court, Brown condemned them as 'an attempt to make this University safe for the sherry party establishment who believe that they, and they alone, can contribute to the running of this University'. (A diary column also noted the 'new distinguished greying appearance' of Alistair Darling, then president of Aberdeen University's SRC.)

Salmond, in common with many other student activists at this time, appears to have fallen a little under the spell of Brown. Contrasting the performance of 'celebrity rectors'[73] at Scotland's four ancient universities with that of 'student rectors' in an FSP editorial, Salmond praised the latter as 'models of diligence and effective representation': 'No doubt some senior academics would like to see the Rectorship reduced to a meaningless accolade – something equivalent to an honorary degree. But if Rectorship is to fulfil its primary function i.e. to safeguard our universities from complete academic autocracy, then we owe it to ourselves to elect people who are willing and able to take the job seriously.'[74] Salmond could only have been writing about Brown's tenure at Edinburgh University, where in 1975 he had edited *The Red Paper on Scotland*, a widely read if not particularly influential tract that included contributions from the Scottish Labour Party MP Jim Sillars and Vince Cable, the future Liberal Democrat MP who was then a Labour member of Glasgow Corporation. Reviewed in the FSP, Bob

Waugh praised it as 'a timely reminder to the S.N.P. of its socialist duty. Let's get organised.'[75]

Partly in response, the SNP produced *The Radical Approach: Papers on an independent Scotland*, which was prominently advertised in the summer 1976 edition of the FSP and described (probably by Salmond) as a work that 'promises to become a standard text. Initial examination of the proofs reveals a high quality of writing, a large proportion of contributions from the "radical wing" of the S.N.P., and, unlike the sexist "Red Paper", a number of contributions by women.'[76]

Edited by Gavin Kennedy and including contributions by left-wingers such as Margo MacDonald, Stephen Maxwell (a contributor to the FSP), Andrew Currie, Owen Dudley Edwards and Isobel Lindsay, *The Radical Approach* was an important early influence on Salmond. Indeed, in February 1977 he helped organise a conference entitled 'Scotland at the Crossroads' with seminars focusing on the SNP's 'radical approach' to political and social questions. Kennedy and Maxwell were speakers, as was the Highlands SNP activist Rob Gibson (yet another contributor to the FSP). It culminated with a university debate on the motion that 'This Government believes that Independence is in the best interests of the people of Scotland'. Speaking on the government side were Stephen Maxwell, Gavin Kennedy and Jim Fairlie, with Malcolm Rifkind, Jenny Chapman (a Liberal) and Dennis Canavan making up the cross-party opposition.

Peter Brunskill remembered it well. 'The old university library had just moved so we asked if we could use Parliament Hall for the debate,' he said. 'It had once housed the old Scottish Parliament and hadn't been used for a debate in centuries.' 'During the debate Dennis Canavan said the trouble with Nationalists was that they believed they were the sole representatives of the Scottish people. Alex intervened and said "We may not be the sole representatives but don't you think we have the soul of the Scottish people?" "Well sonny," said Dennis, "I hope you don't believe in the afterlife." Alex just roared with laughter, he loved that; he thought that was the most brilliant exchange. He lived for the cut and thrust of debate, even when it was against him.'

Salmond was also fully involved with the SNP beyond the St Andrews campus. Brunskill also remembered witnessing an impromptu speech towards the end of a debate on faith schools at a 1976 meeting of the party's National Assembly in Dundee. 'Alex said he wasn't interested in the politics of the debate,' recalled Brunskill. 'He said the party should vote for what it believed in. Then, he said, "the SNP could become something unusual in Scotland, a party that tells the truth". That phrase made BBC Scotland's evening news and afterwards he was invited on to Grampian TV's news programme.'[77] It seems clear that Salmond caught the media bug quite early on. Indeed, he acted as press officer for the East Fife SNP association, while helping on the subcommittee that produced its newsletter.

In September 1977 Salmond also organised St Andrews walkabouts by four leading SNP 'personalities': Stephen Maxwell, Margo MacDonald, George Reid and Winnie Ewing. The last of these was a great success, and a beaming (and very thin) Salmond was pictured alongside Ewing in the 8 October edition of the *St Andrews Citizen*. The wider goal of the SNP's autumn campaign was, Salmond told the newspaper, 'to show how wealthy this country is in actuality and how, properly used by a Scottish Government, this wealth can eradicate unemployment'. By 'wealth' he did not simply mean oil. 'We also mean our wealth of energy,' added Salmond in a remarkably prescient outline of one of his favourite themes as First Minister 30 years later. 'How many countries have the potential choice of Hydro-electric, wave, solar and wind power to heat their homes and supply their industries with reliable sources of non-pollutant electricity?' He continued:

But above all, by wealth, we mean the people of Scotland. We are universally known as one of the best educated and most highly-skilled peoples in the world, yet almost 9% of our fellow-countrymen are jobless. In the past, London's answer to Scottish unemployment was emigration and, through that, we have lost almost one million people since the war. The SNP does not intend to stand idly by while our people drift in one direction in search of jobs and the wealth which could create these jobs drains down the greedy gullet of the British Treasury. All the Scots need is the self-confidence that knowledge of their country's wealth can give them – and the Scottish Government to make the wealth work for them. Our slogan 'Get the strength of Scotland's wealth around you' may sound terribly un-British to the comfortable mandarins of Whitehall. To almost two hundred thousand unemployed in Scotland it is a message of hope.[78]

After two years at the helm, Salmond resigned as editor of the FSP in June 1977. 'I have decided to make way for a younger man', he joked, 'but more seriously I think two years in one job is long enough and it is time for the paper to have a fresh approach. I will continue, of course, to write for the F.S.P.'[79] Launching and editing a Scotland-wide student newspaper had been an ambitious undertaking for Salmond, but amply demonstrated – even in his early twenties – his self-assurance, campaigning flair, journalistic talent and capacity for hard work. He was, as Brunskill recalled, 'a phenomenal multi-tasker'.[80]

Another of those tasks was as a member of the St Andrews University SRC. It is not exactly clear how much time Salmond actually spent on the SRC (he failed to win a place, for example, in elections on 24 February 1976, despite polling 179 votes), but he was certainly one of a small band of SNP members who spent five years trying to outwit a dominant Conservative contingent. (Membership of the FSN in 1976–77 was 72 compared with 509 in the Tory club.)

'I can recall him sitting at the back of the lecture theatre which was used for SRC meetings,' recalled Peter Jones, a fellow SRC member. 'Lecture room 4 in the Old Quad if I remember correctly, and flouncing out when he lost some vote or other.'[81] In debate Salmond was already formidable but, according to Jamie Stone, later a Liberal Democrat MSP, 'had no lightness of touch': 'If you scored a lighthearted point he would come back with all guns blazing. He was fully in command of the facts during a debate, indeed he was feared, if not the most feared speaker. He would always enter debates late on and come in quickly and make the killer points. He was savage; spoke without notes. During a short pause you could see his mind whizzing and that was the moment he would formulate the attack.'[82] Likewise, Alistair Hicks recalled: 'He was always jumping up to intervene, often on a point of order. He could usually be relied on to make it difficult for the ruling clique. His rhetoric was not as well-honed as it is now, and he had a hankering repetitive tone that made some of his audience doze off, as they thought they had heard it all before. That said, he was a good abrasive element on the St Andrews scene.'[83]

Tim McKay, however, remembered Salmond's rhetoric being polished and apparently spontaneous. 'I remember asking him what he was going to say and he replied: "I never know what I'm going to say until I stand up", then it just sort of came to him.' 'He was a serious politician even then,' added McKay, 'and it was obvious that's what he wanted to pursue. I remember debating Proportional Representation with him and Alex saying "PR's not a policy, it's just a procedural issue.'[84]

Again, these debates, particularly those with the emerging Thatcher-ites in the Conservative Party, were formative experiences. 'I had a glimpse of the future,' reflected Salmond in 1988, 'and it was enough to make anyone swallow.'[85] The budding Nationalist politician also aired his rhetoric beyond the confines of the SRC. One contemporary remembered accompanying him to an SNP meeting in 1977: 'He was in his early twenties but he was already a leader. The meeting felt like a gathering of a revolutionary cell in St Petersburg before the Russian Revolution. It was full of wild ideas and unrealistic people. Alex stood out because he was realistic and he could speak. People twice his age loved him for what they thought he could do. He was capable of sounding like a firebrand, hell bent on immediate independence and nothing less, but his mind was already in control of his emotions.'[86]

At around this time Salmond also asked Willie MacRae, a solicitor and the SNP's candidate in Wester Ross, if he could speak at a series of public meetings MacRae was holding as part of his campaign to win the seat. Jim Fairlie, the party's Dundee West candidate and a member of the party's National Executive Committee, remembered giving Salmond a lift from St Andrews and witnessing his first contribution: 'Now Alex attempted to tell a joke; it was supposed to be at the expense of Margaret Thatcher, who'd recently referred to the economy being strangled by the "tentacles of an octopus". Alex said "I thought she'd said the testicles of an octopus." That went down like a lead balloon; I could almost see the blood draining from their faces, because these people took their religion very seriously. The only person who laughed was Alex. Afterwards, Willie said to him: "You've just lost me 10,000 votes." But Alex never lacked, even then, self-confidence or self-belief.'[87] Peter Brunskill also remembered Salmond telling him that MacRae said: 'Alex, a word of advice, no genitalia north of Perth. He loved that.'[88]

The St Andrews SRC was also a very social body, although the consensus is that Salmond remained aloof from that side of student life. 'When the SRC finished quite late at around 3 or 4 a.m. some of us would go to the bakers' to get a roll,' recalled Jamie Stone, 'but he was never part of that. There was also a drinking element in the SRC, which was held on the top floor of the Union; he was never part of that. I don't recall him being involved in any of the more humorous episodes.'[89] Similarly, Tim McKay remembered that Salmond was 'sociable with a few political people, but never mixed with Tories or Labour people. He wasn't a social animal; he wouldn't go out drinking a lot although he liked to drink. You didn't see him out in the pubs for a session.' The fiercely private side of Salmond's personality was already evident. 'He kept himself to himself,' added McKay, 'In some ways he didn't open up a lot to people so I couldn't say what it was that motivated him.'[90] This did not mean that Salmond was unpopular. As Dave Smith put it, 'he wasn't the life and soul of the party but he was a good guy'.[91]

Des Swayne, however, recalled a more convivial impression of Alex: 'He was a really nice guy. We were poles apart politically but we could not have been better friends. I recall cycling from Edinburgh to St Andrews having missed the last train to Leuchars one night and he passed me on the way back from some crucial by-election in 1978 on some windswept moor and he and Margo MacDonald insisted on cramming me and my bike into their little car. He was a very persuasive speaker but also something of a party animal. He was very left wing and a unilateralist but an excellent fellow to have a pint with.'[92] Recalling his student days in 2006, Salmond revealed that his favourite tipple had been Southern Comfort and milk. 'Somebody told me this was a health drink,' he said. 'I went off it but I thought it was very hip at the time.' He also admitted to a penchant for pies: 'My favourite memory was going on the back of my Honda 50 from my flat to the baker at three o'clock in the morning for half a dozen Scotch pies.'[93]

There were, of course, also girlfriends. One was Marion Macdonald, the daughter of a local SNP activist called Dennis Macdonald (whom Salmond and Brunskill tried very hard to get elected to North East Fife District Council at a May 1976 by-election). Described invariably as 'a complete doll' and 'absolutely gorgeous', Brunskill remembered staying with the couple at Salmond's parents' house 'and them both leaning out of the window to smoke – he smoked a lot – and it wafting into the flat'.[94] Likewise, Tim McKay remembered Marion being 'very pretty'. 'I remember thinking "you've done very well there Alex". The thing was he didn't see much of his girlfriend because he was always away at political things, and for about two years he didn't have a girlfriend at all.'[95] It seems the Macdonald residence became something of a 'home from home' for Salmond, and he 'organised and planned many of his political activities' there.[96]

As already mentioned, Salmond's closest friend throughout his student days was Peter Brunskill, who was the only other Nationalist member of the SRC. Both considered running for president in February 1977, but decided to pull out at the last minute, Salmond claiming that 'due to pressure of work he would be unable to give enough time to the campaign'. In Brunskill's case there was a distinct possibility of failing to graduate, but for his partner in crime this was obvious code for 'I won't win'. *Aien* had a bit of fun spoofing this joint withdrawal as the 'Society wedding of the year'. 'After a courtship of five years, Alex Salmond and Peter Brunskill finally took the plunge and bluffed their way to the altar,' the article spoofed. 'Both bride and bridegroom withdrew their nomination forms shortly before the five o'clock deadline as their respective campaigns would have "interfered with their honeymoon."'[97]

Instead, Salmond decided instead to stand for the education vice-presidency, probably with the intention of using it as a launch pad for the SRC presidency the following year. With Brunskill he produced a campaigning news-sheet entitled 'Gallery Retort', an allusion to a publication produced by Michael Forsyth called 'Gallery Report'. This prompted a twin attack from two Conservative opponents in the pages of *Aien*. The first, by Steve Masty, questioned Salmond's literacy, while the second came from the SRC's arts convener Chris Mann, who accused Salmond of resorting 'to what can only be described as a smear campaign in order to win the Education Vice-Presidency'.[98]

Whether or not Salmond ran a 'smear' campaign is academic: he won, and in the context of student politics that was all that counted. The main issue that preoccupied him during his year in office was a long-running problem with failure rates among first-year students in the science faculty. Even 30 years later he sombrely recalled the 'huge fights' he had with St Andrews, and it was a battle with Nationalist overtones. In short, Salmond believed that the students 'weren't failing because they weren't clever. They were failing because the course structure in the 70s at St Andrews was oriented towards [English] A Levels, despite the fact that it was a Scottish University'.[99]

The issue reached a head just before Christmas 1977 when statistics revealed the extent of the failure rates. Interviewed by *Aien*, Salmond said the 'prevailing attitude among some departments' seemed to be to 'take the least possible action and thus the amount of concern shown is directly related to the amount of press publicity'. The ball, he added, was 'now quite firmly in the University's court'. 'It's time for certain departments to stop asking what's wrong with their students', Salmond concluded, 'and to start asking what's wrong with the courses they provide.'[100]

Early the following year Salmond drafted a paper for the SRC urging action. 'It was a huge scandal', he reflected in 2009, 'and then it was sorted because the University decided to reconnect itself with what it was meant to be doing in the first place.'[101] These negotiations also brought Salmond into close contact with the university authorities. 'He's always been a very confident guy,' recalled Tim McKay. 'Even in his dealings with the university he had a certain authority. He dealt with a chap who was master, Stuart McDowall, a well-known economist and establishment figure, and you could see that he was dealing with Alex as an equal.'[102] In December 1977, meanwhile, Salmond was nominated, along with two other members of the SRC, to join St Andrews Community Council, his first taste of non-university office.

Another contemporary political event that impinged upon St Andrews was the bitter Grunwick dispute, a long-running battle for trade union recognition among employees of the Grunwick Film Processing Laboratories in Willesden, North London. In early 1978 the campus Conservative Association invited George Ward, who ran the plant, to make his first public speech since the dispute began. Salmond responded by tabling a motion at a meeting of the SRC that condemned Ward's visit 'since it was likely to lead to violent demonstrations'. Des Swayne, however, introduced another amendment welcoming Ward that was eventually passed. 'Indubitably,' observed a correspondent in *Aien*, 'Mr. Salmond was wrong to introduce his motion in the first place. The private affairs of affiliated societies are surely no business of the SRC.'

Salmond had, arguably, overstated the prospect of violence, although a group of about 20 people from Dundee, thought to be from the Socialist Workers' Party, were refused entry to the union, while two Labour members had to dissuade them from attacking guests awaiting transport for a post-speech dinner. Meanwhile there were chants of 'Tory Club – Fascist Club', while Ward warned inside that Grunwick had shown 'the unacceptable face of trade unionism'. 'A smoke bomb was thrown,' reported *Aien*, 'though no damage was done.'

Salmond, however, sought to extract maximum political capital from the meeting, accusing the Tory Steve Masty of using Ward's visit as 'a crudely engineered publicity stunt depending on a violent demonstration for its success'.[103] The accusation of publicity seeking was a little ironic considering Salmond's own flare for self-promotion, and his exploitation of the Grunwick affair has to be considered in the context of his bid for the SRC presidency, which was then under way.[104]

Indeed, Salmond's manifesto appeared in the same edition of *Aien* that covered Ward's speech. 'The job of SRC President is basically one of an advocate,' he wrote. 'Two things are crucial if the job is to be done well. First, realising that priority should be given to things the SRC can change rather than to things which are outside its control and second having a good idea of what your priorities are.' Salmond's priorities included weekend library opening, 24-hour visiting in halls of residence (if two-thirds of occupants were in favour), financial help for self-funding students and keeping up the pressure on failure rates among science students. 'These things can be done this year and will be done if the arguments are put clearly and forcibly,' concluded Salmond, 'which is the way to get a positive response from the University.'[105]

Salmond's campaign flyer (entitled 'Are YOU sitting on the Fence?') took a more humorous approach:

Dear Student,

In this leaflet I have tried to steer clear of the usual ridiculous drivel found in SRC leaflets, what a nice guy I am etc. What is surely more relevant is what my record is and what my policies are.

One final point. The basic division in student politics is not between left and right but between students and their own representatives. The one way that gap can be closed is for the SRC to be seen to be achieving results. That is what I pledge myself to ensure.

Yours aye,

Alex Salmond.

He continued by reminding students that he had implemented the manifesto upon which he had stood as education vice-president the previous year. 'Is there another candidate in this election, in any SRC election,' he wondered, 'who can claim to have met all his election promises?'[106] Although Salmond was well known on campus as chairman of the FSN, he stood for the SRC presidency on a 'Broad Left' platform.

At this point there was only one other candidate, a postgraduate divinity student called Bill Hogg who was also the SRC's publicity officer. He was, in Salmond's retrospective opinion, the best candidate. 'I always remember his hustings speech,' he later recalled. 'Bill made a speech saying because Peter was chairman of the Tory club and I was chairman of the Student Nationalists, standing for the broad left that "the issue in this election is not left or right but up or down". He should have won just on that phrase alone.'[107] 'Peter' was Peter Bainbridge, who posed a much bigger threat to Salmond's chances of success.

As with his battle to become education vice-president, Salmond was not afraid to fight dirty. The race, however, failed to excite the wider student body, with only thin attendance at traditional 'SRC hecklings' the week before polling. 'The usual political banterings were exchanged by the Swayne/Masty/Blacklocks/Salmond sectors', reported *Aien*, 'though most effort was wasted since there were probably only one or two dozen people in the theatre who had actually gone along to hear what all the candidates had to say.' 'Alex Salmond got the best general reception,' continued the report. 'Pete Bainbridge was applauded mainly from one corner of the room, while Bill Hogg got off fairly lightly.'

The final result in what *Aien* described as 'the closest ever fought presidential election'[108] was nail-bitingly tense. Although Salmond pulled into an early lead of more than 100 votes, a new voting system meant Bill Hogg's votes were reallocated according to his supporters' second preferences. Initial reallocations were fairly even but after three hours of counting it became clear that Bainbridge was ahead, and he won by only 54 votes out of a poll of 1,311. On the face of it, however, Salmond had performed extremely well considering the relative strength of Nationalists and Tories on campus. Anticipating this, Salmond had enlisted virtually all the foreign students at St Andrews, who voted as a block, but it still had not been enough. Salmond came to refer to it as the only election he ever lost. 'It serves me right because I called him Braindamage throughout the campaign,' he reflected in 2008. 'Last I heard of him he was an executive with BP, doing very well.'[109]

Bainbridge, in fact, went on to work at RMIT University in Vietnam. He remembered Salmond being sharp ('not an intellectual but savvy and hard working') and possessing a 'caustic sense of humour and a clear determination'. 'I believe he lost because of the slowness and the coverage of his canvassing,' he recalled. 'I heard that he got bogged down on the doorstep talking about policies. The election was obviously quite a setback for Alex at the time in terms of morale.'[110]

Indeed, Bainbridge also has 'faint memories of Alex storming out of the count quite vociferously'[111] following the declaration, something later denied by Salmond. 'Peter . . . acted like St Andrews Tories in those days in thinking they had a divine right to win every election', he recalled in 2011. 'I had no hard feelings at all.'[112] Peter Brunskill also remembered Salmond's temperament in this sort of situation. 'I said to Alex once that he wasn't a good loser,' he recalled. 'He quoted Jackie Stewart: "Show me a gracious loser, and I'll show you a loser." He really felt it because he'd thrown everything into it. It was personal to him; he didn't think there was any need for graciousness in defeat.'[113] Salmond, meanwhile, believed he could have won had he had just one more dedicated campaigner, Brunskill having by that point graduated and moved back to England.

It must have been all the more galling that Bainbridge, by his own confession, was a political 'amateur with no real interest in a political career', although he 'enjoyed the cut and thrust of political debate'.[114] Bainbridge did, however, contest the Clydesdale constituency for the Conservatives at the 1983 general election, abandoning active politics thereafter. Salmond later pinned a photocopy of the front page of *Aien*, which announced the result, to the wall of his office at Westminster.

Salmond's defeat coincided with the beginning of a steep decline in the SNP's electoral fortunes. This was clear from its performance in the May 1978 local government elections, as well as in three Parliamentary by-elections throughout the year. For Salmond, however, the experience was invaluable in both personal and political terms, and also belied a growing inclination to take calculated risks. If the 1977 SRC presidential election had represented a tactical retreat, then that in 1978 had marked an ambitious attempt to seize the university's biggest political prize. 'Everything he did, even then, was calculated as to what was in it for Eck [Salmond],' reflected Brian Taylor. 'He was driven by two things: calculation and mischief; he just couldn't resist an opportunity for mischief.'[115]

One such opportunity presented itself at around the time of the SRC elections, when the Young Liberal magazine *Liberator* alleged that the Scottish wing of the Federation of Conservative Students had agreed to draw up blacklists of left-wing students for employers concerned about giving jobs to known troublemakers. 'Even Alex Salmond, not noted for his right-wing affinities,' reported *Aien*, 'conceded that no legitimate organisation unless it was ridiculously naïve would associate itself with such politically suicidal underhand activities.'[116]

Salmond had colluded with Brian Taylor, *Aien*'s editor, to get the story on the campus newspaper's front page, which was then picked up by the *Dundee Courier & Advertiser*. 'It concerned, of course, the outrage of Scotland's oldest university keeping tabs on potentially disruptive students,' Salmond joked in August 2008. 'There was a modicum of vested interest for Brian and I in exposing this story, it should be said . . . In retrospect I can find and see that it was an entirely sensible precaution. But the university's authorities were dressed up by Brian to look like a major sinister conspiracy.'[117]

The months leading up to Salmond's graduation were busy politically as well as journalistically. The sitting MP was Sir John Gilmour, whom Salmond defeated in a debate (assisted by Willie MacRae and the SNP MP Hamish Watt) on the Union in February 1978, while the prospective Liberal candidate was Menzies Campbell, and the Labour hopeful Henry McLeish. At an FSN day school Salmond (still its vice-president) launched a bitter attack on the economic policies of successive Tory and Labour governments. 'The Scottish economy has reached the point of no return,' he said. 'A generation of Westminster bungling and indifference has reduced Scotland, a country with immense economic potential, to the status of an underdeveloped region. The message coming from Westminster is quite clear – Labour government works, 200,000 Scots don't. The message we should send back is that only a Scottish Parliament with economic muscle and full control over Scotland's resources can pull Scotland out of the Westminster cycle of unemployment and emigration.'[118] The similarity of Salmond's language to that used decades later is quite striking.

There were also regional council elections that May, at which Dennis Macdonald and Salmond's friend David Hunt stood for divisions in St Andrews, and the Hamilton by-election on 31 May, at which Salmond once again campaigned for Margo MacDonald. More prosaically, that year saw him earning some extra cash by ball spotting for the Royal and Ancient golf club.

Salmond collected his MA degree in Economics and Medieval History on 6 July 1978, having been awarded second-class honours (St Andrews did not sub-classify in those days). Almost 30 years later, and just a few months after becoming First Minister of Scotland, Salmond took to the same stage in the Younger Hall to deliver the graduation address in November 2007. St Andrews University, he told them, was a 'massive success story in Scotland'.[119]

Chapter 3

'WEST LOTHIAN LEFT'

In the months preceding the Referendum of 1979 I remember in particular three utterances by members of the Scots upper middle class. A distinguished scientist solemnly assured me that 'we are a very poor country and always have been'. The head of a well-known girls' school declared that 'we have never been good at governing ourselves and managing our own affairs'. An eminent philosopher of advanced age asked me: 'What is going to happen to my pension?' These statements I judged to be the quintessential voice of the Scots bourgeoisie.[1]

Geoffrey Barrow, from his inaugural lecture at the University of Edinburgh, *The Extinction of Scotland*, 11 December 1980

Salmond left St Andrews University with the basic political beliefs and tactical instincts that would remain with him for the rest of his career. As Brian Taylor has said, 'he was almost a fully-formed politician even at that stage'.[2] It is difficult, however, to assess Salmond's mood in the summer of 1978 but it seems likely that, despite his natural optimism, it was not good. Losing the SRC election had been a blow to his morale, while Salmond's bad luck continued after his graduation, producing more personal and political disappointments.

It seems Salmond struggled, at least initially, to find work. After graduating he moved back to his parents' house in Linlithgow – as is clear from a steady stream of letters to his local newspaper[3] – and immersed himself in West Lothian politics, chairing the SNP's Linlithgow branch while applying for jobs. He most likely pursued several posts, but was particularly keen on a career in journalism. 'In the SNP at that time, George Reid for example, were lots of people who'd been journalists and I think Alex thought it would be a good thing to build a public profile with,' remembered Peter Brunskill. 'Alex wanted to be a journalist. He applied for a job with BBC television after graduating. He got a fairly long way along the process but didn't quite make it; he was devastated when he didn't.' Indeed, journalism appears to have been a longstanding ambition. As Brunskill also remembers, 'he was looking to write for a living from the first time I met him'.

At this time Salmond had a slight speech impediment: a lispy delivery that meant his 'ths' came out as 'fs', something that had not been rectified by childhood elocution lessons organised by his mother. 'He was quite self-conscious about it and it initially limited his opportunities to speak in public,' recalled Brunskill. 'After his 1976 National Assembly triumph I remember him saying to me after that he just wished the word "truth" hadn't come out as "troof". I think he might even have thought that it had scuppered his chances of getting the BBC job.' It is also possible that Salmond considered becoming a candidate for either the UK Parliament or the proposed Scottish Assembly. 'I remember talking to him about parliamentary constituencies and selections and all of that,' remembered Brunskill. 'George Reid had visited the university and told us that Westminster was no longer the only game in town, and that we should all be thinking about Assembly seats.'[4] There is no evidence, however, that this idea progressed very far.

By November, nearly six months after graduating, Salmond was still without a job. When a couple of English readers accused him of calling Scots émigrés 'unpatriotic' in a letter to the *Linlithgowshire Journal and Gazette*, Salmond replied that such a charge was 'ridiculous' given that 'the vast majority of the million Scots who have emigrated since the War have been forced to through lack of employment opportunities', and particularly so because he 'too will shortly, in all likelihood, be joining this sorry procession'.[5]

Since Salmond has always listed his employment at the Scottish Office as having lasted from 1978 until 1980, it appears that he found work with the Civil Service just as he was preparing to join that 'sorry procession' south of the border. The language is telling. While many of Alex's university contemporaries were perfectly content to head to England for employment (Michael Forsyth, for example, worked in PR before becoming a councillor in Westminster), Salmond certainly was not.

Salmond entered the Scottish Office – Whitehall's northern outpost – having gained one of 20 places from among 200 candidates in the general Civil Service exam. He ended up at the Department of Agriculture and Fisheries for Scotland (DoAFfS), which had a large Economic and Statistics Unit (ESU). He clearly found the work tedious and longed for something more stimulating and, one suspects, high profile. To make matters worse he was based at Chesser House, a grim government building on the outskirts of Edinburgh.[6] Later, Salmond would regale people with stories of how he had devised 'a new forecasting technique for the Scottish sheep flock by counting the number of 23 buses lumbering up Gorgie Road in any half-hour period',[7] while explaining that although his title, Assistant Agricultural Economist, sounded reasonably grand, he had been in fact 'the lowest form of life in the Governmental economic service', carrying 'little pay and precious few privileges'.[8] Tim McKay, a university friend, remembers Salmond visiting St Andrews at around this time and talking about his Civil Service work. 'It was obvious,' he remarked, 'that it didn't inspire him.'[9]

However pedestrian, the Civil Service also provided useful experience for an ambitious young economist. Working in the ESU, for example, gave Salmond the opportunity to contribute to 'an estimable and serious journal entitled *Scottish Agricultural Economics*', published annually by HMSO. Salmond recalled being 'somewhat in awe of this official digest although sensible enough to realise that the rest of Scotland was not necessarily queuing at the bookshops awaiting [its] publication'.[10]

Work also took Salmond to England for the first time since a Hearts match back in 1971, representing the Scottish Office at quarterly forecasting meetings in Whitehall. He remembered these trips with typical humour: 'I was delighted to find that while I was too lowly to justify a single-sleeper compartment, the documents which accompanied me were very important indeed and could travel only by first class. Thus I travelled back and forth to London with my comfort secured by the sensitivity of the forecasts on Scottish sheep numbers. If these had fallen into the wrong hands then the integrity of the state could well have been placed in jeopardy!'[11]

'The first thing that struck us was that he was scruffy,' recalled David Dalgetty, a colleague with whom Salmond would lunch almost daily for the next year and a half. 'He had on an open-necked shirt and jeans, although this was not long after you got told off for not having your jacket on in the corridor at St Andrew's House. None of us looking at him at that time could have imagined he would become an undersecretary, let alone First Minister.'

Another regular luncheon companion was Tony Cameron, whose political outlook was closer to Salmond's and who had also worked in the ESU. Together the trio usually discussed politics, and indeed there was plenty to talk about: the Labour government of James Callaghan had just been humiliated by the International Monetary Fund, while in October 1978 Callaghan had ducked calling a much-anticipated general election. The economic situation was bleak, the notorious 'winter of discontent' was imminent, and the age of Thatcher was less than a year away.

'I remember Alex being derisory about the socialism of the Labour government,' recalled Dalgetty. 'He was more socialist than they were; they weren't socialist enough, but I could never make up my mind just how serious he was about his own professed socialism. He made that common mistake of assuming Scotland was a socialist country and had concluded that the SNP could only achieve independence by calling themselves socialists.' Salmond's Nationalism, however, struck Dalgetty as much more sincere: 'There was something in the soul of the man [Salmond] that burned with a sense of injustice to the Scots – everything was the result of exploitation or neglect of Scotland by governments in London. But when you went through all the arguments you were left with the impression that he didn't know if Scotland would be better or worse off as an independent country. All that mattered was that Scots should rule themselves. I was wasting my breath with arguments against.'

As for Salmond's work as a civil servant it was 'low-grade stuff' without any 'serious economics'. More to the point, he was not around long enough for anyone to take a determined view as to how far he might progress, soon leaving to work at the Royal Bank of Scotland. 'He was a relatively quiet person and had none of chutzpah and bumptiousness he's developed since,' recalled Dalgetty. 'He was also softly spoken. I remember thinking at the time that he was moving to more congenial territory.'[12] The Royal Bank, he meant, almost certainly paid better than the Scottish Office.

Salmond's brief first career did, however, produce at least one valuable legacy. Also working at the DoAFfS as an executive officer was Moira French McGlashan. A motor engineer's daughter from Peebles, on 6 May 1981 she would become Mrs Alex Salmond following a service at St Cuthbert's Parish Church in Colinton, Edinburgh. Conspicuously, the *Linlithgowshire Journal and Gazette* carried no photograph of the happy couple, simply reporting that Alex was now 'settling down to married life'.[13]

The newlyweds soon moved to a new home at Rivaldsgreen House on Linlithgow's Friars Brae, Salmond having finally moved out of his parents' house at 101 Preston Road. Everyone who knew either Alex or Moira at this time recalls them being a perfect match, while their 17-year age gap was barely perceptible. Although not the political animal her husband was, Moira had significant political influence. She was among those unfailingly credited in pamphlets edited by her husband, while Salmond would later acknowledge her shrewd advice and unswerving support. She was certainly devoted to her husband, even teaching him to drive shortly after their marriage, while she would happily feed grateful groups of firebrand Nationalists whenever required.

Some contemporaries, however, regarded Salmond's marriage to Moira with 'bemusement'. 'It was so out of character, so out of style with Alex generally,' recalled one, 'this young radical working class person marrying someone not only 17 years older than him but, by her own admission, of a more Conservative-leaning background and so much more proper than he was.'[14] It certainly must have been a big decision for Salmond to make, not least in terms of family: by marrying a woman in her early 40s he was more or less deciding that children would not be part of his life. But while these considerations would intrigue journalists and, indeed, biographers, it is difficult to reach any conclusion other than that Salmond was deeply in love with Moira and wanted to spend the rest of his life with her.

When Salmond first met Moira, presumably in late 1978, Scottish politics was about to enter one of its most turbulent periods. Not only was the Labour government of Jim Callaghan in its death throes, it and every other party north of the border was preparing a referendum on Scottish devolution, to be held on 1 March 1979, as well as an imminent general election.

The prospects for the SNP, and particularly its eleven MPs, did not look good. Opinion polls demonstrated the Nationalist tide had turned, while there were also internal tensions between the party's Westminster representatives and its Edinburgh-based leadership. One such flashpoint concerned how the party ought to approach the 1978 Queen's Speech.

Salmond weighed in to the debate in a lengthy, and typically well-written, article for the *Scots Independent*, a monthly journal read by many Nationalists although independent of the party. Salmond criticised a recent article by Douglas Henderson, the MP for East Aberdeenshire, as representing 'attitudes that can only bequeath the SNP missed opportunities in the present and serious problems for the future'. 'For surely what matters about the now key position of our MPs in the Westminster political arithmetic is *not* the event of how they vote on the big day in November', wrote Salmond, 'but the process of how they use, or fail to use, the opportunity of intense media interest to drive home the SNP message to the people of Scotland.'

A more 'fruitful strategy', argued Salmond, was

> to be actively attempting to influence what is in the Government's programme and more importantly telling the public what the SNP believe should be in the Queen's Speech. Let's be quite clear about this. I'm not talking here about pacts or agreements, formal or informal. That idea would be rejected out of hand by all responsible nationalists. But what I am talking about is the difference between positive and negative policies. The difference between passively reacting to what the Labour Government decides to offer in 24 hours in November (which is what the Parliamentary Group appear to be doing) and positively seizing the political initiative by stating and restating what the SNP believe should be in the Government's programme (which is what I believe the Parliamentary Group should be doing).

Salmond said the SNP's MPs should be pushing for 'an oil fund for the Assembly, an early date for the referenda ..., Government action to stop land speculation and safeguards against nuclear dumping, further action on fishing limits, etc'. The 'press speculation' – already important to Salmond – 'would then not be on how the SNP were going to react to the Queen's Speech but whether or not the Government were going to cave in to SNP demands. Then when the big day dawns, if the Queen's Speech has met a substantial part of the SNP programme our MPs could keep the Government in power safe in the knowledge that they had provided the Scottish public with devastating proof of our claim to be "Good for Scotland". If, on the other hand, the Government refused to meet the SNP priorities our MPs could bring them down safe in the knowledge that they had clarified the issues on which the election in Scotland could be fought and won.'

Salmond would advocate remarkably similar tactics three decades later. He was also concerned by Henderson's statement that 'the Parliamentary Party welcomes advice and counsel from party candidates, office-bearers, executive committees and so forth but will itself, as a group, make the decision'. This, he assumed, meant they were asserting their independence from the party leadership in Scotland. 'Tensions between the leadership at home and the leadership at Westminster should come as no surprise to the SNP,' wrote Salmond. 'However, the issue of split leadership is one which will have to be settled within the Party and settled quickly otherwise we shall be continually treated to absurd spectacles like the three directly conflicting SNP statements inside 24 hours of Callaghan's no election broadcast.' He continued:

No one is denying that the Parliamentary Group must be free to determine Parliamentary tactics but the question of the vote on the Queen's Speech is not one of tactics but of fundamental Party strategy. Surely that is something which, in our Party, is determined by the Party executive as elected by our conference. If not, then it is easy to see a situation in a few months time where there will be four separate branches of SNP leadership – one for Westminster, one for the EEC Parliament, one for the Assembly and one for the rest of us. That farcical position is the likely outcome of the attitude reflected in Douglas Henderson's article.

Salmond concluded by apologising if he seemed 'over-critical of the Parliamentary Group. No one would acknowledge sooner than I the enormous problems they face operating in a hostile Parliament reported by a hostile press.' But the issues he had raised needed 'discussion *now* if present and future Westminster balance of power positions are to be made to work for us rather than allowed to work against us'.[15] Salmond's preferred approach to the Queen's Speech demonstrates how essential he regarded tactics to keeping the SNP relevant in tough political times.

Nor did Labour politicians escape Salmond's caustic pen and forensic analysis. Commenting on the continued flip-flopping of his local Labour Party on the devolution issue, Salmond wrote: 'So the cat is finally out of the bag and West Lothian Labour Party have finally declared their Devolution Policy which is apparently that they have no policy. A far cry from the halcyon days of October, 1974, when they hung on, if tenuously, to their majority by campaigning full tilt for self-government behind the then pro-devolution Mr Dalyell. At least we know now that the local Labour Party are every bit as unscrupulous as their MP. "Sic a parcel o' rogues in a nation!"'[16]

The pages of the *Linlithgowshire Journal and Gazette* also provided Salmond with ample opportunities to defend and promote the aims of the SNP. Responding to one letter from a Mr Simpson, he became positively evangelical:

Unionists, like Mr Simpson, seem quite pleased with the state of the country and see it as a matter for celebration that things are better than in

1950. Nationalists, on the other hand, want Scotland to achieve the same degree of economic success and social progress of every independent European nation. To that end the SNP have developed and published the most comprehensive and detailed policy programme ever offered to the people of Scotland. Mr Simpson claims never to have heard of SNP policies. Well, if he cares to visit the SNP rooms in Linlithgow any Saturday morning, I will personally present him with the SNP policy statement on any aspect of Scottish life he cares to mention.

Furthermore, Mr Simpson would 'look in vain if he wishes to label the SNP as Tory or Labour, who will be perfectly capable of presenting their own shop-soiled policies in an Independent Scotland. What he will find is a programme based on radical democratic reform and social justice, designed to propel Scotland out of its present provincial backwater and back into the mainstream of world affairs as a free and prosperous country.'[17]

Salmond's analysis of Scotland's economic problems was also reasonably well developed: 'In the modern economy around 70 per cent of industry is "footloose", i.e. it can locate virtually anywhere for similar costs. Far from being disadvantaged in a geographical sense Scotland is in an excellent strategic position for world trade in the American and European markets with unrivalled deep-water facilities . . . Scotland's fundamental economic problem is not distance from markets but distance from Government and the lack of the social and economic infrastructure that it is the duty of governments to provide.'[18]

Unsurprisingly, Salmond saw the solution to Scotland's economic woes primarily in constitutional terms. He expanded further on this in a letter to the *Guardian* in September 1978. An article by Terry Coleman, wrote Salmond, had presented the reader 'with one gem of post-imperial delusion – "an influence on the world was better than mere independence," he declared, as if it were an obvious truth'. Yet, 'If "Coleman's law" thus explains crippling rates of unemployment, emigration and social deprivation as the price Scotland should pay for having "influence in the world," I can't see this proposition having much support in Scotland. I, for one, would settle for a little Scandinavian-style democracy and prosperity to replace British-style poverty and hypocrisy.' Coleman's article, he continued, was also 'symptomatic of the complete failure of the English "quality" press to seriously analyse the political revolution that has occurred in Scotland over the past 10 years'. 'How many of your readership', asked Salmond, 'have been informed of the motivation and philosophy of the party'?

The 40 per cent rule, under which 40 per cent of the Scottish electorate were required to vote yes in order for a Scottish Assembly to be established, was a particular bugbear for Salmond, and indeed for any serious supporter of devolution. 'I suggest that if democracy was being so abused in a UK referendum,' Salmond added in his *Guardian* letter, 'then you would be screaming criticism from every leader. I would have a care ... the philosophy of ballot rigging could soon be applied south of the Tweed.'[19]

Elsewhere, Salmond called this 'the most disgraceful distortion of democracy in Britain since the rich were able to vote twice', and that ballot-rigging 'by which everybody who doesn't vote be they dead, on holiday or at home in the bath is counted as being against Devolution' was 'something which the Scottish people are unlikely to forgive or forget'.[20]

'I cut my political teeth in West Lothian,' recalled Salmond in 1994, 'where local politics has always been a "take no prisoners" affair.'[21] When, however, in January 1979 Salmond was appointed press officer for the West Lothian 'Yes for Scotland' (YFS) campaign (an offshoot of the national all-party 'yes' campaign led by the former judge Lord Kilbrandon), hostilities were put on hold. In advance of a public meeting at Linlithgow Burgh Halls to launch the campaign, Salmond demonstrated his willingness to work with other political parties when he called it a campaign 'for people of all political parties and those of none'. 'Anyone who cares about Scotland's future is welcome in this campaign,' he said. 'We intend to win this fight on the strength of the overwhelming arguments in favour of Devolution and to demonstrate by the breadth of support we attract, just how negative and extreme Mr Dalyell's position is.' He explained:

Above all we hope to get across three specific points. Firstly that the Assembly will improve the efficiency of government in Scotland by abolishing the monster [local government] regions and by providing, for the first time, democratic control of the Scottish Office bureaucracy. Secondly that the Assembly will improve the standard of government in Scotland by providing the opportunity for improved legislation on Scottish education, health, local government, law and the many other domestic affairs which Westminster has simply lacked time to consider properly. Thirdly the Assembly will be a voice and a political force working for Scotland, in a way which no Westminster MP or group of MPs could hope to emulate, ensuring that Scotland's interests are not neglected in London or in Brussels.[22]

Again, Salmond's arguments for devolution would remain largely unchanged between 1979 and the second devolution referendum of September 1997. He was instinctively a 'gradualist' who believed that devolution was a staging post on the road to full sovereignty. Indeed, SNP campaign material from the period promised that a 'Scottish Assembly' would be the 'first step to independence'.[23] Also remarkably consistent was Brian Wilson, the chairman of Labour's Vote No Campaign, who wrote in Salmond's local paper that 'Under an Assembly, the real problems of Scotland – poor housing, unemployment, deprivation – would be no less grim than at present'.[24]

Salmond was clearly in his element. The *Scotsman* journalist Neal Ascherson later recalled watching as a campaign team run by Salmond 'deftly' slid 'its message into local papers and radio stations'. 'This group was a coalition of SNP, Tories, Liberals, Communists, the National Union of Mineworkers and some of the brightest survivors of the "Sillarsite" SLP,' added Ascherson. 'They took turns haranguing the shoppers in the Steelyard at Bathgate, who took pains not to be impressed.'[25]

An inactive local Labour campaign (on account of Dalyell's opposition) also led to some covert activity which would no doubt have infuriated some local Nationalists. 'The Labour Party nationally were campaigning yes, but in West Lothian they were not campaigning,' recalled Stewart Stevenson, by then chairman of the West Lothian SNP. 'So Alex and I arranged to collect the leaflets and posters for the Labour Party and we ran a virtual Labour Party campaign on their behalf.'[26] As an academic account of the campaign noted, it was 'clear that the SNP activists were the mainspring of many local YFS groups as well as of the SNP Yes campaign. But many Party members felt that the trumpet gave forth a more uncertain sound than might have been expected.'[27]

Indeed it did. On 1 March, both the Lothian and Central regions of Scotland voted 'yes', but only just. In Lothian, 187,221 voted 'yes' to 186,421 voting 'no', while in Central, 71,296 voted 'yes' and 59,105 'no'; 34 per cent in both regions, meanwhile, did not vote at all. The result nationwide was similarly close and, having failed to secure a 'yes' vote from 40 per cent of the Scottish electorate, the Scotland Act – and with it the Scottish Assembly – was effectively dead. It would not be the first time Salmond was disappointed by the electoral behaviour of his fellow Scots.

To make matters worse, he had not been able to cast his vote. Salmond later explained to his local newspaper that his 'name had been entered by mistake on the absent voters' list. Something which it is impossible to check before polling day and impossible to do anything about on polling day, and no doubt, something which applied to many other non-voters round Scotland.'

Moving on to the political ramifications of the result, Salmond asked if it was 'too much to expect that Mr Dalyell will now put aside his personal viewpoint and accept the majority vote in Scotland and the resounding Yes majority from those people in West Lothian who were fortunate enough to be able to vote in the referendum?'[28] The answer from both Dalyell and James Callaghan's government was essentially 'no'. After cursory attempts to salvage the Scotland Act through cross-party talks, the Labour government lost a motion of no confidence on 31 March by just one vote. In a decision that was to haunt them for decades, the SNP's 11 MPs joined the Conservatives in the 'no' lobby.

This, claimed Labour in West Lothian, meant the SNP had voted against devolution, something swiftly rebutted by Salmond: 'The truth is, of course, that the SNP voted against the Government because the Prime Minister could not even promise to try and put the Devolution Act through the Commons ... However much the SNP and the Liberals might like to accept the responsibility of bringing down a Government which has doubled unemployment and prices (and which is now engaged in strike-breaking against public sector unions) the fact is that Jim Callaghan was brought down by his own back-bench MPs. For Mr Dalyell and his fellow anti-devolutionists made it quite clear that they would rather see the Government fall than vote for the Devolution Act.' Salmond concluded with his usual pop at the local MP. 'Mr Dalyell is not a bad MP for West Lothian because he is an aristocrat,' he wrote. 'He is a bad Labour MP for West Lothian because on issues like Devolution and the EEC he has ignored the democratic decisions of the Labour Party and the majority wish of his constituents.'[29]

The use of the word 'aristocrat' belies Salmond's Marxist leanings during this period. 'I was the antithesis of much of what he believed,' reflected Dalyell several decades later. 'I think Alex may have reacted, understandably, against that. Part of his embracing of the Scottish National Party was a reaction against the Unionist establishment epitomised by me, everything that irritated him.' Even the fact that Dalyell was a Black Bitch ('Alex and I are males of the species'[30]) did not absolve him, leading Salmond to conclude that on the issues of devolution and Europe 'he will be defeated at the coming election'.[31]

That proved to be wishful thinking. At the general election held on 5 May Billy Wolfe was again the SNP candidate, but was again defeated by Tam Dalyell, this time by a decisive 36,713 votes to 16,631. In the rest of Scotland just two SNP MPs survived the electoral cull. Within days Salmond was articulating what was to become the stock SNP charge against the new Conservative government of Margaret Thatcher. 'Despite attempts to persuade us otherwise,' he wrote, 'Scotland did say "Yes" in the referendum by a majority of over 80,000. 52% of those voting said Yes and 48% said No.' He continued: 'The Conservative Government who, with the collaboration of Mr Dalyell, are about to repeal the Scotland Act received only 23% of the electoral roll in Scotland. Of those voting 70% voted against their policies and only 30% for them. If they do not consider a clear majority constitutes a mandate to implement the Devolution proposals how can they consider their massive minority gives them a mandate to destroy the Assembly Act?'[32]

A few weeks later Salmond offered his analysis of the election result, admitting that the SNP had taken 'a real hammering': 'I would suggest that the main reason for the election result here, and elsewhere, was a general attempt to "stop Thatcher" by voting Labour, and the lesson that Scots should take from the results is that you cannot thwart a Tory majority in England by voting Labour in Scotland ... West Lothian voted Labour and Scotland voted Labour, and [as] a result we have a Tory Government and a quasi-Tory MP.'[33]

Completing an electoral hat trick were the first direct elections to the European Parliament in June 1979, at which the SNP polled a respectable 19.38 per cent of the vote, enough to elect Winnie Ewing in the Highlands and Islands. 'During that period I think Alex and I were surviving on about three hours' sleep a night,' recalled Stewart Stevenson. 'I lost a lot of weight and so did Alex, although he was already skinny, and it probably didn't do his health an awful lot of good.' He added:

> At the end of the campaigning day we'd go back to my house in Linlithgow and we'd work on the next day's press release, which I'd type up with several carbon copies. That would take us up to 1 a.m. and the next day I'd drive through to Edinburgh and distribute them to the media ... Alex had a flair for organisation. He had a very clear idea that campaigning was a business activity with measurable inputs and measurable outputs and that it

could and should be done in a professional way, that nothing you did was without a purpose. Yes you had to create the political environment that enabled people to vote for you but at the same time you had to identify the people likely to vote for you on the day and make sure that they did.[34]

Salmond, therefore, found the referendum and general election results profoundly depressing, later referring to 1979 as 'that *annus horribilis* in British politics'.[35]

Indeed, the referendum experience had a deep impact on the SNP as a whole. The 'experience of 1979 when the SNP had campaigned full tilt for an inadequate Labour scheme, while Labour campaigned half-heartedly,' reflected Salmond in 2000, 'had soured many in the party to the idea of being "entrapped" in the devolution process.'[36] It also convinced many Nationalists that no UK government could be trusted with consultations on Scotland's constitutional future, a suspicion that would cause Salmond problems as leader of the SNP more than a decade later. 'With the drumbeat of self-determination silenced,' he later observed bleakly, 'Scotland lapsed into a dark political decay of acrimony and recrimination.'[37]

Salmond, meanwhile, was busy carving out an alternative, this time political, career for himself within the SNP. He did not choose a conventional route. While others pounded the streets, kept their heads down and drafted dull but worthy resolutions for the party's National Council, Salmond took a much riskier option.

It was the Australian-raised Scot Roseanna Cunningham who, together with her brother Chris, first floated the idea for what became the '79 Group' during the February referendum campaign. Both then worked at the SNP's HQ, Roseanna as assistant research officer, and they named the group after the year of its formation. On the Saturday following the referendum 'defeat', Margo MacDonald, the party's deputy leader, also made an influential speech at a meeting of the party's National Council.

MacDonald's analysis was simple: while working-class Scots had voted 'yes' in the referendum, Scotland's middle classes had voted 'no'. The SNP, therefore, had to look to the former in order to build future support. Although this interpretation of the referendum result was flawed, eight Nationalists sympathetic to MacDonald's viewpoint met in Edinburgh on 10 March, and between 30-35 attended a second meeting at the city's Belford Hotel on 31 May. There, the clumsily named 'Interim Committee for Political Discussion' became the 79 Group with three spokesmen, Margo MacDonald, Andrew Currie and Alex Salmond. Salmond later assumed responsibility for publicity, regularly dispatching 79 Group badges from his home in Linlithgow.

Although not the group's leader as such, the former Lothian Regional councillor Stephen Maxwell quickly became an influential figure. 'I remember going to lots of meetings at Friars Brae in Linlithgow,' he recalled, 'Alex and Stewart Stevenson used to live very close to one another.' 'Stewart Buchanan would be there, Alex, Stewart, quite often the Cunninghams and Kenny MacAskill, for 79 Group committee meetings. Alex would be friendly and chummy and keen to be friendly, not just as a political colleague, but I don't remember him ever being very intimate or giving much away. There was a sense that he was holding back to some degree. He was involved but not that involved.'[38]

On the fringes of the Group was Billy Wolfe, whom Salmond had known for nearly a decade via West Lothian politics. Though no longer SNP leader following the 1979 general election, he became a sort of father figure to the 79 Group (or 'as their stooge',[39] according to Arthur Donaldson, a former party leader). 'Not only did the West Lothian members enjoy the prestige of West Lothian SNP's long and vigorous challenge to the Labour Party in an industrial constituency', observed Maxwell in 1985, 'but they were well organised and led by two of the 'discoveries' of the Group: Alex Salmond . . . and Ken MacAskill.'

The latter was a radical young lawyer whom Salmond had persuaded to join the SNP following years of intermittent activism. Maxwell called this contingent the 'West Lothian Left', which also included Stewart and Sandra Stevenson, who hailed, like MacAskill, from Linlithgow. 'Their influence within the Group', added Maxwell, 'helped to confirm a model of Scottish society in which the industrial working class figured as the only potential challenger to the British state.'[40] More widely, however, neither Salmond nor MacAskill were, at this stage, particularly prominent.

In an early paper for the 79 Group, meanwhile, Salmond penned a critique of the SNP's performance in the late Parliament. 'There is a distinction to be drawn between policies and philosophy,' he observed. 'I would suspect that the Parliamentary Group of Oct 1974–May 1979 would come out rather well if an examination were made of the number of specific SNP policies they voted against . . . And yet I would say that, by in large [sic], SNP elected representatives have not presented an image consistent with Party feeling.'[41] Later, in 1982, Salmond would reflect that 'the "all things to all men" approach, further muddied by the voting habits on ... of our Parliamentary Group, drove us to complete defeat in the class-dominated election of 1979'.[42] Throughout the short life of the 79 Group, Salmond would often indulge in such simplistic Marxist analysis.

The 79 Group's three guiding principles, meanwhile, were Nationalism, socialism and republicanism. As James Mitchell recalled of a conversation with Salmond, 'he agreed with certainly one of the three objectives of the 79 Group – independence; [had] some sympathy with the second – socialism; but not a lot of sympathy with the third – republicanism'.[43] Salmond's attitude towards the monarchy was tactical rather than ideological. Peter Brunskill remembered Salmond refusing to attend a meeting of the Scottish Republicans at university, explaining 'that in terms of the future of Scotland, republicanism wasn't going to make any difference to how the country was governed. He said it was irrelevant so I'm not going to bother with it.'[44]

In the context of the 79 Group Salmond continued to view it as a distraction, or an issue that at the very least ought not to be treated as a priority.[45] Rob Gibson, another member of the group, recalled that Salmond, MacAskill and Sillars 'were more pragmatic and had a difference of emphasis, they didn't see the monarchy as the highest priority'.[46] Indeed, Salmond later told the journalist Arnold Kemp that he reckoned the group's biggest mistake had been its espousal of republicanism.

In Salmond's eyes the SNP's recent problems were not only tactical, but also structural. He was especially critical of the 'haphazard process' by which elections for party office were held. 'The result is to favour seniority and notoriety regardless of politics and, one suspects, merit.' In terms of the Group's prospects, he added in a 79 Group paper, 'A lot will depend now on how we organise ourselves within the Party and how other interests respond to our presence. I would have thought that the role of the "79 Group" includes organising backing for specific people and motions within the Party's councils, and some thought should be given as to how this can be best achieved.'

He also dwelled upon the notion of representative democracy. 'The general feeling of the "79 Group" would be against the notion of political freedom for elected representatives and towards the idea of a delegate role accountable to the Party,' he wrote. 'British politics provides a fine example of how the concept of an M.P. being the representative of all his constituents is actually used as a pretext for M.P.s being responsible to nobody.' Salmond, well known for his lack of interest in political ideology, clearly had not read his Burke.

As for the SNP, Salmond continued, a 'remarkable feature' of the party had been 'that it has been more of an apolitical party than a political one ... political uniformity has not brought unity and conflicts have emerged on a personal level rather than a political one. It may be unfair, but it is certainly revealing, to point out that the most passionate speech at the last National Council, climaxed by a Party Vice-President "gesticulating" at the audience, was not over some philosophical divide but because someone had suggested he was "heartless".[47]

Salmond, meanwhile, remained active in his local party. In April 1980 he was unanimously re-elected chairman of the Linlithgow branch while it geared up for district council elections in which the SNP hoped to secure a second term. Jimmy McGinley, an SNP councillor to whom Tam Dalyell remembers Salmond being quite close, was contesting the town for the first time, while Stewart Stevenson was also a council candidate.

The campaign quickly became bitter, especially when Salmond ('himself a professional economist') publicised unflattering statistics about the previous Labour-run district council in a propaganda sheet called the 'West Lothian Standard'. 'Labour are on the run from the facts in West Lothian,' wrote Salmond. 'They have no answer to the figures which show that the SNP have done more and asked for less since taking control of the council in 1977.'[48]

In the event, McGinley lost to the independent Jim Clark while Labour regained control of the council. Demonstrating an emerging talent for presenting defeat in the best possible light, Salmond said the Labour Party were 'now on a hook of their own devising'. 'It is clear ... that Labour won the election by ... concentrating on the general argument that they could somehow protect Scotland from the Thatcher Government'. Labour, therefore, had 'sown the seed of their own destruction by promising to achieve something they are so clearly unable to do. We shall see if the Labour promises made in this campaign will stand in the political winds which will blow over the next few years.'[49] The young Salmond also had, it seemed, a penchant for cliché.

Salmond warmed to this theme at the Rothesay SNP conference in June 1980. 'The Labour Party are political eunuchs who have neither the will nor the means to stop Mrs Thatcher,' he told delegates. 'Despite having a clear mandate from the people of Scotland, they have failed to prevent the worst excesses of Thatcherism. They have failed to prevent cuts which have closed wards in our hospitals; they have failed to prevent the disruption of our children's education, with Labour councillors actively supporting Tory policies which have led to chaos in our classrooms. And these so-called "champions of the working people" are standing idly by while Scottish dole queues grow even longer.'[50]

Tam Dalyell, meanwhile, remained a regular target. 'Scotland is now totally helpless against a Government we did not elect but was forced upon us by the Tory voters of the south-east of England,' wrote Salmond. 'And the disgraceful truth is that Mr Dalyell would rather see Margaret Thatcher ruin Scotland from Westminster than even the Labour Party govern Scotland from a Parliament in Edinburgh.' He continued:

> If we had a Scottish Assembly operating in Edinburgh today, even of the type proposed by the Labour Government, the political situation in Scotland would be a good deal brighter. Not only would the Assembly have been able to directly control Scottish housing, education and criminal justice to name but three areas, where the Tories are foisting their minority viewpoint on the rest of Scotland, but the institution of a Scottish Parliament could have provided the bulwark Scotland needs against Tory economic policies. Margaret Thatcher's Government, with the support of little more than 20 per cent of the Scottish electorate, would have found the greatest difficulty in running full-square against the views of a directly-elected Assembly speaking for Scotland.[51]

This critique was to remain virtually unchanged over the next decade, that of a 'feeble' block of Scottish Labour MPs unable to deliver a tangible response to, or protection from, Thatcherism, although Salmond was always careful not to rubbish the spirit of the Labour movement. 'While many of us, as socialists, are attracted to the original aims of the Labour Party,' he said in late 1979, 'we cannot stomach the sort of hypocrisy at national level, incompetence at local level, and corruption at both, which has disgraced Labour administrations over the past 25 years.'[52]

The aims of the 79 Group, meanwhile, were outlined in seven publications called, rather ostentatiously, the 'SNP 79 Group Papers'. These varied in quality but two, *The Case for Left-Wing Nationalism* (No. 6) and *The Scottish Industrial Resistance* (No. 7), came closest to fleshing out the bones of the group's thinking. The former, written by Stephen Maxwell in 1981, proclaimed that 'the SNP must look to the urban working class to ... establish itself as the radical Scottish alternative to the Labour Party'.[53]

The Scottish Industrial Resistance, meanwhile, attempted to explain how. This included an account of the Plessey dispute – during which more than 200 workers had 'occupied' the Bathgate electronics plant in protest at its planned closure – by Kenny MacAskill, who had given the workers creative, and ultimately successful, legal advice. This, according to an introduction by Salmond, was a key event in his party's development. The SNP's track record on industrial politics, he lamented, had not 'been a distinguished one' with no attempt to preach 'nationalism on the shop floor as well as on the doorstep'. As a result of 79 Group agitation, Salmond argued, the 1981 SNP conference had recognised 'that a real Scottish resistance and defence of jobs demands direct action up to and including political strikes and civil disobedience on a mass scale'. Although this sort of engagement was not new (Billy Wolfe's Association of Scottish National Trade Unionists had been established in the 1960s and revived in the 1970s), the 79 Group took it to a more public level.

It is clear that this was the 79 Group strategy Salmond took most seriously. Writing to the *Glasgow Herald* in January 1982, he took issue with the 'argument that factory occupations damage the economy': 'Are you seriously saying that there would be production now at Lee Jeans and Robb Caledon if their respective workforces had not fought for their jobs? The mythology that militancy is a problem in Scottish industry conceals the reality that apathy has been the real weakness. And, given the impotence of their present political representatives, working people are starting to mount their own "Scottish Resistance".'[54]

It is therefore worth dwelling on Salmond's analysis of the SNP's 'new attitude' towards industrial engagement that he identified as having followed the 'crushing defeat' of 1979:

Firstly the emphasis on courting popularity and respectability, which had been a dominant trend in the Party after it achieved its electoral break-through, was devalued by the debacle of 1979. Similarly, the pious belief that Westminster would deliver the goods on devolution/independence as soon as a ballot box majority was achieved was looking threadbare. After the 'fixing' of the referendum on devolution only the most unimaginative in the Party clung completely to the nostrum that all the SNP need concern itself with was fighting elections. A third change of emphasis, like the others heavily promoted by the leftist '79 Group, was the growing acceptance of the idea that the SNP could only build stable political support if the desire for constitutional change and the demand for social change could be forged together. All of these factors combined to lead the SNP into a position favouring involvement in industrial disputes.

Salmond concluded this Marxist analysis with a characteristic historical flourish: 'In 1812 Marshal Kutuzov startled his Czar by arguing that Napoleon's occupation of Moscow was irrelevant because "Russia is the army". In 1982 with our economy and political life still in tatters Scotland is our factories. For it is there that a real Scottish resistance has begun.'[55]

The driving force behind the 'Scottish Resistance' and 'civil disobedience' campaigns was Jim Sillars, who joined the SNP (and the 79 Group) just days before the 1980 SNP conference. Formerly the Labour MP for South Ayrshire and a hard-line Unionist, Sillars came to the party via his own breakaway grouping, the pro-devolution 'Scottish Labour Party'. Highly personable, but seemingly plagued by a restless energy, Sillars' oratory blended humour, personal testimony, passionate advocacy and anger in the best tub-thumbing Ayrshire tradition. Salmond was captivated. At this stage, the relationship between Sillars and Salmond was, according to the SNP activist Isobel Lindsay, akin to that of 'mentor and protégé'.[56]

'He is without question one of the most eloquent figures in Scottish politics and will prove an immense asset to the SNP,' Salmond told his local paper shortly after Sillars joined the SNP. 'His decision to join the SNP now reflects the fact that the issue of Scottish self-government will not go away as the Tory and Labour leadership fondly hope. Jim Sillars represents someone of intelligence and courage who has been convinced of the necessity for independence by the force of argument. I believe that many others will follow him into the SNP with the growing realization that 44 Labour MPs and thirty-odd Labour-controlled councils are helpless in the face of a Thatcher majority at Westminster.'[57] 'He had a tremendous messianic speaking style,' Salmond recalled of Sillars in 2001. 'They say . . . a diplomat's someone who can tell you to go to hell and leave you looking forward to the trip; if you listen[ed] to a Jim Sillars speech you could come to believe just about anything.'[58] As the 79 Group's orator-in-chief, Sillars frequently worked his magic at meetings in West Lothian, at Salmond's invitation, and around the country.

Salmond, meanwhile, had spoken in support of the civil disobedience policy at the 1981 SNP conference. He told delegates:

> What we should consider is the difference in the political position occupied by the Labour and Conservative parties in Scotland, because it is in the political position that the rationale and the justification for Civil Disobedience lies. This is a powerful and a very carefully-phrased resolution, but the justification is that we face a Tory Government with less than a third of Scottish MPs; less than a quarter of the Scottish electorate behind them at the last election; one recent opinion poll put it as low as 12 per cent. It's a government of occupation that we face in Scotland, just as surely as if they had an army at their backs, and when you think about it, perhaps they have.[59]

He urged delegates, however, not to blame the Conservatives exclusively for Scotland's economic plight, for the 'Scots Tories may have betrayed their country, but Labour have betrayed their class.' Salmond also betrayed a certain chippiness when he described the reluctance of certain Scottish Labour activists to be used as 'fodder for the Oxbridge elitists who run the Labour Party in England'.[60]

This was the firebrand Salmond, willing to use militaristic imagery to convince Nationalists of his argument. But although endorsed by conference, the twin campaigns enjoyed only a fleeting ascendancy. They ran for only a few months, by Salmond's own admission, 'before being overtaken by public opposition in the Party leadership'.[61] Nevertheless, he pointed to a brief push above 20 per cent in the polls in November 1981 as proof the strategy had enjoyed public support, however briefly.[62]

Although Gordon Wilson, SNP leader since 1979, thought civil disobedience was 'likely to backfire . . . particularly if some of the fringe elements get to work'[63] and shrewdly made Jim Sillars responsible for the policy, it was Salmond who drafted the proposals to put the conference resolution into practice. This, observed Arnold Kemp, 'showed a subtle mind at work'. 'The campaign was within the law and it was aimed at the Labour grass-roots,' observed Kemp, 'bypassing the leadership.'[64] 'While senior figures in the Labour movement twitched nervously as workforce after workforce voted for occupation the SNP were unambiguously committed to supporting such actions,' wrote Salmond. 'It was this commitment which brought the Party together with the Plessey workers to establish an historic legal victory for the Scottish working class.'[65]

Salmond also drew inspiration from the nascent Solidarity movement in Poland, where the Polish flag had played a prominent symbolic role. 'From the shipyards of Gdansk to the coalfields of Silesia,' he said, 'the flag is hoisted to show solidarity with the struggle against an unwanted regime. We in the SNP call upon the people of Scotland to show something of the resistance displayed by the Poles, and raise the Saltire on Sunday [St Andrew's Day] in protest against the unwanted government, foisted upon our nation by the pampered south-east of England.'[66]

At the 1981 Aberdeen conference, the 79 Group appeared to be on a roll, with Andrew Currie elected vice-chairman for organisation and Sillars vice-chairman for policy. These were influential positions, while the group and its allies came within one vote of having a majority on the party's governing National Executive Committee (NEC), including a place for Salmond, at the age of only 26. He attended his first NEC meeting on 21 June 1981, during which he was elected to the SNP's Demonstrations Committee, along with Jim Sillars, and also its Election Committee, beating Winnie Ewing on a tie.

This prompted an angry letter from Margaret Bain, the former MP for East Dunbartonshire, which betrays how many in the party perceived Salmond at this time. 'I am extremely angry at the exclusion of Winnie from that committee in preference to someone like Alex Salmond – most definitely the 79 Group's nominee,' she wrote to Gordon Wilson, 'and whom I regard as a lackey to the anti-MP faction within the party.' 'I now believe we are in a situation that candidates selected by the current composition of this committee', continued Bain, 'will be devolutionists, extreme lefties concerned (so they say) with the West of Scotland, and who will give no real cutting edge to the Scottish dimension.' Bain was clearly feeling the pressure from a sustained 79 Group campaign against her. 'Margo [MacDonald] said two years ago she would change this party within two years to such an extent people wouldn't recognise it,' she concluded. 'This has most certainly been achieved; I don't recognise it.'[67]

Salmond, meanwhile, told his local paper he was 'highly pleased' with his election. 'The SNP have returned to the youthful exciting image which brought us success in the mid-1970s,' he added. 'We have also come clean with the Scottish people and owned up to our distinct left of centre position on the political spectrum ... the SNP will inevitably gain support as the only real Scottish resistance against Thatcher.'

And we intend to take a much more militant line against the industrial destruction visited on Scotland by the Tories. The task for the SNP now is to build up the coalition of stable electoral support from the urban working class, the rural working class and the progressive section of the middle class which will win Scotland its independence. And it is only independence which can guarantee that Thatcher or her like will never ruin our country again.[68]

During his year on the NEC Salmond was a positive and reforming member to some, and a nuisance to others. Iain More, initially the SNP's research officer before becoming director of its HQ, recalled Salmond being the former, believing 'the party needed a breath of fresh air'.

Alex was (and is) a risk taker and the biggest risk we took was changing the party political broadcasts from just talking heads to a mini play with actors, a script and professional production values. Alex was very support-ive of that. The response to the first broadcast was amazing but there was a real problem with change in the SNP's organisation. Alex was a supporter of change. I also organised a series of conferences with Alex's support, although only one happened, on unemployment and health, which was a great success. Alex thought that was great because we got Labour-inclined speakers to come along.

This, however, was precisely the sort of ecumenical activity that aroused suspicion among the Old Guard. 'To that particular group, Winnie, Douglas Henderson, et al,' commented More, 'Alex Salmond was anathema because he was progressive, articulate and ambitious.'[69] More and Salmond got along well despite both having applied for the post of SNP research officer in mid-1980. Although Salmond was deemed to be of 'high quality',[70] given the sensitivity surrounding HQ staff (many of whom had helped form the 79 Group), it is likely that Salmond's political associations counted against him. When More resigned from the party two years later, Salmond said it was 'one of the tragedies of the Scottish National Party ... that they don't make it easy for extremely competent achievers to have their head and get on with the job of building up the party.'[71] One imagines that Salmond included himself in that category.

The 79 Group's hubris following the Aberdeen conference, mean-while, was understandable, yet misplaced. The issue of Europe, for example, divided even 79 Group members, with Sillars as strongly pro as Stephen Maxwell was anti (Salmond was by then supportive). There were other tensions. At a meeting in February 1980 Roseanna Cunningham proposed 'that the 79 Group opposes the [John] Corrie Abortion Bill in all its provisions as detrimental to women's rights in society'. That this was backed by a majority vote did not prevent Salmond querying 'the political relevance to the Group of this issue'.[72]

Finally, there was the 'national question', on which Salmond remained a resolute gradualist. Beyond these considerations, however, he appeared to have grown bored of lengthy discussions about political ideology. Salmond had 'no interest in the theories of nationalism,' recalled Stephen Maxwell. 'His eyes used to glaze over when we started discussing Gramsci, and I remember him once confessing [that] he'd never heard of him.'[73]

On 16 October 1981 Jim Sillars and five other members of the 79 Group broke into Edinburgh's old Royal High School building. As an act of 'civil disobedience' the symbolism was obvious, but tactically disastrous. Salmond was not among them but did attend a demonstration to commend the act, telling the crowd that the 'SNP is committed to ensure that those who are prepared to undergo personal sacrifice in the pursuit of our policy of non-violent civil disobedience will not suffer any financial sacrifice'. Billy Wolfe then led 71 volunteers who sought entry to the building but 'staged a dignified and peaceful sit-down protest in front of the barbed wire gates'[74] when they were refused.

The damage was only compounded, this same autumn, by the suggestion of formal links between Provisional Sinn Fein (PSF) and the 79 Group. The SNP's National Council had passed a motion of non co-operation with Sinn Fein in 1980 but the 79 Group had discussed a request from the PSF to send a speaker to its annual conference. The 79 Group's executive, however, scented trouble. 'In response to the PSF letter, Alex Salmond, seconded by Chris Maclean [sic] moved that we do not grant the PSF request,'[75] recorded minutes from a meeting in August 1981. Unfortunately for the 79 Group, a record of this meeting was then leaked to the *Glasgow Herald* via William Houston, vice-chairman of the SNP's Craigton branch, who was in the midst of a vigorous one-man campaign against the 79 Group.

There was obvious tension when the leak was discussed at the next meeting of the SNP's NEC. While Salmond 'said the minutes had not been ratified and contained several inaccuracies', Winnie Ewing claimed she 'had been contacted by Mr [Chris] McLean, Chairman of the 79

Group and he was satisfied that these minutes were substantially correct'.[76] Whatever the case the 79 Group was sufficiently concerned to make Salmond, Sillars and Maxwell available to answer questions about the incident over a 'pie-and-pint' lunch at the SNP's National Council. At the height of the Troubles in Northern Ireland, and with controversy surrounding the republican agenda of the 79 Group, this was hardly helpful coverage for its members.

Indeed, when the Campaign for Nationalism in Scotland (CNS) launched itself at the June 1982 SNP conference in Ayr, it pointed to the PSF incident and the Royal High School break-in as irrefutable proof that the 79 Group was destroying the party. 'I am now fighting back for the survival of my party,' cried Winnie Ewing at a CNS fringe meeting. 'For the triumph of evil, it just takes good men to do nothing.'

The 'civil disobedience' policy, meanwhile, was being laid to rest. Salmond warned delegates that he SNP would be adopting 'a defeatist and cringing mentality'[77] if it foreswore the use of civil disobedience on matters of principle, citing the Plessey dispute to support his argument. 'Hostility to the policy was abated when the conference heard of Salmond's successful campaign aimed directly at the workforce,' observed Arnold Kemp, 'and this reduced the size of the majority by which the policy was abandoned.'[78]

Later, writing in *The Scottish Industrial Resistance*, Salmond called the conference decision 'perverse'. 'The Scottish character flaw that enables us to face difficult or even hopeless challenges bravely but proceed then to fluff the short putts in an agony of self doubt is a major psychological phenomenon,' he mused. 'Nothing is more terrifying than the prospect of success.'[79]

Then, on 4 June, long-running internal tensions came to a head. Despite the absence of any formal motion to proscribe the 79 Group on the conference agenda, in the midst of his keynote speech, Gordon Wilson said he was 'now convinced that the party will not recover its unity until all organised groups are banned'. 'Those of us who put Scot-land and the party above narrow personal or political obsession', he added, 'cannot and will not tolerate behaviour which is divisive and harmful.'[80]

With that, dozens of delegates rose to their feet to clap and cheer, while a few dozen members of the 79 Group marched out of Ayr's Dam Park Pavilion in protest, although Salmond was not among them. Significantly, the walkout overshadowed the main thrust of Wilson's speech, what the *79 Group News* described as 'an innovative strategy for a Scottish Elected Convention to draw up proposals for self-govern-ment'[81]. So personalities, more than policies, had brought the 79 Group to its knees. 'I don't think anybody going into the conference ... thought that [it] would end with the party effectively in two armed camps,' reflected Salmond in 2001, 'of which it would have to be said that the armed camp against the 79 Group was bigger than the armed camp for it.'[82]

Wilson, however, had deliberately polarised the debate and in doing so, cleverly outmanoeuvred the 79 Group. He not only forced delegates to vote for or against the 79 Group, but by implication also for or against his leadership of the party, a bold move that generated some rare positive headlines. 'After an impassioned debate,' recalled Wilson in his memoirs, 'my resolution, seconded by Alan Clayton who was on the left of the party spectrum, defeated by 413 votes to 189 a counter-motion by Alex Salmond seeking to remit the decision to a Special National Council.'[83] The majority for proscription – 308 votes to 188 – was deci-sive without being overwhelming, although the mood was strong enough to sweep Salmond, Rob Gibson, Kenny MacAskill, Roseanna Cunningham and Owen Dudley Edwards from the NEC on 19 June.

For the next few months the SNP's internal battles were played out in the letters pages of the *Scotsman*, as well as in private party meetings. In a long letter published on 24 June, Salmond accused certain SNP members of 'running away from political reality'. Instead, he argued, the 'reality of Scottish politics in 1982' amounted to the prospect 'of a Labour Scottish majority permanently isolated from power in Westminster'. 'In these circumstances', he continued, 'two things may happen':

First, the Labour Party itself, and this is the process argued by Messrs [George] Foulkes, [George] Galloway and others, could move decisively in a nationalist direction to meet the frustration of their supporters. That strategy faces formidable problems and opponents.

Secondly, the SNP could position itself to be a real alternative to Labour – not by borrowing voters as in the past, but by winning activists, shop stewards and stable political support to the Leftist nationalist programme which meets the aspirations of the majority of the Scottish people.

It should be noted, however, that these two trends – the nationalist one in Labour and the Leftist one in the SNP – are not mutually exclusive and indeed could be of substantial benefit to each other and to Scotland.

These three paragraphs effectively laid out Salmond's political approach for the remainder of the decade. He rejected, meanwhile, the sugges- tion by Kenneth Fee, another *Scotsman* correspondent and later editor of the *Scots Independent*, that the 'settled conviction' of the party was an 'Independence – Nothing More' approach. 'This is, in fact,' Salmond wrote, 'neither settled nor the conviction of all but a minority in the party.' The 'all things to all men' approach, meanwhile, must continue 'to be irrelevant in the Scotland of the 1980s'.

There was besides the point raised by Jim Sillars – 'What will be done when Westminster says "No" to a Scottish demand for self- government whether expressed through the SNP or the Labour Party?'. 'In these circumstances', argued Salmond, 'only a party willing and able to call for civil disobedience, primarily through organised labour, will be able to effectively back a democratic Scottish majority for a Parlia- ment. At present the SNP are neither able nor willing to face that eventually while Labour are probably more able but certainly less willing.' Finally Salmond turned on Gordon Wilson's leadership. Although the Dundee East MP had 'correctly defined the SNP policy position' as 'moderate Left of Centre', 'most people in Scotland remain unaware of it and he seems hardly in any position now to strengthen the party's radical image'.[84]

Nor, however, was the 79 Group. When more than 100 members of the group met in Edinburgh's North British Hotel on 28 August 1982, a motion was passed disbanding the group as of 30 August. Crucially, that meeting also took the decision to simultaneously re-form under the same name, but with a wider membership drawn from other political parties. Wilson warned that members of this new organisation (subse- quently called the Scottish Socialist Society, or SSS) were 'following a high-risk policy which could place in jeopardy their continuing membership of the SNP'.[85]

A few weeks later, on 21 September, Salmond received the follow- ing letter by first-class recorded delivery:

Dear Alex

Annual Conference 1982 – Resolution regarding organised political groups

I refer to your letter of 18 September 1982 in response to my letter of 13 September conveying to you the decision of the National Executive

Committee in regard to organised political groups within the Party. As you have not indicated your resignation from the Interim Committee of the 79 Group Socialist Society, I have to inform you that you are expelled from membership of the Scottish National Party with effect from the date of this letter.

In terms of Clause 67 of the Constitution and Rules you are entitled to exercise a right of appeal against this decision.

Yours sincerely

Neil R MacCallum
National Secretary[86]

Six others, Stephen Maxwell, Chris Cunningham, Douglas Robertson, Brenda Carson, Kenny MacAskill and Andrew Doig all received identical missives. 'The Scottish National Party,' stormed Owen Dudley Edwards in the *Scotsman*, 'by expelling Mr Stephen Maxwell, Mr Alex Salmond and their five associates, have committed intellectual suicide.'[87]

For the next few decades Salmond made light of his involvement with the 79 Group, in 2008 dismissing his expulsion as the result of being a 'brash young man'.[88] At the time, however, he found it deeply traumatic, while his already cool relationship with Wilson never really recovered. Having been added to the SNP's list of approved candidates in June 1982, meanwhile, Salmond now had little chance of being selected to fight a seat at the forthcoming general election.

Idealist, but never practical and finally most damaging, the 79 Group proved an endeavour more worthy than wise. Always small in number – there were never more than 100 active members – it was tactically naïve, most notably over civil disobedience, while the assumption that every vote for Labour in 1979 was explicitly 'socialist' proved misguided. Even had Salmond et al. succeeded in convincing the SNP to declare itself 'socialist' in an attempt to displace Labour as Scotland's main political party, there was little evidence that it would have worked. In Wales, for example, Plaid Cymru had done precisely that in 1981, achieving little electoral benefit.

The 79 Group's Marxist interpretations, meanwhile, were often backward looking, particularly as Scotland's old industrial economy was clearly in terminal decline, something MacAskill appeared to acknowledge during a 1990 interview: 'Yes, of course, Alex and I were in the

79 Group. But lots of folk active in the 79 Group weren't socialists. It was really an opposition group, a counterweight to the ruling party establishment, which tried to put forward fresh ideas on policy and strategy. It was oppositionist; it didn't have firm views on ideological issues.'[89] Nevertheless, Salmond always considered the central thrust of the 79 Group as correct. 'I regarded the issue of political identity and of arguing that case,' he later reflected, 'and also intervening in political issues, as the most important thing and I thought the work that the 79 Group, and the 79 Group members, [did] in supporting workers' occupations, in Bathgate for example, was absolutely fundamental.'[90]

Salmond's involvement with the 79 Group also helped hone his media, propaganda and tactical skills, while consolidating some long-lasting alliances, most notably with Stewart Stevenson, Kenny MacAskill and Roseanna Cunningham. All became ministers in his first and second ministerial teams in 2007–09 when, under Salmond's renewed leadership, the SNP finally attained power. The experience also marked him out as a pragmatist. 'Some in the Group felt you had to polarise the debate in order to edge forward,' recalled Stephen Maxwell, 'others took a more pragmatic approach, of which Alex was one. At no point was he simply a careerist just looking for personal advancement. He's not particularly profound – he's never written very much for example – but he was always quite keen on persuading people that they needed to think and analyse where Scottish politics was at, rather than indulging in reflexive nationalism.'[91]

Despite Salmond's best efforts, however, the 'reflexive' attitude of the SNP had resulted in his expulsion from the party of which he had been a member for less than a decade. But the future First Minister was nothing if not a great political survivor, and for this 'brash young man' his time in the wilderness would not last long.

Chapter 4

'THE PRAGMATIC LEFT'

The main thrust of strategy must be to maintain the party in a Left position and to develop its thinking to the point where our collective response to any issue is guided by philosophy and instinct, that puts us unerringly on the side of labour and progressive opinion no matter the issue that lands unexpectedly before us.[1]

Jim Sillars in *The Case for Optimism*

'I mean I get emotional about some things but I'm not a hyperemotional person', reflected Alex Salmond in 2001, 'and therefore I was surprised at myself to the extent that even after a few years in the SNP I'd become extremely loyal and passionate about the party, and was extremely disconcerted not to be in it.'[2] Salmond later told the journalist Andrew Marr that the whole experience 'was traumatic enough to give him a strong desire to expel no one from the modern SNP'.[3] The use of the word 'traumatic', however, surprised Stephen Maxwell, who recalled that he 'obviously never believed it would be anything other than a short-term affair'.[4] 'After the 79 Group expulsion he was much more willing than the rest of us to build bridges,' he recalled, 'he was the one keenest to remain in touch with the mainstream party.'[5] Salmond was not, and had never been, what one senior Nationalist called 'a natural martyr', while he had also benefited from the fact that while 'he may have been a naughty boy, he was our naughty boy, unlike Jim Sillars and Alex Neil'.[6] The whole however, meanwhile, noticeably hardened his character, fostering a determination never to appear vulnerable or weak.

His expulsion, along with four others, was effective from 20 September 1982, by which date Salmond and his allies had failed, as directed, to repudiate the Scottish Socialist Society (SSS) in writing, the committee of which was largely identical to that of the 79 Group. Gordon

Wilson later argued that Salmond and the others had made a tactical mistake. 'A more intelligent course would have been for them to disband and several months later launch a Scottish Socialist Society with an independent membership,' he wrote. 'This ill-judgement likely stemmed from arrogance and pique. If they had been patient, there is no way the Party could have extended the ban to a genuine multilateral body, clearly independent of the SNP.'[7]

Salmond chaired the SSS's inaugural meeting, which took place at Glasgow's North British Hotel on 30 October 1982. Writing in *Radical Scotland* a few months later, he declared that the SSS could 'play an increasingly important role in Scottish politics', explaining: 'If Scotland's Left majority continues to be isolated from influence at Westminster then a major rethink of political strategy by socialists is inevitable. What is certain is that, as of now, no one political party (or part of one) has the definitive answer on how to face rampant Thatcherism in second term. In that period of fundamental political reassessment people may well wish to take to each other across the party divide without prejudicing their own positions. What better forum than the Scottish Socialist Society.'[8]

Indeed, there was much talk of a realignment among the Scottish left, the grand yet elusive design of socialists since the 1920s. There were even tentative gatherings at the New Town home of the political scientist Malcolm Anderson, attended by Salmond, Stephen Maxwell and Isobel Lindsay from the SNP, and figures like George Foulkes and Robin Cook from Labour. 'He always stated that once Scotland had a degree of political autonomy there would be a realignment of the centre left and the emergence of new political groupings to take policy forward,' recalled Salmond's university friend Peter Brunskill. 'This was why he was always relatively inclusive of other political strands, and was what led to his problems in 1982–3.'[9] Nothing, however, came of New Town meetings, although Salmond continued to tease Foulkes about them for years afterwards.

Jim Sillars, meanwhile, tried to persuade the SNP's ruling National Executive Committee to rescind the expulsions, while Salmond and Stewart Stevenson embarked upon a tour of selected SNP branches, screening a self-produced video of events at the Ayr conference. 'It was just a response to what had happened,' recalled Stevenson. 'It was Alex's idea – he persuaded me to find a video camera, which I did and we filmed some links. I put it together using three Betamax machines, although we were careful to put both sides of the argument.'[10]

The NEC and the party, however, were in no mood to forgive and forget, particularly when Wilson and others learned about Salmond's video roadshow. The expulsions were confirmed at a National Council meeting in Glasgow on 5 December, an act that struck many present as short-sighted. 'I remember sitting in the Moir Hall in Glasgow in late 1982 when the national council voted to expel the 79 Group, one of them being Alex Salmond', recalled John Swinney 18 years later, 'and sitting there with my head in my hands thinking: "What on earth have we done? What are we doing to ourselves? We've lost the plot here, we've totally lost the plot."'[11]

Those expelled decided to appeal and Salmond asked Jonathan Mitchell, a young advocate and fellow 79 Grouper, to represent them. The Appeals Committee then met for seven Sundays between December 1982 and March 1983, taking some 40 hours to consider their case. Salmond gave much of the evidence himself, mostly during the committee's third session, and also in writing:

Q If your expulsion is confirmed, will you reapply for membership in two years' time?
A I don't anticipate the premise coming to pass and I don't forecast the future.

Q If you are reinstated, will you agree not to encourage all of the three activities which characterise 'grouping' and which the Party outlawed at Ayr?
A My attitude to Conference policy (which is to abide by it) has remained consistent and is not conditional on my reinstatement. The Party has voted against 'organised political groups within the Party' and I will observe that decision as long as it remains Party policy.

Q Are you a member of the Scottish Socialist Society? If it is proscribed by the Party, will you resign from the Party or the Society?
A Yes. There is nothing in the current policy or constitution of the SNP which would allow proscription of the SSS.

Q Does the SSS have Scottish independence as an objective?
A No.

Q What relationship does the SSS have with the London SS?
A None.

Q Do you agree that an SNP member with so-called Right-Wing views
   is as welcome in the SNP as a member with so-called Left-Wing
   Views?
A I have never disputed this. I have never argued or voted for expulsion
   of anyone from the SNP on political grounds.[12]

Not for nothing did Kenny MacAskill liken the Appeals Committee to
a 'Star Chamber' in the *Glasgow Herald*, while Jonathan Mitchell called
it a 'quick little kangaroo court'.[13] When, on 6 March, the Lanark
National Council voted by 97 to 91 to hear their appeals from the floor,
contrary to the wishes of the Appeals Committee, Salmond echoed
their sentiments: 'Six of the 12 members of the Appeals Committee are
former members of the Campaign for Scottish Nationalism, which was
bitterly opposed to us. Some members of the committee have deliberately prolonged the hearings to prevent us from standing for national
office or for Parliamentary seats. The majority of the party voted today
to hear us. It is a tragedy for the S.N.P. that this divisive issue could
ramble on until a possible June election.'[14]

Indeed, the 15-strong Appeals Committee was an unsettling mixture
of friend and foe. Stewart Stevenson, whose minority report ultimately
secured the return of Salmond and others to the party, was an ally,
although his colleagues included Kenneth Fee and Bill Houston, both
sworn enemies of the 79 Group. Yet there was some wider goodwill to
the arraigned. Salmond's place on the SNP's Standing Orders and
Agenda Committee was even kept open during the appeal hearing
because it 'was felt that replacing Mr Salmond on the Committee would
pre-empt [his] appeal against expulsion'.[15]

Billy Wolfe, meanwhile, intervened on behalf of his West Lothian
protégés. 'Until Alex Salmond and Kenneth Macaskill [*sic*] were expelled
last autumn,' he wrote to Gordon Wilson, 'W.L.C.A. never had a single
serious clash or division – and certainly no expulsions. These two young
men – one a lawyer who reminds me of another young lawyer [he meant
Wilson] whom I met for the first time 21 years ago next month – have
been great nationalist workers.' Chris McLean, the SNP's press officer,
also wrote to Wilson calling the Appeals Committee's report 'a travesty'
and urging him to be conciliatory, adding that from 'conversations I
have had with one or two of the appellants'[16] they would accept expulsion up to 30 April as a compromise.

The Appeals Committee, however, upheld the expulsions by nine
votes to two, presenting its decision to the Larbert National Council on

30 April 1983. It concurred, by 157 votes to 138. 'The debate was reasonably restrained, but tense,' recalled Gordon Wilson, 'and Alex Salmond, speaking for the appellants with a complete absence of nerves, made a notable contribution.'[17] The performance also improved Salmond's long-term prospects, with Wilson later reflecting that he had been 'incredibly impressed by his confidence, his articulacy. He spoke very smoothly and strongly and made mincemeat of the convener of the committee. That's when for the first time I took the view that he was a person who could play a leading part in the development of the party in future, if he behaved himself.'[18]

Neil MacCormick then put forward a creative compromise regarding the sentence. This would be commuted from outright expulsion to temporary suspension (from 21 September 1982 until 25 May 1983) with the proviso that each suspended member wrote to the party's National Secretary accepting the National Council's position and requesting their suspension be lifted. Any appellant refusing to do so would remain expelled. 'This was accepted by an overwhelming majority and a sense of relief by delegates,' remembered Wilson. Although not all of the 'seven' agreed with these terms Salmond did, and was thus readmitted to the party.

'Despite the ending of the surface conflict,' reflected Wilson. 'I was under no illusions. There was a deep-seated animosity in the higher levels of the party leadership and a running debate over the future direction of the Party.'[19] Indeed, when the NEC tried to prevent Kenny MacAskill becoming a Parliamentary candidate, Salmond felt compelled to telephone Wilson and ask him to intercede. He did, and MacAskill duly fought Livingston at the 1983 election. With that endorsement, four years of ruinous infighting finally ended. 'The 79 Group then disappeared,' wrote Peter Lynch in his history of the SNP, 'though it had a considerable legacy in terms of personalities and the ideological outlook.'[20]

Salmond duly returned to the SNP fold at the end of April, but that did not mean he abandoned the Scottish Socialist Society. On the contrary, having been formally launched at the Mitchell Theatre in Glasgow on 29 January 1983, its membership soon reached 250, 35 per cent of whom were from the SNP, 30 per cent from Labour, 6 per cent Communist and 'two members of other parties'. The *Sunday Standard* even praised it as 'a fascinating cross-party Scottish group'.[21]

'While the Scottish voter has remained electorally loyal to the Left-Wing and anti-Tory cause,' wrote Salmond and Stephen Maxwell in a press release distributed a few days before the first meeting, 'Scotland has made little response to the propaganda offensive by the Right over the last few years in support of market forces, privatisation, greater inequality and Great British chauvinism. The Scottish Socialist Society aims to marshall [*sic*] Scottish opinion for a counter-offensive against Thatcherism. The Tory attack on the health and social services, on comprehensive education and on the trade unions will intensify up to and beyond the next election. If an effective Scottish response is to be worked out, then the different strands of Left-Wing thinking in Scotland must work together to strengthen their ideas and their educational work on behalf of the socialist alternative.'[22]

Salmond, Maxwell and MacAskill, meanwhile, were elected to the SSS committee just two weeks before their appeals against expulsion were due to be considered by the SNP, a risky move in the circumstances. Once that issue was resolved, however, the Society began to produce a steady stream of literature devoted to articulating its 'socialist alternative'. Salmond contributed his editorial and journalistic skills to a professionally produced SSS Newsletter, while a series of conferences attempted to put tactical flesh on rhetorical bones.

Salmond's professional and political careers, meanwhile, began to overlap. Not long after narrowly missing out on the job of SNP research officer in mid-1980, he had secured a position as an assistant economist at the Royal Bank of Scotland (RBS), where he would remain until entering Parliament seven years later. This, rather than the humdrum world of the Civil Service, was much more to Salmond's liking. He rose steadily through the ranks, becoming an oil, or energy, economist in 1982; and, from 1984, combining those duties with that of Royal Bank Economist.

The Royal Bank of the early 1980s was not the global giant it later became. Rather it was a little more than a provincial high-street outfit of proud history but few pretensions to British, far less global, dominance. Its vulnerability was evident early in Salmond's tenure when the Hong Kong and Shanghai Banking Corporation, or HSBC, moved to absorb the Royal Bank, followed by an outright takeover bid from Standard Chartered. Salmond recalled:

Both bids were referred to the Monopolies and Mergers Commission, and I found myself as a very young junior economist fetching and carrying for the bank team who were attempting to argue the impossible, i.e. one takeover was bad and should be disallowed while the other was good and should be given the OK . . . As luck and rumour would have it, in the early eighties Honkers and Shankers [HSBC] were non-U as far as the Bank of England were concerned, even if it would have been diplomatically inconvenient to tell them that directly. To rule out their bid while accepting Standard Chartered would have made that pretty obvious. And therefore, lo and behold, the MMC alighted on the Scottish interest and delivered a ringing endorsement of the argument in favour of the retention of headquarters operations in the Scottish economy. Whatever the motivation, the outcome was highly satisfactory.

'After it recovered from the shock of being saved from itself', noted Salmond with some satisfaction, 'the Royal Bank marched from strength to strength through the 1980s.'[23] This experience consolidated Salmond's economic and political thinking, chiefly a belief in government intervention, particularly that with a Nationalist undercurrent.

Working at the Royal Bank also planted a neo-liberal seed in Salmond's mind. 'I remember as a young economist working in the financial sector,' he recalled in 2010, 'how new financial instruments and innovative techniques had earlier been developed to exploit North Sea oil and gas.'[24] Not only would the wealth of the North Sea convince Scots to support independence, Salmond's argument ran, but the exploitation thereof could lead to even greater riches via the wizardry of the financial services sector.

Until the ignominious near-collapse of RBS in 2008, this portion of Salmond's CV was an invaluable political tool with which to counter political criticism of the economic case for independence. Salmond not only talked the language of economics but also had practised it professionally, and although the Royal Bank was not a big financial player between 1980 and 1987, it was respected. Salmond was also part of the Royal Bank's public face, broadcasting and writing extensively on oil and gas economics for the Fraser of Allander Economic Commentary, and is such journals as *Petroleum Review*, *Opec Bulletin* and the *Three Banks Review*.

One of Salmond's projects also allowed him to indulge his historical interests. In 1983 he researched and compiled *The Royal Bank in Glasgow 1783–1983*, a pamphlet commemorating the Bank's bi-centenary in that city. Salmond revealed himself to be talented historian with an eye for a good quotation, and an engaging writing style that betrayed obvious affection for the Royal Bank, its history and character.

He was particularly good, not surprisingly, on politics. Quoting Lord Cockburn on the 'old Edinburgh bankers', Salmond could also have been thinking of himself: 'So they all combined banking with politics. Not that they would discount a bad bill to a Tory, or refuse to discount a good one to a Whig; but their favours and graciousness were all reserved for the right side.'[25] Salmond was particularly taken with Robert W. Service, a Scots-born poet and former Royal Bank employee who penned the following epitaph:

> I have no doubt that the
> devil grins,
> As ink on page I splatter.
> May God forgive my
> lit'ry sins.
> The other kind don't matter.

'Some years ago I came across these lines while writing a pamphlet describing two centuries of the Royal Bank of Scotland's activities in the great city of Glasgow,' recalled Salmond in 1997. 'Unable to write in too much detail about the more interesting and controversial banking events of this century on account of the fact that some of the customers concerned were still alive, kicking, and potentially litigious, I was driven towards the past for new material.'

He discovered that Service had begun his career as a clerk in the Glasgow office of the Commercial Bank of Scotland, which later became the National Commercial Bank, and later still the Royal Bank of Scotland. 'The apocryphal story goes that Service, deciding to seek fame and fortune in Canada, broke the news to his startled manager that he was off on the next boat west. "Dinnae be daft, laddie. If ye mind yoursel' here you'll be a senior clerk – in aboot 20 years or so." Service replied that he was firmly decided on emigration and, after a pause, his manager responded: "Ah weel, if I wis 20 years younger, I'd come wi' you."'. Service, continued Salmond, 'went to Canada and found fame and some fortune, leaving Glasgow still bustling as the second city of the Empire'. What struck Salmond about these accounts of 19th-century banking 'was the absolute confidence they displayed in the economic progress of the city and of Scotland': 'The Royal Bank was itself not immune from the flowering of entrepreneurship and the young gentlemen of the bank were frequently AWOL down at the docks – quite literally waiting for their ship to come in. This behaviour caused ripples of anxiety in the higher echelons at the time but not, I suspect, as much as the bank would display now if their current employees were caught freelancing in personally stimulating trade or commercial venture.'[26]

Salmond no doubt saw a little of himself in Robert Service, while his obvious enthusiasm hints at his own future incarnation, slightly in awe of people and institutions that made vast amounts of money. Even in the early 1980s, there existed political tension between two different Alex Salmonds: one a self-professed socialist, the other a liberal-minded financier.

Salmond, however, would have done well to draw some uncomfortable lessons from his own research. He went on to touch upon the Royal Bank's record of 'Bad and Doubtful Debts', while describing the mid-19th century as a period 'of rapid growth, marked by the familiar "boom and bust" cycle. It was a time when speculation and occasional bouts of over-optimism were endemic in the fabric of commercial life.' Even more pertinent was his account of the collapse of the City of Glasgow Bank in 1879:

> It was widely regarded as the most progressive of all the banks, in respect both of its branching policy and of its international expansion. Its international links became its undoing. These took the form not only of substantial direct interests in speculative ventures in the Far East and North America, but also a heavy concentration of its domestic lending to a few individuals and firms, including notably the 'India houses' of merchants and traders. As these began to decline from the mid-1860s, the bank's controllers resorted to ever riskier ventures and ultimately to outright fraud to maintain an appearance of stability and prosperity. In this they succeeded right up to the end.

When the collapse came, wrote Salmond, 'it rapidly became evident that Glasgow, and the whole of Scotland, had suffered a commercial disaster and fraud of considerable magnitude', although the aftermath at least 'produced a number of changes which strengthened the Scottish banking system'.[27]

Even though Salmond's activities at the Royal Bank were far removed from the less genteel world of Scottish politics, he consciously acquired deeper economic knowledge while working there, poring over oil and energy statistics in the Bank's library, realising it would prove useful should he eventually take up elected politics. Everything he did was calculated towards the ultimate goal, what one long-standing friend called a desire 'to change the nature of Scottish Nationalism'.[28]

'It was Alex's job to write, on yellowing paper, a weekly report on oil prices for those who were interested,' recalled the journalist and historian Michael Fry, who was a regular visitor to the Royal Bank's St Andrew Square HQ. 'That was his job, other than standing in the Abbotsford [an Edinburgh bar] with Grant Baird.' Baird, a chain-smoking St Andrews graduate and former Bank of England economist, was not only Salmond's immediate boss as chief economist, but also a political ally. 'The fact that he was a Nationalist was Alex's essential qualification as far as Grant was concerned,' judged Fry. 'Bright young men leaving university, who were also Nationalists, were pretty thin on the ground in those days.'[29]

Baird was clearly very fond of his discovery, recalling later that he had done 'a lot of excellent work on the oil industry which not only gathered favourable publicity, it also ensured that the oil industry holds him in high regard. He perhaps had a less sure touch on purely financial matters, but he has a very cool head and the ability to play a long game.'[30] Baird was also influential ideologically, persuading Salmond to view the European Community as an opportunity rather than a menace.

Almost as if to illustrate this intermingling of political activism and banking, the office Salmond shared with Baird was decorated with a poster from the magazine *Radical Scotland*, featuring Tom Nairn's dictum that 'Scotland will be reborn the day the last minister is strangled with the last copy of the *Sunday Post*'.[31] When the journalist Andrew Marr let slip this adornment years later, 'Salmond was attacked by Conservatives in his traditionally minded constituency as a bloodthirsty enthusiast for the garroting of Kirk ministers!'[32]

Fry, as well as BBC Scotland's economics correspondent Peter Clarke, were frequent visitors. 'I would just turn up at their office and argue about economics,' remembered Fry. 'I was a monetarist and Alex was a Keynesian. He wasn't much of an economist but was obviously a talented student who could absorb information and argue about it.'[33] Fry also remembered Salmond being impressed that he knew the former French student rebel leader Daniel Cohn-Bendit, later an MEP, with whom Fry used to have lunch while he worked in Brussels. Similarly, Clarke remembered lunching with them 'most weeks'. 'They were a good duet, him and Grant Baird,' he said. 'If you needed a quote they gave you one; and unlike most men in suits they didn't dribble on in corporate prose. Alex pulled rank a wee bit because he loved being on radio and television, but he was what you might call a natural.'[34]

It was Clarke who came up with the idea that the Royal Bank's Economics Office (where Salmond worked alongside Baird) should compile a monthly 'oil index', a statistical commentary on the latest trends in the North Sea oil market. In January 1983 it was launched by Salmond, who later recalled: 'A couple of years ago we were asked ... if we could develop an oil index. When he [Clarke] also told us that another Scottish bank had already tried and failed, it presented a challenge we could not refuse. After a few months of preparation we secured the co-operation of all the oil companies and were ready to go public in January of last year. Since then the Index has gone from strength to strength.'[35] Indeed, Baird remembered that 'we went all over Aberdeen and saw all the big oil companies. All of them signed up except BP, so Alex said to them, "Well we've got Esso, Shell and so on; if you won't agree we'll publish it anyway and say you wouldn't co-operate". So he actually persuaded them. One of the great things about him was a very good tactical sense, a very good tactical brain.'[36]

The index acted as a month-by-month guide to the level of oil production, while the commentary used that information to place a value on output and to forecast the effects of oil on government revenues and the Balance of Payments. 'We look to appeal not just to the specialist but also to the general public,' explained Salmond on its first anniversary. 'For example we don't just talk about Government oil revenues being worth £9,500 million in the current fiscal year, but point out that this figure represents over £1m every hour of every day through the year.' 'This approach is proving its worth', he added proudly, 'with regular publicity not only in all the national media but also in the international press and in local newspapers throughout the UK.'

The index's high point came when it successfully predicted that the government was underestimating oil revenues (in 1984) by £1,000m. 'The Treasury seemed quite pleased that we had found the money for them,' commented Baird. 'Unfortunately they didn't offer us the usual finder's fee of ten per cent.'[37] This quote helps explain why Baird and Salmond got on so well. Salmond liked people who were sharp and amusing – Baird was both.

But however much Salmond enjoyed his work at the Royal Bank, politics remained his primary focus. 'It was his life,' remembered Grant

Baird's wife, Glynne. 'That was his driving force.'[38] Similarly, Peter Brunskill remembered visiting Alex and Moira in Linlithgow in around 1983. 'They were great together,' he said. 'I remember Alex showing me videos of all his political activities over the previous few years, but Moira was definitely the political wife who was as interested in all the stuff Alex was showing me as I was, whereas my wife thought the whole thing was boring.'[39] By then, Salmond had an impressive collection of political footage stretching back to the late 1970s, preserved for posterity using a Philips Video 2000 recorder.[40]

Although the Royal Bank allowed its staff to engage in political activity, his activities in this arena must occasionally have furrowed brows in the boardroom. Perhaps conscious of this, Salmond billed himself as an 'economist', or an 'economist working in the financial sector', when writing for *Radical Scotland* or the *Scottish Government Yearbook*. For both, Salmond made a special study of British Leyland's management at Bathgate, which he concluded had been deliberately run down since 1981, while making use of his Royal Bank expertise in talks to branches of the Federation of Student Nationalists. Occasionally he could kill two birds with one stone. In 1985, Salmond co-wrote *The Oil Price Collapse* with Dr Jim Walker of the Fraser of Allander Institute, who would succeed Salmond as Royal Bank Economist in 1987.

From 1983 the SNP began to rebuild under the steady if unflashy leadership of Gordon Wilson. Determined to maintain a broad church, Wilson stressed that the party had 'always had a radical, left of centre bias',[41] although this had clearly become a little too inflexible for his liking. Three policy positions were within Wilson's sights: the SNP's anti-NATO policy, its antipathy to membership of the European Community and finally its inflexible constitutional stance of 'Independence – nothing less'.

The results of the 1983 general election demonstrated what a monumental task Wilson faced. The SNP lost 54 deposits and slipped from 17.3 to 11.8 per cent of the vote, squeezed by the SDP/Liberal Alliance (analysis showed it attracted a fifth of those who had voted SNP in 1979) and a surprisingly resilient Tory vote. Of the nine SNP MPs defeated four years before, seven contested seats in 1983 but not one was returned. This ensured that not only did Gordon Wilson remain leader, but that figures such as Salmond and Kenny MacAskill were able to rise within the SNP without much competition from what they perceived as a reactionary Old Guard.

Wilson, meanwhile, faced internal opposition to his recovery strategy, although ironically this came from fundamentalists and those concerned about his uncharismatic performances, rather than from left-wingers. 'The most difficult part I had to play over the next few years', reflected Wilson in 2009, 'was to cajole and coerce all the leaders of the Party to work together despite their deeply rooted antipathies.'[42]

To this end he set up a Commission of Inquiry to examine the party's organisational structure, largely unchanged since Billy Wolfe's reforms of the 1960s. Neil MacCallum, who was to convene the Commission, wrote to Wilson on 21 July 1983 suggesting possible members, speculating that 'the Party would have justifiable grounds for criticism, if a prominent member of the former 79 Group was not included'.[43]

Wilson took on board that advice, inviting Alex Salmond to join Alasdair Morgan and John Swinney ('all of whom were rising in the Party'[44]) as representatives of the SNP's National Council on the Commission. Salmond was responsible for drafting section 8 of its report, covering the role of the party's branches and constituency associations. He concluded that the latter should receive more resources and greater representation at the annual conference, while district and regional associations ought to be abolished. Salmond also reflected that the SNP's 'lack of organisation in workplaces may be one reason why our strength in the country has not been reflected in the trade union movement'.[45]

The previous year's SNP conference at Rothesay, meanwhile, had proved central to Wilson's strategy of nudging the party back into political reality. A resolution easing opposition to the European Community[46] was moved by Salmond, supported by Winnie Ewing, shored up with effective speeches from the Jims Fairlie and Sillars, and endorsed overwhelmingly. But Wilson's proposal for an elected 'Scottish Convention' to determine Scotland's constitutional future did not fare as well, despite the backing of Salmond and Sillars. Already proposed in 1980, 1982 and on the eve of the 1983 election, it was defeated by 173 votes to 141. Given Salmond's background in the 79 Group, his support for a softer line on devolution was invaluable from Wilson's point of view, although his contribution was overshadowed by a memorably epic oratorical battle between Sillars and Fairlie on the same subject. Nevertheless, on reflection Wilson thought 'the 1983 Conference was one that altered the course of the Party radically and in my view for the better. The gamble had paid off. The separatist, isolationist image had been shattered.'[47]

★   ★   ★

From 1984 most prominent Nationalists agreed on central strategy, even if there were varying personal emphases. 'The most notable political figure to emerge during this period was Alex Salmond,' judged the academic James Mitchell. 'His view that the SNP required to project a clear position on socio-economic matters did not lead to the party changing its policies so much as presenting them more coherently. The "moderate left of centre" label, pro-European position and advocacy of a constitutional convention were widely accepted.'[48]

The constitutional convention, usefully, could conclude in favour of either full independence or devolution, neatly reconciling so-called 'gradualists' and 'fundamentalists' within the party. Tentatively, meanwhile, the SNP began to engage with the Campaign for a Scottish Assembly (CSA), a cross-party group it had hitherto shunned. Salmond thought this attitude reflected his party's lack of self-confidence. 'It is my opinion that when the SNP is about to make a leap forward and grow it takes a relaxed attitude to self-government,' he observed in 1984, 'but when it is on the defensive it adopts a tight, narrow attitude.'

Salmond was one of the delegates chosen by the NEC to meet with the CSA's executive, but when motions supporting both the campaign and Wilson's Scottish Convention proposal were endorsed at the SNP's 1984 Inverness conference, Jim Fairlie, the party's deputy leader, resigned, declaring that the party had 'to declare once and for all whether it is going for independence or some form of gradualism'. Nationalists, he said, were in danger of withdrawing to 'the fringe of Scottish politics ... part of an anti-Tory coalition'.[49] Jim Sillars – newly returned from working in the Middle East – and Salmond, however, were jubilant. The SNP was now committed, albeit with dissent, to an ecumenical approach to devolution. Thus emboldened, Salmond urged the NEC, which he had rejoined in late 1983, to continue the party's engagement with CSA meetings. 'They are not earth shattering in importance but do provide a useful method of focussing debate,' he reasoned. 'Not to go would confer a political penalty, which, of course, is why the Labour Party have started to attend albeit in a semi-official capacity.' The NEC agreed, and for the next two years Salmond acted as the SNP's main liaison with the CSA.

The 'pragmatic left', as Roger Levy called it, was in the ascendancy. Their aim was to target the Labour vote on a number of specific social and economic issues while gradually softening the party's position on constitutional reform. There were signs of progress in June 1984 when the SNP managed to beat the Alliance's share of the vote in elections to the European Parliament. Salmond, meanwhile, urged 'that sustained discussion of the political options facing the Party is necessary at Executive level. Such debate is not useless, silly (unless we choose to make it so) or a waste of time but necessary if we are to sustain a political challenge over the next few years. Knowing what you are doing and why is not a sufficient condition for electoral success but, in the medium term, it is a necessary one.' Salmond added that trends since the 1983 general election 'support the view that the fulcrum of Scottish politics lies on the left of centre', so if the SNP was to 'double our vote by the next General Election we will have to win the support of a substantial number of Scots currently voting Labour'.

His strategy for doing so involved putting Labour on the defensive by flagging up a series of cross-party anti-Tory campaigns, thus putting 'Labour in the position of either having to accept them and thus raise the Scottish dimension and Scottish expectations or (by far the most likely course) to reject them and engender discontent among the many people in the Labour Party who care about what's happening to Scotland'. For such an approach to work, he added, 'the SNP itself would have to be confident and relaxed about its own position particularly on the independence devolution convention debate'. That, he accepted, was 'an open question at the moment'. But when Salmond's strategy document was discussed at the NEC on 14 July it simply 'noted the paper and thanked Salmond for leading the discussion'.[50]

Responding to an opinion poll suggesting that a third of Labour voters supported independence, Salmond instead took his strategic battles to the *Scotsman* letters page. There was, he said, an 'opportunity for the SNP to substantially increase its vote which is what internal debate in the party should be about':

> The position of the SNP Left is broadly as follows: the fact that people who support independence vote for the Labour Party confirms the pre-eminence for most people of social and economic issues over constitutional ones. This may be irritating to many in the SNP but it is unlikely to change. One solution ... [is] for the SNP to present a stronger political profile, not, I repeat not, by adopting 'extreme Left' policies but rather by being prepared to accept a Left of Centre label on the radical policies the SNP already largely possesses. This should both help voters to identify the SNP more clearly as a *political* party and also assist the SNP's leadership in making judgments on the day-to-day issues on which there can be no detailed policy.

In essence, concluded Salmond, 'what the Left of the party are saying is that a first target for dramatically increasing the SNP constituency should be to win over the independence voters currently supporting Labour'.[51] But Salmond's analysis was simplistic. Not only did it rest too heavily on one opinion poll; it implied a degree of engagement with independence from a section of Labour voters that arguably did not exist.

'Our economic policies are radical but our social policies are conservative, because that's the way Scotland is,' was how Jim Sillars characterised the SNP's 'pragmatic left' grouping to the *Toronto Star* in August 1986. 'That's why we wear suits. The striped-jersey style of British, leftist, polytechnic lecturers doesn't go over here.'[52] Both Salmond and Kenny MacAskill did indeed wear suits; usually grey ones with red ties, perhaps in an effort to resemble Labour apparatchiks of the time. MacAskill, meanwhile, contributed to *The Case for Scottish Socialism*, an important pragmatic left document published in early 1986.

In his own book, *The Case for Optimism*, published the same year, Sillars urged the 'growing number of young people who are breaking through into leadership positions' in the SNP 'to look back coolly and not in anger'. Central to the Salmond/Sillars analysis was that Scotland and England were different. As the 1980s progressed, they reasoned, England became an inescapably Conservative country, whereas Scotland resisted and, if anything, became more socialist. Sillars identified the consequence as 'an active and progressive nationalism, not ugly, not born of a desire to do down anyone else, with a wish to free the energies and attributes of the Scottish people so that they can engage not only on the reconstruction of our own society but on the problems that keep the vast mass of humanity in a miserable existence'.[53]

In early 1985, meanwhile, the Commission of Inquiry into the SNP's organisation finally published its report. National Secretary Neil MacCallum said the party had become 'too bureaucratic, too introspective and too conservative'[54] and recommended abolishing the National Assembly and strengthening the party's central leadership by appointing a general convener and general secretary while streamlining the NEC. The *Glasgow Herald* hailed Salmond and Kenny MacAskill as the comeback kids, 'highly articulate and full of talent',[55] determined to seize executive control of the party. A key battleground was the admission of political groups within the SNP, such as the CND, a proposal guaranteed to revive troubled memories of the 79 Group.

That, together with almost every other proposal in the 42-page report, was thrown out by a special conference in Stirling on 23 February. After almost two years' work and hundreds of hours devoted to gathering evidence, Salmond felt understandably resentful, particularly towards Gordon Wilson, whom he believed should have utilised more fully the fruits of his labours. In a surprising volte-face, Wilson explained that he had established the Commission in a panic following the 1983 general election, and now that the party had stabilised the need for radical organisational reform had passed.

Salmond, however, remained active on the party's unreformed NEC, developing an already keen, and occasionally devious, tactical style. 'I remember him asking me to push this line for him at an NEC meeting he couldn't attend,' recalled Isobel Lindsay, 'and he said "if it looks as if you won't get the votes try and leave it to the next meeting". Now I didn't feel particularly strongly about it but I got it postponed to the next meeting. Alex then came in the following month and said "I see, looking at the minutes, that at the last meeting Isobel and someone else took rather extreme positions so let me try to find a compromise!"'56 In this, the political thrillers of the Tory politician Douglas Hurd perhaps inspired Salmond. 'There's a clear understanding of cabinet government and how a prime minister had to emerge with a consensus he'd manipulated,' he later said of Hurd's protagonist, Patrick Harvey. 'And at various points Harvey is trying to get the results he wants from a cabinet meeting so he balances one member against another and then comes to a conclusion that he wanted all along.'57

In 1985 Salmond also beat Lindsay to become the SNP's vice-convener for publicity, succeeding the journalist Colin Bell who had decided to concentrate on his career at the BBC. Salmond had long coveted the post, first standing against Lindsay in 1982 (he had lost by 373 votes to 161). His manifesto from that contest, which appeared in the *Scots Independent*, is worth noting:

Publicity direction – the main emphasis should be on persuading Labour supporters that Independence is the only option to a succession of Tory or Tory/Alliance UK Governments. Publicity style – We should:
(a) Continue to innovate, e.g. on P[arty]P[olitical]B[roadcast]s
(b) Stick to our yellow and black colours
(c) Aim more publicity at specialist interest groups
(d) Produce two leaflets for each … campaign and offer branches a choice
(e) Give more publicity back-up to our youth and trade union campaigns58

Salmond tried again at the September 1983 SNP conference, this time standing against Colin Bell, Pat Kennedy and his old enemy Kenneth Fee, but did not, for some reason, submit a statement to the *Scots Independent*. Although Salmond made it to a second round of voting, Bell defeated him by 251 votes to 177.

The party, however, seemed conscious that Salmond's abilities were not being put to good use. In May 1984 Gordon Wilson asked him to act as campaign research director ('not only preparing material for press conferences but also participating in the public presentation'[59]) for that year's autumn 'Save Scotland Campaign', while in August 1984 Colin Bell included Salmond's name on a list of potential party broadcasters. By the time Salmond was elected publicity vice-convener in 1985, however, he was already a polished television performer, while his elevation was further evidence of his restored prospects within the party hierarchy. Just two years ago he had not even been a member, and had only rejoined the NEC 18 months before. Gordon Wilson was not yet disturbed by Salmond's rise, noting in his memoirs that he 'was already an experienced and skilful politician'.[60]

He also benefited from having to seek election at the party's National Council rather than its annual conference due to Bell's sudden midterm resignation. Not only did he have fewer delegates to win over, but Isobel Lindsay failed to secure the backing of Jim Fairlie, which virtually guaranteed Salmond's victory. 'What swung it for him is that he'd produced a lot of his own literature prior to the election which was better than the official party material,' recalled a senior Nationalist, 'and had it distributed to local associations, which was a bit cheeky but did the trick.'[61]

The position played well to Salmond's strengths as an articulate advocate for the SNP as well as its most talented propagandist. He had recently fretted over the general thrust of party campaigning, quietly deploring the previous autumn's line, 'Independently we're winners', at an NEC meeting on 11 August 1984. 'We've had some difficulty with recent campaign slogans,' he observed a few months later. 'One problem we may or may not be fully aware of it that, after 20 years as part of the political furniture, the SNP is not as exciting or as different as we once were.' Salmond wanted to concentrate more on direct-mailing techniques, as well as an SNP letter-writing club to circulate supportive comments to the press. He also had 'reservations' about the 'exact style' of the new logo developed in 1984 (this was a more casual version of the traditional thistle motif, looking as if it had just been painted on a wall), although he accepted 'the underlying idea of updating our symbol'.[62]

Salmond wasted no time on assuming office. On 9 March he told the NEC that he would breakfast every Friday with Chris McLean, now SNP press officer, and Alan McKinney, the National Organiser, to plan and co-ordinate short-term activity such as press releases. Meanwhile, Salmond asked Jim Sillars, John Swinney and, interestingly, Isobel Lindsay to assist him as members of the party's Publicity Committee, which he now chaired. 'This post – probably the most important of the Party's five Vice-Chairs – also includes Campaigns and PPBs,' observed an approving *Radical Scotland*, 'which effectively makes Salmond's 8-person sub-committee into the SNP's Saatchi & Saatchi.'[63] It did not, however, include control of the *Scots Independent*, which Salmond had tried to seize via the ill-fated Commission of Inquiry.

Following his first spring campaign in charge of publicity, Salmond was full of confidence, telling conference that the

> SNP's campaigning strength has been renewed. We are once more a cred-ible political force – and self-government is once again on the Scottish political agenda. Through the summer, our Autumn Campaign and into next May's Regional election we will drive home the message that only a Scottish Parliament can offer renewed hope and opportunity – and only the SNP can and will deliver that. Our Spring Campaign has sought to demonstrate the need for self-government as a prerequisite for the sort of society the vast majority of Scots want. We have shown that only with Independence will Scotland have the policies, the resources and the ability to create a caring and compassionate community.[64]

The following month Salmond presented his strategy for the next autumn campaign to the NEC. This must be positive, he said, 'present-ing the SNP and our vision of an independent Scotland'. His answer was 'The New Scotland Campaign', with the slogans 'SNP – New Ideas for a New Scotland' and the more concise 'SNP For a New Scot-land'. Salmond also addressed 'the SNP's perennial problem of having little or no social and economic profile'. He wanted to campaign on a 'limited number' of issues to combat this, including Scotland in Europe ('We should move on to the offensive with our new EEC policy'); a renewed oil campaign ('Hardly a new issue but it can be revamped'); the Scottish Convention policy ('Important to indicate SNP are exam-ining the mechanics of transferring power from Westminster to

Scotland'); and 'One Social Issue' ('Probably housing is the issue which provides the most scope for developing in a variety of ways').

This was familiar territory for Salmond, building on his rejected proposals from the previous year. 'It is important to define our objective in these attacks', he concluded, 'apart from our understandable desire to be nasty to our opponents.'[65] The *Free Student Press*, created by Salmond as a student in 1975, was to be relaunched, while he sought longer annual conferences in order to maximise party publicity.

Though there remained a 'fundamentalist' and 'gradualist' divide in the SNP, the 'pragmatic left' held the advantage. 'From this period on,' observed Gordon Wilson, 'there was relative unity within the party as it entered a series of political campaigns over the steel industry, coal and education.'[66] These demonstrated that the SNP, with Salmond running publicity, had returned to its (and the 79 Group's) industrial strategy of the early 1980s and its attempt to build working class and trade union support for the party. To this end Salmond met with Campbell Christie, the new general secretary of the Scottish Trades Union Congress and an articulate devolutionist. He also persuaded the NEC to back a new publication, *SNP News*, partly to compete with the *Scots Independent*. By January 1986 this was self-financing, with circulation having risen from an initial run of 30,000 to 45,000.

By March 1986 Salmond was busy preparing campaigns on the future of Dounreay, British Steel at Gartcosh and the controversy surrounding the government's cold climate allowance and its application in Scotland. It was, arguably, during the period 1985–86 that the Conservative government lost the political initiative north of the border, the miners' strike, teachers' strike and the cold climate allowance row conflating to generate the impression that Conservatism was hostile to any concept of 'Scottishness'. Most elements of the Salmond strategy were in place by the regional local government elections of April 1986, in which the SNP's slogans were 'Turn the Tide for Scotland', 'Save Scottish Steel' and 'Play the Scottish Card'.

It appeared to pay off, with the SNP polling 18.2 per cent of the vote, up nearly 5 per cent on the 1982 poll. 'This year's Regional Election Campaign demonstrated the importance to the SNP of a good campaign with a clear theme,' Salmond reported to the NEC in August. 'In that campaign we offered a distinctive and relevant message to the electors and were rewarded with second place in the overall vote.' By now a great believer in sustaining political momentum, his sights were now set on an autumn campaign ('designed to build on that success'), that would also serve as a launch pad for the general election expected in 1987. 'Our job is to produce the Scottish dimension to that debate', he urged, 'but at all costs we must avoid being pushed to the fringes of what are perceived to be the 'real issues' of the campaign.'

Even at this stage, however, Salmond was not without his critics. In September 1986 one vice-convener 'expressed concern about the method of preparation of Autumn Campaign material',[67] while he also clashed with John Swinney, then the SNP's acting National Secretary, over who would lead a press conference launching that year's confer- ence agenda. Although Swinney was supposed to fill this role, it seems that Salmond decided he would do the job better. 'I spoke with the Executive Vice Chairman who indicated that although unwilling to "pull rank", he had every intention of doing so,' complained Swinney to Gordon Wilson. 'He said it was necessary to have an elected Office Bearer leading the Press Conference as I held office only in an appointed capacity. He refused to acknowledge any merit in the argument that as Convener of the Standing Orders and Agenda Committee I was enti- tled to lead the Press Conference. He also made no comment on the fact that I executed all functions of the National Secretary's position without question or quibble yet was being denied this opportunity to fulfil the post.'[68] It was typical of Salmond to spot a weakness in anoth- er's position – in this case Swinney's lack of party mandate – and exploit it to ruthless effect. The upshot was, however, that Salmond had made an enemy of Swinney, who would remain so for the next four years.

This spat also illustrated Salmond's fondness for getting his face on television, although his use of non-party members to assist in prepar- ing campaigns and television broadcasts also got him into trouble. Technical assistance for the autumn campaign had come from two leading lights in Jim Sillars' defunct Scottish Labour Party, Bob Brown and Alex Neil, the latter a future MSP, Salmond opponent and finally a minister in his government. The *Glasgow Herald* quoted a 'leading right-winger' thus: 'Mr Salmond might be happy with his choice of advisers but I suspect many in the party will look askance at his deci- sion to consult such eminent Left-wingers.' The publicity vice-convener defended himself vigorously, arguing that Brown and Neil were both 'sympathetic to the SNP'. 'I ask advice from a wide range of people, many outwith the party, for professional reasons, and obviously it is done on a private and confidential basis. What is arrived at in terms of the campaign is entirely my decision. I approve the campaigns and leaflets and I put them to the national executive for approval. It is my decision and my responsibility and I carry the can whatever way it goes.' 'That is the way I work and will continue to work,' was his uncompromising conclusion. 'I would consider anyone's skills if it benefited the party.'[69] Reporting to the NEC that October with thinly concealed irritation, Salmond said it was 'quite intolerable that people assisting the SNP should be wilfully placed in an embarrassing position by a Party member gossiping to the papers', while he believed 'the NEC should be concerned about the practice and use of anonymous quotations' which offered 'journalists an enormous power to exaggerate or indeed manufacture divisions where none, of a serious nature, exist'. This complaint, given Salmond's own relations with the media, was a little rich.

Nevertheless, after 18 months in control of the party's publicity machine, Salmond believed he had made considerable progress. 'I remain relaxed about Party morale and unity and the mood at Annual Conference vindicates this viewpoint,' he reflected. 'Relative to the other parties our internal mood is excellent and a complete transformation from the position at the last election.'[70] The SNP, with considerable help from Salmond, now geared up to fight a general election.

From the outset Salmond thought a third Conservative victory was the most likely outcome of the election, although this did not preclude the possibility of the SNP performing well in Scotland. Publicly, however, Salmond promoted the 'hung Parliament' strategy, under which the SNP could extract concessions for Scotland should neither the Conservatives nor Labour gain overall control in the House of Commons, a strategy he would deploy at almost every general election thereafter. 'It is perfectly credible', he argued, 'for us to point out that a Westminster party is more likely to concede certain demands to the Scots and Welsh than to change the structure of British politics.'[71]

Key to this was a proposed alliance with Plaid Cymru, which Salmond unveiled at the September 1986 SNP conference. 'In developing this and in launching the SNP's campaigning programme for the run-up to the General Election,' he told delegates, 'we will demonstrate that a vote for the SNP is the one sure way to guarantee real progress for Scotland in the next parliament.' Otherwise, the conference agenda was cautious. 'The Conference,' he declared, 'will be fine-tuning existing strategy and policies.'[72]

The hung Parliament strategy, however, had its critics. After Gordon Wilson somewhat paradoxically declared that it 'would not make a blind bit of difference if every single person in Scotland voted Labour. Mrs. Thatcher will still be re-elected for a third term',[73] Jim Fairlie, the party's former deputy leader and a strong critic of Salmond, declared the strategy 'dead'.[74]

Undeterred, and after commissioning a £20,000 study of Scottish electoral attitudes, Salmond predicted that the SNP were 'set to oust seven Tory MPs at the coming Election – one third of their total representation in Scotland – and our most spectacular gains will come between the Tay and the Moray Firth'.[75] The survey also revealed that 45 per cent of the electorate might vote SNP under certain circumstances, while 70 per cent wanted to see the party do well. Salmond, therefore, pointed to 'the tantalising prospect that a bridgehead breakthrough might be possible in Central Scotland before the election if the Labour Party is brought under pressure during the Campaign, perhaps due to the increasing likelihood of electoral defeat at U.K. level'.[76]

Accordingly, Salmond had fun taunting what he called the Labour Party's 'dogs of war' (George Foulkes, John Home Robertson and John Maxton), whose continued insistence that Labour could oust the Tories from power, he argued, ignored political reality. 'This time round the trio have something of a credibility problem,' wrote Salmond in the *Scotsman*, 'having barked so much and bitten so little . . . Under these circumstances might not the ridiculous position of the Labour Party in Scotland be described as "Thatcher's Fifth Column"?'[77]

It was during this election campaign that Salmond first pursued the SNP's soon familiar 'anti-Scottish Tory Party' theme. 'Anti-Scottish is the phrase which, better than any other, sums up how the vast majority of Scots view Mrs Thatcher's English Tory regime,' he explained. 'Just a few of the Tories' policies make it crystal clear that they are a Government of the South of England, elected by the South of England, for the South of England.'[78] In May 1987, meanwhile, Salmond stormed that in return for North Sea oil 'the Tories have butchered our industry, severely damaged the social services and left us with appalling and rising unemployment. Not since the Spanish stole the Inca gold has there been a case of robbery on such a grand and international scale.'[79]

Privately, party planning was geared towards winning between eight and ten seats, while in public Salmond predicted at least seven gains (in addition to the two seats already held) and a possible total of 12 MPs. One of the SNP's top target seats was the rural constituency of Banff and Buchan, for which Salmond had been selected two years before. The impetus had been his speech supporting Gordon Wilson's policy of an elected Scottish Convention at the 1984 party conference. 'The chairman of the Banff and Buchan constituency at the time, Alex Sim, saw the speech,' recalled Salmond in 2001, 'and thought this is the kind of guy we should be including in our panel of candidates and approached me at the conference.'

Banff and Buchan had one of the smallest majorities in Scotland, the former SNP MP Douglas Henderson having come within 938 votes of defeating the Tory incumbent Albert McQuarrie in 1983. That Salmond was head-hunted to stand in the SNP's most winnable seat seems remarkable. He had no local connections and just three years before he had been expelled from the party. Even Salmond's rivals for selection, however, knew he was a formidable candidate. Jim Fairlie, who vetted Salmond as a member of the SNP's Election Committee, recalled: 'I put it to Salmond: "if you could be as certain that Scotland would be worse off under independence would you still be a Nationalist?" I always asked candidates that just to see how they would handle it. I was anti-devolution and I wanted independence for the sake of it, even if it meant Scotland being worse off. When I said that, Alex said to me: "I don't think I could be as definite as you. That is something I would have to consider."'[80] Even in 1984, Salmond was hedging his constitutional bets.

In January 1985 his name was added to a short list of four (another of whom was councillor Mike Weir, later an SNP MP) drawn up by the Banff and Buchan constituency association. This led to charges of 'discrimination' against local candidates from councillor Jim Ingram, who told the *Press and Journal* that his name ought to have been in the final four.[81] Douglas Henderson, meanwhile, lobbied against Salmond (something he never forgave) while Jim Fairlie was also urged to go for the nomination.

.   When Salmond was selected a few weeks later by a single vote, Ingram decided not to renew his SNP membership, saying he was 'disappointed with what had been happening in the Constituency Association', while councillors Sam Coull and Ian MacKinnon also quit the party, citing 'growing left-wing influence'.[82] By that, the trio presumably meant Salmond, which goes to show how long the wounds caused by the 79 Group took to heal in some quarters of the party. A key player in Salmond's selection had been Stuart Pratt, who would go on to become his long-serving election agent. 'I feel it is only Tory by default and that being Left is not only compatible but necessary in that seat,' Salmond told the *Glasgow Herald*. 'It was only held by 900 votes last time and if we unite the anti-Tory vote in a constituency with a high working-class population, then it will come back to us.'[83]

Later, Salmond reflected that 'there was some understandable internal resistance to the idea of a left-winger, not long restored to membership after expulsion, standing for a key target seat in the North-east', but reasoned that the fact that two of the councillors who 'had competed against me for the seat may have had something more to do with it. This left us with a grand total of one councillor in the whole of Banff and Buchan. I wasn't too pleased at the time but, in retrospect, it was the best thing that could have happened. In particular, the constituency was united in the belief that the way to win Banff and Buchan was to offer a radical alternative to the Tory incumbent, not some sort of substitute.'

Salmond was on stage at London's Hilton Hotel in speaking on behalf of the Royal Bank at a conference on the world oil price collapse when he heard the news. 'In a quiet moment I was passed a message from the *Press and Journal* asking for my reaction to "the split" in the SNP in Banff and Buchan,' he remembered. 'This was not at all how I had envisaged my entry into representative politics.'

Nevertheless, Salmond must have been delighted to have secured the nomination for one of the SNP's most winnable target seats. 'No one of my generation in the SNP seriously expected to pursue politics as a full-time career as opposed to a passion or a hobby,' he later reflected. 'Lots of people were willing to travel hopefully. Few expected to arrive.' He also claimed to have 'had no real thought of being an MP while I was working as an economist at the Royal Bank. It was only when invited to stand by Banff and Buchan Constituency Association in 1984 that I agreed.'[84] This is not entirely accurate, for Salmond had applied to join the SNP's list of approved candidates back in 1982, from which he was probably removed following his expulsion from the party.

Now he was on course for the House of Commons, however, Salmond wasted no time in transforming himself from an urban socialist into a champion of rural Scotland. At the 1985 SNP conference he styled himself as 'a former DAFS fisheries economist', and drew on that experience to demand a fuel subsidy for the Scottish fishing fleet and 'cheaper marine gas oil'.[85] A few months later Salmond called for an election victory 'so decisive that it will break the Tory grip on this area once and for all'. 'It was the north-east which gave the rest of Scotland a political lead in the 1970s,' he said at a constituency engagement, 'and now the SNP are once again poised to break through in this area.'[86] Having been a loyal Hearts fan since 1972, meanwhile, Salmond engaged 'in the process of transferring his allegiance from Tynecastle to Pittodrie, for obvious reasons'.[87]

The Royal Bank, however, 'was having difficulty in adjusting to the fact that one of its economists wanted to be an MP'. 'This was not an everyday occurrence', Salmond recalled, 'and certainly the idea of standing for the SNP was novel, not to say eccentric.' Grant Baird and chief executive Charles Winter, however, proved to be Salmond's 'friends and protectors'. 'That proved to be necessary because a section of the Scottish Tories organised a letter-writing campaign threatening to withdraw their accounts if the Royal allowed an employee to stand as a Scot Nat. Much later I found out how Winter dealt with the situation and pacified a rather upset and worried Royal chairman in Michael Herries. He contacted a respectable Tory – I think the late Alick Buchanan-Smith – who sent a message that under no circumstances should the Royal bow to underhand tactics from his colleagues.' Winter ('a lovely man, the most successful Scottish banker of his generation') even showed Salmond a bundle of 'sack him' letters in the bottom of a drawer when it was all over. 'At any rate Charles took my news that I wanted to stand as a candidate as some sort of youthful aberration,' mused Salmond. 'After first finding it hard to accept that I really wanted to do it, he stoically refused to believe that I had any chance of winning.'[88]

Those who would determine whether he did or not, the voters of Banff and Buchan, mainly worked in farming, fishing and the oil industry. Through his work, Salmond had grown familiar with all three, and during the campaign made much of the high unemployment – 14 per cent – in Fraserburgh and Peterhead, both fishing ports and two of the most important towns in the seat. The oil slump, meanwhile, had hit the Forties oil pipeline at Cruden Bay and the gas reception terminal at St Fergus.

Salmond's principal opponent was the Tory incumbent Albert McQuarrie, who revelled in his 'Buchan Bulldog' epithet. SNP support was mainly concentrated in the seat's coastal areas but Salmond was confident it would change hands 'on a puff of political wind'. To ensure it did he targeted 4,000 first-time voters with direct mail and the slogan 'Only 938 more to win',[89] a reference to McQuarrie's modest majority. 'Our chief worry is non-voting', said Salmond, referring to a history of low turnouts in Banff and Buchan, 'but our organisation is better than ever before.'[90] Indeed, Stewart Stevenson had developed an early computer system to catalogue every constituent and their voting intentions while Robert Salmond, Alex's younger brother and a fellow SNP activist, took time out from his studies at Aberdeen University to support his brother's bid to become an MP. The Salmond campaign was typically meticulous. The *Scotsman* even noted that his SNP rosette 'had been carefully wrapped in tissue paper' before being pinned to his lapel. 'Then he was ready,' read a diary item. 'He explained that his wife ironed the rosette for him every day and sent him out into the world in the neatest political shape.'[91]

In his capacity as publicity vice-convener, Salmond also put in time at the SNP's national campaign headquarters in Edinburgh. John MacLeod, then a young SNP activist and later a columnist and author, remembered encountering him at that time: 'It wasn't a matter of shining political gifts, outstanding ability, or that charismatic "X factor" which so enchants the modern multitude,' he wrote. 'It was a case of plain kindliness.'[92]

> He was one of the few who oozed ease, serenity, and not-in-a-rushness; of more significance, he was the only who sat down with us, stuffed a few envelopes alongside us, autographed *The Radical Approach* for me, and seemed not only to appreciate our efforts but genuinely be interested in us. He was hard to place. There was an extraordinary calm about him – a self-possession, a security, a centredness that was at once real, sincere, cool, and calculating. A cynic might suggest he already had serious internal ambitions and already aspired to climb higher, and climb soon, and was smart enough to know that fanatical envelope-stuffers might, even that very autumn, be Annual National Conference delegates.[93]

And climb the cool, calm and collected Salmond did. The election also boosted his profile nationally, with appearances on Radio 4's *Any Questions* and the BBC's *Question Time* alongside Ken Clarke, Alan Beith and Denis Healey. Salmond, judged the *Glasgow Herald*'s Julie Davidson, 'is one of our most able young politicians'. 'Relaxed and unintimidated by the heavyweights from Westminster,' she wrote, 'he brought grace and humour to his contribution, as well as fluent intelligence.' 'He will go far,' concluded Davidson wryly, 'but probably not with the SNP.'[94]

Charles Kennedy, then a young SDP MP, also first encountered Salmond during the campaign, together with Michael Forsyth and Gordon Brown 'under Kirsty Wark's watchful eye at the BBC in Glasgow'. He was, recalled Kennedy a few years later, 'highly effective and looked like the sure-fire winner which Banff and Buchan made him a couple of weeks later.'[95]

Salmond won Banff and Buchan decisively, with a majority of 2,441 on a 3.9 per cent Tory-to-SNP swing with a 71 per cent turnout. The full result was:

Alex Salmond (SNP)	19,462
Albert McQuarrie (Conservative)	17,021
G. M. Burness (Alliance)	4,211
J. M. Livie (Labour)	3,281

Salmond's father Robert saw his eve of poll speech, later calling it 'one of the highlights of my life'. Mary Salmond was 'just over the moon' even though she still 'couldn't believe that anyone would really want to be an MP'.[96] Albert McQuarrie, the defeated Tory candidate, was singularly ungracious. He refused to shake Salmond's hand on stage at the count, and announced for all to hear that he would not 'shake hands with scum'. Not only that, but Salmond believed he had won by a much bigger margin than the official result, a suspicion fuelled when the returning officer refused to let him inspect certain bundles of ballot papers.

John MacLeod recalled Salmond and his wife Moira still smarting from both slights at a celebratory function at SNP HQ on the Monday following polling day. 'I remember her softly expressed but ferocious dedication to him,' said MacLeod. 'They were happy, they were proud, but they had two beefs. Moira's anger was still very evident three days later.' Alluding to McQuarrie's behaviour at the count MacLeod told the story of John F. Kennedy's famous crack at Richard Nixon on defeating him in the November 1960 presidential election: 'He went out the way he came in – no class.' (Nixon had refused publicly to concede defeat on television.) 'Alex seemed almost cross,' recalled MacLeod. '"Why didn't you tell me that before?" he asked, "I could have done with it at the count!"'[97] A few days later, when Salmond went to see the Royal Bank's chief executive, Charles Winter, to say his farewells, 'he promptly offered me my job back after the next election'.[98]

Alexander Elliot Anderson Salmond, aged just 32, was now a Member of a Parliament that he did not acknowledge as having any legitimacy to govern Scotland. A discussion paper written by Salmond and Isobel Lindsay hinted at how he was likely to respond once he reached the green benches. 'SNP M.P.s could use Parliamentary procedures to delay legislation,' it suggested, 'certainly the Scottish Grand Committee and the Scottish Standing Committees will need to be exposed as sham institutions or turned into effective ones.'[99] The stage was set for an eventful two years in the life of the new Member for Banff and Buchan.

Chapter 5

'THE INFANT ROBESPIERRE'

To the Russian prince, Robespierre was an upright man of great moral purity whose revolutionary faith never faltered. But he was also a moderate, an administrator, not a visionary – 'careful not to go beyond the opinions of those who were the dominant force at any given time' – whose power stemmed precisely from occupying the centre ground.[1]

Philip Short on Kropotkin's account of the
French Revolution, *La Grande Révolution*

There was the usual convivial atmosphere as Members filled the House of Commons on Budget day, 15 March 1988. While Nigel Lawson, Chancellor of the Exchequer since 1983, settled onto the government benches, the SNP's three MPs – Margaret Ewing, Alex Salmond and Andrew Welsh, all elected the year before – took their usual places opposite. They had something planned, something carefully calculated to make not only a political point, but an intervention that would place Salmond firmly on the UK political map.

By long-standing tradition the Budget statement was heard in respectful silence by Members on all sides of the House, as it was as Lawson worked towards a section – widely trailed in the media – announcing a cut in the basic rate of income tax. 'Lawson was a tease,' remembered Salmond. 'Time and time again it looked like he was coming to the key passage only for him to announce some other gimmick.'[2] As it neared, Hansard recorded what happened next:

Mr Nigel Lawson: The basic rate of income tax for 1988–89 will be 25 pence in the pound. The small companies' rate of corporation tax will similarly be reduced to 25 per cent. This means that the basic rate of income tax and the corporation tax rate for small companies will both be at their lowest level since the war.

Mr Alex Salmond: This is an obscenity. The Chancellor cannot do this. [Interruption]

Mr Deputy Speaker: Order.[3]

Salmond's intervention had been barely audible above the ensuing uproar, although the *Glasgow Herald*'s lobby correspondent reported hearing him shout 'Tax cuts for the rich, the poll tax for the poor' before adding 'a protest about the lack of any extra cash for the NHS'.[4] 'Lawson sensibly ignored me,' recalled Salmond in 2000. 'However, the Tory benches started to roar and the Commons authorities turned my microphone off. Pandemonium broke out. Lawson turned to Thatcher and I could read his lips saying: "This is terrible."' He also remembered the withering look he was shot by the Prime Minister herself. 'I reckon that look was a good reason to keep going,'[5] he later joked.

> It was at that moment I decided not to sit down. If it was terrible for Lawson it would probably be good for us. The man in the Speaker's Chair was Harold Walker, a Labour MP and a real martinet. After a few quick instructions for me to sit down he rapidly raced through the disciplinary procedure from naming me to suspension. However, I was ready for that. To suspend someone from the Commons requires a vote, and a vote takes the best part of 20 minutes. This was before parliament was televised, so in television and radio studios, not to mention stockbrokers' offices, round the country there was confusion as they tried to grasp the significance of why this young Scottish Nationalist was interrupting this sacred Westminster event.

Despite Salmond's later claim that his intervention was spontaneous, it had been planned well in advance as part of the SNP's programme of Parliamentary disruption, as prepared by Salmond and Isobel Lindsay prior to the 1987 general election; they had simply been waiting for an appropriate moment. In an autobiographical piece written 12 years later, Salmond explained the background:

> One of the first things I had done at Westminster was to digest the parliamentary bible Erskine May and Standing Orders to look for opportunities to make an impression. For a party of three MPs out of a parliament of 650

this was not easy. At any rate, I determined that if Lawson went ahead with a tax cut for the rich while the Tories were imposing the poll tax on Scotland then I would intervene. It had never been done, but there was nothing in Erskine May to say the Budget speech had to be listened to in silence. My experienced colleagues Margaret Ewing and Andrew Welsh were at first taken aback by my idea, but then supportive. The only question remaining was whether I had the guts to do it.[6]

Never lacking in self-confidence, Salmond did, although it seems likely that actually pushing his protest to the point of suspension had not been part of the plan. The *Scotsman* reported that 'Margaret Ewing tugged at Salmond's jacket in an attempt to get him to sit down', while the *Glasgow Herald* observed that both Ewing and Dafydd Wigley, a Plaid Cymru MP, 'told him he had made his point'.[7] This was later tacitly confirmed by Ewing when she remarked, 'if someone's mind is determined, he will keep going'.[8] 'You can't imagine the psychological pressure when even your colleagues are tugging at your jacket to get you to sit,' Salmond recalled in 1998, giving the impression that he could have been persuaded to desist. 'It was terrifying.'[9]

Hansard's record continues:

> Mr Salmond: This Budget is an obscenity.
> Mr Deputy Speaker: Order. I name Mr. Alex Salmond.[10]

When the leader of the House, John Wakeham, proposed Salmond's expulsion, there was a great roar of support from both sides of the Chamber. The motion was then put that he be suspended 'from the service of the House' for five days. This was then voted on, with the Labour front bench and the government supporting the Deputy Speaker ('He had been anxious to get me for several months,' recalled Salmond. 'He didn't like me'[11].). A handful of the Labour left (including Scottish MPs Dennis Canavan and David Lambie) joined the Scottish and Welsh Nationalists in the 'no' lobby, where the final figures – 354 to 19 – revealed that most Labour Members had abstained.

As Salmond, Ewing and Welsh left the Commons they were hissed and jeered from both sides of the Chamber. 'A nice policeman suggested it was cold outside and I might want to go back to my office to fetch my coat,' remembered Salmond. 'I have never seen so many cameras as was awaiting me by the time I left.'[12] That, he added in another account, 'gave me my opportunity to explain to a wider audience why the poll tax was a dreadful thing and that they would be hearing much, much more from the SNP.'[13] Reflecting on the incident in his own memoirs, Nigel Lawson said he 'could not help wondering what kind of democracy the Nationalists would establish in Scotland if ever they had the opportunity'.

Salmond's intervention was, however, 'no more than a curtain-raiser'[14] compared to what happened when Lawson announced that the upper rate of income tax was to fall from 60 to 40 per cent. Then all hell broke loose with Militant-aligned Labour MPs creating such disorder (crying 'shame' repeatedly) that the sitting had to be suspended for ten minutes. Indeed, the *Glasgow Herald* speculated that Salmond might have got wind of plans by Labour MPs to interrupt the Chancellor's speech when he reached the well-trailed announcement about the 40 per cent rate, thus seeking to rob them of their moment in the spotlight. 'If that is correct, it would explain the timing of his intervention,' commented the newspaper, 'which looked as if he had jumped the gun slightly.'

Neil Kinnock, the leader of the opposition, then prompted a walkout by one of his own MPs, Dennis Canavan, when he condemned Salmond's actions. 'In this, as in everything else in this democracy,' said Kinnock, 'argument is always superior to the form of action we have seen in the course of this afternoon.' Other Labour MPs were equally critical. Donald Dewar, the Shadow Scottish Secretary, dismissed it as 'a sad little incident' and 'a charade'; John Reid said: 'The man's a twit. It was a calculated and premeditated attempt to grab publicity'; Sam Galbraith called it 'a classic gimmick. They have been stung by the criticism that they are not doing much here'; while Brian Wilson, Salmond's nemesis since the 1979 referendum, said simply: 'A rehearsed stunt; cretinous.'[15]

These responses, however, betrayed more than a hint of irritation that an SNP MP had stolen their oppositionist thunder, while conveniently ignoring the fact that Tam Dalyell had been expelled twice from the Chamber for similarly disruptive antics. Indeed, Salmond enjoyed rubbing salt into their wounds by pointing out afterwards that had Labour's 50 Scottish MPs backed his protest it would have had even more impact. 'This is what Labour's feeble opposition should have been doing for the last nine years,' he told the *Scotsman*. 'The SNP is prepared to lead the fight against this Government and the poll tax, as Labour have shown themselves totally incapable of so doing.'[16]

With that, Salmond, Ewing and Welsh held a celebratory dinner at Vitello D'Oro, a nearby Italian restaurant where the trio most likely chewed over the political consequences. As the SNP's finance spokes-man, Salmond's suspension meant he could no longer take part in the Budget debate, which lasted until Monday (his suspension continued until Tuesday), so the following day he flew to his constituency to catch up with mail and to speak to the Portsoy ladies' circle. The topic, aptly enough, was Parliamentary procedure. Meanwhile, television viewers in the south of England witnessed, for the first time, 'a short, neat young man, soberly suited beyond his years, a little sleek about the jowls, wearing a smile suggestive of some secret and superior knowledge'.[17]

Ewen MacAskill profiled Salmond at length in the *Scotsman*: 'Mr Salmond is smart, single-minded and combative. He is seen by some Labour MPs and by some SNP members as arrogant, abrasive and cold. Anti-social is an adjective he frequently attracts. Not for him the bonhomie of Westminster's Annie's bar, the drab haunt of some jour-nalists and MPs. Even when he does put in an appearance, he is more likely to be drinking orange juice than alcohol.' But his Budget inter-vention, noted MacAskill, 'will have done him no harm in nationalist circles, and increased his already strong chances of leading the SNP'. Indeed, SNP HQ reported a steady number of phone calls. 'I have had only one call against, and about 30 for his action,' reported Peter Murrell, then working in Salmond's Peterhead office but a future chief executive of the party. 'They have been not just from around here, but from all over Scotland.'[18] Even the *Scots Independent* wrote approvingly that he had 'defied the rules of cricket', while the paper's columnist Jim Fairlie, again no fan of Salmond's, said his action 'should be applauded by every Nationalist'.[19]

Indeed, a subsequent opinion poll showed SNP support rising to 20 per cent, which gave the party an invaluable boost ahead of May's district council elections, the SNP's plans for a Poll Tax non-payment campaign and, within a few months, the battle to win the Glasgow Govan by-election. Salmond's belief in creating and maintaining politi-cal momentum was again at play. 'We are giving fair warning that we will indulge in these tactics again if the circumstances arise,' he told the *Scotsman*. 'We are totally united in our willingness and preparedness to strike hard, but we do not wish to telegraph our intentions.'[20]

The disruption of Nigel Lawson's Budget speech was clearly a defining moment in Salmond's political career, and he certainly thought so. 'The Budget intervention from 1988,' Salmond told Bernard Ponsonby in 2001, 'is pretty important on a personal level in terms of reputation.'[21] Although ironic in that Salmond would later support precisely the sort of low-tax business-friendly economics Lawson had outlined, at the time it neatly encompassed all of Salmond's thinking on politics, tactics and publicity. 'His tax cut was daft economically as subsequent events were to show,' was Salmond's rather disingenuous explanation in 2000, 'but it wasn't the economics I was waiting to protest against, just the morality.'[22] With one Parliamentary act, the SNP's deputy leader also became 'known' across the United Kingdom. 'It was a simple demonstration,' he added modestly, 'but one that fitted the times. The mood in Scotland and certainly in the SNP was that someone had finally done something.'[23]

'The House of Commons is a place where new MPs arrive, fresh from real life, knowing almost everything about something,' Salmond wrote in 1994. 'Over time, at best, they end up knowing a little about everything. At worst they know nothing about anything.'[24] He had arrived at West-minster in the summer of 1987 intending not to fall into that trap. The 1987–92 Parliament, as James Mitchell has observed, offered the SNP significant opportunities. Labour was reeling after a third successive defeat; the Tories in Scotland had been reduced to a rump of ten MPs; and although the election had returned just a trio of SNP MPs, within 18 months the party would appear to be on the cusp of an electoral break-through. The new Member for Banff and Buchan appeared to many to embody this new political reality. 'A younger generation of SNP activ-ists,' wrote Mitchell, 'much tougher and more sophisticated, was emerging around Alex Salmond.'[25]

Salmond's maiden speech indicated that he was more than ready to take up the challenge. Assured, articulate and clear-minded, he laid his prede-cessor, Albert McQuarrie, to rest by 'wishing him a long and happy retirement', and waxed lyrical about Banff and Buchan, whose 'robust characters . . . work with their hands and get their faces dirty. They are involved in producing, making and catching things. They are people engaged in the manufacturing and primary sectors who are the real crea-tors of wealth. If Government policy was orientated more to the primary and manufacturing sectors of industry, rather than to the rentier economy produced by the Conservative party, the long-term health and welfare of this country would be better served.' Turning to the constitutional ques-tion, he seriously suggested 'to Conservative Members representing English constituencies that the nations of Scotland and England have a close and long history. Sometimes it has been a troubled history but it has always been a close one. At this juncture in our affairs, when there is a dramatic political divergence between Scotland and England, and indeed between England and Wales, would it really hurt them so much to concede a little justice to the Scottish nation?'[26] Salmond had set out his political stall. The ultimate goal, of course, was 'justice' for Scotland, while political tactics dictated that much of his ire would be directed at what he memorably dubbed the 'feeble fifty', dozens of relatively powerless Scottish Labour MPs.

Salmond had been given special responsibility for maintaining the pressure on Labour at the first meeting of the SNP Parliamentary group on 14 June. His colleagues were just two: Margaret Ewing (née Bain), daughter-in-law of Winnie, who was elected Parliamentary leader, and Andrew Welsh, another of the 1974 intake who was returned for Angus East. One SNP staffer at Westminster, however, found the transition from working with Gordon Wilson and Donald Stewart to this new trio difficult. 'I am getting on all right with the new "team",' a short note informed Wilson in July 1987. 'However, I must admit that I find Alex very difficult. He is very patronising when he speaks to me and that approach does not bring out the best side of my character. I think he is just overwhelmed by the House. I hope he settles down quickly and can perhaps make an attempt to treat me like an equal.'[27]

If Salmond was 'overwhelmed' by the House of Commons, then he disguised it well. Of the three new MPs, however, he undoubtedly had the most ambition and the least Parliamentary experience. Ewing, too, had her eye on the top job and, as Wilson was effectively a lame-duck leader having been defeated in his Dundee constituency, it was only a matter of time before the pair would battle it out for the succession.

The value of a Commons seat in boosting Salmond's profile was immeasurable, even before his Budget intervention in March 1988. Sunday newspaper colour supplements included him among 'MPs to watch', while in November 1987 Salmond even appeared as a guest on Terry Wogan's popular television chat show. Always good at building relationships with individual journalists, Salmond could also be found distributing his own press releases to the Lobby. As the SNP's spokesman on energy (he joined the Energy Select Committee in November 1987), finance, fisheries, trade and industry, meanwhile, Salmond also had a wide-ranging remit which allowed him to comment on major aspects of government policy. In that context his continuing role as the SNP's publicity vice-convener seemed almost superfluous. By October, his ally Mike Russell had taken over, a useful position from which to mastermind Salmond's leadership campaign, which effectively began the moment he became an MP.

A profile of Salmond in the *Glasgow Herald* ('Rising star of SNP faces his toughest test'), written soon after his election, neatly captures the new MP as he prepared to climb the greasy pole: 'At the age of 32, the new MP for Banff and Buchan is clearly the brightest and ablest talent to emerge in the SNP for a long time. He looks destined to become leader of the party, possibly sooner rather than later,' wrote Harry Reid. 'He has hardly put a foot wrong in his career to date, and people speak highly of his niceness and his ability.' Reid, however, set out to discover 'whatever flaws may be lurking beneath his somewhat smooth carapace', adding: 'He is already fleshing out around the jowls, and his dapper, neatly-suited appearance suggests someone who is conservative and hypercautious rather than radical. For someone still in his early 30s, he can seem almost too mature; his style is cool and contained and he is always totally in control ... he can exude just a touch of self-satisfaction ... his political assets are formidable. He is highly intelligent ... He can, and does, work extremely hard. He is not a fiery orator, but he is a good concise public speaker, and he can throw in the odd populist phrase to stir things up.'

Although Salmond maintained, despite the election result, that the 'choice for Scotland is now between Thatcherism and independence', he conceded that 'we can't just say independence is a cure for all Scotland's ills'. Meanwhile, he added, 'we need a consistent political line on current issues like the poll tax and parent power. In other words, the party needs a day-to-day political identity, and I'd define that identity as being moderate left-of-centre.' The profile also quoted Stephen Maxwell on Salmond's political journey: 'It's hard to produce evidence that he's changed, but in the 79 group he argued that it should be a left-wing party with a socialist policy; now I gather it's to be a moderate left-centre consensus party. I am marginally sceptical about the seriousness of his commitment to a left-wing programme. I suspect he's going to be very pragmatic. But he is organised, relaxed and very capable.'[28] But while Maxwell grumbled that Salmond was not left-wing enough, others in the SNP believed his 'socialism', however ill defined, was a bad thing. In the *Scotsman*, for example, the former SNP councillor Sam Coull (who had resigned when Salmond got the Banff and Buchan nomination in 1985) warned that, in his 'Right-of-Centre constituency', 'Alex is going to have a continuous struggle between his political ambition and the impact and cost in lost votes of his Left-wing principles'.[29]

At the 1987 SNP conference in Dundee the divide was a tactical one. The general election result had provoked a predictable bout of internal soul searching, with the argument raging between defenders of the party's election strategy, such as Salmond, and those, like Jim Fairlie, who believed it had been disastrous. Conveniently, both men were also bidding to become senior vice-convener, the de facto deputy leader of the SNP.

Learning, meanwhile, that Gordon Wilson was considering standing down as leader, Salmond invited him 'to lunch and offered his support'. As Wilson recalled: 'This was strange. Alex and I had not been close and although he was not the main irritant during the '79 Group affair, his involvement with the others had almost caused the Party to self-destruct. Nevertheless, since he had just been elected MP for Banff/Buchan, he had the platform to be a future leader. If it came to the crunch, his mentor, Jim Sillars was ahead of him in the queue on the Left. Of course, either would have been up against Margaret Ewing who would almost certainly have been elected at that time.'[30]

Concerned lest Margaret Ewing or Jim Sillars beat him to the leadership, Salmond obviously considered that keeping Wilson in place, at least for the time being, was the best possible scenario. The race for deputy leader, meanwhile, continued between Fairlie, George Leslie (vice-convener for policy) and Salmond. By way of a manifesto, Salmond warned at a fringe meeting: 'It's not enough to argue for independence and nothing else. The constitutional case must not be presented in isolation but as the route to social and economic change in Scotland. The priority is to win the economic argument for independence, but we must also present Scots with a challenging, outward-looking vision of Scotland's potential as an independent state.'[31] Salmond won easily, while Fairlie barely survived as an ordinary member of the party's National Executive Committee. This clearly shook the party's establishment, for at least one newspaper was briefed to the effect that so greatly did Gordon Wilson distrust his new deputy that he would stage-manage his own departure in order to pass the torch to Margaret Ewing.[32]

Wilson's subsequent appeal to his party to be realistic and not to try competing with Labour 'on the far left of the political spectrum'[33] has to be seen in this context. Indeed, Salmond would enjoy, at best, a workmanlike relationship with Wilson over the next few years. There is little evidence of direct correspondence between leader and deputy among Wilson's papers, while some believed that Salmond and Wilson never once spoke by telephone. This seems unlikely given that it was Salmond's preferred means of communication, although Mike Russell remembered the relationship being 'very poor'.[34]

Whatever the case, for the next three years Wilson was occupied with running the party from Scotland ('Those were the best three years of my leadership,' he later recalled, 'my hand was back on the tiller'[35]), while Salmond was equally busy at Westminster. A committee of senior office bearers (known as SOBs) ran the party at that time, and while ordinarily that would have been chaired by the senior vice-convener (Salmond), Wilson shrewdly took the chair himself, realising that Salmond already had a 'platform' from which to secure the leadership. SNP activist Iain Lawson certainly got the impression that as soon as he became deputy leader Salmond was campaigning to succeed Wilson, while Mike Russell later admitted that it was an 'open secret'.[36]

The 1987 conference, meanwhile, backed Salmond's autumn campaign theme, 'The Real Choice – Independence or Thatcher', which was framed partly as a response to Labour's Scottish Assembly Bill, soon to be tabled in the House of Commons. Salmond likened it to the 'Scotland Free or a Desert' slogan of the 1820 radical uprising. 'Both crystallise the stark choice for Scots,'[37] he said, reasoning that: 'One thing is certain, the Bill will go down to defeat. That is one bit on which we will be hanging our campaign, that devolution is no longer an option, having been rejected by Westminster.'[38]

Sure enough, when MPs voted on the Bill on 27 January 1988, the SNP's three MPs backed it while gleefully taking advantage of its subsequent defeat. 'Just as Labour have no plans to prevent the poll tax being imposed,' said Salmond, 'so they have no strategy to deliver a Scottish Assembly once the English Tories vote down their Bill. After tomorrow, the devolution option will no longer be on the table. The real choice for Scots will have crystallised – the status quo and continued English Tory rule, or independence and the Scottish National Party.'[39]

The SNP had, throughout the mid to late 1980s, finessed its position in relation to the European Economic Community (EEC) or European Community. Indeed, James Mitchell reckoned the party's decision to commit itself 'to independence in Europe as its fundamental political goal ... was one of the most significant changes in SNP policy in the 1980s'.[40] It was a significant change that had Salmond's full support. A vehement opponent of the EEC as a student, he had gradually shifted ground together with Jim Sillars, who set out the intellectual case for the new policy in a pamphlet called *Moving On And Moving Up In Europe* (1985), and more notably in his book, *Scotland: The Case for Optimism* (1986).

There, Sillars made the main tactical point in favour of the 'independence in Europe' slogan, that with 'an independent Scotland within
the Community, the charge of separatism disappears'.[41] The slogan was
adopted at a senior office bearers meeting in early 1988, while a crucial
NEC meeting backed, by 14 votes to 4, a motion supporting the Single
European Act (SEA). Finally, on 11 July 1988, the SNP's three MPs
marched into the 'aye' lobby with Mrs Thatcher's Conservative government (for only the second time in that Parliament) to support the SEA,
which compelled the EEC to establish a single market by the end of
1992, while moving towards a common foreign and security policy.

The debate preceding that division found Salmond on eloquent
form:

> I want to look at Scotland's real choice – whether we want to play a bit
> part on the British stage or whether we want to find a new role for our
> nation within the European Community. I find the British state funda-
> mentally unattractive. It is unattractive in the attitude displayed towards
> foreigners and unattractive in terms of the breakdown of social cohesion.
> It is a depressing vision for the Scottish people to have to continue to play
> a subsidiary role within a declining and out-of-date Britain. Steinbeck
> once wrote that Scotland was not a 'lost cause' but a 'cause unwon'. The
> Scottish National party gives notice to the House of Commons that it
> intends to win that cause.[42]

Salmond took up the issue again in the pages of *Radical Scotland*, a left-
wing journal edited by the former 79 Grouper Alan Lawson. He
explored how the SNP had learned to stop worrying and love the EEC,
while sketching out the likely impact of the party's new policy. The
SNP, wrote Salmond, was converted 'tentatively in 1983 and more
firmly since, to a pro-EEC position'. The 'acid test of this change of
heart', he added, would come at 1988's Inverness conference, 'when the
Party addresses not just the EEC policy but its attitude to the Single
European Act. The debate will be a key one because it will dictate how
the national case is argued in 1990s.'

It is clear that Salmond saw the policy primarily in tactical terms, in
that it changed 'the ground rules fundamentally from when independence was debated in the 1970s'. 'There is no question of separation,
economic or personal, within the European context,' he argued. 'Now
it is the SNP who have the intellectual initiative in arguing for independent status within the Community to replace colonial status within

the UK. Of course the conversion to the European cause must be more than a mere tactic for the SNP, however profoundly it changes the perspective of Scottish independence. To win real converts the SNP and the Scottish left in general will require to be convinced that Europe post 1992 will not be an economic straitjacket with all major economic decisions predetermined and increasingly remote from those who take the consequences.'

Addressing the problem of sovereignty, which so offended National-ists like Stephen Maxwell and Jim Fairlie, Salmond conceded that membership of the European Community 'involves a degree of sacrifice of sovereignty', but, he said, 'in Scotland's case it is very much an academic loss since we are starting from a position of no control. The SEA is not without its challenges but the case essentially depends on realpolitik. Scottish independence could be obtained by the mid-1990s and by then the single market will be a reality in some form. Options which used to pertain for Scotland will be closed as indeed is also being recognized by the other small European states outwith the Community. Within the EEC and within the SEA Scotland would still retain the freedom to develop economic, social and international policy in a way which would transcend the British experience.'

Importantly, Salmond failed to outline exactly how far this 'freedom' to develop economic policy would actually extend, a vagueness that would cause him difficulties – particularly in the context of the single currency – later on in his career. 'In the coming polarisation of Scottish politics into those who grudgingly accept Scotland's subsidiary role in a Thatcherite Britain and those who reject it outright,' concluded Salmond, 'independence within Europe offers the vastly superior posi-tion from which to win our cause.'[43]

The Inverness conference endorsed Salmond's stance with a large majority, although an important caveat dictated that, as in 1975, Scots would decide whether or not to remain a member of the European Community via a referendum after independence. The first test of the 'independence in Europe' policy, meanwhile, came at the June 1989 elections to the European Parliament. Salmond played an active role, not least in pursuing his enduring interest in energy policy, now given an added edge by the emergence of 'green' politics. A clean environ-ment, he said, was 'not just a desirable aim from a Scottish perspective – it is also a vital economic necessity'. The SNP's policy was 'to phase out nuclear power as fast as possible',[44] instead utilising Scotland's wind, tide and hydro power to generate electricity.

This positive vision, as well as the party's new slogan, appeared to work, for on polling day the SNP secured 25.6 per cent of the vote, beating the Conservatives into third place and helping make Scotland, at least on the European map, a Tory-free zone. It was the party's best result in a Scotland-wide election since October 1974. Salmond, however, came to resent the identification of Jim Sillars with the 'independence in Europe' policy, later arguing that while he 'did indeed see the significance of the European dimension for Scotland', 'a glance at their [the Scottish Labour Party's] foundation documents confirms that independence was not part of their agenda'.[45] Rather, Salmond claimed figures like Winnie Ewing, George Reid and Neil McCormick had in fact laid the groundwork in the mid 1970s, whatever his personal views at that time.

The Nationalists had achieved another breakthrough, albeit more modest, at May 1988's district council elections, increasing its share of the vote from 1984's abysmal 11.7 per cent to 21.3 per cent, and nearly doubling its number of councillors from 59 to 113, although still nowhere near its 1977 highpoint of 170. The SNP still only controlled one district council, while its performance in Labour's heartland was good but patchy. But given that the SNP's aim, as calculated by Salmond, had been 'obtaining a mandate at the District Elections to lead a mass campaign of non-payment against the Poll Tax',[46] then the outcome was not exactly a triumph.

Also backing non-payment were the Scottish Trades Union Congress, the National Union of Students (Scotland) and a range of other Labour-affiliated organisations, although they focused on frustrating the registration process in order to make the tax administratively unworkable. Brian Wilson, meanwhile, orchestrated Labour's 'Stop It' campaign, which ironically stopped short of advocating non-payment. Donald Dewar, predictably, attacked the SNP's tactics, claiming it made no contribution to the task of challenging the government. 'No less than 71 per cent of Labour voters agree with the SNP on the need for a mass campaign of non-payment to defeat the poll tax,' retorted Salmond. 'The real division over the poll tax is not between the SNP and the STUC but between the Labour leadership and their own supporters.'[47]

Nevertheless, at the end of April the SNP withdrew from the STUC's cross-party Poll Tax initiative. Campbell Christie, its general secretary, claimed the Nationalists had demanded the other parties agree to lead an illegal non-payment drive, while Salmond said they had simply requested a 'modest commitment to preparation'. He added: 'The only way that offers the opportunity of stopping the tax is by enough of us refusing to pay, by organizing a campaign over the next year and building a solid army of non-payers – people who can afford to pay the Poll Tax but won't. The SNP is entitled to seek support for that platform whether the other parties approve or not and whether Campbell Christie approves or not. The STUC may now be reduced to a Labour Party subsidiary but they must not expect the SNP to assume the same position.'[48] Salmond's tactics now switched to a slightly different campaign, under which the SNP would recruit 100,000 wealthy non-payers to declare 'Can pay, won't pay', a policy endorsed by the party's June National Council. 'We want an army of non-payers united with the bulk of public opinion behind them', said Salmond, 'and we are very confident we can achieve that.'[49]

That autumn's annual conference overwhelming supported the non-payment campaign, reminding some present of 1981's 'civil disobedience' policy. 'We will be targeting those people in Scotland who can afford to pay this tax', said Salmond after the vote, 'and can afford to pay the penalties and who can show their solidarity with people who cannot pay.' He also highlighted the inequities of the Poll Tax by contrasting what the Queen would pay for her 'holiday home' at Balmoral, £400, and the £750 a 'postie' in his constituency would be forced to shell out.

The Poll Tax policy was, Salmond later reflected, 'a significant registration of the SNP on the political landscape of Scotland',[50] although it was not necessarily an electorally successful one. Despite being the major issue at the 1990 regional council elections – held when the Poll Tax was a reality rather than a prospect at the 1988 district poll – there was 'little evidence ... that its campaign or policy of ... non-payment ... brought significant dividends in support'.[51] The Conservative vote, meanwhile, actually went up, while the SNP managed only a modest increase from 18.2 to 21.8 per cent of the vote and 42 seats, far short of the 30 per cent Salmond had predicted back in 1987.

At the 1988 SNP conference Salmond was also re-elected, unopposed, as deputy leader. He had by then consolidated his position within the SNP, and was popular with all but a vocal minority on the fundamentalist fringes. A sign of how effective Salmond was at this time can be gauged by the strength of opposition attacks, not only from Labour but from the Conservative government. During a lengthy debate in the Commons on 6 July 1988 Malcolm Rifkind, the mercurial Scottish Secretary (or 'the Walter Mitty of Scottish politics',[52] as Salmond had dubbed him), launched a particularly scathing attack on the Member for Banff and Buchan, whom Rifkind likened to 'the infant Robespierre'. The SNP was, he added 'a party which, apart from its desire for separatism and the break-up of the United Kingdom, does have a coat of many colours. It uses a moderate voice in rural areas, anti-Socialist policies in areas where it believes that that would be popular, and a radical Left-wing Socialist policy elsewhere. The hon. Gentleman [Salmond] expresses puzzlement and points to himself, but since he has been allowed to return to the fold of the SNP he has been less noticeable for his propositions of Socialist policy than he was some years ago. Perhaps that has something to do with representing Banff and Buchan.' There was, nevertheless, a degree of repartee between Rifkind and Salmond, both of whom respected talented opponents. Salmond willingly took up the 'infant Robespierre' mantle, observing later that he had 'started the debate as Robespierre and end by being a moderate. The right hon. and learned Gentleman will have to decide in what role he wishes to place me.'[53]

Just weeks after this light-hearted exchange Bruce Millan, formerly Secretary of State for Scotland between 1976 and 1979, resigned his Glasgow Govan constituency to become one of the UK's European Commissioners in Brussels. The resulting by-election would provide a significant boost to the SNP, Salmond and, not least, Jim Sillars. The seat had Nationalist provenance, Margo MacDonald (by 1988 Mrs Jim Sillars) having captured it – albeit fleetingly – back in November 1973.

Salmond took an active role in the campaign almost from the moment Millan resigned, suggesting seven possible candidates: Gordon Wilson, Jim Sillars, Kenny MacAskill, Mike Russell, Alex Neil, John Swinney or Alasdair Morgan. Given the 'media importance of this by-election', he wrote, 'I think the candidate has to be a politician experienced at national level.' Most importantly, concluded Salmond, the 'by-election should take precedence over all other aspects of Party activity since our performance in Govan will dictate our performance in the Euro elections'.[54]

Always thinking one step ahead, Salmond instinctively realised that a by-election victory in Labour's heartlands could give the SNP invaluable momentum, as well as taking its non-payment campaign to an altogether different level. Once Sillars was selected as candidate, it also meant the return to front-line politics of Salmond's closest colleague in politics.

Salmond personally took charge as convener of the SNP's Govan By-election Campaign Committee, preparing a leaflet on the Poll Tax and accelerating membership growth in the SNP's Govan constituency association. Sillars, of course, was the campaign's biggest asset, otherwise memorable for a particularly weak Labour candidate called Bob Gillespie, whom Salmond said represented 'the Dan Quayle syndrome'.[55] Come polling day, on 10 November 1988, Sillars emerged triumphant with 14,677 votes to Gillespie's 11,123, a swing of more than 33 per cent from Labour to the SNP. That same night, the SNP also came from third place to win a by-election to West Lothian District Council. 'It is an indication that something is happening right across the board,' remarked Salmond, 'that there is outright rejection of Thatcher in Scotland.'[56] 'Govan', Salmond later reflected, 'arrived at exactly the time that people were examining that period looking at the Poll Tax issue and contrasting the Labour Party's lack of stomach apparently to do anything about it and the SNP's new vigorous campaigning style.'[57]

Although many Nationalists hoped, like Salmond, that the Govan result indicated a sea change in support for the SNP, it in fact represented little more than a protest vote against the Poll Tax rather than a genuine realignment of voting patterns. Salmond, therefore, was not complacent, and urged the SNP to review its campaign structure the following month. The ever-confident Jim Sillars, meanwhile, had arrived at the House of Commons denouncing Mrs Thatcher as 'malicious, wicked and quite evil in respect of the policies being pursued in her counter-revolution for the welfare state'.[58]

It did not take journalists long to speculate what form the Sillars/Salmond dynamic would take. 'Some Westminster-watchers say both are on the Left of the party and that they are buddies,' observed the *Scotsman*. 'Others feel Sillars is such an overpowering personality that tension is inevitable.' Salmond was at least able to joke about it. As Sillars prepared to address a rally of supporters outside Parliament, he was spotted in a supporting role, carrying half a dozen precariously balanced glasses and a jug of water. 'See what I've been reduced to?'[59] quipped Salmond.

At this point in the Sillars/Salmond relationship, however, the pair got along well. Sillars probably looked upon Salmond as an indispensable ally – although certainly not an equal – while his campaign in Govan had emphasised tactical themes valued by both, a need for devolution as a stepping stone to independence, a hard line on the Poll Tax and a conciliatory approach to the Labour voters the SNP wanted to attract. But within just two months of Sillars' remarkable victory, he began to shift ground, treating his protégé insensitively and weakening his loyalty as a result.

It is likely that soon after the by-election Sillars began sounding people out about standing for the leadership (something he later denied), which would inevitably have come to the attention of Salmond. There was also the problem of proximity. Although the pair had long worked together, most closely within the 79 Group, they did not know each other intimately, while the rigours of Parliamentary life – of which Sillars had considerably more experience than Salmond – would have produced tensions of its own.

Most striking, however, was Sillars' change of tack politically. During the Govan campaign he had attacked the STUC and co-operation with Labour on Scotland's constitutional future; immediately after his victory he talked about reaching 'out the hand of friendship to like-minded people in the Labour Party in Scotland'; but within weeks of that he had launched a strong personal attack on leading Labour figures, even likening Donald Dewar to 'Uncle Tom' during a speech in Castlemilk.[60]

Sillars, curiously, had ignored his own tactical advice as outlined in *The Case for Optimism*, in which he wrote that 'the SNP has still not learned that a certain style of attack on the Labour movement can be counter-productive'.[61] Always a more consistent and thoughtful tactician, Salmond must, at the very least, have been surprised by Sillars' behaviour. There was at least a welcome distraction in terms of polling data. For around four months after Govan the SNP were riding high, even reaching 32 per cent in January 1989, only 4 per cent behind Labour and the party's best showing since 1977.

The final straw in the increasingly tense relationship between Sillars and Salmond, however, came when the SNP decided to withdraw from ongoing cross-party talks concerning the Scottish Constitutional Convention. Initial negotiations, led by Gordon Wilson, Margaret Ewing and Jim Sillars, had gone well, but gradually the mood began to change. In late January 1989, Wilson began to consult senior office bearers by telephone, all of whom expressed opposition.

Crucially, however, Salmond – as senior-vice convener – was not among those contacted. What exactly happened is unclear but it seems likely that Wilson delegated consultation with Salmond to Sillars, not surprising given that the leader and his deputy were hardly close. Sillars did call him, but failed to mention the impending decision, even though many journalists had already been briefed to that effect. 'It's likely that Jim just didn't mention it,' reckoned a senior Nationalist, 'perhaps to bring Alex down a peg or two, or because he knew what the reaction would be.'[62] That same evening, Gordon Wilson used a Burns Supper at the Edinburgh SNP Club to denounce the composition of the Convention as 'a travesty of reality'.[63]

When asked if he had consulted Salmond about the decision in 2001, Wilson replied, somewhat awkwardly: 'Not directly, no.'[64] Isobel Lindsay, who was contacted, later told Arnold Kemp that Salmond, despite subsequent claims to the contrary, 'wasn't unavailable' on the weekend in question. 'They assumed Alex,' she explained to Kemp, 'would want to participate.'[65] This was broadly correct; although neither Lindsay nor Salmond was starry-eyed when it came to the Convention, having argued in a February 1987 paper that it seemed unlikely that 'a glorified public meeting' could provide the basis for 'a constitutional challenge to Tory rule in Scotland'.[66] Kemp summarised Salmond's position thus: 'Salmond took a different tactical view though there was no strategic disagreement. He felt the SNP should go along with the convention to the point that it could be shown that it would not discuss independence as a serious issue or allow it to be presented to the people of Scotland. He also thought the SNP should argue within the convention for a multi-choice referendum (independence, devolution, the status quo). On these tactics Salmond thought he had the agreement of Sillars.'[67]

Almost a decade later Salmond gave the broadcaster Brian Taylor a similar account, describing it as 'the right decision at the wrong time': 'It was the right decision because I don't think it would have been possible for the SNP to run into the 1992 election on the same platform, effectively, as the Labour and Liberal parties. The wrong timing because if you are going to make a decision like that you have got to be able to demonstrate your case and you can't do that if you apparently, in terms of public perception, flounce out within forty-eight hours of the talks taking place. So it was badly handled in that sense but the decision strategically was the right one.'[68]

On Sunday, 29 January 1989, presumably at around the same time Sillars spoke to Salmond, the SNP issued a press release – drafted by Sillars – which declared: 'Scotland lost out in 1979 because of a rigged referendum. It is our view that the SNP cannot take part in a rigged Convention which can neither reflect nor deliver Scottish demands.'[69]

The press response the following day was universally negative. 'SNP pulls out of Convention', was the *Scotsman*'s front-page headline. An editorial headed 'SNP ought to think again' accused the party of being 'reckless, irresponsible and short-sighted', while the *Glasgow Herald* classified it as 'an old story. Our chronic inability to unite is a national curse.' Journalists had, quite naturally, spent the previous evening locating dissenting voices. 'This is tactically wrong for the SNP and wrong for Scotland,' Isobel Lindsay told the *Scotsman*. 'I think it is going to push us out on the extreme again.' While Professor Neil MacCormick described the leadership's judgment as a mistake. 'The Convention can do the party no harm,' he said, 'even in its current proposed form. It could do the party and the country a great deal of good.'[70]

Salmond, however, was not among those quoted. 'The radio news the following morning was the first many Nationalists knew of the abrupt change,' wrote Andrew Marr. 'That was the moment when the trust between him and Sillars disappeared.'[71] Isobel Lindsay concurred. 'That was the first time I had seen hostility openly expressed between Alex and Jim,' she recalled. 'Before that Alex would never criticise Jim.'[72]

'I couldn't believe it at first,' reflected Salmond several years later. 'I had a conversation with Jim Sillars on the Sunday night I think from my constituency office in Peterhead. By the time I got back down to the Central Belt the Monday papers said the decision had been made.' 'That was the first time that I think our relationship of trust broke down', he added, 'and it broke down not because we disagreed about the issue, which we did; it broke down because I'd had that conversation and he'd pointedly not told me what was going on.'[73]

It is easy to sympathise with Salmond on this point. Sillars was, he believed, a close colleague, yet he had deliberately kept him in the dark as the party, of which Salmond was deputy leader, made a key tactical decision. Their relationship, however, had already cooled by the beginning of 1989, Sillars' behaviour being a manifestation of that rather than the cause. At least in the short term Salmond was vindicated. Although Wilson et al. protested that they had not withdrawn from the Convention, they had merely refused to join it, the impression generated was one of deliberate, and small-minded, sabotage on the part of the SNP.

But in spite of his reservations, Salmond swiftly fell into line, telling reporters: 'The problem with the convention is that it isn't going to get anywhere anyway. The devolution option that the convention will end up with is predetermined and it isn't going to be implemented. If we had gone into the convention as it was suggested we would have ended up going into the next election campaigning for a devolution package, and that would have been a major mistake.'[74]

There was nothing like the zeal of a convert. At a National Council meeting in Port Glasgow five weeks later, Salmond even turned on those, such as Isobel Lindsay, who continued to argue that the party had made a mistake. 'Mr Alex Salmond, MP for Banff and Buchan, launched a stern attack on Ms Lindsay,' recorded the *Glasgow Herald*, 'accusing her of being more of a Unionist than the Secretary of State for Scotland and "more of a Unionist and a Conservative" on the referendum issue than Mr Charles Gray, leader of Strathclyde region.'[75]

As the journalist Iain Macwhirter observed, 'Comparing an SNP executive member to the Labour leader of Strathclyde Region is the most outrageous abuse in the SNP lexicon, and Mr Salmond was taken to task by other speakers'.[76] 'When I look back on it that National Council was not our finest hour,' reflected Mike Russell in 2001. 'Alex can be a very spirited attacker ... I think it was probably the most direct speech he's every made. I think it was probably a bit harsher than it needed to be but I think he knew that too.'[77]

Indeed, Gordon Wilson remembered having to intervene from the chair, so vehement was Salmond's attack, while Jim Fairlie recalled him being 'howled down' by delegates not once but twice during his attack on Lindsay: 'Salmond attacked her personally because I suspect he felt very uncomfortable toeing the NEC line, so his tactic was to have a go at Isobel, who was still regarded with a lot of respect. I remember talking to Brian Taylor [the BBC journalist] about it afterwards and we just couldn't understand it. He [Salmond] seemed to have lost all contact with his audience.'[78]

Recalling the Port Glasgow meeting more than 20 years later, Isobel Lindsay was philosophical: 'I think Alex's attack on me was a mixture of two things. One, that he knew I was right, which often makes people a bit more hostile, but the other thing, perhaps more importantly, was that he possibly felt he had to prove his credentials with his own supporters or with the wider party ... oddly enough it didn't bother me at all, having been used to politics I knew all the rhetorical stuff that goes on.'[79] To his credit, Salmond later sounded a rare note of contrition. 'If I had my time again I'd take back that speech,' he reflected in 2001. 'I think Isobel probably had the rights over that argument.'[80] Nevertheless, the incident demonstrated just how aggressive the once even-tempered Salmond could now be.

The strength of Lindsay's argument, however, did not stop the resolution being crushed by 198 votes to 48. There were a number of factors at play, which went some way to explaining Salmond's behaviour as well as that of the wider party. The devolution debacle of the 1970s still hung over the party, while there was a collective folk memory of the internal strife that followed. 'Everyone in Port Glasgow that Saturday remembered the divisions in the party over the emergence of the 79 group, and the expulsions and bitterness that followed in the early 1980s,' observed Iain Macwhirter. 'The vote on March 4th was not so much a vote against a Convention, as a vote against Labour and a declaration of party unity.'[81] Party unity was certainly at the forefront of Salmond's mind. 'There is a time in politics for holding your nerve and not being stampeded,' he argued during the National Council debate. 'If we buckle under Press pressure now what will we be like when we are approaching independence?'[82]

Privately, however, Salmond believed the political momentum of the Govan by-election had been squandered, a view supported by the SNP's subsequent decline in opinion polls. He and Sillars, meanwhile, attempted to regain the initiative by turning up at a Commons education committee meeting as it considered controversial legislation enabling Scottish schools to become self-governing. Only Margaret Ewing was an appointed committee member, and when her colleagues attempted to 'join' the debate, Conservative and Labour MPs voted to report them to the House and adjourn. Michael Martin, the committee chairman, appealed for the trio to leave, saying that they were not entitled to be present. Salmond, gesticulating at English Tory MPs, retorted: 'I count four of them, and they are sitting over there. They have no right to be here.'

After a ten-minute adjournment the three SNP MPs were reported to the House and the committee halted, with only Ewing voting against. The Scottish Labour MP, Henry McLeish, accused the Nationalists of post-Govan hubris. 'Our fight is with this Conservative Government,' he said, 'not with Parliament.' Undeterred, Sillars then tried to disrupt the 1989 Budget by moving a writ for the Vale of Glamorgan by-election before the Chancellor's speech, which, had it been successful, would have led to a relatively lengthy debate. On 16 March Salmond and Andrew Welsh tried once again to join the education committee, but when Michael Martin prepared to use his new powers of expulsion (as voted on by the Commons), they departed quietly. 'There are opportunities on the floor of the House to pursue our case', said Salmond afterwards, 'which will heavily inconvenience both the Government and the Leader of the Opposition.'[83]

The *Scotsman* speculated that Charles Stewart Parnell, leader of the Irish Parliamentary Party in the 19th century, had been the model for Sillars and Salmond's renewed guerilla action. Such tactics, however, had already outlived their usefulness. The novelty, at least from a media perspective, had passed, while nothing could ever match Salmond's disruption of the 1988 Budget. Although the 1989 SNP conference unanimously congratulated the party's four MPs for 'selective parliamentary disruption which is providing genuine Scottish opposition to English Tory legislation',[84] there were few serious attempts to disrupt Parliament between then and the next general election.

The Glasgow Central by-election, held on 15 June 1989, also demonstrated that the post-Govan momentum had gone. Alex Neil, a former Labour member and close friend of Sillars from the short-lived Scottish Labour Party, had been selected as the SNP candidate, but Labour held the seat convincingly, despite a 20 per cent increase in the SNP's vote share. Salmond responded by promising that the SNP would not hesitate to resort to 'street fighting' in future contests. 'The future for Scottish politics', he declared, 'will be eyeball to eyeball confrontation.'[85]

Salmond was, as ever, putting a brave face on political setbacks, another of which came when an attempt to promote 'independence in Europe' in the House of Commons fell rather flat. It was debated, said a commentator, 'with none of the passion or emotion which there had been in the immediate wake of Govan'.[86] Salmond's contribution, however, showed no evidence of faltering resolve: 'I am a great believer in the self-determination of nations. I believe in self-determination for the Scottish nation, the Welsh nation and the Irish nation ... [The] SNP claims no mandate to run or govern Scotland until it obtains a majority of the seats and has a mandate to negotiate independence. That is in clear contrast with the Tory party, which claims its mandate to run Scotland on a basis of 10 parliamentary seats, no European seats and a vote now reduced to 20 per cent.' The SNP, declared Salmond, would soon 'have a mandate to negotiate independence with Westminster and simultaneously to negotiate with the EEC. The constitutional settlement resulting from that will be put to the Scottish people in a referendum, so the Scottish people will decide.'[87]

★   ★   ★

Perhaps Alex Salmond's most significant contribution during the 1987–92 Parliament, and certainly in the longer term, was his development of what became known as the 'economic case for independence'. In late 1987, he had established the Scottish Centre for Economic and Social Research (SCESR), perhaps inspired by Billy Wolfe's Social and Economic Inquiry Society of Scotland, which had been created in 1962. The academic James Mitchell described the SCESR thus: 'This Nationalist think-tank consists of a number of Nationalist sympathisers, not all members of the party, under the chairmanship of Alex Salmond who intend to commission articles under three specific headings: economic affairs, social affairs and a "1992 Series" on the implications of the Single European Act.'[88] Mitchell himself would later contribute papers, as would the journalist Neal Ascherson and a recent SNP convert called Christopher Harvie, later a Nationalist MSP.

Nervous since his expulsion about upsetting mainstream party opinion, Salmond stressed that the SCESR 'would not interfere in the normal Policy making processes of the Party but would provide valuable information which should be of great aid to the Party in the future'. When Gerry Fisher, not exactly a Salmond supporter, demanded to know who the main contributors were, he replied that revealing them 'would certainly reduce the number and quality of economists taking part' as it would clearly 'affect their normal employment'.[89]

Indeed, Salmond was so secretive about who was involved that Gordon Wilson had to write to him in March 1988, asking for a membership list 'in confidence so that I can assure the media, who have been asking questions lately, that the group really does exist'.[90] He duly obliged, the list including a familiar roll call of Salmond acquaintances such as Peter Murrell (secretary), Christian Albuisson, Robin Angus, Grant Baird, Stephen Maxwell, James Mitchell, Alex Neil, Diarmid O'Hara, Douglas Robertson, Jim Sillars and Jim Walker. Salmond was also careful to invite non-SNP members like the *Glasgow Herald* journalist Alf Young and the economist David Bell to contribute papers, usefully dispelling accusations that the SCESR was nothing more than an SNP talking shop.[91]

To Salmond, fleshing out this area of party policy was a key component of the SNP's strategy following the 1987 general election. In the autumn of that year he had circulated a paper in which 'The Economic Case for Independence' (Phase Three), flowed naturally from attacking 'Labour's Feeble Fifty' (Phase One) and presenting the real choice between 'Independence or Thatcher' (Phase Two). He stated:

We know from our experience that putting pressure on the Labour Party does not automatically translate into SNP votes, and similarly there is no exact relationship between the number of people prepared to express support for Scottish independence and the number of people prepared to vote SNP. Both in the short term and the medium term, therefore, it is the SNP image that needs to be enhanced. When we argue that Labour's fifty MPs are ineffective in protecting Scotland we must be able to show that the SNP can be effective. When we argue that independence is essential to secure any future for the Scottish economy we have to be also able to show that the SNP can bring about such a transformation.

'This will be the first shot in the medium term strategy to solidify the Independence vote,' he explained. 'We will make a serious and sustained attempt to take the initiative in the economic arguments about Independence by the presentation of quality material designed to inspire the confidence first of our own activists, then key opinion formers and through them the people.' 'Credibility', he concluded, 'is still the single most important missing ingredient for so much of what we wish to do.'[92]

There was still scope, however, for good old-fashioned attack and rebuttal. 'I regard the appropriation of Scottish oil revenues', declared Salmond during a Commons debate in January 1988, 'as probably the greatest piece of international larceny since the Spanish stole the Inca gold.'[93] The following year, the SNP also issued its first 'Scottish budget', based on (it claimed) available government statistics and independent analysis. This, said Salmond, 'demolished completely the myth of a subsidised Scotland'.[94]

Salmond's own proposals were published a few months later. 'This is no Marxist budget', he protested, preferring a 'social democratic' label under which commercial success would be encouraged in order to fund anti-poverty and employment programmes. Although the Fraser of Allander Institute gave the proposals qualified support, another economist dismissed it as 'garbage for garbage'. 'You feed hypothetical figures into a model,' he said, 'they'll tell you anything.'[95] Political opponents also questioned Salmond's grasp of economics. 'I can understand why the hon. Gentleman made the most urgent exit from a banking career that he was able to find,' joked Malcolm Rifkind. 'If his understanding of economics is explained in his remarks this afternoon, the longer he stays away from banking, the better for the Scottish banking industry'.[96]

Salmond, meanwhile, fleshed out his critique of Labour's economic policy in a review of Gordon Brown's recent publication, *Where There is Greed . . . Margaret Thatcher and the Betrayal of Britain's Future*. He was not impressed by what the Shadow Chief Secretary to the Treasury had to say. 'The publicity blurb accompanying the book calls the Brown account "informed and impassioned",' wrote Salmond, 'but virtually throughout there is a surplus of information and a debit of passion.' Furthermore, Brown's 'economic indictment of the Thatcher years, although comprehensive, is pedestrian, provoking the thought that for all his parliamentary success against [Nigel] Lawson he may be more comfortable on another brief . . . it seems a poor ideological base from which to confront Thatcherism . . . [reflecting] the now-accepted Labour wisdom that the trouble with the lady is that she is ideological and dogmatic as opposed to having the wrong ideology and the wrong dogma. When Brown writes (effectively) of the beneficiaries of Thatcher largesse he still leaves the distinct impression that it is only the top 1 per cent who need fear any Labour redistribution of income.'[97]

Another emerging economic refrain was Salmond's increasing attraction to the Irish model. At the 1989 SNP conference, both he and Alex Neil had pointed to the Republic of Ireland as an economic example for an independent Scotland, particularly its lower interest rates having joined the European Monetary System (EMS). Inflation, said Salmond, was also down to just two per cent, something he claimed 'was possible in an independent Scotland, too'.[98]

Salmond's reputation within the SNP certainly grew as a result of his articulate espousal of the economic case for independence, and in 1989 he and almost every other office bearer were returned unopposed. A rumoured leadership challenge by Jim Sillars, meanwhile, failed to transpire, leading one insider to refer sardonically to the 'most serious outbreak of harmony for many years'.[99] It was not to last.

On 24 January 1990 Salmond made a speech. 'The 1980s were a period of transition and stagnation in Scotland,' he told an SNP audience in Dollar. 'Above all they showed the folly of relying on United Kingdom general elections to produce a result amenable to Scottish ambitions.' His solution was that whatever devolution blueprint was drawn up by the Scottish Constitutional Convention should, together with 'independence in Europe' and the status quo, 'be put to the test in a referendum of the Scottish people and the constitutional debate brought to a decision'. Westminster opposition to such a poll, he argued, could 'be overcome by the Scottish local authorities organising a simultaneous postal ballot of all electors in their areas'. He continued: 'The advantages of my proposal are manifest. After more than 20 years of constant constitutional debate in Scotland it would allow a proper public test between the main constitutional options facing Scotland. After a year of fundamental transformation in Eastern Europe it would allow the Scottish nation our own opportunity at people power ... I am confident that the case for independence in Europe could carry such a poll but I am willing to trust the Scottish people to make the decision.' 'The SNP should now take the initiative', concluded Salmond, 'and challenge the other parties to do the same.'[100]

The idea of a multi-option referendum was not new, but this speech demonstrated that Salmond was coming into his own as a politician, deliberately pitching the constitutional question to attract the broadest possible support. To opponents, however, it sounded like rapprochement to Labour, and fuelled suspicion of Salmond's motives. As a result, the referendum plan was defeated at the next meeting of the SNP's NEC. Peter Lynch observed:

> Salmond had lost out on this debate to Wilson as well as Jim Sillars, his former ally on the gradualist left of the party, and a major fissure ... opened up between Salmond and Sillars which was both personal and political. Not only were both competing for political influence within the party at the highest levels, but Sillars' strategic outlook within the SNP had changed. Sometime after the Govan by-election, Sillars moved away from gradualism to adopt a more fundamentalist course within the SNP. Sillars' supporters followed and there was a major division within the left of the SNP as a group of neo-fundamentalists were established which the Sillars camp often referred to as 'central belt activists': code for neo-fundamentalist left-wingers who opposed Salmond and his gradualist strategy.[101]

The scene was set, therefore, for an acrimonious fight over the future course of the Nationalist movement. A copy of Salmond's Dollar speech had also found its way to Gordon Wilson, who by mid-1990 was reaching the end of his decade-long leadership. 'The end game approached,' he wrote in his memoirs. 'In early May, Jim Sillars requested a meeting that took place in my office in Dundee. He told me Alex Salmond was likely to make a bid for the leadership and proposed that we stand together on a joint ticket. During the previous two years, he and Alex had drifted apart and relationships between them and their respective teams were, to put it mildly, not cordial. I was non-committal and promised to think things over and let him know. The news was half expected and there would have been no surprise if I had received a courtesy call from Alex to tell me of his intentions.'[102]

Sillars, however, disputed Wilson's version of events, suggesting that Salmond had been minded to make his bid for the leadership the previous year: 'Alex was going to challenge in 1989 but I said no [to supporting him] and that was the beginning of the breach. You're either for him or against him. Margaret Ewing also wanted to stand and I knew she wouldn't win against Alex, and I couldn't stand because I would have split the party from top to bottom. Gordon Wilson wanted me or Margaret.'[103]

Given that Wilson had wanted to resign as leader since 1987, if Salmond had challenged him in 1989 he would, as one senior Nationalist put it, have 'been pushing at an open door'.[104] It is possible, however, that Salmond was genuinely stung by the refusal of Sillars to support a leadership bid in 1989. 'The first year he went for the leadership, there was a heavy-handed refusal from the older and wiser ones like Jim and me,' recalled Margo MacDonald. 'We just thought he wasn't ready yet. Jim had a conversation with him saying "we both think you'll be leader but not yet". I didn't realise just how much he had resented that.'[105] Age was certainly an issue. Seventeen years Salmond's senior, Sillars perhaps felt his chance of leading the SNP was at risk of being scuppered by a younger man in a hurry.

So by 1990 it seems that both Salmond and Sillars had resolved to stand, although Salmond later claimed, unconvincingly, that had Sillars 'stood for party leader in 1990 ... I might well have supported him'.[106] Wilson, meanwhile, knew the game was up. Having been alerted to Salmond's intentions by Sillars, Wilson decided to announce his resignation more quickly than planned. 'A leader should know when to stand, what to do when he is in power and when to call it a day,' he reflected in his memoirs. 'After eleven years, I had reached the last stage. I saw no merit in being involved in what would be a bitter election. The Party needed fresh leadership.'[107]

Salmond, however, was obviously not what Wilson meant by 'fresh' leadership, and he and Mike Russell were virtually the last to be informed of his intentions. Most of those on the NEC also did not want Salmond to run, considering him talented but fractious. Knowledge of this opposition, however, simply made Salmond more determined to stand: 'The argument was put to me last May [1990] that the SNP should not have a leadership election. Far better, it was said, to have an agreed leader, i.e. Margaret Ewing, emerge from the collective leadership and then possibly a contest after the general election. I thought it was a threadbare argument then. I still think so now. The SNP claims to be the voice of Scottish democracy in the 1990s would look silly if we adopted the same system of selecting a leader as the Tory Party discarded in the 1960s.'[108]

Although Salmond's stock was rising in the party – regional council candidates in his constituency had performed particularly well at the May 1990 elections – and he 'had just about persuaded many on the Right to forget his involvement in the 79 Group crisis and the claims that he is not a "real" Nationalist',[109] he was believed to be unprepared for a summer contest. Although Wilson's resignation was not completely unexpected, he had repeatedly spoken of his intention to stay on until after the next general election and Salmond probably had not expected the vacancy to open up quite so quickly. Unperturbed, he declared his candidacy at a constituency meeting on 27 May.

Asked about the gamble he was taking in challenging Ewing, Salmond wielded one of his favourite lines of poetry by James Graham, the 1st Marquis of Montrose:

He either fears his fate too much,
Or his deserts are small,
That puts it not unto the touch,
To win or to lose it all.

'What happened to Montrose?' asked one former SNP MP rhetorically. 'He was hanged for his trouble.'[110] Torn limb from limb in the Grassmarket after falling foul of his supporters, Salmond's opponents expected the same fate to befall him.

And while Wilson remained publicly aloof from the battle to replace him, it was no secret that Ewing was his preferred successor. Not only had she been given advance notice of his intentions (unlike Salmond), Ewing even faxed Wilson the text of her leadership pitch for his comments on 9 July, a privilege not enjoyed by her opponent.

Ewing's campaign, however, quickly ran into difficulties: 'Ewing had some clear weaknesses as a potential party leader,' reckoned the SNP's historian Peter Lynch. 'First, she had no real vision for the SNP in terms of policy, organisation or identity. Salmond, by contrast, had a range of issues and initiatives he was keen to advance as party leader, and was more keenly aware of what needed to be done within the party to improve its position. He was also impatient with the condition of the party under Wilson's leadership in terms of organisation, finance and campaigning. Second, in terms of the leadership campaign, the Ewing candidacy was ill-organised and rather complacent compared to Salmond's.'[111]

As well as being ill-organised it soon became clear that Ewing had two parallel campaigns, one run by her husband Fergus and the other by Jim Sillars. When the latter invited around 50 SNP activists to a 'Left caucus' meeting in Paisley, accompanied by Kenny MacAskill and Alex Neil, he revealed his hand by urging those present to support Ewing. But the meeting, which lasted five hours, also gave rise to some less than gentlemanly remarks about Salmond, emphasising to one journalist with 'shocking clarity just how much of a threat Salmond appears to have become to some of his long-standing comrades'.[112] Salmond later recalled 'a succession of phone calls from people highly embarrassed to have been invited to a "left caucus" meeting in Glasgow where my motives for seeking the leadership were denounced. Trotsky apparently had got off light in comparison.'[113]

Although the disagreements, both personal and political, between Sillars and Salmond dated back to late 1988, they had not previously spilled over into the public domain. The repeated implication from the Sillars camp was that Alex was 'soft' on Labour, and from Sillars himself that, at 35, Salmond was simply too young for the leadership.[114] Salmond must have found some of Sillars' attacks quite hurtful. On 13 August, for example, he indirectly compared Salmond with a former SDP leader. 'David Owen is a superb performer on television. None can match him for style,' said Sillars. 'Yet he and the party that wrapped itself around his style and personality are both finished. A one-man or one-woman band on television is no substitute for the policies, the strategy, and the unity that comes from a collective leadership based on the depth of experience.'[115] Kenny MacAskill echoed this critique the following month. 'If television was the crucial factor in politics,' he said, 'David Owen would be Prime Minister and Gary Hart would be President.'

Sillars, meanwhile, promoted MacAskill as a candidate for the deputy leadership, one theory running that he planned MacAskill to succeed Ewing as leader after a suitable interlude, thereby recreating the 'Scottish Labour Party' under a puppet leader. Interviewed by John MacLeod for the *Scotsman*, MacAskill damned Salmond with faint praise. 'No-one is putting down Alex's abilities, indeed the opposite. His integrity's self-evident and he's vital to our success,' he said. 'But who's doing the writing, the thinking, producing pamphlets? It's Jim Sillars. He's the one with vision. Margaret could unite the party.' The implication was that Salmond was an intellectual lightweight seeking to impose his media-friendly personality upon the party. 'I think, if she becomes leader,' MacAskill also told MacLeod. 'Jim would almost certainly become our parliamentary leader.'[116]

Salmond's restraint was admirable during the campaign, although one supporter told the *Guardian* that he had been 'alarmed' by Sillars' stridency. 'Jim's position has been more fundamental than Alex would have liked,' said the source. 'There's been tension, but I wouldn't describe it as personal bitterness.'[117] Of the attacks, Salmond reckoned party activists were 'well able to separate legitimate campaigning from some of the desperate nonsense which has appeared in print over the last week ... no supporter of ours should allow themselves to be sucked into any exchanges with our colleagues in the opposition.'[118] Ewing, thought Salmond, was 'suffering from having so many influential backers – they were in danger of eclipsing her own personality'.[119]

His campaign, meanwhile, had 'sewn up vast areas of the country before the contest had even started',[120] aided by a small band of committed supporters he had been nurturing since entering Parliament in 1987. From these he selected the party's publicity vice-convener, Mike Russell, who – although dismissed as a lightweight by the Sillars camp – guided Salmond closely throughout the next few months.

He and team Salmond (consisting of ten key individuals[121]) had taken early soundings within the party membership and actively campaigned for the votes of delegates, who would choose Gordon Wilson's successor at the September conference. Always keen on modern campaigning techniques, Salmond and Russell set up a special telephone line where members could listen to a two-minute recorded message about his leadership ambitions, while their slickly produced literature was quickly dispatched around the country.

The youth wing of the SNP, the Young Scottish Nationalists (YSN), was quick to back Salmond's campaign. 'Ewing is a fine parliamentary leader of the party, but we have a definite preference for Alex Salmond,' explained Cliff Williamson, the YSN's representative on the NEC. 'We feel his campaign is striking the right chords with young people not just in the party, but in the population generally.'[122] The YSN's national secretary was then a young activist called Nicola Sturgeon. Another affiliated organisation, the Nationalist trade union group, also backed Salmond, giving him another six delegates for the conference vote.

Salmond deliberately targeted areas like Linlithgow, Livingston and Clackmannan where he was confident of support 'but where people might be undecided due to the strong links with Kenny and Jim'. In these areas, noted Salmond in a campaign diary for *Scotland on Sunday*, the 'hostile reception to the press statements from Kenny *et al.* was tangible'.[123] Gradually the Salmond campaign made progress, and by the end of July its intelligence suggested that, 'at worst', they were level with Ewing.

In terms of ideological differences an outside observer must have found it hard to push a voting slip between Ewing and Salmond's stances. Ewing's campaigners claimed it was the difference between 'bedding down with Labour' (Salmond) and remaining true to the SNP's tradition of being 'the only political vehicle that can set Scotland free' (Ewing).[124] Ewing herself struggled to articulate the difference, telling one interviewer that it was said 'Alex would like to pull back a little on the poll tax non-payment campaign, whereas I think it's vital at this stage to keep up the pressure'.[125] This was hardly the stuff of great ideological battle. To one observer, meanwhile, Ewing exuded the 'fatal' impression 'of not appearing to know exactly why she was running in the first place'.[126]

Salmond, on the other hand, focused on leadership, analysis of the political situation, what action should follow and, most importantly, his ability to deliver it. 'It is the economic case for independence which will be the key for transforming the latent sympathy for our policies into hard votes,'[127] he told a press conference in Glasgow towards the end of the campaign. In Dick Douglas, who had quit the Labour whip in protest at his party's refusal to advocate non-payment of the Poll Tax, Salmond found the perfect case study for another aspect of his campaign. 'If I am elected next month, the SNP will make an explicit appeal to rank-and-file Labour supporters who agree with us on the poll tax, on nuclear weapons and on fighting for the Scottish economy,' he said, having paraded Douglas as his 'guest of honour' at an SNP barbeque in Aberdeenshire. 'The SNP must never forget that our enemy is not the Labour rank-and-file but its grey Scottish leadership, who wish only to keep Scotland quiet and safe for their own private interests.'[128]

This ('rather innocuous') speech prompted a scathing attack from MacAskill and Alex Neil, which simply strengthened Salmond's tactical resolve: 'Mike Russell (my campaign manager) and my wife Moira share the same birthday and that evening we had a car phone conversation on our way to our respective celebration dinners. We agreed that we would continue undaunted on our theme of Labour converts since it went to the heart of our message of whether the SNP of the 1990s was to be a party welcoming new recruits or an exclusive one setting deadlines on when people were allowed to come from the unionist stable to the Nationalist ranks – whether we were to be the electable or the elect.'[129]

In the summer edition of *Radical Scotland*, meanwhile, both leadership candidates set out their stalls. 'The party must present a moderate left-of-centre policy profile,' said Ewing. 'We must never be subsumed in an amalgam of British and Scottish hoodwinking as a Mark II Labour Party or as prisoners of a mock convention.' This was an oblique attack on Salmond, whose declared left-wing strategy would, opponents claimed, split the SNP and make him soft on Labour, leading to engagement with political traps like the Scottish Constitutional Convention. Salmond countered that with polls showing 40 per cent support for independence but only 20 per cent for the SNP. This, he argued, was 'the faultline in Scottish politics' which gave the party something to aim for: the Labour voters who sympathised with independence but could not yet bring themselves to vote SNP.

As if grasping for negatives, the Ewing camp pointed to Salmond's 'arrogance' and 'domineering personality', both of which were true – to an extent – but hardly killer blows. *Radical Scotland* caught the mood of the party well when it referred to its increasing maturity, 'which seems set to show that it wants a modern, pragmatic, and politically talented leader rather than just – as in the past – relying on wishful thinking and Put Scotland First slogans. The final shaking off of the old guard may mark a turning point for the SNP, but it will have considerable repercussions for Scottish politics as a whole.'

In an adjoining article ('Seeking a Leader for the '90s'), Alasdair Morgan, Salmond's running mate for the deputy leadership, played down the new leader's likely impact on the party's fundamental strategy, but said he (or she) would influence 'how Scotland and Scotland's voters see the SNP, and in the longer term how the Party sees and shapes itself'. Morgan went on: 'I am looking for a leader who can break this log-jam and release the pent-up potential within the SNP. In all of his activities, previously as Vice Convener for Publicity in the period before the last election and more recently as convener of the Scottish Centre for Economic and Social Research, the nationalist think-tank, Alex has a proven record of mobilising new talent in the Party's work.' 'He is a nationalist for the 1990s,' concluded Morgan. 'Alex has also proved over the last few years that he can present all our policies tenaciously and with confidence. In an era when television creates the cockpit for electoral success or failure these skills are essential.'[130] Far from being a drawback, went the argument, Salmond's media prowess was his in fact his principal strength in a new political era. Ewing, by contrast, repeatedly stressed her political experience, prompting one of her supporters to quip: 'Maggie offered a CV. Alex offered a manifesto.'[131]

It had the desired effect. As pledges of support came in during August, it became clear that Salmond was attracting greater-than-anticipated support. Panic, therefore, probably motivated Kenny MacAskill and Alex Neil to stage a press conference, of which Ewing was unaware, in which they savaged Salmond, the former referring to him as a 'smooth talker', and the latter likening him to a 'latter-day First World War general'.[132] Ewing appeared confused when asked why her supporters were attacking her opponent, and during the subsequent media row declined interview requests while Salmond accepted every opportunity to state his case.

The campaign reached its final phase as Salmond returned 'well refreshed' from a holiday on Colonsay at the beginning of September. Encouraged by the response of North of Scotland delegations to what he modestly called 'one of the best impromptu speeches of my life', Salmond's confidence grew and by the time of his last campaign meeting on 14 September, 'our information put the margin at 3–1 with the undecided's breaking in my favour'. 'The large rural constituencies where we thought initially our campaign might be badly mauled', he added, 'were enthusiastically supporting us.'[133] A *Scotsman* poll, however, put Margaret Ewing ahead among the general public.

The oratorical showdown came on Thursday, 20 September, at the SNP's annual conference in Perth's City Hall. Ewing took a hard line against the Convention and the Labour Party, receiving ecstatic applause despite her nervous delivery. Salmond, by contrast, used a three-minute slot in a separate debate to deliver what the journalist Peter Jones described as 'a punchy, polished speech larded with statistics designed to show his knowledge of economic affairs'.[134] Both candidates had cause for concern. The signs were that Ewing had not fully swayed uncommitted delegates, while the mood still seemed to be against Salmond's referendum strategy. Thursday's newspapers, however, still gave Ewing the edge. 'The actual voting delegate doesn't seem to have been consulted by the press,' responded Mike Russell in a campaign diary for the *Scotsman*. 'They are clearly sticking by Alex.'

Salmond was nevertheless 'moody'. 'The pressure he and Moira have been under has been tremendous,' wrote Russell. 'Old allegiances based not just on politics but on friendship have been broken by the campaign – although they can and will be reformed.' Indeed, when asked about reports that he had barely been on speaking terms with Kenny MacAskill over the past six months, Salmond said: 'Since I brought Kenny MacAskill into the SNP, I have always recognised his substantial talents. He is going to be a major figure in the SNP for a long time to come.'[135]

In his farewell address as national convener, Gordon Wilson praised both Ewing and Salmond as excellent people, although there was a subtle subtext. 'The convenership is more like being a team captain than a striker, or even team manager,' he said. 'Under our constitution, the convener has plenty of influence and initiative but little power.'[136] Despite assurances to the contrary, there remained a lingering suspicion that Salmond would not be a good team player, that he would be presidential, centralising power and sidelining opponents. Indeed, a 'well informed Nationalist' told the Liberal Democrat Charles Kennedy, that 'all of those who had known and worked with Alex the longest – well, they were all voting for Ewing'.

There were, therefore, gasps of surprise when the result was announced on Saturday, 22 September. Salmond had won, but instead of the 60:40 margin he had privately hoped for, he had managed 70:30, matching almost exactly Mike Russell's prediction from that morning. Although the NEC had backed Ewing 9–3, the 30-strong National Council had supported Salmond 18–2, and he had secured an overwhelming majority among conference delegates. It represented a crushing blow for Ewing, although she was gracious in defeat. 'If there is going to be a change in the party it must be decisive. Alex clearly has the endorsement of the party,' she said. 'His commitment to the collective leadership of the party is important and I will continue as parliamentary leader. The SNP's ultimate goal of independence is much more important than my slightly dented ego.'

In his victory speech – watched by Moira, who had slipped quietly into the back of the hall before the result was announced – Salmond declared that Labour's days of dominating Scottish politics were numbered. 'Labour may win the yuppie votes in the south of England. We are going to win the battle for the hearts and minds of the Scottish people,' he said. 'The SNP is not interested in running a good second. We are not running for a medal – we are going for gold.'[137] Salmond also took care to remind delegates that he considered himself a 'socialist' while sounding an inclusive note: 'The SNP needs to campaign for all Scotland, and all Scotland needs the talents of all the SNP.'[138]

Salmond's parents, Robert and Mary, were driving back to Linlithgow from South Queensferry when they heard the result on their car radio. 'We're very, very proud of him,' Robert told a local reporter, having driven to Perth to join his son's victory celebrations. 'We were always quietly confident that Alex would win the election against Margaret Ewing although some of the newspapers thought otherwise on the eve of the conference,' he added. 'It was a tremendous achievement.'[139]

Indeed it was. Salmond's victory showed him to be an inspired strategist, securing his base in the constituencies before managing an efficient campaign that completely outflanked the combined might of the Sillars-led left, party traditionalists loyal to Margaret Ewing and, not least, the wishes of the outgoing convener, Gordon Wilson. Salmond would no doubt have approved of a parallel with Churchill, who had also been nominated to lead the party that had once spurned him.

Charles Kennedy also saw parallels with Paddy Ashdown: 'Both started as outsiders and, in remarkably short periods, gained the top job.' He also recalled musing with Salmond about political leadership over lunch at Grampian TV in late 1987. 'He put forward the view that British politics, particularly Scottish politics, should stop thinking of leadership as something which occurs in one's 40s or 50s,' recalled Kennedy. 'Why not get, say, a decade of leadership under the belt before that – if time and chance permit?'[140]

Two years later Salmond concluded that 'time and chance' did permit and, that weekend in Perth, he had secured the SNP's biggest prize. Salmond's lunchtime chat with Kennedy was also remarkably prescient in another respect, for he would serve almost exactly a decade as leader before standing down months before his 45th birthday. Perhaps, like Churchill, Salmond had always felt a sense of destiny. 'At last I had the authority to give directions over the whole scene,' read Churchill's famously self-confident account of his becoming Prime Minister. 'I felt as if I were walking with destiny, and that all my past life had been but a preparation for this hour ... I was sure I should not fail.'[141]

Chapter 6

'FREE BY 93'

> Like Alexander I will reign,
> And I will reign alone;
> My only thoughts did evermore disdain
> A rival on my throne.
> He either fears his fate too much,
> Or his deserts are small,
> That dares not put it to the touch,
> To gain or to lose it all.
>
> James Graham, the 1st Marquis of Montrose,
> from his poem 'My Dear and Only Love'

'Within minutes of winning the SNP leadership in Perth in 1990,' observed James Mitchell, 'Alex Salmond's opponents were talking to the media about his overthrow. His demise was predicted and hoped for by some of his erstwhile associates from the '79 Group days.'[1] Indeed, and as Charles Kennedy observed, 'leadership contests do have an uncanny and an unhappy knack of bringing out the daggers'. 'Mr Salmond obviously needs to spend some more time cultivating lesser intellects and stroking oversensitive egos,' he wrote. 'The problem about being a young man in a hurry is that there's never much spare time available for those rather wearying pursuits. And Salmond is someone in a big rush.'[2]

He was indeed, and it would take Salmond a few years to consolidate his position as leader of the SNP although he was, by his own admission, 'a resilient character'.[3] The Jim Sillars camp remained strong while Margaret Ewing – popular and respected despite her defeat – was still in place as Parliamentary leader at Westminster. Nevertheless, it is possible that Salmond underestimated his own strength. Of the SNP's nine

senior office bearers – its 'inner cabinet' – seven were Salmond supporters, an outcome almost as surprising as his margin of victory. 'In short,'
wrote the journalist Peter Jones, 'Mr Salmond asked the party grassroots to give him a team to back him up rather than one which would
cramp his style, and he got it.'[4]

Beyond elected office holders, Salmond also did his best to heal the
wounds of the campaign. 'After he was elected he invited me for a
meeting and said he knew what my views were but that it didn't matter,'
recalled Chris McLean, then the SNP's press officer and a Ewing
supporter. 'He thought I was good at the job and as long as I gave an
undertaking to work with him as leader then we could both go
forward.'[5] Salmond also sought to placate John Swinney, their relationship having turned sour back in 1986. 'Alex knew that John was a very
effective operator,' recalled a senior Nationalist, 'so when he became
national convener he asked John for a meeting so that they could
accommodate their differences. Alex, however, had to take the initiative, something John would never have done.'[6] Indeed, as presiding
officer in the leadership election, Swinney had been in 'a difficult position'. 'Alex and I had up to that time not been terribly close politically,'
he later admitted, 'but that afternoon Alex made a point of saying his
would be an inclusive leadership.'[7]

Salmond's victory, meanwhile, had created a feel-good factor.
'Members believe he can, and want him to, lead them to victory,'
assessed the *Scotsman*, which reckoned the 1990 SNP conference had
'every chance of going down in history as a watershed event'.[8] Also
enthusiastic was the academic Tom Gallagher, later a critic of Salmond
as First Minister: 'Salmond's energy, media skills, and the sharpness of
his thinking means that the identity of the SNP is likely to be far less
blurred in future. To a grassroots membership cheated of sustained electoral success, the prospect of dynamic leadership boosting the appeal of
the party was enough to silence doubts about a responsibility so grave
falling to one so young and, at times, impetuous.' 'If a leader like Alex
Salmond fails to lift the party from the trough it has found itself in since
1979,' added Gallagher cautiously, 'then it is hard to see how it can
emerge as a serious contender for power in Scotland.'[9]

The first test of what sort of leader Salmond would be came just two
months after his election, with by-elections in Paisley North and South.
The selection of the SNP candidate for the former caused the first row of
his leadership, when Salmond was accused of trying to block Iain Lawson
from putting his name forward, something he strenuously denied. Roger

Mullin (the SNP's organisation vice-convener) was chosen, achieving a 16.5 per cent swing and a creditable second place for his party. Lawson instead stood in Paisley South, managing a 13.5 per swing and, again, a good second place. The by-elections were perhaps more memorable for providing an electoral backdrop to the protracted demise of Margaret Thatcher. 'She is fatally wounded', Salmond told reporters following the first Tory leadership ballot, 'and must go as soon as possible.'[10]

Although Salmond had once dismissed Mrs Thatcher as 'this formidable but limited and, in some ways, rather absurd Prime Minister',[11] there was a private respect for her steely resolve and clarity of purpose that perhaps mirrored his own. Recalling her premiership 20 years later, Salmond said he always felt that she 'lacked a sense of humour and compassion', although found himself proven wrong on the former when their paths crossed in the Commons tea room shortly after her defeat. 'I started to call her Prime Minister, as I had always done,' Salmond remembered. 'Pri . . ., pri . . . I stammered. She said, "That's okay Alex, I have exactly the same problem, I cannot get used to not being called it either."'[12]

Salmond's elevation to the top SNP job, of course, had an impact on another important woman in his life – Moira. Already commuting between their constituency home in Strichen, their Linlithgow house (still at Friars Brae) and a Westminster flat, the inevitable demands of leading a party were about to make married life even more complicated. Although Moira had not been completely invisible since her husband's election in 1987, working for a while in his Peterhead office, she remained better known to the party faithful rather than the general public. 'She is invariably cheerful, optimistic, welcoming and friendly, but determined to stay in the background,' wrote Paul Henderson Scott in his memoirs. 'She never speaks to the press or appears on a political platform but it is apparent to everyone who has met her that Alex could not have a more sustaining ally.'[13]

That was certainly true, although Moira was – at least initially – not as reluctant to shun the limelight as has often been stated. For example, in February 1991, she accompanied Salmond to a celebration of his victory in Linlithgow, which was photographed and reported in the local paper, while the previous year she even gave an interview (jointly with Alex) to, of all things, the *Sunday Post*. In the absence of many, if any, competing accounts, this is worth quoting from at some length, not least for its insights into the Salmonds 'at home'.

'I'm no Glenys Kinnock,' Moira told a reporter. 'I married Alex, not politics. That's his life and I am happy to be in the background.' Rather she saw the role of an MP's wife, and that of herself, in the more traditional Tory mould, helping with constituency work, opening flower shows and supervising their three homes, not least their 'tiny' Strichen cottage 'with its open log fire, beams and stripped pine floors', where this interview took place. 'Sometimes I go to make a cheese and tomato toastie in Linlithgow,' said Moira, 'absolutely sure I've got a pound of cheese in the fridge, and then I remember it's in the kitchen in Strichen!' It seems colleagues later teased Salmond about this particular revelation.

There was little expansion, however, upon Moira's political views. 'I share his convictions,' she said firmly, 'but one politician in the family is *quite* enough!' Salmond's new duties, however, meant less time with his wife. 'I do get lonely when he's away all week in Westminster,' she said thoughtfully, 'so our time alone together is very precious. We drive up to Strichen on a Friday and like to potter around the cottage, having meals by the fire and a long leisurely fry-up on a Sunday morning.' The couple also liked playing Scrabble and cards, although it invariably caused rows due to Alex's tendency to change the rules as he went along. 'He gets mad because I invariably win Scrabble,' said Moira. 'The thing is, he can't spell.' At this point in the interview Alex grinned and shrugged his shoulders. 'Even my computer gets confused when I type in certain words,' he said. 'Thank goodness it has a spell check!'

Salmond, it seems, was not really a man for the Nineties. 'He can't cook, is reluctant to do housework and still hasn't put up the new pole for her curtains,' noted their interrogator, 'even though she's had it for six months!' 'Let's just say I'm not inspired by doing household jobs,' he admitted. 'Moira gets on to me for spending a lot of time on other people's problems and never having time for our own.' Then, slipping into uncomfortably Freudian analysis, Moira declared: 'His mum did everything for him and I've just fallen into the same pattern.' Alex did, however, remember anniversaries, although sometimes dinners had to be delayed due to other commitments. Moira also admitted doing all Alex's packing and always making sure he had enough shirts to last a week. 'Sometimes I switch on the six o'clock news and I'm horrified by what he's wearing,' she said with a shudder. 'He hasn't a clue about the colours of ties, shirts and socks. He just puts on the nearest thing to hand.' Alex then broke into another grin: 'She phones me up to give me a telling off!'[14] Indeed, as he prepared to be grilled by Brian Walden in the run up to the 1992 general election, Salmond took care to pull up his socks with his wife in mind. 'I was on Panorama a few weeks ago and I got gip from Moira,' he explained to a bemused Walden. 'I came home and said "how did I do?" and she said, "I could see your legs."'[15]

Moira's hobbies, meanwhile, included collecting antiques, gardening and floral art. 'She's a homemaker with a sure touch for making a room look calm, restful and pretty,' reported the *Sunday Post* in typically homespun style. 'Her feminine influence can be seen around the house, in places like the alcove she made herself, filled with books, old china and flowers. She also enjoys the painstaking job of stripping down doors, waxing and restoring them.' Above all, Moira desired privacy. 'I regard myself as public property,' explained Salmond, 'but I like to protect Moira as much as I can from the limelight. We are not a political couple and I find it refreshing to come home and let off steam to someone who isn't in the thick of it.'

Moira and Alex evidently complemented each other well. 'It has to be said that Alex Salmond is such a good talker,' observed the *Sunday Post*, 'a man with a flow of words and arguments which he delivers with confidence and conviction, that it was a wise move to choose a wife with a gift for listening.'[16] The journalist Kenny Farquharson remembered having lunch with both Mr and Mrs Salmond in the early 1990s, an encounter that captured a more playful aspect of their marriage. 'Alex was obviously playing up to Moira, putting on a show, telling anecdotes and providing mischievous commentary on the events and political personalities of the day,' he recalled. 'Moira had her elbows on the table, leaning forward and lapping it all up, occasionally shooting me an "Oh! Isn't he awful!" look, as if she was an aunt with a naughty favourite nephew.'[17] Such meetings, however, were rare, and it seems that having seen the result of Moira's one and only interview in the *Sunday Post*, Salmond decided there would be no more.

Salmond's honeymoon as leader, meanwhile, was marked by sunny optimism. 'Labour is very vulnerable now in Scotland and that's why I'm convinced the time has come for our party to make a major breakthrough,' he told a reporter towards the end of the year. 'I couldn't have become leader at a more challenging time. There may be a General Election next year and I believe the sky's the limit.'[18]

On the constitutional question, Salmond's stance was already well known: no longer would he pretend that the Scottish Constitutional Convention did not exist (it had published its interim report a week after his election), instead arguing – as he had at the beginning of the year – that its recommendations ought to be put to Scots in a three-pronged referendum. This time, however, Salmond won the backing of the NEC, as well as that of Charles Gray (the same Charles Gray with whom he had earlier compared, unfavourably, Isobel Lindsay), the Labour leader of Strathclyde Regional Council. 'By asking for a referendum', declared Salmond, 'we are throwing down the gauntlet.'[19]

At the SNP's National Assembly in Perth, meanwhile, Salmond continued his journey away from socialism by telling delegates that independence in Europe would 'slash' interest rates, giving Scots a direct say on a single currency and escaping the overheated economy of the south-east of England. 'In terms of economic affairs,' Salmond explained to the journalist Peter Jones, 'I think that as a country on the periphery of the European Community, Scots recognise that the economy has got to be productive and competitive.' He also denied that an independent Scotland would be interventionist and subsidy-dependent. 'I have never believed in anything other than a mixed economy,' he said. 'I am not uncomfortable at all about the market place and about the economy being competitive and productive.' 'I am quite happy to proclaim my socialism in that context,' he declared, 'but that doesn't make the SNP a socialist party.'[20]

The National Assembly also considered a paper by Jim Sillars arguing that an independent Scottish government would have to accept the authority of all existing European institutions and treaty obligations. This led to the creation of 'Sovereignty 90' early the following year, and although around three hundred Nationalists signed its founding charter, including the former SNP MP Donald Stewart, it posed little threat. 'If he [Andrew MacDonald, the movement's founder] wants to form a new political party,' said Salmond, 'he should get on with it.'[21] And, alluding to his own suspension from the party almost a decade before, Salmond reiterated 'a pledge that I will never expel anyone for political reasons'.[22]

As a pragmatist, Salmond was simply recognising that there were strict limits to the degree of independence available within the EEC, while he applied the same analysis to the devolution question. He maintained that the SNP's job was to convince people that only full independence was the most viable option, converting other parties and public opinion to its agenda. 'Now that is an entirely different thing from saying, do I think that a devolved parliament would be better than the status quo? I happen to think it would be,' he explained. 'Would the SNP in Parliament vote for or against a devolution scheme? Well, I think the SNP would vote for it, as being better than the status quo. But we won't argue for that case.'

This position was, at best, contrived, although Salmond was convinced that it put the SNP in a more credible, and therefore potentially electorally successful, position. Interviewing Salmond in February 1991, Peter Jones noted that he was 'much given to talking about undercurrents of opinion, underlying tensions, both here and abroad, and then relating them to scenarios and strategies. Such talk gives him a wily, perhaps cunning, image, not necessarily the image which makes him as trusted by his party . . . but qualities which make him a politician to be reckoned with.' Above all, what made Salmond a politician to be reckoned with was his tactical prowess. 'When the opportunity presents itself, before and after the election,' he told Jones, 'you know where you are going, and you seize it with both hands.'[23]

At a special SNP conference in late March 1991, Salmond put his party on an election footing while laying to rest the three-year-old 'Can Pay, Won't Pay' Poll Tax campaign. 'The battle now transfers to the ballot box,' said Salmond, following a debate in which only his speech and a 'final oratorical flood'[24] by Jim Sillars had turned the tide in their favour. Having been pressured into not speaking in the debate, the party's Poll Tax spokesman (and architect of the non-payment campaign), Kenny MacAskill, was then demoted to defence spokesman. Although MacAskill and Salmond had long since drifted apart, this incident did little to improve relations between the two Linlithgow Academy boys who had once dreamed of a Scottish socialist republic.

There was further bad news for Salmond in April, when a MORI poll put SNP support at just 15 per cent and Salmond's personal rating at its lowest level since becoming leader. Later that month, Salmond also lost a key ally when Mike Russell, the SNP's publicity vice-convener since 1987, stood down due to external work commitments. Salmond paid glowing tribute to someone who had 'contributed so much to building a professional and effective publicity machine and to enhancing the credibility of the party and its message'.[25]

The first year of Salmond's leadership had, according to some, 'produced doubts about his facility for working with other people',[26] just as Sillars, Wilson, et al., had feared back in September 1990. By the summer of 1991 several Parliamentary candidates were also complaining about inactivity and lack of leadership, not to mention the drift in the polls. 'We don't know what we are campaigning for,' complained one. 'There is no energy about the party . . . it's not the strategy that is wrong, but that it is just not being implemented.' The *Scotsman* said 'Their views all add up to the same thing – a growing belief that Salmond is firstly, not providing enough leadership, and secondly, that he does not have a good enough team around him. While he is acknowledged to be in the driving seat, and nobody is going to contest his position, the fear is that he has kept his foot off the accelerator for so long that when he comes to press it, the engine won't respond.'

Although Gil Paterson, a Ewing supporter who was by then in charge of party organisation, thought Alex was 'a hard taskmaster' ('If he thinks you are not putting the work in, he will tell you'),[27] otherwise he had no complaints, while others began to get all nostalgic for the days of Gordon Wilson's unflashy yet capable leadership. Wilson was even pressed to stand for re-election to the NEC, while Margaret Ewing received calls urging her to challenge Salmond at the 1991 conference.

To be fair to Salmond, some of these problems were not of his making – favourable news coverage of his election had been quickly overtaken by the Gulf War and Mrs Thatcher's demise – although others were. His handling of the non-payment policy had offended talented campaigners like MacAskill, for example, while depriving activists of an emotive issue with which to convince voters that the SNP cared about social as well as constitutional matters.

What Salmond called the 'Big Idea' of independence in Europe also suffered from presentational problems. Rather than pitching this as Scotland securing its proper place in the world it emerged as a technocratic idea involving the European Central Bank (which Salmond argued ought to be located in Edinburgh) and incomprehensible monetary mechanisms. And while accusations of 'inactivity' were unfair (Salmond was, if anything else, prodigiously hard-working), he attracted criticism for travelling abroad with the Commons Energy Select Committee instead of attending party rallies. The failure to have an election strategy in place as late as May despite the prospect of a June election also appeared complacent, something Salmond conceded when he told the US consul-general that a June 1991 general election would be 'disastrous'[28] for the SNP.

If all this was not enough for Salmond to contend with, it then emerged towards the end of July that Jim Sillars was planning to challenge Alasdair Morgan for the deputy leadership. 'The Salmond guile, plus the Sillars bombast, makes for an intriguing mixture,' wrote one journalist, 'potentially exciting, but potentially also divisive.'[29] Salmond said he was perfectly relaxed at the prospect of working again with Sillars, although privately he would have preferred there to be no contest. As if anticipating controversy, meanwhile, he warned in a message to SNP members that one requirement of electoral success was 'self-discipline throughout the party and particularly among our prominent members'.[30]

There was, in any case, an uneasy truce between the Salmond and Sillars camps. 'He [Salmond] is still perversely mistrusted by many members for his cool confidence, intellectual certainty and apparent lack of passion,' observed the journalist Julie Davidson in a 1992 newspaper profile. 'And in a party where sociability is important he remains aloof from the fun and games, drinking sparingly and avoiding all choruses of Flower of Scotland. What's more, Jim Sillars wants his job. Waiting in the wings like Lord and Lady Macbeth are Sillars and his wife, the former MP Margo MacDonald, who made a theatrical exit from the SNP ten years ago but has now applied for readmission.'[31]

But whatever his internal and external problems, Salmond soon demonstrated his aptitude for seemingly spontaneous political rejuvenation. On the Monday prior to the 1991 conference the Edinburgh-born actor Sean Connery – whom Salmond had met at the actor's Freedom of Edinburgh celebrations earlier that year – appeared in a party political broadcast urging Scots to support the SNP. It was a notable publicity coup for the media-savvy Salmond, and his reward was a revived opinion poll showing in which the party edged towards the psychologically important level of 20 per cent.

'The way I see the conference is re-positioning the SNP in peoples' minds,' said Salmond, 'getting away from the idea of the SNP as a vehicle for protest towards a view of the SNP as a party which is bidding for government.'[32] Despite his campaigning past, Salmond now believed the SNP could not sustain itself by moving from one isolated campaign to the other, and that the secret of electoral success lay in remoulding it as a 'social democrat' party of government. 'We are evolving a party programme which would be recognisable to any of the great Social Democratic parties in Europe,' he told delegates in his first conference speech as leader, 'not to the right-wing aberration which has fizzled out in the UK – but to European Social Democrats.'

This was a significant departure, not only from the party's ideological past, but also from Salmond's. For more than a decade he had argued that the SNP could only attract disaffected Labour voters from the left, now he was saying it ought to be done from the political centre-ground. But this did not mean old left-wing shibboleths had been ditched. On the contrary, Salmond vowed never to 'desert the cause of unilateral nuclear disarmament' while parading steel workers on the conference platform, alongside middle-class professionals, in order to emphasise the party's broad, but still essentially left-wing, appeal. Salmond also took several smaller gambles, announcing that the party's principal spokesmen, MPs and other supporters would form a 'Scottish cabinet – a government-in-waiting of people with the ability to take Scotland forward',[33] a structural innovation with the added benefit of giving Salmond tighter control over party policy.

Also important, particularly in the longer term, was the SNP's decision at that conference to participate in elections for a Scottish parliament, should one be set up following the next general election. 'I advanced this position', Salmond later explained, 'for I believed the establishment of the parliament would be a defining moment in the process of independence.'[34] Many Nationalists, however, continued to suspect that at heart their new leader was little more than a devolutionist.

Salmond's first conference speech, at least in presentational terms, had been a success, although it was overshadowed by a damaging row over the SNP's target date for independence. At a press conference on 18 September Alex Neil, the new publicity vice-convener, told reporters the SNP had set a target 'to reach independence by 1 January, 1993'. When senior Nationalists expressed surprise, fearing such a date would be seen as unrealistic, Neil insisted it had been agreed in advance, arguing that his wording was simply a logical extension of Salmond's own statement that the SNP would be 'ready to form the government of an independent Scotland after the coming general election'.[35]

Although this incident quickly blew over, the slogan would return to haunt Salmond during and after the 1992 general election, while resentment lingered for much longer. Critics, however, believe Salmond grew wise after the event. '"Free by 93" was agreed by the [National] Executive under the leadership of Alex Salmond', protested Iain Lawson, 'and this again is the rewriting of history to suit political objectives.' 'I thought to myself,' Salmond later recalled of the press conference, 'I didn't realise that was in the script ... Iain's recollections of SNP documents must be larger than mine. I don't recall Executive meetings sitting around saying "Free by 93" shall be our election slogan.'[36] Writing in 2000, Salmond also allocated some of the blame to Jim Sillars. 'The words were not his but the off-stage direction was pure Sillars,' he said. 'It was never an official SNP slogan, nor an election theme. It was just a silly boast to reporters before the conference even began.'[37] At least that silly boast had one great virtue as Donald Dewar memorably quipped, it could be re-used every ten years.

Significantly, rather than dump the phrase as he had the non-payment campaign, Salmond decided to go along with it. 'I think that raises one serious question about Alex Salmond's leadership,' pondered James Mitchell, 'which I think has recurred occasionally and that is his unwillingness to take on his opponents.' Mitchell had a point. 'I don't think it was my most glorious moment of leadership,' concurred Salmond. 'I should have caught on to what was happening quicker and perhaps re-orientated the strategy before it got too strong a hold.'[38] Instead of controlling what he called a 'trite phrase', however, Salmond 'tried to manage the position and set about giving the claim some degree of credibility'.[39]

Also unveiled at the 'Free by 93' press conference was a more angular version of the SNP's traditional thistle-shaped logo, ostensibly to highlight party's new, crisper political message. Commentary instead focused on its resemblance to an early version of the Nazi swastika, while upside down it was virtually identical to that of a German neo-Nazi organisation active in the 1950s and 1960s. The press had a field day, particularly as delegates debated the rise of fascist, neo-Nazi movements throughout Europe. 'The logo is clearly recognisable as a revamped and updated version of the long-established SNP symbol', said an irritated Salmond, 'based on the St Andrew's cross – the Saltire.'[40] Moira Salmond, meanwhile, confessed that she was 'not sure about the logo . . . because it is so sharp; it tends to jab you if worn as jewellery'.[41]

Ironically, another conference fixture – the election of a deputy leader – actually passed off rather smoothly despite widely anticipated trouble. Jim Sillars won by 279 votes to Alasdair Morgan's 184, and although this was interpreted as him putting down a leadership marker following Salmond's difficult summer, the two would actually complement each other well. Sillars was good on detailed policy, carefully addressing lots of hypothetical positions about, for example, Scottish membership of the EEC, while Salmond concentrated on political positioning. 'The SNP put on a skilful, good week,' judged Charles Kennedy in his *Scotsman* column. 'Problems lie ahead but electoral discipline will keep two highly talented individualists like Salmond and Sillars rubbing along well enough meantime. The Cain and Abel phase comes later.'[42] That biblical analogy would prove eerily prophetic.

Fifteen months after becoming SNP leader, and having successfully recovered from a summer of discontent, Salmond now bristled with confidence. 'Because we weren't anchored to a political base, we were vulnerable to being called all sorts of ridiculous names: tartan Tories and tartan Trots at the same time,' he said of his ideological rebranding. 'If you don't own up to a particular identity, you can't complain if someone pins one on you.' And, with a nod to Jim Sillars, Salmond told the *Guardian* his strategy was 'Taking sides in Scotland as well as taking Scotland's side'.

Even former opponents appeared to be warming to Salmond as leader. 'He was never my choice as successor,' admitted Gordon Wilson. 'Alex and I didn't always see eye to eye, but he seems to be growing into the job.'[43] While Isobel Lindsay declared him to be 'far and away the best leader the SNP could have at the moment'.[44] Other critics grudgingly admired his obvious ability ('a cool, professional television performer, the master of the six-second soundbite, who gives no quarter') while pointing out that he could still come across as 'a bit of a smart Alex, a smirker, maybe just a bit too clever'. 'The problem is that Alex is not a natural team player,' said one former senior official. 'He's very bright, a first-class soloist, but it's important for a party to have a good conductor.'

From the Christmas of 1991 up until the general election of May 1992, that 'first-class soloist' was in fine voice. Salmond began to speak 'the language of Edinburgh's alternative business establishment, dispensing oil revenue statistics or trading surpluses to justify Scotland's potential self-sufficiency'.[45] 'We need constitutional change to allow Scotland to move on to a higher economic plane,' he had informed an economics seminar a few months before. 'My message to the business and financial community is a straight one. It should wake from its true blue slumber and start to consider the future. Business should join in the search for the best constitutional future for Scotland and our people.'[46]

Edinburgh's Usher Hall also provided the former boy soprano with the perfect acoustics for a memorable multi-party debate on 19 January 1992. Just two days after British Steel announced it was to close the totemic Ravenscraig, 2,500 people filed into the venue, another 6,500 having been turned away. Salmond had initiated the idea over lunch at the L'Auberge restaurant in Edinburgh, one of the SNP leader's favourite eateries. His guest, the *Scotsman* editor Magnus Linklater, meanwhile, agreed to organise it.

Opening the debate, Salmond appeared uncharacteristically nervous but settled quickly to deliver the most commanding performance of the night. 'Scotland isn't being governed – we're being misgoverned,' he declared. 'We're not represented in Europe but misrepresented in

Europe.' Salmond was also buoyed by a vociferous and, frankly, partisan audience. 'Labour later claimed the SNP had bussed in the audience,' protested Salmond in 2000. 'We didn't. We didn't have the organisational capacity.'[47] He was also effective during a question-and-answer session, scoring points when he asked Donald Dewar to name a single Scottish industry saved by Labour. 'Labour offers us a plasticine parliament. The form but not the substance of power,' said Salmond, although he admitted he would probably back a Labour devolution bill in the House of Commons and also stand in 'plasticine' elections.

Ian Lang, the Scottish Secretary, also came under attack ('The Tories' entire political approach is based on the politics of fear'[48]), and when he tried to argue that the vast majority of Scots had voted for Unionist parties, thus giving the Conservative government a mandate, Salmond demonstrated his agile mind: 'What you're actually saying is what you do is you incorporate the votes of everyone who votes Democrat or Labour into your votes and claim their votes as part of your right to run Scotland? Do you think people who vote for the Democrats or Labour are aware that this is what you intend to do?' Even Lang managed a smile at so clever a riposte. Donald Dewar, meanwhile, freely conceded 'that if the clapometer measured anything then no doubt Alex Salmond would win that European Song Contest tonight', while boiling his political argument down to basics: 'He can't win; we can.'

Interestingly, Salmond was much weaker when challenged about the nature of the country he aspired to govern. When the Scottish Democrat leader Malcolm Bruce asked 'what kind of Scotland' an independent Scotland would be, he dodged the question, while later, when asked what law he would pass first in an independent Scotland, Salmond's response was less than inspiring: 'A law abolishing direct mailings, which come cascading through your letterbox.'

Overall, however, Salmond exuded reason and authority: 'The case for national independence is at heart a simple one and rests on three basic propositions. Firstly, no one, but no one, will make a better job of running Scotland than the people that live here. Government by remote control is, has and would continue to be a failure. Secondly, we have got a distinct contribution to make to the international community; we have a voice well worth hearing and we've a responsibility to make it heard. Thirdly, in the new Europe which is now developing, it offers Scotland an unrivalled opportunity right now to achieve both domestic self government and a defined international role.'[49]

Although Salmond was naturally a good performer, he had clearly rehearsed at length for this much-anticipated debate. 'Close as I was to the preparations, the Great Debate was still an eye-opener,' reflected Mike Russell. 'Meticulous attention to detail, the covering of all the bases, prodigious hard work and then a sparkling performance made it clear that the momentum was all on the Salmond side and with the SNP.'[50]

The so-called 'Great Debate' at the Usher Hall and a later head-to-head with Labour's George Robertson did much to shore up Salmond's position, not least within the SNP. Indeed, the resulting media coverage was virtually unanimous in proclaiming Salmond the winner. 'The debate went well for me and pretty badly for Dewar,' recalled Salmond. 'It was an extraordinary occasion, a throwback to pre-television politics.'[51]

But if this was to be Salmond's first pre-election fillip, there were more to come. On 23 January 1992 the Scottish edition of the *Sun* newspaper, a tabloid owned by Rupert Murdoch that previously supported the Conservatives, declared support for the SNP. 'We have come to the inescapable conclusion that Scotland's destiny lies as an independent nation within the European Community,' declared an editorial, while the front page urged Scots to 'Rise now and be a nation again'.[52] This political conversion, in which Salmond had been influential, clearly had a lot to do with challenging the dominant (and Labour-supporting) *Daily Record*, but still constituted an invaluable boost for a party hitherto starved of such positive coverage.

The icing on the electoral cake came just under a week later when an ICM poll for the *Scotsman* and ITN put support for independence at a staggering, and unprecedented, 50 per cent. 'We are now upping the ante. We are making it clear to the London establishment that this time the Scots are not bluffing,' responded Salmond. 'When nations across Europe are achieving their independence, Scotland will not be left behind. All it takes is for those Scots who already believe in independence to vote for the only party that can deliver it – the Scottish National Party – and we can make this Scotland's Independence Election.'[53] 'I surfed this political tide for all it was worth,' admitted Salmond in 2000. 'At one point in the campaign, when we touched 30% in an opinion poll, it seemed that Scots might just "rise and be a nation again", but we had next to no money and a poor organisation in many seats.'[54]

'Gradualists around Alex Salmond sought a measured campaign which concentrated on maximising the SNP vote and winning key marginals,' observed the 1992 *Scottish Government Yearbook*. 'Fundamentalists around Jim Sillars and Alex Neil sought to present the election as a full-blown campaign for independence.'[55] The SNP's party political broadcast certainly had a fundamentalist tone, depicting the American Revolution in order to drive home the point that no nation had ever celebrated 'devolution day'.

There was an assumption (supported by some opinion polls) that the election would produce a hung Parliament or a Labour victory. Initially, however, Salmond was cautious when it came to forecasting the SNP's performance, predicting that three or four Tory marginals might fall to Nationalist candidates. In one previous Tory marginal, meanwhile, two full-time party workers (Peter Murrell and Richard Lochhead) continued to nurse the constituency that their candidate was about to defend for the first time. 'People hear stories about Alex being a rabid socialist', commented Murrell, 'but when they meet him it's no contest.'[56] Salmond was determined not to repeat Gordon Wilson's experience in Dundee East at the last election.

Salmond kicked off the national campaign at Macduff harbour on a sleet-sodden March day. His transportation was the so-called 'Natmobile', a converted mini-bus driven by Stewart Stevenson, while at a summit meeting of the SNP Scottish cabinet and NEC in Edinburgh, the party's campaign plans were finalised. 'We enter this campaign at a higher level than in any previous election, having already broken through the crucial barrier of 30 per cent support,' said Salmond. 'With a third of Labour voters thinking of switching to the SNP, we can push our vote up to 40 per cent and win a majority and a mandate to negotiate Scottish independence.'[57] Inflated rhetoric, therefore, was not the sole preserve of Messrs Sillars and Neil.

A feature of the campaign was a dramatic increase in television coverage for the SNP, both in Scotland and across the rest of the country, although Salmond was deprived of a UK-wide platform when three ITV companies – Granada, Central and Yorkshire – decided not to screen a set-piece election interview by Brian Walden, arguing that it was of no relevance to their viewers, something the party criticised as 'petty minded parochialism'.[58] Walden vigorously pursued Salmond over an independent Scotland's position within the EEC, which he referred to as a 'beguiling prospect'.[59] By the end of their 50-minute joust Walden clearly had the edge, although Salmond had held his own, gaining valuable coverage during a campaign in which Jim Sillars and Alex Neil had featured more prominently.

An opinion poll released a week before polling day put the SNP just seven points behind Labour, prompting Salmond to claim that his party was now 'surging' to victory. 'We're going to end Tory rule in Scotland, not just for one election,' he said of the government, 'we're going to end Tory rule in Scotland for good.'[60] The campaign, however, was not all plain sailing. Labour launched a damaging attack on Salmond's financial case for independence, branding his analysis 'Toytown economics', while Roseanna Cunningham remembered thinking about halfway through that 'this is not working, we're not doing this, we're not connecting, we're not getting anywhere'.[61]

Unexpectedly, meanwhile, John Major ('certainly the nicest'[62] Prime Minister he had dealt with, admitted Salmond) also fronted surprisingly effective Scottish and UK campaigns centred on a robust defence of the Union. 'If I could summon up all the authority of this office, I would put it into this single warning – the United Kingdom is in danger,' he said at one rally. 'Wake up, my fellow countrymen! Wake up now before it is too late!'[63] Salmond, however, remained upbeat. 'Undoubtedly,' judged the newspaper, '[he] has had a successful campaign and, if unable to bring about the landslide victory necessary to end the Union, would seem to be on course to increase the number of SNP seats.'[64]

But it was not to be. 'In the SNP headquarters, the day after the 1992 election, a mute tableau summed it all up,' wrote Christopher Harvie. 'On a table stood an untouched bottle of champagne and an empty bottle of whisky.'[65] Indeed, despite expectations of a breakthrough, the SNP had won, or rather held, just three seats, the 1987 contingent of Salmond, Andrew Welsh and Margaret Ewing. In Banff and Buchan, Salmond increased his majority to 4,108:

Alex Salmond (SNP)	21,954
S. Manson (Conservative)	17,846
B. Balcombe (Labour)	3,903
R. Kemp (Lib Dem)	2,588

Beyond the Nationalist north-east, an impressive increase in vote-share from 14 to 21.5 per cent was scant consolation for the failure to hold two seats, Dunfermline West (an SNP constituency by virtue of Dick Douglas's defection) and perhaps more damagingly, the messianic Jim Sillars in Glasgow Govan (gained at a by-election in 1988). Although little remarked upon at the time, even more humiliating was the fact that the apparently unelectable Scottish Conservative Party had modestly increased its number of votes and MPs. The general election of 1992 was, in short, a massive anticlimax.

'The 1992 election was an object lesson in how to turn a campaign triumph into a perceived defeat,' judged Salmond, again blaming Sillars. 'In the run-up to 1992 . . . Sillars was obsessed with securing "the mandate" – a majority of 36 seats that would precipitate immediate independence.' This was unfair, given that Salmond himself had spoken of winning an outright majority. 'In addition, as the UK election progressed,' he added, 'we got caught in a political vice. Labour supporters deserted [their party] to keep out the Tories; Tories turned out to keep out the SNP. On polling day, instead of "Free By 93" it was "three MPs in 1993".'[66]

Chapter 7

THE FUTURE OF NATIONALISM

The whole drive of Parnell's policy ... was therefore to conciliate English opinion by demonstrating that Home Rule, so far from being the gateway to separation, meant a different kind of partnership in which the two countries would be linked by friendship, not force.[1]

F. S. L. Lyons on Parnell's brand of Nationalism

'The campaign wasn't a failure – our vote soared', reflected Salmond eight years after the 1992 general election, 'but the perception was disastrous.'[2] Predictably, he received much of the blame, although supporters argued there had been too little time between Salmond's election in September 1990 and an election campaign to sort out a party that was 'underfunded, badly organised and unmodernised as a political organisation'. 'Salmond's impatience with this situation', observed the SNP's historian Peter Lynch, 'was understandable.'[3]

There were, however, upsides. Salmond was widely acknowledged, even by opponents, to have performed well during the election campaign, thus strengthening his position as the SNP's new orator-in-chief, particularly now that Sillars had left the Commons. The loss of such a high-profile figure brought his former protégé mixed blessings. 'My relationship with him had not been easy since he directed the SNP's over-hasty exit from the Constitutional Convention in 1989 and flung away the political initiative gained from his victory in the Govan by-election that year,' Salmond later admitted. 'However we had patched up a decent working relationship and I was genuinely surprised and saddened when he lost his seat. I reluctantly accepted his decision to retire and we parted on good terms. The next I heard was an early morning call from Scottish Television who told me they had an exclusive interview in which Sillars had described Scots as "90-minute patriots", before jetting off to his villa in Portugal. Fielding the substantial fallout, I determined that Jim and I had had our last political conversation and the SNP their last experience on the Sillars roller coaster.'[4]

With those words – '90-minute patriots' – Sillars and Salmond became, as Charles Kennedy had predicted less than a year before, Cain and Abel. But with Sillars now sulking in the political wilderness, Salmond could finally establish himself as leader. 'I think Alex had a number of problems in the early years of his leadership,' reflected Mike Russell: 'He didn't have a programme he wanted to put in place ... I think he had a generalised programme but the nuts and bolts took longer, he had difficulties in knowing exactly where he wanted to go to, and also had problems with other people who had a different view of where they wanted the party to go ... Alex is a very pragmatic politician, he reacts to circumstances as they exist. You have to push Alex a little to make him plan, and make him plan systematically.'[5] Having been in constant campaigning mode for almost two years, with the general election contest out of the way and another unlikely for at least four years, Salmond finally had the opportunity to mould the party he led.

'The debate in the SNP as to whether it was right to support a devolved parliament as a stepping stone to independence goes to the very heart of the party,' Salmond later reflected. 'The assumption, for the greater part of the SNP's 70-year history, was always that independence would be preceded by the setting up of a subsidiary parliament. For a brief period in the early 1980s SNP policy was not "independence nothing less" but "independence nothing else". That changed for the better in Gordon Wilson's term of office. However, the dramatic exit from the Constitutional Convention in 1989 had created a misleading but enduring public impression of a purist SNP unwilling to engage with the political process in Scotland.' Therefore from 1992 on, Salmond and others 'worked to change the SNP's stance as it seemed obvious ... that independence was more likely as a process building from devolution than some sort of instantaneous political "big bang".'[6] Just a week after polling day he sought to persuade a disappointed and divided SNP to back a revived multi-option constitutional referendum while also seeking cross-party co-operation.

An indication of how difficult this would be came when the Scottish Trades Union Congress (STUC) effectively withdraw an invitation for Salmond to address its forthcoming Congress. The SNP released the text of his planned speech anyway. 'The challenge for Scottish politicians is to find a method of divorcing Scotland's constitutional future from that Westminster arena,' Salmond would have said, 'to repatriate not just the debate but the decision to Scotland.' Boldly, Salmond added that the 'SNP does not ask anyone to give up their principles and we have no intention of surrendering ours', although he was prepared, 'in the interest of unity, to go through that process [of co-operation], but let us do it quickly to clear the ground, not slowly as a means of delaying decisions.'[7]

Salmond devoted the next few months to a multi-option referendum with almost missionary zeal, attempting to frame May's district council elections as a second chance to decide Scotland's constitutional future. Gordon Wilson, however, branded the referendum a 'dead duck' at the SNP's Stirling National Council, while Iain Lawson said it was the party's 'job to remove the strength from Labour', which you did not do 'by joining up with them'.[8] Salmond responded by cleverly presenting the referendum as a campaigning device that would expose divisions within the Labour Party. 'The idea of a Scottish-built referendum goes down one of the deepest fault lines in Scottish politics,' he told activists. 'One of our major Unionist opponents is disintegrating before our very eyes. Let's get the lever in and prise them apart.'[9]

With the overwhelming support of his party, Salmond now had the authority to meet with Scotland United and Common Cause, two umbrella groups devoted to Scottish devolution. 'The SNP have been seen to be rather confrontational when a softer approach might have paid more dividends,' Salmond told the *Dundee Courier* in May 1992. 'But in looking at these new organisations, like Scotland United, we have to be extremely friendly in our approach ... I am anxious not to force people into a corner.'[10]

On 29 June 1992 the Labour MP George Galloway (a 'crypto-nationalist' according to Salmond) and the STUC's Campbell Christie led a Scotland United delegation to meet Salmond at the SNP's North Charlotte Street headquarters. With Salmond's tribalistic National Council speech in mind, Donald Dewar accused Scotland United's Labour backers of 'collaborating' with the SNP. This outbreak of cross-party co-operation, however, came too late. By the time Salmond had his party behind him on the referendum, judged the journalist Iain Macwhirter, 'the moment had passed, and the idea was all but dead'.[11]

That idea also came under scrutiny at the 1992 SNP conference, at which Salmond also attempted to avoid a damaging post-mortem of the general election result. Gordon Wilson took advantage of Salmond's temporary absence at Westminster by summing up how he believed the party should deal with its Unionist opponents: 'Attack, attack and attack.' His attitude towards co-operation with Labour members of Scotland United was similarly hard-line. 'I know who our enemies are,' added Wilson, 'I know who the enemies of Scotland are and they include George Galloway.' Margaret Ewing concurred. 'I say to my friends in the Scottish nationalists and to all the voters of Scotland,' she said in her conference speech, 'and to members of this party: there is only one realignment in Scotland's political life which really counts. Are you a Unionist or a nationalist? Because you cannot have it both ways.' Evoking 1979, she added: 'Too often in the past we have manned the marches, provided the banners, but been denied a speech or a presence on the platform. We will not play second-fiddle to anyone, no matter how beguiling the tune.'[12]

Returning to conference the following day, Salmond tried to steer delegates onto considering a new medium-term strategy, a four-year plan highlighting the economic disadvantages of the Union, condemning Labour's refusal to fight for constitutional change, and reviewing the party's organisation, finances and campaigning ability. Salmond also worked hard to consolidate his socially democratic rebranding. 'Our programme clearly places us in the mainstream of social democracy,' he told reporters, 'but if we don't acknowledge the label [then] we are vulnerable to identities laid on us by political opponents, either Tartan Trots or Tartan Tories.' Gordon Wilson, however, reminded delegates that Donald Stewart, who had died the previous month, had 'held social democracy in utter contempt' and Salmond's proposal was rebuffed.[13] The previous conference's proposal for a 'Scottish cabinet', meanwhile, was finally passed, although not by a margin sufficient for inclusion in the party's constitution.

In a combative keynote speech, Salmond reasserted himself, signalling his determination to press on with cross-party co-operation, culminating in a demonstration at the European Summit in Edinburgh later that year. The seasoned Nationalist observer Peter Jones said Salmond's 'supreme asset is his public speaking ability linked to an easy confidence on television, and that, allied to a growing ability to inject humour into his performances makes him a leader with no obvious challenger. Also standing him in good stead is a growing command of the technocratic aspects of politics, represented at this conference by the presentation of a four-year plan of reorganisation and fund-raising to take the SNP up to the

next general election. However, Mr Salmond is sufficiently acute to
realise that pinning all on the next election is not quite good enough,
hence his determination to be linked to the referendum campaigns of
Scotland United.'[14]

The difficult year of 1992 did, at least, end on a high note for
Salmond. On a cold, sparkling winter day in mid-December, some
25,000 people snaked through the centre of Edinburgh while delegates
gathered close by for a European Summit. After speeches by the new
Scottish Liberal Democrat leader Jim Wallace, Salmond and Labour's
Henry McLeish, a young actress – introduced as Scotland's 'unknown
citizen' – read out a 'declaration on democracy' which called upon the
European heads of government attending the summit to recognise the
desire of most Scots for devolved government and a recall of the old
Scottish parliament, adjourned in 1706.

It was a dignified, if ultimately fruitless, gathering, while Salmond's
attempts to maintain the momentum he believed it had generated soon
got bogged down in disputes with the Labour Party. It was desperate to
extract itself from the 'recall' policy and when an otherwise non-
contentious Commons division over the Maastricht Treaty plunged
Salmond's still-fragile leadership into crisis, it duly found an ideal
pretext. It all began in March 1993 when the Conservative government
reached a deal with 21 Liberal Democrat MPs, four Plaid Cymru
Members and the SNP's three to pass an amendment it feared losing
because of rebellious Tory backbenchers. Although the SNP (which
was pro-Maastricht) argued for a second-question referendum on Scottish independence in return for its support, when John Major told
Margaret Ewing (who was leading the talks) that everything was non-
negotiable except representation on the Committee of the Regions
(CotR), a pan-European body for local and regional authorities to be
created post-Maastricht, the discussions focused on that.

Instead of Scottish members of the CotR being chosen by the UK
government, Ian Lang, the Scottish Secretary, offered to let Scotland's
four political parties nominate their own representatives from among
members of local authorities. Labour, however, refused to co-operate
and the SNP – its approach agreed by Ewing, Salmond and Andrew
Welsh – looked forward to a tactical triumph in which they could point
to a major government concession while thwarting Labour plans to hog
all Scotland's CotR seats. The division, however, did not go to plan.
The government lost and, having spotted Salmond et al. in the wrong
lobby, Labour MPs quickly rounded on the Nationalist trio, jeering and

pointing. Wrong-footed, the SNP MPs left the Chamber, Ewing to prepare for a difficult press conference, and Salmond to sign a declaration with Scottish Liberal Democrat leader Jim Wallace calling for the old Scottish parliament to be recalled.

This press conference took place in a meeting room just off Westminster Hall, where Campbell Christie and Bill Spiers of the STUC were also present. Embarrassingly for Salmond, television cameras caught the moment when Henry McLeish looked in and told Christie privately that the cross-party talks were off as a result of the vote. Labour MPs, meanwhile, signed a motion condemning the SNP and calling on Salmond to resign. 'In the morning Salmond called on all Scotland to unite against the Tories,' McLeish quipped during one radio debate. 'In the evening, he united with the Tories against Scotland.' The Labour-supporting *Daily Record* even ran front-page pictures of Salmond et al. under the headline: 'The Three Stooges.'

There was an immediate backlash from ordinary SNP members, many of whom had watched events unfold on Channel 4 News. At a specially convened meeting of the NEC, Alex Neil and Kenny MacAskill submitted a motion condemning the MPs' actions, while Rob Gibson, ordinarily a Salmond supporter, submitted another sympathising with the MPs but regretting their action. (Neil and MacAskill eventually dropped their motion and endorsed Gibson's.) Winnie Ewing and Gordon Wilson, meanwhile, supported Salmond's motion (signed by all three SNP MPs), arguing that being an MP required taking quick decisions.

The first half of the NEC meeting – during which Salmond apologised – had been relatively civil, but during a break it was alleged Salmond had leaned on two youth representatives (Shirley Anne Somerville, a future MSP, and Stewart Hosie, a future MP), who looked set to vote against him. In the second half of the meeting, according to reports, Salmond hit back at his opponents in deeply personal terms. Alex Neil was blamed for bouncing the party into 'Free by 93'; Iain Lawson was criticised for his candidacy in the Paisley by-election, while Roger Mullin was accused of leaking a fax critical of Salmond to the BBC.

In the event, Salmond's motion passed by 13 votes to 11, with the two youth representatives abstaining. 'It seems doubtful that Salmond would have resigned as leader had the vote gone against him,' judged Peter Jones, 'though Ewing might well have resigned as parliamentary leader.'[15] Neil, MacAskill and Mullin, however, all felt Salmond's assault on them meant they no longer enjoyed his confidence and they promptly resigned from his 'Scottish cabinet'. Some SNP branches called upon Salmond to resign, although six of the 11 NEC members who had voted against the MPs – including Gibson, Roseanna Cunningham, Fiona Hyslop and Nicola Sturgeon – asked for the NEC's decision to be accepted in a letter to the *Scotsman*. 'There was an over-reaction within the party because some feared it was a repeat of 1979,' recalled one of those present at the meeting, 'and ironically that over-reaction probably prevented it from becoming so. For the first time the SNP did what Labour had done all the time, allowed its left wing to let off steam while also managing to keep its head.'[16]

Salmond penned a lengthy defence of his actions for that weekend's edition of *Scotland on Sunday*. Pointing out that the SNP-negotiated concession still stood 'regardless of the fate of amendment 28', Salmond argued that having a 'genuine cross-section of the Scottish population' on the Committee of the Regions represented 'a modest but important gain for Scotland'. Conceding that it was 'certainly rare for the SNP to be in the Tory lobby', he remained defiant. 'The SNP must be pro-Scottish, not only anti-Tory,' he wrote. 'If that means holding my nose as I go through the division lobbies then I will do it.'[17]

Jim Sillars, meanwhile, did not miss an opportunity to thunder from the pages of the *Sun*. 'That our MPs should soil the party's soul for a place on a committee which is a unionist invention to be used against independence, is staggering,' he wrote in his column. 'Tears of rage and despair have been shed by SNP workers and our voters are stunned. It never crossed our minds that with the Tory Government in serious trouble, our MPs would hold out a lifeline.'[18] Sillars deliberately prodded the scars of 1979, implying that Salmond had unravelled ten years of SNP attempts to live down Labour taunts of being 'Tartan Tories'.

Although these events had been damaging, at no point was there the prospect of a serious challenge to Salmond's leadership. A few months later, however, he came close to expressing some contrition. 'We tried to gain something for Scotland and failed,' he admitted. 'But there has been no lasting damage, barely any effect in the polls at all. There were some who panicked but they are not lost to the party, only the cabinet. It has been a toughening experience for the party and . . . I suppose there has also been a benefit for those in the party who thought Alex Salmond was infallible.'[19] The incident certainly demonstrated Salmond's instinct for loyalty, deliberately cutting Margaret Ewing some slack because the memory of her defeat in 1990 was still raw. 'If it told you anything about Alex then it was him as a team player,' observed Jim Eadie, who worked for the SNP group at Westminster at that time. 'He didn't attempt to distance himself from the decision or hang Margaret out to dry, as he could have done. Retrospectively he thought it had been the wrong decision, but stood by it in public and took the flak.'[20]

Salmond took more flak at the Perth National Council on 5 June, but by then the heat had gone out of the issue and a critical motion was defeated by 147 votes to 81. 'We have put introspection behind us', declared the SNP leader, 'and [have] decided to attack our opponents instead of navel gazing.'[21] Salmond – leader of the SNP for only two-and-a-half years – had lived to fight another day.

The row over Maastricht lasted nearly three months and effectively killed off any hope of cross-party co-operation on constitutional reform, although Salmond continued to reposition his party in order to take a more constructive approach to devolution. In a broadcast on Channel 4, he said 'recalling' Scotland's ancient parliament could 'challenge the authority of Westminster to continue its undemocratic rule over Scotland', something dismissed as 'ludicrous'[22] by Jim Sillars in another column for the *Scottish Sun*.

Both men knew their history, although Sillars (and his supporters) had long ago begun to doubt Salmond's intellectual capacity as SNP leader. 'You ask anyone if you can remember a big speech Alex has made,' said Sillars. 'When he got elected I took him for lunch in London and said when you lead a national movement you've got to paint a big picture and make six speeches on the economy, housing, etc. He said "good idea" but I don't think he had it in him.'[23]

To be fair to Salmond, he did have it in him, for in the two months leading up to the SNP's 1993 conference, he did precisely that, delivering a sextet of speeches at locations around Scotland. He later claimed to have got the idea not from Sillars, but from surprisingly high attendance at his public meetings. Words like 'competitive', 'pragmatic' and 'social democracy' peppered the texts, words always guaranteed to ruffle purist Nationalist feathers. He explained: 'We need to anchor our image. It's not so much that it is right or wrong but it is not steady enough. The SNP has this habit of veering in a zigzag across the political spectrum in terms of public perception. I've pursued the thought of a clearer political identity for a number of years. We are getting that into the party thinking much more strongly so that if people don't accept the social democratic label – and I think they might – they will at least accept the essence of what the SNP is about.'[24]

Salmond denied, however, that this meant depriving the SNP of its radical edge. 'I think the SNP's cutting edge and radicalism will remain, on issues like nuclear weapons, on a whole range of social policy,' he said. 'But I don't think we can allow sentiment to interfere with the absolute requirement for an economically successful Scottish economy. What the party and Scotland has to realise is that our social programme is predicated on economic success which requires the economic strategy we are outlining. You can't have a hazy belief that it will be OK if we intervene here, nationalise this. If we don't like that sector we'll take it into public ownership. That's silly and stupid. The government's job is to provide the springboard from which our industry can compete successfully.'[25]

'I feel we lost the economic debate when we could have won it,' he said of the 1992 election. 'We got bogged down on . . . the statistics about who subsidises who when we should have been building up people's confidence that Scotland is a wealthy country'.[26] Salmond also drew inspiration from Scotland's Victorian heyday, as had Mrs Thatcher in a different context, arguing that it had become one of the world's most successful economies through social initiatives like the Scottish education system. 'The scientific and entrepreneurial skills that that fed,' he explained, 'were in turn the furnace of the industrial revolution in Scotland.'[27]

It was, as ever, a delicate balancing act. As Salmond removed traditional socialist tenets from the SNP's economic policy, he injected a counter-balancing radicalism into its social agenda. One commentator called Salmond's new approach 'a kind of pragmatic fundamentalism' likely to appeal in a party 'which otherwise tends to fall back on the kind of purist fundamentalism'. 'It means that however much all other policies are pragmatised, the central constitutional line is likely to remain purist,' judged the *Scotsman*. 'Leaders can only take the led so far, and no further.'[28]

Other speeches dealt with housing, Europe and the 1992 election, while the sixth and final oration, entitled 'Independence and Scottish democracy', attempted to tie everything together. 'By voting for independence, the Scots would take their rightful place in the world as a modern, genuine democracy which includes and involves all its citizens,' argued Salmond, 'where the state serves the people and where the people of Scotland always get the Government of their choice.'[29]

Importantly, he also spelled out how Scotland would achieve its freedom: 'The first thing a victorious SNP will do, after winning a mandate for Independence through a majority of Scottish seats at a General Election, is to invite all other Scottish MPs to join us in an interim Scottish Parliament. We shall then open negotiations with both London and Brussels on the exact terms of Scottish Independence. The next step will be to submit these terms and our detailed proposals for the constitution of an independent Scotland to the people for their approval in a referendum. Once the constitution is agreed, we shall then as quickly as possible hold the first democratic elections to a Scottish Parliament.'[30]

All six speeches were issued in pamphlet form at the 1993 SNP conference, let down by a less-than-inspiring title, *'Horizons Without Bars'*, which rather than advocating a drink-free Scotland was a quote from an essay by William McIlvanney. As political manifestos go it was more tactical than philosophical, but it served a valuable purpose, not least in shoring up Salmond's intellectual credentials among the ever-important media. 'I think in [those speeches] you began to see . . . the beginnings and the development of a very clear political philosophy,' reflected Mike Russell in 2001. '[They began] to map out the socially democratic vision for the party [that was] seeking to engage and bring in the widest possible constituency.'[31] The speeches codified existing thinking rather than generating new ideas, but however socially democratic, Tony Crosland's *The Future of Socialism* it was not, although the subtitle was 'The Future of Scotland'. Perhaps Salmond could have called it 'The Future of Nationalism'.

'He [Salmond] is, pretty much, a pragmatist,' judged the *Scotsman* as delegates gathered for the SNP's Dunoon conference, 'but is suspected by fundamentalists of all persuasions of closet gradualism. That is why he does not yet command unstinting rank-and-file support.'[32] Salmond was, therefore, clearly under pressure, one office-bearer remarking upon 'a degree of irritation with him that wasn't there last year'.[33]

That irritation clearly focused Salmond's mind. His constitutional refrain of the previous three years – a multi-option referendum – was abandoned in favour of a strong solo tune. Until 1994's regional council and European Parliament elections, announced Salmond, it was the SNP's 'job to attack our political opponents. The Tory Party for what they have done to Scotland and Labour for what they have not done for Scotland. But our most important task is to present our inspiring vision for Scotland's future.'[34]

Conscious of criticism that his oratory lacked the fire of Sillars or Alex Neil, Salmond brought delegates to their feet with some stirring passages. 'SNP success will send our Unionist opponents into a spiral of fear, fear not of the present but fear of the future,' he declared. 'Neither wants to lose Scotland. The Tories fear the loss of Scottish resources, Labour the loss of Scottish votes.' To roars of applause he also pushed the right nuclear and energy buttons, demanding that 'rotting nuclear hulks' be removed from Scotland while branding the piping of North Sea gas to England as the 'Great Gas Robbery'.

Salmond also took on his critics, slapping down Jim Sillars '90-minute patriots' jibe by declaring that if Scots had failed to vote for change then 'that's my fault for not explaining the case clearly enough, your fault for not winning on the doorsteps, our fault collectively for a lack of resolution. But it's nobody else's responsibility but ours. We are attempting to build a new Scotland for all of the people of Scotland. There is no place in that crusade for scapegoat hunting of any kind.'[35] Salmond's speech earned him a standing ovation, supporters talking it up as a personal triumph while even critics acknowledged that it was just the sort of 'fire in the belly' speech needed to rouse the party following a difficult year. 'Finally,' declared a *Scotsman* editorial, 'Alex Salmond has taken command of the Scottish National Party'.[36]

The last day of conference, however, demonstrated that that command was not yet total. For the second year running Alex Neil topped the poll for the NEC, while two other Salmond critics, Kenny MacAskill and Iain Lawson, were also easily elected. Shrewdly, Salmond hinted that Neil and MacAskill would be brought back into the fold with Scottish cabinet posts. 'As I have said before,' he told reporters, 'there is no such thing as a lost soul.' The party, Salmond added, was in 'fine fettle', while 'this excellent, united and purposeful conference' would act as a 'launchpad for the electoral contests ahead'.[37]

The year 1994 was indeed the year of elections. First up were May's regional council elections, the last before the Conservative government planned to abolish Labour strongholds like Strathclyde Region to make way for 32 unitary authorities. Although the SNP had long supported this reform, Salmond chose a meeting of the standing committee considering the Local Government (Scotland) Bill for his first bout of Parliamentary guerilla warfare since 1989, chiefly to highlight Scottish Secretary Ian Lang's need to 'parachute' five English Tory MPs onto the committee in order to let the Bill proceed.

On 1 February Salmond forced the abandonment of its first session 'by merely turning up, sitting down and (loyally) reading a copy of *The Herald* newspaper'.[38] As in 1989, he was not a member of the committee, and not only did his action wreck detailed consideration of the Bill, it forced the government to pass a resolution preventing Salmond or anyone else taking part. Unlike in 1988–89, however, Labour joined with the SNP in objecting to the presence of English MPs, although Salmond's tactics were, it seemed, subject to the law of diminishing political returns. It 'all comes dressed up in fine points of argumentation, a sophisticated gloss implying a long-term strategic analysis and approach,' sneered the *Scotsman*. 'Of course it is nothing of the kind. It is about headlines, pictures and soundbites.'[39]

Whatever it was, the disruption meant the Local Government (Scotland) Bill was still working its way through Parliament as Scots voted in the regional council elections in early May 1994. The SNP secured 70 seats and 26.8 per cent of the vote, up from 43 and 21.8 per cent in 1990, its second-best result in the two-decade history of regional authorities. The party also captured the Airdrie South ward in the Monklands East constituency. 'Maybe not free by 93, but we have opened the door by 94,' quipped Salmond. 'Labour can feel the ground shift from under their feet in Scotland.'[40]

The ground continued to shift as Scotland's political parties geared up for June's European Parliament elections. With 32.6 per cent of the vote and nearly half a million votes, the outcome was the SNP's best-ever performance in a national election and firmly established it as Scotland's second party. Once again re-elected in the Highlands and Islands, Winnie Ewing was joined in Brussels by Allan Macartney, the party's articulate deputy leader, in North-East Scotland. 'On the basis of the European results in June,' said a buoyant Salmond, 'a number of the new constituencies in the North-east, including the new Gordon seat, become very realistic SNP targets.'[41]

The regional and European elections of 1994 were central to Salmond's bid to restore electoral credibility after the humiliation of the 1992 general election. In that context, the Monklands East by-election of July 1994 – held in the wake of Labour leader John Smith's premature death – was both a setback and an epiphany. 'Nationalism is in the air again in Scotland,' remarked a Labour MP on the eve of the by-election. 'You can smell it.'[42] Unfortunately for the campaign that preceded it, there was also a distinct whiff of sectarianism.

This hinged upon allegations of sectarian bias on the Labour-controlled Monklands District Council, which included the Monklands East constituency. It was alleged that the authority favoured spending in the predominantly Catholic Coatbridge, neglecting the largely Protestant Airdrie as a result. The by-election itself was essentially a straight fight between the SNP's Kay Ullrich (later an MSP) and the former general secretary of the Scottish Labour Party, Helen Liddell, most recently an aide to the disgraced media tycoon Robert Maxwell. Both candidates sought to avoid campaigning on the allegations themselves, although they proved difficult to avoid.

Relishing the prospect of an SNP win in an urban Labour heartland, Salmond was fully involved with the campaign, so much so that he even cancelled 'plans to attend his niece's baptism in Aberdeen, excusing himself on the grounds that he was campaigning in Monklands East'.[43] Two years earlier Salmond had also missed his mother's 70th birthday celebrations in order to attend a CND rally in Glasgow.[44] Usually very much a family man when it came to such occasions, these absences illustrated Salmond's overriding commitment to politics.

Salmond later claimed to have noticed problems with sectarianism while campaigning in Monklands during the regional council elections in May. In the by-election itself, his own 'observations' turned up 'many occasions late in the campaign on which SNP voters – who happened to be Catholic – were told in the clearest terms by Labour canvassers that the SNP would discriminate against them. These voters were told that we would close Catholic schools and – when that argument failed to stick because it was a lie – that we would "create a Northern Ireland".'[45] On the other hand, Labour later claimed that the SNP had indulged in similar tactics. Charge and counter-charge were par for the course, heightening even the usual tensions of a particularly febrile by-election campaign. At the count on 30 June this tension finally burst out into the open. Liddell won, but with a much reduced majority of only 1,640, while Kay Ullrich came second with an impressive swing of more than 19 per cent. In what Salmond later described as 'the most graceless acceptance speech I have ever heard', Liddell accused the Tory and SNP candidates of having 'played the Orange card' during the campaign, something Salmond dismissed as 'absolute rubbish'.

But it was an ill-judged editorial in the following day's *Herald* that really riled Salmond. Headlined 'Tawdry SNP campaign', the newspaper singled out the Nationalists as having 'given great grounds for concern, for it has sought to revive the "Billy and Dan" factor in Scottish politics from which we have fought so hard to escape'. 'Our need for a Scottish parliament speaks for itself', continued the editorial, 'and does not require the dubious endorsement of an odd and sometimes tawdry by-election campaign.'[46]

Although the next edition of the *Herald* admitted being 'unfair' in making 'certain comments' and accepted that 'the official SNP campaign [had] strenuously avoided this question', the damage was done. Salmond was also given space next to the apology, in which he launched a blistering defence of the SNP and its conduct. 'Most of the recent leadership of the party – and many of its members – have their origins in the central belt,' he wrote:

> Their political philosophy was formed by the injustice that they saw in the post-war years in their own communities. They believed then, and believe now, in equality and fairness and they have fought consistently for a country which harnessed the abilities of all its citizens in a common purpose. Margo MacDonald from Lanarkshire, Jim Sillars from Ayrshire, Winnie Ewing from Glasgow, Andrew Welsh from Govan – and myself from West Lothian – the list goes on, but all of those on it are united in this common purpose. We were all forged in the same fire, a fire that sometimes flickered evilly with the tittle-tattle of bigotry and the actual experience of political gerrymandering for religious ends ... Membership of the SNP was for us, and for many like us, a declaration that rejected utterly such wrongs.[47]

Telling by its absence from this roll call of leading Nationalists was Billy Wolfe, the former SNP leader whom Salmond knew well from West Lothian politics. This was not surprising for in advance of Pope John Paul II's visit to Scotland back in 1982, Wolfe had voiced opposition in the pages of the Church of Scotland magazine *Life & Work*. The row that followed ended Wolfe's career within the party and did much damage to the party as a whole. Although Salmond, together with Jim Sillars, had already done some work to repair the damage, most notably on Catholic schools in the late 1980s, there remained much to be done.

Monklands was, therefore, Salmond's epiphany. 'I was very affected by that by-election,' he reflected in 2009. 'The nature of the whole campaign just made you feel dirty.'[48] Indeed, another account has it that 'the behaviour of fringe supporters in Monklands had sickened Salmond to the point of questioning his current vocation'.[49] 'For me, this was a profoundly depressing experience, but one that in retrospect has turned out to be most helpful,' he elaborated in a 1995 speech. 'It made the SNP look very closely at the whole issue of discrimination.'[50]

Within weeks of the by-election both Salmond and Liddell met with Thomas Winning, the Roman Catholic Archbishop of Glasgow, who would be appointed Cardinal in November that year. According to a biography of Winning, he told an 'unimpressed' Liddell that the Labour Party had problems with bigotry, which she denied, but immediately warmed to Salmond, marking the 'beginning of a close political friendship that would bloom over the next seven years'.[51] As Salmond later put it: 'I liked Tom Winning, and I think he liked me.' Winning also reminded him that the Catholic Church in Scotland had always been distinct. 'The church was the anchor, the rock of the independence movement in the days of Wallace and Bruce,' explained Salmond in 2009. 'It was the only institutional force that could be relied upon – it certainly wasn't the nobles.'[52]

'His goal when asking for a meeting with Winning was to convince him of the changed face of Scottish Nationalism,' wrote Winning's biographer Stephen McGinty, 'but when he arrived the door was already ajar.' Privately, it seems, Winning had 'developed into a Nationalist' despite confessing to Salmond that he had voted against a Scottish Assembly in 1979. 'Winning explained to the SNP leader that his ambition was to see Catholics finally accepted as Scottish, their loyalty seen no longer as attached to Ireland or Rome.' Salmond's calculation was, naturally enough, also tactical, viewing Scotland's large Catholic population (representing around 800,000, mostly Labour, voters) as an 'untapped resource'. He duly informed Winning (over spaghetti) of 'his ambition to remove all trace of anti-Catholicism from the party [the SNP] and to provide a natural alternative to the Labour Party'.[53]

Salmond's account was essentially the same: 'I went to see Cardinal Tom Winning – a great cleric with a common touch – after Monklands and I said to him, "Tom, what can we do about this [sectarianism]?" He said two things to me. First, having been a parish priest in Lanarkshire in the 1950s, he said it was nothing like as bad as it was. And, two, he said: "By your deeds are you known."'[54] Salmond's deeds, articulated in a series of speeches over the next year, further repositioned the SNP in just the sort of long-term strategising at which he excelled, and was if anything more successful than his various attempts to rebrand the party ideologically. Not only did Salmond's personal interest in Catholicism deepen significantly, but that, together with political contacts in Ireland, also fed into his economic strategy. 'The SNP is engaged in the process of reinforcing our identity as a civic national party appealing to all of the people of Scotland regardless of origin,' he wrote in his *Herald* column towards the end of 1994. 'We will be judged on how consistently and successfully we pursue that task.'[55]

Having been run ragged during the council, European and by-election campaigns, Salmond was laid low with pneumonia at the end of 1994 and found it hard to shake off the after-effects for several months. For what limited rest and relaxation he and Moira enjoyed, two weeks each August were still spent in Colonsay, one of the quietest and least accessible Hebridean islands, where Alex could indulge his love of golf and the West Highland scenery.

His marriage, meanwhile, remained strong, despite the demands placed upon Salmond as leader. Moira, as Winnie Ewing had informed the 1993 SNP conference, was 'an absolute cracker'. Having campaigned with Mrs Salmond, added Ewing, she could vouch that she was 'dynamic, efficient, totally dedicated and Alex is a very lucky man to have her. And we have an extra weapon, we've Moira as a secret weapon.'[56]

Earlier that year Salmond had helped celebrate the SNP's 60th anniversary by boldly claiming that the party had helped convert Scotland from a Unionist to a Nationalist frame of mind, while attending a dinner in Edinburgh 'at which all four of my extant predecessors spoke in spellbinding fashion'[57] about the party's great strides over the past six decades. That year also saw the publication of an updated version of Christopher Harvie's much-praised 1977 tome, *Scotland and Nationalism*, as well as a new work by the historian Richard Finlay on the origins of the SNP, *Independent and Free*. Despite his love of history, however, Salmond was slow to appreciate the contribution his predecessors had made to the National Movement.

Indeed, when the SNP had been constituted in April 1934 it had advocated a form of Imperial Federation, with Scotland taking its place as a self-governing Dominion within the British Empire. Sixty years on and Salmond was still redefining the nature of independence long after Britain had lost that Empire and struggled to find a role. 'There is no pure independence in this world,' he reflected on the eve of the 1994 SNP conference, alluding to recent Canadian provincial elections in which the Parti Québécois had secured a majority of seats in Quebec's provincial assembly.

'Quebec currently has a constitutional system which is somewhat in advance of devolution,' said Salmond, 'it has much stronger powers

than is promised by Labour for a Scottish assembly. But the point is that
it is unstable – substantial sections of opinion find it unsatisfactory.
Devolution as a system within the UK is equally likely to be unstable.
The one thing about independence is that it is highly unlikely to revert
to un-independence, it is stable.'

He pointed once again to the Republic of Ireland – by now
Salmond's favoured geographical analogy – citing one economic forecast that had Ireland's per capita GDP levels overtaking those of the UK
by 2005. 'It is quite true that an independent Scotland would be
restricted with what you can do,' he conceded. 'You can go back to 5
per cent [VAT on fuel] within the EU rules. You also have the right to
ask to go to zero.'[58] The wider point, added Salmond, was that even
limited room for manoeuvre would not be available in a devolved Scotland. He planned to implant these arguments, meanwhile, in the mind of
the electorate well before the next general election campaign.

The *Herald* dubbed what followed in Inverness 'the most successful
SNP conference in recent times', and indeed it was the least contentious
gathering of Salmond's leadership to date. Following the regional and
European elections, Salmond claimed he now led 'Scotland's party'[59]
locked in a two-horse race with Labour. He attacked John Major as
inconsistent for offering a referendum on the constitutional status of
Northern Ireland but not Scotland, while lampooning his old and new
Labour targets with particular relish. George Robertson was 'Scottish
on the outside, British on the inside. Tartan ties – Union Jack under-
pants', while Tony Blair was likened to the 'South Sea Bubble', 'the
new southern bubble, floating along on hot air, soundbites and photo-
opportunities'.[60]

There was also a constructive aspect to the speech, most notably its
lavish praise for the Catholic faith's contribution to Scotland intellectual
life, in which Salmond now took genuine interest. 'The Catholic view
of social justice informs our attitude to inequality in Scotland and internationally,' he said, contrasting the 'institutionalised religious
discrimination'[61] of the UK Act of Settlement (which barred Catholics
from acceding to the throne) with the status Catholics would enjoy
under a written bill of rights in an independent Scotland.

Reflecting on Salmond's speech in his column the following day,
John MacLeod judged that it was excellent 'on the ground of technical merit. It was well delivered, rather witty, and came over with
unwonted warmth; it was, at that level, the speech of Salmond's life,
and his brethren loved it. I looked not at him [Salmond], but at them:

hundreds and hundreds of clapping hands, adoring eyes, mesmerised smiles, the great roar of the multitude and their intoxicating applause. I wondered, suddenly, how it felt to engineer such emotion. How it felt when it dawns in your mind what you could make people do.' There were also some perceptive asides on the SNP leader's character, still a closed book to all but his closest confidantes. 'The trouble is, in Denis Healey's tilt at Thatcher, that Salmond has little "hinterland",' wrote MacLeod. 'Politics and economics are all he knows and, seemingly, to him all that matters. He is not a man of books and perspective, and seems secular to the core.'[62] The same could not be said of Mike Russell, the ostentatiously cultured Episcopalian who returned to SNP HQ at the end of 1994 in the newly created position of chief executive.

Not only had Russell been a valued ally since the mid-1980s, but the television producer also imbued his new boss with that hitherto absent hinterland. When Salmond had to provide his cultural influences for a March 1995 edition of the *New Statesman*, for example, there are unmistakable elements of both men. Asked which books and authors had had the greatest effect on his political beliefs, Salmond listed 'John Steinbeck for *The Grapes of Wrath* and *Cannery Row*, and William McIlvanney for his range of works', while also offering *Our Scots Noble Families* by Tom Johnston ('a former secretary of state for Scotland's tirade against Scotland's aristocracy') and John Buchan's *Montrose* ('which shows that there were one or two saving graces'). As for his favourite poem and song, Salmond predictably nominated 'A Man's a Man for a' That' by Robert Burns. Intriguingly, when asked who was 'the greatest prime minister we never had and why?' Salmond offered Jim Sillars 'as the most talented politician of his generation',[63] a charitable reference given his former mentor's regular tabloid attacks.

Russell, like Salmond, also possessed a natural journalistic flair, and occasionally ghosted the SNP leader's weekly *Herald* column, as did Kevin Pringle, another key aide who had joined the SNP as research officer in 1989. Although, more often than not, these columns contained rather bland reflections on the week's political events ('occasionally I dabble with normality'[64]), not to mention regular attacks on the 'spivs' who ran privatised utilities, a few were not only well written, but also provoked bulging mailbags in response. One in May 1993 on the golfer John Panton, for example, went down particularly well while, more broadly, the very presence of the column in a serious newspaper like the *Herald* was invaluable for a party still building its profile and respectability.[65]

As the Conservative government of John Major faltered, Salmond spent the next two-and-a-half years attacking the Tories and lamenting Tony Blair's New Labour. And, as talk of a cross-party approach to devolution diminished, Salmond also sought, this time more decisively, to toughen up the SNP's stance on devolution. To that end, an NEC meeting in early 1995 backed a new dual-path strategy entitled 'Highway to Independence', under which a majority of SNP MPs at Westminster or in a devolved parliament would constitute a legitimate mandate for beginning independence negotiations.

Salmond also used an interview with *Scotland on Sunday* to test his party's mood, telling Kenny Farquharson there was no 'holy grail' in terms of how independence was achieved and that the party 'must not get itself hung up on the route'. 'I would only have difficulty in the party on this matter if I stopped arguing for independence and started arguing for devolution,' he said, clearly trying to pre-empt fundamentalist attacks. 'That isn't going to happen.' *Scotland on Sunday*, however, got a little carried away in its interpretation of an essentially tactical change. 'It is the first time since the 1970s that a devolutionary path to independence has been a stated, overt aspect of SNP policy,' it reported. 'This represents a considerable shift in tone, substance and emphasis from SNP tactics in recent years.' The newspaper's banner headline was also the provocative 'Salmond backs devolution'.[66]

This was, at best, an overstatement, for at the 1990 SNP conference delegates had backed a resolution containing the important caveat 'that if an assembly should be set up, the elections to that body would provide an alternative to a UK general election and an SNP victory would constitute a mandate for independence'.[67] Salmond was simply codifying devolution as a key, rather than a grudging, element of party strategy.

There was, however, predictable scorn from the usual suspects. Writing in the *Herald*, Iain Lawson attacked what he called a 'dilution of policy',[68] while Jim Sillars – still 'fighting for independence' according to his byline – used his column in the *Scottish Sun* to declare that 'Nothing more stupid has ever emerged from the mind and tongue of any SNP leader in the party's history'. 'Far from being a stroke of strategic genius,' he stormed, 'it will neuter the independence movement for years to come, debilitate the SNP membership – and it won't work.'[69]

Unable to contain his usual cool, Salmond likened Sillars to 'an old volcano – each eruption is less significant than the last', while describing

Lawson as a 'cross the SNP has to bear'. 'There is no major policy division of any kind,' he argued, 'just a small disagreement on tactics.'[70] Nevertheless, that 'small disagreement' resulted in what was effectively a vote of confidence at the next meeting of the SNP's NEC. Salmond won by 17 votes to 6, which he described as a 'fairly resounding endorsement'. 'In a sometimes heated meeting,' reported *Scotland on Sunday*, 'one executive member even produced a thesaurus to challenge the interpretation of some comments.'[71]

Normally reluctant to pick a fight with his party, Salmond had calculated in this instance that it was necessary to shift its line on devolution, however subtly, although on other matters, such as the SNP's hostility towards NATO, he remained reluctant to instigate reform. 'If he thinks the time isn't right to do anything you cannot make him do anything,' reflected Mike Russell in 2001. 'I have a feeling at some points that his touch on the party was too light; he has a heavy touch on those around him and the structures around them, but he was curiously reluctant at times to have a heavier touch on the party itself which I think is a very interesting aspect of his character.'[72]

In this instant, however, Salmond's heavier touch not only got him off Labour's constitutional hook during a head-to-head debate at Edinburgh's Old Royal High School with the Shadow Scottish Secretary George Robertson, but it handed him an unexpected political gift. It began with a brilliantly simple question from a lady in the audience by the name of Lorraine Mann. 'We all know what the first choice of you gentlemen is, between independence, devolution and the status quo,' she said. 'But what's your second choice?' 'A small, cruel smile appeared on Salmond's face,' observed Neal Ascherson. 'The question, naturally, gave him no problems: his second choice was devolution, as a stepping-stone towards independence. Then he turned to enjoy the spectacle of George Robertson under torture.'[73]

In an obvious quandary, Robertson accused Mann of asking an 'SNP trap question', and replied only that the status quo was 'unacceptable'. His interrogator, however, bridled and insisted she was a floating voter, saying: 'I am the sort of person you need to convince.'[74] 'There has been some surprise expressed that Ian Lang isn't here tonight,' remarked Salmond, moving in for the kill. 'He doesn't have to be because George Robertson has used most of his best lines.'[75]

Salmond went on to score several other debating points. 'That didn't necessarily mean he had the stronger arguments,' observed Andrew Marr the following day. 'Alex Salmond sounded weakest to me when he was trying to explain why the Scots should not try out a devolved parliament and take a careful, step-by-step approach. But he was the better and better-briefed debater who came complete with props, fast quips and killer statistics. He also was supported by the most vocal and sharpest section of the audience . . . Using the crude barometer of applause, heckles, cries of derision and a quick straw poll, the Scottish National Party leader clearly won with the majority of the 300-strong audience.' [76] The fact was that Salmond sounded weak because, in truth, he agreed with devolution as a first step but still felt unable to push the SNP into unequivocal backing for a half-way house. Once again buoyed up by success in a public debate, however, he then geared up for two more elections, to Scotland's new unitary local authorities and in the Perth and Kinross by-election due on 25 May.

The council election campaign was memorable for what Salmond dubbed the 'Great *Panorama* farce', in which the SNP, Labour and Liberal Democrats threatened legal action to prevent the BBC broadcasting a *Panorama* interview with John Major on the eve of polling day, claiming it would prejudice voting in Scotland. In this instant, however, Salmond was curiously unwilling to push the issue. The Scottish Liberal Democrat leader Jim Wallace had a clear memory of Labour's George Robertson being keen to press ahead with a legal challenge, but not Salmond, 'because I suspect he didn't think we'd win'.[77] They did, the Court of Session banning the broadcast in a ruling cited by Salmond 15 years later in the midst of another row over television coverage during an election.

In the event, however, the SNP vote actually slipped slightly, from the 26.8 per cent secured at the previous year's regional council elections to 26.2 per cent, although its 181 seats and control of the new Perth & Kinross and Angus Councils provided a useful distraction. And while the party once again came second, there was no breakthrough – at which previous election results in Monklands hinted – in Labour's heartlands.

The party performed much better, paradoxically, in rural Perthshire, which had been solidly Tory for much of the previous century. After a difficult selection contest involving tabloid revelations about Roseanna Cunningham, she was eventually chosen as the SNP candidate. Another contemporary of Salmond's from the 79 Group, Cunningham was, in the words of one newspaper, a 'left-wing republican feminist'. She was also articulate, striking and a talented campaigner. 'Our candidate has got grace,' said Salmond, as well as 'true grit' and 'gumption'; she was not, he added, 'anybody's else's clone'.[78] The result was an 11.6 per cent swing and a 7,311 majority over Labour's Douglas Alexander.

Although he was certainly not a republican, Salmond had recently launched a strong attack on anti-Catholic bias in the British constitution as part of his continuing mission to detoxify the SNP. The fact that no Catholic could take the throne or marry the heir to it, he told an audience in Stirling, was 'a scandal of immense proportions'.[79] In a lecture at St Mac Nissi's College in County Antrim a few months later, Salmond also sought to flesh out his hitherto technocratic vision of independence: 'At its narrowest, the Scottish Question is the matter of the constitution – the matter of the failure of successive British Governments to address adequately the needs of the ancient European nation of Scotland ... But the Scottish Question is much more than simply that of constitutional government and the correcting of the democratic deficit. The Scottish question ties together all aspects of our lives, and poses the most fundamental of enquiries: where are we going as a nation, and how can we get there together?'[80]

This was something, to be fair, Salmond would try to address in the run-up to the election, although often he felt more comfortable approaching the 'Scottish question' from a clever, if intellectually hollow, angle. There was, for example, a long-running campaign to bully John Major into agreeing or disagreeing with a passage in his predecessor's memoirs (published in 1993), which stated that as a nation, the Scots had 'an undoubted right to self-determination; thus far they have exercised that right by joining and remaining in the Union. Should they determine on independence, no English party or politician would stand in their way, however much we might regret their departure.'

'It was rather more clear and more dignified than anything she had said while in office,' wrote Salmond in the Herald, 'and it started for me a 14-month paper chase as I tried to get the present Prime Minister to endorse the wise words.' Eventually, Major admitted his position was 'essentially the same' as that of Baroness Thatcher. His stance, of course, was self-evidently true but, sensing Major's discomfort, Salmond had moved in for the kill and won a minor political victory. What he failed to explain was why, despite all the supposed faults of the Thatcher and Major governments (not to forget Tony Blair's opposition), Scots still showed no inclination to, in Lady Thatcher's words, 'determine on independence'.

With Tony Blair, Salmond had a curious relationship. In one *Herald* column he praised the Labour leader as 'both an intelligent and engaging politician' who 'handles interviews with style and aplomb . . . Normally he appears like a political general in full command of his forces',[81] but a couple of months later Salmond's attitude had hardened. 'Although I have always found him personally engaging and talented I have never had much time for Tony Blair's politics,' he wrote. 'For some considerable period before the awful truth dawned on sections of his own party, Blair struck me as someone who would be perfectly comfortable leading a post-Thatcher Conservative Party.'[82]

The two leaders had more in common than either would have cared to admit. Both had begun their political careers on the left of their respective parties before reaching the view that only by shedding left-wing shibboleths and modernising their parties could they hope to expand their support. Although there was no real equivalent of Labour's 'Clause 4 moment' for SNP, many of Salmond's pre-1994 reforms anticipated Blair's own approach on becoming leader. There were also striking similarities between both leaders' handling of political presentation, party management and the use of media professionals to hone their respective messages. In short, both men wanted to turn their parties from election losers into election winners.

Salmond reflected on Blair's battle to rid his party of its Clause 4:

Although political leaders have a right – perhaps even a responsibility – to shape the future of the party they lead, 'that right is not an arbitrary or exclusive one. It certainly does not give the leader a special purchase over a party's collective past. No leader starts with a blank sheet of paper and no leader should have the arrogance to believe that he does, or behave as if he did. No leader can attempt to change the essence of a party without very careful consultation and recognition of the shared ownership of the party and its traditions. There is nothing so sensitive, so morale-sapping or so potentially destructive as desperately trying to buy the political future by selling the party's political inheritance.[83]

That, of course, is precisely what many of Salmond's opponents believed he was attempting to do with the SNP, although these remarks demonstrated a sincere belief that his reforms were firmly in keeping with the traditions of his party, as, no doubt, believed Blair of his.

Salmond's diligent courting of Scotland's business community also echoed Labour's so-called 'prawn cocktail offensive' in the City of

London. In July 1995 he told Edinburgh's Chamber of Commerce what independence would mean for them, while his Oban speech the previous year had already done much to reassure business that the SNP was not the tax-and-spend, public-sector orientated party of old. Finally, Salmond's language was not dissimilar to that of the new Blairite class. 'People's confidence and ambition grows if you help them to join in,' he said in September 1995. 'We must encourage and enrol, not set up barriers and artificial tests. In politics the party that does the first achieves its aims. A party that does the second stays second.'[84]

In the run-up to the 1995 SNP conference, meanwhile, Kenny MacAskill – bidding to become party treasurer – attacked the leadership for spending too much time reacting to the Labour Party and not enough campaigning for independence. Salmond responded by attacking 'a small minority of big egos' on the NEC, which he contrasted unfavourably with a 'Scottish cabinet' busy discussing economic policy. He added: 'People are engaged in internal elections at the moment. Therefore they get excited and that's perhaps understandable. But they have to remember the overall obligation they have to the party in how they conduct themselves in election campaigns and that applies to all candidates. Five years ago, Margaret Ewing and I conducted an election for the leadership of the SNP which, for at least the two of us, was a credit to the SNP, and the election campaigns should be conducted as far as possible in that spirit.'

Salmond refused to comment on reports that the SNP had a deficit of around £85,000 (the party, he pointed out, had fought five elections over the past 17 months), although he did rebut MacAskill's criticism of Mike Russell's appointment at a cost of £30,000 a year. 'Changes were made,' said an irritated Salmond. 'They were vindicated by the Perth and Kinross by-election.'[85] Some Nationalists were perhaps suspicious of Russell solely because Salmond appeared to rely upon him so much. One commentator remarked upon 'the lack of strength in depth at a senior level within the party. There are few big hitters intellectually or politically on to whose shoulders Mr Salmond can shed some of the load.'[86] Always a loner and seemingly at odds with some of his party's biggest personalities, Salmond jealously guarded the few confidantes he possessed.

Salmond also faced growing discontent about his change of tack over devolution. Alex Neil and Christine Creech (later, as Christine Grahame, an MSP) reiterated that the SNP ought to aim for independence 'in one go', Creech claiming that devolution could delay it for a 'century or so'. In a carefully worded speech Gordon Wilson also doubted progress towards independence. 'Because the SNP has been so successful in the day-to-day dogfight of political warfare,' he said, 'it has failed to communicate a wider vision. The party should go to first principles to put its case.'[87]

Salmond's view, as articulated in a recent newspaper article, remained unchanged. 'Devolution in any form will not solve Scotland's problems,' he wrote, but 'Suicide for the SNP would lie in either the devolutionist or absolutist approach. In the first we would repeat the errors of the Seventies. In the second we would be derelict of our cause by failing to address the way in which independence could be achieved despite our opponents.'[88] It was Salmond's allusion to the 'errors of the Seventies' that riled more articulate opponents of his gradualist strategy such as the former deputy leader Jim Fairlie. Although he had left the SNP in the early 1990s, Fairlie called Salmond's historical account 'absolute trash': 'Salmond is wrong to believe that devolution will lead to independence. The real tactical error is in committing the SNP to supporting a devolution bill in the House of Commons ... Salmond is now in exactly the same spot and subject to making the same uncomfortable compromises with which the leadership were faced in the 1970s.' 'Salmond calls the "New Gradualist" approach the "Highway to Independence",' concluded Fairlie. 'Scots are more likely find it another cul-de-sac where they will be allowed to debate endlessly while the English decide. There is nothing unusual about that, it is just a gey queer Nationalist who would advocate it.'[89]

Nor was that 'gey queer Nationalist' swayed when two key opponents of the New Gradualism, Alex Neil and Kenny MacAskill, were elected head of policy and treasurer, respectively, at the Perth conference. On the contrary, he almost deliberately provoked them by speculating about a realignment of Scottish politics (a Salmond goal since the early 1980s) within a devolved parliament. 'I think we might see a realignment which puts the Unionists like George Robertson and Michael Forsyth on one side', he said, 'and those arguing for self-determination on the other. If we do not win an absolute majority, there are people, like Dennis Canavan for example, who in the Scottish context would find the principled position we are adopting more attractive than the position of someone like George Robertson. The SNP has to be big enough to say "if you want to journey along with us, then we're prepared to open out the hand of friendship to you".'[90]

Salmond's remarks followed a speech by the former SNP MP George Reid, who had returned to frontline politics following a career with the

International Red Cross, in which he had urged the party to consider working with Labour in an Edinburgh assembly, citing similar coalitions in other European nations. What might have been a tricky conference for Salmond in light of his controversial *Scotland on Sunday* interview was also saved by an opinion poll in the *Herald* that put the SNP at around 30 per cent. If the 'New Gradualism' was good enough for the electorate, Salmond was able to argue, then it ought to be good enough for the party.

Beyond the usual jousting between gradualists and fundamentalists, Salmond's conference speech had capitalised unashamedly upon the recent success of Mel Gibson's William Wallace biopic *Braveheart*, having apparently conquered his previous embarrassment at the 'SNP's annual, flag-waving, bagpipe-playing rally at Bannockburn'.[91] 'Wallace is an inspirational story,' he told delegates. 'Chambers dictionary described him as the founder of Scottish nationalism. Obviously he wasn't, as the Scottish nation was developing before him, but the ... SNP ain't going to disavow William Wallace. I studied this period. I am well aware, as most people are, of the Hollywood history – the inaccuracies in the film – but what you are looking for is the essence of the story. The essence of the story seems to me to come over very strongly.' In a revealing analogy, Salmond said the real villains of the story were the Scottish nobility. 'I'm sure we've all got candidates as to who modern counterparts might be.'

Instead of sheltering from fears among sections of the electorate about what independence might mean, Salmond said he wanted 'to drag them into the open'. 'Let's expose these fears to a bit of sunlight ... a bit like Dracula, they're dissolving as they are dragged in to the sun. So don't hide from fears, debate them. The same with the economic fears and smears, let's debate them openly.'[92]

Salmond's preferred method of dealing with those 'economic smears and fears' was regularly to cite Ireland as a template for an independent Scotland. 'I am very, very influenced by Ireland,' he admitted in 1997. 'Scottish families often know at first hand how well Ireland is doing.'[93] A *Herald* column in March 1996 ('Unleash the power to create our own tiger economy') had also found him in full flow, extolling the many economic virtues of the Emerald Isle before concluding: 'Ireland has only one striking difference from Scotland: it is no longer ruled from London. With the advantage of full independent membership of the European Union it has used that membership to attract resources and invest in the future. And it has used its sovereignty to develop and apply

policies that first of all benefit its own people and its own country.' This
was, of course, a simplification of recent Irish history. Salmond did not
mention the economic and social stagnation that lasted from the grant-
ing of dominion status in 1922 until membership of the European
Community in the early 1970s. Instead, he emphasised the 'difference
between the status quo, devolution, and independence'. 'Power is the
difference – power that can create jobs and prosperity,' he wrote. 'We
will be better off with independence – and Ireland proves it.'[94]

As *The Economist* observed in April 1996,

> Holding Ireland up as a model not only makes the case for Scottish inde-
> pendence more plausible to the outside world, it could also pay political
> dividends at home in Scotland.
>   Scottish working-class who are mostly of Irish origin [*sic*], have always
> been hostile to the SNP, fearing that an independent Scotland would be
> Protestant and anti-Catholic. Poverty has also glued them to Labour. Mr
> Salmond hopes that his admiration of Ireland and his efforts to assure
> Catholics of the SNP's anti-sectarian credentials (he writes a column in
> the Glasgow diocese's monthly newspaper) may woo some away from
> Labour.[95]

Thus two separate strategies neatly dovetailed, while the Irish model also
filled some of the gap left by the gradual neglect of the once-mighty
'independence in Europe' cry. Since the European summit in Edinburgh
in 1992 the SNP had failed to deal with the post-Maastricht development
of the reformed and renamed European Union (EU), not to mention the
electorate's Euro-sceptic turn, and had been less willing to advance pro-
European arguments as a result. What seemed positive and forward looking
in the late 1980s now appeared negative and regressive. 'The SNP's real
problem about Europe has been one of political and intellectual leadership,' judged the academic Peter Lynch in September 1995. 'Put simply,
the SNP has not given much thought to the European Union since Maastricht. In the late 1980s, it was Jim Sillars who would have seized these
opportunities. Who will fill his shoes in the mid-1990s is less clear.'[96]

It was a fair criticism. 'Independence in Europe' had never been
much more than a slogan, a tactic which shot the Labour fox, for
Salmond, and slogans – however cleverly crafted – were difficult to
adapt when political circumstances changed. Ireland was much more
attractive, and rewarded Salmond's interest with invitations to speak at
seminars and summer schools (he visited Ireland six times in 1996–97).

Speaking at one in Ballina, County Mayo, in the summer of 1996, he contrasted Ireland's growth-rate of between 8–12 per cent with Scotland and the UK's annual 2 per cent, concluding that Scotland ('Europe's invisible nation', in Christopher Harvie's phrase) was being stifled by 'the dead hand of Westminster'.[97] Such talk obviously went down well in a nation that had shaken off that 'dead hand' more than 75 years earlier.

Salmond also developed the economic case for independence in other areas. Michael Forsyth, Scottish Secretary since 1995, had recently published Government Expenditure and Revenue in Scotland, or GERS, statistics to demonstrate that high public spending north of the Border amounted to a direct subsidy from the Treasury. This dovetailed with John Major's regular invocation of the benefits of the Union. 'There is no doubt about the advantages, both to the UK and to Scotland, of Scotland being a full part of the UK,' he said during Prime Minister's Questions in early 1995, prompting a noisy interruption from Salmond. 'The hon. Member for Banff and Buchan clearly has not studied it [the benefits] because he does doubt that,' stormed Major, turning on Salmond: 'That is because he wants an independent Scotland disunited from the UK, in the middle of a European Union where it would have little or no influence, and that would damage the interests of Scots, the interests of Scotland and the wider interests of the UK. That is why his party must never be put in power in any way in Scotland or elsewhere.'[98]

Sensing that this sort of attack touched a nerve, Salmond stepped up his efforts to scrutinise the GERS figures and therefore expose them as bogus, recruiting a young civil service economist called Andrew Wilson to the SNP's full-time research staff in Edinburgh. Having worked for the Scottish Office in Edinburgh, Wilson knew how it operated and set out to pre-empt the next edition of GERS by producing the SNP's own version, backdated through the oil-rich years to produce very different results. He recalled:

We spent a lot of time tabling Parliamentary Questions to the Treasury via Andrew Welsh on the deficit question. William Waldegrave was chief secretary to the Treasury and I'd asked about the deficit going all the way back to 1978 and for some reason the Treasury had responded, effectively conceding that Scotland would have been in surplus had it been independent. The *Herald* splashed on this and Alex was delighted. Then Michael Forsyth came back with quite a clever retort questioning the

methodology, but when I tabled some more questions, thinking I was
being clever, Salmond at first gave me a bollocking ('never underestimate
how clever your opponents are, these are serious people') until the
responses, which actually strengthened our position, came chuntering
out of the fax machine. He just looked at me and said 'you were lucky'.[99]

That Salmond took care to promote Wilson as the economic marksman
behind the GERS ammunition, rather than himself, also demonstrated his
generosity when it came to encouraging young political talent, although
they hard to work incredibly hard in return. 'He pushed us all so hard that
it actually caused angst,' recalled one bright young thing based at Westminster. 'It was great for us, as we were all given an enormous boost by
working closely with Alex but the party at large got hacked off about that,
thinking "we've been campaigning for 20 years" and who are these bright
young things he's surrounding himself with.'[100]

Even Treasury figures and bright young economists, however, did not
appease all the SNP's critics. In the run-up to the election, for example,
the Liberal Democrats published a pamphlet entitled *Alex in Wonderland*,
which rubbished a series of Economic Policy Papers published by the
SNP under the banner 'For the Good of Scotland'. Although it recognised that independence was 'a perfectly legitimate aspiration', it
questioned the SNP's commitment to spending 'huge amounts of additional money', paid for 'by the revenues from an exogenous boost to the
Scottish Economy arising from Independence'.[101]

In June 1996, meanwhile, the Leader of the Opposition also dropped
a constitutional bombshell upon which Salmond was quick to leap.
Tony Blair announced that before establishing a Scottish Parliament, a
Labour government would hold a two-question referendum on devolution, a reversal of the party's existing policy that prompted the
resignation of several front bench spokesmen including the Dundee MP
John McAllion. 'For years Labour have said that a referendum was
totally unnecessary since the constitution would be centre stage in a
general election, but they are now set to do a cynical U-turn under
Tory pressure,' blasted Salmond. 'Tory pressure is dictating new Labour
policy on the constitution.'[102] As the SNP had long argued, Labour
could not be trusted with Scotland's constitutional future.

In truth, however, the U-turn put Salmond in an awkward political
position. 'How will you urge SNP supporters to vote in the referendum?' soon became a question he could not avoid. Initially, Salmond
simply refused to answer, knowing how divisive the issue remained

within his party, while preparing privately for the inevitable. The 1979 debacle still loomed large, yet the dynamic was palpably different. Not only was there greater public support for devolution in 1996 than there had been in 1979, but on offer was a more cohesive, powerful settlement. Crucially, and Salmond undoubtedly sensed this, the political climate was such that it would pay political dividends for him and the SNP to appear ecumenical.

Publicly, however, Salmond kept his cards close to his chest and simply repeated that until the general election the SNP would not state its view on what he described as a 'rigged referendum', exactly how he had always referred to the 1979 ballot. Nevertheless, with the SNP doing well in opinion polls, Salmond was upbeat as he geared up for his last conference before the imminent general election. 'We're cooking with gas,' he told Arnold Kemp. 'This is the best we've been going into a conference. At the last election, the SNP fought an all-or-nothing campaign. This time it's an all-or-something campaign.'[103] It was also clear that he intended to avoid the mistakes of the 1992 campaign, focusing on around a dozen marginal seats instead of spreading resources thinly across as many as possible. A combination of donations, bequests and celebrity donations (most notably from Sean Connery) also meant the SNP's election fund stood at £500,000, instead of £100,000 as in 1992.

'I think we're close,' Salmond told the *Toronto Star*. 'In fact, I think we're very close.' 'Since the 1992 election,' he added, 'we've concentrated not just on being a political party, but on shaping a movement.'[104] That civic Nationalist 'movement' now included Pensioners for Independence, Business for Scotland and New Scots for Independence. 'Part of the project of my leadership of the SNP has been to accommodate legitimate concerns that people have,' he said. 'People felt excluded from the national movement, sometimes by perception because the SNP hadn't tried hard enough.'[105] Perhaps the most important, in Salmond's mind, of the new internal groupings were Scots Asians for Independence. 'It is the members of Scotland's Asian communities who are, in many ways, the most patriotic of all Scots,' wrote Salmond the following year. 'Nor do I find this completely surprising. Many have direct family experience of self-determination struggles, and they appreciate the dignity and promise which Independence brings.'[106] Another Salmond refrain at this time was not to blame the English for Scotland's woes. 'I think Scots have a predilection to have a chip on their shoulder,' he said. 'I'm saying we should get the chip off their shoulder. It hasn't always been like that, this phenomenon of the whingeing Scot is a relatively new one.'[107]

Salmond's attempt to present Scottish Nationalism as a positive movement was, however, derailed slightly when, at the 1996 Inverness conference, Alex Neil (still vice-convener for policy) compared George Robertson with the Nazi propagandist Lord Haw-Haw. Salmond had not been in the conference hall for Neil's speech but demanded an apology. 'He was trying to get across the point that George Robertson and many other Unionist politicians run Scotland down,' explained Salmond, having rejected demands to sack Neil. 'He chose an unfortunate way to do it. That's over.'

Lasting damage was, fortunately for Salmond, minimal, while he recovered ground with another successful conference speech in which he issued a 'come and join us' call to all those who wanted change in Scotland. 'I have the greatest sympathy for the thousands of Labour and Tory voters in Scotland who have stuck by their parties through thick and thin because they believed that those parties would help Scotland and our people,' Salmond told delegates. 'But the reality now is that each of them is exposed as being, in policy and presentation, totally London-dominated. It is the Westminster game that counts for the Unionist parties.'[108]

'What makes Alex Salmond tick?' asked *Scotland on Sunday* at the beginning of 1997, answering with a quote from a recent Salmond interview: 'Some people can look at a picture and recreate it, capture in their mind a flower or a mountain – I've always been able to capture a row of figures.'[109] The comment, judged the newspaper, summed up Salmond's greatest strength, his command of economic statistics, and also his biggest weakness, a perception that he was little more than a political number cruncher with no real vision or passion. This could be termed the Sillars critique. 'Alex's interest is in political tactics but he doesn't get angry about unemployment,' he was to say in 2009. 'He knows he has to be but there's no authenticity there.'[110]

While that was undoubtedly the view of some in the SNP, Salmond's relationship with his party had changed significantly over the past six years. 'Salmond is more relaxed now than ever he was,' observed the academic James Mitchell. 'This is largely because, with Sillars gone, he is in undisputed control of his own party. When first elected leader, the party had respect for him. Now there's an affection as well, which I never thought would happen, frankly. That has changed the relationship not only with the party but also with the audience outside.' That audience had recently watched Salmond take part in a television debate about the monarchy, generating a notably positive reaction among English viewers. An internal Labour survey, meanwhile, revealed that most Scots 'accepted without question that he [Salmond] understands the Scottish psyche', while a *Scotsman*/ICM poll in February also ranked him as the 'toughest' of Scotland's four party leaders.

There was, nevertheless, another public perception of Salmond as 'Smart Alex', an undoubtedly clever politician who was perhaps a little too aware of his own talents. This he had managed to control, particularly at the 1996 conference, although not his temper, 'which as any senior party official or activist will privately testify, is notoriously short'. 'Both the Tories and the Labour party are aware that when they encounter Salmond in public debate their main job is to rile him into an angry outburst,' said one observer. 'An angry Salmond who has lost the rag is not a voter-friendly sight.'[111]

With less than four months until an important election, however, Salmond had to keep his cool as he dealt with the referendum question. Speaking in Brussels on 30 January he said the SNP would 'not obstruct devolution', comments Mike Russell felt compelled to play down as simply 're-stating party policy'.[112] 'The SNP have had as policy since 1983 the clear position that we have independence at the centre and heart of our campaigns,' explained Salmond the following day. 'The policy asserts the primacy of independence, while not obstructing devolution.'[113] Such would be the line until polling day, although Salmond continued to doubt Labour's sincerity on devolution. 'If Scotland votes yes in Labour's proposed referendum, the election to the assembly would take place mid-way through a Westminster government a couple of years from now,' he said. 'The chances of an SNP majority is one reason I seriously doubt there's any real intention on the part of the Labour leadership to fulfill their commitment.'[114]

'Returning from a huge meeting in Crieff,' wrote Salmond in early April. 'I catch sight of the Hale-Bopp comet, lighting the sky above the Wallace Monument. This, I decide, must be an omen for the campaign.'[115] The theme of that campaign was, anticipating Barack Obama in 2008, 'Yes We Can'. 'Our message to the Scottish people is: "Yes, we can win the best future for Scotland",' said Salmond at its launch. 'We are better organised, better financed and more solidly based than ever before and our freedom message will prosper between now and polling day.'[116]

Tony Blair had recently handed Salmond a political gift by comparing the powers of his proposed Scottish parliament to that of an English parish council. 'Out of the mouth of King Blair have come the words I've been trying to get into the Scottish consciousness for some considerable time,' Salmond told the journalist Hugo Young. 'He's a marvellous man.' Blair had also proclaimed that 'sovereignty rests with me as an English MP'. 'It's megalomania,' added Salmond. 'He didn't even say the Queen in Parliament!'[117]

Launching the SNP's manifesto a few days later, Salmond wisely refused to predict how many seats the party would win, or when Scotland would achieve independence. 'The SNP have established themselves as Scotland's second party,' he said. 'We're going into the general election campaign trying desperately to become the first party of Scotland.'[118] The lessons of 1992 had, of course, been learned. Salmond presented the manifesto as a combination of prosperity and social justice, enterprise and compassion, head and heart. 'The SNP's vision is of an enterprise economy and a compassionate society,' he had said the previous month, 'both going hand in hand with the other.'[119] It was a positive, upbeat campaign which appeared to be vindicated when a *Sunday Times* poll towards the end of April put the SNP at 28 per cent, rising to 38 per cent when people were asked how they would vote in elections for a Scottish parliament, its highest-ever opinion poll rating. Salmond placed a £500 charity bet that the SNP would win between 7 and 40 seats. William Hill's agreed to donate at evens; if successful, Salmond's winnings were destined for *The Big Issue* magazine.

The sole gaffe of the campaign, oddly enough, concerned Salmond's mother Mary. 'People across the political spectrum in Scotland', he said at a press conference in London, 'including my mother who has voted Tory since 1945 – believe Cedric Brown [the head of British Gas] should be contributing a bit more', thus revealing for the first time that Mrs Salmond had been a lifelong Conservative. Seeking to manage the situation, Salmond then issued a press release, purporting to be from his mother, which said she was concerned about 'fat cat salary awards and corporate greed at a time when vital services like health and education are being starved of funds'. 'I think people like Cedric Brown, the greatest fat cat of them all, should be asked to pay a little bit more to keep society together,' Mary Salmond's statement continued. 'Therefore, for the first time in my married life, I will be voting the same way as my husband.' That was, of course, SNP.

Not only was the language rather unconvincing, but when door-stepped by a reporter several hours later, it became clear that no one had informed Mary Salmond of her new voting intentions. 'I'll make up my own mind on the day when I cross the road to the polling station,' she said at her home in Linlithgow. 'I'm not a political person to be perfectly honest, just a busy little housewife who prefers fresh-air, the countryside and a bit of gardening.' There was, at least, an endorsement of sorts. 'If I was in Alex's constituency,' added Mary, 'I would definitely vote for him because I think he is a superb MP and I think he listens to people.'[120] Always protective of his family, Salmond was genuinely annoyed that the *Daily Record* had involved his mother in the campaign. He remained close to his parents, first-footing them each Hogmanay as he and Moira saw in the New Year at their home in Linlithgow. 'In the ensuing parties, faither is prevailed upon to sing the Red Flag,' Salmond had written as 1997 dawned. 'He knows every verse, and is word-perfect – more than can be said for Tony Blair.'[121]

The incident with Mary Salmond, however, was but a minor distraction from a broadly successful campaign, which must have made the result on 1 May even more disappointing. 'I have said it before, but the days of boom-and-bust nationalism are over,' Salmond had commented the previous September. 'I'm fed up with going up like a rocket and down like a stick. In the last period I have tried to build on pretty solid foundations. Inspiration is important in politics, but perspiration is vital as well, and the SNP has never been short of both.'[122]

But despite blood, sweat and tears, the SNP got just 22.1 per cent of the vote, representing only a modest improvement upon the 21.5 per cent of 1992; although this time it was masked by an increase in seats from three to six. Not only did Roseanna Cunningham achieve a Nationalist first by consolidating her 1995 by-election gain in Perth and Kinross, but the party also gained Tayside North (John Swinney) and Galloway & Upper Nithsdale (Alasdair Morgan), largely due to a collapse in the Conservative vote that left Scotland a Tory-free zone. Closer analysis, however, revealed that the SNP had lost ground in Scotland's four cities while at least holding their vote share in most other areas. Banff and Buchan, as ever, was the exception to the rule. There, Salmond's majority nearly trebled to 12,845:

Alex Salmond (SNP)	22,409
William Frain-Bell (Conservative)	9,564
Megan Harris (Labour)	4,747
Neil Fletcher (Lib Dem)	2,398
Alan Buchan (Referendum)	1,060

The overall result encapsulated the paradox of the first phase of Salmond's leadership, and perhaps of his whole career. Although the 1990s were to some extent the Salmond decade, in which the SNP's new young leader slowly transformed his party into a mainstream political force, electoral reward was patchy (the 1994 European elections representing the high watermark) and, if gauged between the 1992 and 1997 general elections, modest to the point of being non-existent. Salmond's personality, media performance and work ethic had propelled him and the SNP to a new level of political prominence, but frustratingly for both, there had been no corresponding change in voting patterns.

Salmond's achievements, therefore, were both personal and politically subtle. Not only had he successfully altered the parameters of political debate within the UK, he had – after an uncertain start – stamped his authority on the SNP. As in the first few years of Robert Bruce's kingdom, Salmond's authority had constantly been challenged. Bravely, therefore, he had consistently pushed his party, nudging it into gradualist (but still pro-independence) positions it did not necessarily like, while rebranding its political ideology and transforming its organisational capacity. Most importantly, perceptions of the SNP had shifted substantially since 1992, and if that did not produce immediate electoral dividends then Salmond's considerable self-confidence had not necessarily suffered. 'I am the eternal optimist,' he had remarked as the SNP celebrated its diamond jubilee in April 1994, 'always hopeful that trumps are about to be revealed, and just occasionally they are.'[123]

Chapter 8

'THE SPIRIT OF 97'

The mair they talk, I'm kent the better,
E'en let them clash;
An auld wife's tongue's a feckless matter
To gie ane fash.

'A Poet's Welcome To His Love
Begotten Daughter' by Robert Burns

With a landslide Labour victory, a devolved Scottish Parliament was by May 1997 an imminent reality rather than an esoteric dream. That real-politik, meanwhile, transformed the dynamic of Scottish politics, and therefore also within the Scottish National Party. As Alex Salmond later wrote, 'theory confronted practice and the SNP had to confront the reality of a devolution referendum'.[1] Ironically, the SNP's modest performance in the election ('a sobering lesson on how realistic objectives bring real polit-ical reward'[2]) actually strengthened Salmond's hand in working with the new government when it came to the forthcoming referendum.

The weeks following polling day, however, did not show a naturally disappointed Salmond at his best. Beyond the usual talking up of a modest result ('The SNP have made advances in terms of seats and votes, making the 1997 general election one of the most successful ever'[3]), he ignored the outcome completely in his first *Herald* column after polling day, instead launching a rather silly attack on Brian Wilson, his arch-nemesis since 1979, whom he claimed intended to scupper devolution from his new ministerial berth at the Scottish Office. 'The new Labour team at St Andrews House', said Salmond in another broadside the following week, 'seem to have hit the ground dawdling instead of sprinting.'[4]

That charge was unfair, but Salmond's suspicion had been fuelled by recent statements from Wilson to the effect that any move towards full

independence would be via Westminster rather than through the Scottish Parliament. Salmond and Mike Russell, who began talks with
Scottish Office ministers soon after the election, feared any such caveat
in the devolution white paper would amount to a 'glass ceiling', thus
making formal SNP support in a referendum campaign impossible.

Given the subtleties involved, the appointment of Donald Dewar as
Secretary of State for Scotland, rather than the less sympathetic George
Robertson, had been an important development. Brian Wilson's view
was that there was no need to formally invite Salmond back inside the
'devolution tent' which, ironically, Wilson had reluctantly entered via
the Scottish Constitutional Convention (SCC), from which the SNP
had abstained. 'I was strongly of the view that Donald should resist this
in order to maintain a clear distinction between what Labour was offering and what Salmond was after,' recalled Wilson. He added:

> Donald, and even more so, Gordon Brown, were terrified of losing the
> referendum – hence the rush to get the Bill through and hold it as quickly
> as possible off the back of Labour's election victory. Donald was persuaded
> that they needed the Nats' support in order to deliver a 'yes' vote. I argued
> that they would get that support anyway because, when it came to the bit,
> SNP voters were not going to sit on their hands when it came to a refer-
> endum on a Scottish Parliament. What we should not do was welcome
> Salmond back like the prodigal son and allow him to pretend forever
> thereafter that he had not contributed nothing but abuse to the process
> leading to devolution via the Constitutional Convention.[5]

Wilson had a point – Salmond had, for obvious reasons, airbrushed the
SCC from his political CV – but even so, Dewar's inclination towards
a bigger tent prevailed. Tactically, for the SNP, it was also a no-brainer.
Campaigning for a 'no-no' vote was out of the question; campaigning
'yes-no' on the grounds that the fiscal powers were inadequate was
untenable; while urging SNP supporters to write 'independence' on
their ballot papers would have looked absurd (although that is precisely
what SNP activist Christine Creech proposed to do). Therefore,
concluded Salmond, 'The most important thing was to get the Secretary of State as saying quite unequivocally that if the people of Scotland
wish to move to independence through their default Parliament then
that's exactly what they could do'.[6]

Dewar did just that in the House of Commons on 21 May 1997: 'Even
though the hon. Gentleman and I may have differences of interpretation,

I hope that he will accept that I should be the last to challenge the sovereignty of the people or to deny them the right to opt for any solution to the constitutional question which they wished. For example, if they want to go for independence, I see no reason why they should not do so. In fact, if they want to, they should. I should be the first to accept that.'[7] There had been a degree of choreography in this pronouncement, which Dewar reiterated on 4 June and 24 July, but it was enough to satisfy Salmond, who revealed three years later that although he could have pressed for Westminster to cede more economic powers or responsibility for broadcasting, persuaded that Dewar was not in a position to deliver, he had settled for a removal of the 'glass ceiling' instead. 'Instead of going for more powers,' stormed Jim Sillars in response, 'the price he sought and extracted for SNP support was Donald Dewar saying, thrice, that if Scotland votes for independence then it should get it.' Rather than revealing 'a series of his astute manoeuvres in an important period of Scottish history', Salmond had shown 'how the Westminster professionals took the pants off a Scottish amateur. The result: a parliament shorn of power he could have obtained for it. That's his epitaph.'[8]

For Salmond the tricky bit came not with Sillars, but in squaring political realities with Nationalist aspirations. Salmond prepared the ground by holding five secret regional meetings with around 1,000 activists in the weeks following the election, successfully calming the fears of those who still harboured bitter memories of 1979. He later described this process as being 'like therapy',[9] and the therapy worked. Just three days after the devolution white paper was published on 24 July, the SNP's National Executive Committee unanimously endorsed co-operation with 'Scotland Forward', yet another umbrella body charged with delivering a 'yes-yes' vote in the September referendum, and therefore an implicit endorsement of devolution. Putting his usual deft spin on the decision, Salmond said the white paper opened a 'door of opportunity'[10] for the Scottish people to move towards independence. The only dissenting voices were Gordon Wilson, still bearing the scars of 1979, and, less surprisingly, Jim Sillars, who warned of a Labour trap from his *Sun* column.[11]

On 2 August, a Perth National Council endorsed the NEC's decision. It was the vindication of a long-running campaign by Salmond, both before and during his leadership of the party and, for the first time, gave him absolute authority over the SNP. 'It is the time to put the baggage of the 1970s back in the cupboard,' he told constituency representatives. 'This is an historic opportunity and we must seize it. Once

Scots taste power, they will want the whole thing.'[12] As Salmond later reflected: 'We all seem to have become gradualists now.'[13] Later still, he recalled:

> That night [2 August] I reflected hard about the nature of the day's events. Even traditional sceptics about devolution accepted that it was the right decision. No one seriously believed that the SNP could have campaigned for a No-No vote. Only an embittered and estranged Jim Sillars believed that we could call for something as ridiculous as mass abstention. However, there was an enthusiasm about the decision in August 1997 which took even me by surprise. And it was based on more than political calculation. Whatever the ebbs and flows of politics, whatever the intricacies of political debate, when push comes to shove, the SNP delegates will always do the right thing by the people of Scotland.[14]

In short, judged Salmond, the vote had been 'the single most important decision in my tenure of office'.[15]

The relationship between Salmond and Dewar was crucial to the referendum campaign that followed. Despite their political differences, Salmond believed that

> without question Dewar was a Scottish patriot and I like to think it was this desire to do the right thing by Scotland ... which persuaded him to embrace the joint campaign with the SNP' in August and September 1997. He was well aware that the decision created party difficulties for me just as it created internal problems for him. We therefore worked out a position we could adhere to throughout the campaign and one which was based on principle as well as convenience. We both argued that what brought the devolutionist and independence positions into a joint campaign was our overriding belief in the right of the Scottish nation to determine our own constitutional future whatever it may be.

Salmond called this the 'spirit of 97',[16] and indeed the agreement by Labour, the SNP and the Liberal Democrats to put aside their differences and campaign for a 'yes-yes' vote represented a remarkably outbreak of unity given the usual tenor of Scottish politics over the last two decades.

The first Scotland Forward press conference on 19 August, however, was overshadowed by questions arising from the suicide of Paisley South

MP Gordon McMaster almost three weeks before. (McMaster had left a note blaming party colleagues, including the neighbouring MP Tommy Graham, for spreading smears about his private life.) Instead of being impressed by the unprecedented sight of the three party leaders sharing a platform, journalists wanted to know how Labour was going to react. 'At one point, when things were going particularly badly for Dewar,' recalled Salmond. 'I intervened with a totally straight face to point out that all party leaders had to face occasions where natural justice precluded comment.'[17] The referendum campaign would, contrary to what some critics claimed, prove that Salmond was capable of working with other people, and those from different parties at that. He was in no doubt that he was doing the right thing. 'It will be seen as a step forward to a new Scotland,' replied Salmond, when asked how history would judge the referendum experience. 'It won't quite be the light of day – but it will be a New Dawn.'[18]

Then, on 30 August 1997, Diana, Princess of Wales, died following a car accident in Paris, temporarily putting the referendum campaign on hold. 'What we are doing is looking after Saturday', proclaimed Salmond as campaigning resumed, 'and towards the most intensive, active and participative 100 hours of political campaigning in Scottish political history.'[19] Even Sean Connery played a part, taking a boat trip across the Firth of Forth with Gordon Brown, later joining Dewar, Salmond and Wallace at New Parliament House (the proposed location for the Scottish Assembly in 1979), where Connery recited passages from the Declaration of Arbroath. When he reached the passage 'it is not for glory or riches but for liberty alone' Salmond felt the hairs standing up on the back of his neck. 'It had turned out to be the most fruitful day's campaigning of the referendum,' he later assessed. 'However, "Connery Day" was immensely important. It set the tone for the final few days of campaigning where the Yes-Yes camp were totally dominant and the No-No rivals were blown away completely.'[20]

The initiative in involving Connery had come, curiously enough, from Peter Mandelson, a key architect of New Labour and now Minister Without Portfolio in Tony Blair's Cabinet. 'Mandelson believed apparently, that the campaign was in trouble,'[21] recalled Salmond a few years later. Connery and his wife Michelle subsequently had lunch with Dewar and Salmond in a private room at L'Amico, a restaurant on London's Horseferry Road, to discuss Connery's potential role. Much later, when it emerged that Dewar had personally blocked a suggestion to honour Connery with a knighthood, Salmond believed the decision to have been taken before this meeting. 'We sat down to lunch and Donald had already knifed him,' he told the journalist Brian Taylor. 'It was a breach of trust. It was a surprise. I didn't think he would do something like that.'[22] Salmond made it known that the affair had damaged his long-term opinion of Dewar.[23]

None of this, however, was public knowledge at the time. Following the successful 'Connery Day', Salmond, Dewar and Wallace took part in a Scottish TV debate against 'no' campaigners Tam Dalyell, the advocate Donald Findlay and Tory grandee Michael Ancram in front of 600 people at Glenrothes. 'In arguably the best political debate ever screened in Scotland, the outcome was decisive,' judged Salmond. 'Dewar, Wallace and myself performed as if we had been playing on the same team all our days while the "No-men" couldn't get their act together.'[24]

Polling took place on 11 September. 'All day Thursday I was in Banff and Buchan', recounted Salmond in his *Herald* column, 'and while I was as certain as I could be that the first question was won and won well, the second question seemed, at least in some rural areas, to be touch and go.'[25] He need not have worried. More than 74 per cent of Scots backed the first question, that there should be a Scottish Parliament, while 63.5 per cent backed tax-varying powers in the second. Following the official declaration, Salmond and Jim Wallace emerged from the Edinburgh counting centre and punched the air with delight.

Finally, after more than 18 years, the constitutional sins of 1979 had been absolved and Salmond's vigorous pursuit of gradualism vindicated. Writing three years later, Mike Russell reflected that Salmond's role in the referendum campaign 'was his outstanding moment in a decade of many outstanding moments'.[26] Even Jim Sillars praised Salmond's performance as 'brilliant', although he qualified his praise by effectively calling him a quisling. 'It never seems to have struck the SNP that when your generals are given medals by the other side,' he said, referring to the opposition praise heaped upon Salmond, 'they've probably been firing at the wrong targets.'[27]

'We had many planning meetings together in Scotland and London,' recalled Salmond of his dealings with Dewar, 'and I regard that period as one of the most fruitful and productive during my time as leader of the SNP.'[28] The relationship endured long enough for Salmond and his wife to be invited to the Secretary of State's Christmas party later that year. At Bute House, while Salmond was talking to Muir Russell, then permanent secretary at the Scottish Office, he looked around but could not see either

Dewar or Moira. 'Muir said, "They've gone up to the private apart-ments,"' recalled Salmond jokingly. After heading upstairs he discovered them coming out of a cupboard. It was, of course, perfectly innocent; Dewar had merely been showing Moira the Bute House library. 'You want to be careful with Moira,' joked Salmond to the future First Minis-ter. 'You don't realise she's got a measuring tape in her handbag for the curtains.'[29]

The referendum result also provided a perfect backdrop for the SNP's autumn conference. The outcome, said Salmond, had been the 'first, decisive step' towards independence. Scots had 'broken through the biggest psychological barrier,' he added. 'Self-confidence has triumphed over self-doubt. Scotland has crossed the Rubicon.'[30]

Speaking to the *Scotsman* before the conference began, Salmond went out of his way to stress that the SNP would not seek to wreck the new parliament, which he clearly believed was the only political game in town. 'Everything has changed. The gravity of Scottish politics has now shifted,' he said. 'We are now fighting on a Scottish agenda. The key elections are no longer the elections for the next Westminster parliament; the key elections are 1999 and the elections for the Scottish parliament.'

Despite Salmond's tactical triumph vis-à-vis devolution and the referendum campaign, the 1997 conference demonstrated that his rela-tionship with the SNP remained a curious one. A motion demanding a referendum on the monarchy post-independence was imminent, and Salmond was clearly irritated. 'I'm not troubled by it, no,' he protested to the *Scotsman*. 'I think it would be a mistake to move from the posi-tion of the people's monarchy idea as the SNP viewpoint.'[31] This was enshrined in the 1995 paper 'Citizens Not Subjects', a rather curious document that proposed that the Queen would remain head of state but that the speaker of the Scottish Parliament would assume her duties when she was out of the country.

Despite Salmond's best efforts, however, conference voted by 177 votes to 164 to reject his advice that the motion backing a referendum should be sent back to the NEC for further consideration. During the debate, Salmond argued that committing the SNP to fight a 'second referendum [on the monarchy] during the first independence referen-dum ... would be a foolish mistake'. The Perth MP Roseanna Cunningham, however, had other ideas, arguing that not only should the party campaign *for* an elected head of state, but that few activists would openly support the status quo. 'There are gey few of you who would be out there,' she told delegates to rousing applause. 'I know that, you know that, the press know that and the public know that too and most of them think we're already a Republican party and are not bothered about it. We should uphold the two principles of honesty and democracy.'

As usual, Salmond put on a brave face. 'When political leaders insist on having every delegate agree with them on every iota of a party's policy, as some do,' he said, 'that assumes the leader is the only one with any intelligence and that the rest of the party is brain dead.'[32] He took some solace, meanwhile, when an amendment calling for the SNP to campaign openly *against* the monarchy fell following a 208–153 vote.

A couple of months later Salmond also announced, during a dinner hosted by the European Movement, that the SNP would back Scottish membership of the European single currency. 'It is time that those in favour of progress upped the ante and confronted not just the jingoistic Euro-scepticism of the Tory rump in Parliament,' he wrote in the *Scotsman*, 'but also the incompetence of New Labour in government.'[33] Although hardly commented upon at the time, this decision would lead to discontent later on.

It is worth going local for a paragraph, if only to rectify more modest achievements often neglected by political biographies. On 1 October 1997 a fishing trawler called the *Sapphire* sank a few days after sailing from Peterhead in Salmond's constituency, leaving skipper Victor Robertson the only survivor. When the government refused to recover the vessel, families of the victims set up the Sapphire Trust to raise the money, estimated at £380,000, required to hire a giant floating crane to lift the boat from its resting place in 270 feet of water. Salmond was fully involved, drawing upon his formidable skills of networking, cajoling and organisation. The cash was raised in just four days and on 14 December Salmond was with the families as the trawler returned to her home port with the bodies of Bruce Cameron, Victor Podlesny, Adam Stephen and Robert Stephen. 'When we look back, this is an extraordinary story,' he said. 'It is a story of guts, resolution and determination by four families, the like of which I cannot easily remember.'[34]

Less rewarding had been the Paisley South by-election on 6 November sparked by Gordon McMaster's suicide. Despite a swing of 11 per cent to the SNP, its candidate Ian Blackford (who would later fall out, very publicly, with Salmond) failed to take the seat from Labour, whose candidate Douglas Alexander secured it with a comfortable majority of

2,731. The result provoked another attack on Salmond from Jim Sillars. Under the headline 'Go Now, Alex', Sillars blamed Salmond for the 'debacle' in Paisley South, and called for him to resign. 'The abysmal result is a devastating reflection on a man who, on becoming leader, promised independence in a short space of time,' he wrote. 'He's had his time. Now it's time for someone else.' 'Jim's a journalist now and can write what he likes,' Salmond told BBC's *Good Morning Scotland*. 'I just think that Jim's getting a bit crabbit in his old age.' Even so, judged Peter MacMahon in the *Scotsman*, 'for a leader with a degree of control over his party that his predecessors would have envied, it is clear that this kind of criticism from a former colleague still hurts.'[35]

Salmond had always been a gambling man, both personally and politically, and in early 1998 he took over from Robin Cook as the *Herald*'s racing tipster. 'Herald readers should know that I'm starting as the only newspaper tipster in the world with a 100% record,' he joked before his debut column. 'I once tipped Rough Quest in the Grand National for another newspaper and it won and I've never tried again. But I don't expect this record to last much longer.'[36] Any profits from the 'Salmond Selections' were to go to Shelter in Scotland and the Scottish Catholic International Aid Foundation.

Away from the turf, the SNP's internal divisions came back with a vengeance. The catalyst, or so the *Scotsman*'s version of events had it, was the party's failure to submit its accounts to the Neill inquiry into political party funding. It eventually had to disclose its level of donations, including those from Sean Connery, while the lapse was 'passed off as a glitch or an error of communication', the implication being that party treasurer Kenny MacAskill was to blame. Given the well-known differences between MacAskill and Salmond, the *Scotsman* (according to the SNP) ran 'an aggressive' front-page story 'designed to test the internal unity of the party'.

The next morning Mike Russell, the SNP's chief executive, faxed MacAskill's legal practice in Edinburgh suggesting that he make no comment. 'This was designed to ensure that the story was killed off in one day,' explained Salmond's account to the National Council, later leaked to the press. MacAskill was having none of it, accusing Russell of 'spinning' the story to damage him and refusing to rule out speaking to journalists. The situation then deteriorated to such an extent that Salmond 'instructed the staff members involved to make a written record of their conversations with the national treasurer'. MacAskill then spoke to the

Scotsman, his remarks appearing under the headline 'Civil war breaks out in SNP ranks'. The story included criticism of Russell and other senior party officials, whom Salmond ordered not to respond. Salmond also met with MacAskill, who apologised to a number of those named, but not Russell, forcing Salmond – according to his account – to take the matter to the National Council.

The result was the imposition of a strict disciplinary code to avoid further rows, chiefly collective responsibility among office-bearers, a ban on office-bearers impugning the integrity of staff or speaking to the press about party business without either Salmond's permission or that of the vice-convener for publicity. 'Over the course of the next year our party discipline will be tested as never before,' warned Salmond, 'and I have no intention of going into this year fighting front and back.'[37] The National Council backed the three-point code but, as the *Scotsman* observed, it made Salmond's frequent criticism of Tony Blair for not tolerating internal dissent look a little ironic.

There was further in-fighting when Salmond secured the NEC's backing for Russell to stand as a candidate in the forthcoming Scottish Parliament elections despite being a full-time official, a charge of favouritism repeated when Stewart Stevenson's rejection by a candidate vetting committee (by eight votes to one) was overturned on appeal. At a special party conference in Perth in June 1998 Salmond also urged delegates to reject a New Labour-style one-member one-vote system of selecting candidates, claiming it would be cumbersome and open to manipulation. His preferred method was a series of regional selection meetings at which branches and associations with an equal delegate voting entitlement would select party list candidates. It was via this method that Russell was to secure a place on the South of Scotland list. Salmond won this particular battle, although his proposal for 'zipping' party list candidates to ensure an equal number of men and women was defeated. When the journalist Ron Mackenna reminded Salmond that he had 'been accused of a bit of control freakery', his reaction was to exclaim 'Me?' in astonished innocence. 'You don't have to look too far on our candidate list to see a range of people, who, if I behaved like Tony Blair, would not be on it,' he added more seriously. 'Yes I am powerful enough in the SNP to stop people if I want to do it. But my view is that if you do that people will just reappear in a less constructive form.'[38] As if to demonstrate his humility, Salmond also moved to abolish his 21-member 'Scottish cabinet' in August, the source of so much discontent in the early 1990s, creating instead a smaller team in charge of seven 'superministries'.

Unusually, however, these internal tensions did not appear to affect the opinion polls. Throughout 1998 the SNP were riding high, with one System Three poll in March putting the party on 38 per cent, just one point behind Labour, a buoyant showing that lasted until July. It seemed that Salmond could do no wrong, an impression confirmed by other polls that showed him to be the preference of Scottish voters as the first First Minister of Scotland. 'We are not in a sprint, we are in a marathon,' Salmond told the *Daily Record*. 'And while we are pleased with the position we are in, we intend to work hard to preserve that position. We are not counting any chickens.'[39] Shortly after, Salmond unveiled yet another new SNP logo – which closely resembled that of the early 1980s – and a new slogan, 'Scotland's Parliament needs Scotland's party'.

The New Labour government had not done itself any favours since the previous year's memorable election win. Lone parent benefits had been cut (prompting Malcolm Chisholm's calculated resignation from the Scottish Office), proposals for student tuition fees had proved controversial, while the Sean Connery knighthood affair had made Labour appear deceitful and petty. Logically, therefore, Salmond sought to portray the first devolved election as a straight fight between the SNP and its traditional enemy, while doing his best to sound positive. 'The SNP's strategy for the next year is very simple,' he wrote in the *Scotsman*. 'We will articulate the practical policies we believe will make a difference to our country. And we will promote the right of Scotland to grow in confidence, ability and standing so that we can move forward as a nation.' Only, he concluded, 'such a successful parliament can lead us to independence'.[40]

That prospect looked even more likely when another opinion poll in July showed support for independence at 56 per cent, up four points on a similar survey the previous month. 'Labour are on the verge of hysteria,' said Salmond. 'They're just not used to being challenged in Scotland, let alone falling behind.'[41] This political dynamic inevitably boosted Salmond's confidence. 'The SNP leader has grown in stature and command and treats the front bench with contemptuous disregard,' observed Matthew Parris of Salmond's Westminster appearances. 'Labour hate him. They squeak and mutter when he speaks.'[42]

Panicked by this sustained Nationalist bounce, Labour resolved to do more than mutter and squeak. When Tony Blair was interrupted by the ringing of a photographer's mobile phone during a Scottish visit, he quipped: 'It's probably Mr Salmond calling to say he's discovered an SNP policy.'[43] Labour also accused the SNP of removing a host of costly policies from the relevant section of its website. 'No democratic western European political party has ever fought an election on its previous election's manifesto, said Salmond, laughing off the charge. 'Times and events change.'[44]

Times and events did indeed change, as did perceptions of Salmond himself. He had always possessed chameleon-like instincts, not least during his transition from urban socialist to rural pragmatist following his election in Banff and Buchan. There was also an ostentatious attempt to become a sort of Scottish everyman. The journalist Alan Cochrane was not alone in noticing a subtle adoption of colloquialisms: 'We increasingly hear him saying, among other things, "dinna", instead of "don't" and "mair" instead of "more".'[45]

The journalist Peter MacMahon, meanwhile, commented that the 'slightly awkward mateyness, the mock punches on the arm for voters in Fraserburgh, the hand on the knee of a wheelchair-bound woman in Peterhead hospital, though genuine, appear to betray a rather reticent man behind the public bravado'.[46] There was also increasing commentary upon a darker side to Salmond's character. 'Let us not mince words: despite his resemblance to a hamster, Alex Salmond is quite a nasty piece of work,' observed the Guardian's Ian Aitken. 'This comes across most clearly when he faces up to Labour's Secretary of State, Donald Dewar. Poor Dewar, though brainy and decent, is no match for Salmond's verbal cruelties.'[47] Often accused of having a short temper, meanwhile, Salmond would only admit to 'an occasional exasperation'.[48]

Salmond's love of football, meanwhile, also fitted neatly into this new 'everyman' persona. In June 1998 he jetted off to France to join the Tartan Army during the World Cup. When it emerged that the French TV channel Canal Plus was not planning to show the match between Scotland and Morocco, even though more than 10,000 Scots had gathered in the square at St Etienne expecting to see it, Salmond took decisive action. 'We got through to the office of the managing director of Canal Plus and I said, "I am Alex Salmond, leader of the Scottish National Party",' he recalled a few years later. 'We got nowhere whatsoever. Then I said I was Alex Salmond, the President of the Republic of Scotland, and I wanted to speak to him right now. He came out of his board meeting and I managed to save the game. For three hours I was the President of Scotland.'[49]

As well as fuelling Salmond's delusions of grandeur, the trip produced a memorable photograph of him wearing a Scotland shirt, floppy tartan hat and a jaw-splitting grin. 'I think that's a great picture and I love to see that picture,' he said, a touch defensively. 'If *The Scotsman* wants to publish that picture with this article they will get no complaint from me. I think it's far more genuine than two new lads enjoying a can of beer in No 10 Downing Street.'[50] (This was a reference to rather contrived television footage of Tony Blair and Gordon Brown watching a World Cup match.) It was also that picture, joked the former STV and BBC Scotland journalist Lorraine Davidson, that prompted her to quit the media and join the Scottish Labour Party as a spin doctor.

Despite Salmond's disparaging references to Blair, comparisons between the SNP leader and Prime Minister were frequently made as the decade drew to a close. 'He used to be an advocate of high social spending, increased taxation on the rich and renationalization,' wrote Iain Macwhirter, making precisely that analogy. 'Now we understand that he is going to cut business taxes to the lowest in Europe; hold business rates down; and make Scotland a haven for what he might once have called "multi-national super-profits".' 'Alex Salmond is a "modernizer", in the best Blairite tradition,' added Macwhirter. 'He has transformed the Scottish National Party from an introverted, fractious club for romantic nationalists into a highly effective political opposition. His "project" now is preparing for power.'[51]

Recent critical remarks from Mike Ross, the chairman of Scottish Widows, and Iain McMillan of CBI Scotland had, therefore, caused Salmond consternation. Just as Salmond had moved to neutralise suspicion of the SNP among Catholic voters following the Monklands East by-election, he now prepared to tackle a perception among Scotland's business community that the economics of independence did not quite add up. Salmond established another pseudo-lobby group, Business for Scotland, while pledging to reduce corporation tax in an independent Scotland to as little as 12.5 per cent. The model, as ever, was Ireland, with Salmond becoming a devotee of the 'Laffer Curve', the phenomenon by which Ireland had actually increased its revenue by cutting business taxation.

Although Salmond had first cast his eyes westward in the late 1980s, a key event had been a lecture at the 1997 SNP conference by John D. FitzGerald, an eminent Irish economist and son of the former Taoiseach Garret FitzGerald. Salmond chaired the lecture, at which FitzGerald's arguments immediately persuaded him, Andrew Wilson and others to be more pro-business and more pro-Ireland. The governor of Ireland's central bank, Maurice O'Connell, later took the contrary view, telling the *Scotsman* that emulating the Irish model could cause 'considerable disruption'[52] of an independent Scotland's financial system. Salmond, however, regularly wielded a letter from Professor Laffer himself, making positive noises about his plan, while Garret FitzGerald openly endorsed the notion of Scottish independence within the European Union in a short film the SNP leader fronted for STV. 'We share much in common with Ireland; what we lack is independence,' he said on location in Dublin. 'Ireland is doing so much with so little while Scotland does so little with so much.'[53]

Salmond's affinity with Ireland, however, went deeper than economics. Having forged a strong friendship with the Scottish cardinal Tom Winning in the wake of the Monklands East by-election back in 1994, he had become convinced that the Emerald Isle was a good model for Scotland in several other respects. Not only did he want to emulate Dublin's lobbying prowess in the US and in the EU, but in a talk to the Humbert Summer School Salmond heaped praise upon the forthcoming creation of a British–Irish Council (a feature of the recent Good Friday Agreement), or the 'Council of the Isles' in his own parlance, chiming as it did with his attempt to reformulate Scottish/British identity. The Irish model, therefore, also extended to constitutional change. Asked to cite political heroes, Salmond often mentioned Michael Collins who had – of course – taken a gradualist approach to Irish independence. Winning, meanwhile, rewarded the SNP's courting with a public endorsement in late 1998.

Looking wider afield, Salmond brushed aside criticisms of his proposed admission of an independent Scotland to the European single currency, the details of which he believed to be 'trivial', or issues of 'management'. 'It's our policy to seek entry,' he stated simply, 'because we think it's in Scotland's economic interest to do so.'[54] But it remained a 'no' to control via the European Central Bank. 'We're very pro-EMU, and we'd probably make do with the European Monetary Institute in Frankfurt,' he told the *Independent* on the eve of the SNP conference. 'It would be to everybody's convenience to maintain parity with sterling until entry, although I wouldn't want to venture into EMU at the current rate of sterling.'[55]

Sensing a chink in the Nationalist armoury, Labour tried another attack. Gordon Brown, the Chancellor, accused Salmond of being 'economically illiterate', a calculated insult to a former professional economist, while Donald Dewar – as of August 1998 the de facto leader of the Scottish Labour Party – pointed to what he claimed was a £1.5 billion hole in the SNP's plans for taxation in an independent Scotland. Salmond dismissed this with ease, not least because surveys showed nearly half of Scottish voters believing the SNP to be 'the friend of business and enterprise'.[56] Dewar, he claimed, did not understand the demands of a modern economy.

The SNP's annual conference, meanwhile, got under way against a backdrop of familiar claims that Salmond had engineered a deliberately bland agenda while watering down party policy in order to attract more voters. Indeed, notable by its absence was any debate on the monarchy, no doubt, suspected cynics, because a meeting with Prince Charles was now a more pressing concern. This, it has to be said, was a notable coup for Salmond. The date was set for 13 October and Buckingham Palace asked for secrecy, although Salmond took care to give Roseanna Cunningham, the SNP's most prominent republican, advance notice. Nevertheless, the story was broken by *Sunday Times* Court correspondent, Christopher Morgan, who by chance had been a university contemporary of Salmond's.[57]

Other sections of the press then had fun speculating about what Salmond might raise when the unlikely duo met at Birkhall, the Queen Mother's home in the grounds of Balmoral. Writing in the *Mirror*, Salmond said he would raise the SNP's 'views on the right type of role for the royals in an independent Scotland' among 'many other things'. Salmond also acknowledged existing SNP policy, as voted on at the 1997 conference, for a referendum to decide between a monarchy and an elected head of state should Scotland become independent. 'Both positions are perfectly respectable,' argued Salmond, adding that 'SNP policy is not, however, for a republic'.[58]

Describing the meeting a few years later, Salmond recalled forgetting to bow before indulging in the required small talk:

I knew the Prince swore by chiropractors and thought a conversation about our common affliction might help get things moving. And so it proved. He gave me some incredibly useful advice on posture and some totally useless advice on not having an operation – I subsequently did and it proved a great success ... Eventually, an hour after we first sat down, we got round to discussing the future of Scotland. He asked me if I was committed to independence. I said that I was. He then asked a tentative question about the prospects for the monarchy in that circumstance. He

seemed comforted by my explanation of support, with the important
proviso that the people of Scotland must so wish.

'My overall impression of the Prince was favourable,' judged Salmond.
'He has a genuine love of Scotland. The Scotland that he loves may not
be real, and certainly not typical, but that doesn't make his affection for
it any less sincere.'[59]

This marked the beginning of a new Salmond strategy, emphasising
the positive aspects of change through independence, while also stressing continuity, in this case that which 'the monarchy brings': 'I'm
interested in presenting the case for Scottish independence in a way that
doesn't unnecessarily confront or upset people south of the Border. I
don't think anybody would say if you are starting with a clean sheet of
paper you would write in a royal family. I wouldn't do it. I don't think
most sensible people would. But we're not starting with a clean sheet of
paper.'[60] Retaining the monarch, Salmond argued, would 'secure a
living link with our neighbours in the south, with whom we seek
equality and social union'. It was probably at this point that he moved
towards embracing the retention of the 1603 Union of the Crowns
while repealing the 1707 Act of Union. 'Maybe that [the question of
keeping the Union of the Crowns] was something I learned at that
meeting,' he admitted in 2007. 'It is fair to say, obviously, those matters
were discussed.'[61]

An independent Scotland, claimed Salmond, would 'get rid of what
is bad' while making better 'those things that have served us over the
years'.[62] This constituted yet another ideological guise for the pragmatic
Mr Salmond, this time as a Burkean conservative. Indeed, many of his
political heroes were, curiously enough, centrist Tories, including John
Biffen ('the purest voice of Englishness in the Commons') and Ted
Heath ('his dogged streak, his stamina'), although his own ideology
remained vague and ill defined. 'I've always wanted to call it the Scottish Independence Party,' he confessed to an interviewer. 'It's a much
better encapsulation of what we're about. Independence is our idea, and
our politics are social democrat. I'm a post-nationalist.'

Opinion polls, meanwhile, continued to show support for independence hovering at around 50 per cent, while Salmond pointed to
another finding that showed two-thirds of Scots believing that Scotland would eventually become independent. 'When something
becomes the currency of inevitability,' he said, 'you're well on the
way.' The leader of the SNP could be forgiven for being upbeat,

particularly after such a good summer. 'He is an approachable, ebullient figure, chubby, with prominent dark brown eyes,' judged the *Independent*'s Stephen Fay. 'Words bubble up in him and pour out. Salmond is a compulsive talker – he admits that he sometimes talks too much. But he is generous with his time, and eager to please.' Fay also captured his rather shameless approach to the media: 'We are on the Aberdeen bypass [*sic*] when the public relations man at party headquarters in Edinburgh calls on the mobile to report that Gordon Brown has dropped plans for a new tax on North Sea oil. Salmond instructs the driver to divert to Grampian TV. Arriving unannounced, he offers an interview. Undeterred when Grampian's newsroom rebuffs him, Salmond directs the driver round the corner to the BBC's Aberdeen studios. There he is made welcome, recording an interview that will be broadcast the following morning. On the way out of town, he slips into an independent radio station for one last fix.' Nevertheless, concluded Fay, his 'energy, stamina and commitment are compelling'.[63]

A September *Scotsman*/ICM poll, meanwhile, revealed that Salmond was the SNP's most recognisable figure, leading to his heavy promotion at that year's autumn SNP gathering. 'The SNP conference is about three things,' observed Peter MacMahon. 'Alex Salmond, Alex Salmond and Alex Salmond. Increasingly the SNP is Mr Salmond; policy is largely what he says it is. He dictated the terms of SNP involvement in the devolution referendum. His startling conversion to right-wing policies on taxation and the Laffer curve has been unopposed and largely unremarked. The "modernizing" policy review, which trims on issues such as rail nationalisation and student grants, is being conducted without a voice raised in protest.' Although he had lost a few minor battles, Salmond now dominated his party to an extent unmatched by almost any other political leader. 'Not even the ultimate control freak, Tony Blair,' added MacMahon, 'with whom Mr Salmond is increasingly being compared, enjoys such unchallenged authority.'[64]

By the time Salmond rose to address delegates at the 1998 conference, however, there were already signs that party discipline would not be enough. Another *Scotsman*/ICM poll showed Labour edging ahead of the SNP in both the constituency and party list votes, prompting Salmond to put what he called 'clear tartan water' between the two parties during his keynote speech. This he did in vague terms, appealing for the support of public sector workers while pledging to remove a government-created 'climate of fear'. 'We commit to nothing less than a new democracy in

Scotland,' he said, 'a democracy that involves those who do the job in the decisions about how those jobs should be done ... the SNP offers inclusion, involvement and responsibility.'[65] He also reiterated the three themes of the conference: enterprise, compassion and democracy.

There was, as ever, a conference row. Two days after Salmond promised Scotland would be a 'good neighbour' to England post-independence, Kenny MacAskill referred to the English football team as the 'Great Satan' in his valedictory speech as treasurer, while making it clear he disagreed with Salmond, who had said he would support England should Scotland be knocked out of a tournament. Although the speech was, on the whole, well received, Salmond looked uncomfortable and was the last person on the platform to rise to his feet when it ended with an ovation.

MacAskill went on to top the poll in elections to the SNP's National Council, with the overwhelming support of two thirds of delegates, although he was excluded from Salmond's 'Scottish parliament ministerial team', which was unveiled a few weeks later. This mainly comprised Salmond loyalists such as John Swinney (finance, soon also to become deputy leader), Nicola Sturgeon (education and culture) and Alasdair Morgan (external affairs and the constitution), although there was also space for Roseanna Cunningham (justice) and Fergus Ewing (land, resources and rural affairs). The trouble was, as private polling revealed, these figures were practically unknown to the wider electorate, most of whom only registered Salmond. 'The Scottish election will be fought between Alex and Donald Dewar on presidential lines, and we are happy with that,' a source told *Scotland on Sunday*. 'But there is a problem with the people around him, which creates the perception that the party has no strength [and] depth.'[66]

Salmond, meanwhile, was planning to boost his international profile by making a pre-campaign visit to the United States, supported by the Hollywood pulling power of Sean Connery. Trent Lott, the Republican leader in the Senate, was an obvious target, particularly given his Scottish ancestry and responsibility for the 'Tartan Day' celebrations that took place every year on 6 April, the anniversary of the 1320 Declaration of Arbroath. The SNP had been trying to raise money in the US since November 1993 – an office had even been set up in Portland, Oregon – although without much success.

The SNP leader's stock was, at least on the domestic scene, still high. In November 1998, for example, the *Spectator* named Salmond its Parliamentary Tactician of the Year. 'The new Government thought it could bury, or marginalise, this member,' said the *Spectator* editor Frank Johnson. 'That proved impossible because of his skill at Question Time and his use of the procedures of the House of Commons. He has only to get to his feet for ministerial hackles to rise.' Never one to accept such accolades lightly, Salmond explained that the award showed 'that I'm the real political heavyweight leader of the opposition in Parliament'.[67]

Labour's ministerial hackles were indeed (despite narrowing polls) still prone to rise. It had recently initiated a 'Nat-bashing' strategy, headed up by the strident deputy Scottish Secretary Helen Liddell but begun by Tony Blair in a speech ('stronger together – weaker apart') at Strathclyde University. 'I do not want to be separate from anything,' responded Salmond. 'I want for my country to be joined in co-operation and mutual respect – on a footing of equality – with all the nations of Europe.' He also attempted to depict the divide between the two parties as lying 'deeper than the issue of independence'. It was, said Salmond, 'more than a simple political challenge'. 'It is a contest of approach and ideology and it is a contest that the SNP intends to win.'[68]

Salmond also did his best to tap into the zeitgeist of the 'new Scotland', typified by an upsurge in public engagement with the country's history, culture and politics, while he was also buoyed by victory in the North-East Scotland Euro by-election on 26 November.[69] On St Andrew's Day he said that the recent opening of Edinburgh's new Museum of Scotland by the Queen was 'another sign that our nation is rediscovering itself and, confident in its past, is preparing for its future'.[70]

Salmond, thought Canada's *Globe and Mail*, had much in common with Quebec's premier Lucien Bouchard, being 'seen as an astute politician who only wants to hold a referendum that he can win'. Indeed, when Bernard Landry, Quebec's deputy premier, had visited Edinburgh that September, he met privately with Salmond and Mike Russell and had 'a very enjoyable dinner' (Quebec officials, curiously, denied the meeting ever took place.) George Reid, the SNP's constitutional spokesman, even talked up the comparisons. 'Like the Péquiste [Bouchard],' he said, 'he [Salmond] will choose his moment for the referendum to maximum benefit.'

In recent elections to Quebec's National Assembly, the separatist Parti Québécois (PQ) had won the most seats but without a majority of the popular vote, therefore limiting its options on moving towards separation, a scenario Reid believed could be replicated in Scotland come May 1999. This analogy, however, worked both ways. Earlier in 1998

Sir Malcolm Rifkind had warned that the SNP would use the new Scottish parliament the way the PQ had used the Quebec National Assembly, 'to ferment resentment against our fellow citizens in England and Wales and to sow discord in this island'. The *Scotsman*, which had sent a correspondent to cover the elections in Quebec, also drew its own lessons from the analogy. 'It is surely time for the SNP to recognize that it stands more chance of winning power with a program which aims firstly to run Scotland well,' stated an editorial, 'not to begin another potentially damaging constitutional adventure before the first one has even begun.'[71]

Salmond, of course, was acutely aware of the parallel. 'To argue that this parliament will not – at its start – be fully equipped to meet all such challenges is a far cry from arguing that the parliament will or should fail,' he argued in *Scotland on Sunday*. Rather, its very existence would create 'the inevitable demand that has been experienced by every devolved administration whenever they have been established' for 'more powers'. The 'most potent threat' to the parliament, according to Salmond, actually came from New Labour, 'and from the institutions and government it controls in London'.[72]

Looking back on the past few years at the end of 1998, Salmond claimed to be taken aback at the pace of change in Scotland. 'It's only since the referendum on devolution that I have been certain that independence would happen,' he said. 'Before that I hoped and believed. Now I know.' He also reflected upon his eight years as leader of the SNP: 'When I became party leader I reckoned the SNP had plenty of idealism, plenty of enthusiasm, and plenty of commitment. But I thought it needed a bit more professionalism and a bit more economic and political rigour. I hope I have helped to bring that about. I look at old videos of the party conference. In 1990 they elected me so I can't really complain but I have to say the 1998 version is a lot stronger.'[73]

As a result of that 'stronger' party, Salmond remained genuinely confident of victory in the first elections to the Scottish Parliament, although he took care to hedge his bets. 'I'm not saying we're definitely going to win. I'm not assuming we're going to win,' he told the *Mirror* towards the end of the year. 'I would say we have got a very big chance. We do want to win. We're playing to win.' He conceded, however, that Labour was the 'bookies' favourite'. 'But one thing you learn as a racing tipster is that the favourites don't always win,' he added mischievously. 'If you spent your life backing favourites you would lose a lot of money.'[74]

The New Year, meanwhile, brought further unwelcome news for Salmond. Fundamentalists, most notably Margo MacDonald, began to do well in regional party hustings, while Labour – which had looked so tired and inept a year earlier – began to score remarkable successes, attacking Salmond's understanding of economics and exploiting every inconsistency in SNP policy. Advising Donald Dewar ahead of his first televised debate with Salmond, Labour's spin doctor Alastair Campbell even tried to take advantage of a perception that the SNP leader was 'slippery'. 'I suggested to DD he find an opportunity to say at one point "You are not being honest, Alex",' recorded Campbell in his diary, 'but DD, as ever with anything involving risk or conflict, was ultra-cautious and reluctant.'[75] Polls, however, indicated that Dewar's instincts had not prevented him emerging as most Scots' choice as First Minister, although Salmond's approval ratings remained relatively high. Labour was also concerned when focus groups revealed that Scots believed 'Salmond would get more for Scotland'. [76]

Salmond's memorable triumphs in 1992 and 1995, however, were not matched by a *Scotsman*-sponsored debate in February 1999, chaired by the journalist Andrew Neil. Salmond occasionally appeared evasive, while he failed to tackle trickier questions with his usual aplomb, perhaps still suffering from flu-related symptoms that had recently been plaguing him. 'Donald Dewar and Alex Salmond did Scotland proud with their relish for open, democratic discourse and the high quality of their exchanges,' judged Neil a few days later. 'They were robust without ever being rude. They had policies to proclaim and opponents to declaim. But never once did either raise our spirits or horizons to the finer possibilities that the new Scottish parliament is supposed to herald.'[77]

Salmond also became less sure-footed when it came to policy pronouncements, an area in which he had always been cautious to the point of inactivity. The weekend after his head-to-head with Dewar he committed an SNP administration to meeting in full any public sector pay recommendations from various review bodies ('A huge, great blank cheque,' said Labour), while refusing to say whether it would use the parliament's 3p variable rate. It was, in fairness, a difficult call for Salmond to make, choosing between a straightforward pitch to left-wing voters happy with tax-and-spend policies, and younger swing voters who naturally approved of low taxation. There was also a characteristic lack of detail on other policies such as education, where Salmond floated the idea of a forum of experts and teachers to agree a way ahead, but little more.

A key plank of the SNP's 1999 manifesto, meanwhile, was the Scottish Public Service Trust (SPST), which Salmond launched as the 'first big idea'[78] of the election campaign in February 1999. Devised as an alternative to the controversial Private Finance Initiative (PFI), various trusts were envisaged to manage areas such as housing or health, seeking finance from the private sector in exchange for bonds and bank loans guaranteed by the Scottish government with relatively low interest rates. Once established, these trusts would bid for public sector contracts alongside private consortia, eventually – or so the argument went – squeezing out the latter altogether.

This idea grew out of a lunch Salmond had with an Edinburgh bond trader. 'He said, "Why don't you issue bonds?"' recalled a Salmond aide at that time. 'Of course a devolved government couldn't do that, but we ploughed on nevertheless.' Business leaders who roundly attacked the SNP's proposals upon their publication included Sir Peter Burt, chief executive of the Bank of Scotland, who had agreed to support the SPST on the condition that the language was made more business-friendly. There were other problems, not least communicating the merits of PFI vis-à-vis SPST to voters. 'PFI was the clear dividing line between us and Labour,' recalled the aide, 'but it was impossible to sell to the electorate as it was too complicated.'[79] The Scottish Futures Trust, as it would become prior to the 2007 Holyrood elections, continued to dog Salmond, even as First Minister.

Labour, meanwhile, had successfully been rounding up – and promoting in the press – businessmen critical of the SNP and the likely effect of independence upon the Scottish economy. Salmond's damage limitation strategy in this respect, however, appeared not to be having the desired effect. He pushed champagne nationalism with great bonhomie (and wearing, for the first time, tartan, although trews rather than a kilt) at various swanky functions, while referring to the business vote, with a deliberate *Star Trek* reference, as the SNP's 'final frontier'. He popped in and out of Edinburgh boardrooms while Dennis MacLeod, a US-based mining engineer, promoted events under the auspices of Business for Scotland, and Brian Souter of Stagecoach hosted a private meeting of Salmond and financiers at his Perthshire home.

The SNP leader's immediate circle did, at least, lend these efforts considerable credibility. John Swinney, the finance spokesman, had been a planner at Scottish Amicable, while Andrew Wilson, a Treasury spokesman, had been – like Salmond – an economist at the Royal Bank of Scotland. Some party activists, however, were less impressed, dismissing these business-friendly young Turks as 'Thatcher's children'.[80]

Salmond, meanwhile, also continued to push his pro-English message, most notably in a speech to the London School of Economics. Describing independence as 'the next great adventure', he spoke of wanting 'to see that process of independence fulfilled. And I want to see it shared with those who live next door to us, and who will benefit from it too.'[81] Far from being damaged by independence, he argued, England could benefit from the 'new dynamism' that constitutional change had already released north of the border. This built upon Salmond's notion of a 'social', rather than a political, union between Scotland and England. This was positive and inoffensive stuff, although subsequent remarks to BBC Radio Scotland's *People and Power* programme appeared to be the opposite. Britishness, said Salmond, had been claimed by thugs and racists while Englishness was an 'aristocratic, almost medieval concept', adding: 'It is one of the great problems in English society.' Donald Dewar, sensing an opportunity, accused Salmond of being 'offensive'.[82]

Then, as each of Scotland's parties geared up for their pre-election conferences, Salmond decided to take two calculated gambles. The first, the so-called 'Penny for Scotland', came in the wake of Gordon Brown's Budget decision to lower the basic rate of income tax by 1p. The ortho-doxy until that moment had been that the SNP should not contemplate using the new parliament's 3p variable tax rate through fear of being depicted as a tax-raising party, although Mike Russell had consistently argued for a penny increase. Salmond's position on this had fluctuated, and it seems Brown's Budget changed his mind once again. A deci-sion was needed quickly, as the SNP's Aberdeen conference on 12 March would have to be consulted. Within hours of Brown's Budget statement on 9 March, Russell, Salmond and Swinney were engaged in a series of phone calls to discuss the options.

Accounts differ as to how Salmond handled what amounted to a major policy U-turn. 'There was this very dramatic day at HQ where he [Salmond] called in various senior people and told them what was now happening,' recalled one aide. 'There was obviously a case for the change, but doing it at the last minute and with so little thought was not the way to handle it, although typical of Alex.'[83] Andrew Wilson, however, recalled that Salmond 'didn't railroad it, he won it by the strength of his argument'. 'There was a meeting of the NEC on the tax policy and it was hanging in the balance. John Swinney and I arrived late and Alex reckoned that we would argue against it, but we backed it and it went through.'[84] Whatever happened, by 8 p.m. that evening, the Penny for Scotland was essentially SNP policy.

Salmond then set about swinging conference behind his view with a motion proposed and seconded by John Swinney and Wilson, whom many would have expected to oppose such a move. Delegates overwhelmingly backed the decision, although it soon became clear that the speed with which the decision had been taken had left no time for fleshing out the detail. When asked what the additional revenue raised would be spent on, for example, Salmond did not have a ready response. 'It was too rushed,' recalled someone close to the events, 'so only the price to people was communicated, not the benefit to public services. That was our error.'[85]

The second gamble could not be said to run counter to Salmond's natural instincts. The Allied bombing of Serbia had recently got under way and he had been invited to make a five-minute broadcast in response to Tony Blair's televised address the previous week. It was the first time the SNP had been given such an opportunity and, going out on the BBC just before the Six O'Clock News and later on ITV's three regional stations in Scotland, it was bound to reach a wide audience. Trailed in advance by the *Scotsman*, Salmond said simply that he would voice 'grave reservations' about a bombing campaign he thought was 'difficult to justify'.[86]

'I thought carefully about what I should do,' recalled Salmond the following year. 'On the one hand I was passionately convinced the Nato campaign was making things infinitely worse for the people it was designed to help and was consolidating, not undermining, Milosevic's position in Serbia. On the other, we were in an election campaign and I was under no illusions that with wartime hysteria the press would have no hesitation about turning their guns on the SNP if any substantial criticism was made of government policy.' At one stage Salmond considered 'declining the broadcast rather than indulge in weasel words I didn't believe'. 'I was in the Highlands staying at Scatwell House, the family home of one of the SNP's supporters, Dennis MacLeod,' he remembered. 'After agonising I decided that I would speak the truth as I saw it – election or no election. I broadcast from Scatwell on the Monday morning.'[87]

Salmond's language was pungent, to say the least. He accused Tony Blair and the UK's NATO allies of pursuing a 'misguided' policy of 'dubious legality and unpardonable folly', although he accepted that Milosevic was chiefly to blame for the situation in the Balkans. Salmond went on to argue that the bombing would neither help the Kosovars nor weaken Milosevic. 'In virtually every country which has been blitzed this century, the reaction has been to steel the resolve of the civilian population,' he said. 'This is what happened in London in the Second World War. It is also what happened in Clydebank. Why should we believe that there will not be the same reaction in Serbia?'[88]

Instead, Salmond called for an all-out humanitarian aid effort, a full-scale economic blockade of the Serbs and an agreement that the Rambouillet accord could be policed by United Nations, rather than NATO, forces. The broadcast remains impressive 11 years on – Salmond is composed, sober and authoritative. Monitoring the broadcast at the time, however, Alastair Campbell instinctively ordered an attack of his own. 'Salmond made the mistake of comparing the air strikes – targeted at a dictatorship – with the Blitz of London or Clydebank,' he wrote in his diary. 'Silly boy. Bad judgement and we went for him.'[89]

Went for him they certainly did. Blair branded Salmond's claims 'shameless' while Foreign Secretary Robin Cook, acting on a leaked text of the broadcast, said the remarks would make the SNP leader 'the toast of Belgrade'. There was also more measured criticism from less tribal political opponents. 'Alex Salmond is being incredibly naïve' judged the Scottish Liberal Democrat leader Jim Wallace, 'if he thinks that Milosevic would have given up his barbarous pursuit of the Koso-vars whilst waiting for sanctions to bite.'[90] Wallace also accused Salmond of 'blatant opportunism' in using the broadcast to criticise military action when neither he nor any of his MPs had voiced such opinions before, despite numerous opportunities in and beyond Parliament.

Salmond was unapologetic. 'I am not retreating an inch from my views,' he said the next day. 'I am not going to by silenced by the New Labour spin machine. The fact that they have got to resort to smears is an indication of the weakness of their position.'[91] 'I had steeled myself for press criticism,' Salmond later admitted, 'but the extent of the prop-aganda machine surprised even me.' Only the *Herald* offered qualified support, while retired generals and political heavyweights like Denis Healey and Lord Carrington shored up Salmond's position. 'None was subjected to the propaganda barrage from Unionist politicians and their press patsies,' remarked Salmond. 'Mind you, none of them was fighting an election.'[92] He also cited support from the independent MP and former war correspondent Martin Bell, as well as 'serving and retired service personnel' who had spoken to him or SNP colleagues 'in the last 24 hours'.[93]

It was an impressive and occasionally compelling defence of a contro-versial broadcast, and indeed with the benefit of hindsight it seems clear

that the opprobrium heaped upon Salmond owed more to his unfortunate phraseology rather than the central thrust of his critique. Brian
Taylor later wrote that he should have 'made his intentions clear in
measured, restrained vocabulary'. Instead, however, Salmond had used
the phrase 'unpardonable folly' and therefore chosen 'an absolutist tone
in setting himself apart at that time from other political leaders in Britain
and NATO'.[94]

The row, therefore, focused attention upon Salmond's judgment as
never before. Accounts vary as to the provenance of the text, drafted
the previous weekend by Salmond and Russell. Although the official
line was that it had been Salmond's work with Russell contributing
some of its 'more colourful passages', the *Herald* journalist Murray
Ritchie heard that the broadcast had been written by Salmond 'himself
in a hurry', while Russell later told him that 'he was the author of the
Salmond speech on Kosovo and that Alex changed bits of it. The final
version was a joint effort.'[95] This did not prevent Russell, however, from
describing the broadcast as 'principled, but perhaps impractical'[96] in a
2006 book. George Reid and his deputy as external affairs spokesman,
Paul Henderson Scott, had also communicated their misgivings about
the bombings to Salmond, although Reid had cautioned against appearing to undermine serving personnel.

To imply that the whole thing had been a horrible mistake, however,
would be to do Salmond a disservice. Not only did the NATO action
genuinely offend him, but he believed the broadcast would chime with
a significant portion of public opinion, its anti-war sentiment consolidating the leftward pitch begun with the 'Penny for Scotland' policy. As
Murray Ritchie put it in his account of the election campaign, Salmond
had 'cunningly got himself national UK exposure' by 'breaking the
British political consensus with his outspoken comments'. 'But Salmond
is privately concerned about how his comments will be received,'
Ritchie also recorded. 'He, too, asks me how they are going down.'[97]

In a private email to Mike Russell, meanwhile, Gordon Wilson also
expressed reservations; stressing that Salmond's broadcast should have
concentrated more on the refugee problem. 'By taking a strong line on
the penny tax and Kosovo, the Party has taken the initiative and rescued
us from a period when we were taking punishment,' wrote Wilson.
'But be careful about the rest of the Campaign or we could end up with
another 1992 when the electorate took fright and left us with an
outcome which was less than rosy.' Russell's reply was the slightly
confused: 'Seriously I really take your point. I have already discussed it

with Alex. To some extent we should have avoided this, but it wasn't possible nor would it have been right.'[98]

Asked later if he regretted any of the language used in the broadcast, Salmond replied: 'Yeah. If I had the broadcast again I might have changed a few of the phrases, but I don't regret the broadcast. I didn't really feel I would be able to live with myself if I'd gone onto that broadcast and said nothing because I was frightened to say what I believe in.'[99] A year later, Salmond went further by admitting that the resulting media onslaught had 'dented our election campaign'. 'Undoubtedly the press reaction to my statement on Kosovo stalled the momentum of the SNP election campaign,' he wrote. 'It took us some weeks to recover.'[100] Later events in the Balkans did, however, vindicate Salmond's warnings.

'It is an enormous gamble,' observed *Scotland on Sunday* of the wider strategy, 'the origins of which can be found at the turn of last year. With the polls starting to go in Labour's favour, Salmond and Russell knew that they needed a distinctive identity. Their opportunity came with the Budget and Gordon Brown's income tax-cutting budget. A party which had spent at least the last two years attempting to win from the centre ground of Scottish politics has decided to send out a very different message. Salmond's anti-war, anti-Nato comments were only the most public signal so far that he plans to fight the next four and half weeks on avowedly left wing territory.'[101] With opinion polls showing a strong lead for Labour, Salmond and Russell hoped this tactic would at least deliver them a strong second place, realising – and accepting – that it would take at least one or two Scottish Parliament elections before they could hope to become the biggest single party.

Such was the backdrop to the SNP's manifesto launch on 6 April 1999. There had been much talk at around this time of 'triangulation', an American concept that described the art of presenting a party's ideology as being 'above' or 'between' the traditional 'left' or 'right' sides of the political spectrum, and indeed the SNP's policy agenda was a case in point. Having taken some of its opponent's ideas (tax and spend, being anti-war) and claimed the credit, the 'triangulator', i.e. the SNP, had insulated itself from attacks on those particular issues. 'Alex regularly referred to triangulation,' recalled an aide, 'whereby we said the same as everyone else but with a unique rhetorical twist.' This, however, was not necessarily a good thing. 'The 1999 manifesto,' added the aide, 'never had the expressed desire or inclination to be original or a little bit daring.'[102] There was also controversy over a New Labour-style pledge card. This set out ten manifesto pledges but placing the proposed independence referendum bottom of the list.

'We have the unique combination as Scotland's party,' said Salmond, 'having made the commitment to invest in Scotland's public services and offering people the bridge to the future through the independence referendum. I think that combination will be irresistible over the next four weeks.' Labour, he said, was run by 'remote control' from London while the SNP was 'Scotland's party for Scotland's parliament'. The contrast between the two, he added, would 'be a powerful image throughout these next four weeks'.[103]

Another powerful image throughout the campaign that followed, however, was that of an SNP leader not exactly on top form. The BBC journalist Brian Taylor, also a university contemporary of Salmond's, remembered that on the day of the manifesto launch, 'the party leader did not seem to be at his best. It is difficult to be precise. His opening presentation seemed low-key. He seemed unnecessarily irritated by some of the questions. Certainly, they ranged far beyond the scope of the manifesto itself but that is part of the election process. The sharp leader – and Salmond is incontestably sharp – tackles and rebuts questions, the penetrating and the vacuous, the distinct and the repetitious. That particular day, he seemed to me to be wearying of the task.'

At a photo call held at the Edinburgh's old Royal High School after the launch, Taylor suggested to Salmond that he looked and sounded a little tired. 'I wondered whether a previous problem with back pain had resurfaced,' he later wrote, referring to an operation Salmond had recently undergone. 'Never, he insisted, had he felt better.'[104] Close associates, meanwhile, had mixed impressions. John Swinney thought his boss did not look 'either tired or off form', although Roseanna Cunningham disagreed: 'He was tired. It wasn't jaded or anything. I [just] thought he was exhausted.'[105]

Reflecting upon the election campaign a few years later, Taylor believed that as well as lack of resources and a punishing schedule, there had been an 'additional strain upon the leader':

He was facing persistent pressure from gossip that was circulating privately among politicians and the media. The smear was seen to be without foundation. Not a line was published in any newspaper, despite intensive investigation. However, it destabilised his efforts during the campaign. The smear circulating ... was that he had indulged his interest [in gambling] overenthusiastically, that he had run into debt. The gossip was

Left. Salmond's maternal grandfather, William Milne. 'Mr Milne was a man', noted a newspaper, 'who always said that difficulties and obstacles could be overcome.' Yet in 1941 he committed suicide. (*Courtesy of Lodge Ancient Brazen No. 17, Linlithgow*)

Below. Alex's parents, Mary and Robert Salmond, a 'Winston Churchill Conservative' and 'Uncle Joe', a Stalinist in his youth. (*Courtesy of STV*)

Above. A family snap of Salmond. 'He was a very happy child,' recalled his mother in 2001.

Right. The Reverend (Gilbert) Elliot Anderson, from whom Salmond took his two middle names. 'I have tried to bear that name with pride,' he told the General Assembly of the Church of Scotland in 2009.

OPERA PART FOR ALEX (12)

A young Linlithgow lad took part this week in an operatic production . . . and co-starred among 20 girls.

The production was Callendar Park College of Education's Christmas Opera, "Amahl and the Night Visitors" and the lucky fellow was 12-year-old Alex Salmond.

Alex, of 101 Preston Road, is a boy soprano with St. Michael's Church Choir and he was picked for the part because the composer laid down that the part must be played by a boy.

The show was held in Callendar Park College Hall, on Monday and there was a fine turnout to see it.

Alex will appear with the girls in Linlithgow in January when they bring the show to St. Michael's Church.

Alex fairly enjoyed playing the part and Jean Graham, of the "Falkirk Herald," who saw the show said "Alex is a fine wee singer. He has a very pleasant voice and carried the part very well indeed. He did not seem overawed in the slightest by his female company."

Left. Local newspaper coverage of Salmond's role in Gian Carlo Menotti's opera *Amahl and the Night Visitors.* He was, according to his mother, 'absolutely marvellous'.

Below. The poet R. S. Thomas. Alex identified with Thomas's character, the Welsh hill-farmer Iago Prytherch. (*Courtesy of Bernard Mitchell/National Library of Wales*)

Young Alex: Three early portraits of Salmond by his university friend Peter Brunskill. 'He just had this idea that there was no limit to what he could do,' recalled Brunskill. (*Courtesy of Peter Brunskill*)

Salmond as education vice-president of St Andrews University's SRC, with some of his contemporaries. Back row, left to right: Tim McKay, Pam Beveridge, unknown, unknown, Salmond, Mark Call; front row, right to left: Jamie Stone, Des Swayne, Peter Brunskill, unknown, unknown. (*Courtesy of Peter Adamson*)

Salmond hosting a walkabout with Winnie Ewing at St Andrews in September 1977.

aien

St. Andrews University Newspaper

Vol 17 No8
Wednesday March 1st
10p

Bainbridge 517   **Salmond 506**   **Hogg 288**

CLOSEST ELECTION EVER

Atmosphere was tense in the debating hall on Thursday as the votes were counted for the closest ever fought presidential election.

The final result gave Pete Bainbridge a lead of only 54 votes in a poll of 1311, but it was not until after three hours of counting that it became clear that he would win. Alex Salmond pulled into an early lead of over 100 votes and it was thought that this would be the general trend until the results for University Hall were counted and Pete recouped over 50 of the difference. Again in Chattan he collected 40 votes more than Alex and by the end of the first count he was winning by the narrow margin of 11, Alex having won more polling stations with a ratio of 11:6. Under the new voting system, started last year, Bill Hogg's votes were reallocated according to the second preference given on the ballot papers. Initial redistribution was fairly even until Hall clinched it again, giving Pete a gain of 24 votes, nearly half of his final majority.

NIGHTLINE ST. ANDREWS 5555

V.K. Chapman
jeweller

pewter tankards
clocks and watches
brooches and earrings
21st presents

104 South St. St. Andrews

Attendance at the SRC hecklings last Wednesday night was, to say the least, disappointing. Heavy rain kept away all but 50 students who heard 13 candidates being heckled at School 3 in Quad. A pile of information hand-outs 3'' thick, showing that a better turnout was expected, remained almost untouched. As a result the actual heckling tended to be one-sided, depending on whose side the speaker in question was on. Style and speed of delivery varied greatly, from the lively, fast-talking Dave Applebaum to the more measured tones of Dave Hunt.

The usual political banterings were exchanged by the Swayne/Masty/Blacklocks/Salmond sectors though most effort was wasted since there were probably only one or two dozen people in the theatre who had actually gone along to hear what all the candidates had to say.

There was a certain amount of light relief, with the meanderings of Nigel Callaghan as he tried to form actual questions and the occasional wheeze of amazement from Des Swayne at what someone else had to say.

The presidential candidates within their time limits managed to cover most of the main election issues, which had already been discussed in their publicity handouts, plus their general attitude towards the presidency and what they would like to see done in the future. Alex Salmond got the best general reception, Pete Bainbridge was applauded mainly from one corner of the room, while Bill Hogg got off fairly lightly.

The final results in full are as follows:

P. Bainbridge 517 648 (after redistribution)
A. Salmond 506 594
B. Hogg 288

Services:	O.Ash	689	D. Hunt	445
Education:	D. Swayne	433	S.Blacklocks	653
Secretary:	D. Batchelor	658	D. Applebaum	489
Treasurer:	D. Graham	662	R. Corbett	400

Published fortnightly by AIEN at the Students' Union, St.Andrews. Tel. 3080.

CARS FOR THE BOYS?

News that the SRC is to spend £500-1000 to buy a car to be used exclusively by members of the executive council caused a stir last week. A motion was passed at the last SRC meeting agreeing to such a purchase. A car is to be bought because it will be considerably cheaper than a minibus and because the Union has already just bought another minibus to hire out to students. It is to be used to transport SRC members to and from meetings outside the town, and also to move the large amount of printing materials handled by tghe SRC, as well as distributing and collecting ballot boxes around the town at election time.

SRC member Dave Hunt is to propose a motion at the next meeting that the car be made available for hire to other student bodies such as the societies, after strong views were expressed against the SRC having their own private transport.

However, Pam Beveridge has said that she would have no objections to the car being hired out once the problem of insurance and running costs had been settled.

Aien's coverage of Salmond's defeat in the SRC presidential election of 1978. It still rankled decades later. (*Courtesy of St Andrews University Library Special Collections*)

Salmond forged many long-lasting associations during the 1970s. 'He was able to draw people in,' recalled Stewart Stevenson. 'That was his absolutely key skill.' (*Courtesy of Stewart Stevenson MSP*)

Salmond with the 79 Group. Left to right: Billy Wolfe, Jim Sillars, unknown, Stephen Maxwell, Salmond and Ian Blackford. 'I thought the work that the 79 Group…[did] in supporting workers' occupations', Salmond later reflected, 'was absolutely fundamental.' (*Courtesy of Radical Scotland*)

Salmond shows Grant Baird his oil index at the Royal Bank of Scotland. 'If ever there was an old head on young shoulders,' Baird once said, 'then it's Alex Salmond's.' (*Courtesy of The Royal Bank of Scotland Group*)

Salmond with Jim Sillars in the mid-1980s. For many years their relationship was, according to Isobel Lindsay, akin to that of 'mentor and protégé', although it later turned sour.

As the SNP's publicity vice-convener with Andrew Welsh in 1986. *Radical Scotland* dubbed Salmond's publicity sub-committee 'the SNP's Saatchi & Saatchi'. (*Courtesy of The Scotsman Publications*)

Alex celebrates with Moira after winning Banff and Buchan at the 1987 election. Maureen Watt is second from the right, Dr James Mitchell is third from the left, and Eilidh Whiteford – who succeeded Salmond as MP in 2010 – is to his immediate right.

Salmond as a young MP outside the Houses of Parliament. Malcolm Rifkind likened him to 'the infant Robespierre'.

Above. Salmond celebrates after being elected SNP leader in September 1990. In his acceptance speech he pledged to 'win the battle for the hearts and minds of the Scottish people'. (*Courtesy of STV*)

Left. Alex and Moira Salmond in late 1990, photographed following their one and only joint interview. 'I married Alex, not politics,' Moira told the *Sunday Post*. 'That's his life and I am happy to be in the background.'

The 'Great Debate' at Edinburgh's Usher Hall in January 1992. 'It was an extraordinary occasion,' recalled Salmond, 'a throwback to pre-television politics.' (*Courtesy of The Scotsman Publications*)

Contrary to expectations, Sillars complemented Salmond well as his deputy in the run up to the 1992 general election. 'The Salmond guile, plus the Sillars bombast', assessed one journalist, 'makes for an intriguing mixture.' (*Courtesy of The Scotsman Publications*)

Toasting the 1997 devolution referendum result. Mike Russell reckoned that Salmond's role in the campaign 'was his outstanding moment in a decade of many outstanding moments'. (*Courtesy of The Scotsman Publications*)

Above. Being sworn in as a Member of the new Scottish Parliament in 1999. He promised 'innovative and determined opposition', but his remaining year as SNP leader was neither. (*Courtesy of the Scottish Parliament*)

Right. Salmond embraces his adviser Kevin Pringle after announcing his resignation as SNP leader in 2000. He quoted Harold Wilson: 'It's better to go when they're asking why you're going rather than wait until they're asking why you're staying.' (*Courtesy of The Scotsman Publications*)

Four years later and Salmond announces his comeback at the same Aberdeenshire hotel. He told journalists that he was 'not just launching a campaign to be SNP leader' but his 'candidacy to be First Minister of Scotland'. (*Courtesy of The Scotsman Publications*)

An ebullient Salmond on polling day in May 2007. Later, as it became clear the SNP had won its first Scottish election, he spoke of a 'wind of change' blowing across the country. (*Courtesy of The Scotsman Publications*)

Salmond becomes First Minister following a vote at Holyrood in May 2007. He later remembered it as 'a hell of a moment'. (*Adam Elder/Courtesy of the Scottish Parliament*)

Salmond with his newly enlarged second SNP Scottish Government outside Bute House, his official residence, in May 2011. (*Courtesy of the Scottish Government*)

given added colour by claims that he owed a substantial sum to an Irish bookmaker. Salmond believes, privately, that the smear was spread by political rivals. The problem was that he had no opportunity to rebut the gossip. One newspaper after another investigated the claims and found no substance whatsoever to stand up the story. Not a word was printed and so no rebuttal could sensibly be issued.

Privately, Salmond insisted repeatedly that he had never placed a credit bet in his life, while denying being in debt to an Irish bookie or anyone else. Taylor also recorded 'one particularly febrile weekend – at the mid-point of the campaign – when the Sunday newspapers appeared convinced that one of their number was about to break the story. Salmond and party officials were besieged by phone calls from journalists. Eventually, Salmond broke from campaigning to phone the editor of the paper concerned. He was told that the claims had been investigated some time back, and completely dismissed. For Salmond, this was the worst dilemma possible. He was not facing an enemy he could challenge directly, a political or personal claim he could counter. He was facing an insubstantial rumour, wild gossip without foundation. Little wonder he was under strain.'[106]

Eight years later, during the 2007 Holyrood elections, Salmond still faced similar allegations. 'Do you think it is appropriate given your racing columns that the voters should know what the largest sum you ever won through racing,' asked the *Scotsman*, 'and the largest debt you ever accrued?'. He replied: 'Whether it is appropriate or not, I am not intending to discuss it. I don't think it is a factor in this election. I have been perfectly open about my interest in horse racing, an interest shared by many, many people in Scotland. And, incidentally, I have never had a gambling debt in my life.'[107]

Back in 1999, Salmond also had to deal with more straightforward attacks from his political opponents, not least over his failure to publish, as promised, an 'independence manifesto', as opposed to the 'devolution manifesto' that had only outlined the SNP's plans for devolved policy areas. A defensive Salmond denied backtracking, claiming that when the independence manifesto was produced, it 'will be visionary; it'll also be exciting, people will be able to compare and contrast the two'.[108]

Next were tabloid stories concerning a split between Salmond and Mike Russell over the former's Kosovo broadcast, an unlikely story given Russell's role in drafting it. On 9 April, a 'furious' Salmond telephoned the *Herald* journalist Murray Ritchie to ask if he planned to follow up the story. Ritchie said no; because he did not believe it, and they went on to discuss the SNP's tactics. 'He swears he is convinced he is winning with the Penny for Scotland policy and that his critical comments on Kosovo have not damaged his standing,' recorded Ritchie in an election diary. 'This is not what the opinion polls have been saying, he admits, but he insists he is more impressed by reaction on the streets where his remarks are playing positively.'[109]

Also causing problems were Salmond's declining personal approval ratings. Shortly after the campaign began, these had tumbled to an all-time low of 25 per cent, compared with up to 55 per cent for Donald Dewar, a steep decline of more than 18 points since July 1998. Even the prospect of a coalition with the Liberal Democrats was beset with difficulties, Jim Wallace making it clear that such an arrangement would be conditional upon Salmond giving up his commitment to holding a referendum on independence. 'I believe if we emerge as the leading party there will be enough support in the parliament to enable us to hold a referendum within the four-year term,' responded Salmond. 'I accept we might have to negotiate on timing, and I think that is entirely reasonable.'[110] It was a sticking point between the two parties that would remain unresolved even at the third set of elections to the Scottish Parliament in 2007.

The pressure Salmond was undoubtedly under also manifested itself in some rather careless interviews. 'The Labour Party can be such arse-holes,' he apparently told the *Sunday Mirror*. 'They flew Donald Dewar to Washington to meet Bill Clinton to raise his profile. And do you know how long Clinton allowed him? One minute. Then they flew him home again. Another idea was to take him to the top of the Mound here in Edinburgh for a photo shoot ... and he fell over.' The Prime Minister was also singled out for a personal attack. 'Blair and Brown will be up and down to Scotland like yo-yos. Blair thinks he's their trump card,' he said. 'Give him a message – any message – and he'll sell it. He'd sell his own granny to a glue factory.'

'You operate on pure adrenalin,' Salmond said of campaigning in general. 'The rush is unbelievable.'[111] Yet the usual Salmond rush appeared to be absent for much of the first two weeks of the campaign. When the *Guardian*'s Peter Hetherington put it to him that he was not up to the pressure of Scotland's first 'general election', 'Balls,' was Salmond's blunt response. 'Absolute balls.' 'So what?' he added. 'Let them write what they like ... "The mair they talk, the better I'm kent".'

The SNP leader was, judged Hetherington, 'a private man. He can appear warm and generous on the street; yet critics insist he is cold, calculating, arrogant. But he presents the only credible face of the SNP. He is the party.'[112]

And therein lay the problem with the campaign. Often susceptible to charges of being a one-man band, that one-man band was clearly out of tune. Perhaps the nadir of the campaign came on 22 April when a *Herald* poll gave Labour a 20-point lead over the SNP. The newspaper's front-page headline, 'SNP in Freefall', may have been an exaggeration, but it captured accurately what many Nationalists believed to be a loss of direction. 'The most awful prospect which must haunt Alex Salmond tonight is that perhaps the worst is not yet over,' wrote Murray Ritchie in his diary. 'As of this day his leadership ability is unlikely ever to go unquestioned again.'[113] Salmond also appeared edgy on an edition of the BBC's *Question Time* that evening, while critics of his leadership began to question his position. 'Don't be daft asking me questions about whether I'll go,' said a clearly irritated Salmond. 'I'm 44 years old. I'm laughing this off. All my focus is on the next two weeks and the campaign and I am focusing on nothing else.'[114] Asked about the *Herald* poll at a press conference, Salmond quoted the US naval hero John Paul Jones: 'I have not yet begun to fight.'[115]

Then Salmond demonstrated his remarkable capacity for turning things around. Boldly unveiling a two-week strategy he said would be 'vital, urgent and barnstorming', he cancelled daily press briefings in favour of a campaign that would take the fight for votes direct to the streets. 'As far as this campaign is concerned, the SNP have not yet begun to fight,' said Salmond. 'Our response to unfavourable opinion polls is to get our jackets off and get stuck into this campaign.' To pacify fundamentalist critics, meanwhile, he branded the SNP 'Scotland's independence party', and promised to publish the long awaited 'independence manifesto'.[116] In short, declared Salmond, there would be more political 'razzmatazz': 'We will be here, there and everywhere.'[117]

The first constituency to experience that razzmatazz was Glasgow Govan, where Nicola Sturgeon was hoping to repeat previous Nationalist successes in 1973 and 1988. Shadowed by a small army of journalists, two policemen and a plainclothes officer, Salmond stormed the streets looking for hands to shake. 'It's not the press who are going to dictate the circumstances of this campaign,' he said later, 'it's the people of Scotland.'[118] This was Salmond at his best, noted the *Sunday Herald*'s Torcuil Crichton, even if he remained a little off-colour. 'True, he looks pasty faced, perhaps tired, but winter is long for everyone in Scot-land. In fact the pale skin is at odds with the demeanour, the suit, the aftershave. He does not operate like the usual reticent Scottish MP. His style is more continental. He shines in public, professional and assured, insincere but effective. He has a backslap here for an influential journal-ist, a wave for a lorry driver, cutting a path though minders and media to make contact with an individual in the crowd.'[119]

The Times' sketch writer, Matthew Parris, also captured the 'mechan-ical ferocity' of the occasion: 'A Salmond walkabout moves at about eight miles per hour, chased by cameras and reporters and trampling the weak and unsuspecting underfoot as, eyes blazing, Scotland's best campaigner ricochets from handshake to photo opportunity. He spots a chip shop, dives in, buys a token portion, admires each chip – "Scottish chips" – signs a plastic Scottish flaglet, shakes a hand, and dives out.' 'I saw Salmond campaigning in Galloway in 1997,' remarked Parris more soberly. 'That Alex was on a roll. This one is not. He dives back into his battle bus like someone in retreat. There are photographers at the door. He neglects to wave.'[120]

'So, it has come to this: a last desperate throw of the dice, staking all on the personality of Alex Salmond,' observed Iain Macwhirter. 'It's a weary political metaphor, but the SNP leader is a notorious gambler, and this will be his biggest gamble of all. A hectic, 10-day take-the-country-by-storm appeal to the Scottish nation. If he's tired, off-form, crestfallen or subdued, he wasn't letting on as he began his meet-the-people (avoid-the-press) tour in Govan on Friday. From here on, it will be Alex braveheart versus the Scottish fainthearts. Or as he puts it, hope against the politics of fear. So far, he concedes, fear is winning.' 'The SNP seemed to undergo something like a collective breakdown on Thursday, a loss of self-belief,' continued Macwhirter. 'The Herald poll was only that – a poll. It shouldn't have led to such a drastic collapse of morale.' Problems had, of course, been building over the previous fortnight 'as SNP candi-dates were hammered, day after day, on the war and tax – first by the tabloids, then on the doorsteps. From seeming to do nothing wrong, somehow nothing was going right.'[121]

On Monday 26 April, the beginning of the last full week of the campaign, the SNP relaunched with Sean Connery at the helm. The suite at Edinburgh's International Conference Centre was packed and the atmosphere electric; for the first time during the campaign the SNP had matched Labour with an effective and slick operation. Connery arrived amid a sea of mini-Saltires and delivered a rousing speech, attacking Labour control freaks he claimed had destroyed the enthusi-asm that had marked the referendum campaign. If it had not been for the murder of television presenter Jill Dando the same day, however, the event would certainly have dominated the day's media.

Then came publication of the much-anticipated Economic Strategy for Independence, which Labour had been hounding Salmond about for several weeks. He tried to manage the event by unveiling it at a gathering of favourable businessmen, but even a sympathetic journalist thought Salmond and John Swinney proceeded to 'make an inglorious hash of their press conference. Alex simply refuses to put a figure on the cost of – or benefit to – an independent Scotland from the year 2000. He is asked several times and tries to dodge the question, inviting other people to ask other questions (which they do not) and he tries to offload the questions on John. But eventually after much needless obfuscation he admits that an independent Scotland would be £1.5 billion in the red in its first year, but that it would quickly move into the black in subsequent years.'[122] It actually fell to Andrew Wilson to work out the figure, which was initially given as £1.7 billion, but later corrected to £1.5bn. 'Well you know', Salmond later admitted, 'I don't think that was the finest press conference we held in the history of my political career.'[123]

Again, Labour went to town, Gordon Brown condemning the document as lacking even a shred of credibility and Tony Blair lambast-ing it at a charity lunch in Glasgow. During Blair's speech Salmond – who was also sitting at the top table – smiled, reached into his pocket and pulled out a folded orange card. This, emblazoned with the word 'BLUFF' in large letters, was then held up for all to see, cleverly under-mining Blair's speech without actually making a coherent – or very mature – point.

Opinion polls began to indicate the SNP was clawing back support, a trend the party tried to consolidate by launching its own four-page newspaper – *Scotland's Voice* – later that week. Distributed by party activists in a quixotic attempt to bypass the mainstream media, the SNP claimed that circulation, which began at 50,000, peaked at 120,000 on the Monday before polling day. But it was clearly propaganda, and expensive propaganda at that, and the initiative fell flat tactically.[124] Salmond, meanwhile, 'who for the first three weeks was off-colour, grumpy and aggressive', had only in the final week regained 'his usual talismanic form'.[125] Similarly, Murray Ritchie reckoned that the *Herald*'s 'SNP in Freefall' headline had 'galvanised' Salmond, whose 'disposition became much sunnier immediately after our second poll was published and he has been firing on all cylinders ever since. On several television debates in the past few days he has easily outshone Donald Dewar.'[126] By then, however, it was too late.

Even as polls continued to suggest Labour would comfortably emerge as the largest party, Salmond did not falter. 'Not for one moment,' observed Alan Taylor, who followed him in the last few days of the campaign, 'did he show a flicker of doubt that victory was within his grasp.' A headline in the *Scotsman* captured this well: 'Convinced of Victory Against The Odds.' 'Certainty and self belief are attributes which any leader must have to survive in the brutal, judgemental and egocentric world of politics,' wrote Peter McMahon. 'Salmond has all these attributes, in spades.'[127]

On polling day, Salmond embarked upon a hectic tour of his picturesque constituency. Alan Taylor reported:

> Throughout the day, the SNP leader was accompanied by his wife, Moira, a familiar face in these parts. A veteran of several general election campaigns, she is his unsung strategist, a formidable force at local level . . . Though trailing in the polls nationally, Mr Salmond remained buoyant, insisting that victory was still not beyond the party's grasp. Through a loud hailer, he proclaimed: "Good afternoon. Good afternoon. My name is Alex Salmond. Today is polling day; let's make it Scotland's day. Vote SNP – one, two and three." Eight seconds, he says is the optimum time he has to deliver his message, which he rattles off with machine gun consistency. Stephen Noon, who runs Mr Salmond's Westminster office, said: "Alex always judges his chances by how quickly and positively people are waving at him."[128]

He must have misinterpreted the waves for shortly before 1.40 a.m. the morning after polling day, Noon picked his way through the crowd on the viewing balcony of Macduff Town Hall, tapped Salmond on the shoulder and whispered: 'We've lost Govan.' It was, Salmond later admitted, his worst moment of the election.[129] 'Dawn was breaking over Macduff harbour as Alex Salmond and his wife Moira emerged from the town hall,' observed Alan Taylor. 'But if anyone expected him to show disappointment they were mistaken. While all around exhibited signs of fatigue, Salmond insisted on returning to the Banff Springs hotel and cracking open a bottle of the champagne he had won as *The Scotsman's* best performer in the grinding election battle.'[130] 'I said we would drink this – win, lose or draw,' he told a group of close aides and friends. 'I'll drink now to a win.'[131]

At the historic first elections to the new Scottish parliament the SNP had won 28.7 per cent of the constituency vote and 27.3 per cent on the regional list, giving the party a total of 35 seats, five short of the threshold fundamentalists had warned was required for Salmond to remain as leader. And although Labour's share of the vote declined by 6.8 per cent compared with the 1997 election result, it still managed to secure 56 seats. In short, with a vote increase of 6.6 per cent, it was a reasonable result for the SNP, just not good enough, while the weight of expectation obscured a significant swing and real progress in Scotland's cities.[132] In Banff and Buchan, meanwhile, Salmond secured 16,695 votes and an impressive 11,232 majority.

It had been a curious campaign, dominated by events in a faraway country of which most Scots knew nothing, and one that saw neither Labour nor the SNP truly shine. Donald Dewar had been sidelined while the SNP had the opposite problem, depending too much on Salmond as its public face. The same dynamic, however, had not existed in terms of press coverage. The *Herald* aside, which had made much of its attempts to treat the SNP in a balanced way, the Scottish media had been uniformly hostile, displaying editorial viciousness that had caught the SNP unawares. Apocalyptic Labour broadcasts, meanwhile, depicted the UK breaking apart, while one billboard campaign screamed 'MORE TAX', the 'X' emerging from the SNP's thistle logo. The New Labour observer Andrew Rawnsley rightly suspected that although Salmond had repeatedly complained of 'a London-controlled campaign, based on a deeply negative agenda', his 'real grievance was that it was working'.[133]

That said, there had obviously been faults with the SNP campaign that could not be blamed on the media, chiefly ill-prepared press conferences and spokespeople who often appeared not to know the detail of basic SNP policy. 'I don't criticise the campaign organisation or platform,' Salmond later reflected. 'I'm the leader of the party. Obviously there were shortcomings – I'm responsible for whatever shortcomings there were.'[134]

Chapter 9

'DYNAMIC OPPOSITION'

This is about more than our politics and our laws. This is about who we are, how we carry ourselves ...We are fallible. We will make mistakes. But we will never lose sight of what brought us here: the striving to do right by the people of Scotland; to respect their priorities; to better their lot; and to contribute to the commonweal.[1]

Donald Dewar's speech at the opening
of the Scottish Parliament, 1 July 1999

A devolved Scottish Parliament was the leitmotif of a whole political generation, representing the hopes, aspirations and ambitions of those from all movements and none. Alex Salmond was as much a part of that generation as Donald Dewar and Jim Wallace, having campaigned since his student days for a Scottish Assembly, albeit as one step on the long road to independence. Curiously, having waited so long for its creation, it was a forum in which neither Salmond nor his contemporaries would thrive.

As the electoral dust settled upon those historic first elections to the Scottish Parliament, Salmond put, as ever, a brave face upon the outcome, a task made easier by the presence of 35 SNP MSPs – a greater number of elected representatives than at any point in the party's Parliamentary history. He stated: 'For the first time ever, the SNP are the second party in each of Scotland's four main cities – a powerful base from which to build future progress in urban Scotland. The SNP campaign reflected the nature of a PR election. We piled up votes around Scotland, and piled up seats on that basis. As the official opposition – a new status for Scotland's Party – the SNP will be a powerful force in the Scottish Parliament, introducing innovative policy ideas to make it work for the people of Scotland, including measures to abolish the scandal of tuition fees.' The SNP, assured Salmond, would seek a fresh mandate for independence 'at the first available opportunity'.[2]

Looking back on the election a decade later, however, Salmond was more sanguine. 'It was a fairly towsy election,' he told the radio journalist Colin Mackay. 'Expectations were sky high and probably unrealistic.'[3] Inevitably, there was post-election self-flagellation. Margaret Ewing blamed Salmond's Kosovo broadcast, Alex Neil his and Mike Russell's election strategy, and Margo MacDonald the party leader's neglect of the core independence message. The truth was probably a combination of all three, as well as that rarely attributed factor of plain old bad luck. The SNP had, after all, been subjected to remorselessly hostile press coverage, often in concert with a ruthless and efficient Labour operation that had co-opted Ed Miliband and Charlie Whelan from London.

The new Parliament, in which so many hopes and aspirations had been invested since the late 1980s, met for the first time on 12 May 1999. Following nearly a week of negotiations, Labour and the Liberal Democrats had agreed a coalition deal with relative ease. Salmond prefaced his oath of allegiance by stressing that the SNP group's 'primary loyalty lies with the people of Scotland, in line with the Scottish constitutional tradition of the sovereignty of the people'. He then added, somewhat presumptuously: 'I know that all members of this Parliament will share that view.'[4]

The following day saw the formal election of the First Minister, during which Salmond singularly failed to rise to the occasion. 'I am making the fourth speech, and that rather makes the point that this is a Parliament of minorities,' he told MSPs. 'Some are bigger than others, but none the less it is a Parliament of minorities.' When it came to the vote, every SNP MSP backed Salmond, although the Labour MSP Mike Watson later claimed that two had told him they ought to have backed Donald Dewar, so inevitable was his victory and to demonstrate that the new Parliament was not like Westminster.[5] Indeed, at an SNP group meeting Duncan Hamilton and Andrew Wilson urged precisely that but lost by 33 votes to 2.

Salmond struck a more constructive note as he congratulated Dewar and ruminated on the 'nature of opposition': 'There has been some debate about how we can have the new consensus politics and still have vigorous debate. I suggest that we can have both. Those of us who have served in Westminster know full well what people mean when they talk about yah-boo reflex reaction politics. It is possible for us to avoid that in this new chamber. Therefore, as Leader of the Opposition, let me say that when the Administration proposes things that we think are in the interests of the Scottish people, we will not criticise for the sake of it.' Finally, Salmond dedicated his party 'to being an innovative and determined Opposition'.[6]

Salmond's year as leader of that opposition, however, turned out to be neither innovative nor, or so it seemed to observers, particularly determined. Although officially termed 'Shadow First Minister', Salmond rarely looked like a leader in waiting, while his Shadow Cabinet – unveiled towards the end of May 1999 – seldom had the potential to be the next Scottish Executive. Of Salmond's critics, only the former lost soul Kenny MacAskill made it to the first SNP front bench team as transport and environment spokesman. Alex Neil was given social security, an important portfolio albeit one not devolved to the Scottish Parliament, while Andrew Wilson – one of Salmond's bright young things – was given the crucial finance portfolio. 'The party is united,' declared Salmond, seeking to bury once and for all the tiresome fundamentalist/gradualist hatchet. 'The constitutional debate within the SNP was whether devolution was a route to independence. Since the devolution Parliament is now a reality, that debate now ceases.'[7]

That particular debate did cease, more or less, although following elections to the European Parliament in June (in which the SNP won 27.2 per cent of the vote), internal debate instead focused – predominantly but not exclusively – upon Salmond's handling of the SNP's finances, both internal (donations) and external (its tax policies). The opening salvo between Ian Blackford, the party's national treasurer, and the party leader came in July when questions were raised about the fundraising activities of Business for Scotland (BfS), a pro-independence group of entrepreneurs that had been established the previous year.

It began when the founder of Stagecoach, Brian Souter, found himself at the centre of speculation that he had donated £200,000 to the SNP prior to the 1999 election. Suspicious that BfS was being used to channel donations from people who did not want publicity, Blackford (who had been elected treasurer – defeating Andrew Wilson – in order to 'bring higher standards of scrutiny' to SNP accounts) was only given access to its accounts after he threatened to resign. Salmond refused publicly, however, to say whether money raised for BfS included any contributions from anonymous donors, i.e. Souter. Furthermore, he maintained that he was under no obligation to reveal such donations if they had been made before 14 January 1999, at which point new rules on party funding had been agreed in accordance with Lord Neill's committee on public standards.

This Blackford/Salmond spat was to last nearly a year and only cease when Salmond resigned as SNP leader. When the list of SNP conference motions was published that August, it emerged that the Edinburgh Newington branch (of which Blackford was a member) had tabled a motion calling for a rethink of the Penny for Scotland policy. Salmond, at least initially, tried to play it cool. 'I want a competitive tax policy and one that's also fair in terms of social justice,' he said. 'The motion doesn't utter a word of criticism of the election campaign or the Penny for Scotland. It's totally innocuous and uncontroversial.'[8]

Blackford, meanwhile, insisted that the motion was not intended as an attack on the SNP's taxation policy, but when it emerged that Billy Wolfe – the party's former leader – was preparing to challenge Blackford for the treasurer's post at conference, it seemed clear that Salmond had interpreted it that way. To put the dispute in context, both men had shifted their positions when it came to the Scottish Parliament's tax-varying powers. Salmond had, since the mid-1990s, advocated a low-tax model for Scotland, only adopting the Penny for Scotland policy as a response to Gordon Brown's March 1999 Budget. At the conference debate which endorsed the shift, Blackford had expressed 'concerns and reservations' about the proposal, but said he believed these could be overcome using presentational tweaks. In the wake of the election result, however, he now considered it a barrier to future success. 'The resolution is about independence and about raising the debate on Scotland's economic potential post-independence,' Blackford explained. 'It is about how we can encourage people to invest in Scotland and how we can create a successful economy.'[9] He went on to table another motion, this time critical of Salmond's stance on the Euro, as outlined six days before the election.

'Alex told me that he had a conversation with Billy [Wolfe] and put Billy up to it,' Blackford told the *Daily Express*. 'We have not been happy with each other. We discussed this thing and have drawn a line under it. I would like to think I have got the support of the leadership. I expect to be re-elected.'[10] But Salmond was not so easily appeased, particularly when details emerged of a report by Blackford that was to be presented to conference. Without naming either Salmond or Mike Russell, this clearly blamed the duo for a £200,000 budget overspend in the Scottish Parliament election campaign. The SNP's finances were indeed in a parlous state. Its overdraft was running at £500,000; it had just appealed to party members for interest-free loans until the end of 2000, and it was preparing to sell its Edinburgh New Town HQ in order to raise around £300,000.[11]

'The scenario runs like this,' summarised Robbie Dinwoodie in the *Herald*. 'Alex Salmond, a notorious gambler, took on several bets too many during the election campaign. His party burst the budget and plunged into debt, he risked a politically damaging personal inter-vention on Kosovo, and then staked all on the Scots' innate communitarian spirit by asking them to pay an extra penny in tax.' Blackford was, therefore, attempting to hold Salmond to account over two of those bets, without, he claimed, any wider motive. The trouble was, as Dinwoodie continued, Blackford was 'now being portrayed, because of a longstanding friendship with Margo MacDonald and her husband Jim Sillars, as being used as a tool of their dissent, based on resentment and personal enmity with Alex Salmond'. The idea of Salmond being ousted as leader, however, was 'inconceivable'[12]

'I remember some time ago when I was appointed to the SNP Cabinet that Alex Salmond gave me a useful piece of advice, which was to be my own man,' wrote Blackford in response to Dinwoodie's article. 'It was advice that I was happy to accept, and I believe I have acted as my own man ever since.' 'All that I am concerned about in the SNP is delivering effective stewardship of the SNP's finances,' he added, 'and to that end I will be answerable to the party at its September conference.'[13]

It was a valiant attempt to plead unity, but the Scottish media now sensed a 'crisis' and willingly lapped up dissent. Margo MacDonald, since May an SNP Lothians list MSP, duly delivered. 'It was a mistake,' she said of the party's tax policy. 'The electorate associated "A Penny for Scotland" with them paying money out of their own pockets. It was confusing and muddled. Tactically it was a non-starter. We were bounced into it by Alex Salmond.' And for good measure, MacDonald added: 'Fundamentalists do not get sucked into the unionist system. Alex Salmond unfortunately lacks my clarity.'

Salmond retorted:

Total hot air. This is silly season nonsense ... Every year is a testing time for every political leader, but I'm going to lead the party into the next election in Scotland and we are going to win it. The May results are the best electoral results in SNP history. I would love to have won the election, but in a deeper sense we did because we became the opposition – and parties who become opposition become the government. We are not resting on our laurels. We expect to be challenged and examined, but in terms of political progress there can be few political parties in history who have made that advance from political fringe to centre stage so quickly.[14]

Salmond's analysis of the election result was more convenient than convincing, but preceded a spirited fight back. At a press conference to unveil the SNP's strategy for the first year of the new Parliamentary session, he declared that independence was now 'inevitable', explaining: 'The Scottish parliament is now the focal point of our politics – it is our route, our avenue for progress to independence. Our position is that, by the success of the parliament, we will build confidence in the ability of Scotland to run its own affairs. If the parliament succeeds in running education and health then the natural conclusion that people will come to is that we should be running the economy and macro-policy as well.' In other words, the Scottish Parliament – the 'focal point' of Scottish politics – was now the only game in town. Salmond, who was 'tanned and healthy-looking' at the press conference, was clearly back on form. He also batted aside questions about MacDonald's recent critique of his election campaign, describing the SNP's MSP group as 'very cohesive'. 'I don't think that Margo has changed her opinion of me greatly over the last few years,' he joked. 'A group has to be big enough to tolerate dissent and the SNP has always put a premium on self-discipline.'[15]

Salmond's stance, however, shifted just a few days later as he announced new rules banning criticism of group decisions in the press. 'People expect SNP members to follow SNP policy. I don't know of any political party that doesn't have rules of procedure for members to abide by.'[16] It was clear, however, that Salmond was finding many of his MSPs inexperienced and difficult to manage. 'It certainly had one drawback,' he later admitted to Colin Mackay, of the group. 'It had six or, I think, seven people of Parliamentary experience and that is a difficulty.'[17]

The Blackford versus Salmond fight, meanwhile, took another surprising turn when Billy Wolfe decided to pull out of the contest for national treasurer, leaving Blackford unopposed. Salmond continued to defend the Penny for Scotland, while others speculated about how long he could remain leader. Alex Bell, who had worked for Salmond in the run-up to the 1999 election, said that if the SNP leader did not return from his summer break 'as the feisty, bonny fechter of Scottish politics ... then people will begin to say, well if he doesn't have his aggressive qualities, is he the right man to be leading this party now? He's done it for ten years and the clock is certainly ticking on his leadership.'[18]

Speculation over Salmond's future – the first since 1993 – hung over the SNP's annual conference as delegates gathered in Inverness. Mike Russell, spoken of as a possible successor, felt compelled to tell reporters that Salmond was the 'best leader the SNP has ever had. He is the leader who will take us to independence', while Salmond said he was 'absolutely certain' the party had 'never been more united'.[19] Speaking to the *Scotsman* on the eve of conference, Salmond also echoed Harold Wilson's message to his plot-ridden party: 'I know what's going on – I'm going on.' Still looking tanned and relaxed, he declared his back problem 'cured', citing his improved golf as evidence. 'I am now hitting the ball further than I was with my old back.' He also claimed to be 'enjoying this parliament enormously'. 'I have spent a lot of time in the last ten years running round looking like a crowd,' he quipped. 'Now we are a crowd. We are now 35. We are many. And it's important that the many get the opportunity to show what they can do.'

In other words, the SNP was no longer a one-man band. Salmond heaped praise on Andrew Wilson, who had recently claimed a sense of 'Britishness' could survive Scottish independence. 'Nobody in Scotland must feel excluded from voting for independence,' responded Salmond. 'Andrew takes the position in a slightly different context than I do, but then he is entitled to put forward that view.'[20] Did he not feel at all British himself? 'No I don't. I feel Scottish and European. I am entitled to my identity ... The question you want to ask is can you feel British and still vote for the SNP and the answer is "yes, of course you can".'

Salmond also expanded upon his political identity: 'I am a social democrat and I don't regard social democracy as old politics. I think it is very successful politics in a number of European countries, particularly smaller European countries. I think it works best when it is freed from its corporatist tendency which it can have in larger countries ... It combines interest in an enterprise economy with a collective wish for the provision of public services and to a great extent that represents Scotland or a large group in Scotland of people who believe in both – a dynamic, thrusting entrepreneurial economy [with] decent public services.'[21]

In advance of Salmond's keynote conference address, meanwhile, Ian Blackford cleverly branded his Scottish Parliament-focused approach 'unpardonable folly'. 'There are those in the SNP who argue that the route to independence is solely through the Scottish parliament,' he wrote in the *Scotsman*. 'This can be compared to consigning yourself to taking the A road and ignoring the faster motorway link.'[22]

Salmond was duly dismissive. 'I have not spent too much time reading Ian's thoughts,' he said. 'He thought the party was under-performing – that's a position which does not carry much support.'[23] Blackford's attack, combined with the fallout from Andrew Wilson calling the Union Jack an 'offensive symbol'[24] of colonialism, would have had more damage had it not been for a surprisingly good result in the Hamilton South by-election, which took place – in deliberate timing by Labour – during the conference.[25] Instead of reducing Labour's majority to around 2,500, as predicted, it scraped home by just 556 votes. Salmond's troubles seemingly evaporated while the media, no longer in pursuit of Wilson, was left bemused. Politics, much like gambling, relies upon a mixture of skill and good fortune; at Inverness in September 1999 Salmond had been dealt a lucky hand.

As he prepared to take the stage for his speech the following after-noon, Salmond was 'at his most self-contented'. Instead of being forced to make a defensive address as a leader damaged by internal bickering and a Labour by-election victory, Salmond was able to argue – with justification – that the old enemy was on the run in one of its safest seats. He also gambled by naming a date for independence, shedding memories of 'Free by 93'. 'The Union whose boasted advantages grow ever more feeble has had its chance. It will not see its 300th anniver-sary,' he told enthusiastic delegates. 'Our hour, Scotland's hour, is at hand.' Speaking after the speech Salmond underlined his point by adding: 'That's our target, that's our ambition. It's done in a way which is not a glib slogan but a serious declaration of intent.'

Salmond also used his strengthened position to defend the election result and his policy agenda, arguing: 'An independent parliament in Europe would control 98 per cent [of its economy] – everything save the VAT contribution. In that difference – the difference between 10 per cent financial control and 98 per cent – in economic terms lies the difference between devolution and independence. And therein lies the opportunity to create not just a prosperous economy, but a just society – a free Scotland which will free Scots.'[26] It was a clear riposte to Ian Blackford, and indeed the by-election result made the treasurer's depic-tion of an under-performing party machine appear wide of the mark. Salmond's position was further strengthened when Kenny MacAskill, hitherto a persistent critic, made a public call for the infighting to cease. 'I'm not challenging, there is no vacancy', he said of recent press specu- lation, 'and I'm happy to work with Alex who I believe is running a very good and tight ship at present.'[27] With those words, MacAskill was welcomed back into the Salmond camp after a lengthy absence.

Salmond, meanwhile, began to gaze across the Atlantic. In November 1999 he finally undertook a long-planned visit to the United States with a view to replicating the lobbying power of Irish- Americans. 'This is a trip to familiarise Americans with the changes that are taking place,' he explained, 'that Scotland is heading towards independence but in an impeccably democratic and constitutional manner.'[28] The visit followed the recent inauguration of 'Tartan Day' by the US Senate and encompassed all-important media interviews as well as lectures at Harvard and Princeton. Salmond, meanwhile, developed a strong rapport with Alison Duncan, a Scots-born corpo- rate lawyer based in Washington DC. She shared his 'determination to climb to the mountain-top'[29] and became a key fixer in Salmond's burgeoning relationship with the US.

It is easy to see why Salmond appeared to be smitten. Not only did he see fund-raising potential in the US, but he enjoyed being feted at world-class institutions like Harvard and being taken seriously by movers and shakers on Capitol Hill. Yet he stood apart from other poli- ticians in having no obvious interest in the world beyond Scotland. There is no record of Salmond having travelled as a student, or even in his 20s, his only holiday each year being two weeks in Colonsay. Even as an MP he does not appear to have taken much advantage of the usual perks. Only after a few years as SNP leader did he begin to engage, at first with Ireland, then with the US. Despite, or perhaps because of, his intervention over Kosovo, he was not as sure footed when confronted with questions about international affairs, dodging questions about a possible Scottish withdrawal from NATO and relying instead upon charm and quick thinking. Why would Salmond want an independent Scotland, asked an American reporter during his visit, because 'when something isn't broken, why fix it?' 'I think,' replied Salmond, 'that's what George III said, too.'[30]

Back on home turf, where internal criticism had (for the moment) ceased, Salmond appeared equally confident. Asked for an analysis of the situation he would chuckle and offer some folksy Scots wisdom to characterise his opponents' difficulties, yet there were, as ever, chal- lenges. The first related to his own performance as 'Shadow First

Minister'. Although Salmond and his MSPs appeared content with his weekly jousts against Donald Dewar, the opinion in the press gallery was that he was yet to land a blow on the First Minister. During one exchange Salmond attacked Dewar on the basis of quotes in a six-day-old newspaper article, prompting the First Minister to accuse the SNP leader of 'boring him'. 'I am not sure that I was emotional or tired last night,' was another memorable Dewar retort, 'but I certainly was not sitting at 1 am looking at Ceefax ... [that] was a distinctly alarming piece of information from the leader of the nationalists.'[31]

To be fair, as First Minister Dewar had more back-office support than the leader of the opposition, yet even then there was criticism that preparation work by Noel Dolan, a former television producer and effectively Salmond's chief of staff, was inadequate. Although Dewar, as a result, found Salmond easy to deal with, he also found his aggressive style difficult to stomach. 'Donald Dewar respected Alex Salmond but did not like the sharp invective to which he was subjected,' reflected Henry McLeish. 'Salmond's style is cocky, divisive and very adversarial, the kind of person and politician Donald just did not like.'[32]

The nadir came in May 2000 when Salmond faced not Dewar, who was recovering from heart surgery, but Acting First Minister Jim Wallace, the Scottish Liberal Democrat leader. Although Wallace came under heavy fire from MSPs in general, when Salmond attempted to divide the Executive parties over the issue of British entry into the Euro, Wallace successfully turned the tables on the SNP leader. The exchange went:

Mr Salmond: Will the acting First Minister agree that the failure to enter the euro and the failure to have a strategy to enter is a missed opportunity and has cost thousands of jobs? Will he tell the Prime Minister to stop shilly-shallying on this issue?

Mr Wallace: Mr Salmond supports entry into the euro but he's pretty vague on when that should happen. I think if anyone shilly-shallies it's the man who postures but never gives us any answers himself ... We hear more about the euro from Mr Salmond than independence, but on both issues he's vague about how it's going to work in practice.[33]

In total Wallace filled in for Dewar nine times at First Minister's Questions and came out on top against Salmond on almost every occasion. The Labour MSP Mike Watson was not alone in being 'genuinely surprised that Alex Salmond, with more than a decade's experience in the House of Commons, did not make a better job of it'.[34] Always regarded as an excellent Westminster performer, with a firm grasp of procedure and ready one-liners, Salmond was clearly having difficulty making the transition from guerilla leader to battalion chief.

There was also a growing sense that however well equipped and resourced, that battalion lacked discipline and direction. Reports suggested that Salmond had adopted an Army-style exercise regime in an effort to lose some of the weight he had acquired over the past few years, fitting in sit-ups and rounds of golf meeting engagements, but the old killer instinct – once so feared by Labour – appeared to have deserted him. In short, Salmond appeared to lack any genuine interest in the Scottish Parliament for which he had long campaigned. 'It is perhaps a pity that Alex Salmond became leader a decade ago, because in today's terms that is about the limit any political leader can survive,' commented Margo MacDonald, albeit with an obvious agenda. 'Look how tired and worn out [Bill] Clinton is after eight years and it's getting close to Alex's limit.'[35] Salmond, as usual, affected nonchalance. 'Every political leader will get this occasionally,' he said. 'Donald Dewar gets it every day. I think you ignore it.' Dismissing reports that he was preparing to quit politics for a highly-paid oil industry job, he joked that things could be worse: 'I could be Donald Dewar, Tony Blair or even William Hague. I just shrug it off.'[36]

Perhaps the only issue that Salmond made any running on during this period was over the Scottish Parliament building fiasco. Although in 1993 he had accepted that in 'an independent nation we would have to be realistic and accept the requirement for a modern, purpose-built parliamentary complex in Scotland's capital',[37] by 1999/2000 circumstances had changed and Salmond sensed Donald Dewar's vulnerability. He referred to the Holyrood site as 'Donald's Dome' and made repeated attempts to link the First Minister with covering up the projected costs of the project. These failed to stick, while the whole affair became damaging not just for Dewar, but the devolution project in general. Salmond was so keen to see Labour get the blame that he blocked George Reid's appointment as chairman of the Holyrood Progress Group. 'Reid had the skill, authority, determination and experience to make a go of the [Enric] Miralles building,' observed Iain Macwhirter. 'But Alex Salmond said no. The reason? It's Dewar's hole, so why should a Nationalist MSP dig him out of it? Better a failure under Labour than a success under a Nat.'[38]

Later, Salmond also claimed that the Holyrood building fiasco ('I was pretty scunnered') had contributed to his decision to quit as SNP leader. 'I didn't think that people would wait 300 years to get a parliament and then concentrate on building a parliament. I just didn't believe that,' he lamented in 2007: 'The vote we took in 1999 [to abandon the Holyrood site] I thought we'd win. I thought we'd turn it over in the first parliament. There were only four votes in it. Donald said, of course, he'd resign. He told his MSPs he'd resign. But I did come up with a good phrase. I said the parliament could meet in a hut and be a parliament if it kept the respect of the people. It could meet in a palace and not be a parliament if it lost the respect of the people.'[39]

It was probably the arcane detail of the affair that appealed most to Salmond. When the independent expert John Spencely briefed the four party leaders on the proposed design in 2000, the SNP leader grilled him with typical rigour. 'He was cross-examining me, and I didn't find that an entirely enjoyable experience,' recalled Spencely. 'He was the only person who turned up with an assistant ... who sat and wrote down every answer. I didn't take to Mr Salmond, I have to say.'[40]

Beyond this ongoing issue and the weekly First Minister's Questions – memorably dubbed 'hamster wars' by one bored correspondent – Salmond's profile had been uncharacteristically low-key since the previous May. 'He was the face of the party on television, the voice of the party on radio and the only Nationalist really known to the public,' observed the *Scottish Daily Mail*. 'But since the Scottish parliament elections, many MSPs and activists feel he has almost faded from view.'[41]

Rumours of another leadership challenge began to do the rounds, with Alex Neil, the shadow social security minister, admitting he had been approached to take on Salmond at the September conference. Brian Souter's support for a campaign to prevent the repeal of Section 28 (or Clause 2a as it was known in Scotland), which banned the 'promotion' of homosexuality in schools, also caused the SNP leader problems, particularly as the Stagecoach tycoon had bankrolled the party just a few months previously. 'There is a wider interest than the SNP or Labour,' said Salmond, attempting to elevate the controversy above party politics. 'There is an issue about Scottish society and how people regard change ... I'm much more concerned with finding a solution and drawing some of the heat out of the debate rather than spending my time berating the Labour party or the Clause 28 campaigners for their information.'[42] The active support of some SNP MSPs for retaining Section 2a, meanwhile, also did not help.

Beyond these little local difficulties, however, Salmond continued to concentrate on the bigger picture. Having reiterated his target of Scotland becoming independent by 2007, Salmond announced that a majority at the polls – either at Westminster or the Scottish Parliament – would no longer mean the SNP had an automatic mandate to negotiate independence. 'Independence must be achieved by a referendum and that should be conducted by the Scottish parliament, not by Westminster,' explained Salmond. 'We believe that the Treaty of Union will not see its 300th anniversary, and we are setting in train the detailed organisation, political and financial targets to achieve that objective of national freedom within the next seven years.'[43] This, in retrospect, had been an important change of emphasis. Responding to the realpolitik of devolution, Salmond was not only seeking to further dampen fears about what the SNP would do should it win a majority in the Scottish Parliament, he was firmly shifting the centre of gravity from Westminster to Edinburgh.

Almost three weeks later, at a tense meeting of the SNP's National Council, Salmond did not manage to carry the whole of the party with him, but enough (149 votes to 112) to win the day. 'It [independence] will be the highest of our priorities,' a relieved Salmond told the BBC. 'Our general election campaign will be a clear clarion call for independence. There is no doubt in anyone's mind that the SNP will evangelise the independence issue.'[44] Although there had been criticism from Gordon Wilson ('Referendums are useful things as tactics, but let's not put too much faith in them.') and Alex Neil ('No party has gone into a general election campaign saying "vote for us and if we win the election we won't implement the central part of our policy".'), John Swinney, who drafted the new policy, backed the move ('We need to present to the people of Scotland a credible method of winning independence.') as did, more usefully, Kenny MacAskill ('Any suggestion this is a dilution of our principles or policy is misguided, wrong and, I have to say, downright insulting.').[45] Nevertheless, an initial vote had been close, so much so that according to one of those present, 'even Moira looked worried'.[46]

Ian Blackford, meanwhile, told a closed session of the SNP's next National Council that the party was £400,000 in debt, presenting a financial plan that was unanimously endorsed.[47] Although Salmond denied the figure when questioned by reporters after the meeting, Blackford readily confirmed it. Then, at a meeting of the SNP's National

Executive Committee the following week, Salmond instigated a vote of no confidence in Blackford, who had been unable to attend the meeting. In his absence, Salmond set out the case against Blackford, that he was an incompetent treasurer who had become a destabilising influence. Press reports also suggested that Salmond blamed Blackford for the election overspend. If true, it had the desired effect. The NEC endorsed the vote of no confidence by 18 votes to 3.

Blackford, however, was determined not to take his dismissal lying down. He told the *Scotsman*:

> We had national council a week ago, so if he wanted to challenge me he should have done it then. But I think Alex realised he would not have won. It was an act of political cowardice to challenge me when I was not there to answer allegations being made against me. Natural justice has not taken place, nor has it been seen to be done. This is a clear example that Alex Salmond has not learned lessons from Tony Blair's dismal handling of the situation with Ken Livingstone and Dennis Canavan. What he wants to do is surround himself with yes men who are 100 per cent loyal and reject anyone else with a different opinion. The support I am getting from the party is enormous – Alex Salmond has made a big mistake.[48]

A frequent criticism of Salmond had been his unwillingness to take on his critics, but following his swift – even brutal – removal of Blackford he appeared to have overcome such reluctance. 'I am not like Tony Blair, a control freak,' he had remarked a year earlier. 'If you can't win arguments by persuasion, you can't win them by expulsions.'[49] Another critic, meanwhile, was also targeted. Margo MacDonald stood accused of two serious breaches of party discipline – missing a vote in Parliament without permission and criticising an SNP group decision in a newspaper – and had been ordered to face an internal disciplinary hearing. An emboldened Salmond was trying to lance several boils at once.

One of the boils, however, was not so easily lanced. Having been advised by lawyers that he had 'an open-and-shut case', Blackford decided to sue Salmond for defamation. When he contacted Blackford asking him to resign following the vote of no confidence, meanwhile, the treasurer refused, explaining to the *Scotsman*: 'I have no wish to damage the SNP; this action will be taken against Alex Salmond personally. And while it is ongoing I will remain in position. I have enough support in the party to do so. Salmond has brought this upon the party himself with his control freakery; personally I am happy to work with anybody and everybody in the SNP.'[50] Salmond responded by invoking emergency rules to suspend Blackford as national treasurer, while John Swinney took care to emphasise that the dispute revolved around a 'breakdown in relationships' rather than 'professional issues' in an attempt to avoid legal action. Blackford, however, pressed on, warning that he planned a sustained campaign to win the hearts and minds of SNP activists 'in all sections and all geographic parts of Scotland'.[51]

What, then, had motivated this untypically brutal purge? 'I'm sure there must be a strategy somewhere,' a senior party figure told the journalist Ian Swanson. 'I don't know what it is. But knowing how Alex and John operate, there must be some purpose in it.'[52] The consensus was that Salmond was trying to make the party safe for gradualism, and therefore safe for John Swinney, who was considered likely to succeed him. The Scottish media, however, was always inclined to interpret any internal SNP splits as a feature of the great fundamentalist/gradualist divide, when in truth that was an inadequate political yardstick, seeing issues in black and white rather than shades of grey. Salmond, generally speaking, was sensitive when it came to negative press coverage. Swanson, who regularly (and accurately) reported what critics of his leadership were saying, remembered walking past his office as Salmond cried: 'Spreading any more poison today?'[53]

It seems more likely that personalities rather than ideology were at play. Salmond simply did not like Blackford, whose strict spending controls constrained his ambitions for future campaigning. Blackford could also not escape blame. Despite protestations that his concern was more about the party's finances and future direction than Salmond himself, his accusation of 'unpardonable folly' in the pages of the *Scotsman* had not only been highly personal but also politically damaging. Salmond, however, went over the top. Accusing someone who worked for a prestigious international bank of financial incompetence had simply not been credible, while it also risked the disastrous prospect of senior SNP figures being compelled to justify such slurs in court.

It also looked set to be a damagingly long-running battle. The NEC was due to review Blackford's suspension on 8 July 2000, while in September there would be an inevitable showdown as he fought to remain in post as treasurer. Although not an ideal scenario for Salmond, in reality he had little to fear. 'Salmond's greatest asset is his tenure at the top,' assessed the journalist Kenny Farquharson. 'Most SNP members are stubbornly loyal to the leadership, regardless of whether the incumbent is to their personal taste. When it comes to a crunch vote, their instincts are usually to back the boss.'[54]

Salmond's week from hell, meanwhile, got even hotter. The defection to the SNP of a former Tory candidate, Tasmina Ahmed-Sheikh, backfired when it emerged she had been strongly critical of the SNP as a member of the Labour Party as well as the Conservatives, while Lloyd Quinan, the former STV weatherman turned MSP, resigned from the SNP's front bench due to 'mounting unhappiness at the direction in which the party is going'.

Criticism also continued to be heaped upon Blackford. His poor attendance record at NEC meetings – one out of four – was cited as evidence of his incompetence (he claimed to have attended two), while his decision to address an innocuous Conservative-alligned political dining club was also held against him. 'This seems at the least surprising,' remarked Salmond, while one of his supporters characterised the Tuesday Club as 'a hard right-wing faction within a party moving increasingly to the right'.[55] On 8 July the NEC extended its temporary suspension of Blackford, who was unable to put his side of the story due to a family commitment. The hearing was instead due to take place at the next executive meeting on 12 August.

Then everything changed. On Friday 14 July Salmond summoned his deputy, John Swinney, to his office, Room 2.24 in a temporary office block on the Royal Mile. Although Swinney was preparing to go on holiday, Salmond informed him he would be resigning as SNP leader the following Monday. 'I can't say it was the most surprising piece of news that I'd ever heard,' Swinney told the author nearly three years later, 'because I had got the impression for a little while before that that Alex was thinking in this direction.'[56] On Sunday Salmond told his constituency party the same news ('They were stunned,' he said later. 'I could hear a sob from the audience. It brought a lump to my throat.'[57]) and on Monday morning he despatched a letter to every SNP MSP explaining his decision. He strongly denied any connection with the party's financial problems or the ongoing battle with Ian Blackford, arguing that it was simply time to 'pass the torch' to somebody else. Timing, as ever, was key. 'This will knock Gordon Brown's spending review off the front pages,' a gleeful Salmond told journalists as they assembled at a press conference in Aberdeen's Marcliffe Hotel.

'It was a hugely difficult decision,' admitted Salmond. 'I love this job. I've had a great time. Therefore it will be a wrench.' He dismissed allegations that he had quit because of the SNP's financial problems as 'absolutely rubbish'. 'We are putting the financial situation right in the SNP,' he added. 'We are dealing with it. It will be dealt with in a way that will leave Ian Blackford and his views looking isolated.' With Moira by his side, Salmond also alluded to the impact of the leadership on his lifestyle. 'I've made a great effort over the last year to curb the habit of a lifetime in terms of me always being in front of the TV cameras and microphones,' he said. 'Is it not right that someone else gets a chance to show what they can do? There is a wealth of talent in the SNP. The tradition in the SNP is that you do not pick your own successor, but the party does – although I do have my own private thoughts.' Finally, asked about his legacy to the SNP, Salmond paused only briefly before replying: 'When I became leader we were at 14 per cent in the polls and had three MPs, we are now at 36 per cent and we have 35 MSPs. I think it's fair to say we have made fairly substantial progress.'[58]

Many senior Nationalists were surprised, to say the least. Party president Winnie Ewing said it was 'totally unexpected',[59] while Roseanna Cunningham later recalled that she 'had absolutely no advanced knowledge or warning ... it was absolutely gobsmacking'.[60] Others, however, were relieved, having lobbied behind the scenes for Salmond to quit, as he had clearly 'run out of steam by 2000'.[61] When Salmond told his mother the news, meanwhile, she said: 'Well you've done your ten years.' 'I remembered his first speech ten years before', Mary later explained, 'when he said I'll give it ten years and if Scotland isn't independent I'll pass the torch.' Her husband Robert, however, would have preferred his son to carry on: 'I think he's made the SNP the force it is now.'

This explanation, however, appears to have owed more to hindsight than reality. There is no reference to a ten-year limit in his first speech as SNP leader, nor was there any reference in newspaper reports from that period, beyond a vague aside to the Liberal Democrat MP Charles Kennedy. 'I had always planned on being about 10 years in the job,' insisted Salmond. 'The late Kenny MacIntyre, the BBC Radio Scotland journalist used to ask me, even after one year when I would step down. And I said that I would step down as the SNP leader after 10 years.'[62]

Salmond, meanwhile, quoted Harold Wilson: 'It's better to go when they're asking why you're going rather than wait until they're asking why you're staying.' 'I think there's a time for everything in politics and it wasn't the case that I wasn't enjoying things still, because I was,' he reflected a few months after his announcement, 'and it wasn't the case that I was scunnered with politics, but I could see coming a period when I was not going to be enjoying things.'[63] The Wilson analogy was apt. He, too, had taken his party and the country by surprise by resigning as Labour leader and Prime Minister in 1976, and he, too, claimed it had been premeditated.

Despite Salmond's protestations, the political rumour factory went into overdrive. He was seriously ill; he had gambling debts; he was about to be pushed, all of which Salmond brushed off with aplomb. Reports also implied that it had not been a spontaneous decision, Salmond having tried to quit twice since the May 1999 elections, once just before the September 1999 conference, and again as recently as March. 'He had to be talked out of it then,' said a source. 'This time he left it so late that there was nothing that could be done by anyone. He had made his mind up.'[64] This seems unlikely, and indeed Duncan Hamilton, an MSP at that time and a close colleague of Salmond's, later said he had 'no memory'[65] of previous resignation attempts, an impression backed up by his then colleague Andrew Wilson. This version of events, therefore, was most likely a cover story contrived to lend coherence to an otherwise incoherent event.

The truth probably lies in a combination of factors. Beyond a natural desire to spend more time with Moira, the Blackford affair had been both stressful and damaging, while Salmond probably did not relish the prospect of a showdown at conference which may have made his position untenable. The journalist Peter Jones, always an astute observer of the SNP, reckoned there was a 'good case for thinking that he jumped now before he was pushed next year'. 'A new leader could shrug off [a] general election reverse' in 2001 or 2002, he reasoned, 'blaming lack of money and lack of interest by Scots in Westminster', whereas Salmond could not. He had, therefore, 'quite probably done himself and his party a service'.[66]

The dominant reason, however, appears to have been Salmond's genuine concern that the SNP was, as critics had so often claimed, a one-man band. Although he had always taken care to nurture younger political talent, the only way to solve that perception of the party was for him to quit, leaving space for others to emerge and grow. He explained to the journalist Colin Mackay nine years later:

When I became SNP leader way back in 1990 ... I was a pretty young guy and you could extend [to an] extraordinary range of things,', [but] there was a second reason ... [that] prevailed very heavily upon me. I'd had a pretty good run with the Scottish press corps over the period I'd been an MP, pretty much a charmed existence, especially given that most of them, all of them didn't support the SNP, I'd had a pretty good run. The coverage changed for the 1999 election campaign and some of the stuff we were subjected to was pretty extraordinary . . . when that sort of coverage continued after the election . . . I began to believe that perhaps the SNP would get a better crack of the whip if someone else [took over] . . . there seemed to be a feeling around that perhaps with me as head of the SNP it wouldn't get the coverage it merited.

'I mean, well okay, I quite like being in the limelight I suppose,' he added, 'but you began to wonder how much of that was because of the issue, how much of it was because of the SNP, and how much was because I said it?'[67]

The 1999 election campaign had certainly coloured Salmond's view of the Scottish press corps, or at least a significant portion of it, which he came to see as a necessary evil rather than something to be cultivated. Whatever the explanation for the resignation, however, it is worth noting that, at the time, very few journalists accepted Salmond's version of events. It was just too sudden, too unexpected and too out of character. As Andy Nicoll of the *Sun* put it, leading Scotland to independence had been 'his dream since student days and it's astonishing that he's given it up so easily'.[68]

Nevertheless, the press response to Salmond's resignation was generally sympathetic, even from normally critical publications. The *Scottish Daily Mail* praised his 'remarkable contribution' to the SNP. 'Nationalism without Salmond is Hamlet without the Prince,'[69] declared an editorial. Similarly, the *Scottish Sun* said: 'Think of the SNP, and you think of Alex Salmond. It's hardly overstating the case to say Alex Salmond IS the SNP, and the SNP IS Alex Salmond.'[70] 'The resignation of Alex Salmond is the end of an era in Scottish politics but also inevitably the start of a new one,' assessed another editorial, this time in the *Scotsman*. 'The SNP under Salmond's leadership has helped to transform both Scotland and, though he might not fully appreciate it, Britain as well. He has single-handedly rescued what was a demoralised, factious party a decade ago and transformed it into an effective official opposition. His unswerving commitment to an inclusive and humane, civic-style nationalism has brought a sense of maturity to the independence debate. Where Alex Salmond has failed in the balance is rather in his inability to offer a more compelling vision of a new Scotland, post independence.'[71] More sanguine commentators, however, also made the important observation that despite obvious advances, Salmond had failed to significantly increase support for independence, as distinct from support for the SNP.

Political opinion was, inevitably, mixed. Charles Kennedy, the Liberal Democrat leader, was the most generous. 'Alex Salmond played an important role in Scottish politics,' he said. 'He will no doubt be terribly disappointed that he failed to deliver independence for Scotland, but he has performed the difficult task of keeping the different factions in his party together.' Brian Wilson, still at the Scotland Office, was less charitable. 'Everyone is entitled to move on and it would be no surprise if the attractions of permanent Opposition have waned,' he sneered. 'Mr Salmond leaves his party where he found it – sound-bites and protest votes but going nowhere.' Donald Dewar, meanwhile, described him as a 'doughty opponent'. 'I have considerable respect for his ability', he said, 'and I'm sure he will be missed from the centre stage role he has occupied.' [72] Less than a month later, Salmond paid a similar tribute to Dewar after his premature death following a massive brain haemorrhage. Despite ups and downs, a 'desperately sad' Salmond said he would 'miss the debates and miss the arguments'. [73]

Within the pages of the *Scots Independent*, meanwhile, there were some unusually generous tributes. James Halliday, like Salmond a youthful SNP leader in his day, wrote that with him the SNP 'came of age – not by chance, but because his personal qualities proved to be exactly what the times called for. He knew his stuff, and we all knew that he did; and so confidence spread throughout the ranks. He feared no opponent; he deferred to no professional politician; and he proved himself more than a match for all the champions sent against him. He gave us a new experience – the feeling of being on the winning side, and the guid conceit o oursels that victory brings.'

Ian O. Bayne, meanwhile, reckoned Salmond had left 'an inspiring and constructive legacy'. 'It is up to all of us – and not just to his aspiring successor – to make the most of it in the long war of attrition still ahead,' he wrote in his regular column. 'Meanwhile a standing ovation from us old SNP trade unionists is surely in order. The boy done good.' [74] Two of Salmond's closest political colleagues, the MSPs Andrew Wilson and Duncan Hamilton, also penned glowing newspaper columns on his legacy, which they later framed and presented to him over dinner at his favourite Linlithgow restaurant.

Jim Fairlie, a long-standing critic despite no longer being an SNP member, took a less charitable view. 'Throughout his political career,

Salmond is a man who has been driven by his own overweening personal ambition,' he wrote in the *Perthshire Advertiser*. Not only that, but he had left behind a party 'riven on policy issues', not to mention a 'suspended treasurer and an overdraft running to several hundreds of thousands of pounds'. Salmond had become obsessed with making the SNP 'respectable', added Fairlie, and in the process had 'removed the soul of the SNP and replaced it with a belief in nothing other than the desire for a political presence, however limited, on the stage of the political mishmash that is the EU.'[75]

A letter from 'an ordinary grassroots supporter of the independence movement' in the *Herald*, meanwhile, perhaps summed up the views of many activists. 'Leading the SNP is no easy task, especially given the massive entrenched advantages of the Unionist parties and the anti-SNP bias which pervades most of the Scottish media,' wrote Philip J. Sands. 'Mr Salmond took the SNP from being a fringe party at Westminster to centre stage in a restored Scottish Parliament, playing a crucial role in the re-establishment of that Parliament along the way ... When the SNP's next national convener leads Scotland to independence, he will be standing on the shoulders of honest patriots like Alex Salmond.'[76]

The resignation of Alex Salmond as leader of the SNP – whatever his legacy – marked the end of an era in Scottish politics. That summer, the Plaid Cymru president Dafydd Wigley also stood down after nine years at his party's helm. Like Salmond, he was an experienced politician with a solid Westminster reputation. Having led their respective parties into the Scottish Parliament and the National Assembly for Wales, both men looked strangely out of place in the new devolutionary world.

Their successors then slugged it out to represent the next generation. In Wales, Ieuan Wyn Jones competed with Helen Mary Jones, while in Scotland, John Swinney (a protégé of Gordon Wilson) took on Alex Neil (a Jim Sillars man). The latter swiftly declared that whoever became the next SNP leader should not lead the party as a 'one-man band',[77] while urging to party to renew its drive for independence. Neil, however, was forced to disassociate himself from the usual Sillars onslaught, which came the day after Salmond's resignation. He refused to 'join in the hypocritical praise that will be heaped upon Alex Salmond now that he has snuffed out his political life at the top'. 'He was never big enough for the times,' continued Sillars. 'He was only a spin machine, spinning in a policy vacuum.'[78] And while Salmond declined to back publicly any candidate for leader or deputy, it was generally understood that John Swinney was his preferred candidate.

Salmond, however, clearly had no intention of taking a back seat, although he was careful to avoid giving the impression that he would, like Margaret Thatcher, become a back-seat driver. He told the *Sunday Herald* that he planned to 'remain very much part of the political scene'. 'I'm not giving up politics,' he said. 'I'm still going to be an MSP in the Scottish parliament.'[79] His preferred role was one developing and articulating the economic case for independence, although he wrote in *Scotland on Sunday* that he would be 'available for any task our new leader believes appropriate'. Salmond also remained the MP for Banff and Buchan, although it was understood at this point that he would relinquish his Commons seat at the next general election.

'Over the last ten years I've felt that my presence as party leader was necessary to the SNP's progress,' reflected Salmond as the SNP's annual conference approached. 'That may be a piece of vanity, but nevertheless that's what I felt.'[80] His Inverness swansong, however, was overshadowed by another strong attack from Ian Blackford, still hoping to be re-elected national treasurer. He accused a senior party figure (by implication, Salmond) of using SNP cash to pay for his wife to accompany him to Brussels the previous February. Blackford also claimed taxi bills of £1,000 a month had been the norm while agreed limits on hotel bills had been flouted despite the party being heavily in debt.

Salmond angrily denied the allegations, admitting that Moira had accompanied him on a speaking engagement to Brussels but claiming that the European Institute had later refunded the £450 cost of her flight. 'I have claimed a fraction of the expenses I would be entitled to claim as leader,' protested Salmond. 'Anyone who knows me knows that . . . The party paid for very few of my hotel bills, but if I am doing events for the party, that's obviously [a] legitimate expense.'[81] Although he admitted taxi bills of £9,960 and £8,854 over the last two years, Salmond said it 'would be incredible if the leader of the SNP was driving himself around Scotland at election times'.[82] Blackford, he said, was a 'busted flush', while his chances of being re-elected treasurer were 'sub-zero'. The fact that Moira had been dragged into what had hitherto been a purely internal party affair infuriated Salmond. 'I do not regard it as important. I do not regard Mr Blackford as important,' he said with obvious fury. 'It is my estimation that the delegates will give him his just deserts on Saturday.'[83]

In Salmond's final keynote address to conference after a decade in office, he tried hard to rise above yet another troubled gathering. 'It has been a privilege to lead you part of the way,' he told delegates. 'I look forward to helping my successor and you complete our journey.'[84] 'Generations of our predecessors gave their all for this party, for this movement, with little realistic expectation of success. In contrast, our political cup runneth over. New Labour are now vulnerable, the Tories ain't trusted, the Liberals are moths caught in Labour's flame. Independence will arrive in this political generation.'[85] An emotional speech was marred only by a security warning, which resulted in the police asking delegates to evacuate the conference centre as Salmond finished his oration. An ICM poll for the *Scotsman*, meanwhile, illustrated the outgoing leader's mixed legacy. Although an impressive 76 per cent of those questioned believed he had been a good leader, support for independence had fallen to just 24 per cent, three points down on the most recent poll and nine points lower than peak support in 1998.

When the leadership result was announced on 23 September, meanwhile, John Swinney won easily.[86] Salmond, he said, had 'passed on to me a party in great shape and great heart'. 'In the years of Alex Salmond's leadership we have moved from the fringes of Scottish politics to the centre stage,' he added in his victory speech. 'We have made such progress that I believe I stand here as the first leader in the history of the SNP who has a hard-headed opportunity to lead our party into government and our country on to independence.'[87] Jim Mather, meanwhile, humiliated Ian Blackford in the contest for national treasurer, ousting him by 632 votes to 143, while Salmond easily topped the poll in elections to the NEC.

'The media have moved on from Alex Salmond now,' wrote Norman Harper in the *Aberdeen Press and Journal*. 'The man who has been feted these last few days at the SNP conference is not the man of this morning. For the first time in more than a decade, he must take the back seat.'[88]

Chapter 10

'THE KING OVER THE WATER'

Oh I hae seen the guid auld day,
The day o' pride and chiefain's glory,
When Royal Stewart bare the sway,
and we ne'er heard tell o' Whig or Tory,
Tho' lyart be my locks and gray,
auld age has crook't me doon, what matter,
I'll dance and sing ae ither day,
That day oor King comes o'er the water.
                    'Lady Keith's Lament' by Lady Mary Drummond

Mystery surrounded Alex Salmond's resignation as SNP leader for some time, although media attention quickly shifted to John Swinney. There was a general, if unspecific, assumption that Salmond would not be gone for long. At the House of Commons in London, which of course he had never actually left, Salmond became, in the eyes of many, the 'King o'er the water', the old political pretender just waiting for the right time, the perfect moment to make his comeback.

Shorn of the burden of leadership Salmond visibly relaxed. Jim Eadie, who had worked for the SNP at Westminster a decade earlier, remembered having dinner with him during this period and never having 'seen him so relaxed, bantering with everyone around him and making jokes at his own expense'.[1] Similarly, the Labour MP George Foulkes recalled being invited for a drink. 'He let his guard down for once', he remembered, 'and said dealing with his MSP group had been like "herding cats". I was very struck by that phrase.'[2]

There were fewer cats to herd in the House of Commons, where Salmond effectively assumed the leadership of five SNP MPs, all of whom were expected to stand down at the next general election having also been elected MSPs in 1999. It soon emerged, however, that the Member for Banff and Buchan had other plans; in a bold volte-face that dominated the headlines for several weeks, Salmond decided to ditch the Scottish Parliament and instead remain at Westminster. Stewart Stevenson, a friend of Salmond's since the mid-1970s, was poised to inherit his Scottish Parliament seat.

Salmond was initially coy as the news leaked out, memorably inform-ing Karen Rice at the *Edinburgh Evening News* that 'this dog won't hunt'[3] when presented with the scenario. Indeed, even as he campaign-ing in the Falkirk West by-election in December 2000, Salmond still played down the move. He admitted to the *Scotsman*:

> I have always liked the chamber of the Commons. It's a good place to raise issues and there's a big job to be done there, although I've done the travel-ling up and down the country for 13 years and it's not something I look forward to . . . [The matter] will have to be discussed at a local and national level. Over the last three weeks I have covered Westminster for the party and have made more speeches in the last three weeks than I have in a long time. There has not been a decision taken and as yet I'm unconvinced. There are a lot of arguments in favour but I have yet to be convinced myself. The real problem is I would have to leave the Scottish Parliament.[4]

Salmond, of course, could hardly admit that far from being sorry to leave the Scottish Parliament, he had never quite taken to the new insti-tution's makeshift accommodation on Edinburgh's Mound. The key sentence, however, had been that about making 'more speeches in the last three weeks than I have in a long time'. Having spent most of his time since 1997 in Scotland, Salmond had simply rekindled his love affair with the House of Commons and did not want to leave; particu-larly now he was no longer leader. 'He thrives on the confrontation of Westminster,' a colleague told *Scotland on Sunday*. 'When he hears the heckling and the shouting there is a gleam in his eye. He loves being heckled and heckling back. I just don't think he ever took to Holyrood in the same way.'[5]

Although this U-turn had to be sanctioned by Salmond's local party and the National Executive Committee, there was little prospect of any serious opposition. Stan Tennant, the convenor of Salmond's local party, gave what would become the standard explanation, that Salmond was needed to 'guide' new but inexperienced SNP MPs at Westminster after the next general election. There was also added spin to the effect that John Swinney had asked his reluctant predecessor to stay on in the Commons, although that is hard to take seriously.

Swinney also put Salmond in charge of the SNP's general election campaign. 'Alex has formidable campaigning skills, which will now be deployed at the centre of the SNP's campaign,' he said. 'His candidacy and continued presence at Westminster will strengthen our General Election campaign.' There were further changes afoot, although of a more domestic nature. Salmond announced that he was to make Strichen his main base, having moved between homes in London, Linlithgow and his constituency for the past 13 years. He was now selling the Linlithgow and Strichen properties in order to buy Mill o' Strichen, a converted property not far from his old cottage. 'When I was party leader I needed a base in Central Scotland to fulfil engagements,' he explained. 'That doesn't apply now and when Mill o' Strichen came on the market Moira and I decided it was too good a chance to miss. I'm sure we will be very happy there.'[6]

On Sunday 14 January 2001 the Banff and Buchan SNP confirmed Salmond as its Westminster candidate for the next election. Labour had a field day. Brian Wilson accused him of 'dipping his toe in Scottish political water and quickly deciding he didn't like it'. He added: 'Now he's saying "I'll go back to Westminster but I'll leave my driver behind because the Scottish parliament is so important".'[7] This was a reference to Stewart Stevenson, who was to succeed Salmond in the Scottish Parliament, although his contribution to the SNP had been more substantial than simply driving Alex around during the 1997 election. 'Along with the late Donald Dewar, I think I have helped establish a standard of debate there,' protested a defensive Salmond. 'Now that the Scottish Parliament is under new leadership with John Swinney and Henry McLeish for Labour, I have been asked to do a job which remains at Westminster and I'm willing do to that job.'[8]

The SNP's general election campaign launch in May 2001, meanwhile, was its slickest ever. 'Scotland's share of public spending fell under the Tories, has continued to fall under New Labour, and will be cut even further and faster after the election if John Prescott gets his way,' declared Salmond. 'We need SNP MPs at Westminster to stand for Scotland, protect our schools and hospitals from London Labour cuts.'[9] Salmond had also been working on cutting his weight, having lost seven pounds since the beginning of his fourth election campaign in Banff and Buchan.

The independence message, curiously, received greater prominence in the 2001 Westminster campaign than it had in the Scottish Parlia-

ment contest two years previously. 'There is a thing more powerful
than all the armies of the world,' wrote Salmond in the *Scotsman*,
quoting Victor Hugo. 'It is an idea whose time has come.' 'Our core
belief as a party is that we stand for Scotland becoming a normal independent country,' he explained. 'We stand for Scotland putting its
wealth to work for the people, and taking its place as an equal partner
in the community of nations.' It could do that, claimed Salmond, by
investing surplus oil revenues in a 'Scottish Fund for Future Generations' based on the Norwegian oil fund model. While Norway's was
managed by the Norwegian Central Bank, 'there is absolutely no reason
why ours could not employ the talents of the Edinburgh fund management sector. What a great advert for that sector to have billions of
pounds worth of government business on their books.'[10]

The campaign also marked a decisive shift in the SNP's economic and
constitutional thinking, perhaps the most important since the adoption of
'independence in Europe' more than a decade earlier. The seeds had
been sown a year or so before by party treasurer Jim Mather, who had
urged SNP MSPs to stop focusing on the deficit issue and instead engage
with economic growth. Andrew Wilson, an MSP since 1999, who had
advised Salmond on UK economics at Westminster, had been particularly impressed and by 2001 was convinced that the SNP ought to be
promoting full fiscal autonomy. Not only would it give the party a
more positive message but it also had the potential to attract cross-party
support, elements within Labour and the Scottish Conservative Party
having toyed with the concept since the late 1980s.

To that end, Wilson not only convinced Salmond to throw his
weight behind the change – although he was careful to do so in a way
that did not upset John Swinney – he managed, against extraordinary
odds, to get 12 prominent Scottish academics and financial experts to
sign a letter endorsing fiscal autonomy in the *Scotsman*. Led by Professor
Andrew Hughes Hallett of Strathclyde University, they claimed Scotland had been subsidising the rest of the UK and that devolving control
of taxation and revenue was the only way of 'delivering accountability
and responsibility'[11] to the Scottish Parliament. The SNP, meanwhile,
presented it as a solution to the so-called 'Barnett squeeze', the phenomenon by which Scotland's share of UK public spending was gradually
being reduced.[12]

This intervention enlivened an otherwise dull election campaign,
put Labour on the back foot and, although the issue of fiscal autonomy
did not figure prominently in the 2003–07 session of the Scottish Parlia-

ment, it had introduced an important new dimension to the constitutional debate, and one that conveniently fitted into Salmond's ecumenical approach. Mather and Wilson kept it going with a successful 'Economics of Independence Road Show' in the summer of 2002, while the debate informed a Liberal Democrat policy commission chaired by Lord Steel between 2003 and 2006. Finally, in 2010, Salmond would take the fiscal autonomy debate to a different level by endorsing it as First Minister.

Despite this abundance of ideas, the 2001 election turned out to be yet another disappointment for the SNP. Its share of the vote was down slightly on 1997 while it won just five seats, losing Dumfries and Galloway to the Conservatives. In Banff and Buchan, meanwhile, Salmond's vote held up with an impressive majority of 10,503:

Alex Salmond (SNP)	16,710
Sandy Wallace (Conservative)	6,207
Ted Harris (Labour)	4,363
Douglas Herbison (Lib Dem)	2,769
Alice Rowan (Scottish Socialist Party)	447
Eric Davidson (UK Independence Party)	310

Neither Salmond's Westminster experience nor, it seemed, the novelty of a new SNP leader had improved the party's electoral virility. Yet there was a role for Swinney's predecessor on the London stage. 'With the Tories in disarray and Liberal Democrat leader Charles Kennedy still pinching himself at doing better than Paddy Ashdown on June 7,' observed the seasoned Westminster watcher Bill Jacobs, 'Mr Salmond has filled the vacuum.'[13]

Salmond did so not just in the House of Commons, but also in an ever-expanding 24-hour news market that was shaping political life in new and demanding ways. 'It's good, isn't it?' later chirped a contented Salmond. 'There's a lot more opportunities. I'm sort of resident on Sky.'[14] There was another niche for the king over the water. As the SNP's 'international ambassador', Salmond embarked upon a whistle-stop lecture tour of the United States shortly after standing down as leader. During this trip he, Duncan Hamilton, Sir Sean Connery (and his adviser James Baron) spent an hour and a half at the White House in the company of the newly elected president, George W. Bush, and his wife Laura. Salmond was impressed by Bush's handling of an incident involving a US spy plane that had crashed in China, while the president regaled him with tales of his booze-fuelled visits to Scotland. 'I was impressed. We've all been misled about Bush,' Salmond later told the Labour MP Chris Mullin. 'He's calm in a crisis, self-deprecating, humorous,' adding hastily: 'Of course that doesn't make him right about Iraq.'[15]

Salmond's positive impression of Bush did not prevent him launching a strong critique of US foreign policy at the 2001 SNP conference in Dundee. 'We cannot fight terror against innocents by visiting it on other innocent people,' he said just ten days after September 11. 'Let there be no more financing of one monster to take on another enemy.' War was not 'easy, surgical and decisive' added Salmond. 'It is more likely to be nasty, messy and long. This is not a struggle against Islam. President George W Bush's eloquent words that those attacking mosques represent "not the best of America but the worst of humanity" hold true in Scotland as well.'[16] It was a barnstorming performance that many felt upstaged Swinney's own keynote speech.

In his speech and in print, Salmond was also surprisingly positive about the US president, perhaps influenced by his personal encounter. 'Some people sneer at his folksy speaking style, complain[ing] that he doesn't have the panache of a Clinton,' he said. 'But the world right now does not need a showman or an orator – but a steady hand at the tiller.'[17] And far from rushing to drop bombs, 'the indications are that Bush is prioritising the necessary but inevitably lower profile tasks of evidence gathering, closing off terrorist finance and alliance building, and eschewing the temptations of a quick hit and easy headlines.'[18]

All of that, of course, would change, but Salmond now possessed a credible stance on foreign affairs that would be particularly valuable during another conflict a few years later. Meanwhile, he also kept up his interest in the more humble, yet nobler sport of kings, welcoming the removal of betting tax on 6 October 2001. 'Gordon Brown [the Chancellor] has seized the bull by the horns and abolished the imposition as of today,' wrote Salmond in his *Scotsman* racing column. 'Forget the Brown formula of "endogenous growth-cycle theory". This time Gogs, as I'm sure he was called at school, has actually done something useful. Today, in the immortal words of "mighty" Mac McCririck, is "punters' freedom day".'[19]

There was also praise, of a sort, for Henry McLeish, Donald Dewar's embattled successor as First Minister. Indeed, so embattled was McLeish by late 2001 that it is difficult to believe that Salmond had no regrets about his own self-imposed Westminster exile. Consumed by complex questions about equally complex financial arrangements for his Westminster constituency office, McLeish's nadir came on an edition of the BBC's *Question Time* in early November. During this Salmond, also a guest on the programme, had come to his rescue, gently suggested that McLeish publish his details in full and that no one thought he was dishonest. Despite protests of a 'muddle not a fiddle', however, McLeish resigned a few days later, having been felled by a lack of confidence, media hostility and unsupportive Labour colleagues. 'Whatever our differences, I have seldom doubted that he had Scotland's interests at heart,' wrote Salmond in a generous yet sincere tribute. 'I happen to think that, within political limits, Henry was trying to do the right things in policy terms by distinguishing his programme from that of Westminster. It is a pity that he didn't get the chance to better develop that work.'[20]

None of this, however, made life much easier for John Swinney, who barely had a honeymoon period as SNP leader before getting a rough ride from both the press and his party; some believed he had never recovered the pace from having to assemble a leadership campaign in just two days following his predecessor's sudden resignation. Salmond's absence from Edinburgh had been intended to make things easier for his successor, but when the Scottish Parliament decamped to Aberdeen for a week in May 2002, not only was Salmond present in the gallery when Swinney endured a particularly bad First Minister's Questions, but he also led a team of petitioners protesting at the closure of Peterhead prison in his constituency. Given that prison policy was devolved to the Scottish Parliament, some believed – unfairly in retrospect – that Salmond had overstepped the mark. He chided Brian Taylor for the 'tone' of a report that implied his presence had significance beyond prisons. 'More generally,' recorded Taylor, 'he also ridicules the notion that he envisages a comeback as leader.'[21]

The suspicion that Salmond was plotting a comeback was further fuelled when, in an interview with the *Scotsman* on 10 May 2002, he revealed that he planned to resume his career as an MSP via the northeast Scotland list in 2007. 'I was asked to do a political job, to bring some experience to a totally new Westminster group,' he said. 'But this is a job with a timescale. Not this coming election, but the one after, we should have plenty of experience.' When asked if he had made a mistake in leaving the Scottish Parliament, he replied: 'Not in the slightest.'[22]

The SNP has a tendency to overreact to otherwise innocuous announcements, and this was no exception. Salmond was accused of deliberately destabilising Swinney's leadership, although the criticism came mainly from the usual suspects. Salmond, of course, rejected suggestions that he was 'breathing down the neck' of Swinney: 'When John asked me to go back to Westminster to lend some experience to our new parliamentary group it was always an assumption and agreement between us that I would come back to the Scottish Parliament at some stage. The earliest stage I would do that is 2007 and nobody in their right mind believes that I am anything other than a strong supporter of John Swinney and a strong supporter of John Swinney's leadership.'

This, of course, was slightly disingenuous, as Salmond had actually indicated in 2000 that he hoped to return to the Scottish Parliament once independence had been achieved, rather than before. The sale of his Grade B-listed, 18th-century Georgian home in Linlithgow, meanwhile, also appeared suspicious. Salmond quite correctly denied any connection, the announcement having been made almost two years earlier. 'Last year we bought our mill home which we had been eyeing up for eight years until it became available,' he said. 'The reason for the delay is that we have been renovating our Linlithgow home before we sell it.'[23] It eventually sold a few months later; the Salmonds having lowered the asking price from offers over £250,000 to a fixed price of £215,000. 'And if my hopes are realised and I return to the Scottish Parliament in a few years' time', he added, 'I would have to have a base somewhere near Edinburgh – maybe Linlithgow again. Once a Black Bitch always a Black Bitch.'[24]

The extent to which Salmond still wielded influence within the SNP was, however, revealed when *Scotland on Sunday* reported that Sir Sean Connery had requested that the former leader have a role in deciding his activity on behalf of the party. To be fair, Sir Sean did not really know Swinney while Salmond had introduced the actor to James Baron, who had become his adviser in the US. 'Sean needed someone to give him steady, solid advice in the USA and Scotland,' recalled a source. 'Sean trusted Alex entirely although there was no question of him having a veto. Connery also got along very well with James, who took forward the Scotland agenda in the USA in a non-partisan inclusive manner, which was the trick the SNP missed in the early 1990s.'[25] Baron, a republican, was also a good example of Salmond's ability to appeal to a wide range of people.

John Swinney, meanwhile, had problems. He warned his critics to 'put up or shut up' as a row over SNP list rankings rumbled on, giving notice that he intended to change a system he believed had created a 'cauldron of tension'.[26] George Reid, Mike Russell and Andrew Wilson were soon to be put to the boil, receiving such a low ranking as to make re-election in 2003 apparently impossible, all of which made Salmond's successor all the more determined to introduce one-member-one-vote for candidate selections. Swinney probably lost less sleep over the fate of Margo MacDonald, otherwise known as Mrs Jim Sillars, who had been ranked fifth in the Lothians, again making it impossible for her to continue as an MSP.

Always an independent spirit, MacDonald chose a remedy unavailable to either Russell or Wilson: she resigned as the SNP candidate for Edinburgh South and announced she would stand in the Lothians as an independent. 'It's true I'm the only SNP leader Margo's ever been able to live with,' responded Salmond with caustic wit. 'She resigned under Gordon Wilson, she stayed in under me and she resigned under John Swinney. She's been in out, in out, it's like the hokey cokey, and now, presumably, she's going to shake it all about.'[27]

If the departure of MacDonald marked a break with the SNP's past, then John Swinney's 2002 conference speech marked a little-noticed departure from the Salmond years. He wanted to move from repeatedly stressing what could not be done under devolution, to emphasising what could be done via independence, summed up in the slogan 'Release Our Potential'.[28] Swinney, however, found himself wasting valuable political energy on further rumours about Salmond's comeback plans. 'Alex and I have been close political associates for many, many years,' he said in February 2003. 'Alex has made it perfectly clear that he would view it as ludicrous to come back into the SNP leadership.'[29]

It seems unlikely that Salmond, at any point, deliberately sought to undermine his successor. Instead, he stuck to his post-resignation commitment and spent most of 2003 re-examining the economic case for independence, which he had been exploring ever since joining the SNP in 1973. Two things helped in this task: his appointment as visiting professor of economics at Strathclyde University and the recruitment of the American Jennifer Erickson, previously an intern, as 'senior economic adviser' to the party. In February and March 2003, he also delivered the grandly titled 'Alex Salmond Lectures'.

'It [the economy] was not the only rationale for the Union,' Salmond declared in the first of three lectures, 'particularly not on the English side. Nor is it now the only argument for independence, or even the most important one, but it is none the less a key debate and one as old as the

Union itself.' Inevitably, Salmond focused upon the annual 'Government Expenditure and Revenue in Scotland' (GERS) figures:

> The conclusions and methodology of GERS have ... been widely criticized. However, on the government's own figures, Scotland had a cumulative £24 billion surplus over the past 20 years, over a period when the UK was £418 billion in deficit. Ah, but the chorused complaint is that this Scottish 'surplus' includes oil and gas revenues. But then so does the UK deficit. It is not extraordinary to include oil and gas revenues. What is extraordinary is the exclusion of these revenues from the annually published headline figure. More importantly, the context that the government never provides in GERS is that all but three OECD countries have averaged deficits over this period. Indeed, on Treasury forecasts, the UK itself will be £100 billion in deficit over the next five years.

Salmond then addressed his central question: 'How is Scotland's economy performing within the Union compared with how it could be outside the Union?' His answer to the first part of that question was not very well and, to the latter, 'could be better'. 'It is growth', he said, 'that counts in economics.' He added: 'Since Labour took over at Westminster, the UK has performed almost twice as well as Scotland. Since Labour and the Lib Dems came to power at St Andrew's House, the UK has performed three times better than Scotland. If these differences in growth still seem esoteric, consider these facts from the DTI's recent State of the Regions. Of the constituent nations, Scotland has the highest unemployment, the highest proportion of income support claimants, and the lowest business survival rate.' 'Despite the [Scottish] Executive's posturing, real control over the economy remains with Westminster,' continued Salmond. 'However you measure it, Scotland controls less than 15 per cent of its finances; London controls the rest.'

Could things be different, asked Salmond, if Scotland were a small country outside the UK? Since 1999, he replied, each of the European Union's seven small countries had outperformed Scotland, averaging growth five times higher than in Scotland. The difference, he argued, lay in the fact that those small nations could 'legislate for their own interests, establish a tax system that suits them, and can argue their own cases within the EU'. 'Estimating how much better off Scotland could be outside of the Union is not an exact science,' he concluded. 'But as Keynes once said, it is better to be vaguely right than precisely wrong.

And of one thing there can be no question – the Union is not working for the Scottish economy.'[30]

Salmond continued the growth theme in his second lecture, lamenting that over the past 25 years, Scotland's economy had grown at 1.7 per cent compared with the UK's 2.3 per cent, a figures that had deteriorated further under Labour since 1997. 'The first and most important thing the Scottish economy needs is a political body with a sense of ownership for its fate and the power to do something about it,' argued Salmond. 'It is pretty obvious that Westminster no longer views the specifics of the Scottish economy as its charge; when there is a mess to be cleaned up then it is Scotland's responsibility, as the current fishing crisis illustrates. That implies having financial autonomy. Of course, having financial independence, in and of itself, does not guarantee that things will be better. What it guarantees is that politicians will have to raise their game, grow up, and pay attention to the economy.'

'So having won financial independence,' continued Salmond, 'what should Scotland do with it?' Part of the answer lay in retaining much of the Scottish Executive's Smart Successful Scotland strategy, investing in research and education. In addition to that, business rates had to be lowered, transport infrastructure improved, and broadband targets extended. He went on: 'However, after we have addressed these anti-competitive situations, we will still need something else and something significant. For this, we should substantially lower corporation tax. Low corporation tax would draw businesses – especially much needed decision-making centres – to Scotland. The likely net result of this reduction would be to increase overall corporation tax revenues. The reason is simple: the government would collect less tax from each individual company, but would be collecting that tax from more companies overall – exactly the policy already successfully pursued by Ireland, Sweden and Finland.'

'Art Laffer's famous curve is alive and well,' added Salmond, 'but for business rather than personal taxation. It thus makes substantial economic sense to argue for fair personal taxation to fund public services but certainly for small countries, low business taxation to secure a competitive edge.'[31] This conversion to neo-liberal economics, of course, was not new, Salmond's 1993 Millport speech having marked the first substantial shift in that direction.

The third and final lecture returned to Salmond's favoured Irish analogy, albeit one less concerned with 'social democracy' than in 1993. 'Traditionally a poor and predominately rural economy, Ireland has done what must have been unthinkable when the Free State was established in 1921,' he said, it has 'become wealthier than the UK':

How did it do it? It invested in education, knowing that many would leave. But Ireland reasoned that if it got other things right, those talented people would come back. It also embraced its position within the EEC, got its public finances under control, gained a national consensus allowing it to make difficult decisions and stopped its debt cycle. To woo businesses, the corporation tax was dropped. In addition to bringing in business and with them bringing back Irish citizens, the net effect was to more than double in real terms the overall corporation tax take to the exchequer. In the last 25 years, Ireland has had an average annual growth rate of 5.3 per cent. The past ten years showed an average growth rate of 7.8 per cent.

And it was not just Ireland that had achieved this economic miracle. 'Like the Scottish Parliament, US state legislatures are responsible for issues such as education and the courts,' added Salmond. 'Unlike the Scottish Parliament, the US states also have a high level of fiscal autonomy. The state of Mississippi raises 65 per cent of its revenue directly. The state of Nevada raises 76 per cent. In Scotland, by contrast, less than 15 per cent of the revenue base is controlled by the Scottish Parliament.'

Salmond concluded his lecture series by invoking Scotland's 'great relative economic success at the turn of the late 19th century, with arguably, for a time, the highest GDP per capita in the world'. 'There is no reason why we could not achieve that pinnacle again if we face reality and make serious changes,' he said, going on to quote Keynes. 'The difficulty lies not in the new ideas, but in escaping the old ones.'[32]

There were, however, few new ideas in The Alex Salmond Lectures, which was disappointing given the rationale behind his return to Westminster. Indeed, far from re-examining the economic case for independence, Salmond had simply reiterated several old arguments chiefly revolving around the Irish model. The emphasis, however, had been more ostentatiously business friendly, while it built upon the fiscal autonomy line pushed by the SNP during the 2001 election campaign.

But as the lectures explicitly acknowledged, there was little hard evidence that an independent Scotland could actually achieve higher growth, merely that it presented an opportunity at least to try. 'Salmond is correct to argue that growth is the real issue facing the Scottish economy,' acknowledged Professor Brian Ashcroft of the Fraser of Allander Institute, later to become Mr Wendy Alexander. 'He is also right to point out that Scotland's growth performance on average over the past 20 years has been weak.' However, he continued, 'it would be wrong to believe, as he claims, that the growth rate of Scotland has languished permanently in the basement of world economic growth during this period. During the 1990s, Scottish growth averaged 2.2 per cent per annum, faster than in the 1970s and 1980s. This growth rate was close to the UK average of 2.3 per cent during the period.'[33] There were, of course, lies, damned lies, and economic statistics, and Salmond preferred to stick to a figure of 1.8 per cent.

The lectures were published later that year in a volume edited by Jennifer Erickson entitled *The Economics of Independence*. A dedication read: 'For my late mother, Mary Salmond, who attended every lecture.'[34] She had died, aged 81, while out walking with the Linlithgow Ramblers (of which she was honorary president) near Glenmore. A significant figure in Salmond's childhood, not to mention throughout his life, Salmond paid tribute to 'a remarkable woman [who had been] a picture of health and vitality'. 'It is a shock,' he added, 'but we are comforted that she died peacefully among friends, doing something she loved most of all.'[35]

Much later, Salmond admitted he felt guilty about the last time he saw his mother alive. 'I was going out canvassing, and I was rushing to get out,' he told the broadcaster Kirsty Young. 'I've always regreted not spending more time ... I've always regretted not saying, "Och well, the canvassing can wait half an hour." Of course I wasn't to know ... she was an incredible women. For every boy, the mother is the most important person.'[36]

Just a few days before the death of Mary Salmond, voters had gone to the polls to elect the second Scottish Parliament. Although John Swinney had presented his manifesto with flair and endured a reasonable campaign, his party secured 23.8 per cent of the constituency vote, a fall of nearly 5 per cent, and just 20.9 per cent on the regional ballot, a fall of more than 6 per cent. This resulted in the loss of ten list MSPs, including Mike Russell and Andrew Wilson, both key Salmond allies. Margo MacDonald, meanwhile, popular but unmanageable, survived only by standing on the Lothians list as an independent (as she had said she would), where she gained enough votes to elect two Margos. The SNP had seriously underestimated the threat from the political fringe as the Scottish Socialist Party and Scottish Green Party won six and seven seats respectively, mostly at the expense of Nationalists.

The result considerably weakened Swinney's leadership of the party, as did the revival of a row over the party's commitment to a pre-legis- lative referendum on independence, as initiated by Salmond shortly before he resigned as leader. The party's fundamentalist wing, for once, actually did something rather than sniping from the sidelines and fielded Bill Wilson as a stalking horse, prompting a spirited defence from Salmond. He wrote in the *Scotsman*:

> If I can offer one solitary piece of advice to the challenger in the leadership contest, historically the SNP has little patience for 'holier-than-thou' arguments which attempt to divide the party into the 'true believers' while the rest of us are less than pure. If the SNP were the largest parliamentary party in Holyrood, party critics of existing policy believe that there should be no independence referendum, and by implication that we should stand aside from the responsibility of governing Scotland. Now that would really impress the people of Scotland: 'Vote for us and we'll do nothing except stay in permanent opposition.' Ah, but the critics say, we could start 'negotiations' with Westminster, either from a minority of votes and seats in Holyrood, or a minority of votes in a Westminster election. You don't need a crystal ball to know what the response of Westminster would be.

Salmond, as ever, had a point, and one that the fundamentalists found hard to contradict convincingly. 'The job of a political leader is not just to paint a vision of a better future, but also the practical means of getting there,' added Salmond. 'Thus, John Swinney is right to highlight the referendum policy – just as he is the right person to lead the SNP.'[37]

Salmond's article provoked what was perhaps the last great war of correspondence in the *Scotsman*, which is worth quoting at some length. Campbell Martin, an SNP MSP for the West of Scotland, fired the opening salvo on 28 August:

> In arguing for the party's current policy of a pre-legislative referendum on independence, Alex asserts that it is now unlikely that the SNP, on its own, can win a mandate for independence. The SNP must be honest with the people of Scotland. We have to say to the electorate: we cannot change Scotland for the better without the powers that come only with independence – and independence is what we will deliver if you vote for us. Under the current leadership, the SNP argument is dishonest. What we said to the people of Scotland at the Scottish Parliament election in May was that they could vote SNP in the knowledge that this wasn't necessarily a vote for independence, because if we formed the Scottish Executive we would hold an 'are you sure?' referendum.

'Meanwhile, the members of the devolved SNP administration would still be able to call themselves ministers and be ferried around in ministerial cars,' concluded Martin. 'It's a simple way to further the careers of the very small number of MSPs who form the current leadership clique. Independence, unfortunately, comes a poor second in the current career-path leadership strategy.'[38] Campbell's article was significant, leading eventually to his expulsion from the SNP, Swinney's resignation and, ultimately, the return of Salmond as leader.

The king over the water responded a few days later:

> The argument between 'gradualism' and 'fundamentalism' is not something that arose in the 1990s. It is almost as old as the party itself, and ... As a serious debate ... ended in 1997 with the devolution referendum and the achievement of the Scottish Parliament. What we have now is a mere aftershock. If a total victory were to come about, the difference between Campbell Martin and myself would be purely tactical. He would advocate the SNP holding negotiations with Westminster and then having a referendum. I think that would be inviting prevarication and obstruction on the part of Whitehall, along the lines of what happened with devolution in the 1970s. I would argue that any referendum is better held on principle by the Scottish Parliament to remove the incentive for delay and obstruction. That was the effect (although probably not the intent) of the pre-legislative devolution referendum in 1997.

'Finally, however wrong I believe Campbell Martin to be, he has a perfect right to make his points,' concluded Salmond. 'What is unacceptable is the manner in which he describes his MSP colleagues. They are neither "dishonest", a "clique", or weak on independence. Perhaps they have just thought about things for a little longer and a little more carefully than he has.'[39]

Martin responded in a conciliatory tone:

> I have the greatest respect for Alex Salmond and for the progress made by the SNP under his leadership, and the party owes him a great deal. Having said that, I hope his letter had more to do with a feeling that he must be loyal to the leadership he helped put in place, than on what he believes to be the political reality the party and Scotland face. I joined the SNP in 1977 because I believed that only independence could transform Scotland and deliver a better quality of life and standard of living for our people. I still believe that, and I believe the SNP should be fighting to deliver inde-

pendence in the shortest possible timescale, not asking to be allowed to form a devolved administration, which is the strategy adopted by the current leadership and Alex Salmond.[40]

'First, I don't argue these points out of loyalty to the party leadership,' replied Salmond, 'which was not put in place by me but democratically by the SNP as a whole. In any case, the referendum policy was not devised by the current leadership of the SNP. It wasn't even put in place by me. The SNP has always accepted that a referendum would be required to change the status of Scotland to that of an independent state. The difference is rather that we now argue that such a referendum should be on principle and held by the Scottish Parliament, not post-negotiation and conducted by Westminster.' 'Our referendum policy was devised to allow Scotland a democratic way out of that Unionist trap, a straight vote on the principle of national freedom,' concluded Salmond. 'Having escaped from the snare, it would seem strange to walk back into it.'[41]

At this point, the correspondence degenerated into an almighty slanging match between Jim Sillars and Salmond. 'If the SNP cannot command an absolute majority of seats, how is it to get the referendum on principle through the parliament?' wrote Sillars, applying his usual cold logic.

'If, however, it does gain an absolute majority, then it doesn't need a referendum to provide the mandate to negotiate independence, as that will have been given by the people in the election. In his debate with Campbell Martin, Mr Salmond is displaying the same surprising lack of understanding of the independence issue as he did when he led the party to its first Scottish Parliament defeat; he put independence tenth on his list of priorities.'[42]

Salmond replied, not altogether convincingly:

The answer is that there may well be MSPs who support independence, but not the SNP, and others who do not agree with independence but favour the issue being settled by the people. I know some of those in the latter category and I think he [Sillars] knows some in the former. He repeats the canard that I put independence tenth in my priorities in the 1999 election. The reality is that the independence referendum was presented as a vital step to a new Scotland, and the manifesto related every single substantive issue within it to the importance of moving on to independence. I have spent my entire adult life arguing for independence. He spent the first half of his political career arguing against it, and the past ten years attacking those who argue for it on the basis that we don't believe in it as much as he does.

'I recognise the zeal of the convert, but the sad fact is that his contribution for many years has been entirely negative,' concluded Salmond woundingly. 'His talent could have been really important for Scotland's cause. What a pity that he wasted it.'[43]

Sillars remained unconvinced:

He says there 'may well be' MSPs from outwith the SNP who support independence, and others who, while against it, will back a referendum. 'May well be' also means 'may well not be', a dangerously loose peg on which to hang party policy. Mr Salmond objects to my 'canard' of his placing independence tenth on his list of priorities. A canard is a false rumour. It wasn't a rumour. He did place it tenth. As for my attacks, these have not been on those genuinely seeking independence, but on those holding up that banner to the party faithful while surrendering to devolution and its electoral 'trap' – Mr Salmond's own word – that he led the party into.[44]

'The advantages of the current SNP policy are manifest – his position leaves the SNP having to gain an absolute majority in a proportional system before any action is taken,' responded Salmond. 'Alternatively, a minority SNP administration could mobilise a referendum majority in the parliament to allow the Scottish people the chance to determine our own future. His all-or-nothing approach seems unattractive, certainly to those of us who don't believe in going off in a grand huff every time we fail to convince the people. He claims that he only attacks those who are not genuine about independence, but as I recall the entire population was once condemned as "90-minute nationalists" [sic].' 'Jim Sillars' strategy changes with every re-emergence from his periodic political slumber,' continued Salmond, clearly getting into his stride. 'In a previous letter, I pointed out he has been both fiercely unionist and passionately nationalist. I missed out his pro-devolution and anti-devolution phases, his pro-convention and anti-convention periods and his bewildering conversion from anti-European to Euro-enthusiast and now to reborn Eurosceptic. Perhaps if his talk had even a smidgeon of consistency, then I might believe that he plans any action at all beyond a long, self-indulgent girn.'[45]

Sillars retorted:

The nearer I get to the deep flaw in the SNP's position on a referendum, the greater grows the personal abuse from Alex Salmond. An SNP with an absolute majority negotiates from the strength of a clear mandate won on the principle in an election. A referendum post-negotiations will detail the agreed terms of divorce from the United Kingdom, enabling a final judgment by the people based upon certain knowledge about the currency and its relationship to sterling (of critical importance to the financial services industry and to those in private pension funds held on a UK basis); trade relations with our biggest market, England; our position within the European Union; pensions; social security; defence, and the division of state assets.

'A referendum held by a minority SNP administration on only the principle of independence,' he continued, 'even if allowed by Westminster, cannot, by definition, put any certainties before the electorate. The difference in these two approaches is clear. The first gets an incontestable majority for the principle, and then guarantees the test of the detail of a negotiated settlement in a referendum. The second puts the SNP's policy in the hands of other parties, and risks the distinct possibility of losing the referendum. A lost referendum on the principle would sink independence, which is no doubt one of the reasons why, as Mr Salmond claimed, Unionist parties might back the minority SNP in holding one.' 'But perhaps I am wrong,' finished Sillars. 'Perhaps the present SNP leadership does understand that, and knows that losing a referendum will leave it free to abandon independence openly, and become the devolution party, as which it fought the last election.'[46]
Salmond replied, having spotted an inconsistency:

While previously he told us the Scottish Parliament wouldn't, or even couldn't, hold such a poll, the real problem is now that we would lose. He then goes on to suggest that such a defeat is the real cunning plan of the SNP leadership. If we leave to one side the last bit, which takes conspiracy theory a long way, even for him, his arguments are similar to those he deployed against the pre-legislative devolution referendum of 1997, in which he campaigned for a national abstention. In reality, that process was altogether more successful than the long-delayed, post-legislative 1979 referendum, in which politicians of his generation allowed the self-government issue to be prevaricated into the sand.

'The point of personal criticism I have made of him is quite different, and, in a way, much more damning,' he concluded, 'no one in recent

Scottish politics has had more God-given talent, and sadly he has wasted it.'[47]

'Mr Salmond seems to believe his policy will keep Westminster out of the independence issue,' responded Sillars in the final letter to appear in the *Scotsman*. 'How naive. The fact is that, so long as the SNP is in a minority in a devolution setting, Westminster calls the constitutional shots. The only way the SNP can remove the obstacle in the Scotland Act, the trap into which Mr Salmond led the party, is by achieving a majority, giving it the mandate to negotiate. The political force of an independence mandate and the temper of the times it would demonstrate, would create a new realm of realpolitik in which control of events would lie in Scotland, and not London. There is no other way.'[48]

Sillars got the last word. Yet although he would be vindicated on the referendum numbers game following the SNP's election victory in 2007, his alternative strategy was, as had been the case with much fundamentalist criticism over the years, quixotic.

John Swinney, meanwhile, survived Bill Wilson's leadership challenge by 577 votes to 111, the last time an SNP leader would be elected by conference delegates, while the Scottish political press pack soon shifted their cynical gaze to an inquiry into the Holyrood building project chaired by the former Conservative minister Lord Fraser.[49] Among those called upon to give evidence were Salmond, and he did not disappoint. 'The true costs of Holyrood were hidden,' he alleged, 'and there was a deliberate effort to make Calton Hill appear to offer less value for money – when the exact opposite was the case . . . there was a deliberate attempt to conceal key costs.'[50]

It was, at least from the media's point of view, 'a stunning return to Scottish political life', underlined by Salmond's confirmation that he would be standing for Holyrood in 2007. He joked to the *Sunday Herald*:

> At a time when the parliament is under assault, then hopefully it's encouraging that somebody wants to be part of it again. I don't want to sound arrogant about it, but it's a vote of confidence. Not because of what the parliament is, because I think the parliament must do much better, but because of what it could become. To help it become that thing, what people expected, what people have a right to deserve and expect, then you don't have to be a party leader. As long as you can help the parliament on that road . . . I am not standing as SNP leader again. I did 10 years, I

loved it. I had a whale of a time, but I really like not being SNP leader as well and I've had a whale of a time the last few years doing all sorts of things I couldn't have done when I was SNP leader. I did that bit, so that's not my wish or intention.[51]

The June 2004 European Parliament elections, however, effectively ended Swinney's leadership of the SNP. Although the party retained two Scottish MEPs despite a reduction in seats from eight to seven, there was a further decline in vote share, something Salmond later described as 'a pretty ropey result'.[52] After another spate of fundamentalist and media attacks – including a dire warning from Mike Russell that 'men in grey kilts' might call upon the SNP leader – Swinney resigned on 22 June 2004. Shortly afterwards, Salmond made his famous declaration that nothing would persuade him to enter the contest: 'If nominated, I would decline. If drafted, I will defer and, if elected, I will resign.'

Explaining his decision in an impassioned speech to a Stirling National Council, Swinney hit out at his critics. 'The small and vocal minority must understand this – our leader is democratically elected and once elected should be supported by every single member,' he said. 'I want you to do something about it – to make sure that those people who put their personal interests above the party's are brought down not a peg or two but a good number of pegs.'[53] Swinney argued that he simply could not remain leader amid continued speculation over his future, which was certainly a more convincing reason than any provided by Salmond four years earlier.

Although Swinney did not believe his predecessor had been anything other than loyal ('I am grateful to Alex Salmond for his loyalty and steadfast support throughout my time as leader'[54]), the usual suspects implied that he had been pulling the strings in concert with Mike Russell. The leadership race soon took shape, with the Salmond-backed Nicola Sturgeon competing against Roseanna Cunningham and Mike Russell, the last of whom was not even an MP or MSP. Although once extremely close, Salmond and Russell had recently drifted apart, while his decision to stand most likely eroded their relationship to the point of no return. All three leadership candidates, interestingly, had been Salmond allies at various points over the past 25 years. Alex Neil, a long-standing critic, had planned to stand but withdrew after claiming Salmond had effectively 'vetoed' his candidacy by declaring on television that he 'would find it difficult to have somebody as leader who has been busy undermining John Swinney over the last four years'.[55]

Then, on 15 July 2004, Salmond took one of the biggest gambles of his political life. After nearly four years of speculation, he declared his intention to contest the SNP leadership for the second time in 14 years. In an impressive scoop for the *Herald* newspaper, it emerged that Nicola Sturgeon was to step aside and stand as his running mate. 'Champany Inn in Linlithgow will now be etched in the annals of SNP history,' observed the *Herald*, 'as the place where Alex Salmond persuaded Nicola Sturgeon to step aside and let the king return from across the water.'[56] Salmond had phoned Cunningham and Russell the evening before in a 'gung-ho' mood, telling them he believed he could 'turn the situation round'.[57] With perfect timing, his announcement came just before nominations closed; Moira's being the first name on his papers. As Salmond later explained, his wife had had 'an effective veto' over his decision to stand. 'If Moira had said no, that would have been that,' he said. 'Luckily for me, and possibly the party, she said yes.'[58] Salmond was being perfectly genuine. 'In 2004 he was out, he was clear, and from her point of view there was great celebration that he was free from the constant media coverage,' recalled a former aide. 'To deliberately choose to go back to all that was a big call for both of them.'[59]

With deliberate symmetry, Salmond formally announced his comeback at his favourite hotel, the Marcliffe of Pitfodels, the same venue he had used to reveal his resignation almost exactly four years before. The press conference, wrote Fraser Nelson, 'was staged like a De Gaulle-style comeback. Aides created an aisle for him to walk up, and cheered as he passed. It was a homecoming hero.' 'Almost four years ago I announced that I was standing down as SNP leader,' he said. 'I did not expect to ever be doing that job again. But I didn't anticipate that, after waiting 300 years for a Parliament, it would allow itself to sink into something approaching disrepute.' As well as presenting himself as the saviour of devolution, Salmond also alluded to an American Civil War general to explain his volte-face. 'I was quoting William Sherman,' he said. 'He was turning down the Republican nomination. He sent a telex [*sic*]. I admit, I should have quoted General MacArthur, who said: "I shall return."'

'Did you not think my batteries have been recharged in four years?' he asked Fraser Nelson in a post-press conference interview. 'I'm a professor of politics at Strathclyde Economics. And I'm a member of Inverallochy golf course ... I have a greenhouse, I have eight Muscovy ducks [an expensive South American breed] a river, two bridges and other stuff.' So why was he giving all that up? 'How can I tell you,' he replied, 'without sounding mawkish? When old-age pensioners write to you and describe how much they've done for the party over their life-time and how much of their savings they have put to the party, and say "we really do think that it's quite disappointing that things haven't advanced more". It makes you think that you have to do that extra help.'[60]

It was not just old ladies imploring Salmond to return, but also senior figures in the party. Annabelle Ewing, daughter of Winnie, urged him to reconsider in a phone call, while Andrew Wilson and Angus Robertson reinforced Salmond's own inclination to stand during several curries at the Top Curry Centre in Pimlico. At one such gathering, the Labour politician Charles Clarke even briefly joined in the conversation, without offering, however, a view on what Salmond should do. 'By that stage it was pretty obvious where the lay of the land was,' recalled someone close to these events. 'It was obvious we needed to get some momentum back into things. We wanted it to be the right change and I think that was pretty obvious to him, albeit privately.'[61]

There was an assumption that Salmond only agreed to stand because it appeared that Roseanna Cunningham (despite a fumbling perfor-mance on a recent edition of *Question Time*, which Salmond must certainly have seen) would beat Sturgeon, an outcome he believed to be undesirable. As he put it in 2009, 'Things weren't developing as I'd hoped'.[62] 'What was he thinking in 2004? That Nicola wasn't going to win, Mike Russell wasn't in a great place and I think Alex was genu-inely reluctant,' recalled a source. 'The party's finances were also in disarray. He was genuinely worried about what might happen, that the party might implode.'[63]

Later, Salmond would present his comeback as part of a grand elec-toral strategy, although those close to him say he did not, at that point, expect to win the 2007 Holyrood elections. 'The politics of the UK were changing in such a way as people would be pretty fed up with the New Labour Government at Westminster,' he explained to the radio journalist Colin Mackay in 2009, 'and also there was a new confidence emerging in Scotland that perhaps the Parliament could be different as well. I thought these things would come together and the SNP would give it a pretty fair crack and I was prevailed upon to believe I was the best-placed person to put the SNP into a challenging position to try to win the 2007 election.'[64]

So when Salmond told journalists gathered at the Marcliffe that he was 'not just launching a campaign to be SNP leader' but his 'candidacy to be First Minister of Scotland' he was taking a stab in the dark, adding mischievously that if he 'could nearly beat Donald Dewar' in 1999, he could 'certainly beat Jack McConnell'[65] in 2007. It was also pushing things too far to imply, as some did, that Salmond had planned his comeback all along. It 'was not calculated,' confirmed Salmond in 2008. 'I didn't think "I'll resign, come back again, win the 2007 election". Nobody can calculate like that.'[66]

Salmond's other commitments quickly began to suffer. '*Scotsman* racing columnist Alex Salmond is a non-runner in today's paper after his late entry for the three-horse race to become the new leader of the Scottish National Party,' joked the *Scotsman*. 'The odds-on favourite to succeed John Swinney will be back with his column next week.'[67] Elsewhere in the same newspaper, Jim Sillars was predictably scathing:

> After ten years of Alex's leadership, and his continued manipulative dominance, the party Gordon Wilson led in his final years, with a mass membership, financially solvent, a happy, united team capable of campaigning with vigour and imagination, has been turned into a poisonous cabal, operating with one controller, with a membership shrunk in numbers and confidence, and its only asset [its New Town HQ] long sold off.[68]

One former Sillarsite, however, was more easily persuaded. 'The leadership of the SNP is not about personal ambition,' said Kenny MacAskill as he bowed out of the deputy leadership race. 'My ambition is for the future of the SNP and for the future of Scotland. I believe that the Salmond/Sturgeon team is the best to unite the party and take the SNP forward.'[69]

This statement completed MacAskill's long political journey from fundamentalism to gradualism. 'The way forward will be incremental,' he wrote in a book on 'post-devolution Nationalism' that year, 'building up both the Parliament as an institution and the powers to be exercised within it.'[70] Although Mike Russell essentially agreed with MacAskill's analysis, he vowed to fight on. 'There is no such thing as a coronation in the SNP,' he declared. 'I am not afraid of a policy debate with Alex – not least because I used to write the lines for him.'[71]

Salmond gave an interview to *Scotland on Sunday* the weekend after his dramatic announcement which caused old fears about his 'arrogance' to resurface. Jack McConnell, the First Minister, was dismissed as 'an apparatchik who has been put into the sunlight and . . . turned to dust', his former referendum ally Jim Wallace was described as 'pretty appalling' as a minister, while he urged the Scottish Conservatives to ditch David McLetchie as leader and replace him with the 'far more impressive' Annabel Goldie (which they did a year later, although in disagreeable circumstances). Salmond was more positive, however, when it came to his joint ticket with Sturgeon. 'If Nicola and I win then we are both agreed that everyone in the Scottish National Party starts from day one,' he said. 'There's no grudges, grievances, no prior record. Everybody starts with a clean slate and we will use all the talents available.'

Salmond, surprisingly, was actually the youngest of the three leadership candidates at 49 (Russell and Cunningham were 50 and 52 respectively). 'I just hope they don't try to use my youth and inexperience against me,'[72] he joked. They did not, although both repeatedly stressed the impracticality of having a party leader based at Westminster. 'Let us not forget the distance between Westminster and the Scottish Parliament,' warned Cunningham in a televised leadership debate from which Salmond was absent. 'The SNP in Westminster are about getting noticed, they are about making a stooshie and getting some attention. The SNP in the Scottish Parliament is about winning and holding power. It is only by doing that in the Scottish Parliament that we will be able to deliver independence.'[73]

Such attacks did Salmond's campaign little harm, particularly as he and Sturgeon were engaged in a policy blitz. An education convention, public involvement in choosing Holyrood debates, a bullet train between Edinburgh and Glasgow and the dualling of the A9 between Perth and Inverness – paid for by a trust fund based on private and public investment – were all unveiled in the joint Salmond/Sturgeon manifesto. 'The past is a great thing but you can't live in it,' responded Russell. 'No matter how much we all admire Alex Salmond, the time has come for the SNP to think new thoughts and do new things.'[74]

Salmond's was, unsurprisingly, a smooth and well-organised campaign, marred only by one minor gaffe. Leigh Arnold, a shrewd Press Association reporter, managed to steer Salmond into criticising his predecessor. 'As an SNP leader with a hostile press one of the things you have to be able to do is have a television rapport and I think John wasn't as strong in that aspect of politics,' Salmond told him. 'And therefore when the press gave him a rough time he didn't have the skills or the salvation I had when I was in the same position.' There was also a subtle, if clumsy, swipe at Swinney's 'Release Our Potential' slogan. 'I think there was a slogan last year that Scotland had to "realise our potential". Well we haven't realised our own potential as a party. Maybe we should realise our own potential as we ask Scotland to do likewise.'[75]

Speaking to journalist Catherine Deveney as ballot papers made their way to SNP members, Salmond chose his words a little more carefully as he looked back on his resignation in 2000. 'I began to think, "I am the problem." I thought maybe if we could present a softer image, less abrasive, less history, less baggage, they'd give us some credit,' he said. 'It was a ridiculous misjudgement. If anything, John [Swinney] got it worse than I did. They sensed blood, which they never did with me.' Asked about his reputation for arrogance, meanwhile, Salmond exclaimed: 'Good God ... It would be very difficult to survive as leader of a minority party unless you had a good conceit of yourself. Because, believe me, if you don't, you'd get knocked about, swept aside.'[76]

Salmond also admitted he may have been 'too young' on becoming SNP leader for the first time. 'I've got long trousers now and I will express all parts of my personality,' he told Leigh Arnold, 'some of which I think will help inject some dynamism and vigour into the SNP's campaigning.'[77] 'In my first tenure I was cocky, and that was quite deliberate,' he also admitted to Deveney. 'And provocative, and that was also deliberate. But you're leading a party with four members, and the first priority is to get yourself noticed.'[78]

Indeed, Salmond repeatedly stressed to journalists how much he had changed:

> If you're leading me to suggest that as a 49-year-old, I might be less brash and individualistic, then the answer's yes. You learn lessons as life goes on. I was a young man in a hurry 14 years ago, and now I'm a middle-aged man in a hurry ... What else did I learn? I learned to put things in the right context. I don't know if my skin's thicker, but my sense of proportion is greater ... My style will be much more collective, because I have more people to be collective with. Even in 1999, with 35 MSPs elected, only six had parliamentary experience. Most were learning their trade. A lot of them have.[79]

Salmond, however, was typically vague when asked about his vision of an independent Scotland: 'I don't believe everyone thinks the things I do, or wishes for the things I wish for. But I think there is a shared vision. I would like us to articulate through our institutions a vision of Scottishness that we can aspire to. It's a bit like religion in a way: we can aspire to being good and all fall short, but it's not a question of failure if you don't get there. It's a good thing to try, a really good thing.'[80]

Salmond got there, as widely expected, at the 2004 SNP conference, attracting 75.8 per cent of the 4,952 votes cast, more than 60 per cent of the party membership. Nicola Sturgeon, meanwhile, took 53 per cent of the vote in the deputy leadership contest, a more convincing victory than many had expected. 'It's good to be back,'[81] Salmond told cheering supporters. The gamble had been won, however bad the odds, and won decisively.

Chapter 11

SALMOND REDUX

It is in truth not for glory, nor riches, nor honours that we are fighting, but for freedom – for that alone, which no honest man gives up but with life itself.

From the Declaration of Arbroath

'We intend to lead with the head, the heart, and touch the soul of Scotland,' declared Alex Salmond as he embarked upon his second term as leader of the SNP. The Swinney years, meanwhile, were swiftly buried, as Nicola Sturgeon announced a policy review and Salmond set a target of raising £250,000 to fight the next general election campaign. Given that the party's debt was around £750,000 at that point, it was a tough challenge. He also promised to recruit 1,000 new members over the next three weeks. 'I will be leading it [the SNP] from around Scotland – every nook and cranny, every village and town and city,' he said, 'as we rouse this nation to make progress next year, and secure victory in 2007, and then on to Scottish independence.'[1]

With Salmond at the helm, cries of social democracy were never far behind. In another series of speeches outlining a new policy platform for the SNP, he called for an ideological compromise: 'In Scotland today we pay social democratic rates of taxation, we have social democratic levels of spending but we do not have social democratic standards of service. The challenge for those who are concerned with the Common Weal of Scotland is to propose public service reform in Scotland which rejects both the neo-Thatcherite changes South of the Border but also the total inactivity of the Scottish Lib/Lab Executive. We need to find a way – the Scottish Way – to avoid being sucked in to the Blair agenda South of the Border but to ensure first class standards of delivery and service.'

This was the latest incarnation of Salmond's brand of social democracy, 'a competitive and successful Scotland' that was also committed 'to excellence in the delivery of public services'. Again, Ireland was the model, and this time in terms of domestic policies as well as its tiger economy. 'We should look to our near neighbours in Ireland for an example of a complete transformation of an education system from being one of the worst performers in Europe to one of the best,' he said. 'That was achieved by a Convention, by consensus and by a social contract between government and people. It wasn't brought about by the top-down imposition of the latest wheeze from some Downing Street policy geek.'[2]

The key challenge, Salmond told journalists, was to 'refresh' the SNP's 'social democratic message'. As ever, delving any more deeply proved frustrating. 'Defining these clichés is tough because Salmond says different things to different audiences,' observed Paul Hutcheon in the *Sunday Herald*. 'His acceptance speech in Edinburgh was slick, centrist and controlled. Later on in Dundee, his pep talk at the adoption meeting was populist, left-wing and folksy.'

And having clung on to the Penny for Scotland policy until the day he resigned as leader, Salmond no longer believed it was necessary to increase income tax. 'There is now a different perspective where we have seen reasonable increases in public spending,' he explained. 'There is an extra £5 million to spend over the next spending review. It is now a question of delivery.' Salmond also agreed with Nicola Sturgeon, who said the SNP's policies had become too 'centrist', something they planned to rectify by making health boards and other public bodies partly elected.

Most SNP activists, however, were glad to have him back. When Salmond appeared at Stewart Hosie's adoption meeting in Dundee East on the evening of his leadership victory, 'all hell broke loose. Folk laughed, old women cheered and the room lit up. It was as if a celebrity had entered the building.'[3] Elsewhere, there was inevitable criticism from Labour, which delighted in reminding Salmond of Mike Russell's remark about him being an 'absentee laird'. 'I congratulate the hon. Gentleman on his good fortune in being elected leader of his party for the second time,' remarked Alistair Darling at the first Scottish Questions following Salmond's return. 'It is good to see him leading from London, and we look forward to his doing that for many months.'[4]

With time, however, the Sturgeon/Salmond joint leadership gathered momentum. 'The idea of team leadership is new to me, and it will work,' admitted Salmond. 'She'll take care of [Jack] McConnell and I'll impeach the Prime Minister at Westminster.'[5] Again, he took care to stress how much he had changed. 'First time around it was seen as just me,' he said. 'This time it's a team because politics is a bit like football – it's not just about having a striker, it's about a team that can play at the highest level.'[6]

The 2004 SNP conference, meanwhile, gave Salmond his first outing as leader since 2000, and the keynote speech was one of his best, 'displaying the pace and extreme self-confidence activists have come to expect'. 'He combined his disparate themes of Iraq, devolution and renewable energy with skill,' judged the *Scotsman*, 'while the passages of serious politics were interlaced with well-delivered humour and quips at the expense of his political opponents.'

Salmond also sought to distance his party from the perceived failures of the Scottish Parliament: 'Devolution is yesterday's news. It has not responded to today's reality, never mind the challenges of tomorrow. There are basically two explanations why devolution has been one big let-down. Either there is something wrong with Scotland, or there is something wrong with the leadership that Scotland has been getting. To put it simply, either Scotland's rubbish or Labour's rubbish. I prefer to think that it is New Labour who are the problem, and new leadership is the answer. We campaigned, shoulder to shoulder, for home rule because we believe in Scotland. We celebrated devolution because it promised to usher in a new era of politics.' Instead, concluded Salmond, 'we have seen our parliament devalued by a government which doesn't understand the very concept of public service, which dulls the expectations of our nation and which seeks to bore the electorate into submission'.[7]

Salmond's conference speech also highlighted the plight of Kenneth Bigley, a Liverpudlian engineer who was being held hostage in Iraq. 'Blair once said that he would be prepared to pay the blood price for standing shoulder to shoulder with the United States of America,' he said in what one newspaper called a 'searing passage' of his speech. 'But he hasn't paid the blood price. Fourteen thousand Iraqis, more than 1,000 Americans, 66 British soldiers, 69 from other countries, hostages – these are the people who have paid and are still paying Blair's blood price.'[8]

Tony Blair had been feeling the wrath of Salmond for nearly a year. 'Prime ministers and politicians lie about all sorts of things . . . But nobody – nobody in recent politics – has ever lied about the reasons for going to war,' he had said in November 2003, betraying genuine anger about the war in Iraq. 'That may just be the lie too far for Mr Blair. And as you can probably detect, I won't be at his political funeral – or if I am, it will just be to make sure that he's politically dead.'[9]

Salmond was convinced that Iraq would bury Blair politically, and set about spearheading an effective – if ultimately unsuccessful – campaign to ensure that this happened. He believed that academic research clearly demonstrated that 'on many occasions before, during and after the war, the Prime Minster clearly lied about the information he had received'. And given that Blair would not resign voluntarily, 'the only option left is to support a motion of impeachment', a procedure 'clearly set out in parliamentary rules' but unused since the 19th century. 'The Prime Minister', declared Salmond, 'has a case to answer.'[10] The Member for Banff and Buchan, of course, had been a master of Parliamentary procedure since first setting foot in the House of Commons in 1987.

On 24 November 2004, 23 MPs laid a motion before the House of Commons calling for a select committee to examine the case for impeaching the Prime Minister. 'This is not just a matter of Parliament being misled – as we know now it was,' argued Salmond. 'There were no weapons of mass destruction in Iraq. This is also an issue of whether the Prime Minister was in a position to know that his statements were wrong.'[11]

Salmond, however, was careful not to present himself as a pacifist. 'I think what Tony Blair did over the war with Iraq was appalling, not because there wasn't an argument for taking part in an invasion, but because he misled people as to the reasons for the invasion,' he told a television audience during the 2005 general election campaign. 'The argument is not an argument against war, the argument is one in abiding by the rule of international law and the will of the United Nations.'[12]

Salmond launched the SNP's campaign for that election in January 2005, although he did so refusing to set even a modest target in terms of seats. 'I have learned a number of things in politics,' he explained. 'And one of them is, if I'm going to hypothecate [sic], I'll do it on success rather than failure.'[13] Further evidence of this cautious approach came as Salmond revived his hung Parliament strategy, first used at the 1987 general election and at almost every Westminster poll since.

As the election approached, however, Salmond became a little bolder. Launching the SNP's pre-election economic strategy in March, he promised to cut business taxes to 20 per cent in an independent Scotland, giving it a competitive edge over England. It was an important argument and well presented by Salmond, but the political journalist Peter MacMahon sensed something amiss. 'The self-confidence based on a good conceit of his own ability – which some mistake for arrogance – was still there,' he assessed in the *Scotsman*. 'The economist's brain that could have made him a small fortune in the private sector if politics had not become his vocation was still ticking over. And yet ... there was something missing. Perhaps it was the dim lights of the Discovery Centre lecture hall, perhaps the lack of audience response, perhaps it was just a bad day out of the office. But the Salmond of old – the combative, sometimes aggressive performer, the passionate advocate for his cause of independence – seemed to be absent without leave.'[14] MacMahon had identified an interesting phenomenon – Salmond redux was not yet up to par. There were also untypical verbal slip-ups. 'An overwhelming majority of people in Scotland want more powers for the [Scottish] parliament, not necessarily for independence,' he told the ITN News Channel in March, 'although a substantial proportion of people do, but none the less want more power for the parliament.'[15]

Although this was simply a statement of fact, it was unlike Salmond to admit as much. Perhaps sensing weakness, the Chancellor Gordon Brown singled him out for criticism at the Scottish Labour conference. 'He has lost the power of communication', said Brown, quoting (misquoting according to Salmond) Shelley, 'but not, alas, the gift of speech.'[16] When a Scottish Opinion poll showed Labour leading the SNP by 52 per cent to 17 per cent, Salmond said simply: 'We have to work harder to get our message across.'[17]

That message had an historical bent when Salmond launched the formal SNP campaign on 6 April 2005, a date rather tenuously chosen to coincide with the 685th anniversary of the signing of the Declaration of Arbroath, which had first articulated the 'vision' of Scottish 'freedom' in 1320. 'We, as the inheritors of that vision and that ideal of setting the country free,' declared Salmond, having quoted from the document, 'want to stand in equality with the other countries of the world.'

Salmond, therefore, proposed making both St Andrew's Day and 6 April public holidays in Scotland, the latter as it would 'eventually become our independence day'.[18] The SNP campaign was briefly aided, meanwhile, by the launch of a new pro-independence newspaper, the *Scottish Standard*. This carried a column by Salmond, who used the short-lived title's first edition to announce, or rather re-announce, his policy of cutting corporation tax from 30 to 20 per cent. This, claimed Salmond, was an 'independence bonus' that would generate an additional £19 billion by 2015.[19]

The 2005 general election campaign, however, was, as an aide recalled, 'very badly run': 'Alex was also unwell; he had a lingering cold. He just wasn't right and a really inexperienced team was running the show. Moira was quite unhappy about it and Alex was unhappy about it. If you compare the '05 and '07 campaigns there's quite a difference. At the first he spent very long periods away from home and we were sending him all over the country; in '07 he was never away from home for more than two nights.'[20] If the 2005 general election was the first electoral test of Salmond redux, therefore, then the result was disappointing. The SNP got just 17.7 per cent of the vote, its poorest showing since 1987 and a decline of 2.4 per cent since 2001, when John Swinney had been at the helm. Even so (and considering the number of Scottish constituencies had been cut from 72 to 59 in line with the Scotland Act), the party managed to take two seats from Labour, giving them a total of six, one more than in 2001, the result of an electoral strategy that had focused limited resources in a handful of constituencies.

The Liberal Democrats, however, beat the SNP into third place in terms of seats and vote share, which given the symbolic merit Salmond had always placed in being Scotland's second party, was certainly a setback. In Banff and Buchan, meanwhile, Salmond's majority held up at 11,837 despite a small swing to the Liberal Democrats:

Alex Salmond (SNP)	19,044
Sandy Wallace (Conservative)	7,207
Eleanor Anderson (Lib Dem)	4,952
Victor Ross (Christian Vote)	683
Kathleen Kemp (UK Independence Party)	442
Steve Will (Scottish Socialist Party)	412

Salmond, as ever, talked up the result, insisting that the SNP's victory in Na h-Eileanan an Iar (the Western Isles), where the SNP achieved an 8 per cent swing, could act as the template for a 2007 election win. 'We start the campaign today from an excellent position,' he declared, without explaining why, 'better than any other party in Scotland.'[21] Indeed, Salmond was genuinely pleased as he was driven from Strichen

to SNP HQ, listening to Dougie MacLean's 'Caledonia' as he explained
to an aide that the result was good enough to give him a real shot at
becoming First Minister two years later.

This analysis, however, proved difficult to impart to political opponents, particularly in the House of Commons when it reconvened
shortly after the election. An early exhange went:

> Alex Salmond: Does the Prime Minister still intend to serve out a full
> term? In any circumstances will he change his mind?
>
> The Prime Minister: I have already dealt with that, in the course of the
> election campaign and afterwards. I think that my leadership of my party
> has been a bit more successful than the hon. Gentleman's leadership of his
> party. I say frankly, and probably to the delight of my colleagues, that
> when I do leave the leadership, I will not be coming back again.[22]

Salmond redux, it seemed, still had a lot to prove.

Towards the end of 2005, Salmond retained a low profile, his keynote
conference speech managing to appear confident without being one of
his finest. While keeping its 'social democratic' heart, he told delegates,
the SNP needed to add an edge of 'economic efficiency'. 'Our political
strategy is crystal clear,' he said. 'We intend to win the elections of
2007.' Remaining a 'social democratic' party, meanwhile, would mean
that 'we match and marry economic efficiency with a social programme
which shapes the public purpose'.[23]

There was more electoral woe shortly after the Aviemore conference
when the SNP failed to make any headway in two by-elections, one
caused by the death of Labour MP Robin Cook (Livingston) and
another by the imprisonment of Labour MSP Mike Watson (Glasgow
Cathcart) for fire-raising at an Edinburgh hotel. Although Labour's
majority went down in both, the governing party were triumphant.
'The Nationalists are on a downward slide under Salmond's leadership,'
Alistair Darling told a press conference in Glasgow, provoking an
amusing rejoinder from Salmond: 'As Denis Healey said of Geoffrey
Howe, "it's like being savaged by a dead sheep". Being attacked by
Alistair Darling is being savaged by a dead sheep.'[24]

The results proved to be the final straw for Bruce McFee, an SNP
MSP for the West of Scotland since 2003. He announced his intention
to leave Holyrood at the next election, saying he could not 'in all

honesty put myself forward to fight on a policy and a direction I don't believe in'. Of Salmond's target of winning an additional 20 constituency seats in 2007, McFee said the 'difficulty will be filling in the gap between the announcement and the actuality'. 'The feeling I have from most members is that we are staggering around like a blind man,' he added for good measure. 'We have become a party that simply rallies the troops and shouts about independence at the conference.'[25] Although McFee was being unduly gloomy, his remarks represented a genuine strand of opinion in the SNP at that point.

Continuing to shout about independence was Salmond, who unveiled *Raising the Standard* towards the end of 2005, a 28-page document he said constituted the most comprehensive explanation of the process of independence ever published. By publishing this 18 months before the Holyrood elections, Salmond was cleverly pre-empting any Labour charge of putting it on the backburner, although the document focused on the 'how' of independence rather than the arguably more important 'why'. 'We will take full control of Scotland's resources, levy our own taxes and conclude our own international treaties,' said Salmond. 'Our nation will, after 300 years, rejoin the world as an equal nation state. The Scottish Parliament will then have all the powers it needs to make a difference to the lives of the people of Scotland.'[26]

With the constitutional question out of the way – for the time being – Salmond then prepared for another gamble. Rather than standing on the north-east Scotland regional list in 2007, as he had indicated in 2004, Salmond announced that he had accepted an invitation to contest the Gordon constituency, not exactly an easy target for the SNP. In 2003, the Nationalist candidate had come third with almost 4,500 fewer votes than the Liberal Democrat incumbent Nora Radcliffe. On the swing required (7.75 per cent), Gordon ranked 18th on the SNP's target list. But by standing here, instead of on the list, Salmond was demonstrating that his target of winning an additional 20 constituency seats was a serious one. 'I have never lost a constituency election in my life and I don't intend to start now,' he remarked. 'I'm not just running for a constituency – I'm running to be the first minister of Scotland.'[27]

When the SNP suffered another bad result in the February Dunfermline and West Fife Westminster by-election – beaten into third place by the Liberal Democrats – it appeared that Salmond's gamble might have been a foolish one, along with his 20-seat target. That, wrote Gordon Wilson in the *Scots Independent*, was 'regarded as absurd by members'. Wilson also accused his party of having become stuck in 'a devolution honey trap', squandering its energies on 'parish pump politics and sterile nit-picking'. 'The party has lost its way, morale and, with it, membership has fallen,' wrote Wilson. 'Local organisations have become emaciated. Members no longer believe independence is possible.'[28]

Then, in April 2006, Salmond's luck began to change. Not only did the SNP decisively retain the Moray seat in a Holyrood by-election (caused by the death of Salmond's 1990 leadership opponent, Margaret Ewing), but a YouGov poll commissioned by the SNP detected 28 per cent support for an SNP–Lib Dem coalition, compared with 25 per cent for a Labour–Lib Dem alliance. More significantly, it also found that 56 per cent of the public agreed with the statement: 'The Labour Party has been in power too long in Scotland; it is time for a change.' 'This is a watershed result,' proclaimed Salmond. 'It is the first poll for a generation which indicates that Labour is not the preferred government of Scotland. It shows the public mood is that it's time for a change.'[29] That sentiment, and more specifically the words 'it's time', would later form the basis of the SNP's 2007 Scottish Parliament election campaign.

Salmond then tried to maintain what he saw as valuable political momentum by using the summer of 2006 for a series of policy announcements, including the slashing of small business rates and £100 million to abolish student fees and debt. This policy blitz created the impression of a dynamic party preparing for government, as well as cleverly neutralising areas of weak SNP support, although detail in some areas was lacking as well as ideologically vague. Campbell Martin (now an independent MSP) interpreted it as the SNP turning 'hard to the right', while Jim Sillars believed 'an independent Scotland must be right-thinking'.[30]

This tension over the SNP's political direction was laid bare when Mike Russell, out of frontline politics since his quixotic bid to become leader in 2004, published a policy manifesto (co-written with Dennis MacLeod, whose home had provided the backdrop for Salmond's Kosovo broadcast) called *Grasping the Thistle*. This proposed a broadly right-wing agenda while the most interesting, and therefore also the most controversial, proposal in the book was the concept of a 'New Union'. This envisaged sharing responsibility for foreign affairs and defence with England while concentrating on full fiscal powers as a precursor to independence.

In light of Salmond's future thinking on the nature of independence, this part of the book was remarkably forward-looking, although other aspects were unrealistic, for example a proposal for Scots to directly elect the First Minister and other Cabinet members. As the BBC's Brian Taylor put it in a review: 'I found the book impressive, intriguing and well-argued although, to lodge a caveat, it was seldom all three at once.'[31]

Although Salmond refused to comment on the book, his private thoughts emerged shortly after when the resourceful journalist Paul Hutcheon obtained private correspondence. 'Russell sent a copy of the "first" [proofs of the] book to the SNP leader, who then telephoned the author to convey his horror at the content,' wrote Hutcheon. 'The SNP leader warned Russell that he would not be the party's candidate in Dumfries next year if the book was published. Salmond then sent the former MSP a five-page bundle of notes, which the *Sunday Herald* has obtained, outlining the parts he disagree with. The barbs, which were written on House of Commons notepaper and signed "Alex", broke the criticisms down into special code.' This was as follows: 'VD' stood for 'very dangerous', 'D' for dangerous, while 'RH' meant 'relatively harmless'. One passage deemed 'VD', for obvious reasons, was as follows: 'A leader brilliantly suited to guerrilla opposition but much less well attuned to the disciplines and demands of any new politics was followed by a technocratic party manager who was unable to invigorate the national debate and take it in new directions.' It was removed from the published version of *Grasping the Thistle*, while Russell also inserted an 'author's note', in which he claimed that none of his policy proposals were 'indirect or implied'[32] criticisms of the SNP.

But this incident, which most likely destroyed what little had been left of a once-strong friendship, did Salmond and the SNP little harm. Another YouGov poll in August had placed the SNP four points ahead of Labour and, significantly, Salmond as the favoured candidate to become the next First Minister. The party now appeared to have the momentum necessary for electoral victory the following year. 'On form,' declared the *Scotsman*, 'Mr Salmond remains the most formidable politician operating in Scotland.' The Kwik-Fit founder, Sir Tom Farmer, agreed, and kindly donated £100,000 to the SNP's campaign.

Salmond did not disappoint in his final conference speech before the Holyrood battle commenced. 'We have work to do. We can determine the future of Scotland in the next six months, Scotland is there for us to take,' he declared. 'But whether we do so or not depends on what we do; it is in our hands.'[33] Salmond also indicated his intention to run a presidential campaign when he told the *Herald* that Jack McConnell did not 'carry the authority that perhaps a First Minister should'.[34]

This approach, as well as a more positive campaigning style, could be traced back to a gathering of bright young(ish) things at the Craigellachie Hotel on Speyside in June 2005. There, Angus Robertson, Peter Murrell, Stephen Noon, Alasdair Allan, Angus MacNeil and Kevin Pringle (who had recently left Salmond to work for Scottish Gas), identified five priorities, 'communications, governance, message, organisation and resource', allocating teams comprising staff and politicians to each. Under 'governance', the main message was: 'To be ready for government before 3 May 2007, and in government thereafter.'[35]

This dovetailed with a process of reform already under way at SNP HQ in Edinburgh and appeared to have been borrowed from New Labour's 1997 election guide. Indeed, a defectee from Labour, a computer expert called Gordon Guthrie, had just designed an enhanced version of the 'Activate' software used by Labour to identify existing and potential supporters. Such a professional statistics-based approach had been a feature of Salmond's campaigning since the late 1970s, and it was to be of considerable value in the electoral battle ahead.

With the September 2006 conference speech, Salmond's press coverage also changed for the better. 'I haven't seen Alex Salmond in this kind of form for years,' wrote Andy Nicoll in the *Sun*. 'This is the old-time, "come on if you think you're hard enough" Alex Salmond.'[36] 'For Alex Salmond, now in his fifties, it is his greatest chance,' agreed John MacLeod in the *Daily Mail*. 'His biggest strength is his security: assured, thick-skinned, Salmond has no patience with lesser politicians who, as he once told me, "store up all sorts of grudges, remember and brood on every slight". His is a ruthless profession, but he is far from a malicious man, and his passion for nationhood is closer to the surface than people think.'[37]

A panicked Labour Party, wrong-footed by positive polls and a positive SNP message, responded by co-coordinating a wave of attacks north and south of the border. 'He didn't fight for the parliament, he didn't build the parliament, he didn't struggle to have it established and he did not even stay with the parliament,' said John Reid in a highly personal attack. 'He would like to run the parliament now that it suits him. I tell you, Alex – dream on.'

Douglas Alexander, meanwhile, depicted Salmond as 'an old man in a hurry'. 'The tides of history and modernity are against the SNP's cause,' he said. 'The only consistent thing about Alex Salmond is that he always goes back on his word. His promises are cheap, but his deeds would be costly for Scotland.' 'I will try during the coming election campaign', retorted Salmond, 'not to use his [Alexander's] youth and inexperience against him.'[38]

Salmond sought to depict Labour in Scotland as 'incapable of running their own campaign without remote control from their London masters',[39] while capitalising upon a perception that Labour had been in office, in London and Edinburgh, for too long, and giving the war in Iraq a Nationalist twist, arguing that Scotland had been 'dragged into enough foolish, costly and illegal wars'.[40]

Jack McConnell believed that Salmond's momentum largely derived from a sustained period of political 'good luck', a combination of the war in Iraq, the resignation of Charles Kennedy as Liberal Democrat leader (which shifted anti-Iraq opposition to the SNP) and the ongoing battle between Blair and Brown. McConnell later reflected:

> The Labour Party in Scotland was actually in better shape than it had been for a while. But that battle plagued the Scottish campaign for months. We started to feel as if we were swimming against a tide, we were on the back foot. For the first time since devolution he [Salmond] was at the centre of it [at Westminster] and I wasn't. During the campaign itself they [the SNP] picked up on the fact that Scots wanted to hear positive stuff so they ran with a very positive campaign and we ended up on the other side of that, sounding negative. They picked up the ball and ran with it. The momentum was obviously with them.[41]

Indeed, an unintended consequence of Salmond redux had been his ability to take a perceived weakness – his presence at Westminster – and turn it into a strength. Events south of the border, in other words, had conspired to put the SNP and its leader at the eye of the political storm.

SNP strategists, meanwhile, hit upon the inspired idea of marketing its leader as a brand identity, using the term 'Alex Salmond for First Minister' rather than 'Scottish National Party' on ballot papers for the regional list vote. Not only would this ensure that it came first on alphabetical ballot papers, but it would capitalise upon Salmond's huge personal popularity. Jim Sillars later described this approach as 'Scotland's first-ever experience of the cult of personality'.[42]

'It does seem,' remarked Salmond in a mystical frame of mind, 'that circumstances like stars in the heavens are conjoining to create an event which gives us a fantastic opportunity.'[43] Sir George Mathewson, the respected former chairman of the Royal Bank of Scotland, proved to be such a star. 'The reality is I have been somewhat disappointed for some time with work of the Scottish Parliament,' he told the *Scotsman* in March 2007. 'Alex Salmond and the SNP offer the best choice.'[44]

It was a major coup for a delighted Salmond, who had learned of Sir George's support the previous month, but shrewdly convinced him to delay the announcement in order to coincide with a visit to Edinburgh by Tony Blair. It had the desired effect, particularly when the Prime Minister carelessly dismissed Mathewson as 'self-indulgent'.[45] Also happy to indulge himself was the Stagecoach founder Brian Souter, who donated £500,000 to the SNP's campaign. 'The time has come for Alex Salmond to deliver a dynamic government in Scotland which will respect our past,' said Souter, 'respond to our present problems and reflect the future aspirations of the Scottish people.' Souter's donation, however, incurred the wrath of gay rights campaigners; chiefly because of the tycoon's involvement in the pro-Section 28 'Keep the Clause' campaign back in 2000. 'The SNP would never accept a donation from an avowed racist,' pointed out Peter Tatchell, 'so why are they accepting funding from a man who is so clearly homophobic?'[46] Although there was no suggestion that the SNP was about to reinstate Section 28, it did foster the impression that it was edging towards social conservatism. Salmond also had sympathy with the Catholic Church's line on gay adoption, and had personally supported lowering the time limit on abortion since the late 1980s.

Salmond, meanwhile, published an American-style plan of action for his first 100 days in office, while talking up his UK credentials. 'I want a more mature relationship with the government of the UK,' he said at the Glasgow Science Centre, 'a relationship of equals.'[47] Warming to his theme, Salmond also referred to the 'manifest unfairness' in the way England had been governed post-devolution. 'Scotland and England would both be far better off with a new 21st-century relationship,' he wrote in the *Daily Telegraph*, 'a real partnership based upon equality of status.'[48] Salmond had recently compared the potential separation of Scotland and England with that of Slovakia and the Czech Republic, prompting Tony Blair to brand him as 'politically, economically, historically and culturally ignorant'.[49]

Salmond was self-evidently none of those things. He was, however, clearly overweight and had embarked on yet another campaign diet. 'I'm not about to win Slimmer of the Year and I have a long way to go, but my wife is happy about it,' he joked, pledging to cut down on curries, swap much-loved Lucozade for smoothies, while eating porridge for breakfast. 'This isn't for health reasons – although it is probably doing me some good – it's a television thing,' adding that he had never been 'vain' or 'sizeist'.[50] It was clear, however, that Salmond's weight bothered him. He took little or no exercise and was driven everywhere (he claimed he could no longer travel by train because of back trouble), with the result that the 52-year-old SNP leader's frame bore no resemblance to that of the lean (not to mention more left-wing) Alex Salmond of the 1970s.

And although Salmond possessed no self-consciousness about his combative style, party strategists insisted upon media training to make him appear less confrontational during interviews. The SNP MSP Brian Adam later inadvertently revealed that Salmond had found changing his behaviour a 'major challenge'. 'We all had coaching,' he told a group of American students. 'We were all presented with a bag of pennies. Every time we said anything negative we had to put a penny in the middle of the table. This was to stop us saying negative things. It was a major change in approach, not just for the party, but for the party leader, who has a wonderful line in put-downs. He is not known as Smart Alec for no reason. He is a very very able politician ... but he had to change the way, not only [how] he presented himself, but the way he behaved, and it's been a major challenge for him.' Salmond, concluded Adam, was a charismatic but divisive figure. 'People either love him or they hate him.'[51] Another of those present at this coaching session, however, recalled Salmond 'getting it from the start'.[52] Run by Claire Howell from a company called Red Co., the point was to learn how 'to perform effectively, consistently and efficiently in a wide range of conditions'. 'It's a combination of knowing where you want to go and being able to get there,' explained Red Co.'s website. 'Whatever the context, coaching is about unlocking a person's potential so that they maximise their own performance.'[53] Winning the 2007 election, the argument ran, came down to positive thinking.

Salmond was certainly in a positive frame of mind as he hit the campaign trail during April. 'The great jowls split in a vast grin; the soft, chocolate eyes suck us in with the air of an adoring spaniel,' observed John MacLeod in the Western Isles. 'He falls on the Faithful first, with Alasdair Allan, the local candidate, skipping behind him like a happy rabbit. The flesh is pressed. Shoulders are squeezed. Backs are robustly slapped. And the wee wumman gets a vacuuming kiss after all.'[54]

On that trip to the Western Isles, Salmond also had to deal with the fallout from a minor sex scandal involving the incumbent MP, Angus

Brendan MacNeil. He had recently initiated a police investigation into the so-called 'cash for honours' scandal (a phrase coined, according to the Labour official Peter Watt, by Salmond), following a tabloid expose that everyone who had donated more than £1 million to the Labour Party had received either a knighthood or peerage. Salmond made much of the running, branding it 'an incredible abuse of the system' and accusing Tony Blair of 'stuffing' the House of Lords with cronies instead of modernising it as he had promised to do in 1997.[55]

This provided further momentum as Salmond launched the SNP's 2007 manifesto, promising protection for local hospital services, smaller class sizes, more police, help for first-time buyers, a Local Income Tax and a referendum on independence in 2010. 'For the first time in Scottish political history, the SNP are publishing our election manifesto when we have a clear lead in the polls,' said a triumphant Salmond. 'This is more than a manifesto – it is a programme for government, with a real opportunity to be implemented in government.'[56]

Salmond believed his time had come, and quoted the title of Jim Callaghan's memoirs – *Time and Chance* – to the writer Ian Rankin in order to make this point. 'Like Callaghan before him, Salmond thinks the time just feels right; it is a matter of external events, rather than personal success.'[57] Salmond's role, of course, was more important than that, and although polls still gave him a strong lead over Jack McConnell, internal surveys suggested he was seen as too abrasive. 'I've always enjoyed debate and sometimes winning arguments ... Scots are like that,' he protested on being challenged about his public image. Was he perceived as arrogant and smug, asked STV's Bernard Ponsonby. 'None of us are perfect, Bernard.'[58]

Indeed not, although it was something Salmond had been fully prepared to address. 'I came to the conclusion some time ago that I had to seek to build maximum consensus in a number of ways,' he told *Scotland on Sunday*. 'Lots of Scots – not just me – love winning arguments; and sometimes you love winning arguments even when the arguments aren't even about very much; disputatiousness is part of our character: the game becomes more important than the objective. But for me this objective is so important that I am not going to allow the enjoyment of the game to interfere with the outcome, if I possibly can. I am trying to keep my eye on the prize.'

Once again this was Salmond in the guise of a Scottish everyman; his personality traits simply reflected that of the nation as a whole. 'The job of a national party and as the leader, potentially, hopefully, as First Minister, is not just to talk to the folk who agree with me,' he argued. 'It's my job to reach out to people who don't. I think most national parties have to represent, as far as they can, the whole of the country.' What influence did his wife Moira have in this respect? 'Very substantial,' he replied. 'She tells me not to take myself too seriously.'[59] He also committed Moira to occupying a more high profile role should he become First Minister. 'I certainly couldn't do that job without her,' he said. 'My wife has enormous grace and style.'[60] Kevin Pringle, a long-standing adviser who had returned to the SNP fold in January 2007, was acknowledged as the brains behind Salmond's new persona. 'The reason for the success of the partnership is perhaps in the contrast of personalities,' observed the *Scotsman*. 'Where Salmond hogs the limelight, the modest Pringle shuns it.'[61]

Eddie Barnes, meanwhile, judged that Salmond's commitment to independence remained 'utterly concrete', although in truth he was already introducing caveats, making it clear that although he would prefer a straight 'yes' or 'no' referendum question, he would accept another on additional powers for Holyrood. 'I haven't ruled that out so long as I can present the case of independence to the people of Scotland,' he said. 'I have demonstrated that I could be flexible even more on content, on timing, on approach, and even on the question formulation that might be asked. That seems to me to be moving a long way.[62]

Such sentiments were clearly designed to reassure the Liberal Democrats, still considered the most likely coalition partner were the SNP to emerge as the largest party. At a debate in Glasgow, Salmond also pledged that a 'no' vote in an independence referendum would put the issue on hold for around 20 years. 'You can only have another referendum if the people so allow in a future general election,' he said. 'In my view it's a once-in-a-generation thing. There was a referendum on devolution in 1979 and then the next referendum on devolution was in 1997 and that seems to me to be the overwhelming likelihood.'[63]

This was all part of a wider strategy to separate support for the SNP from support for independence, two phenomena polls had always suggested did not necessarily overlap. Voters were being urged to give the SNP a chance while Salmond reassured them that if they did, then it did not necessarily mean independence would follow. He even suggested in one interview that independence was 'not a one-way street', such was Scotland's 'right of self-determination'. 'It can vote to become independent and it can vote if it so chooses to become un-independent,' Salmond told GMTV's *Sunday Programme*, 'that's the prerogative of a nation and Scotland, of course, is a nation.'[64]

Jack McConnell, meanwhile, stepped up his attacks on Salmond by claiming he would 'not be a fit person'[65] to be First Minister of Scotland. There were, however, several high-profile Scots who disagreed, for example the Respect MP George Galloway, the comedienne Elaine C. Smith, Archbishop Keith O'Brien and, more unusually, the historian and former Tory candidate Michael Fry. The press also turned in the SNP's favour, the *Scotsman*, *Sunday Herald*, *Sunday Times* and *Scotland on Sunday* all concluding that an SNP role in government, or an SNP-led coalition, was the best outcome. It did not represent an unqualified vote of support, but it did signify a major shift compared with 1999.

On the 300th anniversary of the Act of Union, meanwhile, Tony Blair, Gordon Brown and Salmond traded commemorative insults. Speaking in Edinburgh, the Prime Minister said it was not the moment 'to shatter [the Union] and go back to the petty rivalries of the past', while Brown said he could not work with, or at least could not 'support' a party that wanted to 'break up Britain'. 'I can understand after winning every election for 50 years then it's perhaps a bit upsetting to be facing defeat in the current election,' responded Salmond. 'But there is no divine right to rule Scotland. The divine right of princes was written out of history some considerable time ago and no political party has such a divine right.'[66]

On polling day, Salmond cast his vote at the Ritchie Hall in Strichen, not for himself but for Stewart Stevenson, who was standing for re-election in Banff and Buchan. Exit polling in Gordon soon revealed that he was heading for victory, and after a day of final campaigning Salmond installed himself at the Marcliffe Hotel outside Aberdeen to watch the results come in and field calls from advisers.

Salmond arrived at the Aberdeen Exhibition and Conference Centre shortly before 3 a.m., having delayed his entrance to the last possible moment. As the result was declared and Salmond's name called, his arm shot up in the air while his face broke into a trademark smile, although it was an expression of relief rather than triumphalism. He had won, against the odds, but he had won:

Alex Salmond (SNP)	14,650
Nora Radcliffe (Lib Dem)	12,588
Nanette Milne (Conservative)	5,348
Neil Cardwell (Labour)	2,276
Donald Marr (Independent)	199
Dave Mathers (Independent)	185
Bob Ingram (Scot. Ent. Party)	117

With a 10.6 per cent swing from the Liberal Democrats, Salmond's majority was a modest but decisive 2,062. Given that Gordon had been placed 18th on the SNP's list of targets, it was an impressive personal result for Salmond. In 'a manner faintly reminiscent of Gladstone at Midlothian in 1880', observed the historian Ewen A. Cameron, Salmond had 'had to surmount a clear challenge to emphasise his credentials'.[67] And, like the Grand Old Man, the much younger Salmond had pulled it off.

Eloquently, Salmond invoked Harold Macmillan. 'There is a wind of change blowing through Scottish politics,'[68] he declared, before promising an inquiry (should he become First Minister) into the night's ballot paper chaos that had disenfranchised around 100,000 Scots. That afternoon the SNP leader flew to Edinburgh by helicopter, Prestonfield House Hotel having been pre-arranged as the landing site.

With a Saltire fluttering behind him and the SNP's election slogan, 'It's Time', static beneath his lectern microphone, Salmond pointed out that, however the last few seats to declare fell, the SNP had won the popular vote. 'Scotland has chosen a new path,' declared Salmond at his most eloquent, 'one which echoes the hopes and aspirations of a new culture of politics':

> We will lead with verve and imagination but always mindful that we serve the people – all the people – of this proud and ancient nation. The Scottish writer Alasdair Gray put it well when he wrote – 'work as though you lived in the early days of a better nation'. My commitment to Scotland is this – we will work, and these are the early days of a better nation.[69]

Back inside Prestonfield House, Salmond calmly awaited the final results. It all hinged on the last count for the Highland regional seats, but after some initial confusion the SNP had won two seats, beating Labour nationally by just one seat. It fell to Geoff Aberdein, the SNP leader's aide and golfing partner, to break the news to his boss. 'That's excellent. Great,'[70] exclaimed Salmond, as party workers crowded into the room. He was untypically generous with his praise, saying, 'Commentators have often given the SNP credit for always being a couple of steps ahead of our opponents, but that's just because you guys have been four or five ahead of them.'[71]

Angus Robertson then drove Salmond and Moira to The Hub, an arts venue at the top of the Royal Mile, near Edinburgh Castle. The atmosphere inside was electric: 'Small children covered in SNP stickers clung to their parents as adults hugged and kissed each other, punching the air in victory and stamping their feet,' observed one reporter.[72] Then, having entered the building from a side entrance, Salmond appeared, 'surrounded by cameras and with a smile as wide as the Dee'.[73] 'I heard a rumour,' he informed his rapturous supporters. 'I think we won the election.'[74]

To form a majority Scottish Executive, Salmond needed not only the Liberal Democrats (with 16 seats) but also the Greens (with two seats), a prospect he had called a 'progressive coalition . . . to move Scotland forward'.[75] He encountered Nicol Stephen, the Liberal Democrat leader and outgoing Deputy First Minister, at a television studio in Aberdeen the morning after polling day, and later claimed they both made the 'working assumption' that there would be some sort of coalition.[76]

But when they met in Edinburgh, most of the 16 Liberal Democrat MSPs were not inclined to coalesce with the SNP, but agreed to negotiate if Salmond agreed to drop his pledge to hold an independence referendum. Salmond and Stephen eventually spoke at around 7 p.m. on the Saturday but failed to reach a compromise. Following further conversations, in which the SNP leader stressed the possibility of a 'creative' solution to the referendum impasse, Stephen called Salmond for the last time on Sunday evening, saying his group's position remained unchanged.

'I have had discussions with Alex Salmond,' said a disappointed Nicol Stephen in a statement. 'I made it clear to him that unless and until the SNP removes the fundamental barrier of a referendum on independence there can be no coalition . . . In these circumstances it seems likely there will be a minority SNP government.' That, said Salmond in a radio interview, was 'not an entirely bad thing', while repeating that a coalition remained his favoured outcome. These negotiations had taken place exactly 26 years after Alex's marriage to Moira. 'He will not be doing anything publicly today,' said a spokesman rather unconvincingly. 'It's his wedding anniversary.'[77]

The following day brought further disappointment for Salmond when he failed to lure the Greens into a formal coalition following two hours of formal talks. Although these were 'very cordial', according to Salmond, the Greens opted instead to support the SNP only on an informal basis. 'At one point he leant close to me,' recalled the Greens leader Robin Harper, 'touched my arm, looked me straight in the eye and, stealing a trick from Tony Blair, said: "Robin, let's forget all these bits of paper. Just trust me.'"[78] Harper did not. 'My working assumption now is that the SNP may go into a minority administration,' said Salmond later. 'I am disappointed not to get into talks with the Liberals. I suspect it's a political position about where they want to be.'[79]

On 9 May Salmond was the first MSP to take the oath at the start of the new session of the Scottish Parliament. As in 1999, he declared that his party's 'primary loyalty' was to the Scottish people rather than the Queen, and beamed proudly as he watched an army of new SNP MSPs follow suit. A week later, once it had become clear that the Liberal Democrats were not prepared to change their minds, Salmond was elected First Minister at exactly 11.11 a.m., by 49 votes to 46.[80] As the result was announced, Salmond looked typically serene while Jack McConnell appeared strained, as if political reality had only just set in. The new First Minister then shook hands with those around him, hugged Nicola Sturgeon, soon to be his deputy, and embraced Bashir Ahmed, Scotland's first Asian MSP.

Salmond then rose, buttoned his jacket and, in a well-judged acceptance speech, declared that he and every other MSP had 'a responsibility to conduct ourselves in a way that respects the parliament the people have chosen to elect'. He added: 'That will take patience, maturity and leadership. My pledge today is that any Scottish government led by me will respect and include this parliament in the governance of Scotland over the next four years. In this century, there are limits to what governments can achieve. But one thing any government I lead will never lack is ambition for Scotland. Today, I commit myself to leadership wholly and exclusively in the Scottish national interest. We will appeal for support policy by policy across this chamber.' 'That is the parliament the people of Scotland have elected,' concluded Salmond, 'and that is the government that I will be proud to lead.'[81]

There was, noted the *Herald*, 'applause in the chamber – muted on the Labour benches, raucous among his MSPs and thunderous in the public gallery'.[82] Among those in the VIP gallery had been Salmond's wife Moira ('radiant in an exquisitely tailored oatmeal jacket, a tapered and fashionable skirt and immaculate jewellery'[83]), as well as Robert Salmond and Gail Hendry, his sister. 'My father has never seen me in the chamber because he always refused to set foot in the Palace of West-minster,' Salmond had remarked in his speech, 'Some people say I should have heeded his advice.'[84] Robert, however, could not bring himself to join in the applause, instead gazing upon his son, as John MacLeod observed, 'through full wet eyes, in a moment held so hard it could bruise', while his daughter Gail asked: 'Did you hear, Dad? Could you hear Alex, could you hear what he said?'[85]

Once formal proceedings were over, Salmond walked from the Chamber to the Garden Lobby, clutching Moira's hand tightly as he descended the stairs. 'I must admit I feel proud,' said his father after the vote, 'I hope that he does well as First Minister . . . I never thought this day would happen actually, it took a long time but he managed it.' Salmond's sister Gail agreed. 'Very very proud of him,' she said. 'The whole family is.'[86] After leaving the chamber, even the normally controlled Salmond was emotional. 'You think you can imagine what it's going to be like,' he told supporters, 'but, when you imagine, it's never quite the reality. It's a wonderful day.'[87] More than a year later, he described it more concisely as 'a hell of a moment'.[88]

But just how important had Salmond been to that moment and the election that preceded it? Interestingly, two academic studies of the 2007 Holyrood election reached different conclusions. John Curtice et al reckoned the SNP's tactics 'and the popularity of its leader in particular'[89] had mobilised voters committed to constitutional change, while Robert Johns et al concluded that 'opinions of the SNP leader had no significant effect on willingness to vote for his party', which was all the more surprising given his star billing on the regional list ballot paper. That said, they did not rule out an 'indirect effect'. 'Insofar as Salmond was responsible for laying the cornerstones of the party's success – its favourable ratings on competence, commitment to Scottish interests and campaign tone – then he may still have had a key role in the SNP's victory.'[90]

Chapter 12

'IT'S TIME'

Work as if you live in the early days of a better nation.
Alasdair Gray, from *The Book of Prefaces* (2000)

The British constitution had always been a remarkably flexible crea-ture, and there was no way the election of an SNP minority government was going to upset it. Having won the backing of MSPs, Alex Salmond left Holyrood and drove to St Andrew's House where he met Sir John Elvidge, permanent secretary to a newly slimmed down and reorganised Scottish Executive, the members of which the First Minister unveiled soon after (to be known as 'Cabinet Secretar-ies' rather than 'Ministers'). He took a congratulatory call from Douglas Alexander, the Scottish Secretary, although not the Prime Minister, Tony Blair. That evening, Salmond held a celebratory dinner at the Raj restaurant in Leith, run by his friend, the chef Ajman 'Tommy' Miah.

Her Majesty, meanwhile, safe in the knowledge that her future would not yet be subject to a referendum, signed a warrant appointing Salmond First Minister. His first official event had been the UEFA Cup Final in Glasgow, at which Salmond met the Crown Prince of Spain and the president of Catalonia. His first official engagement was a more prosaic environmental announcement at Longannet Power Station. The following Saturday Alexander Elliot Anderson Salmond – named after the Kirk minister who had christened him – attended the opening of the General Assembly of the Church of Scotland. Cardinal Keith O'Brien, head of the non-established Catholic Church in Scotland, meanwhile, was full of praise: 'I am sure that he will work for the good of all the people of this country.'[1]

Salmond faced all of this with his usual serenity, almost as if he had expected it since the election campaign had begun. He was naturally pleased – as is evident from television footage of those days – but not overly so; the self-control he had affected since earlier that year was still in place. He was, at least for the time being, in an unassailable position. As First Minister of a minority government he was fuelled not only by political novelty, but also by obvious public goodwill. Salmond also had some 'powerful cards' as leader of the SNP. 'That he is first minister and has presided over the party's most successful election campaign', judged the journalist Peter Jones, 'gives him more authority over his party than perhaps any SNP leader has had.'[2]

Salmond's first acts as First Minister were populist and consensual. Potentially dangerous ship-to-ship oil transfers in the Firth of Forth were halted, A&E units at hospitals in Ayr and Monklands reprieved, while in his first formal policy speech to the Scottish Parliament on 23 May, he put economic growth at the heart of the Scottish Executive's programme for the next four years. 'It is time to get down to business. Scotland's new politics starts now,' he told MSPs, insisting that he wanted to usher in a 'new style of government' which would be neither 'dogmatic nor intransigent'.[3]

To that end Salmond established a US-style Council of Economic Advisers ('Salmond', mused SNP MSP Chris Harvie, 'seemed to regard the Edinburgh financial establishment as an ersatz foreign office.'[4]), while cutting business rates for small businesses, championing renewable energy and ceding control of Scotland's 12 Local Enterprise Companies to local authorities. At this point, Salmond was already talking about the need for 'fiscal autonomy'. 'We are faced with incontrovertible evidence of sustained and damaging economic underperformance,' he wrote in the *Scotsman* at the end of June. 'Perhaps the greatest frustration I feel as an economist and as First Minister is the failure to appreciate the seriousness of that problem.' He continued: 'Successive economic strategies have tried – and failed – to snap us out of this groove of mediocrity. My commitment, and the commitment of my government, is to create the right environment for business to prosper. But it is also about a shift in mindset – a final understanding that no-one owes Scotland a living and that the competitive world of international business is an unforgiving place. That shift in mentality and the aspiration to be the best in the world is what the business men and women of Scotland can help us to achieve.'[5]

There had been no sign, as yet, of the cold winds about to blow. The following evening, a silent Salmond leaned forward with a slight smile as he shook hands with his Monarch. 'The meeting at the Palace of Holyroodhouse, just before 5pm, was formal, brief and largely ceremonial,' noted the *Scotsman*, 'but symbolically and politically, it was momentous.'[6] On 22 June, Salmond told the SNP's National Council that the last few 'remarkable' weeks had provided some 'wonderful experiences'. 'That marks a watershed for our party,' he added. 'Today we can say something we have always wanted to say: The Scottish National Party is now a party of government.'[7]

Labour, meanwhile, displayed signs of finding the election result a little hard to digest. In the House of Commons the Labour MP Anne Moffat compared Salmond's election (as a result of PR) with that of Adolf Hitler in 1933, while Tony Blair was less offensive but almost as rude. 'He has been to Washington and Iraq and has been rather busy,'[8] said his official spokesman, explaining why Blair had yet to congratulate the First Minister. As Salmond put it during First Minister's Questions at Holyrood: 'He never phones, he never writes.'[9] Perhaps Blair was depressed. 'I knew once Alex Salmond got his feet under the table,' he later wrote in his memoirs, 'he could play off against the Westminster government and embed himself. It would be far harder to remove him than to stop him in the first place.'[10]

Relations between Blair and Salmond also plummeted when details emerged of a 'memorandum of understanding' between the UK and Libyan governments on prisoner exchange. Although the Prime Minister insisted it did not cover the convicted Lockerbie bomber, Abdelbaset Ali Mohmed al-Megrahi, Salmond responded swiftly (thanks to an 'eagle-eyed civil servant'[11]), demanding clarification about the status of al-Megrahi, who was serving a life sentence at Gateside Prison in Greenock, and making an emergency statement at Holyrood. Reminding MSPs that the Scottish Criminal Cases Review Commission was reviewing al-Megrahi's case, he condemned the UK government's lack of consultation with Holyrood as 'clearly unacceptable'. 'This government is determined that decisions on any individual case,' he added, 'will continue to be made following the due process of Scots law.'[12] Salmond had captured perfectly the mood of most MSPs, while successfully presenting himself as the defender of Scotland's best interests.

These events were also important in the context of a decision on al-Megrahi that Salmond would authorise nearly two years later. On 13

July 2007 he had breakfast in Edinburgh with Jack Straw, the Justice Secretary, at which it was agreed al-Megrahi would be excluded from any Prisoner Transfer Agreement (PTA). The 'nature and description of the clauses' were agreed on 26 July and, by 19 December, as Salmond later told a Commons committee, 'we were content then with the position'. Then everything changed, with Straw informing Kenny MacAskill, the Justice Secretary, that 'the overwhelming interests of the United Kingdom' had to take precedence. This implied trading agreements, and indeed the fact that major commercial deals between the UK and Libya were then in the process of being signed was, said Salmond, 'only one of the reasons . . . why the Scottish Government was so suspicious of the PTA'. The Scottish Government was itself lobbied, not by BP but by the Qatari government, which, added Salmond, had 'raised the issue and were told what the formal process [relating to al-Megrahi] was'.[13]

To say that Salmond's handling of this issue, as well as his first few weeks in office generally, received a good press would be an understatement. 'The effect of the last six weeks has been devastating,' declared Iain Macwhirter, who quickly became the First Minister's biggest media cheerleader. 'The SNP hasn't so much hit the ground running as lapped the political field on an almost daily basis. Opposition MSPs have been blown away at what has been happening.'[14] The *Edinburgh Evening News*, meanwhile, reckoned Salmond had 'eased into his new role . . . as if he's been in the job for years'.[15]

Salmond also excelled at the weekly First Minister's Questions (FMQs), perhaps feeling more comfortable in a Chamber somewhat more impressive than that he had known during his initial term as an MSP, arguing that the 'ambiance of the place' had taken 'time to develop'.[16] Over time, however, his performances would become more erratic and often aggressive. 'I do bite my tongue just occasionally,' he admitted after a hundred days in office, in order to avoid saying something that 'might cause needless offence'. 'I've always enjoyed political debate,' he added in his defence, 'FMQs could have been made for me.'

Despite the SNP's honeymoon, Salmond soon faced challenges. On 27 June his government was defeated for the first time over an amendment to keep Edinburgh's tram project on track, while three days later a jeep loaded with gas canisters was driven into the main terminal building at Glasgow Airport, bursting into flames as it collided. Salmond was with Sir Sean Connery in Bute House, now his official residence, following the official opening of the Scottish Parliament by the Queen when he was informed. Shortly after Salmond spoke to Gordon Brown, only three days into the job as Prime Minister, to co-ordinate Scottish Executive involvement in a COBRA briefing being convened that evening, while he opened the Scottish Executive Emergency Room (SEER) to co-ordinate the purely Scottish response. 'Life in Scotland will continue,' he said at a press conference that evening. 'The people of Scotland will be satisfied and secure that their Government is taking the appropriate level of precaution.'[17] The First Minister later admitted that he 'felt a bit daunted' in the aftermath of the attack. 'The daunting bit was, it wasn't just about watching [the news on television],' he told the blogger Iain Dale. 'I was expected to do something. You realise it's not some other person that's behind the eight ball, it's you.'[18]

As a result of the incident, Salmond arrived late at a special perform-ance of the Gregory Burke play *Black Watch* at the Pleasance in Edinburgh, which he had been supposed to see with Sir Sean Connery and Moira. Indeed, Salmond's family must have been much on his mind during this period, as the impact of being First Minister on his domestic arrangements sank in. In July 2007 he established 'The Mary Salmond Trust', to which he planned to donate one third of his MSP's salary (which he received on top of his MP's wage and another sum for being First Minister) in order to fund community projects in the north-east of Scotland.

There was also Moira to consider. She had kept a typically low profile since May's election, only emerging from the shadows when Salmond joked privately that Bute House was 'minging' and that Moira had been 'on her hands and knees'[19] scrubbing the floors in the Charlotte Square townhouse. The Georgian townhouse also aggra-vated the asthma from which Salmond had suffered since childhood, triggering mild attacks and causing him to wake in the middle of the night.

Newspapers, meanwhile, tried in vain to produce some original copy on Moira Salmond, but so fiercely did Salmond protect her privacy all they could find were bland off-the-record quotes to the effect that she was 'chic and witty'[20]. Some anecdotes also scraped the barrel of absurd-ity. At 'the Edinburgh branch of Slater Menswear,' reported the *Scottish Daily Mail*, 'an emphatic Mrs Salmond was overheard telling her husband quite simply: "You will not be getting those trousers."'[21]

Salmond opened up a little more when interviewed by the *Guardi-an*'s Ian Jack in early 2009, who thought the 'most interesting thing about Salmond is that he has flourished in politics without the conventional prerequisites of a public family life'. 'There has been very little intrusion, so little that most people, even in Scotland, are surprised (and, believe me, fascinated) when they learn of the 17-year difference in ages between husband and wife,' wrote Jack. 'The English press wouldn't have been so well-behaved.' Salmond concurred: 'There are certain essential differences between Scottish politics and politics down south and one of them is that. I don't think that, to use Gordon Brown's phrase, politicians have ever paraded their family in Scotland. Donald Dewar didn't. John Smith didn't until he was persuaded to by [Peter] Mandelson, and that was probably a mistake; certainly he [Smith] thought that. I remember the Smith girls were announced at a Labour conference and the next day they were busted in the *Sun* for being in a nightclub or something – the usual process.' Salmond, of course, had no children on whom the tabloids could prey. 'Moira does stuff. She does events, races, dinners, all the things that a political spouse does – the most exacting and unrewarding profession you could have,' he told Jack. 'It's a lot of trouble for absolutely no reward whatsoever, but she does it gracefully and willingly.'[22]

In fact, Moira's engagement with public events had been stepped up the previous year, beginning with her own programme of events at the US Scotland Week celebrations in April 2008. But beyond another couple of low-key engagements and a trip to Sri Lanka when Glasgow was bidding to host the Commonwealth Games, Moira preferred privacy to photocalls. When details emerged of her travel expenses – £6,159 over two years – the Labour MSP George Foulkes argued that if she was going to enjoy the perks of being a first lady, she should at least make herself known to the Scottish public.

Moira was present, albeit not publicly, when Salmond visited Europe for the first time since becoming First Minister. 'I believe that it is time to transform the nature of Scotland's representation and impact in Europe tonight,' he told a Brussels audience. 'My message is clear and unambiguous – this is the time for Scotland to assume our obligations and responsibilities and to help mould the world around us to rediscover the sense of internationalism which once defined our nation.'

The journalist Iain Macwhirter thought such remarks, which technically exceeded Salmond's constitutional remit, demonstrated that he was 'a man in a hurry, who has to seize every opportunity to make an impact before being closed down by the logic of the parliamentary arithmetic in Holyrood'. 'I was determined not to end up like Donald Dewar,' admitted Salmond. 'That was constantly in my mind.' His real role model, however, remained a former Labour Prime Minister: 'I'm a great fan of Harold Wilson, you know.' Indeed Wilson, as Macwhirter observed, was, like Salmond, 'a brilliant political improviser'.[23]

During the summer of 2007, meanwhile, there were other blasts from the past. In August there was a run on the English mortgage bank Northern Rock, the first since the traumatic failure of the City of Glasgow bank back in 1878. Salmond was aware of the historical analogy from his time at the Royal Bank of Scotland, although the repercussions of Northern Rock's collapse, and subsequent nationalisation, were yet to sink in.

'Since the heady days of the election,' wrote Salmond after the summer recess, 'I believe that we have governed responsibly and imaginatively, with the consent of people and Parliament . . . we do so as an administration that has put substantial chalk on the board – with an early record and pace of delivery that has left the opposition gasping to keep up.'[24] Indeed, it became increasingly clear that the Liberal Democrats had miscalculated in not having coalesced with the SNP. 'We thought minority government would be so difficult,' reflected a senior Liberal Democrat, 'that they [the SNP] would come running to us by October.'[25]

Salmond, however, did not feel the need to go running to anyone as he skilfully spun his first 100 days in office as dynamic action twinned with dynamic intent. This led to accusations of triumphalism from his predecessor, although the First Minister increasingly saw minority government as a help rather than a hindrance. 'Play the ball as it lies, as my dad used to tell me when I was trying to kick the ball out of the rough at golf,' he mused in an STV documentary. 'He used to say play the ball as it lies, and the ball as it lies is with minority government.'[26]

The final, and perhaps most important, aspect of Salmond's first 100 days was the publication of a white paper on independence. The First Minister, however, tread carefully, refusing to set out a clear timetable for actually holding the referendum ('Rome wasn't built in a day,' he joked, 'not even 100 days') while calling upon his opponents to take part in an 'open, robust and dignified' debate on Scotland's future constitutional direction. Scotland's 'tectonic plates', he claimed, had shifted in favour of strengthening Holyrood's powers.

Scotland's opposition parties, however, had not felt the earth move, at least not yet, and pre-empted the white paper with a co-ordinated attack, accusing Salmond of having an 'obsession' with independence (rather like accusing Keir Hardie of having an 'obsession' with socialism) and questioning his mandate for pushing the independence argument. 'Divergent views are the very essence of democracy,' tempered Salmond. 'The exchanges, the criticism and the debate will be passionate but let those contributions be based on fact, reason and logic rather than smears, allegations and misinformation.'[27] This was to be the so-called 'National Conversation' with the people of Scotland. Although a typical piece of Salmond pragmatism, the publication of the white paper represented a further concession in the independence debate. By conceding that a straightforward 'yes/no' referendum bill was unlikely to attract majority support, the First Minister was opening up a third option and, ultimately, a third referendum question on additional powers for Holyrood, or so-called 'devo-max'. Ten years earlier this would have caused ructions within the SNP and possibly threatened Salmond's leadership. Only Pete Wishart, the SNP MP for Perth and North Perthshire, warned that 'independence has become just an option when it should, of course, be the option'. The SNP, he continued, had to be 'careful that this key choice does not become obscured in a plethora of other options'.[28]

Salmond, meanwhile, cleverly gave the impression of independence by stealth when he rebranded the Scottish Executive as the 'Scottish Government', something Henry McLeish had attempted during his tenure as First Minister but abandoned amid internal Labour hostility. 'Scottish Government surely is something which expresses what we are,' Salmond explained shortly after. 'Scottish Executive sounds like a briefcase or something, it's a ridiculous description, a sort of bureaucratic nothingness.'[29] The new name first appeared on Salmond's maiden legislative programme, which he unveiled on 4 September, announcing 11 largely unremarkable bills covering predictable administrative reforms. The reality of minority government had kicked in, and while the abolition of bridge tolls, scrapping the graduate endowment and direct elections to health boards (all manifesto commitments) were to be dealt with legislatively, other pledges like deploying 1,000 extra police officers and writing off student debt were not.

Opposition cries of 'broken promises' intensified when John Swinney, who had turned out to be an effective Finance Secretary, presented his first budget on 14 November. Although it implemented the pledge to freeze council tax for a year (as an interim measure towards creating a Local Income Tax), there was no sign of the £2,000 grant for first-time house buyers, nor was there any commitment to match

Labour's school-building programme. Opinion polls, however, continued to show considerable support for the SNP, whatever the atmosphere
inside the Chamber.

The First Minister was also aided by the failures of his political opponents. Although Annabel Goldie, the leader of the Scottish Conservatives,
had forged a constructive relationship with the SNP since the election,
the Liberal Democrats – led by former Deputy First Minister Nicol
Stephen – had often appeared listless, while Wendy Alexander, Jack
McConnell's successor as Labour leader, had quickly been consumed by
a row over donations to her leadership campaign. She managed to
recover some ground with a St Andrew's Day speech, in which she set
out an imaginative plan to develop devolution through an independent
Scottish Constitutional Commission.

A 'grand, if informal, Unionist coalition'[30] comprising the Conservatives, Labour and the Liberal Democrats, endorsed Alexander's
proposal at Holyrood on 6 December 2007. To an extent this was, as
one Tory MSP later put it, a knee-jerk reaction to the SNP's election
win earlier that year, although no one could doubt the Labour leader's
commitment to strengthening a devolution settlement that Alexander
had, after all, helped formulate back in 1997. With every party at Holyrood now accepting the need for greater powers, the exercise had also
been a testament to Salmond's ability to alter the terms of political
debate.

On the same day as this vote, Salmond intervened in the ongoing row
over Wendy Alexander's leadership campaign donations, saying that a
police inquiry was now 'inevitable' and that she should step aside until
such an investigation was finished. The First Minister also had troubles of
his own. In December 2007 Aberdeenshire Council's strategic planning
body rejected Donald Trump's plan for a £500 million luxury golf resort
in the north east of Scotland. Salmond, who had backed the project
before becoming First Minister, decided to 'call in' the application the day
after meeting with one of Trump's representatives at the Marcliffe Hotel
near Aberdeen. 'As the [Gordon] constituency MSP not only am I absolutely entitled,' he explained, 'but I have a bounden duty under the
parliamentary code to meet people on all issues of importance to my
constituency.'[31] In an intervention at First Minister's Questions, however,
Liberal Democrat leader Nicol Stephen said Salmond's involvement
'smells of sleaze'.[32]

Salmond's actions, on the other hand, earned glowing praise from
the American tycoon. 'I hardly know Alex Salmond, but what I know

is that he's an amazing man,' gushed Trump. 'He's a person who believes strongly in Scotland and he wants economic development in Scotland.'[33] Holyrood's Local Government Committee, meanwhile, twice questioned the First Minister over his handling of the affair. He acquitted himself well, or rather the committee failed to land any blows, and when it reported in May 2008 Salmond was charged with having taken a 'cavalier' approach to his involvement with Trump's application, displaying, 'at best, exceptionally poor judgement and a worrying lack of awareness about the consequence of his actions'.[34] Although Salmond had done nothing illegal, his preferred working methods – telephone calls and face-to-face meetings – had very nearly landed him in hot political water.

Salmond played a defter hand as negotiations over his first budget continued into early February 2008, telling Kevin Pringle, perhaps his most influential adviser, to slip into his post-Cabinet briefing a warning that the First Minister would quit and force an election if the budget was defeated. 'I'll quit, warns Salmond' was the message on many front pages the following day, and that afternoon the budget passed with Conservative support, no mean achievement for a minority government. A key component of the budget was a so-called 'historic concordat' with Scotland's 32 local authorities to freeze the council tax. Although criticised for disproportionately benefiting the well-off and therefore directly contradicting, as Professor David Bell argued, the SNP's 'cherished aim of reducing inequality',[35] it was, not surprisingly, hugely popular with the all-important electorate.

Although Salmond was still riding high after almost a year as First Minister, he had still failed to make much headway on an independence referendum. Having refused to back a third question on additional powers the previous August, launching 'Phase II' of the National Conversation on 26 March 2008 – a day after Sir Kenneth Calman was announced as chairman of the Commission on Scottish Devolution – he made another key concession. 'I am happy to test support for enhanced devolution, along with support for independence for Scotland,' he told an audience of businessmen, trade unionists and educationalists. 'And I say to those who oppose the restoration of Scottish independence that just as I respect absolutely their right to hold that view, so in return I feel able to require of them a clear alternative which can be put onto a ballot paper and held up to public scrutiny and be available for a decision by the Scottish people.'[36] This, added Salmond, would be carried out using the Single Transferable Vote, a system the *Daily Mail* argued amounted to 'gerrymandering'.[37]

In a surprising U-turn in May 2008, however, Wendy Alexander announced her conversion to an independence referendum live on the BBC's *Politics Show*, famously urging the First Minister to 'bring it on'.[38] On the face of it, this was a brave and imaginative move that in different circumstances would have caused serious problems for Salmond. The timing, however, had not been ideal. Gordon Brown, reeling from bad local government elections in England, pointedly refused to endorse Alexander's plan in the House of Commons, enabling Salmond to fend off her attack. On 28 June Alexander resigned as a consequence of the donations row, effectively killing her referendum argument, while a few days later Nicol Stephen also announced his departure as Liberal Democrat leader.

The Salmond momentum, meanwhile, continued when the SNP's John Mason spectacularly won the Glasgow East Westminster by-election on 24 July. The First Minister had predicted a 'political earthquake', and although it proved to be more of a tremor (Mason's majority was 365), the political aftershocks were felt for several weeks. Not only was Labour's candidate, the popular MSP Margaret Curran, humiliated (although she would take the seat two years later), but a beleaguered Gordon Brown had to endure yet more negative headlines and leadership speculation.

The result was also a personal victory for Salmond, who had been a constant presence in Glasgow during the campaign, although he probably knew better than to believe prophets bearing political gifts. The Glasgow East result turned out to be a false dawn in terms of fulfilling Salmond's long-cherished goal of beating Labour in its urban strongholds, much like Hamilton in 1967 and Govan in 1973 and 1988. In the summer of 2008, however, it made Salmond appear unstoppable. 'Who within his party can now gainsay our Alex?' wrote the columnist Ian Bell, who added that Salmond had 'crushed all internal rivalry'. Had Scottish Nationalism, he wondered, actually been reduced to mere 'Salmondism'?[39]

It was all change at Holyrood following the 2008 summer recess. The MSP for East Lothian and former minister Iain Gray was elected Labour's new leader in the Scottish Parliament, while the Shetland MSP Tavish Scott succeeded Nicol Stephen as leader of the Scottish Liberal Democrats. Salmond, meanwhile, sailed serenely on, into his fourth year as SNP leader and his 18th in front-line politics. He did so despite growing criticism of his proposals for a Local Income Tax (LIT) to replace the 'regressive, unfair, deeply unpopular'[40] council tax, ostensibly backed by the Liberal Democrats. The two parties, however, disagreed as to whether this should be set locally – as the name implied – or nationally at 3p in the pound as the Scottish Government advocated.

Salmond also faced problems with his proposal for a Scottish Futures Trust (SFT), which the SNP had sold as a radical new way of financing major public sector projects. Although the respected financier Sir Angus Grossart had been persuaded to chair the SFT – demonstrating that the First Minister's talent for making friends and influencing people was undiminished – it came under attack from two SNP-inclined economists, Jim and Margaret Cuthbert. 'The present Scottish Government dislikes PFI, quite rightly, and has attempted to move on,' they wrote in the *Scottish Left Review*. 'But in doing so, it has made the disastrous mistake of not taking on board key lessons to be learned from past experience with PFI.'[41] Even where ministers had opted for conventional public funding – as with the £500 million Southern General hospital in Glasgow – the Cuthberts pointed out that ministers had, by only offering large contracts, effectively frozen out Scots-based firms.

'I suppose', an unconcerned Salmond told the blogger Iain Dale in a September interview, 'I have tried to bring the SNP into the mainstream of Scotland.' He went on: 'We have a very competitive economic agenda. Many business people have warmed towards the SNP. We need a competitive edge, a competitive advantage – get on with it, get things done, speed up decision making, reduce bureaucracy. The SNP has a strong social conscience, which is very Scottish in itself. One of the reasons Scotland didn't take to Lady Thatcher was because of that. We didn't mind the economic side so much. But we didn't like the social side at all.'[42]

The final sentence proved to be a rare Salmond gaffe. Under heavy fire from Labour politicians and, as usual, Jim Sillars, for daring to claim that Mrs Thatcher's economic reforms had been necessary, the First Minister took the extraordinary step of calling up the BBC's *Good Morning Scotland* radio programme to explain himself. 'I was commenting on why Scots, in particular, were so deeply resentful of Thatcher,' he said, 'and I think here her social message . . . cut against a very Scottish grain of social conscience. That doesn't mean that the nation liked her economic policies, just that we liked her lack of concern for social consequences even less.'[43] Salmond, of course, had said precisely the opposite in his interview with Iain Dale, but contradicted himself with such self-assurance that hardly anyone noticed.

Dale had also asked Salmond about Adam Smith and his legacy in a Scotland perceived as being over-dependent upon the public sector. 'I think that betrays Adam Smith,' he responded, continuing: 'He was not just a friend of economics. He was a moral philosopher. Margaret Thatcher could have only ever read the Penguin edition of *Wealth of Nations* and she missed out the moral sentiments. I would absolutely defend the reputation of Adam Smith against the Adam Smith Institute. I said to Eamonn Butler [Deputy Director of the ASI], if Adam Smith could sue, you'd be in real trouble.'[44]

Also in trouble were UK banks, although Salmond's response to the crisis was not exactly worthy of Adam Smith. A reporter had recently asked him where he saw Scotland in ten years' time, to which he replied that it would be 'an independent, successful country, part of the European Union and would join the arc of prosperity of small, highly successful independent countries about their shores'.[45]

When the Edinburgh-based HBOS was compelled to merge with Lloyds TSB following a share price plunge, however, a banking crisis sparked off a series of events that made Salmond's 'arc of prosperity' seem a distant prospect. The First Minister, meanwhile, condemned the merger as a 'shotgun marriage' driven by 'a bunch of short-selling spivs and speculators in the financial markets'.[46] The language proved to be badly chosen, not least because it later emerged that the chairman of Salmond's Council of Economic Advisers, Sir George Mathewson, was not only a dab hand at short-selling but happily defended it as a financial activity.

Trouble at the Royal Bank of Scotland (RBS), meanwhile, posed particular problems for Salmond. Not only did he feel its pain as a former employee, but his political connections with the Edinburgh-based banking group – Mathewson and Andrew Wilson, who had returned to an RBS career having lost his Holyrood seat in 2003 – almost seemed to put it beyond criticism. 'It is in Scottish interests for RBS to be successful,' Salmond had written to its chief executive Sir Fred Goodwin shortly after becoming First Minister, 'and I would like to offer any assistance my office can provide. Good luck with the bid.'[47] This was for the Dutch bank ABN Amro, a purchase that precipitated RBS's problems. When Salmond's former employer announced its second-largest loss in banking history, meanwhile, he optimistically stated that he was certain it would 'overcome current challenges to become both highly profitable and highly successful once again'.[48]

The BBC's Jon Sopel also challenged Salmond about a recent 'catastrophic fall' in the RBS share price. 'What about the position of the Chairman [*sic*], Sir Fred Goodwin,' he asked, 'can he carry on?' Salmond replied: 'Well I don't actually think it's the most sensible thing in the world right now, when we're trying to stabilize the financial sector ... to speculate ... on the future of individuals. I would have thought that you would want the people who are doing the negotiations to guide the institutions into safer times and I cannot think that it is helpful in any sense in any way, to turn this into who should go and who should stay.'[49]

Less than 24 hours after that interview, Gordon Brown and his Chancellor, Alistair Darling, announced the part-nationalisation of RBS and the departure of Sir Fred as chief executive. Confronted with his comments on *Newsnight Scotland* that evening, Salmond appeared untypically lost for words. And when invited to condemn either RBS or bankers in general, he refused to do either, simply commenting that there ought to be 'no scapegoats'.[50]

Salmond's previous pronouncements on Scotland's financial sector also came back to haunt him. In February 2008 he had declared that 'Scottish banks are among the most stable financial institutions in the world',[51] while another quote, which undermined Salmond's claim that an independent Scotland could have responded more effectively to the crisis, surfaced from *The Times* of April 2007: 'We are pledging a light-touch regulation suitable to a Scottish financial sector with its outstanding reputation for probity.'[52]

Labour's Jim Murphy, who had proved himself a match for Salmond as Scottish Secretary since his appointment in October 2008, repeatedly mocked what he called the First Minister's 'arc of insolvency' line, while Salmond resorted to blaming the UK government. 'This is London's boom and bust,'[53] he said towards the end of October, adding that it had nothing to do with bankers.

Salmond attempted to recover some ground with an article in *The Times*, chiefly in response to a recent editorial that had questioned the economic viability of an independent Scotland: 'Contrary to the assertions in a leading article in this newspaper, the case for independence has always been on a sound financial footing. The events of recent weeks have merely strengthened the case for Scotland to be given more control of its economy to protect jobs, investment and stability. The economic maelstrom now sweeping the globe is affecting all countries large and small.'

Even so, added Salmond, the IMF had predicted that the economies of Norway, Denmark, Finland and Sweden – 'all smaller European nations' – would keep on growing economically over the next two years. He continued: 'Seizing on the particular problems of Iceland, the argument has lapsed from fear and smear into outright slander. The unedifying spectacle of Gordon Brown and Jim Murphy, the Secretary of State for Scotland, hitting the airwaves to besmirch the achievements of the likes of Ireland and Norway is surely the nadir of new Labour diplomacy. For the Prime Minister, it also amounts to breathtaking hypocrisy. For it was Gordon Brown who, as Chancellor for a decade, presided over the age of irresponsibility in the City. That age has come to a shattering end. And Mr Brown's boast of "no return to boom and bust" is left looking ridiculous.'

Salmond, of course, had offered little criticism of that 'age of irresponsibility' at the time. The Irish model, he argued, remained a good one: 'Ireland may have moved into recession – but only after many years of fantastic growth, easily outscoring the UK. As a result, it is now nearly 40 per cent more prosperous per head than the UK. Ireland was also able to act quickly and decisively to bring stability to its banking sector by guaranteeing all deposits. It was to Ireland that many in Britain turned when the UK Government did not offer a parallel guarantee. Dublin's actions were a clear demonstration of just how effective smaller independent nations can be when the going gets tough.'[54]

Salmond's initial response to the financial crisis had not been his finest hour, although the reasons for this were clear. As a former professional economist he had been content to present himself as an ally of the Scottish financial sector, relying on its reputation to shore up the economic case for independence when the economic climate was good, and therefore floundering when it took a turn for the worse. Only several months later was Salmond willing to venture even mild criticism of bankers. 'Parts of the financial sector, we now know, were run on a false prospectus,' he told the General Assembly of the Church of Scotland in May 2009, 'with the rewards to some individuals completely divorced from basic ideas of fairness, or service. And, as it transpires, sadly those rewards were also divorced from any reasonable notion of lasting value. That could not be sustained. And it was not sustained.'[55]

Whatever Salmond's view, his Scottish Government was not idle in reacting to the crisis, bringing forward £100 million in capital expenditure while arguing for a second financial stimulus. 'On the one hand, the Scottish government has campaigned for a sustained public expenditure-led response to the economic crisis,' observed Stephen Maxwell, Salmond's former 79 Group contemporary. 'On the other hand, it has offered no policy response to the collapse of the greater part of the Scottish banking system. None of its economic spokespersons – neither Salmond, Finance Secretary John Swinney or Industry Minister Jim Mather – has made any public statement about the lessons to be drawn for the future shape and regulation of Scotland's financial services, except for vague murmurings that it must be consistent with reform of the international system.'[56] Maxwell viewed this as part of a wider political malaise, pointing out that 'as the SNP's social heart has become more attached to social democracy, its economic head has inclined to neo-liberalism'. 'Had the SNP taken a more detached and critical look at what was happening in the Scottish-based banks,' argued Isobel Lindsay, another contemporary of Salmond's, 'it would have been in much stronger position today.'[57]

There had been talk of Salmond's honeymoon ending since the end of 2007, but in truth it did so in the autumn of 2008, buffeted by cold financial winds and the Glenrothes by-election, which Labour easily held amid talk of local 'SNP cuts' and Gordon Brown's steady hand at the tiller. This contest was to the SNP what the Glasgow Central by-election had been to the party back in 1989, proof that an apparent breakthrough in Labour strongholds like Glasgow Govan and Glasgow East had in fact been chimeras, an illustration of essentially fickle SNP support.

After nearly 18 months in office, Salmond was also tired. The *Guardian* journalist Ian Jack thought he looked 'a lot less chipper … puffy and grey-complexioned and suddenly slower on his feet'.[58] Despite frequent attempts at dieting, the First Minister's weight had also increased noticeably since May 2007. In time, however, Salmond bounced back – as he usually did – particularly when the SNP 'won' the June 2009 European elections in Scotland with more than 29 per cent of the vote, a result Salmond hailed as 'historic'.[59]

In December 2008, meanwhile, the Calman Commission had published its interim report, upon which Salmond poured pre-emptive scorn. Based 'on what we have seen so far,' he judged, 'no one should expect anything remotely matching the substantial new powers Scotland needs.'[60] This, now, appeared to be the direction of political travel, or 'centre of gravity' as Salmond would later describe it: a debate between Nationalists and Unionists as to the extent of Holyrood's powers within a consensus that it ought to have more, rather than the old argument between independence and the devolved status quo. This new thinking manifested itself in a lecture Salmond delivered at Georgetown University during another trip to the United States in February 2009. Although his oration concluded with the usual independence rallying cry, his emphasis was more on additional powers for the Scottish Parliament: 'Later this week, in London, I will meet with the UK Prime Minister, Gordon Brown, to discuss the economic crisis. At that meeting I will advance the case for new financial freedom for Scotland's government. And in particular I will make the case for Scotland to have the same ability to borrow as other nations, and indeed the US States, have in order to do our bit to inject demand and confidence into the economy.' In 'unprecedented economic times', added Salmond, it was 'perfectly reasonable that Scotland would reassess its own constitution in light of today's pressing economic imperatives'. It was, he said, 'a pivotal moment', 'time for a Scottish Parliament with the ability to respond to the global economic challenges and protect the interests of our people'.[61]

Shortly before his trip to the United States, Salmond had suffered his first defeat in a Holyrood division since the Edinburgh trams vote in his first few weeks as First Minister. Having failed to appease two Green MSPs over a home insulation scheme, the Scottish Government's second budget fell on 28 January 2009 following a tied vote in which the Presiding Officer had cast his vote, as per the Parliament's standing orders, against.

'The government cannot stay in office unless we can get a Budget through,' said a rattled Salmond. 'Because of the economic crisis we find ourselves in, we have an obligation to get the Budget through.'[62] John Swinney, the equally stunned Finance Secretary, promised to introduce a revised budget as soon as possible, although the Labour MSP group, which had voted against, threatened to table a motion of no-confidence in the First Minister should that meet a similar fate. Salmond, in response, repeated his threat from the 2008 budget. 'If the budget can't get through then the government cannot remain in office,' he told reporters. 'Under these circumstances, the normal thing would be to have an election and that's what I would welcome.' For that reason, he added with a dramatic pause, 'I'm putting the SNP on an election footing tonight.'[63]

That, of course, did not prove necessary, and when the budget was introduced for a second time it passed with near unanimous support from all but the two Green MSPs who had scuppered it in the first place. Not long after this close shave with the budget, the Scottish Government also announced its plan to jettison the Local Income Tax policy, citing lack of Parliamentary support. Iain Gray, who tore up a copy of the 2007 SNP manifesto at First Minister's Questions in order to highlight 'broken promises', said Salmond had been 'caught redhanded selling short Scottish voters – his own definition of a spiv and speculator' and ought to apologise. On the contrary, replied the First Minister, apologies were 'required from the council tax cabal of Labour and the Tories, who have voted to uphold the council tax in Scotland'.[64]

That same week, Salmond reshuffled his Cabinet for the first time since taking power, replacing three junior ministers in the process. Mike Russell, now almost rehabilitated following the 2004 leadership race, was promoted to replace Linda Fabiani as culture minister (his environment portfolio was taken by Roseanna Cunningham), while Keith Brown took over from Maureen Watt as schools minister and Alex Neil succeeded Stewart Maxwell as housing and communities minister. Salmond behaved sensitively, stressing that there had 'been no failures in the ministerial team' but that he had wanted to give other 'colleagues an opportunity to show what they can contribute'.[65]

The appointment of Cunningham and Neil took many by surprise, not least the new ministers themselves. Having briefly been the favourite to succeed John Swinney as leader in 2004, Cunningham had long since settled into life as a perennial backbencher, as had Alex Neil, who was so sure of a similar status that he placed a bet with STV's Michael Crow that he would never join the SNP front bench. Yet their appointments demonstrated several aspects of Salmond's character: an inability to hold long-standing grudges against those he believed had been disloyal, and also a genuine desire to have as capable a ministerial team as possible, thereby defying his reputation as a 'one-man band'. Salmond must also have had in mind a historical precedent he had once researched himself: the 1860 US presidential election. Having won the race, Abraham Lincoln proceeded to award cabinet posts to his defeated rivals.

'The timing was very important,' observed someone close to the First Minister. 'He was waiting to see what they would do, whether they would become fundies or whatever.'[66] Interestingly, Cunningham also boosted the 79 Group contingent that now numbered four, including the First Minister, Justice Secretary Kenny MacAskill and transport minister Stewart Stevenson. 'The 79 Group was a product of

its time,' reflected MacAskill a week before the reshuffle. 'The attitudes of Alex Salmond and I have changed because we live in a
different society. Left-wing nationalism needed [then] to have a voice,
now it's got a government.'[67]

Perhaps the biggest focus of that government – beyond, if not including, the pursuit of independence – had been the development of
Scotland's renewable energy capacity. Salmond had always demonstrated great consistency in his views on certain policy areas, and indeed
on renewables he could even claim to be something of a visionary.
'How many countries have the potential choice of Hydro-electric,
wave, solar and wind power to heat their homes', he had asked as a
student in 1977, 'and supply their industries with reliable sources of
non-pollutant electricity?'[68]

More than three decades later and Salmond remained just as engaged.
'Energy is one of the things that enthuses him the most, perhaps even
more so than the constitution' said a source. 'It's not just token. He
really gets into the detail of that and thinks we're on the cusp of a big
turning point.'[69] Indeed, in speeches on renewables Salmond often cited
the discovery of North Sea oil. 'When I started in the Oil and Gas
sector as an economist in the 1980s,' he told the Edinburgh Chamber of
Commerce in March 2010, 'people still harked back to a 1972 SCDI
Conference in Aviemore [where there was] a particularly inspirational
talk by John Raisman, the then Chairman of Shell UK, which articulated and brought home the opportunities for the financial sector offered
by North Sea oil and gas.'[70] Renewables, he told the SCDI itself in
March 2009, was 'a new energy revolution'. 'With firm resolve, shared
purpose, and wise decision-making, we can ensure that the promise of
renewable energy matches that of North Sea oil and gas.'[71]

Marking the second anniversary of his administration in the *Scotsman*, the First Minister had devoted a whole article to energy, boasting
that the Scottish Government had approved 'no less than 20 major
renewable projects', mainly wind farms, while the Saltire Prize had
been designed to 'spur innovation around the world' in terms of marine
projects, not least in the Pentland Firth, which Salmond called the
'Saudi Arabia of marine renewables'. But the old hostility towards
nuclear energy remained. 'The green energy revolution is being developed, built, tested and established – real jobs, real technology, happening
in Scotland now,' he wrote. 'By contrast, nuclear power is unreliable and
unwanted in Scotland.'[72] Salmond saw his role as facilitating the renew-

able revolution via the Scottish Government, as he said (paraphrasing R. S. Thomas) in a slightly different context 'light needs a window to enter a darkened room'.[73]

Salmond took a similar message to the Copenhagen summit on climate change in mid-December, arguing that his ambitious target for cutting carbon emissions should allow him to take part in the main negotiations. Although this was not granted ('I'm not a head of state, I'm not leading a delegation,' conceded Salmond. 'Scotland is not an independent country.'), the First Minister flew to Denmark anyway, with plans to attend fringe events. This attracted cries of 'grandstanding'[74] from political opponents, further fuelled by Salmond's boast that he was set to share a platform with Arnold Schwarzenegger, the Californian governor, Ban Ki-Moon, the UN Secretary General and Boris Johnson, the mayor of London, a high-level meeting that embarrassingly failed to transpire. Instead, Salmond signed an agreement to work with the Maldives to tackle the impact of global warming and help the island archipelago become the world's first 'carbon-neutral country'.[75]

Throughout his term of office Salmond zealously pursued renewable energy initiatives, bending ears everywhere he went and convincing Scottish firms, for example Scottish and Southern Energy, to team up with international firms like the Japanese engineering giant Mitsubishi to co-operate on a range of projects, from developing electric cars to promoting a new generation of offshore wind farms. Even the normally hostile *Daily Record* praised Salmond's 'realistic vision'. 'He deserves great credit for personally driving forward the vision and championing the country's green future,' acknowledged the newspaper in 2010. 'It could prove his greatest legacy to Scotland.'[76]

Other sectors of the Scottish economy, meanwhile, were struggling. In July 2009 the drinks giant Diageo announced controversial proposals that threatened 900 jobs at the Johnnie Walker packaging plant in Kilmarnock and the Port Dundas grain distillery in Glasgow. Salmond's reaction did not show him at his best. After a hastily arranged meeting with Paul Walsh, Diageo's chief executive, the First Minister cancelled at 15 minutes' notice so he could appear as 'guest of the day' on the BBC2 programme *The Daily Politics*. Given that Salmond had earlier referred to the possible job losses as 'cataclysmic', it had been an odd way to behave.

Salmond was again accused of 'grandstanding' when he personally led a march through Kilmarnock protesting at the job losses, while Iain McMillan, director of CBI Scotland, said Diageo had been the target of 'unusually aggressive behaviour by politicians which was simply inappropriate'. A Scottish Government rescue package was then rejected as not having adequately addressed the need for economies. Salmond bluntly rejected criticisms that his negotiating technique had made a compromise impossible, saying his Government was 'not neutral between employment and unemployment'. 'Our plan was extremely detailed and we gave it our best shot,' he added philosophically. 'Sometimes it is successful, sometimes it is not. But we always have to make the effort.'[77]

Almost two months later Salmond was accused of trying to 'bully' another drinks firm, the French company Pernod Ricard, into supporting his plans for a minimum alcohol pricing scheme. Following an unpublicised meeting in Paris with Pernod Ricard's chairman and chief executive, 'senior industry insiders' told the *Scottish Daily Mail* that the First Minister 'was unwilling to listen to reason when the topic was discussed'. 'Salmond went over there and was quite aggressive,' said one. 'His behaviour could be considered as bullying. The people at Pernod were shocked by his behaviour.' Salmond's office strongly denied these reports, claiming the meeting had in fact been 'very positive'.[78] Whatever had happened at that Paris meeting, Salmond could certainly be abrasive in meetings, and occasionally patronising. During an exchange of views on the cancellation of the Glasgow Airport Rail Link, for example, he told Stephen Purcell, leader of Glasgow City Council, to 'behave like a grown-up'.[79]

Salmond also faced scrutiny over his Commons finances as well as his behaviour, as the Westminster expenses row dominated headlines in May and June 2009. The *Sunday Herald* reported that as well as claiming rent on a flat in the prestigious Dolphin Square, Salmond had claimed almost £1,100 for staying in London hotels while on government business. ('The hotels were used for many business meetings, as well as for accommodation,' explained a spokesman, not unreasonably. 'This would not have been possible in the rented flats at Dolphin Square.'[80]) The same newspaper also reported that Salmond claimed expenses for a period in which the Commons was in recess, together with £1,751 for food between April 2007 and March 2008 despite rarely being in the UK capital. Salmond claimed he had done nothing wrong, pointing to an external audit by Sir Thomas Legg that, it has to be said, eventually exonerated him.

Every party was affected to some extent (Angus Robertson, for example, was required to repay the cost of a home cinema system), while Salmond cleverly deflected criticism by urging Westminster to adopt Holyrood's more open expenses system. Despite recent events, Salmond retained a Teflon coating as he entered his third year as First Minister, benefitting from a rare phenomenon – an electorate willing to give a senior politician the benefit of the doubt.

Although Justice Secretary Kenny MacAskill's announcement that convicted Lockerbie bomber Abdelbaset Mohmed Ali al-Megrahi, who had been diagnosed with terminal cancer, was to be released on compassionate grounds had been widely trailed following an impressive BBC Scotland scoop, the actual confirmation in late August 2009 still generated political shockwaves. Having begun his term of office by condemning Tony Blair's Prisoner Transfer Agreement (PTA), Salmond's government had now authorised al-Megrahi's release under a different legal mechanism.

As criticism of the decision grew both nationally and internationally – not helped by television pictures of jubilant crowds waving Scottish saltires as al-Megrahi arrived home in Tripoli – Salmond told the BBC 'it was the right thing to do in terms of the Scottish justice system'. 'We understand the upset. We understand the disagreement,' he added. 'But we have to do what is right in terms of our legal system, that is what we are duty-bound to do. No-one, I think, seriously believes that we made any other decision except for the right reasons.'[81] Indeed, Kenny MacAskill consistently argued that he had, in his quasi-judicial capacity as Justice Secretary, considered al-Megrahi's application for release on compassionate grounds based purely upon medical advice. The Scottish Government, however, persistently refused to disclose that evidence in full, perhaps the only weakness in an otherwise watertight position.

As for the question of al-Megrahi's guilt, Salmond made no public comment although it was not in his nature to indulge in conspiracy theories. Whilst the 1985 death of his SNP associate Willie MacRae, for example, had certainly been unusual, Salmond went along with the prosaic explanation that he had simply killed himself rather than been assassinated by agents working on behalf of Nirex, the nuclear waste agency against whom MacRae had been campaigning. Similarly, Salmond most likely believed that al-Megrahi was guilty as charged. Indeed, the BBC journalist James Cook recalled asking the First Minister about his own view shortly after the release. Salmond replied that one of his first acts on coming to office had been to request all the papers relating to Lockerbie which, having read them, led him to believe al-Megrahi's conviction was sound. And while MacAskill ostensibly reached the decision to release him, it seems likely that Salmond took the lead. Indeed, interviewed a year after the decision, MacAskill wrongly remembered that responsibility for responding to lobbying from the Libyan British Business Council had been 'taken away from me so I would not be coloured'.[82]

There were also wider considerations. Although the decision to release al-Megrahi attracted international condemnation, it also drew attention to a devolved Scottish Government that had made an important decision under a distinct legal system, a system Salmond portrayed as a proxy for Scotland as a whole. 'Some people say that the Scottish system has too much compassion,' he said, defending the decision exactly a year later. 'At the end of the day, I think I'd rather be First Minister of a society with too much compassion than be First Minister of a country with too little compassion.'[83] US news networks carried MacAskill's statement – with its invocation of the Scots as 'a compassionate people' – live, while Obama's condemnation was balanced out by Nelson Mandela's praise. That, it might be said, had done more for Scotland's profile, not to mention that of the SNP, than innumerable marketing campaigns.

Having had their ups and downs since their association via the 79 Group, Salmond and MacAskill had once again become extremely close, a relationship demonstrated by the First Minister's robust defence of his colleague during a difficult period. 'Kenny MacAskill made the right decision for the right reasons,' he told delegates at the 2009 SNP conference. 'He showed that there is a place for compassion in the administration of justice.'[84] On another occasion, when MacAskill faced with a no-confidence vote in May 2009, Salmond had even shored up his position by threatening to resign if it was successful.

Perversely, the decision caused more problems for the Prime Minister, Gordon Brown, who had nothing to do with the decision. It seems that Peter Mandelson and some Scottish MPs advised Brown not to comment on Megrahi's release for a week or two in the belief that this would put pressure on Alex Salmond and embarrass the SNP. This backfired, and Brown's silence (although a statement had been drafted saying he respected the Scottish Government's decision) was taken as evidence he had been involved in the controversial decision.[85]

All went quiet on the Libyan front until the summer of 2010, when a US Senate inquiry engineered, it was presumed, to distract attention from President Obama's domestic woes reignited the Megrahi affair. After a lengthy correspondence, in which Salmond demonstrated his attention to detail (often alleged to be lacking) and ability to present a lucid, consistent account of his Government's actions, he attempted to draw a line under the issue by claiming the Senators conducting the investigation – who had alleged that commercial interests had played a part in Megrahi's release – were either 'unable or unwilling' to understand the separate legal processes involving compassionate release and the UK's Prisoner Transfer Agreement (PTA).[86]

There was, of course, no evidence that the Scottish Government had had contact with the oil company BP in relation to decisions made about Megrahi. Even when the WikiLeaks phenomenon gave light to diplomatic cables concerning the affair, these simply served to vindicate Scottish Ministers, while leaving the previous UK Labour government increasingly exposed. 'Julian Assange, the WikiLeaks' founder, would wish us to conclude that all governments are cynical,' observed Professor James Mitchell in an article for the *Herald*. 'The evidence suggests otherwise. The Scottish Government and judicial processes emerge well.'[87]

Indeed, such was the cynicism surrounding Tony Blair's role in the whole affair, that even when the US magazine *Vanity Fair* alleged that Salmond had offered Jack Straw (the then Foreign Secretary) a quid pro quo (helping end a raft of law suits in relation to 'slopping out' in Scottish prisons) in return for dropping his objections to al-Megrahi's release, almost everyone accepted the First Minister's swift rebuttal. 'Balderdash,' was his Boris Johnson-like exclamation.[88] Straw later hit back, arguing that Salmond had been careful not to accuse him of lying, 'because I'm not'.[89]

The First Minister's hand was strengthened yet further when a UK Government review confirmed that its policy had shifted in the autumn of 2008 to favour the release of Megrahi, while maintaining publicly that there was no such position. This, declared an understandably smug Salmond, was conclusive proof that Tony Blair's government had been 'complicit in the greatest orchestrated political hypocrisy in Scottish ... history'.[90]

What better platform could the SNP leader have wished for on which to 'stand up' for Scotland? That the Megrahi affair vindicated Salmond was a personal victory, and although opinion polls suggested a majority of Scots believed his release to have been a mistake, as with so many other things it did not damage the First Minister's standing. Even when a clearly dying Megrahi became a political football in the final moments of the Libyan regime, Salmond batted aside legitimate criticism with ease. 'What has been proven in every enquiry,' he said in August 2011, 'is that the Scottish Government – almost alone among people acting in this – always acted in good faith and according to the due process of law.'[91]

Salmond, meanwhile, waded through the usual constitutional quagmire. Despite apparent lack of Parliamentary support, he announced his firm intention to press ahead with legislation for a referendum on independence. 'Others have different views on Scotland's future,' the First Minister told the Foreign Press Association at Chatham House. 'But we should be able to develop a consensus in Scotland that the people have a right to their say on what that future should be.' The case for a referendum, claimed Salmond, was 'unassailable'. It was a clever tactic, presenting the three Unionist parties as seeking to deny the Scottish people a democratic say over their constitutional future.

Salmond also told his Chatham House audience that 'a vote on Scotland's future is now a case of "when" rather than "if"',[92] elaborating on what could only be described as a Whig interpretation of Scottish history. A couple of days later he mapped out the series of incremental advances that would culminate in full independence, or at least full independence as now defined by the SNP: 'Step one was the restoration of the Scottish Parliament after three centuries – the nation's democratic heartbeat – and the SNP played our full part in the Yes-Yes campaign. Within a decade of the new Parliament, step two was the election of an SNP administration to provide bold and effective leadership – recognising that Scotland needs a real Government, not a peely-wally "Executive". And step three is achieving the full opportunities and responsibilities that come with independence. And that too will be achieved, because we are now in an irreversible process of independence, and closer to it than ever before.'[93]

Salmond also believed the apparently inevitable election of a UK Conservative government would further aid step three of this unstoppable march, not only through Scottish resentment of Tory rule but the election of 20 SNP MPs in the forthcoming general election. 'There's a vast, overwhelming majority of people in Scotland, regardless of political preference, who rather like the idea of the Westminster parliament being hung by a Scottish rope,' he told the *Daily Telegraph* as he prepared for the SNP's annual conference in Inverness. 'I don't think a Tory majority is a shoo-in by any means. I think a hung parliament or a balanced parliament of some kind is still more than an arithmetic possibility.'[94]

Opinion polls, however, told a different story. Almost in spite of sustained high approval ratings for Salmond as First Minister, his party continued to slide behind Labour in terms of Westminster voting intentions. The Glasgow North East by-election, prompted by the resignation of Commons Speaker Michael Martin (whom Salmond had consistently defended against often vociferous attacks), on 12 November 2009 was a case in point. Following a troubled SNP campaign Labour's Willie Bain won a decisive 59 per cent of the vote, the SNP candidate David Kerr trailing in a poor second place. 'We fought the Glasgow East really well, we fought the European elections spectacularly well, but we lost our way a bit in Glasgow North East and for that I am of course responsible,' conceded Salmond a few months later. 'But it was nothing to do with our candidates. Our candidates were excellent. It was the direction of our campaign. Plus, of course, some hills are higher to climb than others.'[95]

Support for independence remained stagnant at around 30 per cent of those polled. Undeterred, Salmond unveiled yet another constitutional reform white paper on St Andrew's Day, this time setting out four possible options: the status quo, more devolved powers as recommended by the Calman Commission, greater fiscal autonomy known as 'devomax', or the SNP's preferred option of full independence. 'The debate in Scottish politics is no longer between change or no change,' Salmond said at the launch, 'it's about the kind of change we seek and the right of the people to choose their future in a free and fair referendum.'[96]

This represented a further compromise, yet another departure from the purity of the SNP's 'big idea'. Salmond, ever the realist, realised he needed to get at least one opposition party on board – most likely the Liberal Democrats – if the referendum bill was to stand any chance of getting through Parliament. Not only was he no longer 'wedded' to the idea of a vote taking place on St Andrew's Day 2010, but he also indicated that the Scottish Parliament would be free to frame the wording of any third question. 'If the parliament, after deliberation, does not pass the referendum bill,' he warned, 'then I suspect this issue of the right of people to have their say and determine their own future will be a huge, perhaps dominating, question in the 2011 Scottish elections.'[97]

Salmond even softened his line on the Calman Commission, which had recently recommended a limited degree of fiscal autonomy (enabling MSPs to control 10p within each income tax band) as well as devolving responsibility over air guns, drink-driving and speed limits. 'We welcome many of the Calman recommendations,' he wrote in *Scotland on Sunday*. 'Nonetheless, the overall Calman proposals fall far short of what Scotland needs. At a time of recession, when the country needs real economic and fiscal levers to boost growth and take advantage of the opportunities which will come with recovery, the Calman suggestions on tax are at best half-baked, and at worst damaging.'[98]

Salmond assumed direct responsibility for constitutional issues following a limited reshuffle in which Education Secretary Fiona Hyslop had been demoted in order to draw a line under a long-running row over the SNP's election pledge to reduce class sizes. Despite these little local difficulties, some observers believed all was not lost. Murray Ritchie, the *Herald*'s former political correspondent, wrote that 'Polls and scandals and reshuffles and by-election successes and failures come and go and are merely the punctuation in Scotland's political story. The narrative only becomes interesting when the SNP is making waves and that has been the storyline now for more than a decade.' 'History shows you should expect the unexpected with the SNP,' added Ritchie, arguing that Salmond's record demonstrated 'gradualism in practice'. 'If the high road via a referendum next year is closed,' he continued, 'then it is only sensible to take the low.'[99]

Salmond began 2010 with a lecture optimistically entitled 'Choosing Scotland's Future'. Quoting from an essay by his 'favourite economist' John Maynard Keynes ('I hesitate to claim that if Keynes were alive today,' he quipped, 'he would have been a natural SNP voter'), the First Minister outlined the Scottish Government's economic vision: 'Like him [Keynes], we see economic growth as achievable notwithstanding occasional economic downturns and disruption. Like him, we see economic growth as a means more than an end in itself. A means towards what he called living "wisely, agreeably and well", and we call having "opportunities for all to flourish". The only difference between us – reflecting our greater appreciation of the effects of economic development on the environment – is that where Keynes sees living wisely as something that you move on to after the economic problems have been solved and maximum economic growth secured, we would see living wisely as contributing to economic growth.'[100]

Although the qualification 'occasional' belied Salmond's relaxed analysis of the recent financial crisis ('The productive potential of the economy has not been lost,' he told journalists a few months later. 'That can be recovered – perhaps not to the same extent – but it can be recovered'[101]), this was a reasonably clear statement of economic intent. Then, drawing on his memories as a 'young economist' working at the Royal Bank of Scotland, he pointed to 'real opportunities in the development of new financial instruments that harness resources from emerging economies to promote sustainable economic growth and reliable returns for the investor'. Scotland's financial sector would rise again, while a 'key part of choosing Scotland's future will be in how creatively we respond to the opportunities offered by the emerging economies'.

Salmond often demonstrated a wider point by showing visitors to Bute House a silver plate that had been presented to the former Prime Minister Ramsay MacDonald. This was engraved with the signatures of fellow delegates at the Imperial Conference of 1930, convened in response to the economic crisis following the Great Crash. 'At the time, the British Empire represented at the Conference included perhaps a quarter or a third of the population of the Globe,' Salmond explained in his lecture. 'Who would have thought then, that by another 20 to 30 years later, all that would have vanished?' Salmond meant this as a 'visual' demonstration of his Whig outlook:

> For example we have the signature of Desmond FitzGerald, at the time the Foreign Minister of the then Irish Free State. Twenty years on, Ireland would leave the Commonwealth. Fifty or so years on, his son Garret would, in his father's old job, organise the first Irish presidency of the European Council of Ministers and then as Taoiseach put relations with the United Kingdom on a new footing through the Anglo-Irish Agreement. Or again, we have the signatures of the Indian delegation. When I met Mahatma Gandhi's grandson recently at Bute House, where the plate is usually kept, he recalled meeting two of the delegates as a boy with the Mahatma, who within twenty years of the Imperial Conference had led India to freedom.

Similarly, the 'end of colonialism in the 1950s and 60s was followed by resurgence of interest in devolution and independence in the late 60s and into the 70s', and therefore 'we see the future for the nation of Scotland simply as the standard future for any nation, and what was historically the position of Scotland for many centuries: as a nation governing itself in its own state'.[102]

Progress on that front, however, remained sluggish, and without the luxury of majority public support as in Ireland and India. An independence referendum bill had been cleared by the Scottish Cabinet towards the end of January 2010, the year in which Salmond had pledged to hold the ballot, although the bill itself was not published on Burns Night, as had been expected. The First Minister said the priority was passing his third budget, although when it came to the referendum, matters were 'very far advanced'.[103]

But when the three Unionist parties vowed to kill off any referendum bill the following week, Salmond announced another consultation on his proposals (which he had published only in draft form) in order to prevent, by his own admission, the bill's early death. 'It was the intent, in my estimation, of the Labour, Tory and Liberal Democrat parties to grab control of the Referendum Bill and dispose of it as quickly as they possibly could,' the First Minister told a press conference. 'Therefore I think it's far better that the people of Scotland get the opportunity over the next two to three months or so to look at the shape of the Bill.'[104] The proposed date of the referendum, meanwhile, slipped further.

It was, of course, all about tactics. By trying in his own words 'to out-manoeuvre the manoeuvrers',[105] Salmond was targeting what he saw as the weak spot in the pan-Unionist front, believing that the Liberal Democrats in particular could be persuaded to support the 'devo-max' option in a referendum rather than the Calman proposals, and therefore help get the necessary legislation through the Scottish Parliament. The party's leader Tavish Scott, well known for his hard line on a referendum, refused to budge, while the emergence of plans for a 'Scottish Referendum Commission' to oversee any poll further fuelled opposition suspicion that Salmond would attempting to 'rig' the poll.

The draft referendum bill finally appeared towards the end of February as a precursor to a consultation that would conclude after the likely date of the 2010 Westminster general election. The document confirmed Salmond's earlier backing for three separate questions, albeit in a slightly different form. Firstly, voters were to be asked to vote 'yes' or 'no' on whether they supported the Scottish Parliament being given new devolved powers, with two alternative wordings, one based on 'devo-max' and another on the Calman proposals. A second, somewhat contrived question, would ask whether the 'parliament's powers should also be extended to enable independence to be achieved'.

'More than 10 years on from the establishment of the Scottish Parliament, the debate in Scotland is no longer about whether or not the parliament should take on new responsibilities,' commented Salmond, who said he would campaign for a double-yes vote. 'It is about the form of change, and that issue underpins the consultation. The people want our parliament to be able to do more, so the debate is now about how much more. And it is time the people had their say.'[106]

Distracting from this further constitutional repositioning had been two 'sleaze' rows that at points threatened to engulf Salmond and his deputy, the able and popular Health Secretary Nicola Sturgeon. The first involved the auctioning of private lunches at Holyrood for SNP donors, apparently in breach of Parliamentary rules, a row that escalated when the *Sunday Herald* obtained video footage of the auction itself, in which Salmond could clearly be seen handling a cheque for £500, while the auctioneer Humza Yousaf, who worked for Salmond and Sturgeon at Holyrood, repeatedly emphasised Salmond's status as First Minister, rather than as leader of the SNP. Whether Salmond had actually done anything wrong was a moot point, but it did not look good.

To make matters worse, Salmond was then forced to defend Sturgeon when it emerged that she had lobbied a sheriff court on behalf of a constituent who also happened to be a convicted fraudster. Writing in her capacity as the MSP for Glasgow Govan, Sturgeon had urged the court to show leniency towards Abdul Rauf, who had admitted benefits fraud amounting to £80,000 and instead consider a non-custodial sentence. Salmond told MSPs that Sturgeon was a 'fantastic' deputy and that she had his '110 per cent' support. Then, with Sturgeon looking strained and tense beside him in the Chamber, the First Minister overdid it, arguing that MSPs had an 'absolute obligation' to represent constituents 'without fear or favour'. 'If members of this chamber don't understand that obligation,' he added aggressively, 'then they shouldn't be representing constituents on anything.'[107] This had been, at the very least, an overstatement. As Mike Dailly of the Govan Law Centre commented, 'Alex Salmond has this horrible propensity to invent these concepts on the hoof'.[108]

This demonstrated Salmond at his best, his instinctive loyalty towards Sturgeon, and also his worst, using poorly chosen language and pushing things a little too far. Both rows eventually died down, the first after a Parliamentary investigation cleared Salmond and Sturgeon of any wrongdoing, and the second following a well-handled apology for her actions from the Health Secretary. Indeed, with that Holyrood performance, Sturgeon probably convinced many that she was ready to succeed Salmond as SNP leader, and even as First Minister, should a vacancy arise. Her relationship with Salmond ('she has the ability to bite her tongue,'[109] explained one aide) was perhaps the most important in the Scottish Government.

Salmond attempted to recover ground by warning that any move by the UK government to cut public spending in Scotland would be 'neither understood nor forgiven' by Scots. This was to be a dominant Salmond refrain over the next few months and particularly during the forthcoming election campaign, but it had yet to resonate with voters. A series of polls appeared to show declining SNP support, while Gordon Brown's approval ratings even surpassed those of Salmond. This, together with an ongoing row over televised leadership debates from which the SNP was being excluded, enabled the SNP to present itself as the underdog in the 2010 general election campaign.

'At this election, more than ever before, Scotland needs champions,' declared Salmond at the campaign launch. 'And so on polling day, we are not just choosing MPs in the House of Commons, we are choosing national champions to stand up for the people of Scotland.' The Unionist parties, he continued, had 'come together to try to cut Scotland and the SNP out of the election debates', just as they were 'trying to carve Scotland out' of the election. 'The more SNP MPs elected the stronger Scotland's position will be,' concluded Salmond. 'Because at this election the message is simple: More Nats Means Less Cuts.'[110]

It was not only ungrammatical but a less-than-inspired campaign slogan, although Salmond's belated reference to 'greedy bankers'[111] at least demonstrated his awareness of what voters expected to hear. The broader election campaign was also unimaginative, reviving Salmond's 'hung Parliament' (or 'balanced Parliament' as he rechristened it) strategy as deployed at almost every UK general election since 1987. 'I have more experience than anyone in these islands,' had become a regular Salmond quip, 'on how to deal with a hung Parliament.'[112]

UK general elections had often been unforgiving places for the SNP, and so it proved during a memorable campaign in which Salmond often appeared to struggle, reluctant to acknowledge imminent spending cuts and shackled by a quixotic target of winning 20 seats. It also marked his reluctant departure from the House of Commons as the MP for Banff and Buchan. 'I have enjoyed and relished this Chamber for all of my 23 years here,' he said in a valedictory speech, adding: 'The rest of the Palace of Westminster I can take or leave, but this is a fantastic Chamber and a fantastic place for debate to be joined. It has a great atmosphere and at its best it is second only to the Scottish parliamentary Chamber, which looks better on telly. None the less, this is a fine place to have enjoyed debating. I have met and clashed with a number of formidable debaters and speakers from both sides of the House, and I have enjoyed every minute of doing that.' Salmond concluded by telling MPs that his Commons career simply had strengthened his 'absolute conviction that the case for our having full determination over Scotland's finances and resources has never been more urgent and has never required to be better made than it is now'.[113]

The SNP tried to salvage a sluggish campaign by attempting to have the last of three televised debates between Gordon Brown, David Cameron and Nick Clegg (or Tweedledum, Tweedledee and the Tweedledems, as Salmond put it) banned via the Court of Session in Edinburgh. When the legal action failed, however, a clearly frustrated Salmond had to make do with watching the clash from afar in Birmingham. Observing his reaction to Nick Clegg's performance, a journalist noted that Salmond watched 'with rapt attention and whispered almost under his breath: "I'd destroy him."'[114] The legal challenge had, at least, raised Salmond's profile in the final weeks of the campaign, while feeding into a long-standing SNP narrative about the attitude of broadcasters towards the party and its leaders.

On polling day the SNP managed to hold its six MPs and around 20 per cent of the vote, compared with a relatively impressive result for Labour, which polled 42 per cent, 3 per cent up on 2005. Typically, Salmond made the best of a disappointing result, pointing to his party's exclusion from the televised debates and attempting to seize the initiative by ruling out a formal coalition with either the Conservatives or Labour (the 'balanced Parliament' having come to pass) and 'accepting' Gordon Brown's offer of civil service support for negotiations. Salmond, however, went a little far in claiming that he was also in direct contact with the Labour Party, something the former Scotland Office minister David Cairns dismissed as a 'fantasy'.[115] Finally, he called upon the Liberal Democrats to join a 'progressive alliance' comprising Labour, the SNP and Plaid Cymru, warning that a Liberal Democrat 'stitch up' with the Conservatives could lead to 'the complete collapse of Lib Dem support in Scotland'.[116]

Jim Sillars, unhelpfully, called this tactic 'delusional'. 'What the election result should produce for the SNP is a revolution,' he wrote in the *Scotsman*. 'A revolt by the party to bring the present leadership to heel, or replace it with one that will get the SNP back on the road it never should have left: building the case for independence.' There was, added Sillars, 'absolutely everything to be gained by pushing the "bankrupt Britain" message and telling voters they had a choice to become independent and run their own affairs.'[117] Sillars later claimed that he felt no 'animosity' towards his former protégé. 'If Salmond needed me to help tomorrow,' he told the *Sunday Times*, 'I wouldn't hesitate to help.' Although the duo had not spoken since 1992, if 'they meet in the corridors of the parliament, where Sillars has a pass as a member of his wife's political team, they nod or give a curt wave'.[118]

Despite previously disparaging remarks ('Maybe the wrapping has changed somewhat but I think the leopard is still there[119]), Salmond quickly concluded that David Cameron was a UK Prime Minister with whom he could do business, commenting following their first meeting that he had not spent 'much time today trying to convert David Cameron to the concept of independence for Scotland; he didn't spend any time converting me, not that it would be possible, to the concept of London rule in Scotland. We know we've got huge political differences, but if you can find constructive means of agreement to benefit people in Scotland then surely that's what politicians should do and get on with.'[120] Salmond, however, added the caveat that he would wait to see if Cameron's 'mutual respect agenda' was translated into deeds as well as words, deeds that included releasing almost £700 million in funding for accelerated capital spending, Barnett consequentials from the London Olympics and revenue from the fossil fuel levy, then sitting in a London bank account.

'I have no doubt that Alex Salmond will play an instrumental role in shaping the emerging debate, which is now gathering momentum, on new powers for the devolved Administrations,' said Eilidh Whiteford in her maiden speech as the new MP for Banff and Buchan. 'I have no doubt also that, when future generations reflect on the history of Scotland, Alex Salmond's central place in the story of our own times will be assured.'[121]

That 'emerging debate' was, as ever, shifting ground. 'The centre of gravity in Scottish politics currently is clearly not independence,' Salmond told *The Times* in June 2010. 'It's no contradiction if you're campaigning for what's good for Scotland, which may be less than what you think is right for Scotland, and campaigning for independence. It's not a question of (independence) taking a back seat, it's a question of fulfilling your duty. I regard that as a duty. When the SNP was formed, if I remember correctly, the second aim of the party was to further Scottish interests. I believe it's part of my obligation to further Scottish interests as well as to campaign for independence. It's not either or, it's as well as.'

Salmond then linked the SNP's renewed quest for full fiscal autonomy – first set out during the 2001 general election campaign – to a
grim economic context. 'It's my job to come up with some answers,
along with others,' he explained. 'If you go to the public and say "oh
deary, deary me, isn't this awful", then I'd be failing in my duty to the
people.' It was, therefore, 'really important to be able to say to people
that we can change the circumstances, that we can increase revenue as
well as decreasing expenditure. That is fiscal responsibility if you like, in
terms of transferring [tax] powers to Scotland.'[122]

Responding to the *Scotsman* and *Herald*'s coverage of these remarks,
the First Minister took the unusual step of writing to both newspapers. 'I
did not say in an interview in another paper . . . that independence was
"no longer" the centre of gravity in Scottish politics,' he protested,
directly contradicting his headline quote in *The Times*. 'I was in fact
making exactly the opposite point – that the centre of gravity in Scottish
politics is shifting towards independence, not away from it.' . . . A generation ago it [the centre of gravity] was for an assembly, then for a
parliament, then for Calman, now for fiscal responsibility, which is
currently galvanising a range of opinion across Scottish society. At each
stage in that road, the SNP campaigned in favour of more powers for
Scotland as well as pursuing the independence campaign. There has never
been any contradiction in doing that – nor is there now. Indeed, one of
the essential ingredients of gaining more power for Scotland is the vigour
of the independence campaign. It is the engine which fires the debate.[123]

Salmond clearly believed that full fiscal responsibility represented an
opportunity, perhaps the biggest since the 1997 devolution referendum,
to pursue a consensual approach on constitutional reform. The three
Unionist parties, however, failed to play ball despite containing degrees
of enthusiasm for greater financial powers. As *The Economist* observed,
'Fiscal responsibility is a good cause, but Mr Salmond may find it just as
hard to sell as independence'.[124]

It later became clear that Salmond's 'centre of gravity' remark was
the beginning of a tactical retreat from the independence referendum
bill. First, the Scottish Government confirmed the bill would not be
tabled in time to hold a plebiscite, as planned, on St Andrew's Day 2010,
then Salmond admitted the bill faced certain defeat, telling the *Scottish
Sunday Express* that he would instead 'let the people decide'[125] at the
subsequent election.

Finally, at an away-day gathering of MSPs on 2 September 2010,
Salmond announced his intention to publish the bill, but not put it to a

vote at Holyrood. When news of this *volte-face* was revealed in the *Sunday Herald*, Salmond emailed party members – who had not formally been consulted – arguing that a 'new re-elected SNP government will be in a powerful position to secure passage of the referendum having successfully mobilised the people over the blocking tactics of the Unionist parties'.[126] Despite the best efforts of the media, meanwhile, not a single voice was raised in protest, although the MSPs Sandra White and Bob Doris were reported to be 'lukewarm' about the plan. The journalist Alan Cochrane likened Salmond to the Grand Old Duke of York, having 'marched his men – not quite 10,000 – up to the top of the Bill over his plan for a referendum on the break-up of the United Kingdom and then marched them down again'.[127]

Explaining his decision the following day, Salmond predicted that the independence referendum would be a 'transcending issue' of the election campaign, 'with the additional important key characteristic that the only alternative to a decade of despair, of Tory Westminster cuts, is to have the financial independence for the parliament to generate more revenue, more wealth for Scotland and give us a better future'.[128] But the SNP message had become a little confused. Was the party campaigning for independence, fiscal autonomy or merely a referendum on independence? The opportunity, it seemed, had passed, with Wendy Alexander's invitation to 'bring it on' echoing around the Chamber.

The decision was discussed, or rather rubber stamped, by a Cabinet meeting in Kilmarnock on 7 September and included in the Scottish Government's final government programme the following day. The statement found a below-par Salmond on typically bullish form. 'For make no mistake, devolution, as we know it, is over,' he told MSPs. 'When the money *from* London, or rather delivered *via* London, is being cut, then the game changes totally'.[129]

Many SNP watchers were puzzled by this failure to table the independence referendum bill: surely better to have it voted down by the Unionist parties than not presented at all? 'It's a tactical issue,' was Salmond's only explanation,[130] while a leaked US diplomatic cable even suggested the SNP was preparing around this time to shelve its referendum demand in return for a ballot on boosting Holyrood's powers, something dismissed (probably correctly) by the party as a 'misunderstanding'.[131]

Even when it came to the SNP's renewed focus on securing greater fiscal powers for Scotland, there was political trouble. In November 2010, it emerged that the Scottish Parliament's ability to vary the basic rate of income tax by 3p in the pound – the Scottish Variable Rate (SVR) – had lapsed. It was the Liberal Democrat Scottish Secretary Michael Moore who let it be known, via a letter to Holyrood leaders, presumably with the intention of scoring political points against the First Minister.

On the face of it, the mothballing of the SVR was more of an embarrassment than a serious constitutional issue. Unused since 1999, it was, as Salmond put it, an 'academic issue', not least because his Government had no intention of raising taxes. It did, however, appear as if a normally surefooted administration had taken its eye off the ball; this was, after all, the very power the SNP had proposed using during the 1999 election, the so-called 'Penny for Scotland'. Salmond, naturally, fought back, arguing that Her Majesty's Revenue and Customs had demanded £7 million to set up a new IT system in order to administer the hypothetical tax, a sum the Scottish Government was not prepared to pay. The UK Government, alleged Salmond, was using the issue as a 'Trojan horse' to ensure Scotland paid for the cost of the Calman Commission proposals.[132]

Nevertheless, and under mounting pressure from political opponents and the media, something had to give. The Finance Secretary John Swinney, who had recently implied the SVR remained an 'available' fiscal lever, apologised to MSPs for not flagging up its having lapsed. This also prompted the first Parliamentary apology from the First Minister, for whom sorry often seemed to be the hardest word. 'I join in that [Swinney's] apology,' he informed Holyrood, although he protested that the SVR was 'not in a workable condition' when the SNP came to power in 2007. Pressed further by the Scottish Conservative leader Annabel Goldie, Salmond jokingly declared: 'I am Spartacus.'[133]

Public support for independence, meanwhile, continued to flatline at around a third (although one TNS poll in December 2010 did show a brief rise to 40 per cent). This, argued the former SNP leader Gordon Wilson in a *Scotland on Sunday* lecture, was his party's 'primary weakness'. 'It has prioritised its role in government,' he argued, 'and devoted little of its resources towards presenting a relevant, modern economic case for independence.'[134] Yet Salmond's standard response when pushed on this rather crucial point was to dissemble. Is not independence, asked Kirsty Young on the First Minister's *Desert Island Discs*, 'further off than it's ever been?'

'I disagree,' replied Salmond. 'I think we are closer than ever.'[135]

Indeed, when Pope Benedict visited Scotland in September 2010 – the high point of Salmond's long wooing of the Catholic vote – he even argued that it was a 'validation of Scotland's nationhood'.[136]

Paradoxically, rather than exploiting this weakness, the Scottish Labour leader Iain Gray chose instead to accuse the First Minister of having a 'personal obsession with independence' that was 'daft, deluded, deranged and downright dangerous for this country'.[137]

Salmond, meanwhile, continued to attack the 'extraordinary control freakery' of the UK Government's Scotland Bill, which gave legislative form to the proposals of the Calman Commission, most notably the power to control 10p within each income tax band (while also recognising, for the first time, the 'Scottish Government' nomenclature). Instead of welcoming what amounted to partial fiscal autonomy, the First Minister pointed to an 'inherent deflationary bias' within the proposals, on which he was backed up by two economists, Professors Andrew Hughes Hallett and Drew Scott. It looked, he added, 'like a Tory trap' from a Coalition government intent on 'hanging onto the vestiges of power'.[138] Again, this critique was open to question. If partial fiscal autonomy was risky and might lead to a reduced tax take, argued CBI Scotland and others, then where did that leave the Scottish Government's preferred option of full fiscal responsibility?

There was, all the while, a dual narrative emanating from Salmond on the issue of independence: robust fighting talk about ending London rule to assure the party faithful there would be no deviation from the righteous path, and also lots of ecumenical talk about 'partnership' and the 'social union' to ensure those outside the broad SNP church did not take fright. The oft-repeated pledge to hold a referendum made this task all the easier; the party's *raison d'être* had been ring-fenced, separated from its day-to-day work. And with hindsight, whether the bill to enable that referendum had been presented to MSPs or not did not really matter: constant speculation in the media had embedded the principle in the electorate's mind, arguably more firmly than in 2007.

The other dominant dichotomy of 2010–11 was the best of times in terms of Scottish Government pledges and spending, but the worst of times in the UK public finances, thanks to a pre-election deal with George Osborne (perhaps hoping for a Scottish electoral reward that did not come) that delayed cuts to the Scottish block grant for an additional year. Nevertheless, and after successful maneuvering by the Scottish Conservatives, an Independent Budget Review group set out in late July 2010 what John Kenneth Galbraith said of politics in general, a choice between the disastrous and the unpalatable in 'the face of the most challenging public spending environment since the Second World War'.[139]

Its widely praised findings were completely ignored, for the SNP was not about to identify areas on which the axe would fall, particularly in the run-up to an election. Instead, Salmond appointed his own commission on the future of public services, chaired by the former STUC general-secretary Campbell Christie. Despite the severity of the spending cuts, Salmond argued, the Scottish Government was determined to keep 'the social fabric of Scotland intact'. Usefully, Christie was not due to disclose his recommendations until after the May 2011 election.[140] The Scottish Government, therefore, managed to maintain an aura of business as usual, which even repeated Labour accusations of a 'Salmond slump' pervading every aspect of Scottish life could not puncture.

This did not mean, however, that the First Minister could ignore completely the financial storm about to emanate from Westminster. Ahead of the Chancellor's Comprehensive Spending Review (CSR) in October 2010, he joined forces with his counterparts in Wales and Northern Ireland to reiterate their concern that the UK Government was cutting public spending too fast and too deeply. Later Salmond claimed he had 'levelled' with the public over the impact of the cuts, although considering that Treasury figures indicated the Scottish Government would lose £1.3 billion from its next budget (not to forget around £3bn over the next four years) this was difficult to take seriously. Instead the First Minister used the spending squeeze as a vehicle for re-emphasising his demand for 'control of the levers of growth in Scotland',[141] while conceding that defending his administration's 'social gains [wa]s going to be extraordinarily difficult'.[142] Looking back, however, both Salmond and John Swinney got off lightly. The imminent cuts to Scotland's capital budget were massive, yet still they pressed on with plans to invest £2.3bn in a new Forth crossing, nor did the Finance Secretary seem under any real pressure over public-sector pay, higher education funding or local authority cuts.

The UK Government's proposed defence cuts also handed Salmond yet another opportunity to 'stand up for Scotland' while at the same time putting him in something of a quandary over nuclear power. Ministry of Defence (MoD) proposals to close one, most likely two, RAF bases in Scotland were roundly criticised (Salmond dubbed the potential closure of RAF Lossiemouth 'a litmus test for the respect agenda'[143]) not just by the SNP, but also across the political spectrum. Exploiting this, the First Minister drafted a joint cross-party submission to the Coalition's Strategic Defence Review, which rather optimistically argued that the MoD ought to maintain its entire Scottish footprint.

The SNP's long-standing opposition to the four Trident nuclear submarines at Faslane, however, became a sticking point. Left out of the original draft, for obvious reasons, the other three Holyrood parties successfully argued that its retention should be included. If Salmond's argument was that jobs ought to be protected, then what possible justification could there be for making an exception of those on the Clyde?

The First Minister's long-running campaign of championing the renewables industry found him on a safer political footing. His continued prowess at attracting foreign investment, particularly from China, won deserved praise, while the First Minister presented it as a bigger opportunity for Scotland than North Sea oil and gas. It was, he told an audience of industry figures (with a touch of hyperbole to which he had always been prone) 'a pivotal turning point in human history, on a par with the move from hunter-gathering to settled agricultural communities or the discovery of the New World in 1492'.[144] The Scottish Government's target for the proportion of electricity generated by renewables, meanwhile, grew increasingly ambitious, eventually reaching 100 per cent by 2025.

This was questioned by several energy specialists, while Salmond's personal involvement in securing funding for the ill-fated clan 'Gathering' event in Edinburgh the previous year – the centerpiece of the Scottish Government's 'Year of Homecoming' festival – also came under scrutiny, not least its collapse with debts of £726,000, forcing ministers to write off a secret £180,000 loan. Initially, the First Minister refused to appear before Holyrood's Public Audit Committee, while repeatedly claiming the event had generated £10.4m for the economy (a figure disputed by an independent economist) and pledging to support a repeat performance. Under further pressure to give evidence, an almost humble Salmond did so in early December, accepting that his government should have told other public bodies (which lost out to the tune of £675,000) about the loan. Although the row quickly died down, it did raise issues about how Salmond conducted government business. Perhaps, as the *Caledonian Mercury* speculated, he operated under the belief 'that these are his decisions to take, that he knows best how to work situations, how to handle difficult problems and he does not want to be distracted by others debating, discussing and, most pertinently, disagreeing with him'.[145]

A difficult few months for Salmond and the SNP were rounded off when the Transport Minister Stewart Stevenson came up against particularly harsh December weather, prompting Salmond to admit his government had been 'caught out' by a 'perfect storm'.[146] Continuing the then popular trend for public self-flagellation, Stevenson begged Parliament for forgiveness, as did the First Minister. 'This is fast becoming First Minister's apologies,' quipped Iain Gray during his weakly joust with Salmond. 'We have had apologies for losing our tax varying powers; apologies for losing our money in dodgy loans; and, this week, the Transport Minister's apology for losing the plot and leaving hundreds of Scots stranded in their cars overnight.'[147]

Shortly after the First Minister declared his 'full confidence' in his Transport Minister, Stevenson duly offered his resignation. Salmond, a close friend of more than three decades, urged him to reconsider, but his mind was made up. The official response to Stevenson's letter of resignation pulled no punches. 'I understand your reasons for resigning but frankly I think it is wrong that you should have faced this situation,' wrote Salmond, '. . . just as no man can tether time nor tide, sometimes the elements are beyond anyone's control'.[148]

Beyond the personal connection, it was a blow for a First Minister who did not believe in reshuffles, preferring consistency in order to foster familiarity in the eyes of the electorate. A feature of Salmond's first term in office had been his willingness to stand by ministers under pressure to quit, which was why Stevenson's departure prompted only the third mini restructuring of his administration since 2007. His loyalty towards those who had been loyal to him, such as Stevenson, was beyond question.

Importantly, the SNP kept its cool during its winter of discontent, not least the usually unflappable Salmond. Slowly but surely, meanwhile, he set out his stall for the forthcoming election. Free personal care for the elderly, he stated, would be kept free of charge, while on university funding Salmond was unequivocal, making it clear that whatever 'distinctive Scottish' solution was eventually proposed, it would not involve a graduate contribution. 'The rocks,' he said, deploying a Burns quotation, 'will melt with the sun before I agree to tuition fees' – a line he had first used back in November 2007.[149]

On this, as in so many other areas, it was a tale of two policies. The Scottish Government insisted it could maintain key public services (or in other words keep them free) and deal with £1.3bn of cuts through the panacea of 'efficiency savings', while from local government and university management emanated constant warnings that something had to give. Most agreed that something did, but the SNP was determined that it did not until after the election.

Salmond, meanwhile, cleverly geared everything towards articulating a vision of Scottish society that he had hitherto avoided, preferring a sort of everyman Nationalism that did not offend any substantial section of the electorate. He played catch-up on sectarianism, hitherto Labour's policy domain, declaring that there was 'no place in football for those who let the passion become violence and the pride become bigotry',[150] while branding a UK Government decision to evict up to 600 asylum seekers from Glasgow as 'totally devoid of any compassion or understanding'.[151]

The First Minister even condescended to offer advice to the Prime Minister as he relaunched his vision of a 'Big Society'. Emerging from talks at Number 10 Downing Street, Salmond noted a 'substantial suspicion' that this was simply a cover for cuts, claiming the Scottish Government had a much closer relationship with the voluntary sector than south of the Border (the voluntary sector in Scotland did not necessarily agree).[152] But then the message was implicit: while the Coalition slashed and burned, the SNP were protecting the fabric of Scottish society as best they could in difficult circumstances.

WILL THE REAL ALEX SALMOND
PLEASE STAND UP?

Any attempt to identify him with a particular stereotype will always fail
for the simple reason that there was not one Parnell, but at least four
different Parnells. There was, first, the country gentleman with
his ... love of horses ... Then there was ... the political genius who
achieved his dominance by a tactical skill which was apparently instinctive ... [some] knew also a third, and quite other, Parnell. This was
the engaging companion, happy to relax ... exerting apparently effort-
less charm ... The dark side was exhibited to the full only intermittently
by the fourth Parnell ... in the glare of those strange eyes ... and in
that ability of his to convey ... the impression of ice and fire at the
same moment.[1]

F. S. L. Lyons on Charles Stewart Parnell

'I think he loves Scotland as much as I do. I think that's his greatest
strength,' said the then Scottish Secretary Jim Murphy of Alex Salmond
in January 2010. 'Other than that I don't really know him. I don't know
him as a human being, I know him as a politician.'[2] Indeed, as Winston
Churchill once said of Russia, to most political observers Salmond is 'a
riddle wrapped in a mystery inside an enigma'.[3]

Salmond is an intensely private individual, unusually so for a politician in a political era that demands so much of its protagonists. Like de
Gaulle he keeps his personal and public lives strictly separate,[4] but for
more than two decades the SNP's best-known figure has managed to
maintain both his privacy and a high public profile. There are certainly
hidden depths, feelings and vulnerabilities, but Salmond rarely, if ever,
betrays any of them in public. 'I always tried to get him to give a little
bit more of himself to the Press,' recalled a former aide, 'but he just

couldn't do it.'[5] Introspection, as many a profile has noted, is just not Salmond's thing. As he has said himself: 'I don't have much time for obvious psychological interpretations.'[6]

'I think there are three Alex Salmonds,' said one former aide, 'the deeply private and non-political Alex, Alex Salmond the politician and Alex Salmond's public persona.'[7] Brian Taylor captured well at least two of these. 'Salmond is a complex character who blends intensely private thoughts and emotions with an occasionally jovial outward appearance,' he wrote. 'He can seem sometimes possessed by politics...In company, particularly private company, Salmond can be charming, intelligent, diverting and intriguing. He is without doubt one of the closest and most thoughtful observers of the political scene, acutely aware of potential problems and opportunities for his own party and his rivals. In public, particularly in the political debate, he can occasionally seem over-assured. He dislikes failing or indeed admitting weakness in any form. That can be both advantageous and problematic, occasionally vital for a successful political career, can sometimes spill over into self-confidence approaching arrogance.'[8] 'There are two sides to Alex Salmond,' observed Jim Sillars more negatively. 'The public face and the private manipulator who, because of the dominance he gained over the SNP machine and party, has grown arrogant with that internal power. Hubris is his companion.'[9]

Let us start with the public persona and work backwards to the real Alex Salmond, in as much as this biographer has been able to identify him. 'He is the best natural politician I have ever met and probably the best Scotland has produced in a generation,' reflected Mike Russell some time ago. 'Some have talent, some have intellect; he has both and that's what makes him formidable.'[10] This is not a bad summary of the public perception of Salmond; only very few doubt he has either talent or intellect, while even his staunchest critics rarely question his political ability.

He is, in short, an immensely attractive figure. 'On the doorstep, on the high street and at the hustings, he is a formidable, engaging campaigner,' observed Alan Taylor in the *Scotsman*, 'hand on hips, his caterpillar eyebrows raised in interest no matter how banal the encounter.'[11] To experience one of his impromptu speeches, effortlessly combining anecdote, formalities and the bigger picture, is to witness a political performance of the first rank; to see him wrongfoot his opponents is equally impressive, while to watch Salmond demolish someone in debate may be uncomfortable, but also impressive. 'Like all populists with a passionate cause,' wrote Matthew Parris in a sentence that captures Salmond perfectly, 'he combines an open countenance with an instinct for the low blow.'[12]

Salmond is also impossible to disentangle from his party. 'To most Scots Alex Salmond has been the life and soul of the SNP,' judged Duncan Hamilton in 2000. 'His is the face and the voice people associate with modern nationalism. The SNP and Alex Salmond have become one in the public eye.'[13] Salmond's public persona, therefore, has been carefully contrived. 'What he likes to stress,' observed the journalist Ian Jack, 'is his kinship with ordinary Scotland – a kind of Scottish everyman, affable, plain-speaking, dry-witted, dipping naturally into the idiom of lowland Scotland, "wiz" for "was", "fir" for "for", whenever it suits.'[14] Indeed, Salmond often contrives to speak, de Gaulle-like, on behalf of the entire nation, rising above party politics and utilising the royal 'we'. 'Salmond is very informal and approachable, enjoys a joke, and appears to blend in neatly to any social situation,' judged Tom Gallagher. 'His amiability allows many Scots to view him as "the people's friend", a rare accolade for a politician during an era of mounting scepticism towards their like the world over.'[15] This gives rise to another paradox, the pragmatic, ecumenical Salmond keen to find areas of common ground with opponents yet willing to condemn them at the same time, slipping into tribalistic language that would make even Jim Sillars blush.

Nevertheless Salmond seeks to portray himself as Scotland's guardian, to such an extent that criticism of him can also appear to be criticism of the nation he leads. 'His image of himself,' wrote Richard Crossman of Harold Wilson in 1965, 'is as a gritty, practical Yorkshireman, a fighter, the Britisher who doesn't give in, who doesn't switch, who hangs on.'[16] Substitute 'Black Bitch' for 'Yorkshireman' and 'Scotsman' for 'Britisher' and this comes reasonably close to Salmond's own self-view, eschewing – like Wilson – ostentatious displays of emotion in order to preserve it.

Salmond also shares Wilson's serenity, a complete satisfaction with his own personality and way of life. 'Salmond is an exceptionally secure man,' thought John MacLeod in 2009. 'Cold and sunny, like a nice day in January, he is unfailingly serene, and with a capacity most unusual in his trade to forget slights, insults and minor betrayals and to continue in his steady, clever, calculating way.'[17] Salmond is apparently devoid of any inferiority complex, equipping him with great inner strength and an uncanny ability to endure a succession of political knocks. 'He desires to recreate Scotland in his own image,' judged the academic Tom Gallagher, 'extrovert, self-righteous and contemptuous of criticism.'[18]

Even so, Salmond is a realist, well aware that many Scots have adopted an 'assumed identity', a more attractive way of looking at themselves than reality ought to allow. 'I am not and have never been a "wha's like us" sort of person,' he commented in 2008. 'I am well aware of our nation's faults and shortcomings . . . But equally I am well aware of the nation's abilities, strengths and capacity to imagine the future.'[19] Nothing, meanwhile, makes Salmond angrier 'than people who deprecate the abilities of their own country, their own people. It's insidious and damaging. Patriotism is said to be the last refuge of the scoundrel. The reverse is the last refuge of the scoundrel in politics.'[20]

In this respect, Salmond sees himself as the latest in a long line of Scottish patriots defending the country from English exploitation, even though he has little time for 'symbolic heroes', preferring 'to strike the rational, pragmatic if unromantic figure of a modern politician'. Nevertheless, it is tempting to liken him to Robert the Bruce, bruised by his enemies but taking heart from a spider's attempts to spin its web, telling himself to try, try and try again. The analogy must have crossed Salmond's mind. 'Bruce's tactics at Bannockburn were innovatory,' he said in 1992. 'He won because he avoided fighting an orthodox pitched battle. To do this he had to prevent his troops running downhill towards the enemy, which has always been a Scottish impulse.'[21] By adopting unorthodox tactics, Salmond believes he can echo Bruce's success.

Gordon Wilson once compared Salmond with another historical figure, the man who fought for, but ultimately failed to win, home rule for Ireland, Charles Stewart Parnell. 'I think that's quite a compliment,' said Salmond of the allusion. 'I rather like Parnell.'[22] Indeed, the Parnell analogy captures well Salmond's strengths as well as his weaknesses. Like the Irishman, he has succeeded in linking 'fierce ebullience to a constitutional machinery',[23] compelling his opponents to adapt or die in the process. Salmond has also compromised, echoing Parnell in seeking to bring about home rule on the most conservative basis possible. As he admitted in 1998, 'I've tried to fashion a Scottish independence movement that threatens no one in Scotland. This has been my leadership project more than anything else.'[24] 'Scots are romantic – or some are – as far as history is concerned,' he said in 2010, trying to have it both ways. 'But they're usually quite hard-headed too. And that's what I am. A romantic hardhead.'[25]

'I think the fundamental reason for believing in independence,' Salmond commented more generally, 'is that nations are better when they govern themselves.'[26] Yet at the same time he has gone out of his way to emphasise Burkean continuity, a 'social union' with England as well as a joint head of state. 'On the one hand, Mr Salmond tells Scots that independence is something big: that for some reason of national destiny it is worth the inevitable upheaval,' noted *The Economist* in 1998. 'On the other, he assures them that independence is, really, no big deal.'[27]

This paradox is also reflected in Salmond's electoral record. Although there have been notable peaks under his leadership of the national movement – most notably the European elections in 1994 and Holyrood in 2007 – there was little progress at Westminster between 1992 and 2010, while public support for independence, however defined, rarely shattered a glass ceiling of around 33 per cent. It seems likely, therefore, that Salmond has altered his conception of what sovereignty means as a result. 'My suspicion is that [he] is too much of a realist to go for literal independence,' mused the journalist Peter MacMahon in 1998, 'and that he would settle for a halfway house on Catalonian lines.'[28] Similarly, Jim Wallace has always 'had a hunch that Alex would settle for some sort of devolution max, a substantial amount of independence but still within the UK state'. I always got the impression but his model was Jordi Pujol,' he added, 'he'd be quite satisfied with substantial autonomy with him ruling the roost. He's a realist.'[29]

Of course Salmond could never admit as much. 'If I led the SNP away from independence', he said in 2004, 'I would be doing something fundamentally wrong.'[30] Instead, he has sought to present every tactical shift – be it devolution or full fiscal autonomy – as in keeping with the traditions of his party. In this sense the SNP has to catch up with Salmond, rather than the other way round. But just how successful has this gradualist strategy actually been? A decisive answer is elusive. Although it was a Labour government that delivered devolution in the late 1990s, the success of Salmond and the SNP in the middle of that decade certainly ensured it happened quickly and substantially in terms of powers.

This goes some way towards explaining Salmond's love/hate relationship with the Labour Party, and also touches upon another paradox. Throughout his career Salmond always took great care to attack Labour's leadership rather than its grassroots support, a portion of the electorate that – after all – he wanted to convert to Nationalism. Yet despite this ecumenical bent, most notably in the fight for a Scottish Parliament, deep-seated tribalism was never far away. In almost every conference speech as SNP leader Salmond attacked his Labour opponents in the most deeply personal terms, while as First Minister his contempt for opposition counterparts was openly displayed every Thursday afternoon at Question Time. Even so, Salmond regularly attacked the tribal nature of Scottish politics, arguing in March 2010 that opposition parties had 'lost the ability to differentiate from what they like and dislike',[31] which was more than a little ironic given his own record.

Nevertheless, Salmond's place in history is secure as a result of the 2007 Holyrood election, which was above all a significant personal victory. Although he was forced to form a minority administration, the SNP is now a party of government. No longer can Labour depict it as incapable of governing Scotland responsibly, something of immeasurable value to the party's future. Beyond that, however, genuine progress is harder to detect. 'I've always believed, and I would be astonished if I were proved wrong,' Salmond said in 2008, 'that a success of the SNP and the government will translate into increased confidence in Scotland, increased confidence in the Scottish Government, and increased confidence in the case for independence.'[32] In that case, Salmond must prepare to be astonished, for whatever the achievements of his administration between 2007 and 2011 it has done little to increase confidence in, and more importantly support for, independence.

On that basis – notwithstanding the 2011 Holyrood election result – Salmond has to be judged a failure, at least in terms of delivering his ultimate political goal. Like John MacCormick, another Scottish Nationalist, he 'attempted to broaden the electoral appeal of nationalism, exclude the weirder fringes and give it a strong organizational base' but could end up 'a romantic failure'.[33] Indeed, Keith Webb's 1978 assessment of the Scottish Convention leader (MacCormick) is remarkably reminiscent of Salmond: 'In politics he must be considered a pragmatist. Had he paused amid his vast activity to discuss the nature of politics, he too would probably have called it "the art of the possible". Thus, while he was far from averse to the grand gesture, never being a man to eschew publicity, he was not temperamentally drawn to utopian positions . . . He was consistent only to the end of increased autonomy for Scotland, and was inconsistent in his choice of means to achieve this end.'[34]

Thus the frequent charge, usually levelled by fundamentalists, that Salmond, like MacCormick, has 'sold out' on independence. Yet those same fundamentalists rarely came close to identifying a compelling alternative to Salmond's gradualist approach. That said, Salmond did not invent the independence movement, while the SNP enjoyed considerable success before he rose to prominence. Nor has he really changed the direction of the SNP, just the means by which its aims are achieved. Rather Salmond believes, as did de Gaulle, that Nationalism shapes and explains history.

Many other critiques of Salmond also collapse upon closer inspection, not least the oft-repeated claim that his tactical flair has been at the expense of proper attention to long-term strategy. If gradualism can be considered a strategy, then it has been a broadly successful one, while Salmond's attempt to forge a 'civic Nationalism' – his bold updating of Bruce's 'community of the realm of Scotland' – has certainly paid off. 'Scottishness is not a single concept,' he once wrote. 'There is no one definition. It is something that exists in the heart and in the head.'[35] For this inclusive vision he deserves credit, although one must not ignore a more cynical motive. As he once told Winnie Ewing, 'I didn't necessarily get all the votes I wanted but I neutralised a lot of the voters that would have been against us.'[36] Less successful was his long-standing goal of replacing Labour as the party of urban, working-class Scots. Indeed, having identifed the 'three themes' of his leadership as 'left of centre identity, broad civic approach [and] the process of persuad[ing] the SNP to actively back a Parliament short of independence' – Salmond believed the last of those to be 'the most important'.[37]

Salmond is also less convincing when it comes to presenting himself as a political ideologue. Since the late 1970s he has defined himself as, invariably, a socialist, social democrat and even a post-Nationalist, but his overriding desire was always to place himself and his party in the mainstream. 'I've given the SNP a social democratic identity,' he told the *Guardian* in 1997, 'because that fits the Scottish psyche.'[38] Like another Irish politician, Daniel O'Connell, Salmond is 'essentially a pragmatic politician, ready to change his course according to the wind, and always more likely to be influenced by the prospect of immediate and material benefits than by slavish adherence to abstract principles'.[39] As Salmond admitted himself in 2007, 'I don't have any difficulty with changing, I'm changing all sorts of things.'[40]

It would be unfair, however, to suggest he is devoid of political principle. Salmond certainly occupies the broad centre-left, and has been remarkably consistent in that since his student days. Persistent themes have been energy and the rich potential of Scotland's natural resources, alongside a steady belief in a mixed economy. That said, there are still vestiges of the left-wing radical in Salmond, not least when it comes to war, nuclear power and the public sector. This has often come into conflict with the free market aspect of his character, a respect for moneymen and ingenious financial models that first took hold when he worked for the Royal Bank of Scotland at the height of Thatcherism. He is also, in the opinion of Professor John Haldane, 'something of a social conservative'[41] when it comes to issues like abortion and gay adoption, although free of any inclination to make moral judgements about his colleagues or humanity in general.

Another charge is that Salmond does not 'do' policy. 'He was only a spin machine,' judged Jim Sillars, 'spinning in a policy vacuum.'[42] This, like many of Sillars' criticisms over the years, contains a kernel of truth that has been blown out of all proportion. It is true that most policy areas do not engage Salmond beyond whatever tactical advantage they may offer over his opponents (energy is an exception); indeed, many former aides cannot recall ever having had a detailed policy discussion with their boss. As a result, Salmond does not appear to have thought very deeply about the fundamental nature of Scottish society, preferring to parrot clichéd lines about the superiority of Scottish education and the untouchability of the NHS.

In good economic times, that was not much of a problem, but the true test of a politician comes in the bad. Salmond remains convinced that the Irish model is still fundamentally sound, yet the people of Ireland face deep public spending cuts and a shrinking economy as a result of that model. Faced with similar challenges in a devolved Scotland, Salmond argues that similar cuts are unnecessary and are being imposed by the 'London parties'. This implies that he lacks a deep philosophy to fall back on – little that can guide his hand in good times and in bad – and a corresponding reluctance to reform public services or tackle vested interests. Salmond thus bears a degree of responsibility for what Brian Wilson identified as a 'debilitating weakness in Scottish politics': 'Because the politics of the constitution have become so predominant within Scotland . . . we are left with a choice between centrist consensus and referendums leading to separation. The victim of this unwelcome framework is creative or radical thought, which is what Scotland used to be good at. Everything has to be fitted into the strait-jacket of tedious constitutional debate.'[43] Tedious or not, Salmond is therefore at his weakest when trying to explain what Andrew Marr called the 'why' of independence, rather than the more easily articulated 'how'. As Jim Sillars has argued, 'he doesn't link his belief in independence with any sort of vision'.[44]

This is a tricky one. On one level Salmond's vision of what an independent Scotland would be like is clear – enterprising yet compassionate, statist but efficient – although on another it is, at best, vague and incomplete. 'Two years in office makes it clear that Alex Salmond has precious little idea what ought to follow should his demolition of the Union succeed,' was Tom Gallagher's uncompromising judgement in 2009. 'Alex Salmond wants to end the Union but he and most of his party have no ethical or practical vision which will enable them to construct a durable alternative.'[45]

It is what R. S. Thomas called 'the school and the inn and the church,/ The beginning, middle and end',[46] a holistic view of the world and how it can be improved. 'He doesn't have a view of Scotland, an alternative view of how Scotland would be run on becoming independent,' said one former aide. 'That's not what he's about, he doesn't sit there and think what's an independent Scotland going to look like, he sits there and thinks how he's going to get something through the next National Council meeting or get one over on his opponents. And it's only through the failure of the opposition parties that his lack of vision – beyond Scotland being a smaller version of any other state – hasn't been exposed.'

Once again, an Irish analogy is apt. 'The strength of Parnell was character rather than intellect',[47] judged T. P. O'Connor, while similarly John Morley called him a 'man of temperament, of will, of authority, of power, not of ideas or ideals, or knowledge or political maxims, or even of practical reason in its higher sense'.[48] Indeed, Jim Eadie believed that Salmond lacks Sillars' 'intellectual curiosity'. 'He's not someone who constantly reviews his position on issues,' he said, 'He knows what he believes, although he's very pragmatic with a capital "P".'[49] When faced with four years in which to reflect and rethink from 2000 to 2004, for example, Salmond did little of either, instead repackaging existing views in lecture and pamphlet form as the 'economics of independence'.

Instead he has focused throughout his career upon ideas, a few relatively simple ideas repeated often and usually with panache. Independence in Europe was one, while dramatically lowering corporation tax was another. 'I've always been focused on growth: responsible, environmentally sensitive, but sustainable growth,' he told *The Times* in 2010. 'Because growth enables society to be more cohesive.'[50] Yet Salmond shows scant interest in factors arguably making that society less cohesive. He says little or nothing about benefit dependency, giving the impression that he does not want to 'peer too deeply under the social surface in case what is discovered has a troubling and demotivating impact'.[51] As F. S. L. Lyons said of Parnell, 'what strikes one most about his opinions of other vital topics is not so much that they were conservative as that they were banal or even non-existent'.[52]

All of this comes back to Salmond's love of political tactics. 'Politics for him is a game of chess,' judged Kenny MacAskill in the mid-1990s. 'He doesn't burn with anger and rage about poverty in Scotland. It would be wrong to say he's not genuinely committed, but he's got no fire within him.'[53] Salmond's main preoccupation, therefore, has always been gaining and maintaining political momentum with an eye on the next electoral goal. 'Alex is a great believer in winning by just motoring on,' said a senior Nationalist. 'He's a lucky politician; he's Micawberish, he believes that something will always turn up in the end.'[54] Indeed, hopeful expectation runs through all three of Salmond's personas, the public aspect of which can apparently be changed at will, most memorably during the 2007 Holyrood election campaign.

What of the second Alex Salmond, the politician, colleague and employer? As leader of the Scottish National Party he has, like Harold Wilson, adopted an authoritarian style. 'The party is run along almost Stalinist lines,' said one senior Nationalist. 'Indeed old Josef could have learned a thing or two from Alex.'[55] Jim Sillars has also lamented that 'the SNP that once had a strong executive, and a membership with a collective intellectual apparatus capable of robust analysis of any policy advanced by the leadership, and able to challenge it, is no more ... The party is a vacuum the leadership fills with banalities. The SNP has members, branches, and meets all together on occasion, but to no avail. In blind faith they allow themselves to be led down silly paths. The members have allowed power to be transferred from them to a tiny group around the leader, whose policy pronouncements have all the unchallengeable authority of a papal bull.'[56]

This is an exaggeration. In truth, the SNP's policy-making heyday – a period extending roughly from the late 1960s until the mid-1970s – had long since passed by the time Salmond took over as leader in 1990. It is equally true, however, that he did little to revive it, instead initiating most policy-making himself while discouraging independent thought to the extent that his MSPs have uttered barely a word of criticism since he became First Minister in 2007.

Again, however, there is a curious reticence. Although Salmond has devoted considerable energy to revising policy positions he considers detrimental, for example on the monarchy, there has been no attempt to alter other, equally problematic, party lines such as the SNP's opposition to membership of NATO. 'He just doesn't want to pick fights where he doesn't have to because of the period in which he came through the party in the 1970s and '80s,' recalled a former aide. 'NATO has been discussed, certainly, but Alex is someone who looks for mood and momentum and he just doesn't want to disturb that.'[57]

Likewise with the internal structure of the SNP, all the more curious given Salmond's modernising zeal on Gordon Wilson's Commission of Inquiry in the mid-1980s. 'He could have gone much further with the party,' said another former staffer. 'He didn't go for one-member-one-vote, for example. John Swinney had to do that. He's never been interested in structures; he just doesn't regard them as important.'[58]

This conservatism sits strangely with a politician so willing to take calculated political gambles, a trait that straddles his public and political personas. Indeed, in an introduction to Ian Hamilton's account of the theft of the Stone of Destiny, Salmond wrote approvingly of those 'prepared to take individual risks in order to assert our national rights'.[59] This has been a major feature of his career, from his membership of the 79 Group, seeking the nomination for Banff and Buchan, going for the party leadership in 1990, denouncing the bombing of Kosovo and, most importantly, staking everything on the 2007 elections.

Salmond also shares Mrs Thatcher's affinity with his party faithful, a remarkable feel for what they want to hear and, more importantly, how far he can push them. He is almost held in awe by many activists, their sense of gratitude for his achievements effectively putting him beyond criticism. Even when Salmond resigned as leader in 2000, Andrew Wilson reckoned he had left a party 'immeasurably stronger than when he took over'. 'More Scots now trust the SNP, and therefore themselves, than ever before,' he added. 'They know that, whatever our faults, as Scotland's Party we work for what is best for our country. Our job is simply to build the confidence of the Scottish people in themselves. Alex personifies that confidence because he has to.'[60]

There is a lot of truth in that analysis, and it is perhaps a better summary of Salmond's legacy than any assessment of his electoral record would allow. Why, then, such pungent and regular condemnation from the likes of Jim Fairlie, Kenny MacAskill (in his pre-1999 guise) and Jim Sillars? Often they conflated genuine tactical disagreements with personal animosity, which in Sillars' case also sprang from resentment that his contribution to the creation of Salmond's public persona was seldom acknowledged. Indeed, Salmond remains a product of Sillars – in terms of speaking style, turn of phrase and political confidence – perhaps more than either would care to admit. Once they were close; now it seems that hell hath no fury like a mentor scorned. 'Among his most vociferous supporters ten years ago, you will find today his most vociferous opponents,' Sillars once reflected with obvious hurt, 'all of them wounded when they would not toe the leader's line, all discarded when they showed they had a mind of their own.'[61] Other veteran Nationalists have mixed views. 'I have a tremendous amount of respect for Alex and all that he's achieved,' was how one put it. 'I just don't like him very much.'[62]

For the younger generation, however, it is no exaggeration to describe Salmond as their hero. Another legacy is a whole succession of bright young things who typically started working for Salmond in his Peterhead constituency office, or at the House of Commons, before progressing through the ranks as advisers, spokespeople and, ultimately, MPs, MSPs and ministers. Andrew Wilson, for example, wrote to Salmond in the early 1990s asking if he could help out. 'I got this two-page hand-written letter back on how to go about it and within a year he'd made me, a spotty callow youth, a spokesman on Trident. He did that with certain people, fast-tracked them. No one showed me more kindness as a young activist.'[63] 'For those of us who were in the circle it was great,' recalled another of the chosen few, 'because we didn't have much experience of how grownups operated, and Alex made it very easy for us to learn and become more confident in our own abilities.'[64]

Salmond undoubtedly likes being surrounded by young, driven and, it has to be said, often star-struck, staffers. He is a devotee of *The West Wing*, a television series that follows the US president's senior staff and political advisers, a glamorous arena Salmond has emulated to the extent that one of his own aides, Jennifer Erickson, hails from the land of the free. His talent lies in being the leader of such a team, if not that effective a team player. 'Personally, his strength is loyalty towards individuals,' reflected John Swinney in 2001. 'His weakness I suspect is that he pushed people very very hard, but then he's a political leader.'[65] This is where an important, yet seldom acknowledged, aspect of Salmond's character comes into play. 'It clearly matters how a leader works – or cannot work – with his colleagues,' Andrew Rawnsley said of Gordon Brown, 'whether he responds to crises and setbacks calmly or in a hysterical fashion; and how he treats his staff.'[66]

There is no doubting that Salmond can, and frequently does, treat his staff appallingly. 'Some of the people who worked with him in his

Aberdeenshire office had a really rough time, a hard time,' recalled a senior Nationalist, 'but they survived, they came through. He was explosive in his rage but many of us can be.'[67] Salmond is a demanding boss and, if he feels a desired piece of work or project is not up to scratch, he can be merciless in his criticism. 'It's a crushing thing, a soul-destroying emotional train wreck for an individual,' recalled one former Westminster aide. 'It was draining. He would sit there and say: "This is what I require; this isn't what I asked for."'

Salmond's language, however, often goes beyond bland intimations of disappointment. Part of it is about letting off steam; another aspect is a genuine attempt to get the best out of people, but mostly it is just frustration at the inability of others to keep up with him. 'What he demands of people around him is their absolute best,' recalled another aide, 'which was the great thing about him because you brought yourself to meet his standards because he was never content with half an argument, or half a speech, or half an idea, so you had to work to his level which was a challenge. He has an idea of what he wants and where to take it and the staff's job was to give him the tools to do that. He does the politics and our job was to give him the tools or the facts to take his argument or speech forward. He's clear in his own mind what he wants.'[68] 'He is one of those people who pushes you to the frontiers of your ability,' agreed Andrew Wilson in 2000, 'both in thought and effort.'[69]

'Alex is a great motivator,' agreed Stephen Noon in 1999, 'because you know that however hard you work, he is working harder.' Noon also took this snapshot of Salmond in an office environment:

He will blaze at you for two minutes if you have done something wrong, but then it's forgotten. He also has a way of finding out what's going on in the office by leaving pauses which he knows you will fill. In your anxiety to fill the silence you can end up confessing everything, but I'm wise to this trick now. He has another annoying habit of asking a question he knows that you don't have the answer to; but he also encourages you to challenge him.[70]

Indeed, so challenging is Salmond that one former member of staff 'soon concluded that it wasn't actually possible to work for Alex *and* maintain a serious [outside] relationship'. Phone calls can come at every hour of the day, sometimes from his bath. His temper, however, is not completely irrational and, as some aides privately admit, more often than not he has a point. 'He doesn't harbour hatred and, believe it or not, he's not a particularly argumentative person,' said one. 'He doesn't pick fights for the sake of it.' Even if he does, an outburst is soon forgotten. 'Over time the bollockings don't get to you as much,' said another staffer, 'and you can differentiate the serious ones from the not so serious ones.'[71]

'He's not the kind of guy who bears a grudge,' observed yet another. 'At the time it can be very uncomfortable, but it's forgotten about the following day. He's quite willing to move on. He doesn't blow up over silly little things. It is quite pressured working for him; it's almost as if he's testing whether you're trustworthy or not . . . he expects you to have thought things out as deeply as possible, issues that might arise and also opportunities. He pushes people quite hard but not in an irrational or unreasonable way.'[72] The outbursts, perversely, are also an indication that an employee has Salmond's respect. 'If he's lost confidence in you then he stops being rude,' observed one. 'That's how you know.'[73]

The one thing Salmond cannot stand is a member of staff being insincere. 'He's very respectful if you stand your ground but he doesn't like bullshit,'[73] said a senior Nationalist. 'If he's unhappy you don't bullshit,' agreed an aide. 'You say "I don't know but I'll go away and find out". I think he appreciates people who are being frank. If you do bullshit he'll pursue it relentlessly, he'll play with you.'[75] As Andrew Marr once said, 'his expression combines challenging eye contact with a faintly mocking smile',[76] and indeed when Salmond is unhappy that turns into a 'really direct, deadly stare, he looks right at you'.[77] The Salmond stare, however, can go one of two ways. 'Sometimes his eyes are turned on you and they're fierce,' observed SNP MSP Christine Grahame in 2009, 'but sometimes they can be extremely charming.'[78]

Salmond, however, is no tyrant, self-aware ('I am difficult to work for,'[79] he once admitted) and just as capable of being warm. 'He's the most generous boss I've ever had,' recalled one former staffer. 'He regularly took all the staff out for dinner, and MPs and staff would socialise together on an equal basis. I once brought my mum to Parliament and he was brilliant with her. He can be, and is, just great company – always the centre of attention – but he has that charisma and people like to be with him when he's like that.' Even then, Salmond gives little away, even to his closest aides. 'He can be quite generous with his time, quite open, inclusive, and so on,' said one, 'but large parts of his life are unknown to the people that work with him.'[80]

Interestingly, those who knew Salmond well when he was a young man find it very difficult to reconcile the person he was then with accounts of how he can behave now. It is difficult to identify when the change took place, although his temporary expulsion from the SNP in 1982–83 must have been a key event, while a degree of ruthlessness was apparent by the time Salmond became publicity vice-convener in 1985. Even in 1989, however, he surprised many party colleagues with the vehemence of his attack on Isobel Lindsay following the SNP's departure from the Scottish Constitutional Convention. As leader from 1990, meanwhile, the rigours of party office, not to mention frequent attacks from internal and external opponents, must have hardened the Salmond shell even further.

Yet whatever the extremes, those who work for Salmond display quite remarkable loyalty, none more so than Kevin Pringle, who first joined the SNP in 1989. 'He's as close to the voice of Alex Salmond as you'll get,' said a senior Nationalist. 'He has Alex's total trust.'[81] Other advisers, for example Alex Bell, have even returned to his employ after a less than amicable relationship the first time round. 'He's OK, but, having worked together,' said Bell before the 2007 election. 'I think we're both happy not exchanging Christmas cards.'[82] Nevertheless, in mid-2010 Bell succeeded Stephen Noon as Salmond's senior policy adviser.

'There's some hero worship in there,' admitted one former aide, explaining: 'Alex is the politician's politician, so any aspirant politician would want to work with him and learn from him. I would go back tomorrow just because it was him and even if he wasn't leader. For people it's a positive choice to work with him, knowing full well what he can be like ... they all went to work with him because they want that positive spark.'[83] 'He's really one of the most amazing people I've ever worked for or will ever meet,' gushed another former staffer. 'I would not have the outlook or experiences I have now without him. In the four years I worked for him I experienced more than most people would in 20 years.'

This hero worship has its advantages for Salmond. As with Gordon Brown, to 'admirers, who include people on his staff at whom he has unleashed his furies, those volcanic rages are a price worth paying for his other qualities as a leader'.[84] 'Some are starry-eyed and they'll put up with a lot as a result,' observed a senior Nationalist. 'But he's less good at getting on with people as they get older. Perhaps it's because he hasn't had children so hasn't had to adjust how he deals with people as they age and mature. He's uncomfortable with that. When those bright young things become slightly older, fatter and perhaps less bright, they end up having a slightly sparkier relationship with Alex. He still enjoys being surrounded by them, but finds it difficult at the same time.'[85]

Despite innumerable tales of 'bollockings', public dressings-down and other verbal onslaughts, most take care to refer to Salmond's 'basic humanity'. 'I'm sure we've all had our knocks but that doesn't mean he's a bad person,' reflected Jim Eadie, who worked with Salmond at the House of Commons. 'I'm not a close confidante but despite that I don't subscribe to the view that he's a cold calculating machine.' He continued:

> For instance I left Westminster in 1996 to work for STV, but after eight months I got the sack. I remember Alex coming over to Millbank to see me and asking what had happened, "what's this about you losing your job?" I said it's just one of those things and he said "I think you're being very philosophical, do you want me to phone Gus [Macdonald, chairman of STV]?" I said no, and he said "if there's anything you want me to do, if you need a reference, if I can help in any way let me know and I will". He didn't need to do that, but not only was he commiserating with me but he was also offering to help. Now a cold calculating person would not have done that; others would have said "too bad", but not Alex.[86]

Salmond can also take such personal kindnesses to extremes. On his first visit to the US as First Minister, for example, he learned that his Washingston fixer, Alison Duncan, was suffering from cancer. 'She was bed bound,' remembered Colin Pyle, a former aide. 'He left his advisers, jumped in a cab, bought flowers, arrived at her door on the outskirts of DC, walked in (he knew she left the door open), stood in her lounge and sang an old Burns lullaby until she came down. She was startled to say the least ... but it gave her energy for months.'[87] 'There's a basic humanity there,' observed a staffer, 'and he's always a bit embarrassed if you catch him being nice.'[88] Being nice could, after all, be interpreted as vulnerability, as would conceding fallibility, something Salmond finds very difficult. As he one told the blogger Iain Dale, 'When you're First Minister you probably don't find it wise to own up to mistake after mistake'.[89]

One explanation for Salmond's behaviour is a need to demonstrate that he is in control of any given situation. At press briefings, for example, I have watched aides interrupt breathlessly, reminding him that a live interview or some other pressing engagement beckons.

Salmond does not flinch, instead carrying on and even prompting another question. It is a small thing, but it shows that he is in charge and will decide when it is time for him to go. 'He's also a media bully,' observed Lord Wallace. 'I remember an interview at Millbank when he was explosive with the producer once we'd finished recording, claiming that Donald Dewar had got more air time.'[90]

Indeed, one of my first professional experiences with Salmond illustrated that journalists are often treated no differently from staff members. Preparing to interview him after he had announced his comeback in 2004, my Grampian TV cameraman was presented with the leadership candidate's chewing gum, without so much as a polite request to dispose of it. Similarly, when an STV programme on which I worked wanted to question him about job losses at RAF Lossiemouth (in addition to a pre-agreed questions on other matters), he flew into a rage when I told him that for logistical reasons we could not pose the question to the Moray MP Angus Robertson, as he had requested. Following a torrent of abuse in the back seat of a taxi en route to the STV studios at Cowcaddens, Salmond strode into the building and refused to budge from the green room.

That said, he can also be incredibly charming, shooting the breeze at length, particularly if you engage him on something historical. Salmond, however, prefers the attention of London-based reporters, and particularly relishes jousts with media heavyweights like Jeremy Paxman. For a Nationalist, this is a paradox, and one very much in evidence during the row over televised leadership debates in April 2010. 'Whenever I come across him, or question him at a press conference, he always makes a big drama of it, going overboard about how delighted he is to see me or *Newsnight* there,' said Michael Crick, the programme's political editor. 'In Glasgow East [during the 2008 by-election] he came up and put his arm round me. It's always very flattering, but also highly embarrassing, and I was desperately hoping the scene hadn't been caught by any of my rivals on camera. It's clever tactics, as psychologically it makes it harder to ask tough questions. When I doorstepped him in Glenrothes [during the by-election] and said Labour had got him on the run, and asked if the Thud on their (fuel bills) leaflets, was the thud of a falling SNP vote, one could detect his bad temper and the darker side of his character.' 'He always strikes me as being like two thirds of high achievers,' concluded Crick, 'e.g. Jeffrey Archer, Sir Alex Ferguson, Peter Mandelson, etc., – in being a combination of extreme charm and extreme shitiness.'[91]

But however well Salmond gets along with individual journalists, they – like those who work for him – rarely get beyond a steely and occasionally ebullient façade. 'In the ten years that I've known Alex Salmond, I've hardly known him at all,' observed the *Scottish Sun*'s Andy Nicoll in 2000. 'Salmond has always been careful not to go out with the lads at party conference time, not to get drunk, never to give away confidences. He's a bit dark and a bit deep.'[92]

There is no doubting, meanwhile, that Salmond's political persona is incredibly hard-working. 'Oh definitely, that's never really been one of my faults,' he once said to Colin Mackay. 'I've never been slothful. There's plenty of the other deadly sins that I've been accused of but sloth and laziness hasn't been one of them.'[93] He is not, however, a morning person, preferring to begin the day at around 10 a.m. (one of the many reasons he preferred Westminster to Holyrood), only compromising should the *Today Programme* require an 8 a.m. interview, and then working into the small hours. Always a natural multi-tasker, Salmond works by telephone but is not a particularly good timekeeper, often keeping visitors waiting according to his erratic schedule. 'I am single-minded,' he once admitted, 'very bad at tearing myself away from the next deadline.'[94] Many are also struck by his incredible memory for dates and associated events.

'He's demanding but professional,' judged Sir John Elvidge, Salmond's first permanent under-secretary as First Minister. 'He's courteous, he's focused on the substance of the issue and wanting to find a way forward.'[95] At the outset, Salmond wants all the details relevant to the task at hand, although he will quickly decide what the pertinent ones are. And although he is supremely confident of his own judgement, he does have the ability to take alternative points of view on board, as long as they are well argued. There is also a stubborn streak, particularly noticeable once he has reached a decision. 'When you try to explain something to him he'll pick it up but get the wrong end of the stick,' said one economic adviser. 'It's then very difficult to say "No, Alex, you can't do that," his mind is made up.'[96]

Like de Gaulle, Salmond is comfortable with power and disconcertingly calm in a crisis. 'I've never seen Alex get worried, ever; he doesn't get worried, he gets focused,' recalled one former aide. 'Even during the Glasgow Airport stuff, foot and mouth, Trump and so on, he'd stay completely focused while everyone around him worried about it.'[97] Salmond displayed a similar quality as leader of the SNP from 1990 to 2000. 'When he hit adversity in his leadership he was the first person to bounce back with greater energy than before,' reflected John Swinney in 2000, '[that was] one of the great strengths of his leadership.'[98] Indeed, when Iain Dale asked Salmond if he was at all 'daunted' on becoming First Minister, 'I don't do daunted'[99] was his simple, and unequivocal response.

Salmond also enjoys the trappings of office, running it with the same iron grip that typifies his approach to the SNP. One widely-distributed memo, for example, reminded civil servants that material 'likely to be of significant interest to him' or 'that affects the First Minister's interests and the way in which his business is conducted' had to be cleared by his private office. The First Minister, meanwhile, 'often wants background notes and comparative data', while more generally, it was 'important that all our teams exercise care in support-ing the First Minister's interests and in communicating his views and future commitments'.[100] In meetings with civil servants, meanwhile, Salmond can go on a bit. 'He can be,' said one Scottish Government insider, 'a terrible pub bore.'[101] The First Minister certainly likes telling stories, most often about his earlier careers at the Scottish Office and Royal Bank of Scotland.

'I've been very fortunate. All my life I've enjoyed every job I've done, and I love being First Minister,' he told *The Times* in 2010. 'I love being in the first SNP government in history.'[102] There is also a side to Salmond that likes the helicopters, smart hotels and chauffeur-driven cars that go with the territory. He rarely walks more than a few yards, protesting that persistent back problems prevent train travel for any length of time. And even before he became First Minister, Salmond insisted upon staying at the Caledonian Hotel in Edinburgh and the Marcliffe in Aberdeen at SNP expense. As one former staff member remarked, 'the party paid for Alex Salmond in a way it never had with Gordon Wilson'.[103] That said, he has personally raised more money for his party than any other figure in its history, while criticisms of extrava-gance are hardly specific to the SNP or its leader.

There is also the frequent charge that Salmond is smug or arrogant. 'That smile – it has been called smug, cocky and self-delighted,' observed one newspaper profile, 'infuriates his opponents and exasper-ates his allies.'[104] His self-image, however, does not rely on thinking of himself as clever ('I don't go around counting my IQ'[105]), although he readily admits to confidence in his own abilities. 'To do what I'm trying to do,' he informed the journalist Julie Davidson in 1992, 'you need a good conceit of yourself.'[106]

Others believe Salmond has mellowed with age. 'Alex has the ability to put people's backs up,' commented Mike Russell in 2001, '[although] he doesn't do it as much as he used to.'[107] Iain Lawson, meanwhile, detected a change between his first period as leader and Salmond redux. 'I think Alex Salmond today is quite different from the Alex Salmond of before,' he said. 'He is much more responsible and realises that if he has big plans then he has to have big backers. He's changed. He's improved. I think he's got a lot of humour now – that wasn't a strong point the first time round – so he's learned to manage aspects of his personality. He can now laugh at himself and joke at his own expense, and I no longer see him as the slightly pompous guy he was earlier on.'[108] Indeed, a memorable turn by Salmond during the 2008 BBC Children in Need appeal, in which he acted the part of Rikki Fulton's gloom-laden Reverend I. M. Jolly, demonstrated a sense of humour together with a capacity for sending up not only himself, but by association aspects of the Scottish character. A far cry from what Grant Baird once said of his 1980s persona: 'If ever there was an old head on young shoulders, then it's Alex Salmond's.'[109]

What, then, of the real Salmond, the 'private and non-political Alex'? Writing in 1990, Charles Kennedy captured well the barrier that prevents most friends and colleagues delving that deeply: 'One assumes, almost hopes, that he shares his moments of indecision and doubt with his charming wife Moira; but to the rest of the world is displayed that impenetrable plate-glass visage, that piercing stare which always seems about to go one of two ways – towards coldness or laughter.'[110] As one senior Nationalist often asked: 'What's going on behind the eyes?'[111] The answer, at least according to Salmond, is not much. 'I don't tend to suffer from crises of confidence,' he once said. 'If I have moments of self-doubt they wouldn't be about politics.' So what had been his last non-political crisis, asked a reporter determined to penetrate the Salmond shell. 'Oh,' he murmured in response. 'I have doubts about all sorts of things.' Such as? 'They are personal, to do with beliefs and faith and things like that.'[112]

Again, it is difficult to resist a comparison with Parnell, who was 'neither expansive nor introspective'. 'It is one of the strongest and most curious peculiarities of Mr Parnell,' observed T. P. O'Connor, 'not merely that he rarely, if ever, speaks of himself but that he rarely, if ever, gives any indication of having studied himself . . . It is a joke among his intimates that to Mr Parnell the being Parnell does not exist.'[113]

The real Mr Salmond, of course, does exist; he is just largely hidden from view. Roseanna Cunningham reckoned his 'circle of friends [was] very tiny in the sense [of] people he would let his hair down with', while Isobel Lindsay thought there was something that prevented 'him from having a relationship of relaxed equality'[114] with those around him. 'Jim Sillars apart, I believe he has not looked upon anyone as a genuine equal for some time,' said someone who once knew him well. 'He regards his rightful place at the top of the tree and whilst he nurtures friendships, it is on his terms as leader.'[115]

Indeed, it is difficult to identify many close friends. He often golfs with what John MacLeod called 'his young and biddable aide, Geoff Aberdein, part-special counsel, part-Labrador',[116] as he does with Roger Cherry, his driver and 'unofficial bodyguard' who was even relocated to the north-east of Scotland in order to be closer to his boss. Durable friendships are rare – that with Stewart Stevenson is an exception to the rule – while some, such as that with Kenny MacAskill, have often resembled an emotional rollercoaster. There is also a curious reticence when he encounters friends from school or university, almost as if those parts of his life has been compartmentalised or shut off.

Paul Henderson Scott put this down to Salmond being 'hampered a little by shyness'. 'It makes for a certain awkwardness,' he added, 'or lack of spontaneous warmth, in his dealings with his immediate colleagues.'[117] Indeed, Clarissa Dickson-Wright was 'surprised to notice that for such an extrovert he is rather shy'.[118] There is also a touch of self-consciousness, particularly when it comes to his weight; something not helped by his habit of eating late. Indeed, television news crews are made aware that the First Minister does not like to be filmed getting out of his official car, while he has a habit of positioning himself during interviews so that the left – presumably superior – side of his face is to the fore. There are other, possibly nervous, habits. Whenever Salmond makes his entrance at a press conference or manifesto launch, for example, he always touches his nose with his right hand, as if he feels slightly exposed. Finally, there are indications of compulsive behaviour. He constantly chews gum, frequently washes his hands, and drinks too much Lucozade, a habit that goes back to his student days.

Perhaps Salmond's shyness can be traced back to his formative years at St Andrews University. 'The ego and the arrogance is the armour that you put on to survive in the harsh world of politics,' observed Jim Eadie. 'But I don't think that's who he is and in the world of St Andrews, for example, where you're surrounded by all these people who think they were born to rule, it's a defence Alex inevitably developed. More broadly, it's actually very unusual for someone from his background to be as confident as Alex.'[119] Similarly, another former aide got the impression that lurking in Salmond 'was something of the chippy, working-class boy who made it to St Andrews and has been determined to show how much cleverer he was than everyone else' ever since.[120]

Salmond's self-confidence, therefore, is not complete. Digging even more deeply, this aspect of his character was inevitably shaped by his obviously happy childhood. 'Everything Alex has said over the years suggests that he was brought up in a working-class, or lower-middle-class, Scottish family,' observed Isobel Lindsay, a political contemporary but also a professional sociologist. 'He clearly grew up with a very strong sense of Scottishness, and in certain respects he identifies that Scottishness with the working class because the few English accents he would have heard in those early years would have been on TV or radio, and they would also have been posher voices.'[121]

This also explains Salmond's intolerance of figures like Michael Forsyth, someone who – like him – came from a modest background but – unlike Salmond – chose to align himself with the irredeemably English and middle-class Conservative Party. Yet paradoxically he clearly enjoys the company of men of means, as did Tony Blair and Peter Mandelson, although Salmond leans more towards self-made men – such as Sir George Mathewson and Dennis MacLeod – rather than those with inherited wealth. That said, he has obvious admiration for Prince Charles, and is clearly comfortable with elements of the Scottish Establishment.

Here the Parnell analogy grinds to a halt, with nothing from Salmond's childhood – beyond his grandfather's suicide – leaning towards the unconventional. Almost everything about his family background was relatively normal, from the close-knit family to his schooling at Linlithgow Academy and regular attendance at the Church of Scotland. 'He's incredibly well-rooted,' notes one former aide. 'He has a pretty fixed world view and is quite extraordinarily non-judgemental in terms of morality.'[122] As Salmond himself explained: 'I had a strong church upbringing which I think has been invaluable to me in terms of a moral compass – of some idea of what's acceptable and what is not acceptable. I have a Presbyterian nature in that I like its ideas of individual responsibility and democracy. I'm naturally suspicious of people who wear religion heavily on their sleeves – that's just not me and my style.'[123]

Salmond, in short, was well brought up, and has an instinctive desire to help the underdog, be it small, relatively defenceless nation or a constituent in distress. Colleagues remember him helping out an obviously confused John Hume, the former SDLP leader, in the House of Commons, while Salmond himself tells the story of encountering a similarly bewildered Baroness Thatcher at a Remembrance Sunday event. His chief influence in this respect appears to have been his mother Mary. 'I remember Alex saying how much he respected other men who admitted being close to their mum,' recalled Colin Pyle. 'Perhaps because it meant they were probably a big softie at heart. He clearly grew up loving both his parents but was particularly close to his mum.'[124]

Salmond has, quite naturally, sought to recreate that stable and loving background in his own domestic life. Key to that is his home in Strichen and, of course, his wife. 'He's intensely protective of Moira, not for his own sake, but for hers,' said a close colleague. 'Every time there's a story about her [in the newspapers], it just reinforces to him that he's done the right thing in not parading her in public. As a result, it's been a remarkably durable marriage, unusually so in politics.'[125] 'I don't use my family as a prop in politics,' as Salmond once said. 'I've never done it, I don't approve of it, and I'm not going to start it.'[126]

Moira is equally protective of her husband, ensuring he looks presentable and even warning journalists not to give him a hard time in interviews. 'Moira is his principal gauge of people's character,' said Colin Pyle, 'of those he meets and may need to trust. She is a good judge of people and he relies on that judgement all the time. You underestimate Moira at your peril.'[127] Another former aide concurred: 'She's very kind and generous and very good at looking after people. He enjoys sneaking out for the very occasional cigarette and behaves a bit like a naughty schoolboy; he doesn't want Moira to find out and won't have another one for ages if she does. Moira would suspect he had done so and tell him off. There is something of the cheeky lad in him that enjoys sneaking out for a cigarette behind his wife's back.'[128]

'I think it's been hard, in fact it must be hard for any politician's wife,' said a former aide of the transition from protest to power in 2007. 'She believes in him, she's his number one fan, his confidante. Moira believes in her husband and the party, but she doesn't miss a trick. I know it's cheesy but behind every good man there's a strong woman, and that's certainly the case with Alex.'[129] There is no whiff, meanwhile, of marital infidelity, no Kitty, as was the case with Parnell.[130]

The journalist Alan Taylor once painted an idyllic, almost pastoral vision of Salmond's non-political life: 'He and Moira have a house in Strichen and they are often in the north-east at weekends, revelling in its thrawn humour and wind-blasted landscape ... On Saturday lunch-time he is usually to be found dining on fish and chips at the Pennan Inn, meeting, greeting and watching the North Sea waves roll in.'[131] Colleagues rarely see the inside of Salmond's north-east base, Mill o' Strichen, which many consider to be his 'haven', to which he can with-draw from the media glare (although he is often interviewed outside) and craft his memoirs.

Salmond also enjoys the familial atmosphere of certain restaurants, be it the Champany Inn in Linlithgow or Top Curry Centre in Pimlico. 'He likes going back again and again to these family-run places,' said a close colleague. 'He likes the familiarity of being known.'[132] Salmond is also, contrary to some accounts, comfortable around children despite having none of his own. Mike Russell, for example, recalled having lunch with his wife, son Cailean, Alex and Moira in Callander shortly after a 1994 by-election. 'He and Cailean (aged 9) went missing shortly afterwards, to be discovered in an amusement arcade,' recounted Russell. 'There was a horseracing machine in the centre of the room, and there was Alex intro-ducing Cailean to the mysteries of betting and the sport of Kings.'[133]

'The twist in the whole Salmond tale/tail is that despite the image and the criticism from some he is actually softer, warmer and much more normal than anyone ever believes,' said someone close to him. 'Intellectually he is just faster than most and has taken so much shit from internal and external opponents that he has toughened up.'[134] Little of this warmth, however, reaches the electorate, although there is scant evidence that voters consider Salmond at all aloof. 'Is there a limit to the amount people should know about politicians?' a jour-nalist once asked him. 'I'm in the public eye,' he replied. 'I have never whined or moaned about anything and I don't intend to start whining or moaning now.'[135] 'Alex is actually very substantial but doesn't get that across,' said a senior Nationalist with genuine frustra-tion. 'Instead he does the cheeky chappie routine, which he's not very good at.'[136]

Salmond has, of course, often contrived to reveal something of himself. 'I suspect that most people like to see their politicians with an element of hinterland,' he reflected in 2005, 'the suggestion that we are aware that there is more to life than politics. It makes politicians seem, if not normal, then at least human.'[137] Like Parnell, Salmond avoids the arts and points instead to the less cerebral pleasures of the turf. 'Take away politics and golf,' he said in 1997, 'and horse-racing would be my favourite pastime.'[138] However carefully constructed that comment, the sport of kings is clearly a genuine passion, as is golf and football, his team since childhood being Heart of Midlothian.

The young Alex, meanwhile, clearly valued the music of Paul Robeson and the poetry of R. S. Thomas, whose poems he still re-reads and can quote verbatim. Yet his taste in popular culture is almost charmingly middle-of-the-road. He adores country and western music ('I am a devotee of Tammy Wynette'[139]), avidly watches television series like *Miss Marple* but reads little, limiting himself to political novels by Julian Critchley and narrative history by the likes of Stephen Runciman and Arthur Schlesinger Jnr. He has no demonstrable interest in art beyond the paintings of Gerard Burns, one of which hangs in his Holyrood office, or in theatre, beyond Gregory Burke's *Black Watch*, in which he features, or even cinema, apart from Westerns and Mel Gibson's *Braveheart*.

There is also a geeky quality to Salmond, and not just politically. He 'has a video library of political footage dating back to the 70s',[140] which he often re-watches as if to track his progress, while he has been known to spend Parliamentary recesses reliving old general election nights courtesy of BBC Parliament. His is also, by his own admission, a *Doctor Who* fan as well as an 'obsessive Trekkie'. '*Voyager* was my favourite, that and first series *Star Trek*,' he admitted to the *Radio Times*. 'I've seen them all so many times.'[141] Alan Taylor identified this 'trainspotterish' quality in a 2000 newspaper profile, an 'ability to move from discussing the intricacies of the ERM to the fortunes of Heart of Midlothian, his favoured football club'.[142]

Whatever the extent of these private passions, John MacLeod thought they exuded 'an air that is determinedly anti-intellectual'.[143] This is also reflected in Salmond's Holyrood office, which one journalist noted was 'spartan to the point of frugality'. 'No dreary Victorian canvases of Highland stags, no portraits of long dead nationalist heroes,' observed Andrew Collier, 'just an overblown photograph of some Scottish children at play, [a] couple of trophies on a shelf and a rather lonely looking blue vase. You'd never confuse it with the Oval Office.'[144]

What, then, drives Alex Salmond? There is no doubt that it is an instinctive belief in Scottish independence, however loosely defined. 'The utter, implacable certainty of his convictions,' thought Charles Kennedy in 1990, 'the self assuredness of his stance, is what fuels him along.'[145] Indeed, Mike Russell said walking down a street with Salmond was like witnessing 'a crusade to personally convert every Scottish voter'.[146] When that fundamental point is grasped and accepted – something that is often difficult for the uninitiated to do – most other aspects of Salmond's character fall into place. As Andrew Wilson put it, he 'could have made a fortune as one of the most talented economists of his generation, but he chose public service. He could have been a Labour Cabinet minister or leader, but he chose a cause that wants power for his country, not for himself. In a cynical, political world, his legacy has been selfless service to party and country before personal gain.'[147]

Although overblown, this captures much of what Salmond is about. The result is an element of frustration about what might have been, an alternative career in academia or the City of London that might have brought plaudits, influence and better pay without the frequent personal attacks. But such thoughts occur only in weaker moments. As Duncan Hamilton observed in 2000: 'It couldn't be any other way – politics is what makes Alex tick, it is what excites him and defines him.'[148]

Legacy, meanwhile, is uncommonly important to Salmond, even for a politician. 'What's his driving force?' asked a long-standing associate rhetorically. 'Leaving something useful behind. Remember that he's childless. I just think he wants not to leave nothing.'[149] That said, and given Salmond's rooted sense of himself, it is likely he could exist outside the political sphere. 'I don't think he's obsessed,' said one former aide. 'If something happened tomorrow and he ceased to be First Minister he'd be able to lead quite a happy life. I think he'd miss it but he could go and lecture in the United States, perhaps go into business, but whatever he did it would involve promoting Scotland.'[150]

Let us not forget that Salmond identified as a young man with Iago Prytherch, the fictional hill farmer who helped the poet R. S. Thomas understand himself through his questionings and doubts. Yet Prytherch never gave his creator the whole answer, instead labouring in the same field upon the Welsh hills, just as Salmond has toiled on the Scottish political landscape for more than three decades, 'endlessly ploughing'. Even after he is gone and history has made its judgement, Salmond's presence will still be felt, 'never absent' in the story of the SNP and the wider National Movement, although

> there is no applause
> For his long wrestling with the angel
> Of no name. I can see his eye
> That expects nothing, that has the rain's
> Colourlessness. His hands are broken
> But not his spirit. He is like bark
> Weathering on the tree of his kind.
> He will go on; that much is certain.[151]

Postscript 'a change is coming'

History, which is the study of mankind in Time, is often said to teach us nothing. It is certainly a poor guide for snap predictions. Pundits and journalists who wish to know what will happen in the next six months need not bother. Yet time brings change, and change brings the prospect of growth or decay . . . For the one thing that History does teach us is that all power is transient, all success ephemeral.

Norman Davies, *Heart of Europe: A Short History of Poland*[1]

Albert Sorel divided politicians into two groups: those 'who seek to change the world to suit their ideas' and those 'who seek to modify their actions to suit the world'.[2] He was thinking of Montesquieu, but Alex Salmond certainly belongs in the latter group. The aphorism, meanwhile, is particularly apt when it comes to the SNP leader's interpretation of 'independence'. Paradoxically, the party's main strength since Salmond's comeback in 2004 has been organisational; even after four years in government it remains comparatively weak on political philosophy.

To its credit, the SNP did not try to claim that the 2011 Holyrood election result represented an overwhelming mandate for independence. Despite a relatively low turnout,[3] Salmond argued that it *was* a mandate for devolving more powers, and he redirected his political energies accordingly. 'Full fiscal responsibility', his priority since the previous August, was put on hold, while the Scotland Bill, hitherto dismissed as 'dangerous' and a 'Tory trap', was talked up as a 'substantial' piece of legislation in need of amendment.

Although an independence referendum was now – unlike in 2007–11 – a definite prospect, it remained a distant one. The likely date of the referendum had, during the long election campaign, got further away. Initially, Salmond said he had made a mistake by outlining a timescale in the previous Parliament, but by the end of the campaign he had pledged that a referendum would not be held until the 'second half' of the next five-year-long session, while just days before polling he let it be known that it would be later still, 'well into' the second half of that term.

Why the shift? It was, in essence, what Professor John Curtice called 'an implicit acknowledgement of failure'.[4] Salmond had always argued that once the SNP demonstrated competence in government, support for independence could only increase. That strategy did not work. While the 2011 Scottish Election Study (SES) revealed that the SNP had won the election primarily because it was perceived as 'competent', that perception had not translated into increased support for 'independence'. It depended, as ever, how the question was asked, but the SES found support for 'independence' at just 24 per cent, with the status quo and greater powers tied on 38 per cent.[5] (It should be noted that three polls conducted after the election put support for independence at 37, 39 and 35 per cent respectively, demonstrating an apparent upward trend.[6])

In short, the SNP had not managed to build majority support for independence during four years in government, so it made sense to hold off on a referendum for as long as possible. Salmond justified this by saying he had given a pledge during the election while later arguing that his immediate priorities were jobs and the economy. In other words, the party's position had moved from believing that when it did not have a majority (2007–11) there ought to have been a referendum, but now it did have overall control of Parliament, there was no rush.

This did not stop Salmond claiming just days after the election that 'the destination of independence is more or less inevitable', while adding that the timing was 'entirely a matter for the Scottish people',[7] when of course the opposite was true. The delay also exposed, as STV's political editor Bernard Ponsonby argued, 'that no serious thinking has been done on this subject [independence] in over two decades.'[8] Not since Jim Sillars had reorientated SNP policy towards 'Independence in Europe' had the party grappled with the limitations of Scottish sovereignty in an ever-changing UK, European and global context. Delaying the referendum until 2014 or 2015 gave Salmond much-needed breathing space to do precisely that.

But there were early signs that redefining independence would not be easy. Salmond, to be fair, had since the 1990s done much, if only in rhetorical terms, to flesh out his version of independence, but keeping the party on board was a different matter. Within days of the election, the SNP had floated the concept of 'independence-lite', whereby Scotland would assume full economic sovereignty but 'pool' areas such as defence and foreign affairs with the UK government. This 'thinking on independence', claimed a spokesman, was 'modern and forward looking', unlike 'old-fashioned and backward looking' Unionism.[9] Talk of shared services, however, conveniently ignored the UK dimension. Certain services could only be pooled if both parties agreed, and it was not clear why the rest of the UK (or rUK as some took to calling it) would feel compelled to do so.

There was also movement on the Scotland Bill, the UK government's legislative response to the cross-party Calman Commission (boycotted by the SNP, à la the Scottish Constitutional Convention in 1989). Although it fell far short of devolving the sort of powers Salmond desired, it did at least move in that direction, so actually voting against the Bill's Third Reading on 21 June put the SNP in a quandary. So the party U-turned, although hardly anyone noticed. 'We got away with that,' recalled an adviser, 'but it was like a Gilbert and Sullivan opera, an interesting little diversion that we had to engage with but it didn't really matter. It had no punter traction at all.'

Salmond instead argued the legislation ought to be given 'economic teeth' and additional powers for which, he claimed, there was cross-party support, an extension of his characteristic big tent, or 'big bothy'[10] approach. The so-called 'Salmond Six' embraced everything from broadcasting to excise duty, greater borrowing powers, corporation tax, revenue from the Crown Estate and increased representation for Scottish ministers at EU level.[11]

The UK government, having already promised not to put 'obstacles in the way of any referendum',[12] swiftly compromised on borrowing powers and later announced plans for Treasury-run coastal town funds using Crown Estate assets. Initially, it looked as if Whitehall (having conceded the possibility in Northern Ireland) might also have to compromise on corporation tax, but when the province's First Minister Peter Robinson reminded everyone that lowering the tax would mean a vastly reduced tax take (estimated at around £2.6 billion), the SNP retreated. (Curiously, although Salmond already had control over one major business tax – business rates – he had shown no inclination to pull that 'lever' in order to create a more competitive economy.)

On everything else UK ministers were, for the moment, immovable, demanding detailed proposals from the Scottish Government, which, tellingly, had to be commissioned rather than extracted from a file. Supported by heavyweight figures like Sir Tom Farmer, the resulting paper on corporation tax sheepishly conceded that all options 'would require financing, at least in the short term'.[13] In his first substantive speech following the election, Scottish Secretary Michael Moore accused Scottish Ministers of appearing to 'lack interest in the powers they do have while being obsessed with powers they don't have'. Moore also felt compelled to point out that Scotland had 'two govern- ments – distinct, elected and legitimate',[14] an assertion that betrayed Salmond's dominance of the Scottish political agenda.

It was, too, an indication that David Cameron's government had been caught off guard, lacking, as it did, an holistic constitutional narra- tive. Cartoonist Martin Rowson captured the dynamic well in the *Guardian*, depicting Cameron and George Osborne celebrating their local government gains and AV referendum win atop the crumpled remains of Liberal Democrats while seemingly unaware of Salmond's massive face looming behind them.

For several weeks following 5 May, Salmond got momentum out of very little: pre-planned inter-governmental meetings became summits on his demands for additional powers, at which he waved his 'majority around like a club'.[15] The First Minister also talked repeatedly of 'moving towards independence' while stressing how 'reasonable' his demands were, which by implication meant the UK government would be 'unreasonable' to refuse them. Furthermore, Salmond optimistically predicted that if Osborne said 'no' to the Salmond Six, then the Chan- cellor would 'vastly accelerate the movement of Scotland toward independence'.[16]

Salmond was at least consistent, having argued throughout his lead- ership of the SNP 'that you should welcome any addition to the Scottish Parliament's power and authority while still looking for getting the key powers'.[17] So-called 'fundamentalist' Nationalists had long faded into obscurity, while one of them, Jim Sillars, even endorsed independence- lite in the *Scotsman*. 'Alex Salmond is now in the world of the politics and the art of the possible, not the politics of perfection,' he wrote. 'There is no point in being as pure as the driven snow.'[18]

Having won two elections in a row also meant Salmond's authority within the party was complete. His judgement had brought the party thus far, so why not – reasoned even sceptical activists – stay on board for the next five years? 'Mr Salmond will decide,' observed Ian Bell the day after the election. 'That has become the singular, overarching fact of Scottish politics. His authority is as near absolute now as it could be. He has no rivals in sight, in any party.'[19]

Eager to maintain an air of business as usual, Salmond chose to keep most of his senior ministers *in situ* while promoting Alex Neil and Bruce Crawford to the Cabinet. At Holyrood, meanwhile, the SNP not only dominated its committee system (as was their right), but a Nationalist MSP, Tricia Marwick, was elected the Scottish Parliament's fourth Presiding Officer. The Labour MSP Hugh Henry – who had hoped to occupy that chair himself – invoked Lord Hailsham when he warned of an 'elected dictatorship'. Similarly, the new Scottish Liberal Democrat leader Willie Rennie spoke repeatedly of Salmond's 'steamroller government'.[20]

Indeed, despite considerable goodwill, the new administration's first 100 days was poorly planned (in stark contrast to 2007) and marred by repeated accusations that Salmond had allowed an unprecedented mandate to go to his head; the *Scotsman*, for example, reckoned the SNP had 'hit the ground jogging'.[21] A long-running spat over the UK Supreme Court's right to consider Scottish criminal appeals (under Human Rights legislation), meanwhile, revealed the First Minister at his worst.

Although an argument eventually emerged (a judicial anomaly whereby English courts were not subject to the same procedure), the First Minister lashed out, erroneously claiming that 'Scots Law has never been subordinate to any other legal system'[22] (there was, of course, such a thing as UK and European law), while personalising the debate into 'Lord Hope's law', a reference to the Supreme Court Justice at the centre of the row.[23] Salmond was also forced to defend Justice Secretary Kenny MacAskill's remark about Scottish Government funding for the Supreme Court ('he who pays the piper, as they say, calls the tune'[24]), although privately those words had angered him. Still Salmond dug and, with a rambling outburst in *Holyrood* magazine, dug deeper, losing a hitherto sympathetic media in the process, not to mention the Law Society of Scotland and Faculty of Advocates (who issued a strongly-worded joint statement). The First Minister appointed a committee, which took no evidence, and eventually accepted a face-saving compromise. Lord Steel quit a Scottish Government advisory panel in protest at the 'deteriorating tone' of some ministers,[25] while the *Scotsman* mischievously published an unflattering picture of the First Minister under the headline: 'Sneering and arrogant? Who, me?'[26]

The Scottish Government's decision, in the face of significant opposition, to push through anti-sectarian legislation by the summer recess risked
being perceived in a similar light. Salmond, never impervious to honest
advice, realised that and staged a tactical retreat, delaying the Bill until the
end of 2011 to allow for more consultation. Kevin Pringle later suggested
this demonstrated the 'Prestonfield Principle' in practice, a reference to the
First Minister's earlier claim that although the SNP had a majority, it did
'not have a monopoly on wisdom'.[27] Always capable of switching his character when political circumstances dictated, Salmond had once again
become Mr Consensual following more than a month as Mr Angry.

'A change is coming, and the people are ready,' Salmond informed the
Scottish Parliament in his first speech after the election.

> Whatever changes take place in our constitution, we will remain close to
> our neighbours. We will continue to share a landmass, a language and a
> wealth of experience and history with the other peoples of these islands.
> My dearest wish is to see the countries of Scotland and England stand
> together as equals.

'There is a difference between partnership and subordination,' he added
with uncharacteristic language. 'The first encourages mutual respect.
The second breeds resentment.'[28]
That a majority of Scots felt either resentful or subordinate was, of
course, debatable, but the 'change is coming' line had been an example
of the First Minister's technique of stressing the 'inevitability' of something that was not inevitable at all. 'Will it happen?' Salmond asked the
Foreign Press Association rhetorically. 'I am an optimist, and we have
history on our side. In 1945, the UN was founded with just 51 member
countries. Today there are nearly 200.'[29]
This was broad-brush stuff, but the election result meant the SNP
had to paint a more detailed picture of 'independence' than ever before,
for if they did not their opponents would do it for them, and most likely
in 'fundamentalist' terms. Any cursory reading of Salmond's speeches,
and indeed Scottish Government publications between 2007 and 2011,
revealed that 'independence' was no longer that clear cut. 'Politics in
stable democracies involves shadings rather than absolutes,' observed
Professor James Mitchell. 'Shocking as it may be for some, we may be
looking towards a future in which accommodation is found between
union and independence.[30]

As the historian Colin Kidd argued in an important 2008 book, *Union and Unionisms: Political Thought in Scotland 1500–2000*, the two traditions – Nationalism and Unionism – had more in common than either cared to acknowledge. Just as the SNP had a tradition of 'Unionist' thinking (its original aim had been Imperial Federation), the Conservative Party contained a strain of small 'n' Nationalism, from its 1949 policy document *Scottish Control of Scottish Affairs* to Edward Heath's 'Declaration of Perth' in 1968. As the blogger Alex Massie argued, the 'better kind of Unionism – the confident type – can accept nationalist tools (Home Rule, greater fiscal responsibility) while putting them to Unionist ends (rendering independence unnecessary)'.[31]

Surprisingly, the former Conservative Prime Minister Sir John Major did precisely that in a speech some suspected to be a 21st-century echo of Herbert Gladstone's 1885 'Hawarden Kite' on Irish Home Rule, urging the UK government to implement some form of 'devo-max'. The SNP's election performance, meanwhile, had set the parameters for the race to replace Annabel Goldie (for whom Salmond had genuine respect) as Scottish Conservative leader, as well as that to succeed Iain Gray as Labour's leader of the opposition. Proving that it was a two-way process, the SNP blogger and policy chief Stephen Noon increasingly deployed Unionist rhetoric, talking of pursuing a 'true union of equals',[32] while detailed surveys of the SNP's leaders and membership demonstrated that both were relaxed about subtle accommodations with the *ancien régime*.[33]

Many 'Unionists', however, continued to think in primary colours in the wake of the election result. Although David Cameron called on opponents of independence to 'make an uplifting and optimistic case'[34] for the United Kingdom, by the autumn of 2011 the Coalition's 'Quad' (a policy-making quartet comprising Cameron, George Osborne, Nick Clegg and Danny Alexander) had agreed a 'shift in gear' that involved dire (and hardly original) warnings about the costs and instability independence might bring. Reports suggested a 'Scottish task force' had been convened to 'combat moves towards independence',[35] but it seemed probable they were gearing up for the wrong fight. As Stephen Noon observed in his blog, 'they will be arguing against independence in a way that ignores the reality of what independence would be. They will be attacking so-called separatism when separatism is not on the agenda.' Noon quoted a 2007 speech by Salmond in which he said the 'current parliamentary and political Union would become a monarchical and social union – *United Kingdoms rather than a United Kingdom* [my italics] – maintaining a relationship first forged in 1603 by the Union of the Crowns.'[36]

In other words, the SNP wanted to reconstitute the United Kingdom rather than break it up, as the Unionist caricature still had it. Professor Mitchell's feeling, based on interviews with around 80 senior Nationalists, was that the party's 'notion of independence' was 'in transition'.

> I think we're going to move to an ever looser Union, that's what the SNP will understand; there will always be a United Kingdom in some shape or form. The SNP isn't yet ready to say that, but that's where they're heading, I suspect [to] a more confederal type relationship. Maybe, maybe this election result will give the SNP leadership the courage to say what I believe they already think.[37]

Indeed, Nicola Sturgeon insisted there had been 'no fundamental shift in thinking' on independence within the SNP.[38] Salmond, however, was more frank. 'The SNP, for some time, has been presenting our case for independence in a way which reflects the realities of the modern world,' he told the BBC shortly after the election. 'The resumption of independence is the resumption of political and economic sovereignty. How you then choose to exercise that sovereignty reflects the inter-relationships with principally the other countries in these islands.'[39]

Gerry Hassan called this 'post-nationalism', whereby the SNP had embraced 'a politics of nationhood shaped by shared sovereignty, alliances and flexibility and fluidity'.[40] Salmond and his party were well aware of the international precedents, not least Ireland, which had gradually decoupled itself from the UK over three decades. When Queen Elizabeth opened the new Holyrood session in July 2011, Salmond quoted her recent speech at Dublin Castle, in which she had celebrated 'the ties between our people, the shared values, and the economic, business and cultural links that make us so much more than just neighbours, that make us firm friends and equal partners'. Whatever constitutional path Scotland chose to take, he added, 'we will aspire to be, in your words, "firm friends and equal partners".'[41]

Yet the monarchy neatly illustrated the tensions within Salmond's view of independence. The First Minister's eloquent – and it has to be said, bold – speech in front of his monarch ('your predecessors reigned over two sovereign nations – and there was nothing particularly unusual in that arrangement') maintained the impression that SNP policy was to retain the Queen following independence, when in fact it was to hold another referendum on who ought to be head of state. When the journalist Kenny Farquharson asked the party if its September 1997 conference decision still stood, he was rightly surprised to be told that the independence referendum now included 'the long-standing policy for the Queen and her successors to be head of state'. This 'long-standing policy', Farquharson was told, dated 'back to the founding of the SNP in 1934',[42] which was true, although that conveniently skirted over subsequent conference resolutions. Salmond had simply jettisoned a party position he had never been comfortable with, and in keeping with the SNP's extraordinary post-2007 discipline, there was no internal criticism, not even from known republicans like the Environment Minister Roseanna Cunningham, who had, after all, proposed the 1997 conference resolution.

Since his meeting with the Prince of Wales in 1998, Salmond had been an enthusiastic, even fawning, monarchist. He had attended the wedding of Prince William and Kate Middleton during the election campaign ('I should have had this entire city [Edinburgh] covered in royal standards' he told an interviewer regretfully), and regularly gushed about the selfless devotion of the present 'Queen of Scots'. This led to some curious statements. 'There is a better case for an English republic than a Scottish one,' he told *Prospect* magazine. 'I'm not saying Scotland is a classless society, but I still think inequalities in Scotland are not generally linked to the monarchy.'[43]

Defence also emerged as a policy area on which the SNP was weak. Pathologically incapable of being seen to 'cut' anything, the party got itself into a position of simultaneously arguing for some kind of Scottish defence force, pooling resources with the UK Ministry of Defence (indeed, it argued the MoD's Scottish footprint ought to be bigger) – except for Trident – while making it clear it would not commit Scottish troops to any 'illegal wars'. Christopher Harvie called it 'military Unionism', and indeed it smacked of loving 'both the cake and the eating', as Ian Jack put it: 'no to Trident and ludicrous post-imperial pretension, yes please to aircraft carriers and RAF fighter bases on the east coast'.[44] Indeed, Salmond was in Panglossian mode, zealously seeking the best of all possible worlds.

When UK Defence Secretary Liam Fox unveiled plans to base a multi-role brigade of the British Army outside Edinburgh, he argued it would 'strengthen the union', while Salmond hailed 'Scotland's army returning us to where we should rightfully be'.[45] Stephen Noon believed Fox had made a 'strategic error', making it 'significantly easier to make the independence case'. 'The old argument that Scotland would have to create an army from scratch has disappeared,' he blogged. 'We will have one, it will be there for all to see, created and located right here in Scotland.'[46]

On Europe, too, the SNP moved cautiously. Rejecting federalist thinking that advocated harmonising taxes across Europe, the party ruled out both a separate Scottish currency and immediate membership of the Euro, instead making it clear that keeping Sterling was the most 'stable' option, although this begged obvious questions about just how independent a state could be if its currency was administered from London (or indeed Brussels).[47] What would stop London demanding absolute harmonisation of Edinburgh's fiscal policy to avoid destabilisation of Sterling? The Eurozone crisis had made the independence argument harder in more ways than one.

The currency, defence and pro-monarchy stances were, of course, about closing down potentially disastrous 'Unionist' attacks in the run-up to the referendum. Professor Robert Hazell of the Constitution Unit highlighted the 'potential fuzziness' in such a position. 'Defence, macroeconomic policy and foreign affairs are key features of statehood,' he pointed out. 'Does the SNP want Scotland to be independent or not?'[48] But by stressing such continuity, Salmond was attempting to guide moderate Scottish opinion towards viewing independence as no big deal. His concept of a 'social union', which was little more than a statement of the obvious, did likewise, although SNP strategists were conscious that this strategy could be a double-edged sword: if the party kept stressing how consistent the new Scotland would be with the old, then there was a risk voters would shrug and ask 'what's the point?'

Equally, of course, the electorate might bite the bullet and think, 'well, why not?' and, in this respect, Salmond had been responsible for some significant shifts. Whereas the independence debate had once hinged on economic feasibility, by 2007–11 it was more to do with its desirability, most opponents having accepted that an independent Scotland could pay its own way. Even more importantly, as demonstrated by two successive Holyrood elections, Salmond had managed to persuade thousands of Unionists that it was 'okay' to vote for the SNP. 'The SNP's every modern success,' judged the journalist Euan McColm, 'stems from the First Minister's brilliant salesmanship of the idea that a vote for them is not necessarily a vote for the break-up of the United Kingdom.'[49]

Even so, the SNP still had to explain to Scottish voters exactly where devolution ended and independence began. Towards the end of May

2010 the Scottish Government re-published its 2009 constitutional white paper *Your Scotland, Your Voice* to remind voters and commentators that it had been considering these issues. That paper (by its own admission, neither 'exhaustive' nor including any 'commitments to future action'[50]), however, simply spelled out the difference between the Calman recommendations, 'devo-max' and independence without defining precisely what the last option would look like.

The constitution, observed John Swinney's former adviser Ewan Crawford, was 'one area where work needs to be done'. 'The SNP has started to define independence as being, in part, about winning job-creating powers,' he wrote in the *Scotsman*. 'This message needs to be reinforced.'[51] Similarly, the former MSP Duncan Hamilton said the 'SNP will, and must, define and explain independence . . . That task will keep the SNP fully occupied.'[52] The party's research from the summer of 2010 would continue to inform how that could be achieved and, if shrewdly handled, it would pay electoral dividends. The Labour politician Herbert Morrison once said that socialism was whatever the Labour Party did; by 2011, 'independence' was whatever the SNP – or more accurately what Alex Salmond – said it was. It just seemed a little odd it had taken the party so long to spell it out.

One of Alex Salmond's favourite films was said to be Michael Ritchie's 1972 political satire *The Candidate*, starring Robert Redford as Bill McKay, a clean-cut young progressive running for a seat in the United States Senate. Having won an unexpected victory through slick presentation, McKay is left wondering 'what do we do now?' 'The apparent ridiculousness of this proposition,' recorded one journalist, 'makes Salmond roar with laughter.'[53]

Yet the proposition was not at all ridiculous. As Bernard Ponsonby observed, Home Rule politicians – from all parties – had 'spent a lot of the post-war period articulating the demand for devolution, without actually working out what they wanted to do with it'. Hitherto this had been disguised by the SNP's demands for more powers, which allowed them to appear fresh and innovative, but when an independence referendum became inevitable, it was no longer enough. It was the question once posed by the journalist Andrew Marr: rather than constantly focusing on the 'how' of independence, there needed to be more attention paid to the 'why'.

Senior Nationalists realised that was so. Shortly after the election Nicola Sturgeon talked of it being the party's job 'to paint a picture of what an independent Scotland looks like and what it doesn't look like and to cast that in the very real modern world of today'.[54] Yet it was ministers like Sturgeon and Finance Secretary John Swinney who floundered when asked by journalists for details of what an independent Scotland would 'look like'. Swinney, for example, echoed Salmond's call for the devolution of corporation tax, but prevaricated when challenged to admit that this would mean a smaller tax take. There was a similar story with excise duty; its devolution was demanded, but only under questioning did Salmond say whether it would go up or down.

In terms of left and right, statist or small government, the SNP had long staked a claim to be centre-left or social democratic, but in reality it was a bit of everything, taking its cue from Salmond's determination to situate the party within the 'mainstream' of Scottish opinion. 'The SNP is not a policy-heavy party,' reflected one adviser, 'but they think they represent some sort of core Scottishness. It has a canny mix of small "c" Conservatism, reaching out to the Liberal vote, and also "we are the people" Labourism. It's a fascinating dichotomy: we cover all the bases of Scottish politics.' Policy, consequently, was driven by focus groups and the media agenda rather than any coherent political philosophy.

The unifying factor was a belief in (varying degrees of) independence, but many leading proponents of that 'big idea' held different hopes and aspirations for an independent Scotland. Paul Henderson Scott, for example, wanted it to be pacifist (not a view shared by the SNP's defence spokesman Angus Robertson); Michael Fry to unleash neoliberalism; Joyce Macmillan to salvage social democracy; Gerry Hassan to think big and positive, and so on. The point, as the party frequently insisted, was that 'Scots would decide' what the New Scotland looked like, although it seemed unlikely all of them would be happy with the end result. 'All of us who are sympathetic to independence', wrote one Nationalist blogger with obvious frustration, 'have cause to seriously reconsider the political limits of the SNP's tendency to assume the character of everyman Nationalism, which all too often feigns to face every which way simultaneously, and hopes nobody notices . . . We know that the SNP is for Scotland. What we want to know is, what sort of Scotland are we for?'[55]

This confusion was most evident on the economic front, where Salmond had sought to combine the social democratic and neoliberal models in terms of taxation, something the academic Michael Keating dismissed as 'voodoo economics'.[56] Keating also reminded the SNP there was little evidence that following Ireland's lead on corporation tax would work in Scotland, where 'such a cut would provide a windfall benefit for existing businesses without attracting much more'. Although Salmond had previously suggested halving the levy in Scotland, after the election he refused to be drawn. 'The flaw in the SNP's "arc of prosperity" vision was to mix up very different economic and social models,' added Keating, 'low-tax and low-welfare Ireland to high-tax and high-welfare Sweden.'[57]

The party also had little to say on its preferred employment model for Scotland, appearing to think, in the opinion of trade union expert Professor Gregor Gall, 'that all new jobs are necessarily "good" jobs, no matter their purpose, conditions, prospects or security'.[58] Amazon was a case in point, which provided just the sort of low-skilled, poorly-paid jobs that Salmond had been critical of as a radical young activist, while repeated talk of 'reindustrialising' Scotland through renewable energy also harked back to the 1980s.

Welfare was yet another grey area. *Your Scotland, Your Voice* blandly assured readers that in an independent Scotland 'pension and benefits [would continue] to be paid at a similar level as now',[59] but instead of articulating the SNP's alternative vision for unemployment black spots such as Glasgow, Salmond said nothing, preferring to attack the UK Government's reforms. To the journalist Paul Hutcheon, this was because even so-called 'civic Nationalism' was 'a value-free zone'. 'There is no logical Scottish position on wealth inequality, feminism or reforming public services,' he wrote in 2009. 'Most SNP policies are tactical compromises designed solely with the intention of promoting independence.'[60]

The commentator Kenny Farquharson was only marginally more charitable. 'Once again I find myself wondering why we don't know more about how Alex Salmond's mind works,' he wrote during the summer of 2011, 'and what he thinks about some of the key political questions of the age.'

This is a bizarre position to be in. Salmond has been one of the biggest beasts in Scottish politics for more than two decades. He is part of our landscape. We should know him inside out. Yet we don't. Not even nearly. We know what he thinks about the Laffer Curve, but we have no idea what he thinks about welfare dependency. We know his views on the base load possibilities of Scotland's wind turbines, but we're in the dark about his views on tackling Scotland's appallingly high level of teenage pregnancy.

Farquharson posited that Salmond avoided straying into such territory 'because social and moral issues by their very nature divide opinion'.[61] When, for example, the First Minister appeared to back same-sex marriage in early 2011, it revealed a hitherto discreet social conservatism within the SNP. And when Labour MP Thomas Docherty privately challenged Salmond to repudiate homophobic remarks made by one of his MSPs, he reportedly 'went absolutely crazy', adding patronisingly: 'How long have you been an MP, son?'[62]

When it came to the 2008 banking crisis, meanwhile, the SNP belatedly acquired a narrative, arguing that an independent Scotland would only have been liable for around 5 per cent of the RBS and HBOS bailout, dismissing arguments to the contrary as 'theoretical'. 'The events of the past few years aren't the result of independence,' blogged Stephen Noon 'they are the consequence of the Union,' conveniently ignoring the fact that Salmond had advocated even less financial regulation in an 'independent' Scotland.

Salmond's persistent refrain that a fiscally autonomous Scotland would automatically be more prosperous was also backed up with surprisingly thin evidence. In early 2011, he seized on a claim made by two sympathetic economists, Professors Andrew Hughes Hallett and Drew Scott, that 'a 1% point increase in fiscal devolution . . . might be expected to raise GDP by 1.3% after five years above what it would otherwise have been', although other economists pointed out that the evidence for the potential growth impact of fiscal autonomy did 'not support robust claims in either direction'. It could, in short, go either way and 'depends precisely how powers are devolved and used'.[63]

Always prone to seizing on apparently helpful statistical facts and expounding them *ad nauseam*, Salmond had got a bit carried away. Interviewed by the BBC's Stephen Sackur, the First Minister declared it was 'beyond argument' that fiscal independence would lead to greater growth, while he danced on the head of a pin over the UK National Debt, content that Scotland's share upon independence would be 'much smaller' than what was left of the Union. The difference, according to one analysis, was in fact 0.1 per cent, while both Scotland and the UK would end up with deficits of around 12 per cent.[64]

Indeed, one of Salmond's own economic advisers, John Kay, argued that on 'both politics and economics, the advocates for full independence have tended to overstate their case', although he accepted that an independent Scotland 'would clearly be economically viable'. 'The reality is that Scotland would gain little by full independence,' wrote

Kay in *Prospect*. 'In the modern world, economic sovereignty for small nations is inescapably limited, and political sovereignty is largely symbolic.'[65]

The independence-supporting Neal Ascherson concurred, wondering in an essay what an SNP Scotland would look like, either 'maximally devolved' or independent.

> The strange and sad thing is that it would look very much like a Scottish Labour Scotland – if that party were decisively to loosen its ties with London and follow its heart. Both are made up of leftish social-democrats, who believe in a strong public sector and state regulation to protect capitalism from its own excesses. Both are emotionally anti-nuclear and friendly to renewables.[66]

Even when it came to energy, Salmond was guilty of overstating the potential benefits, however bold and positive his vision of a renewables-fuelled Scotland was. Not only did most economists warn that a volatile commodity such as oil was not a sound basis for an economic policy (annual GERS figures were either good or bad for the SNP, depending on the price of oil), but Kay – together with several industry experts – judged that offshore wind energy was no substitute: 'even though Scotland is wet and windy; it is inherently unprofitable, and viable only through cross-subsidy from electricity consumers, mainly English ones'.[67] Indeed, Brian Wilson (a former UK energy minister) praised Salmond's renewables vision but argued that his whole energy strategy was 'profoundly Unionist in character',[68] so reliant was it on a UK-wide energy market.

So even after four years in government – and indeed Salmond's two decades as leader – the SNP's 'vision' of an independent Scotland remained an incomplete one. To Paul Hutcheon, writing in 2009, the First Minister was 'perhaps the Tony Benn or Enoch Powell of Scottish politics: a maverick politician who, by force of personality, makes unreasonable ideas seem reasonable to large chunks of the population'. 'Take him out of the equation,' added Hutcheon, 'as was the case when he resigned the SNP leadership in 2000, and his party nosedives.'[69]

Unsurprisingly, therefore, Salmond stuck to his preferred broad-brush approach, painting a picture of a 'society' not only different from, but also superior to, England. A deficit-cutting Tory-led government in London provided Salmond with the perfect point of contrast, while Stephen Noon spoke of the new Holyrood term being 'a tale of two countries, of two very different visions of society'.[70] Rather than David Cameron's 'Big Society', Salmond said he was focused on creating a 'fair society'.

The First Minister fleshed this out in his 'Taking Scotland Forward' speech to the Scottish Parliament. 'Elsewhere on these isles, the tolerance of the poor is being tested,' he told MSPs, 'budgets slashed, priorities changed, hope crushed in the braying tones of people who claim to know best.'

> We should aspire to be different. In Scotland the poor won't be made to pick up the bill for the rich. When we control our natural assets as a sovereign power, the profit from the land shall go to all. Too many of them have been ill-served by the union as is currently stands. There is a better way.

Constitutional change, added Salmond, was 'not an end in itself but a means to a better nation'. 'My aim is now, has been in the past, and always will be: to deliver a better society for the people of Scotland.' For good measure, he reminded MSPs of Margaret Thatcher's 'Sermon on the Mound' (which 'sounded to this nation like fingernails being dragged across a blackboard') before declaring: 'There is such a thing as society, and we will protect it.'[71]

Salmond sought to emphasise this contrast in new and occasionally baffling ways. Although Scotland and England shared the same language ('albeit with different accents'), he told one bemused interviewer, 'you couldn't get two more different cultures. Nobody would mistake a Scottish novelist for an English novelist.'[72] And during widespread rioting in English cities during August 2011 the First Minister complained about BBC reports describing the phenomenon as 'riots in the UK' and reminding everyone that there existed 'a different society in Scotland'.[73] How would England react to this sort of rhetorical wedge? The political scientist Michael Keating concluded that rather than the end of the UK being instigated by Scots, it might in fact 'come from the succession of an England that is no longer prepared to pay the political or economic price of union'.[74]

But just how different was Scotland from England? Several commentators, many sympathetic to the SNP, opined that – in office during 2007–11 – the party had been cautious and managerial. Christopher Harvie, the outgoing SNP MSP, wondered aloud if the past four years had not just been 'part of a contest between two versions of Scottish social democracy, partial and flawed, struggling to survive on an unstable British stage'. Ministers, he added, had 'tended towards orthodoxy', while the 2011 SNP manifesto had been another exercise in 'safety first'.[75] As Gerry Hassan argued in the *Scotsman*, 'it has not been a transformational government', rather 'one of caution and timidity'. Although the SNP frequently criticised the nature of the Labour 'network state', in office it had done little or nothing to 'dismantle' it.[76]

Indeed, the record of the first Nationalist Scottish Government contained few hints as to what the party might attempt in an independent or maximally devolved Scotland. The first legislative programme of the second SNP administration, meanwhile, was meagre fare beyond plans to introduce a single police force and reintroduce minimum pricing for alcohol. Instead Salmond's speech focused on the economy, repeating his call for control of more fiscal levers and predicting that the Scottish people would soon become the 'independence generation'.[77]

Brian Wilson, a persistent critic of Salmond and his party, spread the blame more widely with an Irish analogy. 'Scottish politics have been depoliticised,' he wrote. 'Devolved government is managerial rather than ideological.'

> The most remarkable fact about the Nationalists' four years in power is that it has been devoid of any discernible social imperative ... The SNP is Scotland's Fianna Fail. Big tent, non-ideological, populist, everything to be resolved through constitutional change, unembarrassed by where its money comes from since Scottish millionaires are, by definition, part of the same big happy family as the rest of us. And what better-equipped Soldier of Destiny to lead this regiment of Jock Tamson's Bairns than General Salmond?[78]

General Salmond, more than ever, was key to the delivery of some sort of independence, if not the SNP's continued electoral appeal; the 2011 Scottish Election Study revealed the party to be more popular than its leader, although an Ipsos MORI poll in September 2011 found that 68 per cent of voters were satisfied with the First Minister's performance since the election.

During that same period the London-based press went through one of its periodic bouts of adulation, the *Guardian* lauding Salmond as a 'political wizard, weaving the national destiny',[79] while the political philosopher John Gray called him the 'most consistently able operator in British politics'.[80] (A Belgian newspaper viewed him more as a 'Scottish teddy bear',[81] while the Scottish writer A. L. Kennedy said he had the 'eyes of a warm spaniel and the warm potato head of a man who is both undoubtedly Scottish and surely – we must hope – no threat'.[82])

Like Tony Blair in 1997, the election result equipped Salmond with the luxury of not having to fight, negotiate and cajole his way through every vote in the Holyrood chamber. Budgets would look after themselves, while Salmond could look forward to devoting his time and energy to the bigger picture, not least the referendum. It also freed him up to travel more, most likely to China and the Far East. 'He's a salesman,' explained an aide. 'He wants to sell Scotland to the world.'

As a political salesman, Salmond was on top of his game. Although detail had never been his strong point, he remained capable of imbibing facts and figures at short notice, even if his habit of wielding longforgotten quotes at his opponents as if they were killer blows was beginning to wear a bit thin. Interviewers were often surprised to find the SNP leader unfamiliar with his own manifesto, something that also struck Whitehall figures following the election. 'He gives much less thought to things than you imagine,' said one. 'He doesn't display a settled view; he talks in terms of the ballpark.' The detail of 'independence' and the referendum, it appeared, would be for others to labour over. 'He wants to be given something that allows him to make a case,' explained an aide. 'Give him the facts and he'll do the politics.'

Salmond remained an unashamed populist, or as John Lloyd put it, 'politically shallow but brilliantly opportunist'.[83] Indeed, a book published in 2010 had defined populism as an ideology that 'pits a virtuous and homogeneous people against a set of elites and dangerous "others" who are together depicted as depriving (or attempting to deprive) the sovereign people of their rights, values, prosperity, identity, and voice'.[84] It could almost have been written with the First Minister in mind. In Wales, the electorally less successful Plaid Cymru found themselves yearning for a Salmond-like populist who would 'finally grab them by the scruff of their neck and take them to glory'.[85]

There had been speculation prior to the election that Salmond would hand over to his deputy, Nicola Sturgeon, at some point during the 2011–16 Holyrood term, but the overall majority substantially delayed the talented Health Secretary's chances of succession. Asked before the election if, like Margaret Thatcher, he planned to 'go on and on', Salmond quoted his political hero Harold Wilson: 'I know what's going on. I am going on.'[86] Elsewhere he said it was his intention to serve out the full term, then 'see where things take us', but that he was 'committing to substantially longer' than Jack McConnell's six years in Bute House.[87] It was inconceivable that Salmond, unlike in 2000, would desert the SNP now its biggest prize was in sight. It was fascinating, meanwhile, to watch Sturgeon act as the occasional break on her chief, distancing herself from some of Salmond's hastier pronouncements.

In the period 2011–15 it looks likely that Salmond and the UK Prime Minister, David Cameron, will be the major players. Despite the First Minister's public pronouncements, there exists a degree of 'mutual respect' between the two leaders, and indeed in the elections of May 2011 both had played a skillful political hand. Both, reflected one adviser, were 'incredibly lucky politicians'. 'Alex has no sense of entitlement,' he said. 'He works every day with the same level of attention and energy and I don't get that off David Cameron, but then Alex doesn't have children and that completely changes expectations of what you do with your day.'

'He's never off [work],' said another aide. 'He works phenomenally hard and just doesn't stop; he appears to be just as acute at 9 a.m. as he is at 9 p.m.'

It was certainly true that Scotland had not occupied much of the Prime Minister's attention since the 2010 general election, beyond warm words about the 'respect agenda'. Cameron was, according to Whitehall sources, 'alarmed' by the SNP result but quickly grasped its political ramifications. 'Scotland is not something that preoccupies Tory brain cells,' said one. 'It's got the PM engaged with the constitutional question, rather than Scotland. He doesn't want to see Scotland sailing off, as that would be a massive mark against him and his term in office.'

Salmond, of course, relished the prospect of a Conservative Prime Minister (with only one Scottish MP) becoming the default leader of the 'no' campaign. Not only had the Holyrood election demonstrated that the Scottish Conservatives (despite the relative popularity of their leader, Annabel Goldie) remained toxic, but polling indicated that the Coalition was likely to become more, not less, unpopular as spending cuts began to bite. Although Salmond certainly hoped the UK government's unpopularity would peak in advance of a referendum, that prospect did not make him complacent. 'It would be nice to believe we could all put our feet up and wait for David Cameron to propel Scotland to independence,' he mused, 'but I think we might have to exert ourselves somewhat.'[88]

The 'Unionist' parties certainly had a personnel problem: if Cameron was not to head up a 'save the Union' campaign, then who

would? Flatteringly, reports suggested that London Tory strategists had
been impressed with Salmond's ability to present himself as both the
incumbent and a 'change' candidate. 'They view Salmond's campaign,
with its heavy emphasis on the personality of the leader, as a model for
the one they want to fight in 2015,' reported the *Spectator*. 'One
Cabinet minister has even taken to calling the PM "the English Alex
Salmond".'[89]

To borrow a phrase from the 'sovereigntist' politics of Quebec,
Salmond's task between 2011 and 2016 was to create the 'winning
conditions' for independence or 'devo-max'. The nationalist Parti
Québécois had won office in 1976 and held its first 'sovereignty-associ-
ation' referendum in 1980. It lost, but held another in 1995, having
regained office the year before. This also failed, but this time by a
whisker. The depressing lesson was that Quebec nationalism ebbed and
flowed, just as it had in Scotland. 'Salmond would be wise to study
Quebec's travels down the road to independence,' concluded the
academic Françoise Boucek. 'So far, that road has led nowhere.'[90] That
said, would David Cameron be able to emulate Pierre Trudeau in out-
manoeuvring his own secessionists?

An even closer parallel could be drawn between the Scottish experience and Catalonia, the UK and Spain sharing an ad hoc system of
devolution. For more than two decades, the Catalan premier Jordi
Pujol had accumulated more autonomy without full secession. 'Salmond
might be shaping up to become the Pujol of Scottish politics,' speculated the journalist Rob Brown, 'slowly and steadily salami-slicing
sovereignty from London, starting with fiscal autonomy, yet never
quite persuading his compatriots to make the leap of faith to independence in Europe.'[91] The SNP was certainly well aware of the Quebec
and Catalan experiences, frequently meeting with nationalists from
both to 'discuss their respective political situations and exchange information on strategies and tactics'.[92]

As the constitutional historian Peter Hennessy predicted: 'Scotland
will be to the UK what Quebec is to Canada and the UK is to the
European Union, the awkward one spewing out a constant drizzle of
complaint but never pushing it to the point of rupture.'[93] Survey data,
at least for the moment, appeared to bear this out. 'For the most part
people are indifferent or uncertain,' concluded Professor John Curtice,
'rather than convinced that independence would be a disaster,' a state of
mind that posed difficulties for both the prospective 'yes' and 'no'
campaigns.[94] Voters appeared to enjoy being able to have their cake and

eat it, a devolved administration that 'stood up for Scotland' and a Westminster government that supplied the cash.

So in order to convince largely indifferent voters to back radical constitutional change, Salmond, according the former *Economist* editor Bill Emmott, would 'have to define for them the problem to which independence is a solution'.[95] Given that that was not at all obvious, it posed an obvious challenge for the SNP. John Kay reckoned that a referendum campaign, 'unless grievously mismanaged by the UK government and other political parties', was more likely 'to erode support for independence than to increase it, as the risks and complications of separation emerge'.[96] Grievous mismanagement looked a distinct possibility when the Scottish Secretary floated the idea that two referendums might be better than one, while the Prime Minister hinted that he might hold his own independence poll if Salmond did not get a move on. Both options were cursorily dismissed by the First Minister, who posited that 'the real battle in these things is psychological', reasoning that if individual questions were combined – i.e. do you want Scotland to control troop deployment, gas revenues and renewables – 'and there's a majority for each [then] the task and challenge for the SNP is to make people generalise on independence from the particular aims and ambitions of these individual questions'. It was by no means a straightforward or simple task, he added, 'but it's certainly a doable one.'[97]

Angus Robertson, inevitably chosen to run the referendum campaign given his track record in 2007 and 2011, explained that research from those two election campaigns would be used (via the party's Activate software) to target 'swing voters' open to the prospect of 'independence' in a 'modern, project managed' campaign run along similar lines to a Holyrood election. '[T]he benefit that we have is that this [independence] crosses traditional political boundaries,' said Robertson. 'We will work very hard, but we take nothing for granted.'[98]

Unforeseen events could, of course, make that task even more difficult. Since 1999 the Scottish Parliament had operated within a social democratic comfort zone because it had the funds to do so; by 2008 that was no longer possible, although Salmond continued to maintain that cuts were unnecessary if only the UK Government would submit to his 'Plan B' for the economy, something dismissed by Michael Moore as little more than 'a stunt'.[99] Nevertheless, Salmond had to deal with the effect of 'Westminster cuts' on Scotland's 'social contract'. 'The First Minister will discover in the next five years that financial constraints will largely rip up that contract,' predicted Bernard Ponsonby.

Councils will find it impossible (or refuse) to freeze Council tax. The bill for plugging the higher education black hole will be more than £93m. Free personal care, prescriptions and bus passes will become increasingly unaffordable. The belief that you can reform the public sector and have a no compulsory redundancies policy will shatter because it is simply impossible to deliver.

Salmond most likely realised this, speculated Ponsonby, 'but probably bets he can manage his way out of it against a weak and feeble opposition'.[100] Helpfully for the First Minister, polls suggested Scots voters would continue to blame London rather than Edinburgh for any cuts. Even after four years in government Salmond and the SNP enjoyed that most valuable of political commodities – the benefit of the doubt, in the eyes of many voters.

Much also depended on how the SNP's opponents chose to play the referendum campaign. The Calman Commission and Scotland Bill had looked like a clever way of shooting the Nationalist fox, but as the 2011 election result demonstrated, that fox had evaded the Unionists' sights. In 1999 slogans such as 'Divorce is an Expensive Business' had persuaded most Scots to stick with what they knew (i.e. Labour), but it was clear such a strategy was subject to the law of diminishing returns. Indeed, the political scientist David Runciman speculated that in lacking 'a convincing account of the reason different national communities need to be joined together in a larger whole', the UK Labour Party might be 'finished as an electoral force'.[101] The new Scottish Liberal Democrat leader Willie Rennie, meanwhile, cautioned against complacency. 'Independence could happen,' he said. 'Because Alex Salmond is crafty, he may well get people over the edge before they know it. He may well win it.'[102]

Rennie's warning was a clever distraction from his own party's difficulties. Having already attracted almost half the Liberal Democrats' Scottish supporters at the 2011 election, Salmond continued to make a direct pitch to disaffected Liberals with the referendum in mind. 'The old Scottish Liberal Party was the independent party of Home Rule,' he said, adding that 'that honourable tradition' was now reflected by the SNP's constitutional ambitions.[103] The new Scottish Liberal Party, meanwhile, behaved as if its own federalist policy was an embarrassment, while Rennie tried to reclaim 'Home Rule' by establishing a commission to look 'at a settled distribution of powers between London, Edinburgh and local councils'.[104]

The prospect of a second referendum question asking Scots to consider 'devo-max' also put Labour and the Conservatives in a difficult position, for elements in both parties were known to support greater powers for Holyrood. It would be a classic case of divide and conquer, although it left the SNP in the curious position of articulating the main non-independence alternative to the status quo. The First Minister, of course, was careful not to box himself in, and remained vague not only on the referendum date (although he hinted to one journalist that it could be on the same ballot as the 2016 Holyrood election), but whether it would have one or two questions, and even how those questions might be worded.

The First Minister did drop heavy hints, citing the precedence of the two-question devolution referendum in 1997. 'I realise the virtue in having straight questions and straight answers,' he said. 'But I don't limit it necessarily to just one question on one proposition.'[105] He had left that 'open' because he believed there was 'a substantial body of opinion in Scotland' which supported fiscal autonomy. Similarly, when pushed by a Canadian journalist on the subject, Salmond declared:

> Actually, the question will be 'Here is a white paper, which has all the detail of independence; do you wish to proceed along the lines of this white paper and be an independent country?' It's [also] perfectly possible to ask a second question saying: 'Here's another white paper which says maximum devolution, financial freedom – do you want Scotland to have financial freedom?'[106]

There were obvious problems with two questions: what if independence polled 50.1 per cent and 'devo-max' 75 per cent? Or, if the second question easily outpolled the first, could Salmond survive being the SNP leader who had failed to deliver independence when it was within tantalising reach?

In any case, given the concept of 'independence-lite', it looked possible there might not be much separating those two options. Michael Portillo, for one, was sure the former question would not even include the word 'independence',[107] although he nevertheless believed Salmond could pull it off. John Kay reckoned that faced with three options, the chances were most voters would choose the middle course. 'It is also a desirable one,' he added. 'Scotland can get many of the advantages claimed for independence if it negotiates for more autonomy, while still staying part of the Union.'[108] This, to Unionist die-hards such as former

Labour MP Tam Dalyell, meant Salmond could secure a constitutional settlement 'indistinguishable' from independence.[109]

Under either scenario – having modified his actions to suit that small part of the world he had dominated since 2007 – Alex Salmond could claim victory, either 'independence' in a modern context or significantly greater autonomy within the United Kingdom. The task for him, and for his party, was to create the 'winning conditions' needed to secure a mandate for the former, and failing that the latter, by 2016. As the First Minister had said in 2007, an independence referendum was 'a once in a generation thing'.[110]

Could he pull it off? There were certainly good arguments for independence, and equally there was a good case against, although a weak opposition and a neutered media often appeared incapable of presenting the latter with any vigour or originality. As one adviser observed, 'the demise of the Scottish media will always have been part of our success'.

Perhaps all voters would notice would be a good campaign; well funded, beautifully choreographed by the usual talented team, and ably led by the movement's star turn, Alex Salmond. As even Tony Blair's former spin doctor Alistair Campbell conceded, the SNP leader's efforts since 2007 to 'capture the mood' of Scots in terms of values and vision had to be 'judged a success'. Salmond's mood music had generated 'a clever soundtrack to . . . an upbeat, devolved Scotland'.[111] And the fat lady had yet to sing.

ENDNOTES

Acknowledgements

1 *Scotland on Sunday* 1/11/1998.
2 *Sunday Herald* 7/9/2003.
3 *Scotland on Sunday* 15/3/2009.
4 *Sunday Herald* 14/7/2007.
5 Private information.
6 Campbell, Edward Heath, xi.
7 *Observer* 21/2/2010.
8 *Scotsman* 9/10/1999.
9 Crick, *George Orwell*, 31.
10 Pimlott, *Frustrate Their Knavish Tricks*, 157.
11 Ewing, *Stop the World*, 365.
12 Barrow, *Robert Bruce*, xiii.
13 Pimlott, 158.

Foreword to paperback edition

1 Davies, *Heart of Europe*, vii.
2 Kevin Pringle to the author, 10/10/2010.
3 *Scotland on Sunday* 16/1/2011.
4 Kenneth Fraser to the author, 27/10/2010.
5 *Prospect* 6/2011.
6 *Sunday Herald* 19/6/2011.

'Scotland will flourish'

1 Alex Salmond is said to favour this as an independent Scotland's national anthem. 'The song's sentiments are fine and noble,' his official spokesman told one newspaper, 'and it would make a great national anthem for Scotland.' Mail on Sunday 23/5/2011
2 *Independence: The SNP Magazine* May/June 2011.
3 Interview with Angus Robertson MP, 23/6/2011.
4 *Salmond's 100 Days* (STV) 21/8/2007.
5 *Scotsman* 7/5/2011.
6 The SNP received around 15,000 responses from members of the public.
7 *Independence: The SNP Magazine* May/June 2011.

8   *Herald* 8/5/2011.

9   *Beyond Westminster* (BBC Radio 4) 4/6/2011.

10 http://www.snp.org/node/17415

11 http://stephennoon.blogspot.com/2011/01/first-time-for-everything_08.html

12 http://www.snp.org/node/17415

13 This song had started life as the more Unionist 'Let's Stick Together', a favourite of the Los Angeles 1960s rock-blues outfit Canned Heat, while it was also covered by Bryan Ferry. 'Let's Work Together' was performed at the end of the SNP conference by the Edinburgh-based band Jakil.

14 http://www.snp.org/node/17415

15 *Herald* 7/5/2011.

16 *Glasgow Herald* 1/12/1992.

17 http://stephennoon.blogspot.com/2011/02/why-positive-beats-negative.html

18 *Metro* 30/11/2010.

19 *Holyrood* 15/10/2010.

20 *Metro* 30/11/2010.

21 *Portillo on Salmond* (BBC Scotland) 15/5/2011.

22 *Newsnight Scotland* (BBC Scotland) 6/12/2010.

23 *Scotsman* 15/12/2010.

24 *Sunday Herald* 9/1/2011.

25 *Scotland on Sunday* 9/1/2011.

26 On *Newsnight Scotland* on 10 February 2011, Salmond said the SNP's aim was to win an overall majority, but failing that another minority government was the preference. 'That was deliberate, as we wanted to close down speculation about coalitions,' recalled a close adviser. 'Alex ruling that out really freed us up to concentrate on what we'd actually do as a government.'

27 *Scotland on Sunday* 2/1/2011.

28 http://www.notosh.com/2011/05/we-made-history-the-best-new-media-team-in-uk-political-campaigning/

29 http://stephennoon.blogspot.com/2011/01/is-100-days-too-early.html

30 http://stephennoon.blogspot.com/2011/01/curious-case-of-missing-nation.html

31 Hassan, 'Anatomy of a Scottish Revolution' in *Political Quarterly* Vol. 82 No. 3, Autumn 2011.

32 *Scotland on Sunday* 13/2/2011.

33 http://stephennoon.blogspot.com/2011/03/whats-scottish-government-ever-done-for.html

34 SNP press release, 12/3/2011.

35 SNP press release, 22/3/2011.

36 *Sunday Herald* 8/5/2011.

37 *Beyond Westminster* (BBC Radio 4) 4/6/2011.

38 http://stephennoon.blogspot.com/2011/04/one-week-to-go-final-push.html

39 *The Big Issue Scotland* 2-8/5/2011.

40 http://stephennoon.blogspot.com/2011/03/nobody-does-it-better.html

41 http://stephennoon.blogspot.com/2011/03/nobody-does-it-better.html

42 *Herald* 7/5/2011.

43 Interview with Kirk J. Torrance, 11/6/2011.

44 *Independence: The SNP Magazine* March/April 2011.

45 http://www.notosh.com/2011/05/we-made-history-the-best-new-media-team-in-uk-political-campaigning/

46 *Scotsman* 3/5/2011.

47 *Independence: The SNP Magazine* May/June 2011.

48 http://stephennoon.blogspot.com/2011/04/manifesto-final-lap.html

49 Scottish Labour Party, Fighting for what really matters, 2.

50 Kevin Pringle to the author, 8/7/2011.
51 *Sunday Herald* 10/7/2011.
52 *Scottish Sun* 19/4/2011. 'Vote for Alex Salmond, help David Cameron' was the Daily Record's rather crude rejoinder (20/4/2011).
53 *Scottish Sun* 5/5/2011.
54 http://stephennoon.blogspot.com/2011/04/one-week-to-go-final-push.html
55 *Sunday Times* 1/5/2011.
56 *Sunday Herald* 8/5/2011.
57 http://stephennoon.blogspot.com/2011/04/hope-beats-fear.html
58 *The Big Issue Scotland* 2-8 May 2011.
59 *Herald* 4/5/2011.
60 *The Big Issue Scotland* 2-8 May 2011.
61 http://www.notosh.com/2011/05/we-made-history-the-best-new-media-team-in-uk-political-campaigning/
62 *Holyrood Magazine* 28/2/2011.
63 *Sunday Post* 24/4/2011.
64 *Daily Telegraph* 27/4/2011.
65 *Scottish Sun* 7/5/2011.
66 Interview with Angus Robertson MP, 23/6/2011.
67 *Scottish Sun* 7/5/2011.
68 DVL 3943 (STV).
69 *Guardian* 6/5/2011.
70 *Herald* 7/5/2011.
71 *Scottish Sun* 7/5/2011.
72 *Scotland Decides* (STV) 6/5/2011.
73 http://www.guardian.co.uk/politics/2011/may/06/scottish-elections-salmond-historic-victory-snp
74 *Scottish Sun* 6/5/2011.
75 *Scottish Sun* 7/5/2011.
76 *Herald* 7/5/2011.
77 *The Times* 7/5/2011.
78 *Scotsman* 22/6/2011.
79 *Scotsman* 7/5/2011.
80 *Sunday Herald* 8/5/2011.
81 Portillo on Salmond (BBC Scotland) 15/5/2011.
82 DVL 3943 (STV).
83 *Scotland on Sunday* 15/5/2011.
84 *The Times* 7/5/2011.
85 *Scotsman* 7/5/2011.
86 http://www.guardian.co.uk/commentisfree/2011/may/10/time-for-scottish-independence
87 *Sunday Herald* 8/5/2011.

Chapter 1 'A real Black Bitch'

1 *Herald* 29/12/1994. Salmond later wrote of his father's relief at being 'able to welcome his first-born son into the world and then go off to the [New Year's day football] match with a clear conscience if not a clear head' (*Herald* 1/1/1997).
2 *Scotland on Sunday* 15/8/2004.
3 *The Times* 22/7/1957.
4 The minister responsible was the Rev Dr David Steel, who served at St Michael's from 1957 to 1976. His son, also David, was the future Liberal leader.

5 *Independent on Sunday* 8/2/1992.

6 *Linlithgowshire Journal and Gazette* 26/5/1972.

7 Harvie, *Broonland*, 38.

8 *Scotsman* 20/2/2006.

9 Interview with Peter Brunskill, 1/2/2010.

10 This was later corrected to Robert Fyfe Findlay Salmond, the two middle names coming from the minister who christened him.

11 *Scottish Sunday Express* 3/4/2011.

12 http://www.scotland.gov.uk/News/This-Week/Speeches/First-Minister/genassembly09

13 John MacLeod to the author, 19/10/2009. Account of a conversation with Salmond following a hustings meeting in Stornoway on 16/4/2007.

14 William Barclay (1907–78) was an author, radio and television presenter, Church of Scotland minister and Professor of Divinity and Biblical Criticism at the University of Glasgow.

15 *Life and Work* 6/2008.

16 Interview with Peter Brunskill.

17 Devine & Logue, eds, *Being Scottish*, 243.

18 *The Salmond Years* (STV) 18/2/2001.

19 Devine & Logue, eds, *Being Scottish*, 243–44.

20 *Scottish Daily Mail* 31/5/2008.

21 *Herald* 6/9/1995.

22 *Scottish Daily Mail* 31/5/2008.

23 *Scotland on Sunday* 28/2/1999. Salmond later relented. 'I haven't worn the kilt since I was five,' he said in 2004. 'I now have six pairs of very natty trews. It's trews for devolution; kilt for independence' (*Scotland on Sunday* 3/10/2004).

24 *Scottish Daily Mail* 31/5/2008.

25 *Scotsman* 30/10/1996.

26 *Edinburgh Evening News* 17/7/2000.

27 Interview with Margaret Henderson, 22/2/2010. West Lothian had been designated a 'Special Development Area', under which the British Motor Corporation was induced to locate a new truck and tractor plant in Bathgate rather than expand, as planned, its existing Longbridge plant in Birmingham. It closed in 1986.

28 Interview with Margaret Henderson.

29 *Times Educational Supplement* Scotland 25/2/2011.

30 *Scottish Daily Express* 29/4/2011.

31 *Linlithgowshire Journal and Gazette* 5/7/1929.

32 *Linlithgowshire Journal and Gazette* 4/4/1941.

33 'Brother' William Milne was a past master of Lodge Ancient Brazen No 17, Linlithgow.

34 *Linlithgowshire Journal and Gazette* 8/11/1935.

35 Dalyell's grandson Tam also remembered being 'bound up' by Mary Milne, Salmond's mother, at a West Lothian Cricket Club match in 1949; her parents being friends of his grandparents (interview with Tam Dalyell 2/7/2010).

36 *West Lothian Courier* 4/4/1941. Milne's death certificate gives the time of the cleaner's discovery as 7.15 a.m.

37 *Linlithgowshire Journal and Gazette* 4/4/1941.

38 The author is indebted to Tom Gordon for providing these hitherto unpublished quotes, obtained for the *Sunday Times* in the summer of 2008.

39 *Sunday Times* (Scotland) 10/10/2010.

40 *Independent* 29/9/1998.

41 Robert Salmond, Alex's brother, was active in the SNP while at Aberdeen University in the late 1980s. In 2011, meanwhile, Gail Salmond's daughter, Christina Hendry, was

elected a Member of the Scottish Youth Parliament for Ettrick, Roxburgh and Berwickshire.

42 *Scottish Sunday Express* 3/4/2011.

43 *Guardian* 31/1/2009.

44 *Sunday Post* 4/11/1990.

45 *The Salmond Years* (STV) 18/2/2001.

46 *Scottish Daily Mail* 31/5/2008.

47 Interview with Gordon Currie, 8/2/2010.

48 *Daily Express* 2/11/2001.

49 Interview with Mary Salmond, 2/2/2001 (STV B66161).

50 The other two 'great Scottish heroes revered above all others in the Salmond household', according to Alex, were 'King' Willie Bauld and James Graham, the 1st marquis of Montrose (*Herald* 28/7/2009).

51 *Herald* 13/5/1993.

52 *Herald* 28/7/2009.

53 Interview with Robert Salmond, 2/2/2001 (STV B66161).

54 *Scottish Standard* 13/4/2005.

55 *Herald* 3/6/1993.

56 *Scotsman* 16/5/1998.

57 *Scottish Sunday Express* 3/4/2011.

58 Peter Brunskill to the author, 3/3/2010.

59 *Scotsman* 30/7/2005. By 'west' Salmond meant Ireland.

60 *Scotsman* 6/7/2004.

61 *Sunday Herald* 25/7/1999.

62 *Scotsman* 8/2/2003.

63 *Herald* 5/5/1995.

64 *Scotsman* 20/10/2001.

65 *Scotsman* 15/12/2001.

66 *Racing Post* 30/7/2000.

67 *Scotland on Sunday* 25/4/1999.

68 *Scotsman* 2/8/2009.

69 Interview with Mary Salmond.

70 Peter Brunskill to the author, 7/6/2010.

71 Interview with Alex Salmond MSP, 2/2008 (courtesy of Katherine Haddon).

72 *Desert Island Discs* (BBC Radio 4) 16/1/2011.

73 *Independent* 10/8/2008.

74 *Sunday Post* 4/11/1990.

75 *Herald* 21/7/1994.

76 Salmond was also a Boy Scout, although not under Wolfe's guidance. His old scoutmaster, Jim McGurk, later won the lottery in 1995.

77 Lynch, *SNP*, 103–104.

78 *Linlithgowshire Journal and Gazette* 8/12/1967.

79 Lynch, *SNP*, 120.

80 Jamieson, *Linlithgow Academy*, 38.

81 Private information.

82 Interview with Mary Salmond.

83 *Sunday Times* 29/3/2009.

84 Interview with Mary Salmond.

85 *Linlithgowshire Journal and Gazette* 8/12/1967.

86 *Sunday Times* 29/3/2009.

87 Anstey, ed., *R. S. Thomas: Selected Prose*, 31–33.

88 *Scotland on Sunday* 15/8/2010.

89 Anstey, ed., *R. S. Thomas: Selected Prose*, 126.

90 Peter Brunskill to the author, 7/6/2010.

91 Interview with Gordon Currie, 8/2/2010.

92 *The One Show* (BBC) 8/2010.

93 'My relationship with Mr Salmond is not just one of friendship,' MacAskill said later. 'We were at school together' (*Scotsman* 15/8/1990).

94 Interview with Gordon Currie. Alasdair Morgan, later Salmond's deputy as leader of the SNP, started teaching at Linlithgow Academy the year Salmond left.

95 *Scotsman* 5/4/2003.

96 *Edinburgh Evening News* 10/4/1997. After much financial trouble, the College of Commerce merged with Napier College of Science and Technology in 1974, becoming the Napier College of Commerce and Technology.

Chapter 2 'Act of rebellion'

1   Barrow, *Robert Bruce*, 342.

2   Young, *St Andrews*, 262.

3   Salmond had his best return in 1977, teeing off at 5 a.m. so he could get round without having to pay. That, he recalled in 2010, 'was the time of my life. I used to pretend I could play' (http://espn.go.com/golf/blog/_/name/standrews/id/5382836/scotland-first-minister-sees-eden-golf).

4   Young, *St Andrews*, 263.

5   *The Student* 13/1/2009.

6   Interview with Peter Brunskill, 1/2/2010.

7   Interview with Pam Chesters, 5/3/2010.

8   Interview with Dave Smith, 26/1/2010.

9   Peter Brunskill to the author, 3/3/2010. Similarly, Salmond recalled that Sea Pigeon 'probably contributed as much as the Scottish Education Department in getting me through University' (*Scotsman* 14/2/2004).

10 *Racing Post* 30/7/2000.

11 Peter Jones to the author, 22/9/2009.

12 Rod Cross to the author, 7/12/2009.

13 Interview with Charlie Woods, 17/11/2009.

14 *Daily Record* 16/10/2006.

15 *Guardian* 31/1/2009.

16 Webb, *The Growth of Nationalism in Scotland*, 151–52.

17 *Independent on Sunday* 8/2/1992.

18 Devine & Logue, eds, *Being Scottish*, 244.

19 *Scotland on Sunday* 15/8/2010.

20 Geoffrey Barrow to the author, 22/10/2009.

21 Henderson Scott, *A Twentieth Century Life*, 288. Salmond believed Barrow was 'the historian who has perhaps more than any other raised the quality of interpretation of the period' (*Herald* 6/9/1995).

22 http://www.st-andrews.ac.uk/600th/yourstory/

23 Taylor, *The Scottish Parliament*, 163.

24 *Aien* 1/12/1976.

25 *The Salmond Years* (STV) 18/2/2001.

26 *Scotland on Sunday* 14/3/2010.

27 Debbie Horton certainly existed, as Mark Lazarowicz remembered her, but no one knows what became of her after leaving St Andrews.

28 *Sunday Herald* 4/2/2007.

29 *Scottish Daily Mail* 31/5/2008.

30 Interview with Alex Salmond MSP, 2/2008 (courtesy of Katherine Haddon).

31 *Guardian* 31/1/2009.
32 Interview with Peter Brunskill.
33 Peter Brunskill to the author, 3/3/2010.
34 *Guardian* 31/1/2009.
35 Interview with Peter Brunskill.
36 Wilson remembered Salmond telling him that he had helped out during the Dundee by-election, in which case he had been active in the SNP before actually joining the party.
37 Resenting the link with the occasionally violent Scottish Liberation Army, the SNP complained to the BBC and a planned repeat screening was shelved.
38 *Edinburgh Evening News* 31/5/2007.
39 All quotes from 'press' sheets courtesy of Dave Smith.
40 Interview with Peter Brunskill.
41 Peter Brunskill to the author, 3/3/2010.
42 *The Student* 13/1/2009.
43 Interview with Mark Lazarowicz MP, 23/9/2009.
44 Interview with Peter Brunskill.
45 Interview with Robert Salmond, 2/2/2001 (STV B66161).
46 http://www.snp.org/node/16799
47 Wilson, *SNP: The Turbulent Years*, 101.
48 *St Andrews Citizen* 10/5/1975. Salmond was at this time 'EEC Convener' of the St Andrews FSN.
49 Interview with Mark Lazarowicz.
50 *St Andrews Citizen* 27/8/1977. Salmond wanted 10 or 'even' 12 seats.
51 Dalyell, *Devolution*, 307.
52 *Linlithgowshire Journal and Gazette* 27/8/1976.
53 Peter Brunskill to the author, 28/4/2010.
54 SNP, *Scotland's Future*, 31.
55 Interview with Peter Brunskill.
56 Roth & Criddle, *Parliamentary Profiles S–Z*, 1906.
57 Webb, *The Growth of Nationalism in Scotland*, 109.
58 Interview with Mark Lazarowicz.
59 *Holyrood Magazine* 28/9/2009.
60 *Guardian* 20/8/1990.
61 *Independent on Sunday* 8/2/1992.
62 Peter Brunskill to the author, 7/6/2010.
63 *Scotsman* 18/7/2000.
64 *Daily Record* 28/4/1997.
65 *Herald* 13/12/1995.
66 Interview with Peter Brunskill.
67 *Free Student Press* autumn 1975.
68 Peter Brunskill to the author, 5/6/2010.
69 *Free Student Press* autumn 1975.
70 When students voted in November 1977, however, St Andrews opted to remain neutral, affiliating to neither the NUS nor the Scottish Union of Students.
71 Interview with Cllr Tim McKay, 5/1/2010.
72 Interview with Stewart Stevenson MSP, 29/6/2010.
73 *Free Student Press* autumn 1975. During Salmond's time at St Andrews celebrity rectors included the journalist Alan Coren (who had taken over from John Cleese in late 1973), followed by the television personality Frank Muir.
74 *Free Student Press* autumn 1975.
75 *Free Student Press* 10/1975.
76 *Free Student Press* summer 1976.

77 Interview with Peter Brunskill.

78 *St Andrews Citizen* 24/9/1977.

79 *Free Student Press* winter 1977.

80 Interview with Peter Brunskill.

81 Peter Jones to the author, 22/9/2009.

82 Interview with Jamie Stone MSP, 12/1/2010.

83 Alistair Hicks to the author, 13/1/2010.

84 Interview with Cllr Tim McKay.

85 *Scotsman* 17/3/1988.

86 *Daily Record* 10/2/2001.

87 Interview with Jim Fairlie, 27/4/2010.

88 Interview with Peter Brunskill.

89 Interview with Jamie Stone. Brunskill disagrees: 'He could find his way to the pie shop with his eyes closed; he just didn't have drinking buddies with political views he didn't respect' (Peter Brunskill to the author, 7/6/2010).

90 Interview with Cllr Tim McKay.

91 Interview with Dave Smith.

92 Des Swayne to the author, 21/10/2009.

93 *Daily Record* 16/10/2006.

94 Interview with Peter Brunskill.

95 Interview with Cllr Tim McKay.

96 *Scotsman* 19/8/2010.

97 *Aien* 9/2/1977.

98 *Aien* 9/3/1977.

99 *The Student* 13/1/2009.

100 *Aien* 7/12/1977.

101 *The Student* 13/1/2009.

102 Interview with Cllr Tim McKay.

103 *Aien* 15/2/1978.

104 Salmond was nominated by Charlie Woods, his fellow economics student.

105 *Aien* 15/2/1978.

106 Flyer courtesy of Cllr Tim McKay.

107 *Sunday Herald* 4/2/2007.

108 *Aien* 1/3/1978. Bainbridge received 517 votes, Salmond 506 and Hogg 288.

109 *University of Aberdeen Magazine* 12/2008.

110 Peter Bainbridge to the author, 8/3/2010.

111 Peter Bainbridge to the author, 9/3/2010.

112 *Sunday Mail* 1/5/2011.

113 Interview with Peter Brunskill. 'I'm not 100 per cent sure who said it first', said Salmond of the Stewart quote in 2002, 'but my old English teacher was convinced that it was Scotland's world lightweight champion, Ken Buchanan' (*Scotsman* 7/12/2002).

114 Peter Bainbridge to the author, 9/3/2010.

115 Interview with Brian Taylor, 22/9/2009.

116 *Aien* 15/2/1978.

117 http://www.nls.uk/events/donald_dewar_lectures/2008_salmond/transcript.html

118 *St Andrews Citizen* 18/2/1978.

119 http://www.st-andrews.ac.uk/news/archive/2007/Title,17906,en.html

Chapter 3 'West Lothian Left'

1 Barrow, *The Extinction of Scotland*, 7.

2 Interview with Brian Taylor, 22/9/2009.

3 Not content with penning a steady stream of letters himself, Salmond also encouraged his university friend Peter Brunskill to write to the *Linlithgowshire Journal and Gazette*, despite the fact he lived in England. Brunskill even wrote under a pseudonym to maximize his success rate.

4 Interview with Peter Brunskill, 1/2/2010.

5 *Linlithgowshire Journal and Gazette* 10/11/1978.

6 Chesser House, noted Salmond in one of his *Herald* columns, was 'a building later to fall on hard times as Lothian region's chief collection point for the poll tax' (*Herald* 16/8/1995).

7 *Herald* 16/8/1995.

8 *Herald* 30/7/1997.

9 Interview with Cllr Tim McKay, 5/1/2010.

10 *Herald* 16/8/1995.

11 *Herald* 30/7/1997.

12 Interview with David Dalgetty, 25/9/2009.

13 *Linlithgowshire Journal and Gazette* 19/6/1981.

14 Private information.

15 *Scots Independent* 11/1978.

16 *Linlithgowshire Journal and Gazette* 3/11/1978.

17 *Linlithgowshire Journal and Gazette* 27/10/1978.

18 *Linlithgowshire Journal and Gazette* 10/11/1978.

19 *Guardian* 25/9/1978.

20 *Linlithgowshire Journal and Gazette* 27/10/1978.

21 *Herald* 8/9/1994.

22 *Linlithgowshire Journal and Gazette* 26/1/1979.

23 Author's collection.

24 *Linlithgowshire Journal and Gazette* 16/2/1979.

25 Ascherson, *Stone Voices*, 103. The SLP was Sillars' short-lived Scottish Labour Party.

26 *The Week In Politics* (Grampian TV) 5/9/2002.

27 Bochel, *et al.*, *The Referendum Experience*, 19.

28 *Linlithgowshire Journal and Gazette* 16/3/1979.

29 *Linlithgowshire Journal and Gazette* 6/4/1979.

30 Interview with Tam Dalyell, 2/7/2010.

31 *Linlithgowshire Journal and Gazette* 6/4/1979.

32 *Linlithgowshire Journal and Gazette* 8/6/1979.

33 *Linlithgowshire Journal and Gazette* 29/6/1979.

34 Interview with Stewart Stevenson MSP, 29/6/2010.

35 *Herald* 20/3/1996.

36 *Scotland on Sunday* 3/9/2000.

37 *Herald* 19/8/1993.

38 Interview with Stephen Maxwell, 2/3/2010.

39 McIntyre Acc 10090/170.

40 *Cencrastus* summer 1985.

41 Gavin Kennedy Acc 11565/23.

42 *Scotsman* 24/6/1982.

43 *The Salmond Years* (STV) 18/2/2001.

44 Interview with Peter Brunskill. Salmond, recalled Brunskill, took a similar view of Gaelic.

45 The provisional agenda for the 79 Group conference on 18 August 1979 included a talk on 'Republicanism' by Salmond.

46 Interview with Rob Gibson MSP, 3/2/2009.

47 Gavin Kennedy Acc 11565/23. It is not clear to whom Salmond was referring.

48 *Linlithgowshire Journal and Gazette* 25/4/1980.

49 *Linlithgowshire Journal and Gazette* 9/5/1980.

50 *Linlithgowshire Journal and Gazette* 6/6/1980.

51 *Linlithgowshire Journal and Gazette* 31/10/1980. Salmond's use of '20 per cent' to describe Tory support in Scotland was clever, but misleading. The actual figure was nearer 30 per cent, but by using the proportion of the electorate rather than those voting, he was straying into '40 per cent rule' logic.

52 *Linlithgowshire Journal and Gazette* 21/12/1979.

53 Maxwell, *The Case for Left-Wing Nationalism*, 22.

54 *Glasgow Herald* 27/1/1982.

55 Salmond, *The Scottish Industrial Resistance*, 2–4.

56 *The Salmond Years* (STV) 18/2/2001.

57 *Linlithgowshire Journal and Gazette* 6/6/1980.

58 *The Salmond Years* (STV) 18/2/2001.

59 STV North tape L0042.

60 *Linlithgowshire Journal and Gazette* 12/6/1981.

61 Salmond, ed., *The Scottish Industrial Revolution*, 2.

62 At district council elections in May 1982, Salmond also attributed 'a number of significant results for the Party in industrial Scotland' to the SNP's support for industrial action at Plessey and Leyland (*79 Group News* 6/1982).

63 Gordon Wilson Papers Acc 13099/36.

64 Kemp, *The Hollow Drum?*, 167.

65 Salmond, ed., *The Scottish Industrial Revolution*, 4.

66 *Linlithgowshire Journal and Gazette* 28/11/1980.

67 Gordon Wilson Papers Acc 13099/9.

68 *Linlithgowshire Journal and Gazette* 19/6/1981.

69 Interview with Iain More, 23/4/2010.

70 Gordon Wilson Papers Acc 13099/23.

71 *Sunday Standard* 8/8/1982.

72 Gavin Kennedy Acc 11565/23. Corrie was the Conservative MP for Bute and Northern Ayrshire. His Abortion (Amendment) Bill was, although widely supported, unsuccessful.

73 *Independent on Sunday* 8/2/1992.

74 *Linlithgowshire Journal and Gazette* 30/10/1981.

75 Gavin Kennedy Acc 11565/23.

76 SNP Papers Acc 11987/43.

77 *Scotsman* 4/6/1982.

78 Kemp, *The Hollow Drum?*, 169.

79 Salmond, ed., *The Scottish Industrial Revolution*, 3.

80 *Scotsman* 5/6/1982.

81 *79 Group News* 8/1982.

82 *The Salmond Years* (STV) 18/2/2001.

83 Wilson, *SNP: The Turbulent Years*, 213.

84 *Scotsman* 24/6/1982.

85 *Scotsman* 30/6/1982.

86 Gordon Wilson Papers Acc 13099/27.

87 *Scotsman* 27/9/1982.

88 *Total Politics* Issue 3 9/2008. The full quote was: 'I got expelled from the SNP in 1982 as a rather brash young man. I've often reflected that there was a considerable amount of fault on my side.'

89 *Scotsman* 16/9/1990.

90 *The Salmond Years* (STV) 18/2/2001.

91 Interview with Stephen Maxwell, 2/3/2010.

Chapter 4 'The pragmatic left'

1 Sillars, *The Case for Optimism*, 150.
2 *The Salmond Years* (STV) 18/2/2001.
3 Marr, *The Battle for Scotland*, 191.
4 *Glasgow Herald* 21/9/1987.
5 Interview with Stephen Maxwell, 2/3/2010.
6 Private information.
7 Wilson, *SNP: The Turbulent Years*, 214.
8 *Radical Scotland* June/July 1983.
9 Peter Brunskill to the author, 8/8/2010.
10 Interview with Stewart Stevenson MSP, 29/6/2010.
11 *Scotland on Sunday* 17/9/2000.
12 SNP Papers Acc 11987/20.
13 Interview with Jonathan Mitchell, QC, 3/11/2009.
14 *Sunday Post* 6/3/1983.
15 SNP Papers Acc 11987/45.
16 Gordon Wilson Papers Acc 13099/10.
17 Wilson, *SNP: The Turbulent Years*, 215–16. The appeals procedure also meant Salmond missed the wedding of his university friend, Peter Brunskill.
18 Interview with Gordon Wilson, 16/7/2010.
19 Wilson, *SNP: The Turbulent Years*, 217–18.
20 Lynch, *SNP*, 174.
21 *Sunday Standard* 30/1/1983.
22 Stephen Maxwell Papers.
23 *Herald* 15/5/1996.
24 http://www.scotland.gov.uk/News/This-Week/Speeches/First-Minister/Edin-burghlecture
25 Salmond, *The Royal Bank in Glasgow*, 37–38.
26 *Herald* 24/9/1997.
27 Salmond, *The Royal Bank in Glasgow* 11, 38–41.
28 *Independent on Sunday* 8/2/1992.
29 Interview with Michael Fry, 18/3/2010.
30 *Glasgow Herald* 21/9/1987.
31 *New Left Review* May/June 1968.
32 Marr, *The Battle for Scotland*, 217. Salmond's poster came from the first edition of *Radical Scotland*, for which Marr worked as a cartoonist.
33 Interview with Michael Fry.
34 Interview with Peter Clarke, 9/2/2010.
35 *Newsline* 4/1984.
36 Interview with Grant Baird, 22/1/2010.
37 *Newsline* 4/1984.
38 Interview with Glynne Baird, 22/1/2010. Glynne Baird later made it to the SNP's list of approved candidates for the 1999 Scottish Parliament elections but failed to secure a nomination.
39 Interview with Peter Brunskill, 1/2/2010.
40 This was a 'third format' that had been introduced to the European market in 1979. Although considered technically superior to its Betamax and VHS rivals, it was obsolete by 1985.
41 *The Times* 21/9/1982.
42 Wilson, *SNP: The Turbulent Years*, 218.
43 SNP Papers Acc 11987/82.

44 Wilson, *SNP: The Turbulent Years*, 223.
45 SNP Papers Acc 11987/79.
46 This motion supported membership of the EEC following a referendum post-independence.
47 Wilson, *SNP: The Turbulent Years*, 226.
48 *Political Quarterly* 59 4 (1988).
49 Marr, *The Battle for Scotland*, 195, 217–18.
50 SNP Papers Acc 11987/46.
51 *Scotsman* 21/8/1984.
52 *Toronto Star* 31/8/1986.
53 Sillars, *The Case for Optimism*, 79, 95, 145–50.
54 *Guardian* 25/2/1985.
55 *Glasgow Herald* 22/2/1985.
56 Interview with Isobel Lindsay, 23/2/2010.
57 *Scotland on Sunday* 15/8/2010.
58 *Scots Independent* 5/1982.
59 Gordon Wilson Papers Acc 13099/50.
60 Wilson, *SNP: The Turbulent Years*, 227.
61 Private information.
62 *Scots Independent* 6/1985.
63 *Radical Scotland* April/May 1986.
64 *Scots Independent* 6/1985.
65 SNP Papers Acc 11987/47.
66 Wilson, *SNP: The Turbulent Years*, 180.
67 SNP Papers Acc 11987/47.
68 Gordon Wilson Papers Acc 13099/12.
69 *Glasgow Herald* 22/8/1986.
70 SNP Papers Acc 11987/48.
71 SNP Papers Acc 11987/47.
72 *Scots Independent* 9/1986.
73 *Scottish Daily Express* 15/12/1986.
74 *Scots Independent* 12/1986.
75 *Scots Independent* 11/1986.
76 SNP Papers Acc 11987/49.
77 *Scotsman* 9/1/1987.
78 *Scotsman* 8/3/1987.
79 *Scotsman* 20/5/1987.
80 Interview with Jim Fairlie, 27/4/2010.
81 *Press and Journal* 23/1/1985.
82 *Press and Journal* 30/1/1985.
83 *Glasgow Herald* 22/2/1985.
84 *Scotland on Sunday* 3/9/2000.
85 *Scots Independent* 4/1985.
86 *Scots Independent* 8/1985.
87 *Glasgow Herald* 21/9/1987.
88 *Scotland on Sunday* 3/9/2000.
89 *Scotsman* 18/5/1987.
90 *Scotsman* 10/6/1987. The future SNP MP, Angus Robertson, also campaigned for Salmond during this campaign while the young academic, Dr James Mitchell, acted as his press officer.
91 *Scotsman* 4/6/1987.
92 *Scottish Daily Mail* 12/10/2006.
93 John MacLeod to the author, 23/10/2009.

94 *Glasgow Herald* 30/5/1987.

95 *Scotsman* 23/9/1990.

96 Interview with Robert and Mary Salmond, 2/2/2001 (STV B66161).

97 John MacLeod to the author, 23/10/2009.

98 *Scotland on Sunday* 3/9/2000.

99 SNP Papers Acc 11987/49.

Chapter 5 'The infant Robespierre'

1 Short, *Pol Pot*, 74.

2 *Scotland on Sunday* 10/9/2000.

3 Hansard 129 c1008.

4 *Glasgow Herald* 16/3/1988.

5 *Banffshire Journal* 23/3/2010.

6 *Scotland on Sunday* 10/9/2000.

7 *Glasgow Herald, Scotsman* 16/3/1988.

8 *Scotsman* 16/3/1988.

9 *Independent* 20/9/1998.

10 Hansard 129 c1008.

11 *Banffshire Journal* 23/3/2010.

12 *Banffshire Journal* 23/3/2010.

13 *Scotland on Sunday* 10/9/2000.

14 Lawson, *The View From No. 11*, 816.

15 *Glasgow Herald* 16/3/1988.

16 *Scotsman* 16/3/1988.

17 *Independent on Sunday* 8/2/1992.

18 *Scotsman* 17/3/1988.

19 *Scots Independent* 4/1988.

20 *Scotsman* 23/3/1988.

21 Alex Salmond to Bernard Ponsonby, 1/2001 (author's collection).

22 *Scotland on Sunday* 10/9/2000.

23 *Scotland on Sunday* 10/9/2000.

24 *Herald* 7/4/1994.

25 Mitchell, *Strategies for Self-Government*, 222.

26 *Hansard* 118 cc321–25.

27 Gordon Wilson Papers Acc 13099/76.

28 *Glasgow Herald* 21/9/1987.

29 *Scotsman* 16/11/1987.

30 Wilson, *SNP: The Turbulent Years*, 235.

31 *Glasgow Herald* 25/9/1987.

32 Although the author could not trace this article, John MacLeod has a clear memory of its existence (*Daily Mail* 12/10/2006).

33 *Glasgow Herald* 24/9/1987.

34 Interview with Mike Russell MSP, 15/1/2001 (STV B111940).

35 Interview with Gordon Wilson, 16/7/2010.

36 Interview with Mike Russell MSP.

37 *Scotsman* 25/9/1987. The Radical War, also known as the Scottish Insurrection of 1820, was a week of unrest brutally suppressed by the UK government.

38 *Scotsman* 2/9/1987.

39 *Scotsman* 27/1/1988.

40 Mitchell, *Strategies for Self Government*, 185.

41 Sillars, *The Case for Optimism*, 186–90.

42 Hansard 136 c1112.
43 *Radical Scotland* Aug/Sep 1988.
44 *Scotsman* 13/6/1989.
45 *Scotland on Sunday* 10/9/2000.
46 SNP Papers Acc 11987/50.
47 *Scotsman* 22/4/1988.
48 *Scotsman* 29/4/1988.
49 *Scotsman* 6/6/1988.
50 *The Salmond Years* (STV) 18/2/2001.
51 Brown & McCrone, eds, *Scottish Government Yearbook 1991*, 125.
52 Hansard 125 c159.
53 Hansard 136 cc1087–94.
54 Gordon Wilson Papers Acc 13099/40.
55 *Financial Times* 26/10/1988.
56 *Scotsman* 12/11/1988.
57 *The Salmond Years* (STV) 18/2/2001.
58 *Scotsman* 15/11/1988.
59 SNP Papers Acc 11987/50.
60 *Observer* 24/9/1989.
61 Sillars, *The Case for Optimism*, 24–25.
62 Private information.
63 *Scotsman* 30/1/1989.
64 *The Salmond Years* (STV) 18/2/2001.
65 Kemp, *The Hollow Drum?*, 162.
66 SNP Papers Acc 11987/49.
67 Kemp, *The Hollow Drum?*, 162.
68 Taylor, *The Scottish Parliament*, 41.
69 Gordon Wilson Papers Acc 13099/57.
70 *Scotsman, Glasgow Herald* 31/1/1989.
71 Marr, *The Battle for Scotland*, 203.
72 Kemp, *The Hollow Drum?*, 162.
73 *The Salmond Years* (STV) 18/2/2001.
74 *Observer* 5/2/1989.
75 *Glasgow Herald* 6/3/1989.
76 Brown & Parry, eds, *Scottish Government Yearbook 1990*, 29.
77 Interview with Mike Russell MSP.
78 Interview with Jim Fairlie, 19/1/2010.
79 Interview with Isobel Lindsay, 23/2/2010.
80 *The Salmond Years* (STV) 18/2/2001.
81 Brown & Parry, eds, *Scottish Government Yearbook 1990*, 30.
82 *Scotsman* 6/3/1989.
83 *Scotsman* 17/3/1989.
84 *Scotsman* 23/9/1989.
85 *Observer* 18/6/1989.
86 Brown & Parry, eds, *Scottish Government Yearbook 1990*, 17.
87 Hansard 155 cc986–87.
88 *Political Quarterly* 59 4 (1988).
89 SNP Papers Acc 11987/50.
90 Gordon Wilson Papers Acc 13099/13.
91 The SCESR, however, withered on the political vine shortly after the 1992 general election.
92 Gordon Wilson Papers Acc 13099/51.
93 Hansard 125 c531.
94 *Scotsman* 25/2/1989.

95 *Observer* 28/5/1989.

96 Hansard 143 c777.

97 *Scotsman* 20/5/1989.

98 *Scots Independent* 10/1989.

99 *Scotsman* 27/7/1989.

100 Gordon Wilson Papers Acc 13099/14.

101 Lynch, *SNP*, 192–93.

102 Wilson, *SNP: The Turbulent Years*, 246.

103 Interview with Jim Sillars, 17/9/2009.

104 Private information.

105 Interview with Margo MacDonald MSP, 28/6/2010.

106 *The Salmond Years* (STV) 18/2/2000.

107 Wilson, *SNP: The Turbulent Years*, 246.

108 *Scotland on Sunday* 23/9/1990.

109 *Observer* 20/5/1990.

110 *Scotland on Sunday* 23/9/1990. The lines are from Montrose's poem 'My Dear and Only Love', although Salmond often misquoted slightly the third line: 'Who dare not put it to the touch'.

111 Lynch, *SNP*, 193.

112 *Observer* 10/6/1990.

113 *Scotland on Sunday* 23/9/1990.

114 Sillars told Arnold Kemp that he believed Salmond 'was not ready for leadership. He had come into Parliament only in 1987. He was inexperienced. He had not yet learned to handle people' (Kemp, *The Hollow Drum?*, 162).

115 *Scotsman* 14/8/1990.

116 *Scotsman* 16/9/1990.

117 *Guardian* 12/7/1990.

118 *Scotsman* 15/8/1990.

119 *Scotland on Sunday* 23/9/1990.

120 Ewing, *Stop the World*, 244.

121 Two of whom were Peter Murrell, then Salmond's constituency assistant, and Stuart Pratt, Salmond's agent and a senior SNP councillor in Banff and Buchan.

122 *Scotsman* 2/8/1990.

123 *Scotland on Sunday* 23/9/1990.

124 *Scotsman* 9/8/1990.

125 *Scotsman* 28/8/1990.

126 *Scotsman* 23/9/1990.

127 *Scotsman* 30/8/1990.

128 *Scotsman* 7/8/1990. Dick Douglas finally joined the SNP in October 1990.

129 *Scotland on Sunday* 23/9/1990.

130 *Radical Scotland* Aug/Sep 1990.

131 *Scotland on Sunday* 23/9/1990.

132 *Scotsman* 15/8/1990.

133 *Scotland on Sunday* 23/9/1990.

134 *Scotsman* 22/9/1990.

135 *Scotsman* 19/9/1990.

136 *Scotsman* 22/9/1990.

137 *Scotsman* 23/9/1990.

138 *Scotsman* 24/9/1990.

139 *Linlithgow Gazette* 28/9/1990. Inevitably, the *Gazette* concentrated on Salmond's local connections, headlining its report: 'Academy "old boy" now leads SNP.'

140 *Scotsman* 23/9/1990.

141 Churchill, *Second World War I*, 526–27.

Chapter 6 'Free by 93'

1 Mitchell, *Strategies for Self-Government*, 245.
2 *Scotsman* 23/9/1990. Although certainly a 'young man', Salmond was not the SNP's youngest leader, that honour being held by Jimmy Halliday, who had been only 27 when elected in 1956.
3 *Sunday Post* 4/11/1990.
4 *Scotsman* 23/9/1990.
5 Interview with Chris McLean, 22/3/2010.
6 Private information.
7 Interview with John Swinney MSP, 19/1/2001 (STV B102765).
8 *Scotsman* 23/9/1990.
9 Gallagher, ed., *Nationalism in the Nineties*, 1 & 28.
10 *The Times* 22/11/1990.
11 *Scotsman* 20/5/1989.
12 *Banffshire Journal* 23/3/2010.
13 Henderson Scott, *A Twentieth Century Life*, 298.
14 *Sunday Post* 4/11/1990.
15 *Walden Interviews Alex Salmond* (LWT) 15/3/1992. These remarks were made off-air.
16 *Sunday Post* 4/11/1990.
17 Kenny Farquharson to the author, 15/7/2010.
18 *Sunday Post* 4/11/1990.
19 *The Times* 24/9/1990.
20 *Scotsman* 25/2/1991.
21 *Scotsman* 4/1/1991.
22 *Guardian* 2/12/1991.
23 *Scotsman* 25/2/1991.
24 *Scotsman* 24/3/1991.
25 *Scotsman* 23/4/1991.
26 Linklater, *Anatomy of Scotland*, 389.
27 *Scotsman* 12/7/1991.
28 *Sunday Herald* 14/6/2009.
29 *Scotsman* 17/9/1991.
30 *Scotsman* 30/8/1991.
31 *Independent on Sunday* 8/2/1992.
32 *Scotsman* 17/9/1991.
33 *Scotsman* 20/9/1991.
34 *Scotland on Sunday* 23/7/2000.
35 *Scotsman* 19/9/1991.
36 *The Salmond Years* (STV) 18/2/2001.
37 *Scotland on Sunday* 10/9/2000.
38 *The Salmond Years* (STV) 18/2/2001.
39 *Scotland on Sunday* 10/9/2000.
40 *Scotsman* 19/9/1991.
41 *Scotland on Sunday* 22/9/1991.
42 *Scotsman* 23/9/1991.
43 *Guardian* 2/12/1991.
44 *Independent on Sunday* 8/2/1992.
45 *Guardian* 2/12/1991.
46 *Scotsman* 1/8/1991.
47 *Scotland on Sunday* 10/9/2000.

48 *Scotsman* 20/1/1992.

49 *Scotland: A Time to Choose* (BBC Scotland) 1992.

50 *Scots Independent* 8/2000.

51 *Scotland on Sunday* 10/9/2000.

52 *Scottish Sun* 23/1/1992.

53 *Edinburgh Evening News* 29/1/1992.

54 *Scotland on Sunday* 10/9/2000.

55 Paterson, ed., *Scottish Government Yearbook 1992*, 198.

56 *Scotland on Sunday* 1/3/1992.

57 *Edinburgh Evening News* 6/3/1992.

58 *Scotsman* 13/3/1992.

59 *Walden Interviews Alex Salmond* (LWT) 15/3/1992. Walden later disclosed that had he would have supported independence had he been a Scot.

60 *Reporting Scotland* (BBC Scotland) 4/1992.

61 *The Salmond Years* (STV) 18/2/2001.

62 *Scotsman* 28/7/2000.

63 Macdonald, *Unionist Scotland 1800–1997*, 128.

64 *Scotsman* 8/4/1992.

65 Harvie, *Scotland and Nationalism*, 205.

66 *Scotland on Sunday* 10/9/2000.

Chapter 7 The future of Nationalism

1 Lyons, *Charles Stewart Parnell*, 623.

2 *Scotland on Sunday* 10/9/2000.

3 Lynch, *SNP*, 194.

4 *Scotland on Sunday* 10/9/2000. 'I care nothing for Alex Salmond's opinion of me,' responded Sillars, 'or his inventions' (*Scotland on Sunday* 17/9/2000).

5 Interview with Mike Russell MSP, 15/1/2001 (STV B111940).

6 *Scotland on Sunday* 3/9/2000.

7 *Scotsman* 21/4/1992.

8 *Herald* 8/6/1992.

9 *Scotsman* 8/6/1992.

10 Marr, *The Battle for Scotland*, 218.

11 *Scottish Affairs* 1 autumn 1992.

12 *Scotsman* 25/9/1992.

13 *Scotland on Sunday* 27/9/1992.

14 *Scotsman* 28/9/1992.

15 *Scottish Affairs* 5 autumn 1993. The author is indebted to Peter Jones for his detailed account of this episode.

16 Private information.

17 *Scotland on Sunday* 14/3/1993.

18 *Scottish Sun* 15/3/1993.

19 *Scotland on Sunday* 15/8/1993.

20 Interview with Jim Eadie, 13/2/2010.

21 *Edinburgh Evening News* 7/6/1993.

22 *Scottish Sun* 10/8/1993.

23 Interview with Jim Sillars, 17/9/2009.

24 *Scotland on Sunday* 15/8/1993.

25 *Scotsman* 18/8/1993.

26 *Scotland on Sunday* 15/8/1993.

27 *Scotsman* 18/8/1993.

28 *Scotsman* 19/8/1993.

29 *Edinburgh Evening News* 18/9/1993.

30 Salmond, '*Horizons Without Bars*', 57–62.

31 Interview with Mike Russell MSP.

32 *Scotsman* 21/9/1993.

33 *Scotland on Sunday* 19/9/1993.

34 *Herald* 23/9/1993.

35 *Herald* 25/9/1993.

36 *Scotsman* 25/9/1993.

37 *Scotsman* 26/9/1993. Neil was appointed defence spokesman shortly after the conference.

38 *Herald* 3/2/1994.

39 *Scotsman* 5/2/1994.

40 *Herald* 7/5/1994.

41 *Herald* 4/8/1994.

42 *Scottish Affairs* 8 summer 1994.

43 *Herald* 27/9/1994. Salmond's sister Gail was a member of the Aberdeen Free Church.

44 Salmond instead recorded a light-hearted video along the lines of 'my country needs me', while gifting his mother a Swiss Army knife.

45 *Herald* 2/7/1994.

46 *Herald* 1/7/1994.

47 *Herald* 2/7/1994.

48 *The Times* 18/3/2009.

49 McGinty, *This Turbulent Priest*, 337.

50 *Scottish Affairs* 13 autumn 1995.

51 McGinty, *This Turbulent Priest*, 337–38.

52 *Tablet* 25/7/2009.

53 McGinty, *This Turbulent Priest*, 337–38.

54 *The Times* 18/3/2009.

55 *Herald* 6/10/1994.

56 SNP conference (BBC Scotland) 10/1993.

57 *Herald* 14/4/1994.

58 *Scotsman* 21/9/1994.

59 *Herald* 26/9/1994.

60 *Herald* 24/9/1994.

61 *Guardian* 24/9/1994.

62 *Herald* 26 & 27/9/1994.

63 *New Statesman & Society* 10/3/1995.

64 *Independent* 5/1/1997.

65 Salmond was paid £127 per column, a modest rate for the mid-1990s.

66 *Scotland on Sunday* 29/1/1995.

67 *Scotsman* 31/1/1995.

68 *Herald* 1/2/1995.

69 *Scottish Sun* 30/1/1995.

70 BBC Radio Scotland 31/1/1995.

71 *Scotland on Sunday* 12/2/1995. David Kerr, then with the Federation of Student Nationalists, challenged his leader's tactics at the NEC meeting, but survived to become the SNP candidate in the Glasgow North-East by-election of November 2009.

72 Interview with Mike Russell MSP.

73 Ascherson, *Stone Voices*, 122.

74 *Scotsman* 13/2/1995.

75 *Herald* 13/2/1995.

76 *Scotsman* 13/2/1995.

77 Interview with Lord Wallace, 5/3/2010.

78 *Herald* 11/3/1995.

79 *Scotsman* 29/4/1995. Salmond revived his campaign against the Act of Settlement in 2006, this time in partnership with Cardinal Keith O'Brien.

80 *Scottish Affairs* 13 autumn 1995.

81 *Herald* 8/3/1995.

82 *Herald* 17/5/1995.

83 *Herald* 6/10/1994.

84 *Scotland on Sunday* 3/9/1995.

85 *Scotsman* 16/9/1995.

86 *Scotsman* 21/9/1995.

87 *Scotland on Sunday* 17/9/1995.

88 *Scotland on Sunday* 3/9/1995.

89 *Scotland on Sunday* 1/10/1995.

90 *Scotsman* 25/9/1995.

91 *Independent on Sunday* 8/2/1992.

92 *Scotsman* 21/9/1995.

93 *Guardian* 7/4/1997.

94 *Herald* 20/3/1996.

95 *The Economist* 13/4/1996.

96 *Scotsman* 29/9/1995.

97 *Edinburgh Evening News* 23/8/1996.

98 When Salmond demanded a 'right of reply' because the prime minister had started 'bawling' at him, the Speaker Betty Boothroyd accused him of 'making gestures from a seated position and provoking the Prime Minister', adding that Salmond 'got what he deserved' (Hansard 254 cc140–41).

99 Interview with Andrew Wilson, 29/1/2010. The original suggestion for these Parliamentary Questions had come from the journalist George Kerevan.

100 Private information.

101 Scottish Liberal Democrats, *Alex in Wonderland*, 2.

102 *Scotsman* 27/6/1996.

103 *Observer* 25/9/1996.

104 *Toronto Star* 8/9/1996.

105 *Scotsman* 23/9/1996.

106 *Herald* 2/4/1997.

107 *Scotsman* 23/9/1996.

108 *Scotsman* 28/9/1996.

109 *Scotland on Sunday* 27/1/1997.

110 Interview with Jim Sillars, 17/9/2009.

111 *Scotland on Sunday* 12/1/1997.

112 *Scotsman* 31/1/1997.

113 *Scotsman* 1/2/1997.

114 *Scotsman* 6/3/1997.

115 *Herald* 2/4/1997.

116 *Scotsman* 3/4/1997.

117 *Guardian* 7/4/1997.

118 *Scotsman* 8/4/1997.

119 *Herald* 12/3/1997.

120 *Scotsman* 16/4/1997.

121 *Independent* 5/1/1997.

122 *Scotsman* 23/9/1996.

123 *Herald* 7/4/1994.

Chapter 8 'The spirit of 97'

1 *Scotland on Sunday* 3/9/2000.
2 *Scotland on Sunday* 10/9/2000.
3 *Scotsman* 9/5/1997. Salmond also claimed the SNP had won 'nearly' a quarter of the Scottish vote, an exaggeration given an actual figure of 21.5 per cent.
4 *Scotsman* 14/5/1997.
5 Brian Wilson to the author, 28/7/2010.
6 *The Salmond Years* (STV) 18/2/2001.
7 Hansard 294 c725.
8 *Scotland on Sunday* 17/9/2000.
9 *Daily Record* 22/8/1997.
10 *Guardian* 28/7/1997.
11 For once the usually Sillars-aligned Iain Lawson backed Salmond. 'I am totally supportive of the position the party has taken,' he told the *Scotsman*. 'This parliament is the best on offer, and it is the responsibility of the SNP to secure the best on offer' (*Scotsman* 29/8/1997).
12 *Observer* 3/8/1997.
13 *Independent* 20/9/1998.
14 *Scotland on Sunday* 17/9/2000.
15 *Scotland on Sunday* 23/7/2000.
16 Anonymous, *Donald Dewar*, 91–92.
17 *Scotland on Sunday* 17/10/2000.
18 *Daily Record* 22/8/1997.
19 *Edinburgh Evening News* 3/9/1997. Saturday 6 September was to be the day of Diana's public funeral.
20 *Scotland on Sunday* 3/9/2000. Brian Wilson, however, thought the pictures 'nauseating' (Brian Wilson to the author, 28/7/2010).
21 *The Salmond Years* (STV) 18/2/2001.
22 Taylor, *The Scottish Parliament*, 134.
23 Connery was finally knighted in July 2000 at Holyroodhouse. At a celebratory gathering afterwards Sir Sean told Salmond: 'It wasn't long in coming really. After all, the parliament took 300 years' (*Scotland on Sunday* 10/9/2000).
24 *Scotland on Sunday* 17/10/2000.
25 *Herald* 17/9/1997. Salmond's final *Herald* column appeared the following week.
26 *Scots Independent* 8/2000.
27 *Scotsman* 8/5/1999.
28 *Scotsman* 5/11/2003.
29 *Sunday Herald* 4/2/2007.
30 *Guardian* 27/9/1997.
31 *Scotsman* 24/9/1997.
32 *Scotsman* 26/9/1997.
33 *Scotsman* 8/11/1997.
34 *Herald* 15/12/1997.
35 *Scotsman* 13/11/1997.
36 *Herald* 19/2/1998.
37 *Scotsman* 16/3/1998. MacAskill stood down as treasurer in July 1998, after four years in the post.
38 *Mirror* 17/12/1998.
39 *Daily Record* 7/5/1998.
40 *Scotsman* 12/5/1998.

41 *Scotsman* 18/7/1998.
42 *The Times* 22/4/1998.
43 *Scotsman* 18/7/1998.
44 *Edinburgh Evening News* 27/7/1998.
45 *Scotland on Sunday* 12/4/1998.
46 *Scotsman* 10/8/1998.
47 *Guardian* 27/7/1998.
48 *Independent* 20/9/1998.
49 *Daily Express* 2/11/2001.
50 *Scotsman* 10/8/1998.
51 *Scotsman* 11/8/1998.
52 *Scotsman* 21/9/1998.
53 'Poems, Prayers and Profits' for *Platform* (STV) 1997.
54 *Scotsman* 10/8/1998.
55 *Independent* 20/9/1998.
56 *Scotsman* 23/9/1998.
57 Tragically, in 2008 – by which point he was *The Times*' religious affairs correspondent – Christopher Morgan committed suicide aged 55.
58 *Mirror* 4/9/1998.
59 *Scotland on Sunday* 17/9/2000.
60 *Mirror* 17/12/1998.
61 *Scotland on Sunday* 22/4/2007.
62 *Mirror* 4/9/1998.
63 *Independent* 20/9/1998.
64 *Scotsman* 24/9/1998.
65 *Scotsman* 26/9/1998.
66 *Scotland on Sunday* 6/12/1998.
67 *Edinburgh Evening News* 25/11/1998.
68 *Scotsman* 27/11/1998.
69 This had been caused by the death of Allan Macartney, the SNP MEP and the party's former deputy leader, a significant blow for the party at that time.
70 *Daily Mail* 1/12/1998.
71 Quoted in *Globe and Mail* 5/12/1998.
72 *Scotland on Sunday* 13/12/1998.
73 *Mirror* 17/12/1998.
74 *Mirror* 17/12/1998.
75 Campbell, *The Blair Years*, 365.
76 Campbell, *Diaries II*, 687.
77 *Scotsman* 8/2/1999.
78 *Daily Record* 18/2/1999.
79 Private information.
80 *Sunday Herald* 21/2/1999.
81 *Daily Mail* 26/2/1999.
82 Press Association 26/2/1999.
83 Private information.
84 Interview with Andrew Wilson, 29/1/2010.
85 Private information.
86 *Scotsman* 29/3/1999.
87 *Scotland on Sunday* 17/9/2000.
88 *Scotsman* 30/3/1999.
89 Campbell, *The Blair Years*, 372.
90 *Scotsman* 30/3/1999.
91 *Edinburgh Evening News* 31/3/1999.

92 *Scotland on Sunday* 17/9/2000.

93 *Scotsman* 31/3/1999.

94 Taylor, *The Scottish Parliament*, 161.

95 Ritchie, *Scotland Reclaimed*, 73 & 95.

96 Russell & McLeod, *Grasping the Thistle*, 29.

97 Ritchie, *Scotland Reclaimed*, 68–70.

98 Gordon Wilson Papers Acc 13099/65.

99 *The Salmond Years* (STV) 18/2/2001.

100 *Scotland on Sunday* 17/9/2000.

101 *Scotland on Sunday* 4/4/1999.

102 Private information.

103 *Scotsman* 7/4/1999.

104 Taylor, *The Scottish Parliament*, 171.

105 *The Salmond Years* (STV) 18/2/2001.

106 Taylor, *Scotland's Parliament*, 165–66.

107 *Scotsman* 28/4/2007.

108 *Daily Mail* 9/4/1999.

109 Ritchie, *Scotland Reclaimed*, 89–90.

110 *Scotsman* 16/4/1999.

111 *Sunday Mirror* 18/4/1999.

112 *Guardian* 22/4/1999.

113 Ritchie, *Scotland Reclaimed*, 116.

114 *Edinburgh Evening News* 23/4/1999.

115 Ritchie, *Scotland Reclaimed*, 116.

116 *Scotsman* 23/4/1999.

117 *Guardian* 23/4/1999.

118 *Scotsman* 24/4/1999.

119 *Sunday Herald* 25/4/1999.

120 *The Times* 24/4/1999.

121 *Sunday Herald* 25/4/1999.

122 Ritchie, *Scotland Reclaimed*, 133–34.

123 The Scottish Conservatives memorably, if not particularly effectively, portrayed Salmond as a Teletubby 'living in Scot-la-la land' (*Scotsman* 5/5/1999).

124 The models for *Scotland's Voice* were, according to Murray Ritchie, Ireland's Eamon de Valera and Poland's Solidarity movement, both of whom had launched newspapers that eventually became bestsellers.

125 *Scotland on Sunday* 2/5/1999.

126 Ritchie, *Scotland Reclaimed*, 142–43.

127 *Sunday Herald* 4/2/2007.

128 *Scotsman* 7/5/1999.

129 *Scotland on Sunday* 9/5/1999.

130 *Scotsman* 18/7/2000.

131 *Scotland on Sunday* 9/5/1999.

132 In the overlooked local government elections, which took place the same day, the SNP went from 26.2 to 28.9 per cent of the vote, and from 181 to 201 seats, although it slipped from controlling three councils to just one – its stronghold in Angus.

133 Rawnsley, *Servants of the People*, 254.

134 *The Salmond Years* (STV) 18/2/2001.

Chapter 9 'Dynamic opposition'

1 http://www.scottish.parliament.uk/vli/history/donaldDewar/index.htm
2 *Edinburgh Evening News* 7/5/1999.
3 Interview with Alex Salmond MSP, 3/2009 (courtesy of Colin Mackay).
4 Official Report 12/5/1999 Col 1.
5 Watson, *Year Zero*, 14.
6 Official Report 13/5/1999 Col 25–26.
7 *Herald* 27/5/1999.
8 *Edinburgh Evening News* 12/8/1999.
9 *Scotsman* 12/8/1999.
10 *Daily Express* 12/8/1999.
11 The SNP later moved to new premises on McDonald Road.
12 *Herald* 20/8/1999.
13 *Herald* 24/8/1999.
14 *Edinburgh Evening News* 23/8/1999.
15 *Scotsman* 2/9/1999.
16 *Edinburgh Evening News* 7/9/1999.
17 Interview with Alex Salmond MSP, 3/2009.
18 *Scotsman* 20/9/1999. Alex Bell was also the son of Colin Bell, Salmond's predecessor as the SNP's publicity vice-convener.
19 *Edinburgh Evening News* 22/9/1999.
20 *Scotsman* 22/9/1999.
21 *Scotsman* 22/9/1999.
22 *Scotsman* 24/9/1999.
23 *Scotsman* 25/9/1999.
24 http://news.bbc.co.uk/1/hi/uk_politics/456038.stm
25 The by-election had been caused by George Robertson's elevation to the House of Lords after becoming general-secretary of NATO. The SNP, hoping to recapture the magic of another Hamilton by-election in 1967, fielded Annabelle Ewing, daughter of Winnie.
26 *Scotsman* 25/9/1999.
27 *Scotland on Sunday* 17/10/1999.
28 *Scotsman* 16/11/1999.
29 MacAskill & McLeish, *Global Scots*, 153.
30 *Scotsman* 16/11/1999.
31 Official Report 2/7/1999.
32 McLeish, *Scotland First*, 218.
33 Official Report 11/5/2000 Col 589–90.
34 Watson, *Year Zero*, 34.
35 *Edinburgh Evening News* 1/2/2000.
36 *Scottish Daily Mail* 17/2/2000.
37 *Herald* 19/8/1993.
38 *Sunday Herald* 28/5/2000.
39 *Sunday Herald* 4/2/2007.
40 Bain, *Holyrood: The Inside Story*, 97.
41 *Scottish Daily Mail* 17/2/2000.
42 *Mirror* 24/1/2000.
43 *Scotsman* 9/3/2000.
44 *Holyrood* (BBC) 26/3/2000.
45 *Scotsman* 27/3/2000.

46 Private information.
47 Salmond also won backing for his policy on the Euro at this National Council meeting.
48 *Scotsman* 12/6/2000.
49 *Scotsman* 14/6/2000.
50 *Scotsman* 13/6/2000.
51 *Scotsman* 14/6/2000. Kenny MacAskill, who had been treasurer until 1998, stood in for Blackford.
52 *Edinburgh Evening News* 15/6/2000.
53 Conversation with Ian Swanson, 23/6/2010.
54 *Sunday Times* 18/6/2000.
55 *Scotland on Sunday* 18/6/2000. The author must declare an interest, for he is a member of the Tuesday Club, but does not recognise the description.
56 *The Week In Politics* (Grampian TV) 9/1/2003.
57 *Scotland on Sunday* 23/7/2000.
58 *Scotsman* 18/7/2000. This was not quite true. In September 1990 System Three put the SNP at a respectable 24 per cent; the 14 per cent figure more closely reflected the party's 1987 position.
59 Ewing, *Stop the World*, 305.
60 *The Salmond Years* (STV) 18/2/2001.
61 Private information.
62 *Scotland on Sunday* 23/7/2000.
63 *The Salmond Years* (STV) 18/2/2001.
64 *Scotsman* 18/7/2000.
65 Interview with Duncan Hamilton, 21/7/2010.
66 *Scotsman* 21/7/2000.
67 Interview with Alex Salmond MSP, 3/2009.
68 *Scottish Sun* 23/9/2000.
69 *Scottish Daily Mail* 18/7/2000.
70 *Scottish Sun* 18/7/2000.
71 *Scotsman* 18/7/2000.
72 *The Times* 18/7/2000.
73 http://news.bbc.co.uk/1/hi/scotland/967258.stm
74 *Scots Independent* 9/2000.
75 *Perthshire Advertiser* 21/7/2000. Fairlie later joined the Free Scotland Party, which advocated independence from the UK *and* the EU, on whose behalf he contested the 2007 Holyrood elections.
76 *Herald* 19/7/2000.
77 *Scotsman* 19/7/2000.
78 *Scottish Sun* 18/7/2000.
79 *Sunday Herald* 23/7/2000.
80 *Scotsman* 28/7/2000.
81 *Edinburgh Evening News* 22/9/2000.
82 *Scotsman* 22/9/2000.
83 *Mirror* 22/9/2000.
84 *Edinburgh Evening News* 22/9/2000.
85 *Scotsman* 23/9/2000.
86 Swinney secured 547 delegate votes to Alex Neil's 262. Roseanna Cunningham, meanwhile, beat Kenny MacAskill and Peter Kearney to become deputy leader.
87 *News of the World* 24/9/2000.
88 *Aberdeen Press and Journal* 23/9/2000.

Chapter 10 'The king over the water'

1 Interview with Jim Eadie, 13/2/2010.
2 Interview with Lord Foulkes MSP, 4/2/2010.
3 *Edinburgh Evening News* 2/12/2000.
4 *Scotsman* 16/12/2000.
5 *Scotland on Sunday* 14/1/2001.
6 *Aberdeen Evening Express* 15/1/2001.
7 *Scotsman* 15/1/2001.
8 *Edinburgh Evening News* 15/1/2001.
9 *Scotland on Sunday* 20/5/2001.
10 *Scotsman* 30/5/2001.
11 *Scotsman* 21/5/2001.
12 The brains behind this approach had been Jim and Margaret Cuthbert, two SNP-inclined economists.
13 *Edinburgh Evening News* 3/7/2001.
14 *Sunday Herald* 15/8/2004.
15 Mullin, *A View from the Foothills*, 369. Visiting Washington the same day was First Minister Henry McLeish, who got half an hour with the President.
16 *Scottish Daily Mail* 21/9/2001.
17 *Scotsman* 25/9/2001.
18 *Scotsman* 29/9/2001.
19 *Scotsman* 6/10/2001.
20 *Scotsman* 9/11/2001.
21 Taylor, *Scotland's Parliament*, 174.
22 *Scotsman* 11/5/2002.
23 *Scotsman* 21/5/2002.
24 *Edinburgh Evening News* 4/10/2002.
25 Private information.
26 *Scotsman* 10/6/2002.
27 *Edinburgh Evening News* 10/7/2002.
28 *Scotsman* 26/9/2002.
29 *Scotsman* 11/2/2003.
30 *Scotsman* 17/2/2003.
31 *Scotsman* 25/2/2003.
32 *Scotsman* 3/3/2003.
33 *Scotsman* 24/2/2003.
34 Erickson, ed., *The Economics of Independence*.
35 *Edinburgh Evening News* 6/5/2003.
36 *Desert Island Discs* (BBC Radio 4) 16/1/2011.
37 *Scotsman* 16/8/2003.
38 *Scotsman* 28/8/2003.
39 *Scotsman* 2/9/2003.
40 *Scotsman* 4/9/2003.
41 *Scotsman* 6/9/2003.
42 *Scotsman* 9/9/2003.
43 *Scotsman* 12/9/2003.
44 *Scotsman* 16/9/2003.
45 *Scotsman* 18/9/2003.
46 *Scotsman* 19/9/2003.
47 *Scotsman* 25/9/2003.

48 *Scotsman* 26/9/2003.
49 Jack McConnell conceded this early in the 2003 election campaign, perhaps to boost the independent Lothians campaign of Margo MacDonald, who had been urging a probe for some time.
50 *Mirror* 14/11/2003.
51 *Sunday Herald* 16/11/2003.
52 Interview with Alex Salmond MSP, 5/2007 (courtesy of Colin Mackay).
53 *Sunday Mirror* 27/6/2004.
54 *Scottish Sun* 28/6/2004.
55 *Edinburgh Evening News* 10/7/2004.
56 *Herald* 16/7/2004.
57 *Edinburgh Evening News* 15/7/2004.
58 *Scottish Daily Mail* 25/8/2007.
59 Private information.
60 *Scotsman* 16/7/2004.
61 Private information.
62 *Guardian* 31/1/2009.
63 Private information.
64 Interview with Alex Salmond MSP, 5/2009.
65 *Scottish Daily Mail* 19/7/2007.
66 *Total Politics* 3 9/2008.
67 *Scotsman* 17/7/2004.
68 *Scotsman* 16/7/2004.
69 http://news.bbc.co.uk/2/hi/uk_news/scotland/3895575.stm
70 MacAskill, *Building a Nation*, 78.
71 *Scotsman* 16/7/2004.
72 *Scotland on Sunday* 18/7/2004.
73 *Scotsman* 29/7/2004.
74 *Daily Express* 2/8/2004.
75 Press Association 12/8/2004. Salmond later denied making the comments.
76 *Scotland on Sunday* 15/8/2004.
77 Press Association 12/8/2004.
78 *Scotland on Sunday* 15/8/2004.
79 *Sunday Herald* 15/8/2004.
80 *Scotland on Sunday* 15/8/2004.
81 *Edinburgh Evening News* 4/9/2004. Mike Russell received 631 votes, 9.6 per cent of the votes cast, and Roseanna Cunningham 953 votes, 14.6 per cent.

Chapter 11 Salmond redux

1 *Scotsman* 4/9/2004.
2 http://www.snp.org/node/10890
3 *Sunday Herald* 5/9/2004.
4 'I am full-time and elected', retorted Salmond, 'as opposed to part-time and appointed, like him' (Hansard 424 c591).
5 *Sunday Herald* 5/9/2004.
6 *Glasgow Evening Times* 22/9/2004.
7 *Scotsman* 25/9/2004.
8 *Scottish Daily Mail* 25/9/2004.
9 *Sunday Herald* 16/11/2003.
10 *Scotsman* 26/8/2004.
11 *Scotsman* 25/11/2004.

12 *Scottish 500* (STV) 14/4/2005.
13 *Scotsman* 26/1/2005.
14 *Scotsman* 11/3/2005.
15 *Scotsman* 10/3/2005.
16 *Scotsman* 14/3/2005.
17 *Scotsman* 2/4/2005.
18 *Scotsman* 7/4/2005.
19 *Scottish Standard* 9/3/2005.
20 Private information.
21 *Scotsman* 7/5/2005.
22 Hansard 434 cc45–46.
23 *Scotsman* 24/9/2005.
24 Press Association 30/9/2005.
25 *Scotsman* 19/11/2005.
26 *Scotsman* 29/11/2005.
27 *Herald* 17/1/2006. There was also speculation that Salmond would contest Aberdeen Central, then held by Labour's Lewis Macdonald.
28 *Scots Independent* 2/2006.
29 *Scotsman* 18/4/2006.
30 *Scottish Affairs* 57 autumn 2006.
31 *Scottish Affairs* 58 winter 2007.
32 *Sunday Herald* 1/10/2006.
33 *Scotsman* 11/10/2006. The 'It's Time' slogan came from the Golley Slater advertising agency.
34 *Herald* 11/10/2006.
35 *Scottish Affairs* 60 summer 2007.
36 *Scottish Sun* 14/10/2006.
37 *Scottish Daily Mail* 12/10/2006.
38 *Herald* 27/11/2006.
39 http://news.bbc.co.uk/1/hi/uk/6182762.stm
40 http://news.bbc.co.uk/1/hi/scotland/6219745.stm
41 Interview with Lord McConnell MSP, 22/4/2010.
42 *Holyrood Magazine* 29/6/2009.
43 *Sunday Herald* 4/2/2007.
44 *Scotsman* 16/3/2007.
45 *Mirror* 17/3/2007.
46 *Sunday Herald* 18/3/2007.
47 *Scotsman* 19/3/2007.
48 *Daily Telegraph* 20/3/2007.
49 *Edinburgh Evening News* 20/3/2007.
50 *Scotsman* 31/3/2007.
51 *Sunday Herald* 22/11/2009.
52 Private information.
53 http://www.redco.uk.com/coaching.htm
54 *Scottish Daily Mail* 10/4/2007.
55 Watt, *Inside Out*, 43.
56 *Edinburgh Evening News* 12/4/2007.
57 *The Times* 7/4/2007.
58 *Face to Face* (STV) 19/4/2007.
59 *Scotland on Sunday* 22/4/2007.
60 *Sunday Times* 29/4/2007.
61 *Scotsman* 14/7/2009.
62 *Scotland on Sunday* 22/4/2007.

63 *Edinburgh Evening News* 26/4/2007.

64 http://news.bbc.co.uk/1/hi/scotland/6604995.stm

65 *The Times* 23/4/2007.

66 *Scotsman* 2/5/2007.

67 Cameron, *Impaled Upon a Thistle*, 367. There was also a parallel with Charles Stewart Parnell, the Irish home ruler, who stood and won Cork city in 1880 when it was generally assumed he had no chance of taking it.

68 *Scotsman* 4/5/2007.

69 *Daily Express* 5/5/2007.

70 *Scotsman* 5/5/2007.

71 Private information.

72 *Scotsman* 5/5/2007.

73 *Herald* 5/5/2007.

74 *Herald* 5/5/2007.

75 Herald 5/5/2007.

76 Holyrood 15/10/2010.

77 Edinburgh Evening News 7/5/2007.

78 *Harper*, Dear Mr Harper, 131.

79 *Scotsman* 8/5/2007.

80 Salmond was supported by his own MSPs and the two Greens. Labour's 46 MSPs voted against, while the Liberal Democrats and Conservatives abstained.

81 Official Report 16/5/2007 Col 36.

82 *Herald* 17/5/2007.

83 *Scottish Daily Mail* 15/5/2007.

84 Official Report 16/5/2007 Col 34.

85 *Scottish Daily Mail* 15/5/2007.

86 Interview with Robert Salmond and Gail Hendry, 16/5/2007 (STV DVL3037).

87 *Scotsman* 17/5/2007.

88 *Total Politics* Issue 3 9/2008.

89 Curtice, ed., *Revolution or Evolution?*, 120.

90 Johns, ed., *Voting for a Scottish government*, 176.

Chapter 12 'It's time'

1 *Scotsman* 17/5/2007.

2 *Scottish Affairs* 60 summer 2007.

3 Official Report 23/5/2007 Col 58.

4 *Scottish Affairs* 65 autumn 2008.

5 *Scotsman* 30/6/2007.

6 *Scotsman* 25/5/2007.

7 *Sunday Herald* 23/6/2007.

8 *Scotsman* 24/5/2007.

9 Official Report 31/5/2007 Col 315.

10 Blair, *A Journey*, 651.

11 Interview with Alex Salmond MSP, 2/2008 (courtesy of Katherine Haddon).

12 Official Report 7/6/2007.

13 http://www.publications.parliament.uk/pa/cm200910/cmselect/cmscotaf/uc256-i/uc25602.htm

14 *Sunday Herald* 24/6/2007.

15 *Edinburgh Evening News* 9/8/2007.

16 Interview with Alex Salmond MSP, 2/2008.

17 *Salmond's 100 Days* (STV) 21/8/2007.

18 *Total Politics* 3 9/2008.
19 *Edinburgh Evening News* 26/5/2007. This incident also sparked the famous Salmond temper. 'He started ripping into me. He told me never to do anything like that again,' said Angus Blackburn, a press photographer who overheard the remark and decided to publicise it. 'It was not in a balanced manner – he was really, really angry' (*Scotland on Sunday* 27/5/2007).
20 *Daily Telegraph* 10/5/2007.
21 *Scottish Daily Mail* 25/8/2007.
22 *Guardian* 31/1/2009.
23 *Sunday Herald* 14/7/2007.
24 *Scotland on Sunday* 12/8/2007.
25 Private information.
26 *Salmond's 100 Days* (STV) 21/8/2007.
27 *Guardian* 14/8/2007.
28 *Sunday Times* 16/9/2007.
29 *Salmond's 100 Days* (STV) 21/8/2007.
30 *Herald* 8/12/2007.
31 *The Times* 10/12/2007.
32 Official Report 13/12/2007 Col 4434.
33 http://news.bbc.co.uk/1/hi/scotland/north_east/7203148.stm
34 http://news.bbc.co.uk/1/hi/scotland/north_east/7294059.stm
35 *Scotsman* 4/12/2007.
36 http://news.bbc.co.uk/2/hi/uk_news/scotland/7313586.stm
37 *Scottish Daily Mail* 24/9/2009.
38 *Politics Show* (BBC) 4/5/2008.
39 *Herald* 7/7/2007.
40 *Scotsman* 4/9/2008.
41 *Scottish Left Review* 56 Jan. – Feb. 2010.
42 *Total Politics* 9/2008.
43 *Good Morning Scotland* (BBC Radio Scotland) 22/8/2008.
44 *Total Politics* 3 9/2008. Butler had also been a contemporary of Salmond's at St Andrews University.
45 Interview with Alex Salmond MSP, 2/2008.
46 http://news.bbc.co.uk/1/hi/scotland/edinburgh_and_east/7621153.stm
47 *Sunday Herald* 8/8/2010. Salmond later described the ABN Amro deal as a 'huge mistake'.
48 *Sunday Herald* 24/8/2008.
49 *The Politics Show* (BBC) 12/10/2008.
50 *Newsnight Scotland* 13/10/2008.
51 http://news.bbc.co.uk/1/hi/scotland/7224987.stm
52 *Scotland on Sunday* 18/10/2008.
53 *Scotsman* 20/10/2008.
54 *The Times* 20/10/2008.
55 http://www.scotland.gov.uk/News/This-Week/Speeches/First-Minister/genassembly09
56 Hassan, ed., *The Modern SNP*, 132.
57 *Perspectives* 24 winter 2009–10.
58 *Guardian* 31/1/2009.
59 *Guardian* 9/6/2009.
60 *Scotland on Sunday* 30/11/2008.
61 http://www.scotland.gov.uk/News/This-Week/Speeches/First-Minister/FMgeorgetown
62 *Daily Telegraph* 29/1/2009.

63 *Guardian* 29/1/2009.

64 Official Report 12/2/2009 Col 15020.

65 *Herald* 10/2/2009.

66 Private information.

67 Interview with Kenny MacAskill MSP, 30/1/2009.

68 *St Andrews Citizen* 24/9/1977.

69 Private information.

70 http://www.scotland.gov.uk/News/This-Week/Speeches/First-Minister/chamber

71 http://www.scotland.gov.uk/News/This-Week/Speeches/First-Minister/scdi3809

72 *Scotsman* 13/5/2009.

73 http://www.scotland.gov.uk/News/This-Week/Speeches/First-Minister/genassembly09

74 *Daily Telegraph* 16/12/2009.

75 http://www.scotland.gov.uk/News/This-Week/Speeches/First-Minister/Edinburghlecture

76 *Daily Record* 17/7/2010.

77 *The Times* 10/9/2009.

78 *Scottish Daily Mail* 29/10/2009.

79 *Scotsman* 25/9/2009.

80 *Sunday Herald* 27/9/2009.

81 http://news.bbc.co.uk/1/hi/uk/8216589.stm

82 *The Lockerbie Bomber: Sent Home to Die* (STV) 9/8/2010.

83 *Scotsman* 19/8/2010.

84 http://www.snp.org/node/15767

85 Seldon & Lodge, *Brown at 10*, 312–13.

86 *Herald* 13/9/2010.

87 *Herald* 10/12/2010.

88 *Scotsman* 26/1/2011.

89 *The Times* 9/2/2011.

90 *Newsnight Scotland* (BBC) 7/2/2011.

91 Scottish Government Press release, 29/8/2011.

92 http://www.scotland.gov.uk/News/Releases/2009/10/13164214

93 http://www.snp.org/node/15749

94 *Daily Telegraph* 10/10/2009.

95 *Holyrood Magazine* 15/3/2010.

96 *Herald* 30/11/2009.

97 *Scotsman* 1/12/2009.

98 *Scotland on Sunday* 29/11/2009.

99 http://www.scottishreview.net/MRitchie180.html

100 http://www.scotland.gov.uk/News/This-Week/Speeches/First-Minister/Edinburghlecture

101 Author's notes from an election press briefing, 12/4/2010.

102 http://www.scotland.gov.uk/News/This-Week/Speeches/First-Minister/Edinburghlecture

103 *Scotsman* 26/1/2010.

104 *Daily Telegraph* 11/2/2010.

105 *The Times* 12/2/2010.

106 http://news.bbc.co.uk/1/hi/scotland/8535946.stm

107 Official Report 11/2/2010 Col 23791–93.

108 *Scotsman* 12/2/2010.

109 Private information.

110 http://www.snp.org/node/16758

111 Documents released under Freedom of Information later revealed that Salmond had entertained several 'greedy bankers' at Bute House that January.

112 *Andrew Marr Show* (BBC) 21/3/2010.
113 Hansard 508 c710.
114 *Sunday Express* 2/5/2010.
115 http://news.bbc.co.uk/1/hi/uk_politics/election_2010/scotland/8668114.stm
116 *Herald* 10/5/2010.
117 *Scotsman* 10/5/2010.
118 *Sunday Times* 16/5/2010.
119 *Total Politics* 3 9/2008.
120 *Reporting Scotland* (BBC) 14/5/2010.
121 Hansard 511 c111.
122 *The Times* 25/6/2010.
123 *Scotsman* 28/6/2010.
124 *The Economist* 1/7/2010.
125 *Scottish Sunday Express* 29/8/2010.
126 Alex Salmond to SNP members, 5/9/2010, author's collection.
127 *Daily Telegraph* 7/9/2010.
128 *Scotland Live* (BBC Radio Scotland) 6/9/2010.
129 Official Report 8/9/2010 Col 28253 & 28263-64.
130 *HardTalk* (BBC News Channel) 25/11/2010.
131 *Sunday Herald* 20/2/2011.
132 *Scotsman* 20/11/2010.
133 Official Report 25/11/2010 Col 30908.
134 http://news.scotsman.com/politics/Scotland-on-Sunday-lecture-Gordon.6595986.jp.
135 *Desert Island Discs* (BBC Radio 4) 16/1/2011.
136 *Sunday Herald* 19/9/2010.
137 Official Report 30/9/2010 Col 29154.
138 Bute House press conference, 30/11/2010 (author's notes).
139 http://www.bbc.co.uk/news/uk-scotland-scotland-politics-10794298
140 Scottish Government press release, 19/11/2010.
141 *Good Morning Scotland* (BBC Radio Scotland) 19/10/2010.
142 *The Politics Show Scotland* (BBC) 24/10/2010.
143 *The Politics Show Scotland* (BBC) 7/11/2010.
144 Scottish Government press release, 11/12/2010.
145 http://politics.caledonianmercury.com/2010/12/01/does-gathering-loan-show-a-trend-of-secrecy-in-salmond/
146 *Press and Journal* 8/12/2010.
147 Official Report 9/12/2010 Col 31417.
148 Scottish Government press release, 11/12/2010.
149 *Herald* 9/3/2011.
150 *Sunday Herald* 22/11/2010.
151 *Herald* 15/2/2011.

Will the real Alex Salmond please stand up?

1 Lyons, *Charles Stewart Parnell*, 611–13.
2 *The Times* 27/1/2010.
3 Radio broadcast 1/10/1939.
4 Labouring the de Gaulle analogy a little, Madame de Gaulle was said never to have given an interview, rather like Moira.
5 Private information.
6 *Independent* 20/9/1998.
7 Private information.

8 Taylor, *The Scottish Parliament*, 161.

9 *Scotsman* 16/7/2004.

10 *Scottish Daily Mail* 28/4/2007.

11 *Scotsman* 18/7/2000.

12 *The Times* 22/4/1998.

13 *Glasgow Evening Times* 18/7/2000.

14 *Guardian* 31/1/2009.

15 Gallagher, *The Illusion of Freedom*, 130.

16 Crossman, *Diaries of a Cabinet Minister I*, 278.

17 *Scottish Daily Mail* 31/12/2009.

18 Gallagher, *The Illusion of Freedom*, 230.

19 http://www.snp.org/node/14413

20 *Total Politics* Issue 3 9/2008.

21 *Independent on Sunday* 8/2/1992.

22 *Scotsman* 22/9/1999.

23 *Freeman's Journal* 29/9/1906. Salmond's 'National Conversation' document was also prefixed with Parnell's assertion that no one had the 'right to fix the boundary of the march of a nation'.

24 *Independent* 20/9/1998.

25 *Scotland on Sunday* 15/8/2010.

26 *Face to Face* (STV) 19/4/2007.

27 *The Economist* 26/9/1998.

28 *Scotsman* 24/9/1998.

29 Interview with Lord Wallace, 5/3/2010. Jordi Pujol was president of Catalonia from 1980 to 2003, during which time he significantly increased Catalan autonomy within Spain.

30 *Scotland on Sunday* 15/8/2004.

31 *Holyrood Magazine* 15/3/2010.

32 Interview with Alex Salmond MSP, 2/2008 (courtesy of Katherine Haddon).

33 *Herald* 28/5/1994.

34 Webb, *The Growth of Nationalism in Scotland*, 85–86.

35 Rhodes, ed., *Scottishness*, 32.

36 Interview with Winnie Ewing MSP, 12/2/2001 (STV B61582).

37 Alex Salmond to Bernard Ponsonby, 1/2001, author's collection.

38 *Guardian* 7/4/1997.

39 Beckett, *The Making of Modern Ireland*, 333.

40 *Scotsman* 28/4/2007.

41 *Tablet* 10/1/2009.

42 *Scottish Sun* 18/7/2000.

43 *Scotland on Sunday* 21/1/2007.

44 Interview with Jim Sillars, 17/9/2009.

45 *The Times* 18/8/2009.

46 Thomas, *Collected Poems*, 178.

47 O'Conner, *Charles Stewart Parnell*, 221.

48 Robbins, *Parnell: the Last Five Years*, 18.

49 Interview with Jim Eadie, 13/2/2010.

50 *The Times* 25/6/2010.

51 Gallagher, *The Illusion of Freedom*, 221.

52 Lyons, *Charles Stewart Parnell*, 623.

53 *Scotland on Sunday* 27/1/1997.

54 Private information.

55 Private information.

56 *Holyrood Magazine* 15/3/2010.

57 Private information.

58 Private information.

59 Hamilton, *Stone of Destiny*, vii.

60 *Sunday Mail* 23/7/2000.

61 *Scottish Daily Mail* 28/4/2007.

62 Private information.

63 Interview with Andrew Wilson, 29/1/2010.

64 Private information.

65 Interview with John Swinney MSP, 19/1/2001 (STV B102765).

66 *Observer* 21/2/2010.

67 Private information.

68 Private information.

69 *Sunday Mail* 23/7/2000.

70 *Independent* 20/1/1999.

71 Private information.

72 Private information.

73 Private information.

74 Private information.

75 Private information.

76 Roth & Criddle, *Parliamentary Profiles S–Z*, 1906.

77 Private information.

78 *Politics Now* (STV) 5/3/2009.

79 Roth & Criddle, *Parliamentary Profiles S–Z*, 1906.

80 Private information.

81 Private information.

82 *Scotland on Sunday* 22/4/2007.

83 Private information.

84 *Observer* 21/2/2010.

85 Private information.

86 Interview with Jim Eadie, 13/2/2010.

87 Colin Pyle to the author, 8/8/2010.

88 Private information.

89 *Total Politics* 3 9/2008.

90 Interview with Lord Wallace, 5/3/2010.

91 Michael Crick to the author, 9/11/2008.

92 *Scottish Sun* 18/7/2000.

93 Interview with Alex Salmond MSP, 3/2009 (courtesy of Colin Mackay).

94 Roth & Criddle, *Parliamentary Profiles S–Z*, 1906.

95 *Salmond's 100 Days* (STV) 21/8/2007.

96 Private information. Intriguingly, when the handwriting expert Lawrence Warner examined Salmond's signature he concluded that 'Listening skills are not that high – once he has decided on something it is not going to be easy to change his mind' (*Mirror* 2/10/1999).

97 Private information.

98 Interview with John Swinney MSP, 19/1/2001 (STV B102765).

99 *Total Politics* 3 9/2008.

100 'Clearing material relating to the First Minister', 3/2/2010.

101 Private information.

102 *The Times* 25/6/2010.

103 Private information.

104 *Independent on Sunday* 8/2/1992.

105 *Sunday Herald* 10/4/2005.

106 *Independent on Sunday* 8/2/1992.

107 Interview with Mike Russell MSP, 15/1/2001 (STV B111940).
108 Interview with Iain Lawson, 18/6/2010.
109 *Glasgow Herald* 21/9/1987.
110 *Scotsman* 23/9/1990.
111 Private information.
112 *Sunday Herald* 10/4/2005.
113 O'Connor, *Charles Stewart Parnell*, 150.
114 *The Salmond Years* (STV) 18/2/2001.
115 Private information.
116 *Scottish Daily Mail* 31/12/2009.
117 Henderson Scott, *A Twentieth Century Life*, 298.
118 *Scotland on Sunday* 25/4/1999.
119 Interview with Jim Eadie, 13/2/2010.
120 Private information.
121 Interview with Isobel Lindsay, 23/2/2010.
122 Private information.
123 *Tablet* 25/7/2009.
124 Colin Pyle to the author, 5/8/2010.
125 Private information.
126 *Independent* 20/9/1998.
127 Colin Pyle to the author, 5/8/2010.
128 Private information.
129 Private information.
130 *Scottish Affairs* 60 summer 2007. 'But not Kitty,' was Salmond's reaction when Owen Dudley Edwards put the Parnell analogy to him.
131 *Scotsman* 18/7/2000.
132 Private information.
133 *Scots Independent* 8/2000.
134 Private information.
135 *Scotsman* 28/4/2007.
136 Private information.
137 *Scotsman* 13/8/2005.
138 *Independent on Sunday* 5/1/1997.
139 *Total Politics* Issue 3 9/2008.
140 *Independent* c8/2/1992.
141 *Radio Times* 26/4/2010.
142 *Scotsman* 18/7/2000.
143 *Scottish Daily Mail* 31/12/2009.
144 *Tablet* 25/7/2009.
145 *Scotsman* 23/9/1990.
146 *Scots Independent* 8/2000.
147 *Sunday Mail* 23/7/2000.
148 *Glasgow Evening Times* 18/7/2000.
149 Private information.
150 Private information.
151 Thomas, *Collected Poems*, 178.

Postscript: 'A change is coming'

1 Davies, *Heart of Europe*, 311–12.
2 Sorel, *L'Europe et la Revolution Francaise*, 474.
3 For the record, 22.6 per cent of the electorate voted SNP in May 2011, while its total

vote – 902,915 – was 5,477 fewer than voted Labour in May 1999, when the turnout had been a lot higher.

4 *Scotsman* 16/6/2011.

5 http://www.scottishelectionstudy.org.uk/data.htm

6 The first two opinion polls were conducted by TNS-BMRB and the third by Ipsos MORI. The last of those also showed 67 per cent believed MSPs' responsibilities should be extended so they have control over 'all tax-raising powers while Scotland remains part of the UK' (*Scotsman* 8/9/2011).

7 Sky News 8/5/2011.

8 http://news.stv.tv/politics/250107-why-the-snp-victory-exposes-a-lack-of-thinking-in-the-independence-debate/

9 *Herald* 14/5/2011.

10 *Scotland on Sunday* 22/5/2011.

11 A demand that Scottish Ministers be given 'statutory rights' to attend EU meetings was later watered down to them being 'included' in talks on devolved matters (*Daily Telegraph* 8/9/2011).

12 *Sunday Herald* 8/5/2011.

13 http://www.scotland.gov.uk/Resource/Doc/919/0120242.pdf

14 http://www.scotlandoffice.gov.uk/scotlandoffice/15862.html

15 *Scotland on Sunday* 4/9/2011.

16 *Globe and Mail* 4/6/2011.

17 *Today Programme* (BBC Radio 4) 21/6/2011.

18 *Scotsman* 14/5/2011.

19 *Herald* 7/5/2011.

20 *Scotland on Sunday* 21/8/2011.

21 *Scotsman* 25/8/2011.

22 *Scotsman* 1/6/2011.

23 *Newsnight Scotland* 31/5/2011.

24 *Scotland on Sunday* 5/6/2011.

25 *Sunday Mail* 28/8/2011.

26 *Scotsman* 17/6/2011.

27 *Scotsman* 24/6/2011.

28 Official Report 18/5/2011.

29 Scottish Government press release, 23/5/2011.

30 *Holyrood* 16/5/2011.

31 http://www.spectator.co.uk/alexmassie/7205295/nationalist-measures-for-unionist-aims.thtml

32 http://stephennoon.blogspot.com/2011/08/scotlands-new-deal.html

33 Mitchell, Johns and Bennie, 'Who are the SNP Members?', in Hassan, ed., *The Modern SNP: From Protest to Power*, pp 68–78.

34 Hansard 527 c1162, 11/5/2011.

35 *The Times* 15/6/2011.

36 http://stephennoon.blogspot.com/2011/05/stronger-together-as-equals.html

37 *Portillo on Salmond* (BBC Scotland) 15/5/2011.

38 *Holyrood* 30/5/2011.

39 *Scotsman* 16/5/2011.

40 Hassan, 'Anatomy of a Scottish Revolution' in *Political Quarterly* Vol. 82 No. 3, Autumn 2011.

41 http://www.scotland.gov.uk/News/Speeches/scotparlopngJuly1-2011

42 *Scotland on Sunday* 3/7/2011.

43 *Prospect* 6/2011.

44 *Guardian* 14/5/2011.

45 *Herald* 24/7/2011.

46 http://stephennoon.blogspot.com/2011/07/founding-father.html
47 *Scotland on Sunday* 21/8/2011. The SNP MEP Alyn Smith broke ranks to suggest a new Scottish currency pegged to the Euro, à la Denmark.
48 *Scotland on Sunday* 15/5/2011.
49 *Scotland on Sunday* 31/7/2011.
50 http://www.scotland.gov.uk/Resource/Doc/293639/0090721.pdf
51 *Scotsman* 7/5/2011.
52 *Scotland on Sunday* 14/8/2011.
53 *Holyrood* 15/10/2010.
54 *Holyrood* 30/5/2011.
55 http://lallandspeatworrier.blogspot.com/2011/02/historically-snp-has-had-aversion-to.html
56 *Guardian* 26/5/2011.
57 *Scotsman* 15/6/2011.
58 http://www.word-power.co.uk/viewPlatform.php?id=587
59 http://www.scotland.gov.uk/Resource/Doc/293639/0090721.pdf
60 *Sunday Herald* 3/8/2009.
61 *Scotland on Sunday* 14/8/2011.
62 http://news.stv.tv/politics/266655-first-minister-refuses-to-apologise-for-msps-nazi-comment/
63 *Scotland on Sunday* 17/1/2011.
64 *HardTalk* (BBC News Channel) 25/11/2010.
65 *Prospect* 6/2011.
66 *London Review of Books* Vol. 33 No. 11, 2/6/2011.
67 *Prospect* 6/2011.
68 *Scotsman* 13/7/2011.
69 *Sunday Herald* 3/8/2009.
70 http://stephennoon.blogspot.com/2011/05/tale-of-two-countries.html
71 Official Report 26/5/2011.
72 *Prospect* 6/2011.
73 *Courier* 11/8/2011.
74 Keating, *The Independence of Scotland*, 179.
75 *Scotsman* 29/4/2011.
76 *Scotsman* 14/1/2011.
77 Official Report 7/9/2011.
78 *Scotsman* 2/3/2011.
79 *Guardian* 14/5/2011.
80 *Guardian* 16/7/2011.
81 http://archives.lesoir.be/royaume-uni-alex-salmond-plaide-pour_t-20110525-01EQJJ.html
82 *Observer* 28/8/2011.
83 http://www.guardian.co.uk/commentisfree/2006/nov/30/scotsbarbsandenglishcommen
84 Albertazzi & McDonnell, *Twenty-First Century Populism*, 3.
85 *Wales on Sunday* 21/8/2011.
86 *Sunday Times* 1/5/2011.
87 *Sunday Herald* 1/5/2011.
88 *New Statesman* 2/5/2011.
89 *Spectator* 21/5/2011.
90 *Canadian Press* 15/5/2011.
91 *New Statesman* 2/5/2011.
92 *Canadian Press* 15/5/2011.
93 *The Times* 8/5/2009.

94 *Scotsman* 16/6/2011.
95 *The Times* 9/5/2011.
96 *Prospect* 6/2011.
97 *Beyond Westminster* (BBC Radio 4) 4/6/2011.
98 *Herald* 4/6/2011.
99 http://www.scotlandoffice.gov.uk/scotlandoffice/15862.html
100 http://news.stv.tv/politics/250107-why-the-snp-victory-exposes-a-lack-of-thinking-in-the-independence-debate/
101 *London Review of Books* Vol 33 No 15, 28/7/2011.
102 *Scotland on Sunday* 26/6/2011.
103 SNP press release, 8/7/2011.
104 Scottish Liberal Democrat press release, 2/9/2011.
105 *Scotsman* 10/6/2011.
106 *Globe and Mail* 4/6/2011.
107 *Scotland on Sunday* 15/5/2011.
108 *Prospect* 6/2011.
109 *Scotsman* 16/8/2011.
110 *Edinburgh Evening News* 26/4/2007.
111 *Scotland on Sunday* 21/11/2010.

BIBLIOGRAPHY

Archives

Robert McIntyre Papers (National Library of Scotland)
Gavin Kennedy Papers (National Library of Scotland)
Gordon Wilson Papers (National Library of Scotland)
Scottish National Papers (National Library of Scotland)
Stephen Maxwell Papers (private collection)

Published sources

Albertazzi, Danielle, and McDonnell, Duncan, eds, *Twenty-First Century Populism: The Spectre of Western European Democracy* (London 2007)
Anonymous, *Donald Dewar 1937–2000: A Book of Tribute* (Norwich 2000)
Anstey, Sandra, ed., *R. S. Thomas: Selected Prose* (Cardiff 1995)
Ascherson, Neal, *Stone Voices* (London 2002)
Bain, Susan, *Holyrood: The Inside Story* (Edinburgh 2005)
Barrow, Geoffrey, *The Extinction of Scotland* (Stirling 1981)
— *Robert Bruce and the Community of the Realm of Scotland* (Edinburgh 1976)
Beckett, *The Making of Modern Ireland 1603–1923* (London 1981)
Blair, Tony, *A Journey* (London 2010)
Bochel, John, *et al.*, *The Referendum Experience: Scotland 1979* (Aberdeen 1981).
Brown, Alice, and Parry, Richard, eds, *Scottish Government Yearbook 1990* (Edinburgh 1990)
Brown, Alice, and McCrone, David, eds, *Scottish Government Yearbook 1991* (Edinburgh 1991)
Cameron, Ewen, *Impaled Upon a Thistle: Scotland Since 1880* (Edinburgh 2010)
Campbell, Alastair, *The Alastair Campbell Diaries Volume Two: Power and the People 1997–1999* (London *2011*)
— *The Blair Years: Extracts from The Alastair Campbell Diaries* (London 2007)
Campbell, John, *Edward Heath: A Biography* (London 1993)
Churchill, Sir Winston, *Second World War I: The Gathering Storm* (London 1964)
Crick, Bernard, *George Orwell: A Life* (London 1982)
Crossman, Richard, *The Diaries of a Cabinet Minister I* (London 1975)
Curtice, John; McCrone, David; McEwen, Nicola; Marsh, Michael and Ormston, Rachel, *Revolution or Evolution? The 2007 Scottish Elections* (Edinburgh 2009)
Dalyell, Tam, *Devolution: The End of Britain?* (London 1977)
Davies, Norman, *Heart of Europe: A Short History of Poland* (Oxford 1986)

Devine, Tom, and Logue, Paddy, eds, *Being Scottish: Personal Reflections on Scottish Identity Today* (Edinburgh 2002)

Erickson, Jennifer, ed., *The Economics of Independence: Alex Salmond MP* (Glasgow 2003)

Ewing, Winnie, *Stop the World: The Autobiography of Winnie Ewing* (Edinburgh 2004)

Gallagher, Tom, *The Illusion of Freedom: Scotland Under Nationalism* (London 2009)

Gallagher, Tom, ed., *Nationalism in the Nineties* (Edinburgh 1991)

Hamilton, Ian, *Stone of Destiny* (Edinburgh 2008)

Harper, Robin, *Dear Mr Harper: Britain's First Green Parliamentarian* (Edinburgh 2011).

Harvie, Christopher, *Broonland: The Last Days of Gordon Brown* (London 2010)

— *Scotland and Nationalism: Scottish Society and Politics, 1707–1994* (London 1994)

Hassan, Gerry, ed., *The Modern SNP: From Protest to Power* (Edinburgh 2009)

Henderson Scott, Paul, *A Twentieth Century Life* (Argyll 2002)

Jamieson, Bruce, *Linlithgow Academy 1894 to 1994* (Linlithgow 1994)

Johns, Robert; Denver, David; Mitchell, James and Pattie, Charles, *Voting for a Scottish government: The Scottish Parliament election of 2007* (Manchester 2010)

Keating, Michael, *The Independence of Scotland: Self-government & the Shifting Politics of Union* (Oxford 2009)

Kennedy, Gavin, ed., *The Radical Approach: Papers on an Independent Scotland* (Edinburgh 1976)

Kemp, Arnold, *The Hollow Drum? Scotland Since the War* (Edinburgh 1993)

Kissinger, Henry, *The White House Years* (London 1979)

Lawson, Nigel, *The View From No. 11: Memoirs of a Tory Radical* (London 1992)

Levy, Roger, *Scottish Nationalism at the Crossroads* (Edinburgh 1990)

Linklater, Magnus, and Denniston, Robin, eds., *Anatomy of Scotland: How Scotland Works* (Edinburgh 1992)

Lynch, Peter, *SNP: The History of the Scottish National Party* (Cardiff 2002)

Lyons, F. S. L., *Charles Stewart Parnell* (London 1977)

MacAskill, Kenny, *Building a Nation: Post-Devolution Nationalism in Scotland* (Edinburgh 2004)

MacAskill, Kenny, and McLeish, Henry, *Global Scots: Making it in the Modern World* (Edinburgh 2005)

Macdonald, Catriona, ed., *Unionist Scotland 1800–1997* (Edinburgh 1998)

McGinty, Stephen, *The Life of Cardinal Winning: This Turbulent Priest* (London 2003)

McLeish, Henry, *Scotland First: Truth and Consequences* (Edinburgh 2004)

Marr, Andrew, *The Battle for Scotland* (London 1992)

Maxwell, Stephen, *The Case for Left-Wing Nationalism* (Aberdeen 1981)

Mitchell, James, *Strategies for Self-Government: The Campaigns for a Scottish Parliament* (Edinburgh 1996)

Mullin, Chris, *A View from the Foothills: The Diaries of Chris Mullin* (London 2009)

— O'Connor, T. P., *Charle Stewart Parnell* (London 1891)

Pimlott, Ben, *Frustrate Their Knavish Tricks: Writings on Biography, History and Politics* (London 1994)

Rawnsley, Andrew, *Servants of the People: The Inside Story of New Labour* (London 2000)

Rhodes, Mandy, ed., *Scottishness: Reflections on Identity* (Edinburgh 2006)

Ritchie, Murray, *Scotland Reclaimed: The Inside Story of Scotland's First Democratic Parliamentary Election* (Edinburgh 2000)

Robbins, Sir Alfred, *Parnell: The Last Five Years* (London 1926)

Roth, Andrew, and Criddle, Byron, *Parliamentary Profiles, 1997–2002: S–Z* (London 2000)

Russell, Mike, and MacLeod, Dennis, *Grasping the Thistle* (Glendaruel 2006)

Salmond, Alex, *'Horizons Without Bars': The Future of Scotland – A series of speeches by Alex Salmond MP* (1993)

Salmond, Alex, ed., *The Royal Bank in Glasgow 1783–1983* (Edinburgh 1983)

— *The Scottish Industrial Resistance* (Aberdeen 1982)

Scottish Labour Party, *Fighting for what really matters: The Scottish Labour Party Manifesto 2011* (Glasgow 2011)

Scottish Liberal Democrats, *Alex in Wonderland* (Edinburgh 1996)

Seldon, Anthony, and Lodge, Guy, *Brown at 10* (London 2010)

Shinwell, Manny, *Conflict Without Malice* (London 1955)

Short, Philip, *Pol Pot: The History of a Nightmare* (London 2004)

Sillars, Jim, *The Case for Optimism* (Edinburgh 1986)

SNP, *Scotland's Future: S.N.P. Manifesto* (Edinburgh August 1974)

Sorel, Albert, *L'Europe et la Revolution Feincaise* (Paris 1908)

Spicer, Matthew, ed., *The Scotsman Guide to Scottish Politics* (Edinburgh 2004, 2nd edition)

Taylor, Brian, *Scotland's Parliament* (Edinburgh 2003)

— *The Scottish Parliament* (Edinburgh 2000)

Thomas, R. S., *Collected Poems 1945–1990* (London 1993)

Watson, Mike, *Year Zero: An Inside View of the Scottish Parliament* (Edinburgh 2001)

Watt, Peter, *Inside Out: My Story of Betrayal and Cowardice at the Heart of New Labour* (London 2010)

Webb, Keith, *The Growth of Nationalism in Scotland* (London 1978)

Wilson, Gordon, *SNP: The Turbulent Years 1960–1990* (Stirling 2009)

Young, Douglas, *St Andrews: Town and Gown Royal and Ancient* (London 1969)

Ziegler, Philip, *Harold Wilson: The Authorised Life* (London 1993)

Broadcast sources

The Lockerbie Bomber: Sent Home to Die (STV 2010)

Portillo on Salmond (BBC Scotland 2011)

The Salmond Years (STV 2000)

Salmond's 100 Days (STV 2007)

The Scotsman Debate – Scotland: A Time to Choose (BBC Scotland 1992)

Walden Interviews Alex Salmond (LWT 1992)

INDEX